THE COMPLETE BOOK OF THE
TOUR de FRANCE

THE COMPLETE BOOK OF THE
TOUR de FRANCE

**A treasure trove of lore, drama and anecdotes
from the first 100 editions of the
Tour de France**

FEARGAL McKAY

Aurum
Press

First published in Great Britain
2014 by Aurum Press Ltd
74—77 White Lion Street
Islington
London N1 9PF
www.aurumpress.co.uk

Picture Credits
© AFP/Getty Images – 167, 197, 244, 280, 396, 415, 498, 527, 554
© Bongarts/Getty Images - 649
© Gamma-Keystone via Getty Images – 307, 335, 468
© Gamma-Rappho via Getty Images – 510
© Getty Images – 570, 601, 687
© Mondadori via Getty Images – 267
© Popperfoto/Getty Images – 367, 375
© Print Collector/Getty Images – 3
© Roger Viollet/Getty Images – 36, 62, 128
© UIG via Getty Images – 108

Every effort has been made to trace the copyright holders of material
quoted in this book. If application is made in writing to the publisher,
any omissions will be included in future editions.

A catalogue record for this book is available from the British Library.

ISBN 978 1 78131 265 0

1 3 5 7 9 10 8 6 4 2
2014 2016 2018 2017 2015

Typeset in Goudy Old Style by Saxon Graphics Ltd, Derby
Printed and bound by CPI Group (UK) Ltd, Croydon, CR0 4YY

Contents

Introduction

So we beat on, boats against the current, borne back ceaselessly into the past.

~ F. Scott Fitzgerald

Every summer the roads of France are turned into the biggest sporting arena in the world as the cyclists in the Tour de France set out on their annual journey around the country. For three weeks every year the Tour becomes the biggest annual sporting event there is. And, when the three weeks of the Tour are over, the months waiting for the next Tour to roll around are filled with the stories of the race just gone and speculation about the race to come.

The Tour today is contested by just shy of 200 riders. They are supported by a 300-strong entourage of team managers (*directeurs sportifs*), masseurs (*soigneurs*) mechanics, chefs and drivers. Trailing behind them is a press corps that numbers in the thousands. And supporting it all, keeping the show on the road, is a staff of officials, organisers and police that, across the three weeks of the race, can be counted in the tens of thousands. Millions of fans fill the roads of France to watch the race go by, and the global television audience is counted in the billions, touching virtually every country in the world. The Tour de France, it's big. Very, very big.

It is now more than a century since the story of the Tour de France began. Only war has stopped the Tour. In 2013, when the race reached the ripe old age of 110 and 100 Tours had been run, something in the region of 5,000 men had put their names into the Tour's history books, fighting for the final victory, a win in one of the more than 2,000 daily stages that have been raced, glory in one of the classifications that play second fiddle to the final *maillot jaune*, for the opportunity to wear that yellow jersey even if only for one day. Often, the race has simply been to survive, to reach Paris and become a *géant de la route*, for all who finish the Tour are counted as giants of the road.

The idea of this book was to collect the cold data about the Tour. The basic facts: who won what, where and when. The stage winners, the yellow jersey wearers, the winners of the race's other competitions. But that cold data needed more, it needed stories to back it up and tell how the race was won. Each Tour, every single day it generates as many stories as there are people riding it. In 2013, that was 198 riders in 22 teams across 21 stages. The story of each Tour could easily fill a book on its own and it has, in classics such as Geoffrey Nicholson's *The Great Bike Race*, telling the story of the 1976 Tour, or Richard Moore's *Slaying the Badger*, the tale of the 1986 Tour. The stories told here, then, only touch the real story of each Tour.

In order to understand the Tour, though, it is necessary to take a step back from the stories of who won what and how, and try to see the bigger picture. The story of how the race came into being and how the race came to be bigger than all the other races it competes with. The story of how the race came into the possession of its current owners, the Amaury family. The story of the cheating and deception that has been part of the race since the beginning. And, chief among the cheating and deception, that means telling the story of doping.

Since the 1998 Tour – the one that started in Dublin and ended in turmoil – it has been impossible to hide from the fact that the Tour and the whole sport of cycling has had a doping problem. In 2012 the United States Anti-Doping Agency stripped seven-time Tour winner Lance Armstrong of all his Tour titles. But doping didn't begin with the Festina *affaire* and end with Lance Armstrong. Its story is much older, and much deeper, than those two key reference points. In trying to tell the complete story of the Tour de France it is necessary to look at how and when doping came about and to look at what has been done to combat it. And much has been done to combat doping in cycling. I don't think it is naïve to believe that the Tour today is cleaner than it has been in decades, possibly even cleaner than it has ever been. It is not naïve to believe that the sport's culture of doping is changing and that – even as some refuse to get the message and stop doping – there are riders who are winning clean.

I first discovered the Tour de France during the *Nouvelle Éire* of the 1980s, the years when Sean Kelly and Stephen Roche raced against *géants de la route* like Bernard Hinault and Laurent Fignon. My love of the race – with the whole sport – has survived not just in spite of the problems the race suffers from but because of those problems and my attempts to try and understand them. It has also survived because, throughout the race's history, the Tour has created so many so many surprises, so many exploits, so many stories. What follows are just some of those tales.

Feargal McKay
Dublin, Ireland
March 2014

Prologue

The most famous cycling race in the world began with what is probably the most famous lunch meeting in sport. On the Saturday before Christmas 1902, as the citizens of Paris prepared for the festivities to come, Henri Desgrange and Géo Lefèvre sat across a table from one and other in Montmartre's Brasserie du Madrid. Festive cheer was not much in abundance. Desgrange was the editor of the sports newspaper *L'Auto-Vélo* and was much troubled by the poor circulation of his paper.

Launched two years earlier on the back of a political and business dispute between its founder, the aristocratic automobile pioneer Comte Albert de Dion, and the then dominant sports paper *Le Vélo*'s editor Pierre Giffard, *L'Auto-Vélo* was not the success its backers had hoped it would be. Initially circulation had been at or around 30,000 copies – compared with the 80,000 *Le Vélo* was able to rack up at the height of its popularity – but that had fallen to an uncomfortable 20,000. Even when Desgrange and his team borrowed publicity stunts from their rival and briefly boosted circulation they still couldn't get the readers to keep coming back.

In 1901 Desgrange and his team at *L'Auto-Vélo* organised the second edition of the 1,200 kilometres Paris-Brest-Paris race, an event originally created by Giffard in 1891 when he was editor of *Le Petit Journal*. In 1902 they blatantly copied Giffard's 600 kilometre Bordeaux-Paris race, running their edition just one month after *Le Vélo*'s race. Sometimes Desgrange and his team did come up with an idea for themselves, such as the Marseille-Paris race they organised in 1902. But nothing could alter the simple fact: Giffard was beating them hands down in the circulation wars. Soon their backers' patience and money would run out.

In addition to losing in the popularity stakes, Desgrange and his team were losing in court. Giffard had launched a case against *L'Auto-Vélo*, claiming the name was a blatant rip off of *Le Vélo*'s. A judge was soon to announce his decision and it seemed clear that Desgrange would have to lose *vélo* from his paper's masthead. Which, given that cycling was probably the most popular sport in the country at the time, would be a bitter blow for *L'Auto-Vélo*.

Hence, then, that pre-Christmas luncheon in the Madrid. Lefèvre was the paper's cycling editor and he had just suggested to his boss a cycling event the like of which no one had organised before. Why not, he proposed, link up six one-day races – classics – which could be run back-to-back, with the winner being the man who had the shortest elapsed time across all six races? Starting and finishing in Paris and taking in the cities of Lyon, Marseille, Toulouse, Bordeaux and Nantes, the race would be a veritable tour of France. And that was the name Lefèvre proposed giving the endeavour, the Tour de France.

Lefèvre's idea cobbled together ideas that already existed to create out of them something new. Five of the six stages he proposed for the Tour already existed as races in one form or another and the sixth – Marseille-Toulouse – would be an easy thing to organise. The idea of a Tour de France was part of French culture, dating back to the Middle Ages when tradesmen toured the country after serving their apprenticeships. The pioneers of automobile racing had already turned this to a sporting purpose in 1899. And the reason Lefèvre proposed six – not five, not seven, but six – stages was that Six Day racing was already a popular part of cycle sport. And that is what Lefèvre saw his race as being: a Six Day race on the roads of France.

* * * * *

A week before that lunch in Paris, the citizens of New York had cheered home the riders on the last day of the twelfth Madison Square Garden International Six Day Race. Among the entrants had been a number of French and Belgian riders, including Julien Lootens, Jean Dargassies and Lucien Petit-Breton. Whiles Sixes had yet to take off in France's vélodromes, French cycling fans took an interest in the reports of the American races that appeared in their sporting press.

Six Day racing began either in Birmingham in 1875, or in London in 1878. The London Six – held in Islington's Agricultural Hall – was the first to run continuously, starting in the early hours of Monday morning and running through to the late hours of Saturday night (the Sabbath being sacred, there was no racing on Sunday) but most Sixes in the UK were two or three sessions a day, afternoons and evenings, each of three or four hours duration. When the idea was exported to the United States a canny promoter, Tom Eck, found that putting the riders on the track twenty-four hours a day was extremely popular. And that race grew to be the best of its breed: the Madison Square Garden International Six Day Race.

Six Day races were hard, some even called them inhuman. In 1896, the year Teddy Hale – a Briton masquerading as an Irishman – won the Garden Six, Giffard's *Le Vélo* called Six Day racing "a cruel sport" and bemoaned "the lamentable scenes of horror which marked the final hours of this indescribable spectacle." Elsewhere in the French media that 1896 Garden Six was described as having been "one of the worst tortures that one could possibly ask a human being to undergo."

And that was what Géo Lefèvre wanted to put on the roads of France: one of the worst tortures that one could possibly ask a human being to undergo. That anyone was willing to participate is a sign of how hard the riders of that era were.

1903: A Tour is Born

Pierre Giffard, editor of *Le Vélo*, opened 1903 with an important victory over his rival Henri Desgrange: as expected, on 15 January *L'Auto-Vélo* was ordered by a court to take the *vélo* out of its name. Two days later Desgrange struck back, *L'Auto* announcing 14 events they would be organising over the year to come, including 'a bicycle race like no other.' Two days after that *L'Auto* elaborated on that race. Between 31 May and 5 July – 36 days – more than 2,000 kilometres would be covered across six stages, from Paris to Lyon to Marseille to Toulouse to Bordeaux to Nantes and back to Paris.

By the middle of May only 15 entries had been received. Rather than cancel, the organisers tinkered. The start was pushed back and the finish brought forward, cutting the duration of the event in half by the elimination of some of the rest days, leaving just 19 days between start and finish: 1 through 19 July. The prizes were re-jigged, less to the stage winner and more to the placers. The entry fee was halved to 10 francs. And – perhaps most importantly – a five franc *per diem* was guaranteed for the first 50 finishers. As an absolute minimum there was the chance to earn 95 francs from finishing this Tour de France.

By the time the new start day came around 79 people had paid their 10 francs entry fee and, on the afternoon of Wednesday 1 July, 60 of them gathered outside Montgeron's café Au Réveille in the Villeneuve-St-Georges suburb in the south-east of Paris. That morning *L'Auto* had given over the whole of its front page to the Tour and, in an editorial headlined 'The Seed', Desgrange waxed lyrical about the race and the men set to ride it:

With the broad and powerful swing of the hand which Zola in *La Terre* gave to his ploughman, *L'Auto*, journal of ideas and action, is going to fling across France today those reckless and uncouth sowers of energy who are the great professional riders of the world.

Reckless and uncouth the riders may well have been but calling them the great professional riders of the world was, to say the least, something of an exaggeration. Some of them weren't even fully professional, let alone great. Jean Dargassies was a blacksmith who, legend has it, had only just taken up cycling, in order to ride the Tour. Okay, some were like Julien Looten, a Belgian school-teacher who raced under a *nom de guerre*, Samson, and was famous enough to have raced in the Madison Square Garden International Six Day race the previous December. And, for sure, Josef Fischer, Hippolyte Aucouturier and Maurice Garin each had major victories on their *palmarès*, races such as Paris-Roubaix, Paris-Tours, Paris-Brest-Paris and Bordeaux-Paris. But the real stars of the sport were still the men who raced on the track, men like the French sprinter Edmond Jacquelin and the American star Marshal 'Major' Taylor, who would be going head-to-head in the Parc des Princes on 14 July.

Desgrange himself had made a considerable portion of his wealth from the stars of Paris's vélodromes – and was promoting the Bastille Day Jacquelin-Taylor re-match – but promoting the Tour necessitated that he now declare road racing to be the superior form of the sport:

> This type of competition, more than all the great vélodrome races, catches the public's imagination, since it speaks directly to them. It is on his roads, surrounded by his fields, in front of his cottages, that the peasant is to see the Tour de France competitors battling it out. The little local newspapers will tell him which of these men won, and he will never forget him, because he will have seen him.

How many would see the race was, of course, open to question. In Paris, despite all the publicity *L'Auto* had given the race, only a few

La Vie Au Grand Air celebrates Maurice Garin's victory in the inaugural Tour de France, 1903.

hundred spectators descended on Montgeron to wave the men of the Tour off. In front of them, and under the direction of *L'Auto*'s Géo Lefèvre, Alphonse Steinès and Georges Abran, the riders assembled and prepared for the off. It was Desgrange himself who officially called the riders to the start line. At 16 minutes past three o'clock Abran fired his starting pistol and the first stage of the first Tour got underway.

Géo Lefèvre, whose bright idea the Tour had been, was the man responsible for the smooth running of the event. Having seen the riders off from Paris he set off in pursuit, travelling by bike, car and train. Between Nevers and Moulins, at about one o'clock in the morning, he was passed on the road by Maurice Garin and Hippolyte Pagie, who had left everyone else behind them. At Moulins Lefèvre boarded a train and raced Garin and Pagie into Lyons. As the dawn lit up the day the Tour climbed its first col, the 759 metre Col de Pin-Bouchain, north-west of Tarare. At a little before seven thirty the officials in Lyon received a telephone call telling them the first riders were on their way. Quickly they prepared the Vélodrome de la Tête-d'Or for their arrival.

At nine o'clock the sound of bugles heralded the arrival of the first riders and a thousand people cheered them into the vélodrome. At the end of 17h45'13" of racing Garin took the win, 55" ahead of his erstwhile breakaway companion, Pagie. Following them into Lyon was Lefèvre, who arrived in time to see the victory celebrations. He made light of his situation, joking that Garin had form for arriving ahead of schedule, having done so at both Paris-Brest-Paris in 1901 and Bordeaux-Paris in 1902.

By the time the control in Lyon closed at around seven o'clock on the Friday evening – forty hours after the race had left Paris, a minimum speed of 12kph having been required – 37 of the original 60 riders had signed in. The last rider home – Eugène Brange, who has the distinction of being the Tour's first *lanterne rouge* – had arrived just before six o'clock that morning, three hours short of a full day behind Garin.

Friday and Saturday were set aside as rest days, recovery time for the riders, and on Sunday 6 July the second stage of the Tour, to Marseille, got underway. One of the key legends of the Tour de France is Henri Desgrange's alleged belief that the perfect Tour would see just one rider arriving into Paris. The reality is quite different. Fearing that too many riders would be lost along the way during the first Tour the rules permitted riders to return to the race and ride individual stages, though no longer challenging for the overall victory. This rule enabled Hippolyte Aucouturier – *le terrible* – to rejoin the race, stomach cramps having forced him out during the first stage.

The stage to Marseille saw the Tour tackle its first proper mountain, the 1,161m Col de la République, outside Saint-Étienne. Aucouturier broke clear with Léon Georget – who had finished third on the opening stage, half an hour down on Garin – and the two raced into Marseille together, Aucouturier winning the sprint. Garin was in a pack of four riders 26 minutes back, while Pagie crashed out of the race, one of five riders to leave the race that day. The net result of this was that Garin was now holding the green armband that signified the race leader; eight minutes ahead of Georget.

With Monday and Tuesday as rest days the Tour's *peloton* reassembled on Wednesday night for the start of the third stage, taking them to Toulouse. A quick rule change saw the riders there just for the stage being sent off an hour after the main *peloton*. In Toulouse Émile Brange – who had been *lanterne rouge* on the first stage – led home a group of four riders that included Garin. Twenty-eight minutes later Aucouturier raced home alone and claimed the stage win, having covered the stage quicker than those who had arrived ahead of him. Georget's challenge had faded on the road to Toulouse – though he still held on to second – and Garin now held his green armband by 1h58'54". Halfway through the race, the win already looked to be in the bag.

After another couple of days' rest the riders set out for Bordeaux. Again, despite being sent off an hour behind the main pack, it was one of the extras there just for the stage who took the win, the Swiss rider Charles Laeser (the first non-French rider to win a stage in the Tour), while Garin and Georget finished in the same group, the overall lead unchanged. At eleven o'clock the next night – Monday – the remaining couple of dozen riders in the Tour set off for Nantes.

Technically speaking, all riders in the 1903 race were independents, none rode as part of a team. Desgrange and the others in *L'Auto* wanted their race to be one for individuals and – unlike most road races of the era – didn't even want to allow pacers. A rider was supposed to get to the finish by the strength of his own legs and his own legs alone. The reality, though, was that the best riders of the day were signed up to the teams of the main bicycle manufacturers. Marques like Crescent, Gladiator and Cycles JC all had riders in the race. The manufacturer with the most representatives was La Française, for whom Garin rode.

On the road to Nantes three of La Française's riders – Garin, Lucien Pothier and Fernand Augereau – got into an argument over who should win the stage. In the version of the story told by Augereau, Garin had said that he would pay the others to let him win, but he, Augereau, refused to be party to such a deal. At which point there was some argy-bargy and Pothier – known as the butcher of Sens for the rather prosaic reason that he was, well, a butcher from Sens – knocked Augereau to the ground. Then Garin attacked his bike, damaging the forks.

Garin, for his part, said Augereau was delusional and dismissed the story out of hand. But reporters in Nantes' Vélodrome de Longchamp were quick to note that the final sprint was barely contested, the win a formality for Garin. And they found eye-witnesses to support Augereau's version of the tale. At best Garin was facing a penalty that might wipe out his lead (which was now 2h58'02" over team-mate Pothier, Georget having abandoned). At worst he could be thrown off the race. Neither outcome would have looked good for *L'Auto*. Nor would either outcome have looked good for La Française, who happened to have been one the original investors in *L'Auto*. So a certain sense of relief must have been felt by both when Augereau withdrew his story.

That Garin survived the scandal might suggest he was somewhat lucky, and in 1903 luck certainly seemed to be on his side. In May he had been among a number of cyclists who took part in the aborted Paris-Madrid motor rally, during which five competitors and three spectators were killed before the race was halted. Garin was competing in the moped category, cyclists being recruited for this because these early mopeds needed to be pedalled up hill. While Garin survived the event unscathed, other cyclists were not so lucky: Lucien Lesna – a two time winner of both Paris-Roubaix and Bordeaux-Paris – suffered a career-ending leg injury. He would have been a favourite for success at the Tour had he been able to start.

Garin sealed his overall victory in the Tour with a third stage win as the *peloton* raced back into Paris. Reports have 100,000 spectators greeting their arrival, outside the Restaurant du Père Auto in Ville-d'Avray, while the Parc des Princes – where the riders completed a victory lap – was packed to the rafters with another 20,000 fans.

Garin's successes saw him picking up 6,125 francs in prize money, which La Française doubled with bonuses. For Desgrange the success was even more profitable: *L'Auto*'s daily circulation, which had sunk as low as 20,000 copies, averaged 65,000 during the Tour, with 130,000 copies printed for the final stage, of which 100,000 sold. The Tour de France had proven itself as the perfect marketing stunt for the ailing *L'Auto*.

Stage-by-Stage Results for the 1903 Tour de France			Stage Winner	Race Leader
Stage 1 Wed 1 Jul 15h16	Paris (Montgeron) to Lyon 60 starters, 37 finishers	467 km 17h45'13" 26.3 kph	Maurice Garin (Fra) La Française	Maurice Garin (Fra) La Française
Thu 2 Jul				
Fri 3 Jul	Rest days			
Sat 4 Jul				
Stage 2 Sun 6 Jul 02h30	Lyon to Marseille 32 finishers	374 km 14h28'53" 25.8 kph	Hippolyte Aucouturier (Fra) Crescent	Maurice Garin (Fra) La Française
	Major climbs: Col de la République (1,161m) Hippolyte Aucouturier (Fra) Crescent			
Mon 6 Jul	Rest days			
Tue 7 Jul				
Stage 3 Wed 8 Jul 22h30	Marseille to Toulouse 25 finishers	423 km 17h55'04" 23.6 kph	Hippolyte Aucouturier (Fra) Crescent	Maurice Garin (Fra) La Française
Thu 9 Jul				

Stage-by-Stage Results for the 1903 Tour de France			Stage Winner	Race Leader
Fri 10 Jul	Rest days			
Sat 11 Jul				
Stage 4 Sun 12 Jul 05h00	Toulouse to Bordeaux 25 finishers	268 km 8h46'00" 30.6 kph	Charles Laeser (Sui) La Française/Cosmos	Maurice Garin (Fra) La Française
Stage 5 Mon 13 Jul 23h00	Bordeaux to Nantes (Vélodrome de Longchamp) 21 finishers	425 km 16h26'31" 25.8 kph	Maurice Garin (Fra) La Française	Maurice Garin (Fra) La Française
Tue 14 Jul				
Wed 15 Jul	Rest days			
Thu 16 Jul				
Fri 17 Jul				
Stage 6 Sat 18 Jul 21h00	Nantes to Paris (Ville-d'Avray then neutralised to Parc des Princes) 21 finishers	471 km 18h09'00" 26.0 kph	Maurice Garin (Fra) La Française	Maurice Garin (Fra) La Française
Sun 19 Jul				

Prize fund: 20,000 francs (3,000 francs first prize)

Final Classification				
Place	**Rider**	**Team**	**Time**	**Age**
1	Maurice Garin (Fra)	La Française	2,428 km 94h33'14' 25.679 kph	32
2	Lucien Pothier (Fra)	La Française	+ 2h59'31"	20
3	Fernand Augereau (Fra)	La Française	+ 4h29'24"	20
4	Rodolfo Muller (Ita)	La Française	+ 4h39'30"	26
5	Jean Fischer (Fra)	La Française	+ 4h58'44"	32
6	Marcel Kerff (Bel)	Unsponsored	+ 5h52'24"	37
7	Julien Lootens (Bel)	Brennabor	+ 8h31'08"	26
8	Georges Pasquier (Fra)	La Française	+ 10h24'04"	25
9	François Beaugendre (Fra)	La Française	+ 10h52'14"	22
10	Aloïs Catteau (Bel)	La Française	+ 12h44'57"	25
Lanterne Rouge				
21	Arsène Millocheau (Fra)	Unsponsored	+ 64h57'08"	36

1904: Tour de Farce

Maurice Garin set several firsts in winning the 1903 edition of the Tour. Obviously, he was the first overall winner. He was also the first stage winner, the first rider to win the opening and closing stages and the first to lead the race from first to last. On a lesser note, he was also the first winner to have been born in one country but who represented another.

Born in Arvier in Italy's Aosta Valley in 1871, Garin's family had emigrated to France in the 1880s. By the time he was 15 Garin was working as a chimney sweep in Reims, earning him his most enduring nickname, *le petit ramoneur*, the little chimney sweep. Taking up cycling in 1892 he scored his first win the following year, Namur-Dinant-Givet, a victory partly achieved with the help of a rival's bike. Garin was leading the race coming into Dinant but punctured. Seeing a *soigneur* with a spare bike for a rival Garin jumped off his own, grabbed the new bike, and sped off to victory (he did later return the borrowed bike).

The following year Garin turned up for a race in Avesnes-sur-Helpes, near to his home in Maubeuge, which was restricted to professionals. Despite being an amateur he insinuated himself into the *peloton* and took the win. But, because he wasn't a pro, the race organisers refused to give him the 150 franc purse. The crowd took up his cause and raised 300 francs for him.

After that incident the Italian decided to take out a professional licence and his first known pro win came in February 1895 when he rode a 24 hour race behind tandem-mounted pacers. The race – Les 24 Heures des Arts Libéraux – was organised by *Le Vélo* and took place on a track in Paris's Champ de Mars. Only two riders survived the freezing February temperatures: a British rider called Williams, and Garin, with the little chimney sweep having covered a distance of 701 kilometres, about 40 kilometres more than the Briton.

In 1896, when Paris-Roubaix was launched, Garin was in that first *peloton*, finishing third, 15 minutes down on Josef Fischer. A year later he was back for more and this time took the win, beating Mathieu Cordang in a sprint on Roubaix's cement track. And then he came back in 1898 and made it back-to-back wins.

In 1901 Garin – who had just taken out French citizenship – signed to ride for La Française, a Paris-based manufacturer which had taken a small investment in *L'Auto*. Garin proved his value by winning the 1901 edition of Paris-Brest-Paris, at 1,200 kilometres the toughest road race on the calendar at the time. The following year he added *L'Auto*'s edition of Bordeaux-Paris to his *palmarès*. A year on from that he won the Tour. And then a year later he won the Tour for a second time.

Garin's victory in the second Tour was as straightforward as was his first, he again taking the first stage and holding the lead all the way back to Paris. But this second Tour was quite different from the one raced the year before. While the race itself covered the same route – with the addition of a few more rest days for the riders – the excitement of the first race had ignited the passions of France's cycling fans, and they were out in force in 1904, cheering on their favourites and – sadly – doing their best to hamper the chances of the rest.

On the opening stage fans on their own bikes rode with the *peloton*, sometimes accidently causing riders to crash. The bigger problem came at the end of the stage, when the rider who finished third, Pierre Chevalier, was disqualified after it was discovered he had completed part of the stage by car. Lucien Pothier, who finished second, was lucky to escape with a financial fine after it was discovered he had drafted behind the car of La Française's *directeur sportive*, Delattre, as he attempted to rejoin the bunch after a puncture.

On the second stage to Marseille things got worse. On the Col de la République outside of Saint-Étienne, supporters of a local rider, Alfred Fauré, attacked Garin and the Italian Giovanni Gerbi as they led the race over the col. It took the arrival of Géo Lefèvre in his car to break up the mêlée, he firing a pistol in the air to disperse the crowd. For Gerbi, though, Lefèvre arrived too late and the Italian retired from the race with an injured hand. At a hastily re-arranged finish in Saint-Antoine – moved to the outskirts of the city instead of the planned finish in Marseille's vélodrome Larchevêque – Hippolyte Aucouturier won a four-man sprint, with the local boy Fauré leading home the second group of riders, just two seconds back.

By the time the stage to Nîmes got started another rider had been tossed off the race for cheating. This time it was Ferdinand Payan who was accused of having taken pace from riders not involved in the race (pacing was the norm in cycling at this stage and the Tour itself was unusual in banning pacers). Aucouturier, having broken away with another rider, took an easy victory in Nîmes. Over the next few days, as the riders rested, a new controversy arose, when it was claimed that Aucouturier and his breakaway companion had accepted food from a car, something which was banned by the race's rules. That companion was Henri Cornet, born Jardy and known in the *peloton* as *le rigolo*, the joker.

Pothier took the win in the fourth stage, to Bordeaux, with team-mate Garin one second back, in a day apparently devoid of controversy for the organisers. Aucouturier took the next stage, into Nantes – where fans of Payan attempted to disrupt the race – and then it was on to the last lap, which Aucouturier won while Garin celebrated his overall victory. Pothier was the runner up – by a mere 30 seconds – and Garin's younger brother César rounded out the top three.

But the race was not yet over. This was a Tour than ran and ran for months after the finish. Desgrange himself, in the immediate aftermath of the finish, acknowledged that all was not well. In an editorial in *L'Auto* he questioned whether the race had any future, saying it had been 'killed by its own success, the blind passions it has unleashed, the verbal abuse and the dirty suspicions that are given value by the ignorant and the spiteful.' He condemned the riders who were caught cheating, but let the manufacturers who sponsored the riders, and their entourages, off without censure, despite their evident complicity (perhaps wisely, given *L'Auto* relied on those manufacturers placing ads in the paper).

Despite *L'Auto* having penalised a number of riders during the race the French federation felt more could and should have been done. They'd already had to deal with allegations of cheating earlier in the season at Bordeaux-Paris, organised by *Le Vélo*, and the outcome of that was that the first four riders home – Léon Georget, Lucien Petit-Breton, César Garin and Rudolphe Muller – were all disqualified, with the victory re-allocated to the rider who was fifth, Fernand Augereau (the rider who had made allegations against Maurice Garin during the 1903 Tour).

At the end of November, after an extensive investigation, the federation announced the findings of their investigation. Twenty-nine riders were disciplined, including all the stage winners and the first four in the overall general classification. A couple of lifetime bans were handed out to the worst offenders, though these were later reduced on appeal. Most got away with little more than a slap on the wrist.

Garin, though, was made to pay a high price and was stripped of his win. In his stead the victory was awarded to the 21-year-old joker in the pack, Henri Cornet, *le rigolo*. But, for some, Garin was still the winner of that Tour, regardless of what his cycling federation decreed. He was the first man back to Paris and damn the means by which he got there. If everyone was cheating – and even Cornet was reprimanded, though not punished, by the federation – then Garin was still the first among equals. Desgrange had no choice but to accept the judgement handed down, though he made clear his feeling that the federation had over-stepped the mark.

The year was not all bad news for *L'Auto*, with the Tour again boosting the paper's circulation. Even better news came in November when Pierre Giffard's *Le Vélo* shut up shop, handing victory in the circulation war to Desgrange and his backers. Somewhat ironically, given the court case Giffard had launched against Desgrange over the similarity of their two papers' names, a group of investors bought the bankrupt *Le Vélo* and relaunched it as the *Journal de l'Automobile*.

Stage-by-Stage Results for the 1904 Tour de France			Stage Winner	Race Leader
Stage 1 Sat 2 Jul 21h00	Paris (Montegeron) to Lyon 88 starters, 52 finishers	467 km 17h07'06" 27.3 kph	~~Maurice Garin (Fra)~~ ~~La Française~~	~~Maurice Garin (Fra)~~ ~~La Française~~
Sun 3 Jul			Michel Frédérick (Sui) Peugeot	Michel Frédérick (Sui) Peugeot
Mon 4 Jul	Rest days			
Tue 5 Jul				
Wed 6 Jul				
Thu 7 Jul				
Fri 8 Jul				
Stage 2 Sat 9 Jul 23h30	Lyon to Marseille 40 finishers	374 km 15h09'00" 24.7 kph	~~Hippolyte Aucouturier~~ ~~(Fra)~~ ~~Crescent~~	~~Maurice Garin (Fra)~~ ~~La Française~~
Sun 10 Jul			Antoine Fauré (Fra) Sauvinet	Émile Lombard (Bel) Bary
Major climbs: Col de la République (1,161m) Antoine Fauré (Fra) Sauvinet				
Mon 11 Jul	Rest Days			
Tue 12 Jul				
Stage 3 Wed 13 Jul 20h30	Marseille to Toulouse 35 finishers	423 km 15h43'55" 26.9 kph	~~Hippolyte Aucouturier~~ ~~(Fra)~~ ~~Crescent~~	~~Maurice Garin (Fra)~~ ~~La Française~~
Thu 14 Jul			Henri Cornet (Fra) Cycles JC	Henri Cornet (Fra) Cycles JC
Fri 15 Jul	Rest days			
Sat 16 Jul				
Stage 4 Sun 17 Jul 05h00	Toulouse to Bordeaux 34 finishers	268 km 08h40'06" 30.9 kph	~~Lucien Pothier (Fra)~~ ~~La Française~~	~~Maurice Garin (Fra)~~ ~~La Française~~
			François Beaugendre (Fra) Cycles JC	François Beaugendre (Fra) Cycles JC
Mon 18 Jul	Rest days			
Tue 19 Jul				
Stage 5 Wed 20 Jul 22h00	Bordeaux to Nantes 30 finishers	425 km 16h49'40" 25.3 kph	~~Hippolyte Aucouturier~~ ~~(Fra)~~ ~~Crescent~~	~~Maurice Garin (Fra)~~ ~~La Française~~
Thu 21 Jul			Jean-Baptiste Dortignacq (Fra) Elvish	Henri Cornet (Fra) Cycles JC
Fri 22 Jul	Rest day			
Stage 6 Sat 23 Jul 19h00	Nantes to Paris (Ville-d'Avray then neutralised to Parc des Princes) 27 finishers	471 km 19h28'00" 24.2 kph	~~Hippolyte Aucouturier~~ ~~(Fra)~~ ~~Crescent~~	~~Maurice Garin (Fra)~~ ~~La Française~~
Sun 24 Jul			Jean-Baptiste Dortignacq (Fra) Elvish	Henri Cornet (Fra) Cycles JC

Prize fund: 21,000 francs (5,000 francs first prize)

Final Classification

Place		Rider	Team	Time		Age
1		~~Maurice Garin (Fra)~~	~~La Française~~	~~93h06'24"~~		~~33~~
2		~~Lucien Pothier (Fra)~~	~~La Française~~	~~+ h06'28"~~		~~21~~
3		~~César Garin (Fra)~~	~~La Française~~	~~+ 1h51'03"~~		25
4		~~Hippolyte Aucouturier (Fra)~~	~~Crescent~~	~~+ 2h52'26"~~		~~27~~
5	1	Henri Cornet (Fra)	Cycles JC	~~+ 2h59'27"~~	2,428 km 96h'05'55" 25.265 kph	19
6	2	Jean-Baptiste Dortignacq (Fra)	Elvish	~~+ 5h15'36"~~	+ 2h1614"	20
7		~~Philippe Jousselin (Fra)~~	~~La Française~~	~~+ 8h33'42"~~		~~32~~
8	3	Aloïs Catteau (Bel)	La Française	~~+ 12h00'56"~~	+ 9h01'25"	26
9		~~Camille Fily (Fra)~~	~~Veuve Fily~~	~~+ 15h36'42"~~		17
10	4	Jean Dargassies (Fra)	Gladiator	~~+ 16h04'01"~~		32
	5	Julien Maîtron (Fra)	Clement		+ 13h04'30"	23
	6	Auguste Daumain (Fra)	Peugeot		+ 22h44'36"	26
	7	Louis Coolsaet (Bel)	Valante		+ 23h44'20"	19
	8	Achille Colas (Fra)	Davignon		+ 25h09'50"	29
	9	René Saget (Fra)	Cassignard		+ 25h55'16"	
	10	Gustave Drioul (Bel)	Cycles JC		+ 30h54'49"	28
Lanterne Rouge						
	15	Antoine Deflotrière (Fra)	L'Etna		+ 101h28'52"	27

Note: On November 30 1904 the results of the 1904 Tour were re-written by the French cycling federation. Names shown in ~~strikethrough~~ are before the revisions, the others after.

1905: Trading Stages

Faced with the widespread cheating and crowd troubles of 1904, *L'Auto* set about reinventing the Tour for 1905. Out went the 400-plus kilometre stages, which had necessitated racing through most of the night. The 423 km Marseille-Toulouse stage became 192 km from Toulouse to Nîmes and then 367 km from Nîmes to Toulouse. Bordeaux-Nantes (425 km) became Bordeaux-La Rochelle (257 km) and La Rochelle-Rennes (263 km). Alphonse Steinès – who was chiefly responsible for the route the race followed – suggested taking the race into the mountains, and the Ballon d'Alsace in the Vosges was added, which extended the race's eastward march to Nancy, before taking the race southward along the western foothills of the Alps, taking in the climbs of the Côte de Laffrey and the Col Bayard in the Chartreuse Massif, between Grenoble and Toulon.

All these changes brought the number of stages up to 10 (from six) and extended the overall distance to 3,021 km, while shortening the race from 24 days to 23 by the elimination of a few rest days. The biggest change wrought by the organisers, though, was in the way the winner would be decided. Elapsed time was out – and would stay out for the next seven years – and a points system was brought in. Finish first on a stage and you got one point, second got you two, third three and so on. Finish more than five minutes behind the rider in front of you and you got an additional point added to your score. At the end of the race, the rider with the least number of points across all 11 stages was judged to be the winner.

One other innovation was added: the Tour's riders were split into two categories, *coureurs de vitesse* and *coureurs sur machines poinçonnées*. In the *poinconnées*, or stamped, category, riders had to complete the whole Tour on the same bike, fixing problems as they went along, unable to replace any of the parts which had been stamped. The *vitesse*, or speed, riders were allowed to change bikes as they pleased.

The Paris-based bike maker La Française had dominated the first two Tours but in 1905 the baton was passed to one of France's oldest bike builders, Peugeot. Formed in 1810 by three brothers the company soon found a niche in the market producing coffee and condiment grinders before climbing aboard the bicycle boom in the latter half of the nineteenth century, producing the penny-farthing *le grand bi* in 1882. By the turn of the century the Peugeot brothers were building both bikes and automobiles. A couple of Peugeot-sponsored riders had turned up for the 1904 Tour but in 1905 the lion cubs (the company's logo was a lion rampant) arrived in force. And they took the Tour by the scruff of the neck.

Louis Trousselier took the opening stage and the race lead for the lion cubs. For the third year in a row Hippolyte Aucouturier – now also a Peugeot man – was again one of the pre-race favourites, and this time he managed to lose 26 minutes on the opening day, which translated into a seven point gap to his team-mate.

Tack attacks – partisan fans had strewn the road with small nails in order to cause punctures – again blighted the opening stage, and many riders ran out of spare tyres and were forced off their bikes and into cars or trains in order to get to Nancy. So many, in fact, that *L'Auto* – once more fearing there would be too few riders left in the race to make a compelling spectacle – allowed all who had abandoned on the first stage to continue, but with the addition of a 75 point penalty. Lucien Petit-Breton – riding his first Tour, for Cycles JC – had quit the race in consequence of the number of punctures he'd suffered and had returned to Paris by train. But on learning that he could still continue he took another train to Nancy, arriving there just an hour before the start of the second stage, which took in the Ballon d'Alsace.

Despite the fact that the Tour had already climbed one high col before – at 1,161m the Col de la République is just seventeen metres lower than the Ballon d'Alsace's 1,178m – Desgrange and his team still trumpeted the Ballon as the Tour's first mountain. If the results of the 1904 race could be rewritten months after it finished, it seemed the history of the Tour itself could be rewrought too.

The choice of the Vosges and the Ballon d'Alsace, as well as taking the Tour into the mountains and away from the crowds, served a political purpose as well as a practical one, the Ballon looking out over the German occupied territories of Alsace-Lorraine, which France had lost after the Franco-Prussian War of 1870–71 and dreamed of regaining. This political purpose was, of course, denied by *L'Auto*, with Alphonse Steinès writing in 1906 that "God knows that we are free from any political thought, since only the popularisation of sport guides us in organising our great sporting event."

As for the symbolism of whitewashing the Col de la République from the Tour's history, perhaps there was a desire here to forget the now tainted Garin years and start over, anew. Or maybe the hyperbole was just good marketing, no one caring whether it was true or not. Either way, it worked and, even today, most people will tell you that the Ballon was the Tour's first mountain.

For the riders themselves the Ballon was something to be feared. They were riding bikes that averaged about 15 kilograms in weight – compared to modern bikes which have to have ballast added to top seven kilos – and only had a single gear. So at the base of the Ballon most of them switched to new bikes, with lower gears better suited to the gradient. On the climb Henri Cornet, the inheritor of the 1904 victory, went up elbow to elbow with René Pottier (Peugeot), until Pottier darted away from him and crested the climb alone.

As they crossed the crest of the climb the riders who had switched bikes remounted their original machines. Except for poor Cornet, who was left standing at the side of the road for 20 minutes waiting for his Cycles JC team car to make its way up the climb, it having broken down.

Aucouturier caught his Peugeot team-mate Pottier after Belfort and took the stage win, but Pottier won the bigger bounty, taking the overall race lead from Trousselier. On the next stage, though, Pottier was forced out of the race with injuries and thus became the first rider to abandon the Tour while leading overall. In his absence, the green armband of the race leader passed back to Trou-Trou (Trousselier), after he won the stage.

One of the riders punished by the French cycling federation for cheating at the 1904 Tour, Trousselier, like most of the rest – with the exception of Maurice Garin, who would never get to ride the Tour again – had been rehabilitated by 1905 and went into the race on the back of a victory in Paris-Roubaix, now organised by *L'Auto* following the demise of *Le Vélo*. Trou-Trou's control of the 1905 Tour was only challenged briefly, on Stage Four as the riders crossed the Chartreuse Massif and the climbs of the Bayard and Laffrey, with his Peugeot team-mate Aucouturier taking the stage, bringing them level on points. Cornet was once again let down by his support crew, who were delayed in providing him with a new bike with lower gearing at the base of the Laffrey. *Le rigolo* decided to quit the Tour, his chances of defending his title having all but evaporated.

On the next stage, over to Nîmes, Trou-Trou reasserted his authority by taking the win, while Aucouturier was once again laid low by stomach cramps. He held on to second place overall behind Trousselier but was now 17 points behind his team-mate, his hopes of victory gone. Thereafter all Trou-Trou had to do was to defend his lead, which he did successfully, adding another two stage wins to the three he'd already notched up, and in Paris he was crowned the winner.

Reneging on one of the ideals of the first Tour – that it would be a race for individuals – Desgrange and his team permitted the riders to employ pacers for the opening and closing stages. Thus Pottier – recovered from the injuries which had forced him to abandon – was able to return to the Tour for the run in to Paris, to help pace his Peugeot team-mates. Cornet also returned, to provide pace for the Cycles JC riders.

Tour legend has it that Trousselier, who was known to be a gambling man, spent the evening after the race ended holed up in the Vélodrome Buffalo, gambling his winnings away on dice. With the money all gone, the next day he returned to his army posting, having been off on leave in order to ride the Tour.

For *L'Auto* the reborn Tour was, despite the odd hiccough, a success. Cheating had been kept to acceptable minimum and the paper saw its circulation consistently top 100,000 throughout the race – half as much again as had been achieved during the first Tour and a five times the lowly circulation figures *L'Auto* was posting before the Tour was dreamt up.

Stage-by-Stage Results for the 1905 Tour de France			Stage Winner	Race Leader
Stage 1 Sun 9 Jul	Paris (Noisy-le-Grand) to Nancy 60 starters, 45 finishers	340 km 11h25'00" 29.8 kph	Louis Trousselier (Fra) Peugeot	Louis Trousselier (Fra) Peugeot
Mon 10 Jul	Rest day			
Stage 2 Tue 11 Jul	Nancy to Besançon 40 finishers	299 km 10h11'00" 29.4 kph	Hippolyte Aucouturier (Fra) Peugeot	René Pottier (Fra) Peugeot
	Major climbs: Ballon d'Alsace (1,178m) René Pottier (Fra) Peugeot			
Wed 12 Jul	Rest days			
Thu 13 Jul				
Stage 3 Fri 14 Jul	Besançon to Grenoble 36 finishers	327 km 11h14'00" 29.1 kph	Louis Trousselier (Fra) Peugeot	Louis Trousselier (Fra) Peugeot
Sat 15 Jul	Rest day			
Stage 4 Sun 16 Jul	Grenoble to Toulon 32 finishers	348 km 13h19'45" 25.7 kph	Hippolyte Aucouturier (Fra) Peugeot	Louis Trousselier (Fra) Peugeot
				Hippolyte Aucouturier (Fra) Peugeot
	Major climbs: Col Bayard (1,246m), Julien Maîtron (Fra) Peugeot; Côte de Laffrey (900m) Hippolyte Aucouturier (Fra) Peugeot			
Mon 17 Jul	Rest day			
Stage 5 Tue 18 Jul	Toulon to Nîmes 30 finishers	192 km 7h24'00" 25.9 kph	Louis Trousselier (Fra) Peugeot	Louis Trousselier (Fra) Peugeot
Wed 19 Jul	Rest day			
Stage 6 Thu 20 Jul	Nîmes to Toulouse 30 finishers	307 km 12h07'45" 25.3 kph	Jean-Baptiste Dortignacq (Fra) Saving	Louis Trousselier (Fra) Peugeot
Fri 21 Jul	Rest day			
Stage 7 Sat 22 Jul	Toulouse to Bordeaux 28 finishers	268 km 10h12'40" 26.2 kph	Louis Trousselier (Fra) Peugeot	Louis Trousselier (Fra) Peugeot

Stage-by-Stage Results for the 1905 Tour de France			Stage Winner	Race Leader
Sun 23 Jul	Rest day			
Stage 8 Mon 24 Jul	Bordeaux to La Rochelle 26 finishers	257 km 8h25'45" 30.5 kph	Hippolyte Aucouturier (Fra) Peugeot	Louis Trousselier (Fra) Peugeot
Tue 25 Jul	Rest day			
Stage 9 Wed 26 Jul	La Rochelle to Rennes 26 finishers	263 km 10h25'45" 25.2 kph	Louis Trousselier (Fra) Peugeot	Louis Trousselier (Fra) Peugeot
Thu 27 Jul	Rest day			
Stage 10 Fri 28 Jul	Rennes to Caen 26 finishers	167 km 6h33'01" 26.1 kph	Jean-Baptiste Dortignacq (Fra) Saving	Louis Trousselier (Fra) Peugeot
Stage 11 Sat 29 Jul	Caen to Paris (Orgeval, then neutralised to Parc des Princes) 24 finishers	253 km 7h30'00" 33.7 kph	Jean-Baptiste Dortignacq (Fra) Saving	Louis Trousselier (Fra) Peugeot

Prize fund: 25,000 francs (4,000 francs first prize)

Final Classification				
Place	**Rider**	**Team**	**Points**	**Age**
1	Louis Trousselier (Fra)	Peugeot	2,994 km 110h26'58" 27.107 kph 35 pts	24
2	Hippolyte Aucouturier (Fra)	Peugeot	61	28
3	Jean-Baptiste Dortignacq (Fra)	Saving	64	21
4	Émile Georget (Fra)	Cycles JC	123	23
5	Lucien Petit-Breton (Fra)	Cycles JC	155	22
6	Augustin Ringeval (Fra)	Cycles JC	202	23
7	Paul Chauvet (Fra)	Griffon	231	
8	Philippe Pautrat (Fra)	Cycles JC	248	21
9	Julien Maître (Fra)	Peugeot	255	24
10	Julien Gabory (Fra)	Cycles JC	304	25
Lanterne Rouge				
24	Clovis Lacroix (Fra)	Unsponsored	870	
Coureurs de Vitesse				
	Louis Trousselier (Fra)	Peugeot		24
Coureurs sur Machines Poinçonnées				
	Philippe Pautrat (Fra)	Cycles JC		21

1906: The First Grimpeur

For their fourth Tour de France, Henri Desgrange and his team at *L'Auto* reworked the race route and, for the first time, the Tour more or less mapped the outlines of France's *hexagone*. Rolling out from Paris the race went north up to Lille and then swept across the country to Nancy in the east and down to Nice in the south, once again skirting the western edges of the Alps. From there was westward all the way to Bayonne, staying north of the Pyrenees, and up to Brittany, the race travelling all the way out to Brest before turning for the final run up to Paris.

The stages were still mamoth, with only the first and last dropping below 300 km and four of them topping 400 km. This pushed the overall length of the race out to 4,637 km, an increase of more than 1,600 km on the year before and almost twice as long as the 1903 and 1904 Tours. Now with 13 stages – two more than the year before – the race stretched to 25 days, with one rest day between each stage.

During the previous year's Tour there had been confusion over where stages ended, the organisers having moved finishes to the outskirts of towns, sometimes without making entirely clear in advance precisely where the finish line would be. Lucien Petit-Breton had complained about the confusion this caused and in 1906 Desgrange and his team marked the start of the final kilometre of each stage with a red flag: the *flamme rouge* was born.

Another innovation in 1906 was a transfer between the end of stage one in Lille and the start of stage two in Douai, a distance of about 35 kilometres. This fourth Tour was also the first to extend beyond France's borders. The stage from Douai to Nancy took the riders through the German-occupied city of Metz in Alsace-Lorraine. The stage to Nice took them through Switzerland, at Ventimiglia. And the stage to Bayonne took the race into Spain, at Irún.

The climbing revelation of the previous year's Tour, René Pottier (Peugeot), came out tops at the end of the race's circuit of France. While his victory was complete – he won five stages along the way, four of them back-to-back – it was a close run race, partly through a minor tweak in the way points were awarded: the penalty points for time gaps were dropped, meaning the points you earned were solely related to where you finished on the stage. For Pottier, what this meant was that although he put more than two-and-a-half hours into his Peugeot team-mate Georges Passerieu between Douai at the start of stage two and Nice at the end of stage five – Pottier's territory, the mountains – he led by just nine points with eight stages remaining. The London-born Passerieu was down, but he was far from out.

Over the next two stages Pottier lost four points and Passeriu was looking like he was set to come from behind. Then it was Pottier's turn to pull back three points in two stages. The nip and tuck continued all the way back to Paris, Pottier marking Passerieu all the way, ceding a point one day only to gain it back the next. When they reached Paris just eight points separated the two riders. Yes, they were team-mates, and it was unlikely that Passerieu would have been allowed to attack Pottier, but Pottier was still just one *jour sans* away from losing the Tour, right up until the end.

It was in the mountains that Pottier had laid the foundations for his victory and sealed his reputation as the Tour's first *grimpeur*, or climber. This time around the rules had been changed to stop the *coureurs de vitesse* from swapping to lower-geared machines at the base of a climb, with bike changes only allowed in designated zones around the controls riders had to sign in at during the stage. Even that couldn't halt Pottier – who entered the mountains on the back of a stage win in Nancy – and, as he had in the previous year, he crested the Ballon d'Alsace alone. Only Passerieu and Augustin Ringeval (Labor) were able to hold his wheel initially, but they were soon disposed of and, having crested the Ballon alone, Pottier soloed the remaining 200-odd kilometres down to Dijon.

From Dijon to Grenoble Pottier again reigned supreme as the race climbed through the edges of the Alps. From Grenoble to Nice, over the Bayard and Laffrey climbs there was no holding him back and Pothier rode onto the Côte d'Azur alone again, chalking up his fourth victory in as many stages.

For the defending champion, Louis Trousselier (Peugeot), it was a Tour plagued by poor form and too many mishaps. While he was up with the front runners at the end of the first stage, over the next two stages he dropped from third to fifth, only mounting a fight-back in the final four stages, where he was able to regain third following three back-to-back stage wins. For Lucien Petit-Breton – another Peugeot rider – the cause of Trousselier's problems was simple: too many nights in the gambling halls of Paris and too much of the good life since winning the Tour.

With Pottier, Passerieu, Trousselier and Petit-Breton, Peugeot's lion cubs ruled the Tour for a second year running, but this time round they had a rival: the newly created Alcyon team. Alcyon's 1906 roster included one of the rising hopes of French cycling, Émile Georget (who had finished fourth in the previous year's Tour), and Jean-Baptiste Dortignacq, who had won three stages in the 1905 race and finished third overall. Neither, unfortunately, was in the right shape for the 1906 Tour, Georget suffering from boils – a common complaint among cyclists of that era – and Dortignacq being unable to offer anything more than a single stage victory, in Bayonne. And that only came after appealing to the race's commissaires, claiming that Trousselier, who had been first across the line, had changed bikes outside of one of the permitted zones.

Pottier followed his victory at the Tour by taking to the Vélodrome Buffalo's track in September for the prestigious 24-hour race, the Bol d'Or. There he proved he was as good a *pistard* as he was a *grimpeur*, clocking a distance of 925.29 km and taking the victory. Four months later, in January 1907, the 28-old Pottier was found dead, hanged from the hook that normally held his bicycle in the Peugeot garage. His brother, André, said that Pottier was suffering from a broken heart, his marriage having gone awry.

Stage-by-Stage Results for the 1906 Tour de France			Stage Winner	Race Leader
Stage 1 Wed 4 Jul	Paris (Vélodrome Buffalo) to Lille 82 starters, 49 finishers	275 km 10h09'15" 27.1 kph	Émile Georget (Fra) Alcyon	Émile Georget (Fra) Alcyon
Thu 5 Jul	Rest day			
Stage 2 Fri 6 Jul	Douai to Nancy 37 finishers	400 km 14h21'30" 27.9 kph	René Pottier (Fra) Peugeot	Émile Georget (Fra) Alcyon
				René Pottier (Fra) Peugeot
Sat 7 Jul	Rest day			
Stage 3 Sun 8 Jul	Nancy to Dijon 25 finishers	416 km 15h18'41" 27.2 kph	René Pottier (Fra) Peugeot	René Pottier (Fra) Peugeot
	Major climbs: Ballon d'Alsace (1,178m) René Pottier (Fra) Peugeot			
Mon 9 Jul	Rest day			
Stage 4 Tue 10 Jul	Dijon to Grenoble 25 finishers	311 km 10h32'35" 29.5 kph	René Pottier (Fra) Peugeot	René Pottier (Fra) Peugeot
Wed 11 Jul	Rest day			
Stage 5 Thu 12 Jul	Grenoble to Nice 25 finishers	345 km 12h27'00" 27.7 kph	René Pottier (Fra) Peugeot	René Pottier (Fra) Peugeot
	Major climbs: Côte de Laffrey (900m) René Pottier (Fra) Peugeot; Col Bayard (1,246m) René Pottier (Fra) Peugeot			
Fri 13 Jul	Rest day			
Stage 6 Sat 14 Jul	Nice to Marseille 22 finishers	308 km 11h21'17" 27.1 kph	Georges Passerieu (Fra) Peugeot	René Pottier (Fra) Peugeot
Sun 15 Jul	Rest day			
Stage 7 Mon 16 Jul	Marseille to Toulouse 17 finishers	421 km 17h24'00" 24.2 kph	Louis Trousselier (Fra) Peugeot	René Pottier (Fra) Peugeot
Tue 17 Jul	Rest day			
Stage 8 Wed 18 Jul	Toulouse to Bayonne 16 finishers	300 km 10h46'02" 27.9 kph	~~Louis Trousselier (Fra) Peugeot~~ (1)	René Pottier (Fra) Peugeot
			Jean Baptiste Dortignacq (Fra) Alcyon	

(1) Declassified because of an illegal bike change

Stage-by-Stage Results for the 1906 Tour de France			Stage Winner	Race Leader
Thu 19 Jul	Rest day			
Stage 9 Fri 20 Jul	Bayonne Bordeaux 16 finishers	338 km 12h03'00" 28.0 kph	Louis Trousselier (Fra) Peugeot	René Pottier (Fra) Peugeot
Sat 21 Jul	Rest day			
Stage 10 Sun 22 Jul	Bordeaux to Nantes 15 finishers	391 km 15h21'00" 25.5 kph	Louis Trousselier (Fra) Peugeot	René Pottier (Fra) Peugeot
Mon 23 Jul	Rest day			
Stage 11 Tue 24 Jul	Nantes to Brest 14 finishers	321 km 12h54'00" 24.9 kph	Louis Trousselier (Fra) Peugeot	René Pottier (Fra) Peugeot
Wed 25 Jul	Rest day			
Stage 12 Thu 26 Jul	Brest to Caen 14 finishers	415 km 18h25'00" 22.5 kph	Georges Passerieu (Fra) Peugeot	René Pottier (Fra) Peugeot
Fri 27 Jul Sat 28 Jul	Rest day			
Stage 13 Sun 29 Jul	Caen to Paris (Parc des Princes) 14 finishers	259 km 8h04'52" 32.1 kph	René Pottier (Fra) Peugeot	René Pottier (Fra) Peugeot

Prize fund: 25,000 francs (5,000 francs first prize)

Final Classification

Place	Rider	Team	Points	Age
1	René Pottier (Fra)	Peugeot	4,637 km 189h34'00" 24.463 kph 31 pts	23
2	Georges Passerieu (Fra)	Peugeot	39 pts	20
3	Louis Trousselier (Fra)	Peugeot	61 pts	25
4	Lucien Petit-Breton (Fra)	Peugeot	65 pts	23
5	Émile Georget (Fra)	Alycon	80 pts	24
6	Aloïs Catteau (Bel)	Alycon	129 pts	28
7	Édouard Wattellier (Fra)	Labor	137 pts	29
8	Léon Georget (Fra)	Alcyon	152 pts	26
9	Eugène Christophe (Fra)	Labor	156 pts	21
10	Anthony Wattellier (Fra)	Alcyon	168 pts	26
Lanterne Rouge				
14	Georges Bronchard (Fra)	Biguet	256 pts	19
Coureurs de Vitesse				
	René Pottier (Fra)	Peugeot		23
Coureurs sur Machines Poinçonnées				
	Lucien Petit-Breton	Peugeot		23
Meilleur Grimpeur				
	René Pottier (Fra)	Peugeot		23

1907: Tough Rabbits

Over the closed season Alcyon lured 1905's Tour winner Louis Trousselier away from Peugeot, and Trou-Trou opened his account at the 1907 Tour by showing his superiority on the *pavé* en route to Roubaix (he had won Paris-Roubaix in 1905), taking the stage win and the overall lead for the men in the sky-blue jerseys.

The race's second stage once more took the Tour into the occupied lands of Alsace-Lorraine, this time for the race's first 'foreign' stage finish, in Metz. In the sprint for the line it was Trousselier versus two Peugeot riders, his former team-mate Lucien Petit-Breton and Émile Georget, who had taken the opposite route to Trousselier over the closed season and switched from Alcyon to Peugeot. Georget beat Trou-Trou by a tyre but, following an appeal from Alcyon, the result was declared a dead heat.

En route to Belfort Trou-Trou suffered mechanical misfortune and had to borrow a spectator's bike. The best he could manage was sixth, with Georget this time indisputably taking the win, which gave him the race lead. More punctures the next stage for Trou-Trou and another stage win for Georget dropped Trousselier down the rankings to third.

Now it was the Peugeot man's turn to show his stuff. He had briefly led the race the previous year, when in Alcyon's colours he took the opening stage, only to tumble down the general classification as the race went on, boils hampering him as he rode. On the road to Lyon, Mimile – as Georget was affectionately known – marked the 1906 Bordeaux-Paris winner Marcel Cadolle (Alcyon), who took the stage win with Georget hot on his heels. Cadolle made clear at the stage end that he was gunning for the overall win: 'the rider who puts his name on the list of winners of the Tour de France is a tough rabbit and I want to tell you, I am a tough rabbit.'

More mechanical misfortunes blighted Trou-Trou on the road to Lyon, tumbling him down the general classification, any hope of overall victory gone on the wind. Georget's next most likely challengers were Alcyon's Cadolle and his own Peugeot team-mate Petit-Breton who, having won the *poinçonnées* category the year before, was once more riding as one of the riders who had to fix his bike if it broke down and couldn't swap to a new machine. In Grenoble Georget led home François Faber. This pushed his lead over Cadolle from two points to seven. That opened to 10 points at the run down to Nice. With eight stages remaining, Georget was looking good for the win.

For Cadolle, Nîmes saw the end of his hopes to show just how tough a rabbit he was, not just in this Tour, but ever. Sprinting for third place in a group of six he tangled with Augustin Ringeval (Labor) and went down, crashing into a cart of barrels and smashing his knee. Ringeval was also injured in the crash and that evening in Nîmes his *directeur sportif*, Alphonse Baugé, engaged the services of a female masseur to tend to his injuries, enabling him to continue the race.

Ahead of the crash, Trousselier took the points for third place, with Georget already having led home Petit-Breton nearly 40 minutes earlier. This moved Trou-Trou back up to second, 15 points down on Georget. Petit-Breton also moved up, but with 26 points separating him from first place all he seemed to have to ride for was a second victory in the *poinçonnées* category.

Alcyon's bad luck Tour continued on the run across to Toulouse, Trousselier yet again being beset by problems with his bike. Georget made good use of his rival's misfortune and pushed hard, taking his fifth stage win of the race. In a new tweak to the points system, the tallies were recalculated mid-race to take account of riders no longer in the race. The net effect of this and of the day's racing was that Georget's lead on Trousselier rose by just one point, to 16, while Petit-Breton closed his gap to 23 points in arrears.

And then came Bayonne and controversy. Early into the stage Trou-Trou was yet again forced off his bike. Petit-Breton struck out for home alone, putting in a solo break of more than 200 kilometres to take the stage win, while Georget arrived in fourth place with Trousselier in eleventh. This dropped Trou-Trou from second to third, with Petit-Breton leap-frogging him. Georget's lead was now 20 points.

Then Alcyon's *directeur sportif*, Edmond Gentil, decided to lodge a complaint with the commissaires. Georget, he pointed out, had punctured during the stage and taken the bike of his team-mate Pierre-Gonzague Privat. This, Gentil pointed out, happened outside of one of the allowed change zones and was therefore illegal. Gentil demanded that Georget be dropped to last on the stage. With 48 riders having finished that day this would have dropped Mimile down the general classification and brought Trou-Trou back up to second, just three points behind Petit-Breton.

But Gentil didn't just leave it at lodging a complaint, he issued an ultimatum: either the commissaires punish Georget that night or he would pull the Alcyon riders from the race. The race referees refused to be rushed. So Gentil carried out his threat and the sky-blue jerseys of Alcyon were absent when the stage to Bordeaux commenced (which, given all the mechanical mishaps already suffered by Troussellier, probably saved him from further embarrassment).

The commissaires, though, had finally reached a decision on how to punish Georget: Mimile was dropped to last on the Bayonne stage and his points tally adjusted accordingly. The net effect of this and of his finishing third into Bordeaux was that Mimile now dropped to third overall, behind his Peugeot team-mates Gustave Garrigou and Petit-Breton, with the latter now leading the Tour de France. Peugeot's *directeur sportif*, Léopold Alibert, may have been unhappy with the punishment levied on Georget, but at least his riders were still in control of the race.

From there until Paris nothing troubled the Peugeot riders and Petit-Breton rode into the City of Lights as the winner of the fifth Tour de France. Whether he was the toughest rabbit in the bunch or just the luckiest was a question that would have to wait until another year.

* * * * *

Like the Tour winner, Alfred Le Bars was from Brittany, but his Tour was very different to the one enjoyed by Petit-Breton. Riding without support Le Bars crashed on the opening stage and arrived in Roubaix on a borrowed bike. There he was advised by Labor's *directeur sportif*, Baugé, to quit the race and go home. But the Breton insisted he had to ride on, for the Tour would be passing his home, Morlaix, and he had to get there as part of the race, or else he would be taken for a fool. In an act of kindness – or cruelty if you consider that Morlaix would not be reached until the race's penultimate stage – Baugé decided to provide Le Bars with a spare Labor bike and other provisions.

Each day Le Bars – getting visibly thinner and thinner as the Tour rolled on – rode home hours and hours after the stage had been won: four in Metz; two in Belfort; four in Lyon; six in Grenoble; seven in Nice; ten in Nîmes; three in Toulouse; three in Bayonne; one in Bordeaux; four in Nantes; four in Brest. And then he was on the eve of the stage to Caen, which would take him through his hometown of Morlaix.

That evening he went to Baugé's hotel room and requested a new Labor jersey. Baugé assented to the request and there and then the small Breton donned it: "I can still see him standing there," Baugé wrote in a letter to his Labour boss, "looking in the mirror. The joy on his face! He stood straight as a candle. This is a great thing!" And into Morlaix the next day Le Bars rode like a lion, just two minutes behind the leaders of the Tour de France, the crowd cheering him home as much as they cheered for Petit-Breton. It was a victory, of sorts, and Le Bars celebrated it, there, mid-stage, in Morlaix. By the time he arrived in Caen he was 22 hours behind the stage winner. In Paris he was twenty-sixth of 33 finishers, a *géant de la route*. In that, at least, he was an equal of Petit-Breton.

Stage-by-Stage Results for the 1907 Tour de France			Stage Winner	Race Leader
Stage 1 Mon 8 Jul	Paris (Pont Bineau) to Roubaix 93 starters, 86 finishers	272 km 8h49'30" 30.8 kph	Louis Trousselier (Fra) Alcyon	Louis Trousselier (Fra) Alcyon
Tue 9 Jul	Rest day			
Stage 2 Wed 10 Jul	Roubaix to Metz 80 finishers	398 km 13h39'15" 29.1 kph	Émile Georget (Fra) Peugeot Louis Trousselier (Fra) Alcyon	Louis Trousselier (Fra) Alcyon
Thu 11 Jul	Rest day			
Stage 3 Fri 12 Jul	Metz to Belfort 77 finishers	259 km 7h46'18" 33.3 kph	Émile Georget (Fra) Peugeot	Émile Georget (Fra) Peugeot
	Major climbs: Ballon d'Alsace (1,178m) Émile Georget (Fra) Peugeot			
Sat 13 Jul	Rest day			
Stage 4 Sun 14 Jul	Belfort to Lyon 73 finishers	309 km 9h27'02" 32.7 kph	Marcel Cadolle (Fra) Alcyon	Émile Georget (Fra) Peugeot
	Major climbs: Col du Cerdon (595m) Gustave Garrigou (Fra) Peugeot			
Mon 15 Jul	Rest day			
Stage 5 Tue 16 Jul	Lyon to Grenoble 66 finishers	311 km 11h17'00" 27.7 kph	Émile Georget (Fra) Peugeot	Émile Georget (Fra) Peugeot
	Major climbs: Les Echelles (500m) Émile Georget (Fra) Peugeot + François Faber (Lux) Labor; Col de Porte (1,326m) Émile Georget (Fra) Peugeot			
Wed 17 Jul	Rest day			
Stage 6 Thu 18 Jul	Grenoble to Nice 57 finishers	345 km 12h14'00" 28.2 kph	Georges Passerieu (Fra) Peugeot	Émile Georget (Fra) Peugeot
	Major climbs: Côte de Laffrey (900m) Émile Georget (Fra) Peugeot; Col Bayard (1,246m) Émile Georget (Fra) Peugeot; Estérel (314m) Émile Georget (Fra) Peugeot			
Fri 19 Jul	Rest day			
Stage 7 Sat 20 Jul	Nice to Nîmes 51 finishers	345 km 12h26'00" 27.7 kph	Émile Georget (Fra) Peugeot	Émile Georget (Fra) Peugeot
Sun 21 Jul	Rest day			
Stage 8 Mon 22 Jul	Nîmes to Toulouse 49 finishers	303 km 11h02'00" 27.5 kph	Émile Georget (Fra) Peugeot	Émile Georget (Fra) Peugeot
Tue 23 Jul	Rest day			

Stage-by-Stage Results for the 1907 Tour de France			Stage Winner	Race Leader
Stage 9 Wed 24 Jul	Toulouse to Bayonne 48 finishers	299 km 10h18'00" 29.0 kph	Lucien Petit-Breton (Fra) Peugeot	Émile Georget (Fra) Peugeot
Thu 25 Jul	Rest day			
Stage 10 Fri 26 Jul	Bayonne to Bordeaux 40 finishers	269 km 8h07'50" 33.1 kph	Gustave Garrigou (Fra) Peugeot	Lucien Petit-Breton (Fra) Peugeot
Sat 27 Jul	Rest day			
Stage 11 Sun 28 Jul	Bordeaux to Nantes 35 finishers	391 km 14h33'21" 26.9 kph	Lucien Petit-Breton (Fra) Peugeot	Lucien Petit-Breton (Fra) Peugeot
Mon 29 Jul	Rest day			
Stage 12 Tue 30 Jul	Nantes to Brest 34 finishers	321 km 12h23'00" 25.9 kph	Gustave Garrigou (Fra) Peugeot	Lucien Petit-Breton (Fra) Peugeot
Wed 30 Jul	Rest day			
Stage 13 Thu 1 Aug	Brest to Caen 33 finishers	415 km 16h13'30" 25.6 kph	Émile Georget (Fra) Peugeot	Lucien Petit-Breton (Fra) Peugeot
Fri 2 Aug Sat 3 Aug	Rest days			
Stage 14 Sun 4 Aug	Caen to Paris (Parc des Princes) 33 finishers	251 km 8h44'51" 28.7 kph	Georges Passerieu (Fra) Peugeot	Lucien Petit-Breton (Fra) Peugeot

Prize fund: 25,000 francs (4,000 francs first prize)

Final Classification

Place	Rider	Team	Points	Age
1	Lucien Petit-Breton (Fra)	Peugeot	4,488 km 158h45'05" 28.470 kph 47 pts	24
2	Gustave Garrigou (Fra)	Peugeot	66	22
3	Émile Georget (Fra)	Peugeot	74	25
4	Georges Passerieu (Fra)	Peugeot	85	21
5	François Beaugendre (Fra)	Peugeot	123	27
6	Eberardo Pavesi (Ita)	Otav	150	23
7	François Faber (Lux)	Labor	156	20
8	Augustin Ringeval (Fra)	Labor	184	25
9	Aloïs Catteau (Bel)	Unsponsored	196	29
10	Ferdinand Payan (Fra)	Unsponsored	227	37
Lanterne Rouge				
33	Albert Chartier (Fra)	Unsponsored	568	
Coureurs de Vitesse				
	Gustave Garrigou (Fra)	Peugeot		22
Coureurs sur Machines Poinçonnées				
	Lucien Petit-Breton (Fra)	Peugeot		24
Meilleur Grimpeur				
	Émile Georget	Peugeot		25

1908: The Argentine

For some, Lucien Petit-Breton was just the winner by default of the 1907 Tour, the man who profited the most from the misfortune meted out to Émile Georget by the commissaires. In 1908 the man they called the Argentine returned to the Tour again and this time he put in a performance that was so dominating that it silenced all doubters.

Like Henri Cornet before him – who was really Henri Jardy – Lucien Petit-Breton was not born with the name he became famous under. Born Lucien Mazan in Plessé, near Nantes, in 1882, Petit-Breton was put into the care of an aunt while his parents sailed for Buenos Ares and the dream of a new life in Argentina. Two years later the family was reunited and it was in Argentina that Petit-Breton spent his formative years. And it was in Argentina that he developed a passion for cycling, first from reading about races back in France, and then by becoming a star of the local track scene. His father – a respectable watchmaker – not approving of cycling, the son took the name Lucien Breton to ride under and it was with that name that he became the champion of Argentina.

In 1902 Petit-Breton returned to France, to carry out his military service. He also took some time out to race, mostly on the track. There being another rider called Breton, he added a Petit to his name. In 1902 he finished second in the Bol d'Or, an important 24-hour track race. The next year he was entered for the first Tour but failed to take the start. In 1904 he returned to the Bol d'Or and took the win. He was also – originally – second overall in that year's Bordeaux-Paris but had that stripped from him when the French cycling federation took a look at events in that race and rewrote the results.

Riding his first Tour in 1905, in the colours of Cycles JC, Petit-Breton placed well on most stages and finished fifth overall. A month later he set a new distance for the Hour record, riding 41.110 kilometres at the Vélodrome Buffalo, beating the American William Hamilton's seven-year-old record by 329 metres. That feat must have pleased Henri Desgrange somewhat, he having the distinction of setting the first official Hour record in 1893, shortly after the creation of cycling's first international governing body.

In 1906 – now riding for Peugeot – Petit-Breton returned to the Tour and finished fourth overall, as well as being the fastest rider in the *poinçonnées* category. The following year he took a somewhat controversial victory in the newly created Milan-Sanremo race. Riding for Bianchi – riders often switched teams for the day when they raced outside of their native country – Petit-Breton's win had been aided somewhat by Giovanni Gerbi (a Bianchi team-mate) knocking Gustave Garrigou off his bike just as Garrigou looked set for the win. Then came the 1907 Tour, Georget's bad luck and the victory some saw as being tainted.

Petit-Breton had followed his 1907 Tour win by crossing the Atlantic for the Madison Square Garden International Six Day Race, an event he'd previously ridden three times between 1903 and 1905. Doping was widespread – and widely reported – at Six Day races. But, back then, it was a grey area, not the black and white we see it as today. There was no prohibition against it, and the products used were all legally available and widely used beyond sport. Even so, some railed against it, and some pointed the finger at certain riders and said they doped. Petit-Breton – perhaps because of his association with the Sixes – was one such rider. And so he became the first Tour winner who had to publicly deny his use of doping, saying it would have been impossible for him to have survived such treatment for the four weeks of the Tour.

At the 1908 Tour – for which Petit-Breton had specially reconnoitred sections in advance, the better to prepare for victory – the Argentine opened his account with a second on the first stage, his team-mate Georges Passerieu taking the win and the overall lead. The next day the positions were reversed, Petit-Breton

The start of the 1908 Tour.

finishing first with Passerieu second, resulting in the two sharing the overall lead. Then on the third stage Petit-Breton took control as Passerieu fell victim to the bad luck of a broken saddle followed later by a crash.

From there all the way back to Paris, Petit-Breton was fully in control, with no one rising to challenge him. The Argentine added another three stage wins to his tally and rode into Paris to become the second rider to score back-to-back victories – after Maurice Garin's 1903 and 1904 performances – but the first to keep them. The doubters were silenced.

For Louis Trousselier it was another Tour to forget. Though he'd shown he still had the legs by winning Bordeaux-Paris earlier in the season, bad luck – and bad bikes – once again laid him low. Crashing on the opening stage he damaged the frame of his bike. When his bike was checked before the start of the second stage the commissaires realised it wasn't the same bike he had started the race on. The *poinçonnées* experiment of the previous three Tours having worked so well, Desgrange and his team had decreed that all riders had to start and finish on the same bike, with any mechanical problems having to be repaired rather than the rider simply taking a new bike. Trou-Trou was thrown off the Tour. His *directeur sportif*, Gentil, complained, but the decision was final.

Throughout the Tour the London-born Georges Passerieu (Peugeot) had once again shown that one day he might win the race himself. But the real revelation of the race was a docker from the Colombes suburb of Paris, François Faber, who had debuted the year before, a member of the Labor squad bossed by Alphonse Baugé. Born to a French mother and a father from Luxembourg, Faber stood five foot eight inches tall and tipped the scales at close to 90 kilograms, earning him the nickname the Giant of Colombes. In 1908 Faber was a giant among giants, for this was the year that all who finished the Tour were officially recognised as *géants de la route*, a term that Victor Breyer and Robert Coquelle had first coined back in 1899.

For *L'Auto* the Tour was becoming ever more profitable. The paper's ciculation was now up 140,000 copies throughout the year, with that climbing to 250,000 during the Tour. Labor and the tyre manufacturer Hutchinson had also come on board, sponsoring the *meilleur grimpeur* prize L'*Auto* had been awarding since 1906. Perhaps showing just how much the French had taken the race to their heart, the Tour also saw a woman shadow-riding it.

Marie Marvingt was a French adventurer who was rarely afraid to turn her hand to something new. She sought permission from L'*Auto* to enter the Tour, but her entry was refused. (As had, in 1904, a request from one of L'*Auto*'s readers that the paper organise a women's version of the race.) Marvingt was not the type to be put off by such a setback and so she decided to trail the race, setting off behind the *peloton* and following in their wheel tracks.

With five stage wins for Petit-Breton, four for Faber, three for Passeriu and one each for Jean-Baptiste Dortignacq and Georges Paulmier, Peugeot's lion cubs made it a complete whitewash. The other teams – most notably the poorly organised Alcyon and Labor squads – must have wondered if they had any future in the race against such opposition. But Peugeot's bosses were about to make a decision which would quickly change all that. And would see the French riders put in the shade in their own Tour.

Stage-by-Stage Results for the 1908 Tour de France			Stage Winner	Race Leader
Stage 1 Mon 13 Jul	Paris (Pont Bineau) to Roubaix 114 starters, 106 finishers	272 km 8h27'00" 32.2 kph	Georges Passerieu (Fra) Peugeot	Georges Passerieu (Fra) Peugeot
Tue 14 Jul	Rest day			
Stage 2 Wed 15 Jul	Roubaix to Metz 98 finishers	398 km 13h12'00" 30.2 kph	Lucien Petit-Breton (Fra) Peugeot	Georges Passerieu (Fra) Peugeot
				Lucien Petit-Breton (Fra) Peugeot
Thu 16 Jul	Rest day			
Stage 3 Fri 17 Jul	Metz to Belfort 87 finishers	259 km 9h13'00" 28.1 kph	François Faber (Fra) Peugeot (1)	Lucien Petit-Breton (Fra) Peugeot
	Major climbs: Ballon d'Alsace (1,178m) Gustave Garrigou (Fra) Peugeot			
Sat 18 Jul	Rest day			

Stage-by-Stage Results for the 1908 Tour de France			Stage Winner	Race Leader
Stage 4 Sun 19 Jul	Belfort to Lyon 58 finishers	309 km 9h52'03" 31.3 kph	François Faber (Fra) Peugeot (1)	Lucien Petit-Breton (Fra) Peugeot
	Major climbs: Col du Cerdon (595m) Maurice Brocco (Fra) Griffon			
Mon 20 Jul	Rest day			
Stage 5 Tue 21 Jul	Lyon to Grenoble 51 finishers	311 km 11h08'00" 27.9 kph	Georges Passerieu (Fra) Peugeot	Lucien Petit-Breton (Fra) Peugeot
	Major climbs: Col de Porte (1,326m) Georges Passerieu (Fra) Peugeot			
Wed 22 Jul	Rest day			
Stage 6 Thu 23 Jul	Grenoble to Nice 45 finishers	345 km 12h12'00" 28.3 kph	Jean-Baptiste Dortignacq (Fra) Peugeot	Lucien Petit-Breton (Fra) Peugeot
	Major climbs: Col Bayard (1,246m) André Pottier (Fra) Peugeot, Côte de Laffrey (900m) André Pottier (Fra) Peugeot			
Fri 24 Jul	Rest day			
Stage 7 Sat 25 Jul	Nice to Nîmes 42 finishers	354 km 12h05'00" 29.3 kph	Lucien Petit-Breton (Fra) Peugeot	Lucien Petit-Breton (Fra) Peugeot
Sun 26 Jul	Rest day			
Stage 8 Mon 27 Jul	Nîmes to Toulouse 39 finishers	303 km 11h08'00" 27.2 kph	François Faber (Fra) Peugeot (1)	Lucien Petit-Breton (Fra) Peugeot
Tue 28 Jul	Rest day			
Stage 9 Wed 29 Jul	Toulouse to Bayonne 37 finishers	299 km 10h07'00" 29.6 kph	Lucien Petit-Breton (Fra) Peugeot	Lucien Petit-Breton (Fra) Peugeot
Thu 30 Jul	Rest day			
Stage 10 Fri 31 Jul	Bayonne to Bordeaux 37 finishers	269 km 8h25'00" 32.0 kph	Georges Paulmier (Fra) Peugeot	Lucien Petit-Breton (Fra) Peugeot
Sat 1 Aug	Rest day			
Stage 11 Sun 2 Aug	Bordeaux to Nantes 36 finishers	391 km 14h05'00" 27.8 kph	Lucien Petit-Breton (Fra) Peugeot	Lucien Petit-Breton (Fra) Peugeot
Mon 3 Aug	Rest day			
Stage 12 Tue 4 Aug	Nantes to Brest 36 finishers	321 km 11h08'00" 28.8 kph	François Faber (Fra) Peugeot (1)	Lucien Petit-Breton (Fra) Peugeot

Stage-by-Stage Results for the 1908 Tour de France			Stage Winner	Race Leader
Wed 5 Aug	Rest day			
Stage 13 Thu 6 Aug	Brest to Caen 36 finishers	415 km 16h23'00" 25.3 kph	Georges Passerieu (Fra) Peugeot	Lucien Petit-Breton (Fra) Peugeot
Fri 7 Aug	Rest days			
Sat 8 Aug				
Stage 14 Sun 9 Aug	Caen to Paris (Parc des Princes) 36 finishers	251 km 8h41'18" 29.2 kph	Lucien Petit-Breton (Fra) Peugeot	Lucien Petit-Breton (Fra) Peugeot

(1) Born in Paris to a French mother and father from Luxembourg, Faber took the latter's nationality from 1909 forward but in 1908 was riding as a Frenchman.

Prize fund: 30,000 francs (4,000 francs first prize)

Final Classification				
Place	**Rider**	**Team**	**Points**	**Age**
1	Lucien Petit-Breton (Fra)	Peugeot	4,488 km 156h53'29" 28.740 kph 36 pts	25
2	François Faber (Fra) (1)	Peugeot	68	21
3	Georges Passerieu (Fra)	Peugeot	75	22
4	Gustave Garrigou (Fra)	Peugeot	91	23
5	Luigi Ganna (Ita)	Alcyon	120	24
6	Georges Paulmier (Fra)	Peugeot	125	25
7	Georges Fleury (Fra)	Peugeot	134	30
8	Henri Cornet (Fra)	Peugeot	142	24
9	Marcel Godivier (Fra)	Alcyon	153	21
10	Giovanni Rossignoli (Ita)	Bianchi	160	25
Lanterne Rouge				
36	Henri Anthoine (Fra)		512	30
Pneus Démontables				
	François Faber (Fra)	Peugeot		21
Meilleur Grimpeur				
	Gustave Garrigou (Fra)	Peugeot		23

1909: Rivals

At the end of the 1908 Tour Lucien Petit-Breton – who, with team bonuses added to his winnings during the race, had pocketed 30,000 francs for his efforts – announced his retirement and anointed François Faber – now a citizen of Luxembourg – as his successor. But the little Argentine wasn't long enjoying the quiet life before he was coaxed back to the sport. Only it wasn't to ride the Tour. It was to compete in the Tour's first real rival, the Giro d'Italia.

Over the previous six years, *L'Auto* had seen off any challengers in the circulation wars and, on the racing front, established the Tour as the pre-eminent road race of the era. Important enough to attract the attention of Italian journalists, with *La Gazzetta dello Sport* being in attendance to report the 1907 and 1908 races. In August 1908 the *Gazzetta*'s owners announced that they would be launching a Tour of Italy, the Giro d'Italia. And to help their race along they lured Petit-Breton – who had won the first edition of the *Gazzetta*-organised Milan-Sanremo – to once more throw his leg over a bike. And, unlike the Tour which was still nominally a race for individuals, the Giro's organisers were clear from the start: theirs was a race for teams.

Responding to this – and accepting the reality of the previous six years – Desgrange and his team at *L'Auto* decided that they too would have to welcome teams to their race if they were not to be outdone by the Giro. Thus 38 of the 150 starters were riders grouped in the colours of Alcyon, Atala, Biguet, Felsina, Le Globe, Legnano and Nil, with the rest riding as *isolés*, unsupported individuals who had to fend for themselves throughout the race. Missing from that list of teams was Peugeot.

Having won the race four times in a row, the Peugeot bosses decided to take a different approach to promoting their bikes. They decided to ignore the Tour and organise their own race. Or, more precisely, a series of races, the Circuit Français, made up of 15 different races.

The Alcyon bosses, having now put teams into three Tours and not been able to break the Peugeot dominance, seized their opportunity and stepped things up a gear, recruiting some of the best of Peugeot's lion cubs and bringing in a new *directeur sportif*, Alphonse Baugé.

The inaugural Giro d'Italia ended on 13 May and, eight weeks later, its winner, Luigi Ganna, was taking the line at the Tour, ready to add another 4,407 kilometres of racing to the 2,448 he'd raced in Italy. Although he'd come out of retirement to ride the Giro, Petit-Breton opted not to defend his Tour title. The winners of the 1904 and 1905 Tours were there, Henri Cornet riding for the Nil squad and Louis Trousselier once again wearing Alcyon's sky-blue jersey. But the man to watch was one of Trou-Trou's team-mates, François Faber.

Faber dominated the race's early mountain stages, through the Vosges, along the western edge of the Alps and across the Chartreuse Massif, taking five stages in a row between Metz and Nice, a new record for back-to-back stage wins. Even in Lyon, where the Giant of Colombe's chain snapped a kilometre before the finish line, Faber came out on top, running with his bike to cross the line 10 minutes ahead of the next rider home.

After that the Alcyon star was able to show some largesse, allowing his step-brother Ernest Paul – who was riding as one of the unsupported riders – to take a stage. That win helped Paul assure his victory in the *isolé* category, the best unsupported rider in the race. Faber's team-mates Jean Alavoine, Trousselier, Gustave Garrigou and Paul Duboc also took stage wins, and Faber himself added a sixth to his tally.

Faber's victory was the first overall win for a non-French rider – six years after the Italian-born Maurice Garin had taken the first victory for France – and the 1909 race was the first time French riders hadn't dominated the race. Only twice before had non-French riders won stages in the race's brief history: Switzerland's Charles Laeser in 1903 (he had abandoned the race on the third stage and then rejoined the race just for the stage glory) and his compatriot Michel Frédérick in 1904 (only after the results were rewritten). But in 1909 French riders only managed to win seven of the 14 stages, for as well as the six won by Faber, the opening stage to Roubaix had been taken by the Belgian one-day specialist Cyrille van Hauwaert (Alcyon), the first of Belgium's hard men to make an impression on the Tour.

Van Hauwaert already had wins in Bordeaux-Paris (1907 and 1909), Milan-Sanremo (1908) and Paris-Roubaix (1908) on his *palmarès* and his successes had helped drive the popularity of road racing in Belgium, with new races being added to the calendar. The previous year the Liège-Bastogne-Liège classic was revived after a 15-year absence – because of its origins in 1892 the race is today referred to as *la doyenne*, the old lady. Belgians were getting more and more opportunities to prove their toughness.

Asked at the end of the race what he planned to do next Faber replied that he intended to go fishing and not return until the September end-of-season classics.

Stage-by-Stage Results for the 1909 Tour de France			Stage Winner	Race Leader
Stage 1 Mon 5 Jul	Paris (Pont de la Jatte) to Roubaix 150 starters, 142 finishers	272 km 9h18'00" 29.2 kph	Cyrille van Hauwaert (Bel) Alcyon	Cyrille van Hauwaert (Bel) Alcyon
Tue 6 Jul	Rest day			
Stage 2 Wed 7 Jul	Roubaix to Metz 133 finishers	398 km 14h09'00" 28.1 kph	François Faber (Lux) Alcyon	François Faber (Lux) Alcyon
Thu 8 Jul	Rest day			
Stage 3 Fri 9 Jul	Metz to Belfort 105 finishers	259 km 9h28'00" 27.4 kph	François Faber (Lux) Alcyon	François Faber (Lux) Alcyon
	Major climbs: Ballon d'Alsace (1,178m) François Faber (Lux) Alcyon			
Sat 10 Jul	Rest day			

Stage-by-Stage Results for the 1909 Tour de France				Stage Winner	Race Leader
Stage 4 Sun 11 Jul	Belfort to Lyon 93 finishers		309 km 10h44'00" 28.8 kph	François Faber (Lux) Alcyon	François Faber (Lux) Alcyon
	Major climbs: Col du Cerdon (595m) Ernest Paul (Fra) Unsponsored				
Mon 12 Jul	Rest day				
Stage 5 Tue 13 Jul	Lyon to Grenoble 79 finishers		311 km 11h12'00" 27.8 kph	François Faber (Lux) Alcyon	François Faber (Lux) Alcyon
	Major climbs: Les Echelles (500m) François Faber (Lux) Alcyon; Col de Porte (1,326m) François Faber (Lux) Alcyon				
Wed 14 Jul	Rest day				
Stage 6 Thu 15 Jul	Grenoble to Nice 73 finishers		345 km 12h09'00" 28.4 kph	François Faber (Lux) Alcyon	François Faber (Lux) Alcyon
	Major climbs: Col Bayard (1,246m) François Faber (Lux) Alcyon; Côte de Laffrey (900m) François Faber (Lux) Alcyon + Gustave Garrigou (Fra) Alcyon				
Fri 16 Jul	Rest day				
Stage 7 Sat 17 Jul	Nice to Nîmes 72 finishers		354 km 12h43'00" 27.8 kph	Ernest Paul (Fra) Unsponsored	François Faber (Lux) Alcyon
Mon 18 Jul	Rest day				
Stage 8 Mon 19 Jul	Nîmes to Toulouse 71 finishers		303 km 10h10'10" 29.8 kph	Jean Alavoine (Fra) Alcyon	François Faber (Lux) Alcyon
Tue 20 Jul	Rest day				
Stage 9 Wed 21 Jul	Toulouse to Bayonne 69 finishers		299 km 9h59'00" 29.9 kph	Constant Ménager (Fra) Le Globe	François Faber (Lux) Alcyon
Thu 22 Jul	Rest day				
Stage 10 Fri 23 Jul	Bayonne to Bordeaux 68 finishers		269 km 8h02'00" 33.5 kph	François Faber (Lux) Alcyon	François Faber (Lux) Alcyon
Sat 24 Jul	Rest day				
Stage 11 Sun 25 Jul	Bordeaux to Nantes 61 finishers		391 km 12h47'00" 30.6 kph	Louis Trousselier (Fra) Alcyon	François Faber (Lux) Alcyon
Mon 26 Jul	Rest day				
Stage 12 Tue 27 Jul	Nantes to Brest 55 finishers		321 km 11h18'00" 28.4 kph	Gustave Garrigou (Fra) Alcyon	François Faber (Lux) Alcyon

Stage-by-Stage Results for the 1909 Tour de France			Stage Winner	Race Leader
Wed 28 Jul	Rest day			
Stage 13 Thu 29 Jul	Brest to Caen 55 finishers	424 km 15h02'00" 27.6 kph	Paul Duboc (Fra) Alcyon	François Faber (Lux) Alcyon
Fri 30 Jul	Rest days			
Sat 31 Jul				
Stage 14 Sun 1 Aug	Caen to Paris (Parc des Princes) 55 finishers	250 km 8h53'00" 28.3 kph	Jean Alavoine (Fra) Alcyon	François Faber (Lux) Alcyon

Prize fund: 25,000 francs (4,000 francs first prize)

Final Classification

Place	Rider	Team	Points	Age
1	François Faber (Lux)	Alcyon	4,497 km 157h01'22" 28.658 kph 37 pts	22
2	Gustave Garrigou (Fra)	Alcyon	57	25
3	Jean Alavoine (Fra)	Alcyon	66	22
4	Paul Duboc (Fra)	Alcyon	70	26
5	Cyrille van Hauwaert (Bel)	Alcyon	92	26
6	Ernest Paul (Fra)	Unsponsored	95	28
7	Constant Ménager (Fra)	Le Globe	102	21
8	Louis Trousselier (Fra)	Alcyon	114	29
9	Eugène Christophe (Fra)	Unsponsored	139	25
10	Aldo Bettini (Ita)	Unsponsored	142	24
Lanterne Rouge				
55	Georges Devilly (Fra)	Unsponsored	713	
Inependents				
	Ernest Paul (Fra)	Unsponsored		28
Meilleur Grimpeur				
	François Faber (Lux)	Alcyon		23

1910: Assassins!

The 1910 cycling season kicked into high gear on Sunday 3 April, with the fourth edition of Milan-Sanremo classic, organised by the Italian newspaper *La Gazzetta dello Sport*. The weather was atrocious, with 20 centimetres of snow on the Turchino Pass. Of the 65 riders who took the start only four completed the 290 kilometres to Sanremo and it was a man whose name would soon become synonymous with the Tour de France who prevailed: Eugène Christophe.

Christophe had raced the 1909 Tour as one of the *isolés* and his ninth place finish helped attract the attention of Alycon's *directeur sportif*, Alphonse Baugé, who had an eye for talent and the ability to get the best from it (Baugé had written a training manual based on the techniques of the notorious – but highly successful – English trainer James 'Choppy' Warburton). His April 1910 win, though, came at the cost of a month's hospitalisation for the 25-year-old Christophe and he was in no state to start the Tour. His time, though, would come.

The bosses at Peugeot were still of the opinion they didn't need the Tour and, following the success of their Circuit Français series of races the previous year, they took on the Tour with a full stage race, the Tour de France des Indépéndents, a race for the recently created category of riders between amateurs and professionals riding with manufacturer-sponsored teams. This took place after the Tour had ended, between 9 August and 4 September and helped showcase some names that would go on to make an impact on the Tour in future years.

Alcyon, Legnano and Le Globe were the only three manufacturers who fielded 10-man squads for the eighth Tour, bringing with them past winners François Faber, Louis Trousselier (both Alcyon), Lucien Petit-Breton (Legnano) and Henri Cornet (Le Globe). The other 80 riders all rode as unsupported *isolés*.

Émile Georget, riding for Alcyon, was still looking to fulfil the promise he'd shown in earlier Tours and, with victory in May at Bordeaux-Paris, was one of the riders expected to perform. Faber, though, as the defending champion, was the odds-on favourite. He had carried his Tour-winning form into Paris-Tours the previous season after having enjoyed his fishing holiday, adding that to his list of victories. But there was a new kid on the block who was about to upset Faber's applecart: his Alcyon team-mate Octave Lapize, who had won back-to-back victories in Paris-Roubaix in 1909 and 1910.

Faber also had another opponent to deal with: the Pyrenees. The previous year Desgrange, acknowledging the competition the Tour now faced from the Giro d'Italia and Peugeot's entry into the race organising game, noted that the Tour was at a turning point in its history and had suggested that maybe it would have to visit the French-held colonies of Tunisia or Algeria. Or, he said, maybe the race should tackle the Pyrenees in the same way it had been tackling the Alps since 1905. For Alphonse Steinès, the man with most responsibility for the Tour's route, this was the opportunity he was waiting for and, instead of tackling the foothills of the Pyrenees, he suggested taking the race right into their heart.

Steinès was a fan of the mountains that separated France and Spain and his determination to see them included in the race led him to reconnoitring possible routes early in 1910 and seeing if any road improvements were necessary. His determination also led him to getting lost in the snow while crossing the Tourmalet and then sending a telegram back to headquarters which was more than somewhat economical with the *actualité*, telling Desgrange that he'd crossed the Tourmalet and that the roads were in very good condition.

The addition of the high mountains on France's southern border added an extra stage to the race – bringing it up to 15, with only six of them below 300 kilometres. With a rest day following every stage, the overall duration of the race was now stretched out to 29 days, the race virtually filling the whole of July. To help sweep up stragglers – and to monitor events at the back of the race – *L'Auto* added a vehicle to the race convoy, the *voiture ballai*, or broom wagon.

Faber was able to take control of the race on the second stage and, while he wasn't as dominant through the Vosges and down into the Chartreuse Massif as he had been the previous year, he arrived on the Côte d'Azur with a solid lead over his team-mates Gustave Garrigou (12 points in arrears) and Cyrille van Hauwaert (a further three points back). Lapize, who had had a bad day en route to Lyon where mechanical problems caused him to lose 20 points to Faber (he had to finish the stage on foot), was 19 points in arrears arriving in Nice.

Adolphe Hélière, a 22-year-old riding as an *isolé*, had spent most of the race up to Nice finishing with the back markers, long after the stage was won. On the rest day he went for a swim in the Mediterranean where he got into trouble – some say he was stung by jellyfish, others that he had a stroke – and died, the first time the *peloton* had suffered a fatality during the race.

Lapize's gap to Faber closed to 15 points in the two transition stages taking the race to Perpignan, and then the riders were into the high mountains. There Tatave – as Lapize was affectionately known – went on the rampage, taking both stages. As he crossed the Aubisque – where he was chasing one of the *isolés*, François Lafourcade, who had briefly taken the lead on the stage – Victor Breyer sought a quote to add to his report for *L'Auto* and shouted a question to Tatave. To which he received the immortal reply: "You're assassins! You're criminals!"

Lapize came out of the mountains 10 points in arrears of Faber, after the latter had finished third on both stages (as with the previous two Tours, the points tally was again recalculated midway through the race, which benefited Lapize one point more than it did Faber). With five stages remaining, the odds favoured Faber, but Tatave pulled back another three points on the road to Bordeaux. Then, on the twelfth stage, taking the riders up to Nantes, Faber got taken down by a dog, broke his handlebars and lost another six points to his team-mate. Lapize was now just one point in arrears.

Racing out to Brest on the next stage Lapize could see that Faber hadn't fully recovered from the injuries he sustained in his crash. And so he put the boot in. At the stage's end he'd distanced Faber enough to take the race lead, with a margin of three points over his unfortunate team-mate.

Again Lapize went on the attack on the penultimate stage, to Caen, and again he put three points into Faber. On the rest day in Caen he was able to relax and enjoy himself, taking the time to enjoy his first flight in an airplane. Faber spent the day in his bed.

When Lapize punctured just three kilometres into the final stage, Faber returned the compliment that had been given to him the previous two days of racing and attacked his team-mate. And with him went eight other riders. Faber needed seven points to win the race, so all he had to do was get this group to the finish ahead of Lapize and himself finish at least third in the sprint. Faber's Tour hopes were still alive, even at the last gasp.

But, one by one, his breakaway companions fell away, until they were just four. And then Faber punctured, finishing last of the quartet. All that mattered now was how far back Lapize was. Eleven minutes after Faber crossed the line the next rider came home. Aldo Bettini. Another four minutes passed before the next rider appeared. Lapize, his Tour saved in the race's dying kilometres.

With nine stage wins, the first four places on general classification and the best climber title all to Alcyon's credit the men in the sky-blue jerseys were now dominating the Tour in the same way Peugeot had. Four years earlier, when they first came to the race, the company was selling just shy of 10,000 bikes a year. With the successes the team had brought the company – particularly in the last two years – that had now risen to just shy of 32,000. The Tour wasn't just good for selling newspapers.

Stage-by-Stage Results for the 1910 Tour de France			Stage Winner	Race Leader
Stage 1 Sun 3 Jul	Paris (Pont de la Jatte) to Roubaix 110 starters, 100 finishers	269 km 8h54'00" 30.6 kph	Charles Crupelandt (Fra) Le Globe	Charles Crupelandt (Fra) Le Globe
Mon 4 Jul	Rest day			
Stage 2 Tue 5 Jul	Roubaix to Metz 98 finishers	398 km 13h08'00" 30.3 kph	François Faber (Lux) Alcyon	François Faber (Lux) Alcyon
Wed 6 Jul	Rest day			
Stage 3 Thu 7 Jul	Metz to Belfort 83 finishers	259 km 9h07'00" 28.4 kph	Émile Georget (Fra) Legnano	François Faber (Lux) Alcyon
	Major climbs: Ballon d'Alsace (1,178m) Émile Georget (Fra) Legnano			
Fri 8 Jul	Rest day			
Stage 4 Sat 9 Jul	Belfort to Lyon 78 finishers	309 km 9h44'00" 31.7 kph	François Faber (Lux) Alcyon	François Faber (Lux) Alcyon
	Major climbs: Col du Cerdon (595m) n/a			
Sun 10 Jul	Rest day			
Stage 5 Mon 11 Jul	Lyon to Grenoble 72 finishers	311 km 10h43'00" 29.0 kph	Octave Lapize (Fra) Alcyon	François Faber (Lux) Alcyon
	Major climbs: Col de Porte (1,326m) Charles Crupelandt (Fra) Le Globe			
Tue 12 Jul	Rest day			
Stage 6 Wed 13 Jul	Grenoble to Nice 70 finishers	345 km 11h46'00" 29.3 kph	Julien Maîtron (Fra) Le Globe	François Faber (Lux) Alcyon
	Major climbs: Côte de Laffrey (900m) Émile Georget (Fra) Legnano; Col Bayard (1,246m) Émile Georget (Fra) Legnano			
Thu 14 Jul	Rest day			
Stage 7 Fri 15 Jul	Nice to Nîmes 63 finishers	345 km 11h48'00" 30.0 kph	François Faber (Lux) Alcyon	François Faber (Lux) Alcyon
Sat 16 Jul	Rest day			
Stage 8 Sun 17 Jul	Nîmes to Perpignan 63 finishers	216 km 6h14'00" 34.7 kph	Georges Paulmier (Fra) Le Globe	François Faber (Lux) Alcyon
Mon 18 Jul	Rest day			

Stage-by-Stage Results for the 1910 Tour de France			Stage Winner	Race Leader
Stage 9 Tue 19 Jul	Perpignan to Luchon 59 finishers	289 km 10h53'00" 26.6 kph	Octave Lapize (Fra) Alcyon	François Faber (Lux) Alcyon
	Major climbs: Col de Port (1,249m) Octave Lapize (Fra) Alcyon; Portet d'Aspet (1,069m) Octave Lapize (Fra) Alcyon; Col des Ares (797m) Octave Lapize (Fra) Alcyon			
Wed 20 Jul	Rest day			
Stage 10 Thu 21 Jul	Luchon to Bayonne 46 finishers	326 km 14h10'00" 23.0 kph	Octave Lapize (Fra) Alcyon	François Faber (Lux) Alcyon
	Major climbs: Col de Peyresourde (1,569m) Octave Lapize (Fra) Alcyon; Col d'Aspin (1,489m) Octave Lapize (Fra) Alcyon; Col du Tourmalet (2,115m) Octave Lapize (Fra) Alcyon; Col d'Aubisque (1,709m) François Lafourcade (Fra) Unsponsored			
Fri 22 Jul	Rest day			
Stage 11 Sat 23 Jul	Bayonne to Bordeaux 46 finishers	269 km 8h12'00" 32.8 kph	~~Charles Crupelandt (Fra)~~ ~~Le Globe~~ (1) Ernest Paul (Fra) Unsponsored	François Faber (Lux) Alcyon
Sun 24 Jul	Rest day			
Stage 12 Mon 25 Jul	Bordeaux to Nantes 45 finishers	391 km 13h28'00" 29.0 kph	Louis Trousselier (Fra) Alcyon	François Faber (Lux) Alcyon
Tue 26 Jul	Rest day			
Stage 13 Wed 27 Jul	Nantes to Brest 45 finishers	321 km 11h01'00" 29.1 kph	Gustave Garrigou (Fra) Alcyon	Octave Lapize (Fra) Alcyon
Stage 14 Thu 28 Jul Fri 29 Jul	Brest to Caen 41 finishers	424 km 14h38'00" 28.4 kph	Octave Lapize (Fra) Alcyon	Octave Lapize (Fra) Alcyon
Sat 30 Jul	Rest day			
Stage 15 Sun 31 Jul	Caen to Paris (Parc des Princes) 41 finishers	262 km 8h17'30" 30.3 kph	Ernesto Azzini (Ita) Legnano	Octave Lapize (Fra) Alcyon

(1) Charles Crupelandt (Le Globe) crossed the line first in Bordeaux but was demoted to fourth after he was judged to have blocked other riders in the sprint.

Prize fund: 25,000 francs (5,000 francs first prize)

Final Classification

Place	Rider	Team	Points	Age
1	Octave Lapize (Fra)	Alcyon	4,734 km 162h41'30" 29.099 kph 63 pts	22
2	François Faber (Lux)	Alcyon	67	23
3	Gustave Garrigou (Fra)	Alcyon	86	25
4	Cyrille van Hauwaert (Bel)	Alcyon	97	26
5	Charles Cruchon (Fra)	Unsponsored	119	27
6	Charles Crupelandt (Fra)	Le Globe	148	23
7	Ernest Paul (Fra)	Unsponsored	154	28
8	André Blaise (Fra)	Alcyon	166	22
9	Julien Maîtron (Fra)	Le Globe	171	29
10	Aldo Bettini (Ita)	Alcyon	175	24
Lanterne Rouge				
41	Constant Collet (Fra)	Unsponsored	580	21
Independents				
	Charles Cruchon (Fra)	Unsponsored		27
Meilleur Grimpeur				
	Octave Lapize (Fra)	Alcyon		22

1911: Domestique

Gustave Garrigou had enjoyed a degree of success in the four Tours since 1907. In his début ride, as a member of the all-conquering Peugeot squad, he picked up three stage wins along with second overall and winner of the *coureurs de vitesse* category. The following year, still one of Peugeot's lion cubs, he came away without any stage victories but did claim the *meilleur grimpeur* prize and finished fourth overall. For 1909 he switched to the sky-blue jerseys of Alcyon, and took a single stage win while finishing second overall, adding another stage the following year, when he finished third. Each time, the rider who won the race overall was one of Garrigou's team-mates. Eventually, he knew, his day would come.

Looking at the wealth of talent at his disposal in 1911 Alcyon's *directeur sportif* Alphonse Baugé was spoilt for choice when it came to where a likely victory would come from. Over the closed season he'd lost the defending champion Octave Lapize to La Française, who were returning to the Tour once more. But Baugé still had previous winners François Faber and Louis Trousselier, along with Faber's step-brother Ernest Paul who had a couple of stage victories to his credit. And he also had that hardman Eugène Christophe, the winner of the previous year's Milan-Sanremo classic. And he had Garrigou too.

As well as Alcyon and La Française, Le Globe and Automoto also had teams entered for the ninth Tour. La Française had past winner Lapize and Lucien Petit-Breton, the nearly-men Émile Georget and Georges Passerieu and a man who had won a stage the year before (and been stripped of victory in another), Charles Crupelandt. Le Globe had Henri Cornet as well as Constant Ménager, who had a stage win on his roll of honour. Automoto were something of an unknown quantity, this being their first Tour, with Alfred Fauré – who had inherited a stage win in 1904 – and Georges Paulmier, a stage winner in 1910, their most likely sources of success. The race looked like it would be between Alcyon and La Française.

From the off it was advantage Alcyon, with Garrigou profiting from problems for Lapize and Petit-Breton and winning the stage. The next stage finished in Longwy – the German authorities no longer welcoming the Tour in Metz – and in a four-man sprint Garrigou finished third, his team-mate Jules Masselis taking the win and the race lead. Over the Ballon d'Alsace on the third stage Faber flew and Garrigou could only manage third again. This put Faber in the lead, the third Alcyon rider to hold the lead in as many stages. Then the race headed for the high hills, starting with the Faucille in the Jura.

The Tour's experiment with the Pyrenees the previous year had proved to be a success and immediately Alphonse Steinès' eyes turned to France's eastern border and the mountains the race had been diligently avoiding since 1905. The 1,323 metre Col de la Faucille was added between Belfort and Chamomix, while the 1,498m Col des Aravis, the 1,566m Col du Télégraphe, the 2,058m Col du Lautaret and the monster 2,556m Col du Galibier were all to be crossed between Chamonix and Grenoble. The Tour was certainly rising to all challenges thrown at it.

Those challenges continued to come from within and without. Internally, the men behind the Tour wanted not just to maintain their race's status as the premier bike race, but also to ensure that it was constantly testing its participants as hard as it could as they and the sport itself evolved. Externally, the challenges were still coming from La Gazzetta dello Sport in Italy, whose Giro d'Italia completed its third edition four weeks before the 1911 Tour started, and from Peugeot, whose Tour de France des Indépendents was again scheduled to take place after L'Auto's Tour ended. And there was also a new challenge, coming from Alcyon, who launched an eight-day race, Huit Jours d'Alcyon. Between all these challenges, and the new mountains added to the Tour, entries had fallen back to pre-1907 levels, with just 84 riders taking the line in 1911.

Starting into the stage to the Faucille and Chamonix, Garrigou was downhearted. He knew the challenges that awaited him and he could also see that there was a strong challenge coming from within his own team, with Faber leading him by one point and Masselis a further four points back. A few kilometres from the stage finish, things seemed to be turning against Garrigou, when he began to suffer from the hunger knock, but with him at the time was Faber and he too was running out of energy. There and then Garrigou realised this was his chance and he pushed on, leaving his team-mate behind. Crupelandt took the stage for La Française, but Garrigou managed to finish third yet again with Faber two places back. This gave Garrigou the lead by a single point.

Over the high Alps it was, to say the least, a tough day in the office for Garrigou. Georget slipped the leash with his La Française team-mate Paul Duboc and Garrigou was forced to chase, alone. La Française's duo opened up a four-minute lead but, bit by bit, Garrigou began clawing back time. Between the Aravis and the base of the Télégraphe he caught the escapees, only for Georget to jump clear alone and Duboc to give chase. Alone, riding and walking, Garrigou crossed the Galibier, with the snow piled up almost head high and Duboc ahead of him, Georget further still up the road. And that was the order they finished, Garrigou picking up his fourth third place in a row. More than an hour after Garrigou reached Grenoble, Faber rolled home, twelfth on the stage. That put him 10 points behind Garrigou, with Duboc now up to third place, another four points back.

Over the hills of the Chartreuse Massif, en route to Nice, Duboc launched an early attack but was soon overtaken, with Faber breaking away alone to take the stage and Garrigou taking second. At the end of the first round of mountains Garrigou was leading Faber by nine points with Duboc a further seven back.

The two transition stages across to Perpignan, via Marseille, saw Faber's challenge fall away and Duboc claw back to within 13 points of Garrigou. And then came the Pyrenees, and controversy.

The 1,069m Aspet was served up as an entrée on the road to Luchon before the full feast en route to Bayonne. Garrigou slipped to fourth on the stage and, with Duboc taking the victory, his lead fell to just 10 points. The rider from La Française went on the attack the next stage, crossing the Peyresourde (1,569m), the Aspin (1,489m) and the Tourmalet (2,115m) alone. But between the Tourmalet and the Aubisque (1,709m) Duboc suffered a *défaillance* – a complete break down – of epic proportions. Garrigou passed him in a ditch near the town of Arglés and seized the advantage, finishing second to his team-mate Maurice Brocco. When Duboc finally rolled home, three hours after Garrigou, he was twenty-first on the stage and had dropped to 26 points off the lead. The race was now Garrigou's to lose.

Questions were immediately asked as to what had caused Duboc's collapse. Attention soon turned to a bottle that had been passed up to him at the control after the Tourmalet. Had he been slipped a Mickey Finn? If so, by whom? Well, looking at who benefited, it must have been by someone on Garrigou's side. Or so Duboc's fans believed. And when the race reached Rouen, Duboc's home town, even Desgrange agreed that Garrigou should ride in disguise if he was to finish the stage without getting lynched.

When the race finally reached Paris, Garrigou was the clear victor, with Duboc the runner up. He clawed back eight of the 16 points he lost on the road to Bayonne and many felt that, had he been able to win that stage Duboc would have won the Tour.

There was another controversy that day in Bayonne, a town that seemed to attract controversy in the Tour: Brocco's stage victory was a major annoyance to Desgrange. Any slim hope Brocco might have had of winning the Tour evaporated on the race's second stage, when he finished forty-ninth, all but ruling him out of the running save for a miracle. So his next best hope was to save himself and ride for a stage win on a day that might suit him. This alone was enough to infuriate Desgrange, who expected riders to be always trying, never taking it easy.

But Brocco's bigger crime – in the eyes of Desgrange – was that he began to ride for others. That those others included his own team-mates was neither here nor there to Desgrange. He may have accepted teams into his race – and by now the Tour was firmly associated with Desgrange, as much as it was with *L'Auto*, it was *his* race – but he had only done so reluctantly. He still refused to countenance the idea of team-mates working together. So when Brocco rode like a pilot-fish for Faber – his Alcyon team-mate – on the road from Perpignan to Luchon, Desgrange wrote bitterly of him in *L'Auto*, saying he was little more than a *domestique*, a domestic servant. Cycling got a new word added to its lexicon, but Brocco got the fire lit in his belly.

On the road to Bayonne, over the high passes of the Pyrenees, he worked like a Trojan, trailing after Duboc, and then seized his moment when Duboc fell by the wayside. Rather than celebrating a fine performance in the mountains, this only confirmed Desgrange's belief that Brocco had been riding within himself. And so Desgrange ordered that his name be struck from the record, that he be stripped of his stage win, and that he be thrown off the race. Even so, history – and this includes the Tour's official history – still lists Brocco as the winner of that stage. A *domestique* had had his day, no matter how much Desgrange denied it.

Stage-by-Stage Results for the 1911 Tour de France			Stage Winner	Race Leader
Stage 1 Sun 2 Jul	Paris (Pont de la Jatte) to Dunkerque 84 starters, 70 finishers	351 km 12h32'00" 28.0 kph	Gustave Garrigou (Fra) Alcyon	Gustave Garrigou (Fra) Alcyon
Mon 3 Jul	Rest day			
Stage 2 Tue 4 Jul	Dunkerque to Longwy 65 finishers	388 km 13h30'00" 28.7 kph	Jules Masselis (Bel) Alcyon	Jules Masselis (Bel) Alcyon
Wed 5 Jul	Rest day			
Stage 3 Thu 6 Jul	Longwy to Belfort 60 finishers	331 km 10h50'00" 30.6 kph	François Faber (Lux) Alcyon	François Faber (Lux) Alcyon
	Major climbs: Ballon d'Alsace (1,178m) François Faber (Lux) Alcyon			
Fri 7 Jul	Rest day			
Stage 4 Sat 8 Jul	Belfort to Chamonix 57 finishers	344 km 11h46'00" 29.2 kph	Charles Crupelandt (Fra) La Française	Gustave Garrigou (Fra) Alcyon
	Major climbs: Col de la Faucille (1,323m) Maurice Brocco (Fra) Alcyon			
Sun 9 Jul	Rest day			

Stage-by-Stage Results for the 1911 Tour de France			Stage Winner	Race Leader
Stage 5 Mon 10 Jul	Chamonix to Grenoble 50 finishers	366 km 13h35'00" 26.9 kph	Émile Georget (Fra) La Française	Gustave Garrigou (Fra) Alcyon
	Major climbs: Col des Aravis (1,498m) Paul Duboc (Fra) La Française + Émile Georget (Fra) La Française; Col du Télégraphe (1,566m) Émile Georget (Fra) La Française; Col du Lautaret (2,058m) Émile Georget (Fra) La Française; Col du Galibier (2,556m) Émile Georget (Fra) La Française			
Tue 11 Jul	Rest day			
Stage 6 Wed 12 Jul	Grenoble to Nice 47 finishers	348 km 13h17'00" 26.2 kph	François Faber (Lux) Alcyon	Gustave Garrigou (Fra) Alcyon
	Major climbs: Côte de Laffrey (900m) Paul Duboc (Fra) La Française; Col Bayard (1,246m) François Faber (Lux) Alcyon; Col d'Allos (2,250m) François Faber (Lux) Alcyon			
Thu 13 Jul	Rest day			
Stage 7 Fri 14 Jul	Nice to Marseille 45 finishers	334 km 12h14'00" 27.3 kph	Charles Crupelandt (Fra) La Française	Gustave Garrigou (Fra) Alcyon
	Major climbs: Col de Castillon (706m) n/a; Col de Braus (1,002m) Émile Georget (Fra) La Française			
Sat 15 Jul	Rest day			
Stage 8 Sun 16 Jul	Marseille to Perpignan 44 finishers	335 km 11h04'00" 30.3 kph	Paul Duboc (Fra) La Française	Gustave Garrigou (Fra) Alcyon
Mon 17 Jul	Rest day			
Stage 9 Tue 18 Jul	Perpignan to Luchon 40 finishers	289 km 11h10'00" 25.9 kph	Paul Duboc (Fra) La Française	Gustave Garrigou (Fra) Alcyon
	Major climbs: Portet d'Aspet (1,069m) Paul Duboc (Fra) La Française			
Wed 19 Jul	Rest day			
Stage 10 Thu 20 Jul	Luchon to Bayonne 35 finishers	326 km 13h26'00" 24.3 kph	Maurice Brocco (Fra) Alcyon	Gustave Garrigou (Fra) Alcyon
	Major climbs: Col de Peyresourde (1,569m) Paul Duboc (Fra) La Française; Col d'Aspin (1,489m) Paul Duboc (Fra) La Française; Col du Tourmalet (2,115m) Paul Duboc (Fra) La Française; Col d'Aubisque (1,709m) Maurice Brocco (Fra) Alcyon			
Fri 21 Jul	Rest day			
Stage 11 Sat 22 Jul	Bayonne to La Rochelle 34 finishers	379 km 12h58'00" 29.2 kph	Paul Duboc (Fra) La Française	Gustave Garrigou (Fra) Alcyon
Stage 12 Sun 23 Jul	La Rochelle to Brest 31 finishers	470 km 17h40'00" 26.6 kph	Marcel Godivier (Fra) La Française	Gustave Garrigou (Fra) Alcyon

Stage-by-Stage Results for the 1911 Tour de France			Stage Winner	Race Leader
Mon 24 Jul	Rest day			
Stage 13 Tue 26 Jul	Brest to Cherbourg 29 finishers	405 km 13h44'00" 29.5 kph	Gustave Garrigou (Fra) Alcyon	Gustave Garrigou (Fra) Alcyon
Wed 27 Jul	Rest day			
Stage 14 Thu 28 Jul	Cherbourg to Le Havre 28 finishers	361 km 12h01'00" 30.0 kph	Paul Duboc (Fra) La Française	Gustave Garrigou (Fra) Alcyon
Fri 29 Jul	Rest day			
Stage 15 Sat 30 Jul	Le Havre to Paris (Parc des Princes) 28 finishers	317 km 10h40'00" 29.7 kph	Marcel Godivier (Fra) La Française	Gustave Garrigou (Fra) Alcyon

Prize fund: 30,000 francs (5,000 francs first prize)

Final Classification				
Place	**Rider**	**Team**	**Points**	**Age**
1	Gustave Garrigou (Fra)	Alcyon	5,343 km 195h37'00" 27.322 kph 43 pts	26
2	Paul Duboc (Fra)	La Française	61 pts	27
3	Émile Georget (Fra)	La Française	84 pts	29
4	Charles Crupelandt (Fra)	La Française	109 pts	24
5	Louis Heusghem (Bel)	Alcyon	135 pts	21
6	Marcel Godivier (Fra)	La Française	141 pts	24
7	Charles Cruchon (Fra)	La Française	145 pts	28
8	Ernest Paul (Fra)	Alcyon	153 pts	29
9	Albert Dupont (Bel)	Le Globe	158 pts	27
10	Henri Devroye (Bel)	Le Globe	171 pts	26
Lanterne Rouge				
28	Lucien Roquebert (Fra)	Unsponsored	392 pts	21
Independents				
	Paul Deman (Bel)	Unsponsored		22
Meilleur Grimpeur				
	Paul Duboc (Fra)	La Française		27

1912: Freewheeling to Victory

Writing in *L'Auto* in the aftermath of the 1912 Tour's eleventh stage, Henri Desgrange was in a bad mood. He complained that the riders had put pressure to the pedals for barely half of the stage's 379 kilometres. He complained that the riders in the pack were being sucked along 'as if on a sofa.' He complained that the riders had completed the stage without fatigue. 'Is there any remedy?' he asked. 'Are our races seriously threatened with decadence by this infernal invention?' The infernal invention Desgrange objected to was the freewheel.

The freewheel had been available since 1869 and, since it was incorporated into the coaster brake by some manufacturers at the turn of the century had seen widespread uptake among ordinary cyclists. Racers, by and large, still preferred the fixed wheel, but some began to toy with the free. And that included racers at the Tour. In the race's first edition Pierre Desvages is known to have used a freewheel. In later years, Émile Georget is known to have been a proponent of its use: when he won the stage to Grenoble in the 1907 Tour the freewheel had enabled him to distance François Faber – on a fixed – on the final descent.

For reasons that are now unclear, there seems to have been widespread uptake of the freewheel in the 1912 Tour. This may, perhaps, have had to do with the fact that teams were limited to five riders. Even though teamwork was technically forbidden, this still meant that competitors had fewer allies in the *peloton* and so needed every advantage possible.

While Desgrange's ire was aimed at the freewheel, the real problem seems to have been the fact that the riders were sticking together on the road. And this was clear just by looking at the results of stages. In the previous Tours, a bunch sprint for the stage win was made up of four, five, maybe six riders. In 1912, on the road to Perpignan just ahead of the Pyrenees the bunch at the finish was more than a dozen strong. On the other side of the Pyrenees, on the road to La Rochelle – the stage that upset Desgrange so – it was a dozen and a half. Not quite the pell-mell of a full-on field sprint, but not the sort of thing that pleased Desgrange much, who wanted to see riders suffering alone.

One can only speculate as to why teams were limited to five riders, but looking at events in the previous Tour, when Maurice Brocco had worked for a team-mate instead of chasing victory himself and, in consequence, got tossed off the race, a likely reason seems obvious: Desgrange was trying to reduce the possibility of a team's riders working for one and other. The unforeseen consequence of this was that teams began to co-operate more. This was the norm in other races. But Desgrange fought hard against it at the Tour.

The Tour's boss (by now already identified as the father of the Tour – Géo Lefèvre's contribution being overlooked) was not the only one bothered by the way the Tour was evolving. Octave Lapize, the 1910 champion, was also upset. He had left Alcyon in the closed season and signed for La Française, who returned to the Tour after a long absence. Tatave abandoned in Perpignan, claiming that Alcyon's riders were receiving too much help from the other teams in the race. More precisely, he was bitter that the Belgian riders seemed to have rallied around their compatriot Odile Defraye, who was riding for Alcyon and leading the race, and were working toward ensuring he held the lead all the way to Paris. Lapize's remaining team-mates followed him out of the race before the start of the next stage.

With the threat from Peugeot and Alycon's rival races having been defeated – neither the Tour de France des Indepéndents nor the Huit Jours d'Alcyon made it on to the 1912 calendar – the need for innovation at the Tour was gone and Desgrange and his team could focus on perfecting the formula. (*La Gazzetta dello Sport*'s Giro d'Italia was still a threat, but it was increasingly turning into an

Vicenzo Borgarello fixes a puncture during the 1912 Tour.

Italian race for Italian riders, with foreigners given a cold welcome.) The route of the tenth Tour was, more or less, the same as the year before, a couple of flat stages to open the race, a long haul through the Vosges, the Jura, the high Alps and the Chartreuse Massif, a couple of transition stages followed by the high mountains of the Pyrenees, with the final stages being a run of long, relatively flat stages taking the riders back to Paris.

Participating in the race were 10 teams of five riders, along with another 81 unsupported riders, the *isolés*. As well as La Française's return, the tenth Tour also welcomed back Peugeot after their three-year absence, with Léopold Alibert once more bossing the lion cubs. The other teams came from Aiglon, Armor, Automoto, Griffon, JB Louvet, Le Globe and Thomann – plus; the team that had ruled the race for the previous three editions, Alcyon, still bossed by Alphonse Baugé.

Since serving a two-year apprenticeship learning the trade with Labor, Baugé had shown himself to be one of the best team bosses of his generation. He hadn't just won three Tours, he'd won three Tours with three different riders: Faber, Lapize and Gustave Garrigou. Coming into his fourth race as Alcyon's boss Baugé had initially selected five French riders to represent the team, including Garrigou, the 1905 winner Louis Trousselier and the rising talent that was Eugène Christophe. One of Alcyon's Belgian representatives requested that he include a local rider, to help drive Belgian publicity (and sales), and so Baugé added Odile Defraye at the last minute.

On the third stage – after the race had seen an Italian take the lead for the first time, on stage two – Defraye took charge. Even when Christophe made a charge through the third, fourth and fifth stages through the Vosges, the Jura and into the high Alps, taking the wins in all three and drawing level with his team-mate on points, Defraye remained calm. Christophe fell back in the Chartreuse Massif only for Lapize to challenge Defraye, taking the stage to Nice and exiting the first round of the mountains level with the Belgian.

And then came the allegations of other teams working toward an Alcyon win and the Belgians working for Defraye – all unproven but likely as not true – as the race sped across to the Pyrenees, where Lapize withdrew, leaving the way clear for Defraye. He was harried all the way home by Christophe, the new French favourite only losing time on two of the remaining five stages, but at the end of the race the points differential made it look like a commanding win for the Belgian, a gap of 59 points back to Christophe. But when the time taken by each was looked at, Defraye had taken a relatively narrow victory, a matter of minutes. Something, the men at *L'Auto* realised, would have to change.

Stage-by-Stage Results for the 1912 Tour de France			**Stage Winner**	**Race Leader**
Stage 1 Sun 30 Jun	Paris (Luna Park, Porte Maillot) to Dunkerque 131 starters, 127 finishers	351 km 11h39'37" 30.1 kph	Charles Crupelandt (Fra) La Française	Charles Crupelandt (Fra) La Française
Mon 1 Jul	Rest day			
Stage 2 Tue 2 Jul	Dunkerque to Longwy 120 finishers	388 km 13h01'08" 29.8 kph	Odile Defraye (Bel) Alcyon	Vicenzo Borgarello (Ita) JB Louvet
Wed 3 Jul	Rest day			
Stage 3 Thu 4 Jul	Longwy to Belfort 113 finishers	331 km 11h04'54" 29.9 kph	Eugène Christophe (Fra) Armor	Odile Defraye (Bel) Alcyon
	Major climbs: Ballon d'Alsace (1,178m) Odile Defraye (Bel) Alcyon			
Fri 5 Jul	Rest day			
Stage 4 Sat 6 Jul	Belfort to Chamonix 82 finishers	344 km 12h04'17" 28.5 kph	Eugène Christophe (Fra) Armor	Odile Defraye (Bel) Alcyon
	Major climbs: Col de la Faucille (1,323m) Eugène Christophe (Fra) Armor			
Sun 7 Jul	Rest day			
Stage 5 Mon 8 Jul	Chamonix to Grenoble 72 finishers	366 km 13h40'23" 26.8 kph	Eugène Christophe (Fra) Armor	Odile Defraye (Bel) Alcyon
				Eugène Christophe (Fra) Armor
	Major climbs: Col des Aravis (1,498m) Eugène Christophe (Fra) Armor; Col du Télégraphe (1,670m) Eugène Christophe (Fra) Armor; Col du Galibier (2,556m) Eugène Christophe (Fra) Armor; Col du Lautaret (2,058m) Eugène Christophe (Fra) Armor			
Tue 9 Jul	Rest day			

Stage-by-Stage Results for the 1912 Tour de France			Stage Winner	Race Leader
Stage 6 Wed 10 Jul	Grenoble to Nice 68 finishers	323 km 12h09'27" 26.6 kph	Octave Lapize (Fra) La Française	Odile Defraye (Bel) Alcyon
				Octave Lapize (Fra) La Française
	Major climbs: Côte de Laffrey (900m) Odile Defraye (Bel) Alcyon; Col Bayard (1,246m) Octave Lapize (Fra) La Française; Col d'Allos (2,250m) Octave Lapize (Fra) La Française			
Thu 11 Jul	Rest day			
Stage 7 Fri 12 Jul	Nice to Marseille 64 finishers	334 km 12h06'00" 27.6 kph	Odile Defraye (Bel) Alcyon	Odile Defraye (Bel) Alcyon
	Major climbs: Col de Castillon (706m) Giovanni Cocchi (Ita) Unsponsored; Col de Braus (1,002m) Giovanni Cocchi (Ita) Unsponsored			
Sat 13 Jul	Rest day			
Stage 8 Sun 14 Jul	Marseille to Perpignan 63 finishers	335 km 12h47'57" 26.2 kph	Vicenzo Borgarello (Ita) JB Louvet	Odile Defraye (Bel) Alcyon
Mon 15 Jul	Rest day			
Stage 9 Tue 16 Jul	Perpignan to Luchon 61 finishers	289 km 10h24'57" 27.7 kph	Odile Defraye (Bel) Alcyon	Odile Defraye (Bel) Alcyon
	Major climbs: Col de Port (1,249m) Eugène Christophe (Fra) Armor; Portet d'Aspet (1,069m) Odile Defraye (Bel) Alcyon; Col des Ares (797m) Odile Defraye (Bel) Alcyon			
Wed 17 Jul	Rest day			
Stage 10 Thu 18 Jul	Luchon to Bayonne 52 finishers	326 km 14h19'15" 22.8 kph	Louis Mottiat (Bel) Thomann	Odile Defraye (Bel) Alcyon
	Major climbs: Col de Peyresourde (1,569m) Eugène Christophe (Fra) Armor; Col d'Aspin (1,489m) Louis Mottiat (Bel) Thomann; Col du Tourmalet (2,115m) Odile Defraye (Bel) Alcyon; Col du Soulor (1,474m) Eugène Christophe (Fra) Armor; Col d'Aubisque (1,709m) Louis Mottiat (Bel) Thomann			
Fri 19 Jul	Rest day			
Stage 11 Sat 20 Jul	Bayonne to La Rochelle 47 finishers	379 km 13h11'00" 28.7 kph	Jean Alavoine (Fra) Armor	Odile Defraye (Bel) Alcyon
Stage 12 Sun 21 Jul	La Rochelle to Brest 44 finishers	470 km 16h07'39" 29.1 kph	Louis Heusghem (Bel) Alcyon	Odile Defraye (Bel) Alcyon
Mon 22 Jul Tue 23 Jul	Rest day			

Stage-by-Stage Results for the 1912 Tour de France			Stage Winner	Race Leader
Stage 13 Wed 24 Jul	Brest to Cherbourg 43 finishers	405 km 14h45'16" 27.4 kph	Jean Alavoine (Fra) Armor	Odile Defraye (Bel) Alcyon
Thu 25 Jul	Rest day			
Stage 14 Fri 26 Jul	Cherbourg to Le Havre 43 finishers	361 km 12h32'01" 28.8 kph	Vicenzo Borgarello (Ita) JB Louvet	Odile Defraye (Bel) Alcyon
Sat 27 Jul	Rest day			
Stage 15 Sun 28 Jul	Le Havre to Paris (Parc des Princes) 41 finishers	317 km 10h55'51" 29.0 kph	Jean Alavoine (Fra) Armor	Odile Defraye (Bel) Alcyon

Prize fund: 32,500 francs (5,000 francs first prize)

Final Classification				
Place	**Rider**	**Team**	**Points**	**Age**
1	Odile Defraye (Bel)	Alcyon	5,289 km 190h30'28" 27.763 kph 49 pts	24
2	Eugène Christophe (Fra)	Armor	108 pts	27
3	Gustave Garrigou (Fra)	Alcyon	140 pts	27
4	Marcel Buysse (Bel)	Peugeot	147 pts	22
5	Jean Alavoine (Fra)	Armor	148 pts	24
6	Philippe Thys (Bel)	Peugeot	148 pts	22
7	Hector Tiberghien (Bel)	Griffon	149 pts	24
8	Henri Devroye (Bel)	Le Globe	163 pts	27
9	Félicien Salmon (Bel)	Peugeot	166 pts	29
10	Alfons Spiessens (Bel)	JB Louvet	167 pts	23
Lanterne Rouge				
41	Maurice Dartigue (Fra)	Unsponsored	612 pts	34
Independents				
	Jules Deloffre	Unsponsored		27
Meilleur Grimpeur				
	Odile Defraye	Alcyon		24

1913: A Legend is Forged

The eleventh edition of the Tour saw the race going backwards, literally and figuratively. First, the race route was turned on its head and, for the first time in its brief history, the riders circuited France anti-clockwise, tackling the Pyrenees before the Alps (that aside, the route was more or less that of the previous two editions, with minor tweaks). Secondly, Desgrange and his team at *L'Auto* gave up on using points to decide who had won and switched back to the time-based formula they'd used in the race's first edition. Finally, Desgrange carried through on his threat to ban the freewheel on certain stages.

Over the closed season, a couple of the manufacturers' teams went through major shake-ups in their personnel. Peugeot lost the 1905 Tour champion Louis Trousselier, who hadn't made the cut for the 1912 Tour team and jumped ship to JB Louvet. Lucien Petit-Breton also abandoned the lion cubs in favour of the Saint-Étienne-based Automoto. With him went the team's *directeur sportif*, Léopold Alibert, the architect of his victories in 1907 and 1908. The Peugeot bosses responded by poaching François Faber, Gustave Garrigou and Eugène Christophe from Alcyon, and with them the man who had now bossed four different riders to victory at the Tour in four years, Alphonse Baugé. Octave Lapize and Émile Georget stayed with La Française. Odile Defraye stayed with Alcyon, who built a largely Belgian team around the defending champion.

Early in the season Defraye and Faber had both shown form by winning Milan-Sanremo and Paris-Roubaix, but Bordeaux-Paris – like the Tour the previous year – had gone Belgian, to Alcyon's Louis Mottiat. For Belgian cycling it seemed the time had come, with its own calendar now including races such as Liège-Bastogne-Liège (which took place during the first week of the Tour) and the Tour of Belgium, as well as the newly created Ronde van Vlaanderen, these races and more offering Belgian riders the chance to show their worth. And at the Tour they showed their worth in spades.

Entering the Pyrenees, Defraye was leading the race for Alcyon, nearly five minutes up on Eugène Christophe, and ten on Marcel Buysse, both from Peugeot. Their team-mate Phillip Thys was just over twenty minutes off the race lead. On the road between Bayonne and Luchon Defraye had a *jour sans* and abandoned the race at Barèges, at the foot of the Tourmalet, already more than two hours behind the front runners. That meant Christophe – who had led over the Aubisque – looked set to become the leader of the Tour, if he maintained his pace all the way to Luchon.

But on the descent off the Tourmalet, which Thys summited five minutes ahead of Christophe, disaster struck: the French hope's forks broke. Walking down the mountain he arrived at the village of Sainte-Marie-de-Campan and, finding a forge, set to work to repair his bike. Between descending the mountain on foot and the time spent making repairs, Christophe lost the thick end of four hours. Only for the race commissaires to add to his woes with a 10 minute time penalty – reduced to three on appeal – because he'd allowed a young lad operate the forge's bellows for him. The repairs completed, Christophe remounted and rode on to Luchon, where he arrived three hours and 50 minutes behind his team-mate Thys, who had won the stage and taken the race lead, with Buysse second, six minutes off the lead.

On the second of the two Pyrenean stages Buysse usurped his team-mate, taking the stage and the race lead, and now having an advantage of just over six minutes on Thys. Across the two mountain stages the toll on the *peloton* had been heavy, with 27 riders leaving the race. All the Alcyon riders were gone, along with the riders from Armor and Labor. Earlier in the race Lapize's La Française squad had abandoned, as had the Libérator riders. Automoto still had one rider in the race, as had Griffon; JB Louvet had four, and Peugeot their full quota of eight. *L'Auto*, when writing of Christophe's travails on the

Tourmalet, had complimented him for helping ensure that the Peugeot squad would return to Paris complete.

Buysse held his lead as the race headed from Perpignan to Aix-en-Provence, but on the ride across to Nice, in the climbs of the Braus and the Castillon, it was his turn to suffer a mechanical mishap, his handlebars breaking in a crash near Fréjus. Like Christophe before him he was forced to walk until he could find somewhere to effect repairs, costing him about three hours, to which was added another 30 minutes as a penalty for receiving assistance. Thys was now firmly in the lead, more than an hour clear of Garrigou.

Over the remaining six stages Buysse refused to accept defeat, taking four stage wins, but he was incapable of undoing the damage done on the road to Nice, even when Thys lost nearly an hour on the penultimate stage after he crashed. With both Petit-Breton and Garrigou little more than an hour behind him on general classification Thys could have lost the Tour here – and probably should have, had the commissaires imposed a time penalty on him for receiving outside assistance. The best Garrigou could do was close to within 10 minutes of the lead, while Petit-Breton crashed out with a broken knee.

Many years after the fact Thys claimed that, when the Tour had reached Grenoble, his *directeur sportif*, Baugé, suggested he should wear a special jersey to signify he was leading the race. Desgrange being in agreement a suitable garment was found, yellow in colour, the same colour as the paper *L'Auto* was printed on. Before Thys made this revelation, though, it was generally understood that the *maillot jaune* hadn't arrived in the Tour until part way through the 1919 edition of the race. Few doubt Thys' claim, but the proof for it is lacking.

In the crowd of 200,000 Parisians awaiting the Tour's arrival in Paris was *Le Matin's* special correspondent Colette, gathering her impressions of the throng assembled to cheer the riders home. She described it as closing in on the riders likes a field of corn, the crowds closing around the riders, wanting to touch them as they passed. The Tour had clearly passed from being just a sporting contest and was becoming a part of French life.

Stage-by-Stage Results for the 1913 Tour de France			Stage Winner	Race Leader
Stage 1 Sun 29 Jun	Paris (Boulogne-Billancourt) to Le Havre 140 starters, 111 finishers	388 km 14h09'47" 27.4 kph	Giovanni Micheletto (Ita) Griffon	Giovanni Micheletto (Ita) Griffon
Mon 30 Jun	Rest day			
Stage 2 Tue 1 Jul	Le Havre to Cherbourg 101 finishers	364 km 12h20'06" 29.5 kph	Jules Masselis (Bel) Alcyon	Jules Masselis (Bel) Alycon
				Alfons Lauwers (Bel) Libérator
				Marcel Buysse (Bel) Peugeot
				Odile Defraye (Bel) Alcyon
Wed 2 Jul	Rest day			
Stage 3 Thu 3 Jul	Cherbourg to Brest 84 finishers	405 km 13h58'45" 29.0 kph	Henri Pelissier (Fra) Alcyon	Odile Defraye (Bel) Alcyon
Fri 4 Jul	Rest day			
Stage 4 Sat 5 Jul	Brest to La Rochelle 61 finishers	470 km 16h10'16" 29.1 kph	Marcel Buysse (Bel) Peugeot	Odile Defraye (Bel) Alcyon
Sun 6 Jul	Rest day			
Stage 5 Mon 7 Jul	La Rochelle to Bayonne 59 finishers	379 km 12h40'28" 29.9 kph	Henri van Lerberghe (Bel) Unsponsored	Odile Defraye (Bel) Alcyon
Tue 8 Jul	Rest day			
Stage 6 Wed 9 Jul	Bayonne to Luchon 44 finishers	326 km 13h54'23" 23.4 kph	Philippe Thys (Bel) Peugeot	Philippe Thys (Bel) Peugeot
	Major climbs: Col d'Aubisque (1,709m) Eugène Christophe (Fra) Peugeot; Col du Tourmalet (2,115m) Philippe Thys (Bel) Peugeot; Col d'Aspin (1,489m) Philippe Thys (Bel) Peugeot; Col de Peyresourde (1,569m) Philippe Thys (Bel) Peugeot			
Thu 10 Jul	Rest day			
Stage 7 Fri 11 Jul	Luchon to Perpignan 32 finishers	324 km 11h55'40" 27.2 kph	Marcel Buysse (Bel) Peugeot	Marcel Buysse (Bel) Peugeot
	Major climbs: Portet d'Aspet (1,069m) Émile Engel (Fra) Peugeot; Col de Port (1,249m) Marcel Buysse (Bel) Peugeot; Col de Puymorens (1,915m) Marcel Buysse (Bel) Peugeot			
Sat 12 Jul	Rest day			
Stage 8 Sun 13 Jul	Perpignan to Aix-en-Provence 32 finishers	325 km 10h42'16" 30.4 kph	Gustave Garrigou (Fra) Peugeot	Marcel Buysse (Bel) Peugeot

Stage-by-Stage Results for the 1913 Tour de France			Stage Winner	Race Leader
Mon 14 Jul	Rest day			
Stage 9 Tue 15 Jul	Aix-en-Provence to Nice 32 finishers	356 km 13h34'26" 26.2 kph	Firmin Lambot (Bel) Griffon	Philippe Thys (Bel) Peugeot
	Major climbs: Col de Braus (1,002m) Firmin Lambot (Bel) Griffon; Col de Castillon (706m) Firmin Lambot (Bel) Griffon			
Wed 16 Jul	Rest day			
Stage 10 Thu 17 Jul	Nice to Grenoble 30 finishers	333 km 13h08'37" 25.3 kph	François Faber (Lux) Peugeot	Philippe Thys (Bel) Peugeot
	Major climbs: Col d'Allos (2,250m) Lucien Petit-Breton (Fra) Automoto; Col Bayard (1,246m) François Faber (Lux) Peugeot + Gustave Garrigou (Fra) Peugeot			
Fri 18 Jul	Rest day			
Stage 11 Sat 19 Jul	Grenoble to Geneva 29 finishers	325 km 12h01'42" 27.0 kph	Marcel Buysse (Bel) Peugeot	Philippe Thys (Bel) Peugeot
	Major climbs: Col du Lautaret (2,058m) Marcel Buysse (Bel) Peugeot; Col du Galibier (2,556m) Marcel Buysse (Bel) Peugeot; Col du Télégraphe (1,566m) Marcel Buysse (Bel) Peugeot; Col des Aravis (1,498m) Marcel Buysse (Bel) Peugeot			
Sun 20 Jul	Rest day			
Stage 12 Mon 21 Jul	Geneva to Belfort 29 finishers	335 km 12h31'02" 26.8 kph	Marcel Buysse (Bel) Peugeot	Philippe Thys (Bel) Peugeot
	Major climbs: Col de la Faucille (1,069m) n/a; Ballon d'Alsace (1,178m) Marcel Buysse (Bel) Peugeot			
Tue 22 Jul	Rest day			
Stage 13 Wed 23 Jul	Belfort to Longwy 26 finishers	325 km 11h29'23" 28.3 kph	François Faber (Lux) Peugeot	Philippe Thys (Bel) Peugeot
	Major climbs: Col de la Grosse Pierre (923m) Lucien Petit-Breton (Fra) Automoto			
Thu 24 Jul	Rest day			
Stage 14 Fri 25 Jul	Longwy to Dunkerque 25 finishers	393 km 14h21'55" 27.4 kph	Marcel Buysse (Bel) Peugeot	Philippe Thys (Bel) Peugeot
Sat 26 Jul	Rest day			
Stage 15 Sun 27 Jul	Dunkerque to Paris (Parc des Princes) 25 finishers	340 km 12h01'37" 28.3 kph	Marcel Buysse (Bel) Peugeot	Philippe Thys (Bel) Peugeot

Prize fund: 39,900 francs (5,000 francs first prize)

Final Classification

Place	Rider	Team	Time	Age
1	Philippe Thys (Bel)	Peugeot	5,287 km 197h54'00" 26.715 kph	23
2	Gustave Garrigou (Fra)	Peugeot	+ 8'37"	28
3	Marcel Buysse (Bel)	Peugeot	+ 3h30'55"	23
4	Firmin Lambot (Bel)	Griffon	+ 4h12'45"	27
5	François Faber (Lux)	Peugeot	+ 6h26'04"	26
6	Alfons Spiessens (Bel)	JB Louvet	+ 7h57'52"	24
7	Eugène Christophe (Fra)	Peugeot	+ 14h06'35"	28
8	Camillo Bertarelli (Ita)	Unsponsored	+ 16h21'38"	27
9	Joseph Vandaele (Bel)	JB Louvet	+ 16h39'53"	23
10	Émile Engel (Fra)	Peugeot	+ 16h52'34"	24
Lanterne Rouge				
25	Henri Alavoine (Fra)	Unsponsored		23
Independents				
	Camillo Bertarelli (Ita)	Unsponsored		27
Meilleur Grimpeur				
	Philippe Thys (Bel)	Peugeot		23

1914: The End of an Era

In the pre-dawn dark of a summer's Sunday morning, the 145 riders in the twelfth Tour de France rolled out of Saint-Cloud, Paris, where 45 years earlier cycling legend has it the first bike race had taken place. Their passage lit by the headlamps of the race convoy, they were heading for Le Havre. The *peloton* was somewhere around about Le Tréport, 220 kilometres into the stage, when, 1,800 kilometres to the east, in Sarajevo, Bosnia, Gavrilo Princip assassinated the heir to the Hapsburg throne of Austria-Hungary, Archduke Franz Ferdinand, along with his wife. The world stood on the brink of war. At the Tour, the show went on, as it always did.

The internationalisation of the Tour's *peloton* saw Australian riders – Don Kirkham and Iddo 'Snowy' Munro, who were riding for Phébus, alongside the London-born Georges Passerieu – join the fray. The previous year the Tour had welcomed its first Dane and its first Tunisian and the latter, Ali Neffati, was back for more. A couple of Algerians had flown the flag for Africa in 1910. In the main, though, the Tour continued to draw its participants from what had become cycling's heartland: France, Belgium and Italy, with the odd representative from Switzerland, Luxembourg and Germany. The Belgians, in particular, were increasingly coming in force. And dominating the race.

It was a Belgian, the defending champion Philippe Thys, who took early control of the 1914 Tour, taking the opening stage and the lead. The yellow jersey that may or may not have appeared at the previous year's race was still not officially the way the race leader was identified, and he continued to ride in his Peugeot jersey.

Jean Rossius (Alcyon) presented the first threat to back-to-back victories for Thys, taking the second stage and sharing the lead all the way down to Bayonne, the eve of the race's two Pyrenean stages. Arriving into Bayonne the *peloton* was 28 strong as it sprinted for the line – the biggest bunch sprint yet seen in the Tour – and the man who emerged from the mêlée first was Peugeot's Oscar Egg, who had also won the previous stage into La Rochelle. The Swiss star was at this stage famous; since August 1912 he had been trading Hour records with Marcel Berthet (who, in 1907, had broken Lucien Petit-Breton's 1905 record). In 22 months there had been five new records, the distance climbing from 41.520 kilometres to 44.247, Egg having set the latter just 10 days before the Tour started.

Over the Aubisque and the Tourmalet, on the road to Luchon, Rossius's challenge fell away as he lost more than an hour. The man who emerged as Thys's next most likely challenger was the young Henri Pélissier, riding in his second Tour. The twenty-five-year-old Parisian was a graduate of Peugeot's Tour de France des Indépendants, where he won a stage in 1910, and had shown his potential by taking victories in one-day races like Milan-Turin (1911), the Giro di Lombardia (1911 and 1913), Milan-Sanremo (1912), as well as a couple of stages in the Ronde van België (1912), Belgium's mini-Tour.

Pélissier had lost about eight minutes on the Tour's second stage but clawed his way back to within five minutes of the lead come Bayonne. Despite leading over the Aubisque in the first round of Pyrenean climbs he lost half an hour on the day – the victim of the *fringale*, having forgotten to eat – and was 35 minutes off the pace at the stage end. The Frenchman held his own on the second set of mountains en route to Perpignan and, through the Alps and up to the Vosges, launched a fight-back, taking two stage wins. But that was only enough to close to within 32 minutes of the lead as the race completed two ascents of the Ballon d'Alsace. And then on the road to Dunkerque disaster struck Thys and Pélissier was suddenly in with a shout of victory.

The roads of northern France were, at this time, particularly unkind. Thys himself had almost lost the Tour the year before on the road to Dunkerque – the penultimate stage – and that's where he almost lost it again in 1914. The Belgian was leading at the front of the race with team-mates Faber and Pélissier when a Sunday cyclist, who thought it would be fun to play with the big boys, accidently brought him down. In the fall Thys damaged his front wheel and made an illegal change before catching his erstwhile companions. The three Peugeot riders rode into Dunkerque together, with Faber taking the win. And then the commissaires consulted the rule book. The previous year they had been lenient when Thys received outside assistance. But not so this year. They gave him a 30 minute time penalty. Which, conveniently, brought Pélissier to within two minutes of the race lead.

On the final stage Pélissier tried valiantly to take the title, riding into Paris alone and in the lead. But the same crowds which Colette, the year before, had described as being like a field of corn, closed in on him, eager to cheer him to victory but actually impeding his progress and allowing Thys to close in on him. Pélissier had the consolation of the stage win, but once more a Belgian had won the Tour de France.

In the 12 years the race had been running the Tour had come a long way. The six stages of the original race were now 15, the overall distance was now more than twice that covered by the first riders, mountains had been added, the best riders were organised in teams. But in some respects it was still the same Tour. Partisan fans still blighted it with tack attacks – in Grenoble in 1914 many riders punctured because of nails strewn on the road. And some riders were still letting the train take the strain – one of the isolés, Marcel Allain, had done just that on the stage to Brest.

But in other ways the Tour was becoming more modern. Automoto had signed the Italian star Costante Girardengo – who was soon to become Italy's first campionissimo, the champion of champions – and when he pulled out of the race in the Pyrenees, citing fatigue, Desgrange complained bitterly that he had really left the race because he had other commitments in Italy. The day had already come when riders could get value from riding just a portion of the Tour.

The day had come, too, when rumours of doping were associated with certain riders. The day had also come when riders would reconnoitre the whole or parts of the Tour's *parcours*. And the day had come when a rider could dedicate his season to the Tour, as Thys had just done, not bothering with most of the early season races and working solely toward defending his Tour crown.

Doubtless Thys was already looking to the future and planning for a third Tour title as soon as he had won his second. But the chance to claim that win and raise himself above Lucien Petit-Breton's two victories – and the shadow still cast by Maurice Garin – would be a long time coming. Within days of the Tour ending the Great War began, and the Tour was put on hold. Many of the *géants de la route* swapped their cycling jerseys for military uniforms. Not all of them came home.

Stage-by-Stage Results for the 1914 Tour de France			Stage Winner	Race Leader
Stage 1 Sun 28 Jun	Paris (Saint-Cloud) to Le Havre 145 starters, 120 finishers	388 km 13h18'28" 29.2 kph	Philippe Thys (Bel) Peugeot	Philippe Thys (Bel) Peugeot
Mon 29 Jun	Rest day			
Stage 2 Tue 30 Jun	Le Havre to Cherbourg 115 finishers	364 km 12h15'26" 29.7 kph	Jean Rossius (Bel) Alcyon	Philippe Thys (Bel) Peugeot
				Jean Rossius (Bel) Alcyon
Wed 1 Jul	Rest day			
Stage 3 Thu 2 Jul	Cherbourg to Brest 101 finishers	405 km 14h58'06" 27.1 kph	Émile Engel (Fra) Peugeot	Philippe Thys (Bel) Peugeot
				Jean Rossius (Bel) Alcyon
Fri 3 Jul	Rest day			
Stage 4 Sat 4 Jul	Brest to La Rochelle 87 finishers	470 km 16h13'45" 29.0 kph	Oscar Egg (Sui) Peugeot	Philippe Thys (Bel) Peugeot
				Jean Rossius (Bel) Alcyon
Sun 5 Jul	Rest day			
Stage 5 Mon 6 Jul	La Rochelle to Bayonne 84 finishers	376 km 13h25'29" 28.0 kph	Oscar Egg (Sui) Peugeot	Philippe Thys (Bel) Peugeot
				Jean Rossius (Bel) Alcyon

Stage-by-Stage Results for the 1914 Tour de France			Stage Winner	Race Leader
Tue 7 Jul	Rest day			
Stage 6 Wed 8 Jul	Bayonne to Luchon 74 finishers	326 km 14h39'04" 22.3 kph	Firmin Lambot (Bel) Peugeot	Philippe Thys (Bel) Peugeot
	Major climbs: Col d'Aubisque (1,709,) Oscar Egg (Sui) Peugeot + Henri Pélissier (Fra) Peugeot; Col du Tourmalet (2,115m) Firmin Lambot (Bel) Peugeot; Col d'Aspin (1,489m) Firmin Lambot (Bel) Peugeot; Col de Peyresourde (1,569m) Firmin Lambot (Bel) Peugeot			
Thu 9 Jul	Rest day			
Stage 7 Fri 10 Jul	Luchon to Perpignan 72 finishers	323 km 11h47'05" 27.4 kph	Jean Alavoine (Fra) Peugeot	Philippe Thys (Bel) Peugeot
	Major climbs: Col des Ares (797m) Jean Alavoine (Fra) Peugeot; Portet d'Aspet (1,069m) Jean Alavoine (Fra) Peugeot; Col de Puymorens (1,915m) n/a			
Sat 11 Jul	Rest day			
Stage 8 Sun 12 Jul	Perpignan to Marseille 69 finishers	370 km 13h00'00" 28.5 kph	Octave Lapize (Fra) La Française	Philippe Thys (Bel) Peugeot
Mon 13 Jul	Rest day			
Stage 9 Tue 14 Jul	Marseille to Nice 62 finishers	338 km 12h35'38" 26.8 kph	Jean Rossius (Bel) Alcyon	Philippe Thys (Bel) Peugeot
	Major climbs: Col de Braus (1,002m) Jean Rossius (Bel) Alcyon; Col de Castillon (706m) Jean Rossius (Bel) Alcyon			
Wed 15 Jul	Rest day			
Stage 10 Thu 16 Jul	Nice to Grenoble 57 finishers	323 km 13h22'03" 24.2 kph	Henri Pélissier (Fra) Peugeot	Philippe Thys (Bel) Peugeot
	Major climbs: Col d'Allos (2,205m) Firmin Lambot (Bel) Peugeot + Henri Pélissier (Fra) Peugeot; Col Bayard (1,246m) Philippe Thys (Bel) Peugeot			
Fri 17 Jul	Rest day			
Stage 11 Sat 18 Jul	Grenoble to Geneva 55 finishers	325 km 12h29'06" 26.0 kph	Gustave Garrigou (Fra) Peugeot	Philippe Thys (Bel) Peugeot
	Major climbs: Col du Lautaret (2,058m) Henri Pélissier (Fra) Peugeot; Col du Galibier (2,556m) Henri Pélissier (Fra) Peugeot; Col des Aravis (1,498m) Philippe Thys (Bel) Peugeot			
Sun 19 Jul	Rest day			
Stage 12 Mon 20 Jul	Geneva to Belfort 55 finishers	325 km 12h32'05" 25.9 kph	Henri Pélissier (Fra) Peugeot	Philippe Thys (Bel) Peugeot
	Major climbs: Col de la Faucille (1,323m) Henri Pélissier (Fra) Peugeot; Ballon d'Alsace (1,178m) Jean Alavoine (Fra) Peugeot + Henri Pélissier (Fra) Peugeot			
Tue 21 Jul	Rest day			

Stage-by-Stage Results for the 1914 Tour de France			Stage Winner	Race Leader
Stage 13 Wed 22 Jul	Belfort to Longwy 55 finishers	325 km 10h30'44" 30.9 kph	François Faber (Lux) Peugeot	Philippe Thys (Bel) Peugeot
	Major climbs: Ballon d'Alsace (1,178m) Jean Alavoine (Fra) Peugeot + Henri Pélissier (Fra) Peugeot; Col de la Grosse Pierre (923m) Jean Alavoine (Fra) Peugeot			
Thu 23 Jul	Rest day			
Stage 14 Fri 24 Jul	Longwy to Dunkerque 54 finishers	390 km 15h03'16" 25.9 kph	François Faber (Lux) Peugeot	Philippe Thys (Bel) Peugeot
Sat 25 Jul	Rest day			
Stage 15 Sun 26 Jul	Dunkerque to Paris (Parc des Princes) 54 finishers	340 km 13h21'16" 25.5 kph	Henri Pélissier (Fra) Peugeot	Philippe Thys (Bel) Peugeot

Prize fund: 45,000 francs (5,000 francs first prize)

Final Classification				
Place	**Rider**	**Team**	**Time**	**Age**
1	Philippe Thys (Bel)	Peugeot	5,380 km 200h28'48" 26.835 kph	24
2	Henri Pélissier (Fra)	Peugeot	+ 1'50"	25
3	Jean Alavoine (Fra)	Peugeot	+ 36'53"	26
4	Jean Rossius (Bel)	Alcyon	+ 1h57'05"	23
5	Gustave Garrigou (Fra)	Peugeot	+ 3h00'21"	29
6	Émile Georget (Fra)	Peugeot	+ 3h20'59"	32
7	Alfons Spiessens (Bel)	JB Louvet	+ 3h53'55"	25
8	Firmin Lambot (Bel)	Peugeot	+ 5h08'54"	28
9	François Faber (Lux)	Peugeot	+ 6h15'53"	27
10	Louis Heusghem (Bel)	Peugeot	+ 7h49'02"	24
Lanterne Rouge				
54	Henri Leclercq (Fra)	Unsponsored	+ 99h04'45"	
Independents				
	Camille Botté	Unsponsored		25
Meilleur Grimpeur				
	Firmin Lambot (Bel)	Peugeot		28

1915-1918: Mort pour la France

In the 52 months of fighting that were the Great War, something in the region of 10 million soldiers were killed, on all sides. Many sporting stars across the full range of sports went to war and many of them never came home. In cycling, the exact death toll is not known, but several hundred cyclists died over the course of the conflict, most of them unsung heroes of the *peloton*, but many stars of the sport too. The honour rolls of races such as Milan-Sanremo, Liège-Bastogne-Liège, Bordeaux-Paris, Paris-Roubaix, Paris-Brussels, Paris-Tours, the Giro d'Italia, the Giro di Lombardia and many others all include the names of champions who died over the course of the conflict. Track racing's rolls of honour also bear the scars of war.

Upwards of 50 men who rode the Tour de France – out of a corps of nearly 700 riders across the race's first twelve editions – lost their lives. Most famous among them are the winners of the 1907, 1908, 1909 and 1910 Tours, Lucien Petit-Breton, François Faber and Octave Lapize.

Of the three, Faber was first to fall, on 8 May 1915. Having opted to renounce his French nationality in 1909 and become a citizen of Luxembourg – his mother was French, his father from the Grand Duchy – Faber could have sat out the war, but he joined the French Foreign Legion in order to do his bit to defend the country that had helped make him famous. He was killed in action during the Battle of Artois, some say while trying to rescue a fallen comrade.

On Bastille Day 1917, 14 July, Octave Lapize was the next of the three to die. He had enjoyed a flight in one of Blériot's airplanes on the last rest day during the 1910 Tour and taken quite a fancy to flying. When war came he joined the Aéronautique Militaire, the French air corps, and was killed in action, shot down over the front line near Flirey, to the south-east of Verdun.

Petit-Breton's death on 20 December 1917 was more mundane. He was serving with a logistical division of the French army when he was involved in an automobile accident behind the lines, near Troyes, and died.

They were the biggest stars of the Tour to fall, but not all who died were stars. The Tour also lost two *lanternes rouge*, two of the last men home in the race: Georges Bronchard, who was *lanterne rouge* in 1906; and Henri Alavoine, *lanterne rouge* in 1913. They fell in April 1918 and July 1916.

Others who fell had shone briefly at the Tour. Émile Engel had caused equal measures of joy and dismay in the 1914 race, joy when he took the race's second stage, dismay when he was thrown off the race on stage eight after striking a commissaire. He was one of the Tour's first stars to fall, killed in action during the First Battle of the Marne on 14 September 1914 – seven weeks after the Tour had ended – where German forces closing in on Paris were pushed back.

Or there was Pierre-Gonzague Privat, the man from whom Émile Georget borrowed the bike that cost him the 1907 Tour. As well as being a rider Privat sometimes served as a *soigneur* and was also an illustrator and caricaturist, his work appearing in French journals, books and on promotional posters. He was killed in October 1915, during the Third Battle of Artois.

Or there was François Lafourcade, the man who crested the Aubisque ahead of Octave Lapize in 1910 and – some say – may have been guilty of poisoning Paul Duboc in 1911. He fell on 10 August 1917.

You could go on, and on, naming the dead. Marcel Kerff, sixth in the first Tour, fell in August 1914. Anthony Wattelier, who started seven and finished five Tours between 1905 and 1911, fell in December 1915. Camille Fily, the youngest rider to start a Tour, fell in May 1918.

Or one could consider the brothers of Tour riders – some of whom also rode the Tour in their own right – who also fell. The Mazan family lost not just Lucien (Petit-Breton) but also Anselme, who died in June 1915. The Trousselier family lost Lucien, younger brother to Louis, who fell in September 1914. The Pélissier family lost Jean – the second of four brothers who all took to the bike – who died in March 1915.

Not all who died in the war years were killed fighting. The self-styled Baron Henri Pépin, a true knight of the road, died late in 1914. He had started his third Tour that year and, like his previous two attempts, failed to finish, this time having to abandon on the opening stage. In 1905 he had got as far as the seventh stage, to Bordeaux, before pulling out. Perhaps the most famous tale of him comes from the 1907 race, where he engaged the services of two Tour veterans in order to help him round the route (Jean Dargassies, the blacksmith from Grissoles, who had finished eleventh in the first Tour and tenth the next – elevated to fourth after the French federation did their thing; and Henri Gauban, who had entered each of the previous four Tours, without finishing a single one). Years before helpers would come to be described as *domestiques*, Pépin had hired these two servants to perform precisely that task for him. Not that they got him round the full route: he pulled out after just the fourth stage.

* * * * *

One death during the war years probably best shows how far the Tour specifically, and road racing in general, had yet to go. Many of the races we know today were already established – from the Tour to the Giro, Milan-Sanremo to the Giro di Lombardia, Liège-Bastogne-Liège to the Ronde van Vlaanderen, Paris-Roubaix to Paris-Tours – but road racing was not yet the most popular part of the sport. The real stars of cycling were still the men who raced in the crowd-filled vélodromes. And one of their biggest stars, Louis Darragon, fell during a motor-paced event at the Vélodrome d'Hiver in April 1918, and died (he had been discharged from the army after suffering a broken arm). Thousands filled the streets of Paris to watch his funeral cortege pass. Road racing had still to produce a star of that calibre.

1919: The Return of the Tour

In the pre-dawn dark of another summer's Sunday morning, the 67 riders in the thirteenth Tour de France rolled out from the Parc des Princes, Paris, bound for Le Havre. Five years had passed since the twelfth Tour, in 1914. Five years filled with war and death. That twelfth Tour started just hours before the assassination of Franz Ferdinand, which set in train the events that led to 52 months of senseless slaughter. The final signatures on the peace treaty between France and Germany were added just hours before the thirteenth Tour started.

In the seven months in between the end of the fighting and the signing of that peace treaty, cycling slowly returned to the roads of France. One new race added to the calendar was *Le Petit Journal*'s Circuit des Champs de Bataille, a seven-stage affair which ran from 29 April through 11 May and took in various battlefields of the war. As well as the symbolism of remembering the dead, this was a race that, by starting and finishing in Strasbourg, celebrated the return of something long dreamed of: the territories of Alsace and Lorraine, which had been liberated from Germany.

Prior to organising Paris-Roubaix – which of necessity had to cross lands which had been fought over for the previous five years – *L'Auto* sent Victor Breyer out to scout the route and see whether it was still feasible after all the fighting. Breyer's report of what he saw read like something from Dante: 'Shell-holes one after the other, with no gaps, outlines of trenches, barbed wire cut into one thousand pieces; unexploded shells on the roadside, here and there, graves. Crosses bearing a jaunty tricolour are the only light relief.' It fell to his travelling companion to utter a line that would give cycling an immortal phrase: 'Here, this really is the hell of the North.' That travelling companion was Eugène Christophe.

Born in 1885 Christophe had been in his prime before war broke out. His *palmarès* included France's cyclo cross championships six times in a row, as well as that arctic Milan-Sanremo win in 1910. At the Tour, he had three stage wins to his account in 1912, when he finished second overall, followed by seventh and eleventh in 1913 and 1914. His forks failure on the Tourmalet in 1913 had cost him a shot at victory, but it was not yet what he was famous for – it was just another of those hard-luck stories the Tour produced in abundance. In 1919 all that was about to change.

With the French economy only slowly recovering from the hardships of war, the main French cycling manufacturers decided they needed to sign a non-aggression pact if they were not to be driven out of business. Before the war, riders' salaries had been rising, and post-war the sums involved were simply not sustainable. So the major marques – principally Peugeot and Alcyon, along with their subsidiaries and a few others – banded together under the banner of La Sportive. All their riders wore the same grey jersey and all rode the same La Sportive bikes. Between them, they accounted for more than half the field at the 1919 Tour.

Not that the 1919 Tour officially had teams. Once more Desgrange and his team at *L'Auto* took a step backwards, and the riders were simply grouped into A and B categories: the As the aces, the stars of the sport, and the Bs the *isolés* of old, the unsupported individuals. One innovation the Tour did offer was that the race organisers took responsibility for feeding riders during stages, something the teams had had to look after in the past.

Christophe took control of the race on the fourth stage, to Les Sables-d'Olonne (which had replaced La Rochelle), deposing Henri Pélissier. Henri and his brother Francis had won the previous two stages and – as the winner of Paris-Roubaix and Bordeaux-Paris earlier in the season – Henri Pélissier seems to have let all the success go to his head somewhat, and he began to brag a bit. Had he just compared himself to a thoroughbred he might have survived unscathed, but it was saying that his rivals were just cart-horses that really got their backs up. Leaving Cherbourg on the third stage the *peloton* was in the mood to bring the Pélissiers down a peg or two. And when they got the opportunity – Henri Pélissier stopping momentarily – they drove home the lesson by driving the *peloton* away at speed. Though he chased he couldn't catch the fleeing bunch and lost more than half an hour on the day, and the race lead with it.

That put Christophe firmly in charge, with his nearest rival – Firmin Lambot – 50 minutes in arrears. Following largely the same route as before the war the Tour took the riders down France's Atlantic coast – with a new, monstrous 482-kilometre stage between Les Sables-d'Olonne and Bayonne added to the itinerary – and across the Pyrenees before returning to Paris via the mountains along the country's eastern border, with time before the finish to celebrate the liberation of Alsace-Lorraine by having stage finishes in both Strasbourg and Metz.

Christophe's control of the race was efficient, without being spectacular. He was no longer the youthful Cri-Cri of old, he was now *le vieux gaulois*, the old Gaul. Intelligence would have to make up for what age had taken away. Christophe let Lambot chip away at his lead without panicking and, by the time the race arrived in Metz, with just two stages remaining, he still had a 28 minute safety cushion. He also had the *maillot jaune.*

Philippe Thys's claims about being awarded a yellow jersey in the 1913 Tour notwithstanding, official Tour history has long held that Eugène Christophe was the first wearer of the fabled garment. Perhaps as a way to pass time during the run down to Bayonne, La Sportive's *directeur sportif*, the incomparable Alphonse Baugé, once again suggested to Desgrange that really there ought be a way of designating the leader of the race, especially when half the field were wearing La Sportive's grey jerseys. Desgrange took the idea as his own and, three days later, *L'Auto* announced the birth of the *maillot jaune*. By the time the specially ordered yellow jerseys were available the Tour had moved on to Grenoble, and it was there, in the café l'Ascenseur, that Christophe (officially) donned the Tour's first *maillot jaune*.

And it was on the roads of northern France – in that war-ravaged region which he himself had dubbed *l'enfer du nord* just months earlier – that Christophe lost the yellow jersey. And, as had happened in 1913 when he was the virtual leader of the Tour, the reason Christophe lost the race lead was that his forks broke. This time there was no mountain to descend but, even so, *le vieux gaulois* still lost more than hour making his repairs. And then he compounded his losses when he crashed on a level crossing. By the time he reached Dunkerque the crowds who had cheered home stage-winner – and new race leader – Lambot had long since departed and Christophe was third overall.

When they arrived back in Paris race-winner Lambot won the applause of the crowds filling the Parc des Princes, but it was Christophe who won their hearts. Like Émile Georget in 1907, he was the moral victor of a Tour unjustly lost. Money began to pour in to *L'Auto* for him, a few francs here, a few hundred francs there, and when it was all totted up Christophe had the satisfaction of a purse of 13,310 francs to add to his moral victory, substantially more than had been awarded to Lambot.

Initially, 11 men finished the thirteenth Tour, almost half the number who had completed the first race in 1903. A fortnight after the race ended that was reduced to 10, when action was taken against Paul Duboc, he of the poison on the Tourmalet incident in the 1911 Tour. Duboc had damaged his bike on the final stage and taken a lift in a car in order to get to the next control where repairs could be effected. Even though it was the last stage, and even though Duboc gained no competitive advantage, the commissaires decreed that the rules must be obeyed. His name was scrubbed from the list of finishers.

From the first stage of the race the commissaires had been showing their toughness. The Belgian Jean Rossius won the opening stage but was denied the race lead after he was handed a 30-minute time penalty for having passed water to his compatriot Philippe Thys. On the second stage Léon Scieur, who had suffered multiple punctures, was warned that he would be handed a time penalty if he accepted help threading a needle in order to sew up a repaired tyre. Two stages later, on the road to Les Sables-d'Olonne, Francis

Pélissier was warned against pacing his brother Henri as they sought to regain the *peloton* that was speeding away from them up the road. On the road to Marseille Aloïs Verstraeten was thrown off the race for having taken a tow from a passing motorbike. As if the Tour wasn't tough enough the organisers seemed to be taking every opportunity to make it tougher still.

Stage-by-Stage Results for the 1919 Tour de France			Stage Winner	Race Leader
Stage 1 Sun 29 Jun	Paris (Parc des Princes) to Le Havre 67 starters, 41 finishers	388 km 15h56'00" 24.4 kph	Jean Rossius (Bel) La Sportive	Henri Pélissier (Fra) La Sportive
Mon 30 Jun	Rest day			
Stage 2 Tue 1 Jul	Le Havre to Cherbourg 27 finishers	364 km 15h51'13" 23.0 kph	Henri Pélissier (Fra) La Sportive	Henri Pélissier (Fra) La Sportive
Wed 2 Jul	Rest day			
Stage 3 Thu 3 Jul	Cherbourg to Brest 25 finishers	405 km 15h30'05" 26.1 kph	Francis Pélissier (Fra) La Sportive	Henri Pélissier (Fra) La Sportive
Fri 4 Jul	Rest day			
Stage 4 Sat 5 Jul	Brest to Les Sables- d'Olonne 20 finishers	412 km 15h51'45" 26.0 kph	Jean Alavoine (Fra) La Sportive	Eugène Christophe (Fra) La Sportive
Stage 5 Sun 6 Jul	Les Sables-d'Olonne to Bayonne 17 finishers	482 km 18h54'07" 25.5 kph	Jean Alavoine (Fra) La Sportive	Eugène Christophe (Fra) La Sportive
Mon 7 Jul Tue 8 Jul	Rest day			
Stage 6 Wed 9 Jul	Bayonne to Luchon 16 finishers	326 km 15h41'51" 20.8 kph	Honoré Barthélémy (Fra) La Sportive	Eugène Christophe (Fra) La Sportive
	Major climbs: Col d'Aubisque (1,709m) Luigi Lucotti (Ita) Bianchi; Col du Tourmalet (2,115m) Honoré Barthélémy (Fra) La Sportive; Col d'Aspin (1,489m) Honoré Barthélémy (Fra) La Sportive; Col de Peyresourde (1,569m) Honoré Barthélémy (Fra) La Sportive			
Thu 10 Jul	Rest day			
Stage 7 Fri 11 Jul	Luchon to Perpignan 15 finishers	323 km 13h12'43" 24.4 kph	Jean Alavoine (Fra) La Sportive	Eugène Christophe (Fra) La Sportive
	Major climbs: Col des Ares (797m) Jean Alavoine (Fra) La Sportive; Col de Portet d'Aspet (1,069m) n/a; Col de Port (1,249m) Jules Nempon (Fra) Nempon; Col du Puymorens (1,915m) Honoré Barthélémy (Fra) La Sportive			

Stage-by-Stage Results for the 1919 Tour de France			Stage Winner	Race Leader
Sat 12 Jul	Rest day			
Stage 8 Sun 13 Jul	Perpignan to Marseille 13 finishers	370 km 13h50'32" 26.7 kph	Jean Alavoine (Fra) La Sportive	Eugène Christophe (Fra) La Sportive
Mon 14 Jul	Rest day			
Stage 9 Tue 15 Jul	Marseille to Nice 12 finishers	338 km 13h39'48" 24.7 kph	Honoré Barthélémy (Fra) La Sportive	Eugène Christophe (Fra) La Sportive
	Major climbs: Col de Braus (1,002m) Luigi Lucotti (Ita) Bianchi; Col de Castillon (706m) Honoré Barthélémy (Fra) La Sportive			
Wed 16 Jul	Rest day			
Stage 10 Thu 17 Jul	Nice to Grenoble 11 finishers	333 km 13h08'10" 25.3 kph	Honoré Barthéleémy (Fra) La Sportive	Eugène Christophe (Fra) La Sportive
	Major climbs: Col d'Allos (2,250m) Honoré Barthélémy (Fra) La Sportive; Col Bayard (1,246m) Honoré Barthélémy (Fra) La Sportive			
Fri 18 Jul	Rest day			
Stage 11 Sat 19 Jul	Grenoble to Geneva 11 finishers	325 km 13h46'41" 23.6 kph	Honoré Barthélémy (Fra) La Sportive	Eugène Christophe (Fra) La Sportive
	Major climbs: Col du Lautaret (2,058m) Honoré Barthélémy (Fra) La Sportive; Col du Galibier (2,556m) Honoré Barthélémy (Fra) La Sportive; Col des Aravis (1,498m) Honoré Barthélémy (Fra) La Sportive			
Sun 20 Jul	Rest day			
Stage 12 Mon 21 Jul	Geneva to Strasbourg 11 finishers	371 km 15h08'42" 24.5 kph	Luigi Lucotti (Ita) Bianchi	Eugène Christophe (Fra) La Sportive
	Major climbs: Col de la Faucille (1,323m) n/a			
Tue 22 Jul	Rest day			
Stage 13 Wed 23 Jul	Strasbourg to Metz 11 finishers	315 km 11h55'13" 26.4 kph	Luigi Lucotti (Ita) Bianchi	Eugène Christophe (Fra) La Sportive
Stage 14 Thu 24 Jul	Metz to Dunkerque 11 finishers	468 km 21h04'27" 22.2 kph	Firmin Lambot (Bel) La Sportive	Firmin Lambot (Bel) La Sportive
Fri 25 Jul				
Sat 26 Jul	Rest day			
Stage 15 Sun 27 Jul	Dunkerque to Paris (Parc des Princes) 10 finishers	340 km 15h00'54" 22.6 kph	Jean Alavoine (Fra) La Sportive	Firmin Lambot (Bel) La Sportive

Prize fund: 50,000 francs (5,000 francs first prize)

Final Classification

Place		Rider	Team	Time	Age
1	1	Firmin Lambot (Bel)	La Sportive	5,560 km 231h07'15" 24.056 kph	33
2	2	Jean Alavoine (Fra)	La Sportive	+ 1h42'54"	31
3	3	Eugène Christophe (Fra)	La Sportive	+ 2h26'31"	34
4	4	Léon Scieur (Bel)	La Sportive	+ 2h52'15"	31
5	5	Honoré Barthélémy (Fra)	La Sportive	+ 4h14'22"	27
6	6	Jacques Coomans (Bel)	La Sportive	+ 15h21'34"	30
7	7	Luigi Lucotti (Ita)	Bianchi	+ 16h01'12"	25
8		~~Paul Duboc (Fra)~~ (1)	~~La Sportive~~		35
9	8	Joseph Vandaele (Bel)	La Sportive	+ 18h23'02"	29
~~10~~	9	Alfred Steux (Bel)	La Sportive	+ 20h29'01"	27
~~11~~	10	Jules Nempon (Fra)	Nempon	+ 21h44'12"	29

Lanterne Rouge

~~11~~	10	Jules Nempon (Fra)	Nempon	+ 21h44'12"	29

Independents

		Jules Nempon (Fra)	Nempon		29

Meilleur Grimpeur

		Honoré Barthélémy (Fra)	La Sportive		27

(1) Paul Duboc was disqualified after it was found he had completed part of the final stage by car.

1920: The First to Three

Nine years and five Tours after Gustave Garrigou was the last French winner of the Tour, French hopes rested on the shoulders of Eugène Christophe, the moral victor of the 1919 race, and Henri Pélissier, the thoroughbred who had come so close (with a little help from the commissaires) in 1914. French hopes, though, were dashed and – but for three stage wins – the Belgians once again dominated the *grande boucle*.

After having abandoned on the opening stage of the previous year's race Philippe Thys was back in form for 1920. The opening stage saw his key rivals – defending champion Firmin Lambot, Christophe and Pélissier – all lose more than a quarter of an hour. That opening stage saw a group of five riders arrive in Le Havre together – Louis Mottiat, Jean Rossius, Philippe Thys, Félix Goethals and Émile Masson – with Mottiat taking the stage win. All five shared the race lead. Thys took the next stage, but the same five riders still shared the lead. Four of them were still sharing the lead in Brest, where Mottiat fell away and Pélissier took the stage win. The French star made it back-to-back victories in Les Sables-d'Olonne, with Thys and Masson still tied for time and sharing the lead.

On the mammoth 482-kilometre stage from Les Sables-d'Olonne to Bayonne the Tour really kicked off. Pélissier got slapped with a time penalty for throwing away a punctured tyre – riders were supposed to start and finish with the same equipment, and the commissaires decided that included tyres – and once more quit the race. Lambot took the stage win but already his hopes of defending his Tour crown were all but gone, he being more than an hour behind Thys and Masson (who still shared the lead).

In Luchon, at the end of the first round of Pyrenean climbs, Thys was finally alone in the lead of the race, with Lambot – who added the stage to Luchon to his tally – in third and Hector Heusghem in second, 28 minutes behind Thys. Christophe had a bad day in the mountains, losing more than two hours to the leaders and abandoned the race the next day.

Thys's control of the race the rest of the way home was unchallenged. In Nice, he finally got to don the *maillot jaune* – again, if his story of wearing one in 1913 is true – *L'Auto* having, for one reason or another, not been awarding the jersey earlier in the race. The Belgian's passage back to Paris was eased somewhat by the elimination of some of the climbs that normally featured in the final portion of the race.

Back in Paris, the Parc des Princes was once again filled to the rafters to cheer home the Tour's first triple winner. For Alphonse Baugé, Thys's *directeur sportive* at La Sportive, this win really elevated him above Léopold Alibert, the architect of Louis Petit-Breton's back-to-back wins in 1907 and 1908 and, now having guided six riders to seven victories, Baugé was clearly not just the best team boss of his generation, but also the best the Tour had yet seen.

While only a fifth of the *peloton* made it back to Paris, those who did showed their toughness, none more so than Honoré Barthélémy, whose four stages wins the previous year had excited many. He took a tumble in the Alps, fracturing his shoulder and dislocating his wrist. Undaunted, he rode on, only for a stray flint to blind him in one eye. Barthélémy still managed to finish as the best placed French rider, in eighth.

As well as being remembered for producing the first three-time winner, the 1920 Tour is also notable for being the first time the organisers officially addressed the issue of doping. Writing in the pages of *L'Auto* Desgrange reproached riders who thought nothing of doping. His real ire, though, was saved for the members of their entourage – the managers and "certain doctors" – who Desgrange felt were the real cause of the problem blighting the sport. Who he was pointing the finger at is unknown. But the problem he identified would take more than mere words to solve.

Stage-by-Stage Results for the 1920 Tour de France			Stage Winner	Race Leader
Stage 1 Sun 27 Jun	Paris (Argenteuil) to Le Havre 113 starters, 97 finishers	388 km 14h50'46" 26.1 kph	Louis Mottiat (Bel) La Sportive	Louis Mottiat (Bel) La Sportive
				Jean Rossius (Bel) La Sportive
				Philippe Thys (Bel) La Sportive
				Félix Goethals (Fra) La Sportive
				Émile Masson (Fra) La Sportive
Mon 28 Jun	Rest day			
Stage 2 Tue 29 Jun	Le Havre to Cherbourg 84 finishers	364 km 15h17'48" 23.8 kph	Philippe Thys (Bel) La Sportive	Philippe Thys (Bel) La Sportive
				Jean Rossius (Bel) La Sportive
				Louis Mottiat (Bel) La Sportive
				Félix Goethals (Fra) La Sportive
				Émile Masson (Fra) La Sportive
Wed 30 Jun	Rest day			
Stage 3 Thu 1 Jul	Cherbourg to Brest 67 finishers	405 km 16h09'00" 25.1 kph	Henri Pélissier (Fra) La Sportive	Philippe Thys (Bel) La Sportive
				Jean Rossius (Bel) La Sportive
				Félix Goethals (Fra) La Sportive
				Émile Masson (Fra) La Sportive
Fri 2 Jul	Rest day			
Stage 4 Sat 3 Jul	Brest to Les Sables-d'Olonne 48 finishers	412 km 15h59'28" 25.8 kph	Henri Pélissier (Fra) La Sportive	Philippe Thys (Bel) La Sportive
				Émile Masson (Fra) La Sportive
Sun 4 Jul	Rest day			
Stage 5 Mon 5 Jul	Les Sables-d'Olonne to Bayonne 43 finishers	482 km 19h44'00" 24.4 kph	Firmin Lambot (Bel) La Sportive	Philippe Thys (Bel) La Sportive
				Émile Masson (Fra) La Sportive
Tue 6 Jul	Rest day			

Stage-by-Stage Results for the 1920 Tour de France			Stage Winner	Race Leader
Stage 6 Wed 7 Jul	Bayonne to Luchon 31 finishers	326 km 15h15'25" 21.4 kph	Firmin Lambot (Bel) La Sportive	Philippe Thys (Bel) La Sportive
	Major climbs: Col d'Aubisque (1,709m) Firmin Lambot (Bel) La Sportive; Col du Tourmalet (2,115m) Firmin Lambot (Bel) La Sportive; Col d'Aspin (1,489m) Firmin Lambot (Bel) La Sportive; Col de Peyresourde (1,569m) Firmin Lambot (Bel) La Sportive			
Thu 8 Jul	Rest day			
Stage 7 Fri 9 Jul	Luchon to Perpignan 27 finishers	323 km 13h41'50" 23.6 kph	Jean Rossius (Bel) La Sportive	Philippe Thys (Bel) La Sportive
	Major climbs: Col des Ares (797m) n/a ; Col de Portet d'Aspet (1,069m) Firmin Lambot (Bel) La Sportive; Col de Port (1,249m) Philippe Thys (Bel) La Sportive; Col du Puymorens (1,915m) Firmin Lambot (Bel) La Sportive			
Sat 10 Jul	Rest day			
Stage 8 Sun 11 Jul	Perpignan to Aix-en-Provence 25 finishers	325 km 12h12'18" 26.6 kph	Louis Heusghem (Bel) La Sportive	Philippe Thys (Bel) La Sportive
Mon 12 Jul Tue 13 Jul	Rest days			
Stage 9 Wed 14 Jul	Aix-en-Provence to Nice 23 finishers	356 km 16h15'44" 21.9 kph	Philippe Thys (Bel) La Sportive	Philippe Thys (Bel) La Sportive
	Major climbs: Col de Braus (,1002m) Firmin Lambot (Bel) La Sportive; Col de Castillon (706m) Firmin Lambot (Bel) La Sportive			
Thu 15 Jul	Rest day			
Stage 10 Fri 16 Jul	Nice to Grenoble 22 finishers	333 km 14h47'39" 22.5 kph	Hector Heusghem (Bel) La Sportive	Philippe Thys (Bel) La Sportive
	Major climbs: Col d'Allos (2,250m) Firmin Lambot (Bel) La Sportive; Col Bayard (1,246m) Hector Heusghem (Bel) La Sportive			
Sat 17 Jul	Rest day			
Stage 11 Sun 18 Jul	Grenoble to Gex 22 finishers	362 km 15h30'43" 23.3 kph	Léon Scieur (Bel) La Sportive	Philippe Thys (Bel) La Sportive
	Major climbs: Col du Galibier (2,556m) Firmin Lambot (Bel) La Sportive; Col des Aravis (1,498m) Firmin Lambot (Bel) La Sportive			
Mon 19 Jul	Rest day			
Stage 12 Tue 20 Jul	Gex to Strasbourg 22 finishers	354 km 14h19'19" 24.7 kph	Philippe Thys (Bel) La Sportive	Philippe Thys (Bel) La Sportive
Wed 21 Jul	Rest day			
Stage 13 Thu 22 Jul	Strasbourg to Metz 22 finishers	300 km 11h13'24" 26.7 kph	Philippe Thys (Bel) La Sportive	Philippe Thys (Bel) La Sportive

Stage-by-Stage Results for the 1920 Tour de France			Stage Winner	Race Leader
Fri 23 Jul	Rest day			
Stage 14 Sat 24 Jul	Metz to Dunkerque 22 finishers	433 km 18h33'51" 23.3 kph	Félix Goethals (Fra) La Sportive	Philippe Thys (Bel) La Sportive
Stage 15 Sun 25 Jul	Dunkerque to Paris (Parc des Princes) 22 finishers	340 km 14h31'40" 23.4 kph	Jean Rossius (Bel) La Sportive	Philippe Thys (Bel) La Sportive

Prize fund: 80,765 francs (15,000 francs first prize)

Final Classification				
Place	**Rider**	**Team**	**Time**	**Age**
1	Philippe Thys (Bel)	La Sportive	5.503 km 231h07'15" 24.072 kph	30
2	Hector Heusghem (Bel)	La Sportive	+ 57'21"	30
3	Firmin Lambot (Bel)	La Sportive	+ 1h39'35"	34
4	Léon Scieur (Bel)	La Sportive	+ 1h44'58"	32
5	Émile Masson (Bel)	La Sportive	+ 2h56'52"	31
6	Louis Heusghem (Bel)	La Sportive	+ 3h40'47"	30
7	Jean Rossius (Bel)	La Sportive	+ 3h49'55"	29
8	Honoré Barthélémy (Fra)	La Sportive	+ 5h35'19"	28
9	Félix Goethals (Fra)	La Sportive	+ 9h23'07"	29
10	Joseph Vandaele (Bel)	La Sportive	+ 10h45'41"	30
Lanterne Rouge				
22	Charles Raboisson (Fra)	Unsponsored	69h00'05"	30
Meilleur Grimpeur				
	Firmin Lambot (Bel)	La Sportive		34

1921: Belgium, Again

Henri Desgrange was not a happy man as the 1921 cycling season opened. The Tour had not produced a French winner since 1911. He was increasingly annoyed by – what he perceived to be – the lack of effort some riders made in the race. And he was particularly irked by the best cyclist France had yet produced, Henri Pélissier, the man who in 1919 had compared himself to a thoroughbred while his rivals were mere cart-horses. Writing in *L'Auto* Desgrange declared that Pélissier would never win the Tour as he simply did not know how to suffer.

Come the last Sunday of March, and Paris-Roubaix – now nicknamed *l'enfer du nord*, the hell of the north – Desgrange was forced to eat an amount of humble pie when Pélissier reigned supreme. *L'Auto* had no choice but to celebrate the win and even went so far as to declare it a triumph for the thoroughbred, echoing Pélissier's own description of himself. But if anyone believed that that success prefigured glory for Pélissier and France at the Tour they were sadly mistaken. The thoroughtbred decided he couldn't be bothered with a race that best suited cart-horses and so sat it out.

French hopes also soared in May, when the 36-year-old Eugène Christope – *le vieux gaulois* – took the victory in Bordeaux-Paris. Surely this must be a sign that France could once more win the Tour? Though Christophe did make the start of the Tour he didn't make the end and was never in contention.

Hopes soared even more when news came through that both the defending champion Philippe Thys and 1919 winner Firmin Lambot were carrying illnesses into the Tour and were unlikely to present much of a threat. French hopes turned to Honoré Barthélémy, who had shown such spirit the year before when he rode on after breaking his shoulder and dislocating his wrist, arriving in Paris blind in one eye, but still the best of the French riders. And, at the end of the race's first stage, Barthélémy seemed like real contender. Despite multiple punctures he rolled home just two minutes down on Louis Mottiat, who once again took the opening stage and the early lead. With a four minute gap back to his nearest rival surely Barthélémy was looking like he was fit for the victory? Those hopes were dashed the next stage when Barthélémy lost the thick end of an hour and Léon Scieur took the race lead from his compatriot Mottiat.

The 33-year-old Scieur was born in the same Walloon town of Florennes as 1919 Tour winner Firmin Lambot, and it was the Tour champion who had got him into cycling, at the unusually late age of 22. In 1920 Scieur put a stage in the Tour and victory at Liège-Bastogne-Liège on his *palamarès* – his best successes to date – and once he took control of the 1921 Tour he never relinquished it, or the *maillot jaune* which this time the organisers had remembered to organise a supply of ahead of the race.

Through the early stages down along France's Atlantic coast Scieur opened up a lead of nearly half an hour on his only real rival, Hector Heusghem. On the first stage in the Pyrenees, taking in the Aubisque and the Tourmalet, Heusghem took flight and Scieur had to fight to limit his losses, arriving in Luchon with just a four minute cushion over his *maillot jaune* rival. But Heusghem failed to press home his advantage on the second day in the Pyrenees and Scieur exited the first round of mountains still in the race lead.

Over the Braus and the Castillon on the road to Nice Scieur was able to put time into Heusghem, but on the next stage Heusghem seized the opportunity to attack when the yellow jersey suffered a puncture. For years now riders had been taking advantage of others' misfortune and attacking, but for Scieur such behaviour was beyond the pale. Fixing his tyre he chased and caught Heusghem and launched into a lecture on racing etiquette. To drive home his point he drove home alone, dropping his compatriot and team-mate and taking a solo victory in Grenoble.

Despite the fact that *L'Auto*'s circulation was booming – interest in the race was such that more cars had been added to the race convoy to accommodate journalists, especially ones from abroad – Desgrange was not happy with the way his race was unfolding. The riders simply weren't trying hard enough. Scieur had finished the stage to Strasbourg with a broken wheel strapped to his back (a change to the rules allowed riders to replace broken parts, but they had to present the broken part as proof that the replacement was needed). If the riders behind couldn't catch a man handicapped like that, well Desgrange would just have to find a way to encourage them to try harder.

On the stage from Strasbourg to Metz the second-class riders – the *isolés* of old – were sent off two hours ahead of the main *peloton*, Desgrange judging that to be a fair handicap for the aces. Three of them survived the chasers behind and arrived in Metz three-quarters of an hour up on the stars in the main *peloton*. The aces hadn't tried hard enough, Desgrange decided. The fix for that was to send the second class riders off behind the first. At this they rebelled and threatened strike. Desgrange, not wanting to lose them before Paris, had to relent and switch back to the normal way of racing, everyone setting off together.

When the Tour rolled in to Paris, with Belgium chalking up its sixth Tour win, an era closed. In 1903 a twenty-year-old Lucien Pothier finished second in the inaugural Tour de France. The following year he was once again second, until the French federation started investigating what had happened at the race and was one the riders airbrushed from that race's history. He returned to the Tour again in 1909 and 1910, failing to finish the first and just making it into the top 30 in the other. That should have been the end of his story, but there he was again, now 38 and once more riding into Paris at the end of his final Tour de France.

Stage-by-Stage Results for the 1921 Tour de France			Stage Winner	Maillot Jaune
Stage 1 Sun 26 Jun	Paris (Argenteuil) to Le Havre 123 starters, 103 finishers	388 km 15h29'10" 25.1 kph	Louis Mottiat (Bel) La Sportive	Louis Mottiat (Bel) La Sportive
Mon 27 Jun	Rest day			
Stage 2 Tue 28 Jun	Le Havre to Cherbourg 88 finishers	364 km 13h07'50" 27.7 kph	Romain Bellenger (Fra) La Sportive	Léon Scieur (Bel) La Sportive
Wed 29 Jun	Rest day			
Stage 3 Thu 30 Jun	Cherbourg to Brest 76 finishers	405 km 15h08'45" 26.7 kph	Léon Scieur (Bel) La Sportive	Léon Scieur (Bel) La Sportive
Fri 1 Jul	Rest day			
Stage 4 Sat 2 Jul	Brest to Les Sables-d'Olonne 71 finishers	412 km 15h31'41" 26.5 kph	Louis Mottiat (Bel) La Sportive	Léon Scieur (Bel) La Sportive
Sun 3 Jul	Rest day			
Stage 5 Mon 4 Jul	Les Sables-d'Olonne to Bayonne 69 finishers	482 km 18h47'26" 25.7 kph	Louis Mottiat (Bel) La Sportive	Léon Scieur (Bel) La Sportive
Tue 5 Jul	Rest day			
Stage 6 Wed 6 Jul	Bayonne to Luchon 48 finishers	326 km 15h09'36" 21.5 kph	Hector Heusghem (Bel) La Sportive	Léon Scieur (Bel) La Sportive
	Major climbs: Col d'Aubisque (1,709m) Léon Scieur (Bel) La Sportive; Col d'Aspin (1,489m) Hector Heusghem (Bel) La Sportive; Col du Tourmalet (2,115m) Hector Heusghem (Bel) La Sportive; Col de Peyresourde (1,569m) Hector Heusghem (Bel) La Sportive			
Thu 7 Jul	Rest day			
Stage 7 Fri 8 Jul	Luchon to Perpignan 47 finishers	323 km 12h58'15" 24.9 kph	Louis Mottiat (Bel) La Sportive	Léon Scieur (Bel) La Sportive
	Major climbs: Col de Portet d'Aspet (1,069m) Félix Goethals (Fra) La Sportive; Col de Port (1,249m) n/a ; Col du Puymorens (1,915m) Luigi Lucotti (Ita) Ancora			
Sat 9 Jul	Rest day			
Stage 8 Sun 10 Jul	Perpignan to Toulon 46 finishers	411 km 16h06'51" 25.5 kph	Luigi Lucotti (Ita) Ancora	Léon Scieur (Bel) La Sportive
Mon 11 Jul	Rest day			

Stage-by-Stage Results for the 1921 Tour de France			Stage Winner	Maillot Jaune
Stage 9 Tue 12 Jul	Toulon to Nice 43 finishers	272 km 11h26'09" 23.8 kph	Firmin Lambot (Bel) La Sportive	Léon Scieur (Bel) La Sportive
	Major climbs: Col de Braus (1,002m) Firmin Lambot (Ita) La Sportive; Col de Castillon (706m) Firmin Lambot (Bel) La Sportive			
Wed 13 Jul	Rest day			
Stage 10 Thu 14 Jul	Nice to Grenoble 41 finishers	333 km 14h02'30" 23.7 kph	Léon Scieur (Bel) La Sportive	Léon Scieur (Bel) La Sportive
	Major climbs: Col d'Allos (2,250m) Honoré Barthélémy (Fra) La Sportive + Hector Heusghem (Bel) La Sportive; Col Bayard (1,246m) Léon Scieur (Bel) La Sportive			
Fri 15 Jul	Rest day			
Stage 11 Sat 16 Jul	Grenoble to Geneva 39 finishers	325 km 14h04'13" 23.1 kph	Félix Goethals (Fra) La Sportive	Léon Scieur (Bel) La Sportive
	Major climbs: Col du Lautaret (2,058m) Honoré Barthélémy (Fra) La Sportive; Col du Galibier (2,556m) Honoré Barthélémy (Fra) La Sportive; Col du Télégraphe (1,566m) Hector Heusghem (Bel) La Sportive; Col des Aravis (1,498m) Léon Scieur (Bel) La Sportive			
Sun 17 Jul	Rest day			
Stage 12 Mon 18 Jul	Geneva to Strasbourg 38 finishers	371 km 15h07'53" 24.5 kph	Honoré Barthélémy (Fra) La Sportive	Léon Scieur (Bel) La Sportive
Tue 19 Jul	Rest day			
Stage 13 Wed 20 Jul	Strasbourg to Metz 38 finishers	300 km 10h08'30" 29.6 kph	Félix Sellier (Bel) La Sportive	Léon Scieur (Bel) La Sportive
Thu 21 Jul	Rest day			
Stage 14 Fri 22 Jul	Metz to Dunkerque 38 finishers	433 km 17h40'04" 24.5 kph	Félix Goethals (Fra) La Sportive	Léon Scieur (Bel) La Sportive
Sat 23 Jul	Rest day			
Stage 15 Sun 24 Jul	Dunkerque to Paris (Parc des Princes) 38 finishers	340 km 15h25'09" 22.1 kph	Félix Goethals (Fra) La Sportive	Léon Scieur (Bel) La Sportive

Prize fund: 80,000 francs (15,000 francs first prize)

Final Classification

Place	Rider	Team	Time	Age
1	Léon Scieur (Bel)	La Sportive	5,485 km 221h50'26" 24.724	33
2	Hector Heusghem (Bel)	La Sportive	+ 18'36"	31
3	Honoré Barthélémy (Fra)	La Sportive	+ 2h01'00"	29
4	Luigi Lucotti (Ita)	Ancora	+ 2h39'18"	27
5	Hector Tiberghien (Bel)	La Sportive	+ 4h33'19"	33
6	Victor Lenaers (Bel)	Delage	+ 4h53'23"	28
7	Léon Despontin (Bel)	La Sportive	+ 5h01'54"	33
8	Camile Leroy (Bel)	Delage	+ 7h56'27"	29
9	Firmin Lambot (Bel)	La Sportive	+ 8h26'25"	35
10	Félix Goethals (Fra)	La Sportive	+ 8h42'26"	30

Lanterne Rouge

38	Henri Catelan (Fra)	Unsponsored	+ 61h19'57"	26

Independents

	Victor Lenaers (Bel)	Delage		28

Meilleur Grimpeur

	Hector Heusghem (Bel)	La Sportive		31

1922: Another Lucky Win?

La Sportive, the consortium of French bicycle manufacturers created after the war and which had won the last three Tours, came to an end in 1922 as the firms once more decided to race under their own names. In its place they formed a cartel, agreeing to keep costs under control by imposing a salary cap which would keep wages low. This meant that – while officially still not welcomed by the Tour – names like Peugeot, Alcyon and Automoto once more returned to the race.

Aphonse Baugé – post-War now carrying the nickname *le maréchal*, the Marshal – had bossed each of La Sportive's three Tour wins, as well as Peugeot's two immediately before the war and the four racked up by Alcyon before that. And it was to Peugeot he returned in 1922.

The race route was more or less the same as in previous years, with a few more tweaks. A convoy of 15 press cars – five for *L'Auto*'s 600,000 readers during the Tour – was now following the race and reporting how it unfolded. There were still five stages exceeding 400 kilometres – still including the horrendous 482 kilometres from Les Sables-d'Olonne down to Bayonne – but there were now three that dropped below 300 kilometres. The most important of these was the race's tenth stage, which replaced the normal 350 kilometres or so from Nice to Grenoble with a pleasant 274 kilometres from the capital of the Côte d'Azur up to Briançon. Pleasant, that is, apart from the inclusion of the Col d'Izoard, at 2,361 metres a fearsome climb.

After two Tours in which the winner had more or less emerged by the end of the second stage, the sixteenth Tour served up a race in which five different riders wore the *maillot jaune* and the winner did not emerge until the final week of the race.

Peugeot opened the race with the first stage win and the *maillot jaune*, Robert Jacquinot soloing to victory. He held his lead through the next two stages, down to Brest, where he lost more than an hour as a result of punctures and Eugène Christophe (Automoto) took over at the top of the general classification. *Le vieux gaulois*'s lead held through to the Pyrenees,

Jean Alavoine (Peugeot), who had already taken the stage to Bayonne, went on the attack in the mountains – where the ascent of the Tourmalet was cancelled because of snow – putting nearly 40 minutes into Christophe and clawing himself up to within half an hour of the race lead. This he comfortably took when he added the second Pyrenean stage to his *palmarès*, Christophe losing another three-quarters of an hour. Alavoine now led his Peugeot team-mate Firmin Lambot by just under a quarter of an hour, with Christophe 20 minutes off the lead. Alavoine was known for his ability to win stages – he'd racked up 11 before the start of the 1922 Tour – and had finished second overall in 1919, but this was his first time to be leading the Tour.

Philippe Thys (Peugeot), out of contention for the overall victory after a broken wheel in the Pyrenees cost him more than three hours, showed he still had the legs of a winner by taking three stages back-to-back, in Toulouse, Nice and Briançon. After the last of three stages in the Alps, Alavoine held a lead of just under seven minutes over Firmin Lambot and a quarter of an hour over Thomann's Hector Heusghem, having lost time with mechanical problems en route to Geneva. And Christophe had once more broken his forks, this time on the Galibier, and – as he had on the Tourmalet all those years ago – lost three hours walking down the mountain and making his own repairs.

With the mountains behind them, the *peloton* still had nearly 1,500 kilometres to cover before they would hear the cheers of the crowd in the Parc des Princes. Alavoine suffered a series of punctures on the road to Strasbourg, where the man in third place, Heusghem seized the yellow jersey, three minutes clear of Lambot and ten clear of Alavoine.

With two second-place finishes at the two previous Tours, could this finally be Heusghem's chance to shine? No. Damaging his bike on the road to Metz he took a team-mate's – one version of the tale has a commissaire giving him permission to do this – and seemed to have done enough, finishing with the frontrunners in the city the Germans had ruled for so long. But then he got slapped with a one hour time penalty for that bike change and tumbled down the general classification to fourth.

And the man who inherited the *maillot jaune*? That man Lambot, once more still standing while others fell by the wayside, even though he'd actually lost five minutes into Metz and looked like he was ruling himself out of contention. Heusghem took back six minutes on the road to Dunkerque and another two minutes into Paris, but there was no stopping Lambot, who could afford to measure his exertions, his nearest challengers 40 minutes and more off the pace. And so the Belgian once more rode into Paris the winner of the Tour de France, now up there with Lucien Petit-Breton on two wins in the *grande boucle*, and one behind Thys's three.

At 36 years, four months and nine days old, Lambot was the Tour's oldest winner, and also the first to take overall victory without winning a single stage. Making light of his reputation for lucky wins, Lambot declared that to win the Tour you needed first good health, and then good luck. The ability to climb, he said, was only good enough to get you third place.

Stage-by-Stage Results for the 1922 Tour de France			Stage Winner	Maillot Jaune
Stage 1 Sun 25 Jun	Paris (Luna Park, Porte Maillot) to Le Havre 120 starters, 102 finishers	388 km 15h11'48" 25.5 kph	Robert Jacquinot (Fra) Peugeot	Robert Jacquinot (Fra) Peugeot
Mon 26 Jun	Rest day			
Stage 2 Tue 27 Jun	Le Havre to Cherbourg 90 finishers	364 km 15h07'53" 24.1 kph	Romain Bellenger (Fra) Peugeot	Robert Jacquinot (Fra) Peugeot
Wed 28 Jun	Rest day			
Stage 3 Thu 29 Jun	Cherbourg to Brest 73 finishers	405 km 17h34'44" 23.0 kph	Robert Jacquinot (Fra) Peugeot	Robert Jacquinot (Fra) Peugeot
Fri 30 Jun	Rest day			
Stage 4 Sat 1 Jul	Brest to Les Sables-d'Olonne 67 finishers	412 km 15h16'24" 27.0 kph	Philippe Thys (Bel) Peugeot	Eugène Christophe (Fra) Automoto
Sun 2 Jul	Rest day			
Stage 5 Mon 3 Jul	Les Sables-d'Olonne to Bayonne 60 finishers	482 km 19h27'45" 24.8 kph	Jean Alavoine (Fra) Peugeot	Eugène Christophe (Fra) Automoto
Tue 4 Jul	Rest day			
Stage 6 Wed 5 Jul	Bayonne to Luchon 48 finishers	326 km 14h28'44" 22.5 kph	Jean Alavoine (Fra) Peugeot	Eugène Christophe (Fra) Automoto
	Major climbs: Col d'Aubisque (1,709m) Jean Alavoine (Fra) Peugeot; Col d'Aspin (1,489m) Jean Alavoine (Fra) Peugeot; Col de Peyresourde (1,569m) Jean Alavoine (Fra) Peugeot			
Thu 6 Jul	Rest day			
Stage 7 Fri 7 Jul	Luchon to Perpignan 47 finishers	323 km 12h05'43" 26.7 kph	Jean Alavoine (Fra) Peugeot	Jean Alavoine (Fra) Peugeot
	Major climbs: Col de Portet d'Aspet (1,069m) Jean Alavoine (Fra) Peugeot + Honoré Barthélémy (Fra) Automoto; Col de Port (1,249m) Jean Alavoine (Fra) Peugeot; Col du Puymorens (1,915m) Émile Masson (Bel) Alcyon			
Sat 8 Jul	Rest day			
Stage 8 Sun 9 Jul	Perpignan to Toulon 44 finishers	411 km 15h47'18" 26.0 kph	Philippe Thys (Bel) Peugeot	Jean Alavoine (Fra) Peugeot
Mon 10 Jul	Rest day			

Stage-by-Stage Results for the 1922 Tour de France			Stage Winner	Maillot Jaune
Stage 9 Tue 11 Jul	Toulon to Nice 44 finishers	284 km 11h40'12" 24.3 kph	Philippe Thys (Bel) Peugeot	Jean Alavoine (Fra) Peugeot
	Major climbs: Col de Braus (1,002m) Jean Alavoine (Fra) Peugeot; Col de Castillon (706m) Philippe Thys (Bel) Peugeot			
Wed 12 Jul	Rest day			
Stage 10 Thu 13 Jul	Nice to Briançon 44 finishers	274 km 12h50'07" 21.3 kph	Philippe Thys (Bel) Peugeot	Jean Alavoine (Fra) Peugeot
	Major climbs: Col d'Allos (2,250m) Jean Alavoine (Fra) Peugeot; Col de Vars (2,110m) Philippe Thys (Bel) Peugeot; Col d'Izoard (2,360m) Philippe Thys (Bel) Peugeot			
Fri 14 Jul	Rest day			
Stage 11 Sat 15 Jul	Briançon to Geneva 39 finishers	260 km 10h49'14" 24.0 kph	Émile Masson (Bel) Alcyon	Jean Alavoine (Fra) Peugeot
	Major climbs: Col du Galibier (2,556m) Émile Masson (Bel) Alcyon; Col du Télégraphe (1,566m) Émile Masson (Bel) Alcyon; Col des Aravis (1,498m) Émile Masson (Bel) Alcyon;			
Sun 16 Jul	Rest day			
Stage 12 Mon 17 Jul	Geneva to Strasbourg 39 finishers	371 km 15h15'43" 24.3 kph	Émile Masson (Bel) Alcyon	Hector Heusghem (Bel) Thomann
Tue 18 Jul	Rest day			
Stage 13 Wed 19 Jul	Strasbourg to Metz 38 finishers	300 km 12h02'34" 24.9 kph	Federico Gay (Ita) Automoto	Firmin Lambot (Bel) Peugeot
Thu 20 Jul	Rest day			
Stage 14 Fri 21 Jul	Metz to Dunkerque 38 finishers	433 km 17h07'09" 25.3 kph	Félix Sellier (Bel) Alcyon	Firmin Lambot (Bel) Peugeot
Sat 22 Jul	Rest day			
Stage 15 Sun 23 Jul	Dunkerque to Paris (Parc des Princes) 38 finishers	340 km 14h36'57" 23.3 kph	Philippe Thys (Bel) Peugeot	Firmin Lambot (Bel) Peugeot

Prize fund: 80,000 francs (10,000 francs first prize)

Final Classification

Place	Rider	Team	Time	Age
1	Firmin Lambot (Bel)	Peugeot	5,375 km 222h08'06" 24.196 kph	36
2	Jean Alavoine (Fra)	Peugeot	+ 41'15"	34
3	Félix Sellier (Bel)	Alcyon	+ 42'02"	29
4	Hector Heusghem (Bel)	Thomann	+ 43'56"	32
5	Victor Lenaers (Bel)	Automoto	+ 45'32"	29
6	Hector Tiberghien (Bel)	Peugeot	+ 1h21'35"	34
7	Léon Despontin (Bel)	Peugeot	+ 2h24'29"	34
8	Eugène Christophe (Fra)	Automoto	+ 3h25'39"	37
9	Jean Rossius (Bel)	La Française	+ 3h26'06"	31
10	Gaston Degy (Fra)	Peugeot	+ 3h49'13"	32
Lanterne Rouge				
38	Daniel Masson (Fra)	Alcyon	+ 65h53'41"	25
Independents				
	José Pelletier			33
Meilleur Grimpeur				
	Jean Alavoine (Fra)	Peugeot		34

1923: A Thoroughbred's Tour

Gliding noiselessly along the Promenade Anglais in the early morning dark, the remaining riders in the 1923 Tour set forth from Nice, bound for Briançon. Ahead lay the climbs of the Allos and the Izoard. Ottavio Bottecchia – who had débuted at that year's Giro d'Italia, where he finished fifth – was wearing the *maillot jaune*, 15 minutes clear of Peugeot's Jean Alavoine, with his Automoto team-mate Henri Pélissier twice as far back.

Bottecchia had taken the race lead in the Pyrenees, but that fact obscured the reality that he had lost time to Alavoine and Pélissier over the high peaks of the Aubisque and the Tourmalet. Only four minutes to his team-mate, but nearly half-an-hour to his Peugeot rival. Now, with the race heading into the high Alps and the day's major climbs each higher than the Tourmalet, Bottecchia's time in the yellow jersey was drawing to a close.

By the time the race crested the first of the day's major climbs, the Allos, Bottecchia was already two minutes in arrears of Henri Pélissier, who summited the climb at the head of a small group of riders. Between there and the foot of the Izoard Pélissier then proceeded to dispose of his companions. His Automoto team-mate Lucien Buysse was the last to break, surviving until the slopes of the Izoard before dropping away.

Pélissier crossed the alien landscape of the Izoard's Casse Déserte alone before finally cresting the summit of the climb and beginning the descent into Briançon, the stage his, and along with it the *maillot jaune*. Bottecchia was more than 40 minutes behind him by the time he rolled into Briançon, while Alavoine had come into a quarter of an hour earlier, riding one-handed, his arm broken in a fall descending the Izoard. With the Galibier to come on the next stage Bottecchia could be expected to lose yet more time. Alavoine was going nowhere with that arm. Which left Pélissier with a cushion of nearly 40 minutes over his next nearest rival, the Belgian Hector Tiberghien, riding for Peugeot. More than enough. After 12 years and seven races in which Belgians had ruled, the Tour was finally about to be liberated.

Pélissier rose to prominence in 1910, when he took a stage and second overall in Peugeot's Tour de France des Indépendents. A chance meeting the following year on the streets of Paris saw Lucien Petit-Breton taking him to Italy and when Pélissier returned home his *palmarès* carried wins in a number of Italian races, including *La Gazzetta dello Sport*'s Giro di Lomardia.

It was in one-day races that Pélissier really shone. While he did win the 600 kilometre Bordeaux-Paris, it was in races that were usually less than half that distance that he was at his best: as well as three victories in the Giro di Lombardia and two in Paris-Roubaix his list of wins includes races like Milan-Sanremo, Milan-Turin, Paris-Tours, Paris-Brussels, and Nice-Mont Agel.

The Tour at this time rarely featured stages below 300 kilometres. The 1914 race, where – with a little help from the commissaires – Pélissier ran Philippe Thys a close second, had two stages above 400 kilometres, and all the rest were above 300. The six shortest stages were each in or around 325 kilometres. When the race returned in 1919 the number of stages exceeding 400 kilometres rose to four – three of them one after the other between Cherbourg and Bayonne – with still no stages below 300. The shortest stages were still in or around 325 kilometres, but now there were only three of them. The Tour was a race which favoured endurance, in both body and bike. It was a race for cart-horses, whereas Pélissier saw himself as a thoroughbred. Which comment led to his departure from that race and the opening of a rift with Henri Desgrange.

The following year Pélissier again left the Tour early, this time after being penalised a few minutes for having thrown away a punctured tyre. The rules at the time required a rider start and finish with the same equipment, and that included tyres, punctured or

12 Pages   12 Pages

Le Petit Journal

illustré

HEBDOMADAIRE
61, rue Lafayette, Paris

PRIX : 0 fr. 30
29 Juillet 1923

Le Tour de France cycliste

Le hasard a parfois — trop rarement, hélas ! — des attentions délicates. C'est ainsi que la douzième étape du Tour de France, de Genève à Strasbourg, s'est terminée dans cette dernière ville par la victoire d'un Alsacien, le coureur Joseph Muller, en avance de 25 minutes sur ses concurrents les plus proches.

Le Petit Journal Illustré reports Joseph Muller winning the Strasbourg stage of the 1923 Tour.

not. The following two Tours – 1921 and 1922 – he didn't even enter. And perhaps Pélissier wouldn't have entered the 1923 Tour had he not changed teams.

Pélissier had signed for the JB Louvet team in 1922 after having had an argument with *La Sportive*'s boss Alphonse Baugé. Barely a year later it was time to have an argument with Louvet's Pierre Maisonnas, and turn to Automoto. The Saint-Étienne based manufacturer had débuted at the Tour in 1911, to no great impact, even when it had Lucien Petit-Breton riding in its purple jersey in 1913 and Léopold Alibert bossing the riders. But with the end of the manufacturers' consortium, La Sportive, it was coming to the fore. Eugène Christophe had been riding in its colours the previous year when he took the race lead. Riding the Tour, Automoto's bosses made clear to Pélissier, would be a condition of him signing for them.

Which only left the small matter of Desgrange to deal with. The Father of the Tour had written Pélissier off, saying he would never win the Tour as he didn't know how to suffer. But Desgrange needed a French victor, the Belgian domination had gone on too long. And even he realised that, riders like Honoré Barthélémy (who was also riding for Automoto) or Jean Alavoine (Peugeot) notwithstanding, Pélissier might be his best hope of that happening.

And so when it did happen – the lead gained on the Izoard was extended the next stage on the Galibier, and Pélissier made it back to Paris without mishaps – *L'Auto* celebrated a truly classic Tour, "a Tour that provided the swift, noble whippets victory over the hardy, resistant grafters." The yellow jersey had changed hands five times. The Pyrenees had whittled down the likely contenders. The Alps anointed the eventual winner. And there were no thoughts for moral winners or lucky victories. This was a Tour that was won fairly and squarely, on the road, with no outside help.

Or … perhaps not. Among the previous winners riding the seventeenth Tour was Léon Scieur, the 1921 victor. He exited the race in the Pyrenees, claiming to have been slipped a Mickey Finn that was so powerful he had to spend a week recuperating in Lourdes. But Scieur didn't just stop there. He suggested that the defending champion Firmin Lambot had similarly been got at in the Pyrenees. As had others. Beneath the surface, it seemed, the reality of life on the Tour de France was quite different to the version told in the pages of most newspapers, or now being shown on cinema screens in newsreel footage of portions of the Tour.

Stage-by-Stage Results for the 1923 Tour de France			Stage Winner	Maillot Jaune
Stage 1 Sun 24 Jun	Paris (Luna Park, Porte Maillot) to Le Havre 139 starters, 129 finishers	381 km 13h51'56" 27.5 kph	Robert Jacquinot (Fra) Peugeot	Robert Jacquinot (Fra) Peugeot
Mon 25 Jun	Rest day			
Stage 2 Tue 26 Jun	Le Havre to Cherbourg 121 finishers	371 km 14h11'41" 26.1 kph	Ottavio Bottecchia (Ita) Automoto	Ottavio Bottecchia (Ita) Automoto
Wed 27 Jun	Rest day			
Stage 3 Thu 28 Jun	Cherbourg to Brest 101 finishers	405 km 15h44'15" 25.7 kph	Henri Pélissier (Fra) Automoto	Ottavio Bottecchia (Ita) Automoto
Fri 29 Jun	Rest day			
Stage 4 Sat 30 Jun	Brest to Les Sables-d'Olonne 90 finishers	412 km 15h13'30" 27.1 kph	Albert Dejonghe (Bel) La Française	Romain Bellenger (Fra) Peugeot
Sun 1 Jul	Rest day			
Stage 5 Mon 2 Jul	Les Sables-d'Olonne to Bayonne 83 finishers	482 km 20h16'26" 23.8 kph	Robert Jacquinot (Fra) Peugeot	Romain Bellenger (Fra) Peugeot
Tue 3 Jul	Rest day			
Stage 6 Wed 4 Jul	Bayonne to Luchon 63 finishers	326 km 16h05'22" 20.3 kph	Jean Alavoine (Fra) Peugeot	Ottavio Bottecchia (Ita) Automoto
	Major climbs: Col d'Aubisque (1,709m) Otavio Bottecchia (Ita) Automoto; Col du Tourmalet (2,115m) Robert Jacquinot (Fra) Peugeot; Col d'Aspin (1,489m) Robert Jacquinot (Fra) Peugeot; Col de Peyresourde (1,569m) Jean Alavoine (Fra) Peugeot			
Thu 5 Jul	Rest day			
Stage 7 Fri 6 Jul	Luchon to Perpignan 59 finishers	323 km 12h47'58" 25.2 kph	Jean Alavoine (Fra) Peugeot	Ottavio Bottecchia (Ita) Automoto
	Major climbs: Col des Ares (797m) n/a ; Col de Portet d'Aspet (1,069m) Francis Pélissier (Fra) Automoto + Henri Pélissier (Fra) Automoto; Col du Puymorens (1,915m) Henri Pélissier (Fra) Automoto			
Sat 7 Jul	Rest day			

Stage-by-Stage Results for the 1923 Tour de France			Stage Winner	Maillot Jaune
Stage 8 Sun 8 Jul	Perpignan to Toulon 58 finishers	427 km 16h15'35" 26.3 kph	Lucien Buysse (Bel) Automoto	Ottavio Bottecchia (Ita) Automoto
Mon 9 Jul	Rest day			
Stage 9 Tue 10 Jul	Toulon to Nice 54 finishers	281 km 12h10'39" 23.1 kph	Jean Alavoine (Fra) Peugeot	Ottavio Bottecchia (Ita) Automoto
	Major climbs: Col de Braus (1,002m) Jean Alavoine (Fra) Peugeot; Col de Castillon (706m) Jean Alavoine (Fra) Peugeot			
Wed 11 Jul	Rest day			
Stage 10 Thu 12 Jul	Nice to Briançon 50 finishers	275 km 12h45'29" 21.6 kph	Henri Pélissier (Fra) Automoto	Henri Pélissier (Fra) Automoto
	Major climbs: Col d'Allos (2,250m) Henri Pélissier (Fra) Automoto + Francis Pélissier (Fra) Automoto; Col de Vars (2,110m) Henri Pélissier (Fra) Automoto; Col d'Izoard (2,360m) Henri Pélissier (Fra) Automoto			
Fri 13 Jul	Rest day			
Stage 11 Sat 14 Jul	Briançon to Geneva 49 finishers	260 km 9h50'21" 26.4 kph	Henri Pélissier (Fra) Automoto	Henri Pélissier (Fra) Automoto
	Major climbs: Col du Galibier (2,556m) Henri Pélissier (Fra) Automoto; Col des Aravis (1,498m) Henri Pélissier (Fra) Automoto			
Sun 15 Jul	Rest day			
Stage 12 Mon 16 Jul	Geneva to Strasbourg 48 finishers	377 km 15h08'51" 24.5 kph	Joseph Muller (Fra) Peugeot	Henri Pélissier (Fra) Automoto
Tue 17 Jul	Rest day			
Stage 13 Wed 18 Jul	Strasbourg to Metz 48 finishers	300 km 11h36'00" 25.9 kph	Romain Bellenger (Fra) Peugeot	Henri Pélissier (Fra) Automoto
Thu 19 Jul	Rest day			
Stage 14 Fri 20 Jul	Metz to Dunkerque 48 finishers	433 km 18h55'08" 22.8 kph	Félix Goethals (Fra) Thomann	Henri Pélissier (Fra) Automoto
Sat 21 Jul	Rest day			
Stage 15 Sun 22 Jul	Dunkerque to Paris (Parc des Princes) 48 finishers	343 km 15h19'36" 22.2 kph	Félix Goethals (Fra) Thomann	Henri Pélissier (Fra) Automoto

Total Prize fund: 100,000 francs (10,000 francs first prize)

Final Classification

Place	Rider	Team	Time	Age
1	Henri Pélissier (Fra)	Automoto	5,386 km 222h15'30" 24.233 kph	34
2	Ottavio Bottecchia (Ita)	Automoto	+ 30'41"	28
3	Romain Bellenger (Fra)	Peugeot	+ 1h04'43"	29
4	Hector Tiberghien (Bel)	Peugeot	+ 1h29'16"	35
5	Arsène Alancourt (Fra)	Armor	+ 2h06'40"	31
6	Henri Collé (Sui)	Griffon	+ 2h28'43"	29
7	Léon Despontin (Bel)	Peugeot	+ 2h39'49"	35
8	Lucien Buysse (Bel)	Automoto	+ 2h40'11"	30
9	Eugène Dhers (Fra)	Armor	+ 2h59'09"	32
10	Marcel Huot (Fra)	Griffon	+ 3h16'56"	26

Lanterne Rouge

48	Daniel Masson (Fra)		48h31'07"	26

Meilleur Grimpeur

	Henri Pélissier (Fra)	Automoto		34

1924: Tour de Souffrance

Going into the 1923 Giro d'Italia, Ottavio Bottecchia was an unknown, unsponsored rider. He came out of it the best of the independents and fifth overall. Two weeks after that Giro ended he was taking the start in the Tour de France wearing Automoto's purple jersey, there to provide what assistance he could – within the rules that banned all such help – to Automoto's star rider, Henri Pélissier. When, on the race's second stage, he donned the yellow jersey, it was done somewhat sheepishly; he made clear to Pélissier that his tenure at the head of the race would be just temporary.

And temporary it was, just two stages before he was dethroned by Peugeot's Romain Bellenger. But when the race entered the Pyrenees and Bellenger – a sprinter – faded in the high hills, the jersey found its way back to Bottecchia's shoulders and suddenly the Italian neophyte looked like a real challenger. In the Alps, though, Bottecchia's relative inexperience was mercilessly exploited by Pélissier, with Bottecchia choosing the wrong gears for the mountains and Pélissier coming into his own and relieving his team-mate of the *maillot jaune*.

Coming into the following year's race, Bottecchia was the odds-on favourite for overall victory. Pélissier – taking a leaf from his mentor Lucian Petit-Breton's book – had anointed him as his successor. And, when Bottecchia took a leaf from Philippe Thys's book and skipped the early season races in order to dedicate his whole season to the Tour, it was clear that he meant business. So it was no surprise when he took the yellow jersey on the opening stage and held it all the way to Paris (briefly, he had to share it with Théophile Beeckman, on Stages Three and Four, when he drew level on time).

With the experience of the previous Tour, along with his preparations for this, Bottecchia soared in the Pyrenees, and where the previous year he had lost time to his challengers, this time he won both of the Pyrenean stages. In the Alps he measured his effort, following wheels and sacrificing small portions of his lead in order to win the bigger prize. The only rider who came close to unseating him was Alcyon's Nicolas Frantz, but nothing he could do could crack the Italian.

But the story of the 1924 Tour is not the story of Bottecchia's dominating performance. It is the story of a journalist, Albert Londres, who went to the Tour looking for a story and, in a café in Coutances, grabbed it with both hands when it fell into his lap.

Londres was what today would be called an investigative reporter. He had reported on post-revolution Russia and how the reality of life under the Bolshevik regime of Lenin and Trotsky was far from what people thought it to be. His most famous story – *Au bagne* – came in 1923 when he visited the French penal colony in Cayenne, Guiana, and denounced the way the prisoners were being treated. The story Londres told shocked a French nation which thought itself civilised. A year later he followed that up with *Dante n'avait rien vu*, the title of which – Dante saw nothing – suggested that French military battalions in North Africa were even worse than any of the circles of hell depicted in *Inferno*.

Pretty much from the start of the Tour in 1903, *L'Auto* had been portraying its riders as *ouvriers de la pédale*, workers of the pedal, somewhere between obedient industrial workers and independent artisans. Not all agreed with that representation. Quitting the 1919 Tour – after having likened the other riders to cart-horses and classed himself as a thoroughbred – Henri Pélissier threw one final brickbat at his fellow competitors, likening them to *forçats de la route*, the chain-ganged prisoners who cleaned and repaired roads. Far from being workers, they were slaves.

This dichotomy between reality and representation was what Albert Londres sought to investigate when he convinced *Le Petit Parisien* to allow him to cover the 1924 Tour. Over the course of the race he published a dozen articles, each peeking behind the curtain, beyond the myth of *les géants de la route* and considered the reality of the Tour rider's daily existence. In places the articles are what we today would call colour pieces, the Tour as spectacle not sport. But mostly they were about the conditions endured by the riders. The dusty roads of Brittany, the rocky roads of the Pyrenees and the Alps, the *pavé* of France's industrial heartland. Londres wrote of riding through the dark, stages typically starting at two in the morning, some at midnight or ten o'clock at night, the latest starting at six in the morning. He wrote of riding in the heat and riding in the rain. He wrote of cycling as work, hard, hard work. And on the fifth day – the Tour's third stage – he wrote of doping.

The story of that day has become a Tour legend, obscuring reality. Between Cherbourg and Brest, Henri Pélissier had quit the Tour, along with his brother Francis and their Automoto team-mate Maurice Ville. The reason was an argument over cycling jerseys. Legnano's *directeur sportif* Eberado Pavesi had spotted Pélissier discarding a jersey on the previous stage, contrary to Tour rules.

With stages staring in the cold of night and going on through the heat of the day, riders layered up for the night, stripping down during the day. Pélissier simply threw his extra jersey away. Pavesi – who was on his way to becoming the best *directeur sportif* Italian cycling had yet seen, a Trans-Alpine Alphonse Baugé – saw this as an opportunity to undermine Legnano's rivals, and so complained to the commissaires, citing the rule which required a rider to start and finish the stage with the same equipment, which included punctured tyres, and jerseys. Pélissier was given a warning.

At the start of the stage from Cherbourg, a commissaire approached Pélissier and – without asking – checked how many jerseys he was wearing. Pélissier took offence, and then took up his case with Henri Desgrange. The latter was in no mood to listen to Pélissier, and said they'd talk later. Pélissier said there would be no later, he was quitting the Tour.

When Londres discovered that Pélissier – the defending champion and French cycling's brightest star – had quit the race his journalistic instincts kicked in and he went in search of the story. In a café in Coutances, 80 kilometres south of Cherbourg, he found it. Pélissier and his brother, along with Ville, were sitting around a cup of coffee. Londres interviewed them and they explained their story. The indignity of being asked how many jerseys he was wearing was what got to Pélissier, but he then proceeded to rattle off a litany of complaints, the hardships the riders were willing to endure in the name of sport, and those that he felt were simply beyond reason. The three riders compared their lot to Christ on Calvary, noting that there were only 14 Stations of the Cross, but they had to endure 15 stages before their crucifixion was complete. And they showed Londres the drugs that kept them going, pills, potions and lotions that killed the pain or stimulated the brain.

For followers of the Six Day races – Géo Lefèvre's inspiration for the Tour – the use of drugs like chloroform and cocaine were nothing new, their use had been written about for three decades now. But it is those drugs that have – in the years since – become the heart of Londres' story. Yet in the 10 articles that followed, not once did he mention them again. The theme he returned to again and again and again was the level of suffering endured by the riders, and the arbitrary – and seemingly senseless – rules imposed upon them.

Nor was the story Londres filed from Coutances headlined "Les Forçats de la Route," the title legend has given it. The actual headline was far more mundane, a simple statement that the Pélissier brothers, along with Ville, had abandoned the Tour. The convicts of the road phrase had been Pélissier's departing shot when he quit the 1919 Tour, but history has now firmly attached it to Londres' story.

Tour of France, Tour de Souffrance – was used as the headline for one of his later articles, and was later used when they were collected in book form, and the 1924 Tour has gone down in history as that, the Tour of Suffrance.

Londres' articles hit at the vision for the sport promoted by Desgrange, that cycling was all about suffering, hard labour. For those who believed in that vision, such an assault on their beliefs could not be tolerated. The Pélissiers, they said, had quit the race because Bottecchia had them beaten and a noble retreat was better than an ignoble defeat. Londres himself was attacked: he was an outsider, a muck-raking journalist who knew nothing of cycling, a man who did not understand the sport. Even today many still make that claim when talking of the articles Londres filed from the 1924 Tour.

The point made by Londres, that the sport was too tough, did find an audience. And the Tour would, in time, be tamed. But before that could happen, things were going to have to get a lot harder still.

Stage-by-Stage Results for the 1924 Tour de France			Stage Winner	Maillot Jaune
Stage 1 Sun 22 Jun	Paris (Luna Park, Porte Maillot) to Le Havre 157 starters, 139 finishers	381 km 15h03'14" 25.3 kph	Ottavio Bottecchia (Ita) Automoto	Ottavio Bottecchia (Ita) Automoto
Mon 23 Jun	Rest day			
Stage 2 Tue 24 Jun	Le Havre to Cherbourg 125 finishers	371 km 14h34'31" 25.5 kph	Romain Bellenger (Fra) Peugeot	Ottavio Bottecchia (Ita) Automoto
Wed 25 Jun	Rest day			
Stage 3 Thu 26 Jun	Cherbourg to Brest 112 finishers	405 km 15h44'00" 25.7 kph	Philippe Thys (Bel) Peugeot	Ottavio Bottecchia (Ita) Automoto
			Théophile Beeckman (Bel) Griffon	Théophile Beeckman (Bel) Griffon
Fri 27 Jun	Rest day			
Stage 4 Sat 28 Jun	Brest to Les Sables-d'Olonne 97 finishers	412 km 16h28'51" 25.0 kph	Félix Goethals (Fra) Thomann	Ottavio Bottecchia (Ita) Automoto
				Théophile Beeckman (Bel) Griffon
Stage 5 Sun 29 Jun	Les Sables-d'Olonne to Bayonne 89 finishers	482 km 19h40'00" 24.5 kph	Omer Huyse (Bel) Lapize	Ottavio Bottecchia (Ita) Automoto
Mon 30 Jun				
Tue 1 Jul	Rest day			
Stage 6 Wed 2 Jul	Bayonne to Luchon 76 finishers	326 km 15h24'25" 21.2 kph	Ottavio Bottecchia (Ita) Automoto	Ottavio Bottecchia (Ita) Automoto
Major climbs: Col d'Aubisque (1,709m) Ottavio Bottecchia (Ita) Automoto; Col du Tourmalet (2,115m) Ottavio Bottecchia (Ita) Automoto; Col d'Aspin (1,489m) Ottavio Bottecchia (Ita) Automoto; Col de Peyresourde (1,569m) Ottavio Bottecchia (Ita) Automoto				

Stage-by-Stage Results for the 1924 Tour de France			Stage Winner	Maillot Jaune
Thu 3 Jul	Rest day			
Stage 7 Fri 4 Jul	Luchon to Perpignan 70 finishers	323 km 12h40'18" 25.5 kph	Ottavio Bottecchia (Ita) Automoto	Ottavio Bottecchia (Ita) Automoto
	Major climbs: Col des Ares (797m) Lucien Buysse (Bel) Automoto; Col de Portet d'Aspet (1,069m) Théophile Beeckmann (Bel) Griffon; Col de Port (1,249m) Ottavio Bottecchia (Ita) Automoto + Arsène Alancourt (Fra) Armo; Col du Puymorens (1,915m) Philippe Thys (Bel) Peugeot			
Sat 5 Jul	Rest day			
Stage 8 Sun 6 Jul	Perpignan to Toulon 67 finishers	427 km 17h04'45" 25.0 kph	Louis Mottiat (Bel) Alcyon	Ottavio Bottecchia (Ita) Automoto
Mon 7 Jul	Rest day			
Stage 9 Tue 8 Jul	Toulon to Nice 66 finishers	280 km 11h52'08" 23.6 kph	Philippe Thys (Bel) Peugeot	Ottavio Bottecchia (Ita) Automoto
	Major climbs: Col de Braus (1,002m) Jean Alavoine (Fra) Peugeot; Col de Castillon (706m) Philippe Thys (Bel) Peugeot			
Wed 9 Jul	Rest day			
Stage 10 Thu 10 Jul	Nice to Briançon 64 finishers	275 km 12h51'07" 21.4 kph	Giovanni Brunero (Ita) Legnano	Ottavio Bottecchia (Ita) Automoto
	Major climbs: Col d'Allos (2,250m) Nicolas Frantz (Lux) Alcyon; Col de Vars (2,110m) Nicolas Frantz (Lux) Thomann; Col d'Izoard (2,360m) Nicolas Frantz (Lux) Thomann			
Fri 11 Jul	Rest day			
Stage 11 Sat 12 Jul	Briançon to Gex 63 finishers	307 km 12h03'51" 25.4 kph	Nicolas Frantz (Lux) Alcyon	Ottavio Bottecchia (Ita) Automoto
	Major climbs: Col du Galibier (2,556m) Bartolomeo Aimo (Ita) Legnano; Col du Télégraphe (1,566m) Bartolomeo Aimo (Ita) Legnano; Col des Aravis (1,498m) Giovanni Brunero (Ita) Legnano			
Sun 13 Jul	Rest day			
Stage 12 Mon 14 Jul	Gex to Strasbourg 62 finishers	360 km 15h51'02" 22.7 kph	Nicolas Frantz (Lux) Alcyon	Ottavio Bottecchia (Ita) Automoto
	Major climbs: Col de la Faucille (1,323m) n/a			
Tue 15 Jul	Rest day			
Stage 13 Wed 16 Jul	Strasbourg to Metz 62 finishers	300 km 11h36'27" 25.8 kph	Arsène Alancourt (Fra) Armor	Ottavio Bottecchia (Ita) Automoto
Thu 17 Jul	Rest day			

Stage-by-Stage Results for the 1924 Tour de France			Stage Winner	Maillot Jaune
Stage 14 Fri 18 Jul	Metz to Dunkerque 61 finishers	433 km 20h17'51" 21.3 kph	Romain Bellenger (Fra) Peugeot	Ottavio Bottecchia (Ita) Automoto
Sat 19 Jul	Rest day			
Stage 15 Sun 20 Jul	Dunkerque to Paris (Parc des Princes) 60 finishers	343 km 14h45'20" 23.2 kph	Ottavio Bottecchia (Ita) Automoto	Ottavio Bottecchia (Ita) Automoto

Total Prize fund: 100,000 francs (10,000 francs first prize)

Final Classification

Place	Rider	Team	Time	Age
1	Ottavio Bottecchia (Ita)	Automoto	5,425 km 226h18'21" 24.250 kph	29
2	Nicolas Frantz (Lux)	Alcyon	+ 35'36"	24
3	Lucien Buysse (Bel)	Automoto	+ 1h32'13"	31
4	Bartolomeo Aimo (Ita)	Legnano	+ 1h32'47"	24
5	Théophile Beeckman (Bel)	Griffon	+ 2h11'12"	27
6	Joseph Muller (Fra)	Peugeot	+ 2h35'33"	29
7	Arsène Alancourt (Fra)	Armor	+ 2h41'31"	32
8	Romain Bellenger (Fra)	Peugeot	+ 2h51'09"	30
9	Omer Huyse (Bel)	Lapize	+ 2h58'13"	25
10	Hector Tiberghien (Bel)	Peugeot	+ 3h05'04"	36
Lanterne Rouge				
60	Victor Lafosse (Fra)	Remond	45h12'05"	
Independents				
	Omer Huyse (Bel)	Lapize		25
Meilleur Grimpeur				
	Ottavio Bottecchia (Ita)	Automoto		29

1925: Bottecchia, Again

Since 1911, the Tour had been contested over 15 stages. The basic route had been tweaked here and there. One town replaced another, new mountains were added, old ones dropped and the overall distance had only grown by a little, from 5,344 to 5,425 kilometres in 1924. Whereas the 1911 *parcours* had only two stages longer than 400 kilometres, that was five by 1924. Only the two Alpine stages – to Nice and Briançon – dipped below 300 kilometres, but climbs like the Izoard and the Galibier more than made up for the distance lost.

The race rules had also evolved. Following the time penalty handed to Hector Heusghem in 1924 – which had effectively handed victory to Firmin Lambot – riders were now allowed to change broken parts, or bikes, so long as the replacement equipment came from their *directeur sportif*. And, in 1923, in order to try and make the riders race harder, Henri Desgrange had introduced *bonifications* for the stage winners, time bonuses that were deducted from their overall time. In 1923 these had been set at two minutes, in 1924 they were increased to three.

But all the changes couldn't combat the simple reality that, out on the road, riders weren't racing hard the whole stage. This, for Desgrange, was simply not good enough. He had thrown Maurice Brocco off the 1911 race for not trying hard enough, he had tried sending the lesser riders off ahead of the stars in an effort to make them race hard all the way, but all to no avail. The riders rode the way they wanted to ride. So the Tour went back to the drawing board for 1925.

Out went the time bonuses. In – again – came the trade teams, once more officially welcomed to the Tour. Out went the second-class riders; in came *touristes-routiers*, still the *isolés* of old but now with a new name. Out went three of the race's 14 rest days; in came three new stages in their place. Three of the stages that previously exceeded 400 kilometres were gone, especially the mammoth 482 kilometres that since 1920 had been taking the riders from Les Sables-d'Olonne to Bayonne. Seven of the stages now dipped below 300 kilometres, including one that fell below 200. Overall it was a case of easier stages, but more of them, and more often.

There were also modifications to the rules. The replacement rules were relaxed a bit more and a degree of team-work was allowed. One rule change that didn't stick would have seen all the riders being given the same food ration during stages, which was being provided by *L'Auto*. This was a step too far for the *peloton* and they rallied round Henri Pélissier in an early riders' union, threatening to strike if Desgrange carried through on his plan. The Father of the Tour had no choice but to beat a hasty retreat.

So when Pélissier abandoned on the fourth stage of the 1925 Tour, citing injuries suffered at the Circuit de Paris before the Tour, Desgrange went on the attack in *L'Auto*. Few who quit his Tour ever got pity, especially when they were champions, but with Pélissier there were now too many scores to settle. Desgrange told his readers that their hero was simply suffering from a sensitivity of the nervous system. While he accepted that a cyclist needed a calm environment in order to carry out his trade, Desgrange suggested that the praise heaped upon Pélissier the year before – especially by the Communist newspaper *L'Humanité*, which tended to be critical of the Tour – had made Pélissier's life too cosy and he'd gone soft. All he was short of saying, once more, was that Pélissier didn't know how to suffer.

But if Henri Pélissier was on the way out, his younger brother Charles was on the way in, and already walking into Desgrange's line of fire. Charles Pélissier wasn't riding the 1925 Tour, he was there simply as a spectator, to cheer on his other brother, Francis, atop the Tourmalet as the race went through the Pyrenees. With a lack of diplomacy that seemed typical of the Pélissier clan he criticised the state of the roads noting (not entirely incorrectly) that they were just goat-trails. Such roads, Pélissier said, were for cart-horses, not for men of class. Desgrange's response was to mock the youngest Pélissier, noting his barren *palmarès* and – in an attack on the whole family – said that his brothers were peacocks, and all Charles Pélissier had ever done was to snatch feathers from them and glue them to his own back.

But the Pélissiers were just a sideshow in the 1925 Tour, with Ottavio Bottecchia joining Lucien Petit-Breton and Firmin Lambot on two wins, just one behind Philippe Thys on three. Once again donning the *maillot jaune* on the opening stage – he'd led from first to last the previous year – the Italian was fully in control. Even on the third stage, when he surrendered the jersey to Thomann's Adelin Benoît, it looked like he was just passing the load temporarily, to a caretaker. That belief was only confirmed as the race reached Bayonne, the eve of the Pyrenees and the Italian relieved the Belgian of the race lead.

On the first day in the mountains Benoît rose above himself, the mountains and the rest of the racers, taking the stage win and retaking the race lead. Alas the effort took its toll on the next stage and Benoît faded away and down the general classification, leaving Bottecchia to once more lead the race, a lead he held all the way back to Paris.

Bottecchia was one of the first of the post-war generation of riders to shine at the Tour. Thirty in 1925, he hadn't taken up cycling until after the war, having been posted to one of Italy's cycling battalions during the conflict. There, riding between the front and rear lines in the Dolomites, he learned to master the mountains. Apart from his début performance at the 1923 Giro d'Italia, and his performances at the 1923, 1924 and 1925 Tours, his *palmarès* was pretty empty: having found the race that suited his talents, he focussed on that race to the exclusion of others, and then followed up his Tour successes by riding as a star at smaller races, his presence alone drawing a crowd and guaranteeing him a fine appearance fee.

Through his two Tours, only two riders came close to really challenging Bottecchia: Luxembourg's Nicolas Frantz, riding for

Alcyon, and his own team-mate Lucien Buysse. Frantz's fortunes faded in both Tours, but in 1925 it was team orders which stopped Buysse from mounting an attack on the yellow jersey: he was told to ride for Bottecchia and be happy with a couple of stage wins. At the end of the Tour Buysse made clear to one and all that, come 1926, he would be riding for himself.

Stage-by-Stage Results for the 1925 Tour de France			Stage Winner	Maillot Jaune
Stage 1 Sun 21 Jun	Paris (Le Vésinet) to Le Havre 130 starters, 111 finishers	340 km 12h19'02" 27.6 kph	Ottavio Bottecchia (Ita) Automoto	Ottavio Bottecchia (Ita) Automoto
Mon 22 Jun	Rest day			
Stage 2 Tue 23 Jun	Le Havre to Cherbourg 109 finishers	371 km 15h06'00" 24.6 kph	Romain Bellenger (Fra) Alcyon	Ottavio Bottecchia (Ita) Automoto
Wed 24 Jun	Rest day			
Stage 3 Thu 25 Jun	Cherbourg to Brest 96 finishers	405 km 16h22'30" 24.7 kph	Louis Mottiat (Bel) Alcyon	Adelin Benoît (Bel) Thomann
Stage 4 Fri 26 Jun	Brest to Vannes 85 finishers	208 km 8h22'30" 24.8 kph	Nicolas Frantz (Lux) Alcyon	Adelin Benoît (Bel) Thomann
Stage 5 Sat 27 Jun	Vannes to Les Sables-d'Olonne 85 finishers	204 km 7h25'42" 27.5 kph	Nicolas Frantz (Lux) Alcyon	Adelin Benoît (Bel) Thomann
Stage 6 Sun 28 Jun	Les Sables-d'Olonne to Bordeaux 85 finishers	293 km 11h06'51" 26.4 kph	Ottavio Bottecchia (Ita) Automoto	Adelin Benoît (Bel) Thomann
Stage 7 Mon 29 Jun	Bordeaux to Bayonne 80 finishers	189 km 6h35'21" 28.7 kph	Ottavio Bottecchia (Ita) Automoto	Ottavio Bottecchia (Ita) Automoto
Tue 30 Jun	Rest day			
Stage 8 Wed 1 Jul	Bayonne to Luchon 64 finishers	326 km 15h18'56" 21.3 kph	Adelin Benoît (Bel) Thomann	Adelin Benoît (Bel) Thomann
	Major climbs: Col d'Aubisque (1,709m) Ottavio Bottecchia (Ita) Automoto; Col du Tourmalet (2,115m) Omer Huysse (Bel) Armor; Col d'Aspin (1,489m) Omer Huysse (Bel) Armor; Col de Peyresourde (1,569m) Adelin Benoît (Bel) Thomann			
Thu 2 Jul	Rest day			

Stage-by-Stage Results for the 1925 Tour de France			Stage Winner	Maillot Jaune
Stage 9 Fri 3 Jul	Luchon to Perpignan 57 finishers	323 km 13h08'51" 24.6 kph	Nicolas Frantz (Lux) Alcyon	Ottavio Bottecchia (Ita) Automoto
	Major climbs: Col des Ares (797m) Ottavio Bottecchia (Ita) Automoto; Col de Portet d'Aspet (1,069m) Ottavio Bottecchia (Ita) Automoto; Col de Port (1,249m) Ottavio Bottecchia (Ita) Automoto; Col du Puymorens (1,915m) Ottavio Bottecchia (Ita) Automoto			
Stage 10 Sat 4 Jul	Perpignan to Nîmes 57 finishers	215 km 8h44'41" 24.6 kph	Théophile Beeckman (Bel) Thomann	Ottavio Bottecchia (Ita) Automoto
Stage 11 Sun 5 Jul	Nîmes to Toulon 56 finishers	215 km 6h54'07" 31.2 kph	Lucien Buysse (Bel) Automoto	Ottavio Bottecchia (Ita) Automoto
Mon 6 Jul	Rest day			
Stage 12 Tue 7 Jul	Toulon to Nice 55 finishers	280 km 11h02'12" 25.4 kph	Lucien Buysse (Bel) Automoto	Ottavio Bottecchia (Ita) Automoto
	Major climbs: Col de Braus (1,002m) Lucien Buysse (Bel) Automoto; Col de Castillon (706m) Ottavio Bottecchia (Ita) Automoto			
Wed 8 Jul	Rest day			
Stage 13 Thu 9 Jul	Nice to Briançon 51 finishers	275 km 13h05'03" 21.0 kph	Bartolomeo Aimo (Ita) Alcyon	Ottavio Bottecchia (Ita) Automoto
	Major climbs: Col d'Allos (2,250m) August Verdyck (Bel) Christophe; Col de Vars (2,110m) Bartolomeo Aimo (Ita) Alcyon; Col d'Izoard (2,360m) Bartolomeo Aimo (Ita) Alcyon			
Fri 10 Jul	Rest day			
Stage 14 Sat 11 Jul	Briançon to Évian 50 finishers	303 km 11h36'15" 26.1 kph	Hector Martin (Bel) JB Louvet	Ottavio Bottecchia (Ita) Automoto
	Major climbs: Col du Galibier (2,556m) Lucien Buysse (Bel) Automoto; Col des Aravis (1,498m) Ottavio Bottecchia (Ita) Automoto			
Sun 12 Jul	Rest day			
Stage 15 Mon 13 Jul	Évian to Mulhouse 50 finishers	373 km 15h42'45" 23.7 kph	Nicolas Frantz (Lux) Alcyon	Ottavio Bottecchia (Ita) Automoto
	Major climbs: Col de la Faucille (1,323m) Ottavio Bottecchia (Ita) Automoto			
Tue 14 Jul	Rest day			
Stage 16 Wed 15 Jul	Mulhouse to Metz 50 finishers	334 km 13h24'39" 24.9 kph	Hector Martin (Bel) JB Louvet	Ottavio Bottecchia (Ita) Automoto
Thu 16 Jul	Rest day			

Stage-by-Stage Results for the 1925 Tour de France			Stage Winner	Maillot Jaune
Stage 17 Fri 17 Jul	Metz to Dunkerque 49 finishers	433 km 17h07'25" 25.3 kph	Hector Martin (Bel) JB Louvet	Ottavio Bottecchia (Ita) Automoto
Sat 18 Jul	Rest day			
Stage 18 Sun 19 Jul	Dunkerque to Paris (Parc des Princes) 49 finishers	343 km 14h53'06" 23.0 kph	Ottavio Bottecchia (Ita) Automoto	Ottavio Bottecchia (Ita) Automoto

Total Prize fund: 99,000 francs (15,000 francs first prize)

Final Classification				
Place	**Rider**	**Team**	**Time**	**Age**
1	Ottavio Bottecchia (Ita)	Automoto	5,440 km 219h10'18" 24.820 kph	30
2	Lucien Buysse (Bel)	Automoto	+ 54'20"	32
3	Bartolomeo Aimo (Ita)	Alcyon	+ 56'37"	25
4	Nicolas Frantz (Lux)	Alcyon	+ 1h11'24"	25
5	Albert Dejonghe (Bel)	JB Louvet	+ 1h27'42"	31
6	Théophile Beeckman (Bel)	Thomann	+ 2h24'43"	28
7	Omer Huyse (Bel)	Armor	+ 2h33'38"	26
8	Auguste Verdyck (Bel)	Christophe	+ 2h44'36"	23
9	Félix Sellier (Bel)	Alcyon	+ 2h45'59"	32
10	Federico Gay (Ita)	Météore	+ 4h06'03"	29
Lanterne Rouge				
49	Fernand Besnier (Fra)		36h10'50"	31
Meilleur Grimpeur				
	Ottavio Bottecchia (Ita)	Automoto		30

1926: The Longest Tour

The twentieth Tour de France opened with an innovation. On the eve of the race, there was a prologue. Of sorts.

Over the previous few days, the Tour's riders had been assembling in Paris, signing on in *L'Auto*'s offices, having their bikes checked, and letting the public – their public – see in the flesh these men they would be reading about in the pages of *L'Auto* and other newspapers, hearing about on radio, and watching in cinemas on newsreels. When all the formalities were done, the riders assembled at Port Maillot in the early hours of a Friday morning and, wearing suits and ties, paraded to the Gare de Lyon, looking like a *peloton* of office workers. At the station they boarded a chartered train which would take them the 600 kilometres south-east to the spa town of Évian, on the shores of Lac Leman (Lake Geneva).

Henri Desgrange and *L'Auto* had sold the idea of starting in Évian as a way of breaking up the monotony of the Tour's closing stages. No mention was made of Évian having paid to host the Tour, but with the extra cost of transporting the riders from Paris one must presume that some financial arrangement had been reached with Desgrange. The main argument made was that, with the race being won in the mountains, the final three or four stages had become processional. Boring. By starting on Lac Leman and circuiting all the way round the country back to Évian the riders could exit the Alps and get home Paris in just two hops, via Dijon. Évian, it was argued, also had the advantage of throwing the low hills of the Jura and the Vosges at the riders in the opening stages, thus spicing them up.

However, there was a problem with this logic: once out of the low hills the race hit a succession of long, flat stages. In Metz the gallop for the line saw 25 riders duking it out. In Le Havre it was 30. Nineteen in Cherbourg, 29 in Brest, 30 in Les Sables-d'Olonne. Forty-two riders arrived together in Bordeaux, while in Bayonne it was the biggest bunch sprint yet seen in the Tour, 56 riders all hitting the finish together. Nothing was happening on these stages, save for a puncture or other mechanical misfortune. For Desgrange, the riders dawdling through the stage – often arriving an hour or more down on their advertised arrival time – was not the kind of racing he believed in. He wanted his riders racing hard from start to finish, the *peloton* strung out along the roads of France, not riding like tourists on holiday.

And for other journalists too these opening stages of the Tour were a disaster. Some complained that riders were now taking three days to do what could be done in two. This was despite the fact that the number of stages exceeding 400 kilometres had switched back from two to four, and there were now only four stages below 300 kilometres and only one of them falling below 200. Even with one stage fewer than the year before, the race still stretched out to 5,745 kilometres, the longest the Tour had ever seen (nearly 2,500 kilometres longer than that year's Giro d'Italia). But there was some truth in the media's complaints, for, once the race had reached Dunkerque, the lead had barely changed, with JB Louvet's Gustaaf van Slembrouck – a former blacksmith and horse dealer – holding the *maillot jaune* all the way down to Bayonne and the edge of the Pyrenees.

And then the race came alive in what has gone down in history of one the Tour's epic stages, 326 kilometres of riding over four major cols that took more than 17 hours for the winner to complete, two hours slower than was typical for the stage. Through the first half of the race the riders had suffered through dust-filled roads, but in the mountains the rain came, and didn't stop. In Bayonne it was raining when the riders left at midnight, the distant mountains shrouded in cloud. It was a night you wouldn't put a cat out in. But for the 76 riders left in the Tour it was just another day at the coalface.

Wrapped in oilskin jackets they set out together, the roads and the rain thinning them out, the happy bunch of tourists who had

The peloton rolls down the Champs-Élysées prior to boarding a train to take them to Évian and the start of the 1926 Tour.

raced so casually through the preceding nine stages strung out along the road, most on their own, each suffering through his own race. By the time they hit the Aubisque Automoto's Lucien Buysse – the man who had marked everyone's card at the end of the previous year's race and said he would be riding for his own glory in 1926 – was alone at the front of the race. He crested the climb with a lead of two minutes. In the valley Buysse was caught by JB Louvet's Albert Dejonghe. Behind them, struggling in their own private hells, were their ostensible team leaders, the defending champion Ottavio Bottecchia and the man in the *maillot jaune*, Van Slembrouck. Buysse and Dejonghe were now riding for themselves, the former 23 minutes off yellow, the latter a little more than a minute and now the leader on the road, the virtual *maillot jaune*.

At Barège, about half way up the climb, the two Belgians were joined by a third, Dejonghe's JB Louvet team-mate Odile Tailleu, who had started the day ten minutes off yellow. Metre by metre Tailleu opened up a gap on the other two. Then Dejonghe fell behind Buysse, the pace set by his team-mate too much for him, the virtual yellow jersey slipping off his shoulders and onto Tailleu's.

A minute after Tailleu crested the Tourmalet Buysse followed him. In his début Tour, though, Tailleu made mistakes which more experienced riders would have known to avoid. He drank from mountain streams, which left him racked with cramps on the roadside as Buysse rolled past him and climbed the Aspin and Peyresourde alone, finally reaching Luchon a little after five o'clock in the evening.

An hour later and only 10 riders had come home. By seven o'clock that number was up to 18. At eight 26. Thirty-nine riders had arrived by nine o'clock, 43 by ten. By twenty past ten, when the control should have closed, only 47 riders had arrived. Desgrange – who, Tour legend says, favoured a Tour in which just one rider finished – decreed that the control would stay open until midnight, by which time 54 riders were still left in the twentieth edition of the *grande boucle*. Among the 22 riders the Tour lost that day were the defending champion, Bottecchia, and the man who had shone on these same cols the year before, Alcyon's Adelin Benoît.

When Buysse donned the *maillot jaune* in Luchon he had a lead of 36 minutes over Tailleu and 46 over Dejonghe. Not enough, he decided, and on the last mountain of the next stage, Puymorens, he went on the attack again, finishing the day with his lead pushed out to over an hour. From there back up to Évian and then over to Paris the only race was for second place, which Nicolas Frantz won. Buysse had carried through on his promise of the year before and won the Tour.

Stage-by-Stage Results for the 1926 Tour de France			Stage Winner	Maillot Jaune
Stage 1 Sun 20 Jun	Évian to Mulhouse 126 starters, 111 finishers	373 km 14h12′04″ 26.3 kph	Jules Buysse (Bel) Automoto	Jules Buysse (Bel) Automoto
Mon 21 Jun	Rest day			
Stage 2 Tue 22 Jun	Mulhouse to Metz 105 finishers	334 km 13h29′16″ 24.8 kph	Aimé Dossche (Bel) Christophe	Jules Buysse (Bel) Automoto
Wed 23 Jun	Rest day			
Stage 3 Thu 24 Jun	Metz to Dunkerque 93 finishers	433 km 17h11′14″ 25.2 kph	Gustaaf van Slembrouck (Bel) JB Louvet	Gustaaf van Slembrouck (Bel) JB Louvet
Fri 25 Jun	Rest day			
Stage 4 Sat 26 Jun	Dunkerque to Le Havre 90 finishers	361 km 14h57′01″ 24.1 kph	Félix Sellier (Bel) Alcyon	Gustaaf van Slembrouck (Bel) JB Louvet
Sun 27 Jun	Rest day			
Stage 5 Mon 28 Jun	Le Havre to Cherbourg 84 finishers	357 km 14h14′09″ 25.1 kph	Adelin Benoît (Bel) Alcyon	Gustaaf van Slembrouck (Bel) JB Louvet
Tue 29 Jun	Rest day			
Stage 6 Wed 30 Jun	Cherbourg to Brest 83 finishers	405 km 16h12′49″ 25.0 kph	~~Félix Sellier (Bel) Alcyon~~ Joseph van Dam (Bel) Automoto	Gustaaf van Slembrouck (Bel) JB Louvet
Thu 1 Jul	Rest day			
Stage 7 Fri 2 Jul	Brest to Les Sables-d'Olonne 80 finishers	412 km 16h20′54″ 25.2 kph	Nicolas Frantz (Lux) Alcyon	Gustaaf van Slembrouck (Bel) JB Louvet
Stage 8 Sat 3 Jul	Les Sables-d'Olonne to Bordeaux 76 finishers	285 km 12h00′08″ 23.7 kph	Joseph van Dam (Bel) Automoto	Gustaaf van Slembrouck (Bel) JB Louvet

Stage-by-Stage Results for the 1926 Tour de France			Stage Winner	Maillot Jaune
Stage 9 Sun 4 Jul	Bordeaux to Bayonne 76 finishers	189 km 7h38'19" 24.7 kph	Nicolas Frantz (Lux) Alcyon	Gustaaf van Slembrouck (Bel) JB Louvet
Mon 5 Jul	Rest day			
Stage 10 Tue 6 Jul	Bayonne to Luchon 54 finishers	326 km 17h12'04" 19.0 kph	Lucien Buysse (Bel) Automoto	Lucien Buysse (Bel) Automoto
	Major climbs: Col d'Aubisque (1,709m) Lucien Buysse (Bel) Automoto; Col du Tourmalet (2,115m) Odile Tailleu (Bel) JB Louvet; Col d'Aspin (1,489m) Lucien Buysse (Bel) Automoto; Col de Peyresourde (1,569m) Lucien Buysse (Bel) Automoto			
Wed 7 Jul	Rest day			
Stage 11 Thu 8 Jul	Luchon to Perpignan 50 finishers	323 km 12h31'16" 25.8 kph	Lucien Buysse (Bel) Automoto	Lucien Buysse (Bel) Automoto
	Major climbs: Col des Ares (797m) n/a; Col de Portet d'Aspet (1,069m) Théophile Beeckmann (Bel) Armor; Col de Port (1,249m) n/a; Col du Puymorens (1,915m) Lucien Buysse (Bel) Automoto			
Fri 9 Jul	Rest day			
Stage 12 Sat 10 Jul	Perpignan to Toulon 49 finishers	427 km 17h32'32" 24.3 kph	Nicolas Frantz (Lux) Alcyon	Lucien Buysse (Bel) Automoto
Sun 11 Jul	Rest day			
Stage 13 Mon 12 Jul	Toulon to Nice 48 finishers	280 km 11h31'10" 24.3 kph	Nicolas Frantz (Lux) Alcyon	Lucien Buysse (Bel) Automoto
	Major climbs: Col de Braus (1,002m) Marcel Bidot (Fra) Thomann; Col de Castillon (706m) Marcel Bidot (Fra) Thomann			
Tue 13 Jul	Rest day			
Stage 14 Wed 14 Jul	Nice to Briançon 43 finishers	275 km 11h59'55" 22.9 kph	Bartolomeo Aimo (Ita) Alcyon	Lucien Buysse (Bel) Automoto
	Major climbs: Col d'Allos (2250m) Lucien Buysse (Bel) Automoto; Col de Vars (2,110m) Bartolomeo Aimo (Ita) Alcyon; Col d'Izoard (2,360m) Bartolomeo Aimo (Ita) Alcyon			
Thu 15 Jul	Rest day			
Stage 15 Fri 16 Jul	Briançon to Évian 43 finishers	303 km 12h09'08" 24.9 kph	Joseph van Dam (Bel) Automoto	Lucien Buysse (Bel) Automoto
	Major climbs: Col du Galibier (2,556m) Omer Huysse (Bel) Automoto; Col du Télégraphe (1,566m) Léon Parmentier (Bel) Jean Louvet; Col des Aravis (1,498m) Omer Huysse (Bel) Automoto			
Stage 16 Sat 17 Jul	Évian to Dijon 42 finishers	321 km 13h45'57" 23.3 kph	Camille van de Casteele (Bel) JB Louvet	Lucien Buysse (Bel) Automoto

Stage-by-Stage Results for the 1926 Tour de France			Stage Winner	Maillot Jaune
Stage 17 Sun 18 Jul	Dijon to Paris (Parc des Princes) 41 finishers	341 km 14h56'05" 22.8 kph	Aimé Dossche (Bel) Christophe	Lucien Buysse (Bel) Automoto

Total Prize fund: 100,000 francs (5,000 francs first prize)

Final Classification

Place	Rider	Team	Time	Age
1	Lucien Buysse (Bel)	Automoto	5,745 km 238h44'25" 24.273 kph	33
2	Nicolas Frantz (Lux)	Alcyon	+ 1h22'25"	26
3	Bartolomeo Aimo (Ita)	Alcyon	+ 1h22'51"	26
4	Théophile Beeckman (Bel)	Armor	+ 1h43'54"	29
5	Félix Sellier (Bel)	Alcyon	+ 1h49'13"	33
6	Albert Dejonghe (Bel)	JB Louvet	+ 1h56'15"	32
7	Léon Parmentier (Bel)	Jean Louvet	+ 2h09'20"	25
8	Georges Cuvelier (Fra)	Météore	+ 2h28'32"	30
9	Jules Buysse (Bel)	Automoto	+ 2h37'03"	24
10	Marcel Bidot (Fra)	Thomann	+ 2h53'54"	23
Lanterne Rouge				
41	André Drobecq (Fra)	Unsponsored	24h59'03"	
Meilleur Grimpeur				
	Lucien Buysse (Bel)	Automoto		33

1927: Tour de Frantz

For the third Tour in succession, Henri Desgrange and his team at *L'Auto* tinkered with the Tour. While the overall route of the race, hugging the contours of France's *hexagone*, was more or less unchanged, much of the rest of the race was radically different. Out went all the stages that exceeded 400 kilometres. Only four stages exceeded 300 kilometres and of the remaining stages half were below 300 kilometres. Out went another eight of the rest days – leaving just five, all saved for the Pyrenees and the Alps – and the number of stages increased to 24, the overall duration of the race holding steady at 29 days. Also out went the idea of starting the race outside of Paris, the Évian experiment not being repeated.

The biggest change, though, was in the way the stages would be raced. The big bunch sprints of the previous year had annoyed Desgrange, and he decided upon a new formula which would solve that problem once and for all: each of the flat stages, save the stage to Bayonne (the eve of the Pyrenees) and the finale to Paris, was to be run as a team time trial. Teams were to be set off at 15-minute intervals, with the *touristes-routiers* all grouped together at the back of the stage. The teams would have to race hard all the way from start to finish, unable to take things easy for not knowing what the other teams were doing.

The outcome, of course, was that only those with a strong team were in with a shout of victory. But two of the strongest teams in the Tour's history were absent: Automoto and Peugeot. Peugeot had been cutting back its involvement with the sport over the previous few years, the French economy not being kind to their cycling business. For Automoto, the reason was the death of Ottavio Bottecchia, just four days before the Tour started.

Le Maçon de Frioul, the brick-layer from Fruili, as they called Bottecchia, had been found unconscious and with head injuries on the side of a road near his home in Fruili on 3 June. He was taken to a hospital where, 12 days later he died, without having regained consciousness. How Bottecchia came about his injuries is the mystery. The intrigue is in whether they were from a fall from his bike, or whether he was attacked. Few favour the former, more prosaic, explanation. Justifications for the latter abound, with money, sex and politics all entering the mix.

Many years after Bottecchia's death two different men offered up differing death bed confessions. In the first it was claimed that Bottecchia had been the subject of a mafia hit. In the second, a local farmer was said to have thrown a rock at the two-time Tour champion, accidentally killing him. Others insist that he was killed by supporters of the fascist supremo Benito Mussolini, Bottecchia's political beliefs running counter to those of *il Duce*'s supporters.

This left the Tour without its defending champion, Lucien Buysse, only the third time this had happened (after René Pottier in 1907 and Lucien Petit-Breton in 1909). In fact, no previous winners of the Tour took the start in Paris in 1927. Henri Pélissier, the winner from 1923, had more or less retired at this stage, as had Firmin Lambot (the winner in 1919 and 1922), Léon Scieur (1921) and Philippe Thys (1920).

In the absence of the likes of Automoto, the strongest team in the race was the Alcyon squad, now bossed by Ludovic Feuillet and with 1926's runner-up Nicolas Frantz the odds-on favourite for victory. In addition to the main six-man Alcyon squad, the Paris-based manufacturer also fielded three two-man teams representing its subsidiaries Thomann, Armor and Labor (for the purpose of the time-trial stages all four were treated as one). Against Alcyon were an 11-man squad representing JB Louvet, a six-man team from Alléluia and an eight-man team from Dilecta, with the rest of the 142-man field being made up of *touristes-routiers*.

With the Tour lacking in stars of old, Desgrange turned to two old stars and asked them if they would ride: the Pélissier brothers, Henri and Francis. Rather than turn Desgrange down cold they decided to make him an offer he could easily refuse: they would ride, but only on two conditions. The first was an appearance fee of 3,500 francs a day (this at a time when the Tour's winner was pocketing 15,000 francs), the second a promise that when they retired from the race – and it was a when, not an if – L'Auto would be kind and eschew the vitriol normally poured upon them. Neither condition would have been particularly welcomed by Desgrange but he was desperate. At which point Henri Pélissier found a new excuse to stay in semi-retirement while Francis donned the blue and gold jersey of Dilecta and set forth on one more Tour.

Having watched the teams setting off at 15-minute intervals between seven and eight o'clock in the morning of the race's opening Sunday, dedicated cycling fans in Paris that day could have then taken themselves to the Pavillions-sous-Bois to catch the start of the Paris-Reims race. Then, after a light lunch, from two o'clock onwards they could have watched track races in either the Parc des Princes or the Piste Municipale. For the 142 riders in the Tour, though, all that mattered was the road winding northwest from Paris, and Dieppe, 180 kilometres in front of them.

The first team into Dieppe was the Alcyon-Thomann-Armor-Labor combine, Nicolas Frantz leading home four of his team-mates just before the clocks struck a quarter past one. Just after one-thirty Gustaaf van Slembrouck came in with his JB Louvet team-mate Hector Martin. Just before twenty-to-two Alléluia's Julien Moineau came in alone, 10-minutes ahead of any of his team-mates. Hot on Moineau's wheels came the Dilecta squad, Francis Pélissier leading home three of his team-mates. But who'd won the stage?

After the abacus and slide-rule had been taken out Moineau was twenty-fifth, Frantz thirteenth, Van Slembrouck and Martin fifth and sixth and, wearing the first yellow jersey of the 1927 Tour, was Pélissier. Fans watching in Dieppe would have to read a newspaper report – or tune in to one of the broadcasts on radio – in order to have explained to them what they'd just witnessed.

Pélissier held onto his lead until he abandoned on the sixth stage, passing the lead to his Dilecta team-mate Ferdinand le Drogo. JB Louvet took the lead the next day with Hector Martin and he held the *maillot jaune* until the first rest day, in Bayonne on the eleventh day of the race. On that rest day riders and fans alike gasped in awe as the moon eclipsed the sun. The next day, Nicolas Frantz eclipsed everyone as the Tour hit the high mountains of the Pyrenees.

Setting off from Bayonne in the pre-dawn dark it was one of the Italian *touristes-routiers* who seemed to show the most interest in reaching the Pyrenees first. Michele Gordini escaped the *peloton* alone and built up a lead of 36 minutes by Oloron-Sainte-Marie. That ballooned out to just shy of an hour by the base of the Aubisque, the summit of which Gordini crossed just before half nine in the morning.

But by now Frantz had warmed his engine up and was chasing hard. Gordini's lead was slashed back to just 20 minutes by the top of the Aubisque. By the summit of the Tourmalet, Frantz was fully in control, four minutes up on the Italian. Over the Aspin and the Peyresourde Frantz rode alone, hour after tiring hour. More than 16 hours after leaving Bayonne he reached Luchon, 11 minutes up on his nearest rival, team-mate Adelin Benoît. The Luxembourger donned the yellow jersey, with a lead of 1h37'48" over the man who'd worn it that morning, JB Louvet's Hector Martin, and 38'27" over his nearest rival, team-mate Maurice Dewaele.

After that, people were scrapping for seconds, the Luxembourger's Tour all but in the bag. France took solace in the performance of two young riders: Thomann's André Leducq, who ended up with three stage wins added to his *palmarès* and finished fourth overall; and Alléluia's Antonin Magne, who won the stage from Marseille to Toulon and finished in sixth place overall, the first rider home who was not a member of the Alcyon-Thomann-Armor-Labor combine. Two possible stars of the future, hope for a home victory in a Tour that had now seen just one French win in twelve editions. Meanwhile, Luxembourg celebrated its first victory in the Tour since François Faber – also an Alcyon rider – in 1909. They wouldn't have long to wait for their third win.

Stage-by-Stage Results for the 1927 Tour de France			Stage Winner	Maillot Jaune
Stage 1 Sun 19 Jun	Paris (Le Vésinet) to Dieppe (TTT) 142 starters, 107 finishers	180 km 5h55'41" 30.4 kph	Francis Pélissier (Fra) Dilecta	Francis Pélissier (Fra) Dilecta
Stage 2 Mon 20 Jun	Dieppe to Le Havre (TTT) 105 finishers	103 km 3h25'51" 30.0 kph	Maurice Dewaele (Bel) Labor	Francis Pélissier (Fra) Dilecta
Stage 3 Tue 21 Jun	Le Havre to Caen (TTT) 88 finishers	225 km 7h21'05" 30.6 kph	Hector Martin (Bel) JB Louvet	Francis Pélissier (Fra) Dilecta
Stage 4 Wed 22 Jun	Caen to Cherbourg (TTT) 79 finishers	140 km 4h20'46" 32.2 kph	Camille van de Casteele (Bel) JB Louvet	Francis Pélissier (Fra) Dilecta
Stage 5 Thu 23 Jun	Cherbourg to Dinan (TTT) 76 finishers	199 km 6h34'57" 30.2 kph	Ferdinand le Drogo (Fra) Dilecta	Francis Pélissier (Fra) Dilecta
Stage 6 Fri 24 Jun	Dinan to Brest (TTT) 74 finishers	206 km 7h25'47" 27.7 kph	André Leducq (Fra) Thomann	Ferdinand le Drogo (Fra) Dilecta
Stage 7 Sat 25 Jun	Brest to Vannes (TTT) 72 finishers	207 km 6h40'28" 31.0 kph	Gustaaf van Slembrouck (Bel) JB Louvet	Hector Martin (Bel) JB Louvet
Stage 8 Sun 26 Jun	Vannes to Les Sables- d'Olonne (TTT) 65 finishers	204 km 6h03'35" 33.7 kph	Raymond Decorte (Bel) JB Louvet	Hector Martin (Bel) JB Louvet
Stage 9 Mon 27 Jun	Les Sables-d'Olonne to Bordeaux (TTT) 57 finishers	285 km 8h56'34" 31.9 kph	Adelin Benoît (Bel) Alcyon	Hector Martin (Bel) JB Louvet
Stage 10 Tue 28 Jun	Bordeaux to Bayonne 57 finishers	189 km 7h13'40" 26.1 kph	Pé Verhaegen (Bel) JB Louvet	Hector Martin (Bel) JB Louvet
Wed 29 Jun	Rest day			
Stage 11 Thu 30 Jun	Bayonne to Luchon 46 finishers	326 km 16h25'10" 19.9 kph	Nicolas Frantz (Lux) Alcyon	Nicolas Frantz (Lux) Alcyon
	Major climbs: Col d'Aubisque (1,709m) Michele Gordini (Ita) unsponsored; Col du Tourmalet (2,115m) Nicolas Frantz (Lux) Alcyon; Col d'Aspin (1,489m) Nicolas Frantz (Lux) Alcyon; Col de Peyresourde (1,569m) Nicolas Frantz (Lux) Alcyon.			
Fri 1 Jul	Rest day			
Stage 12 Sat 2 Jul	Luchon to Perpignan 45 finishers	323 km 12h10'14" 26.5 kph	Gustaaf van Slembrouck (Bel) JB Louvet	Nicolas Frantz (Lux) Alcyon
	Major climbs: Col de Port (1,249m) Adelin Benoît (Bel) Alcyon; Col de Portet-d'Aspet (1,069m) Nicolas Frantz (Lux) Alcyon; Col de Puymorens (1,915m) Nicolas Frantz (Lux) Alcyon			
Sun 3 Jul	Rest day			

Stage-by-Stage Results for the 1927 Tour de France			Stage Winner	Maillot Jaune
Stage 13 Mon 4 Jul	Perpignan to Marseille 44 finishers	360 km 14h22'37" 25.0 kph	Maurice Dewaele (Bel) Labor	Nicolas Frantz (Lux) Alcyon
Stage 14 Tue 5 Jul	Marseille to Toulon (TTT) 44 finishers	120 km 3h51'44" 31.1 kph	Antonin Magne (Fra) Alléluia	Nicolas Frantz (Lux) Alcyon
Stage 15 Wed 6 Jul	Toulon to Nice 44 finishers	220 km 11h40'02" 24.0 kph	Nicolas Frantz (Lux) Alcyon	Nicolas Frantz (Lux) Alcyon
	Major climbs: Col de Castillon (706m) Nicolas Frantz (Lux) Alcyon; Col de Braus (1,002m) Nicolas Frantz (Lux) Alcyon			
Thu 7 Jul	Rest day			
Stage 16 Fri 8 Jul	Nice to Briançon 44 finishers	275 km 12h58'04" 21.2 kph	Julien Vervaecke (Bel) Armor	Nicolas Frantz (Lux) Alcyon
	Major climbs: Col d'Allos (2,250m) Nicolas Frantz (Lux) Alcyon; Col de Vars (2,110m) Nicolas Frantz (Lux) Alcyon; Col d'Izoard (2,360m) Nicolas Frantz (Lux) Alcyon			
Stage 17 Sat 9 Jul	Briançon to Évian 43 finishers	283 km 11h57'02" 23.7 kph	Pé Verhaegen (Bel) JB Louvet	Nicolas Frantz (Lux) Alcyon
	Major climbs: Col d'Aravis (1,498m) Charles Martinet (Sui) unsponsored; Col du Galibier (2,556m) Antonin Magne (Fra) Alléluia			
Sun 10 Jul	Rest day			
Stage 18 Mon 11 Jul	Évian to Pontarlier (TTT) 43 finishers	213 km 7h09'31" 29.8 kph	Adelin Benoît (Bel) Alcyon	Nicolas Frantz (Lux) Alcyon
	Major climbs: Col de la Faucille (1,323m) Julien Vervaecke (Bel) Armor			
Stage 19 Tue 12 Jul	Pontarlier to Belfort (TTT) 41 finishers	119 km 3h45'30" 31.7 kph	Maurice Geldhof (Bel) JB Louvet	Nicolas Frantz (Lux) Alcyon
Stage 20 Wed 13 Jul	Belfort to Strasbourg (TTT) 39 finishers	145 km 4h19'16" 33.6 kph	Raymond Decorte (Bel) JB Louvet	Nicolas Frantz (Lux) Alcyon
Stage 21 Thu 14 Jul	Strasbourg to Metz (TTT) 39 finishers	165 km 5h24'54" 30.5 kph	Nicolas Frantz (Lux) Alcyon	Nicolas Frantz (Lux) Alcyon
Stage 22 Fri 15 Jul	Metz to Charleville (TTT) 39 finishers	159 km 5h00'29" 31.7 kph	Hector Martin (Bel) JB Louvet	Nicolas Frantz (Lux) Alcyon
Stage 23 Sat 16 Jul	Charleville to Dunkerque (TTT) 39 finishers	270 km 9h09'38" 29.5 kph	André Leducq (Fra) Thomann	Nicolas Frantz (Lux) Alcyon
Stage 24 Sun 17 Jul	Dunkerque to Paris (Parc des Princes) 39 finishers	344 km 13h58'01" 24.6 kph	André Leducq (Fra) Thomann	Nicolas Frantz (Lux) Alcyon

Total Prize fund: 100,000 francs (12,000 francs first prize)

Final Classification

Place	Rider	Team	Time	Age
1	Nicolas Frantz (Lux)	Alcyon	5,398 km 198h16'42" 27.224 kph	27
2	Maurice Dewaele (Bel)	Labor	+ 1h48'21"	30
3	Julien Vervaecke (Bel)	Armor	+ 2h25'06"	27
4	André Leducq (Fra)	Thomann	+ 3h02'05"	23
5	Adelin Benoît (Bel)	Alcyon	+ 4h45'01"	27
6	Antonin Magne (Fra)	Alléluia	+ 4h48'23"	23
7	Pé Verhaegen (Bel)	JB Louvet	+ 6h18'36"	25
8	Julien Moineau (Fra)	Alléluia	+ 6h36'17"	23
9	Hector Martin (Bel)	JB Louvet	+ 7h07'34"	28
10	Maurice Geldhof (Bel)	JB Louvet	+ 7h16'02"	21

Lanterne Rouge

39	Jacques Pfister (Fra)	Unsponsored	30h03'51"	24

Independents

	Secondo Martinetto (Ita)	Unsponsored		32

Meilleur Grimpeur

	Michele Gordini (Ita)	Unsponsored		31

1928: Yellow All the Way

The twenty-second Tour started at the positively decadent hour of nine o'clock on the morning of Sunday 17 June 1928, a good two hours later than any stage of the Tour had ever started, excluding the first stage of the first race. You might almost think that Henri Desgrange and his team at *L'Auto* were going soft. But mostly this was the same Tour as the year before, with a few tweaks which saw two stages being dropped – bringing the overall distance down to 5,377 kilometres – and the number of stages exceeding 300 kilometres rising to seven, with just six below 200. Despite the confusion it caused followers of the race, the team trial format was again used on all stages, except those in the Pyrenees and the Alps and two of the otherwise flat stages, to Marseille and Paris.

Peugeot and Automoto were still absent. Alcyon again fielded two subsidiary teams – Armor and Thomann – along with the main squad, while JB Louvet and Alléluia were the only two other large manufacturers fielding squads. A couple of small manufacturers also fielded teams: Ravat, based in Saint-Étienne; and Elvish, based near Pau, who also fielded a squad in the name of a subsidiary brand, Fontan. As well as the usual trade teams, Desgrange hit upon a new idea: nine five-man regional teams were invited to participate, along with the usual *touristes-routiers*.

The time trial format favoured the richest teams, they being able to field a full complement of 10 riders and so suffering least as riders fell by the wayside. To help the smaller and weaker teams a new rule change was brought it: once the race reached the Alps, substitutes could be drafted in to replace riders who had quit the race.

For the defending champion, Nicolas Frantz and his powerful Alcyon team the time trial format was ideal and left him without serious challengers. Donning the *maillot jaune* on the opening day of the race he led all the way back to Paris. Technically, this was one up on Philippe Thys in 1920 and Ottavio Bottecchia in 1924, both of whom led from first to last but, along the way had had to share the lead with others. And it clearly surpassed Maurice Garin, who led across all six stages of the first Tour, and then all six stages of the next, only to have that second win stripped from him. And, of course, Faber was also carrying into the race the yellow jersey which he had donned on stage 11 of the 1927 race, giving him an unbroken run of 36 days in yellow.

Back in 1907 Alcyon had pulled out of the Tour a little over half way through, with the 1905 winner Louis Trousselier having suffered a series of unfortunate mechanical mishaps. In the 21 years since then the quality of the team's equipment had improved considerably and yet, as fate would have it, the only real challenge Frantz had to surmount in the 1928 Tour came late in the race when his bike broke and he had to ride a borrowed replacement – a ladies' bike complete with mudguards and bell – in order finish the stage.

* * * * *

The twenty-second Tour was notable for the involvement of an Antipodean team, made up of three Aussies and a Kiwi: the Australians Hubert Opperman, Perry Osborne and Ernest Bainbridge, along with Harry Watson from New Zealand. Don Kirkham and Iddo Munro had first flown the flag for Australia in the Tour in 1914, riding for the Phébus squad and finishing seventeenth and twentieth. Since then another Australian, Reggie McNamara, had been making a name for himself on the American and European Six Day circuits and a couple of Australian and New Zealand newspapers decided to organise a fund to send some local riders to Europe and the Tour.

Opperman and his team-mates arrived in Europe in April, and set about acclimatising themselves to the local way of doing things, riding races like Paris-Rennes and Paris-Brussels ahead of the Tour.

For the *grande boucle* the four Antipodeans were supposed to be joined by six local riders, under the Ravat banner, but those would-be team-mates never materialised. This, with the team time trial format employed on the flat stages, left the Antipodean riders weaker than even the five-man regional teams. Even so, three of them made it back to Paris, with Opperman in eighteenth, Watson twenty-eighth and Osborne thirty-eighth.

After the Tour, Opperman showed a glimpse of what might have been, had Desgrange's rules not favoured the big teams, by winning the Bol d'Or 24-hour track race. Having clocked up a distance of 950 kilometres in the race his manger and the fans convinced Opperman to continue on and break the record for 1,000 kilometres, which the Australian did. *L'Auto*'s readers showed their appreciation for Oppy's performances by voting him their most popular sportsman of the year.

* * * * *

Five months after the Tour ended, Swiss cyclist Henri Collé got his collar felt by local coppers.

Collé rode his first Tour in 1921, as one of the independents, and came back for seconds in 1923, when he finished sixth overall and was the best of the independents. On his third participation, in 1924, his was one of the stories told by Albert Londres in *Le Petit Parisien*, Collé having to abandon in the Alps, just as the race came close to his home town of Geneva. The following two Tours he was back for more, riding for the JB Louvet subsidiary Jean Louvet. His sixth and final participation had come in 1928, when he was back with unsponsored independents. As with all the independents, the time trial format did him no favours and he abandoned the race at Évian, close to his home in Geneva.

In November 1928 the 35-year-old Collé was one of six people arrested by Swiss police, charged with having robbed the safe of a local boxing promoter. A cycling career which had reached its zenith at the Tour de France came to a sad end.

Stage-by-Stage Results for the 1928 Tour de France			Stage Winner	Maillot Jaune
Stage 1 Sun 17 Jun	Paris (Le Vésinet) to Caen (TTT) 162 starters, 141 finishers	207 km 6h29'03" 31.9 kph	Nicolas Frantz (Lux) Alcyon	Nicolas Frantz (Lux) Alcyon
Stage 2 Mon 18 Jun	Caen to Cherbourg (TTT) 135 finishers	140 km 4h12'29" 33.3 kph	André Leducq (Fra) Alcyon	Nicolas Frantz (Lux) Alcyon
Stage 3 Tue 19 Jun	Cherbourg to Dinan (TTT) 124 finishers	199 km 6h29'17" 30.7 kph	Gaston Rebry (Bel) Alcyon	Nicolas Frantz (Lux) Alcyon
Stage 4 Wed 20 Jun	Dinan to Brest (TTT) 122 finishers	206 km 6h47'58" 30.3 kph	Pé Verhaegen (Bel) JB Louvet	Nicolas Frantz (Lux) Alcyon
Stage 5 Thu 21 Jun	Brest to Vannes (TTT) 116 finishers	208 km 6h43'36" 30.9 kph	Marcel Bidot (Fra) Alléluia	Nicolas Frantz (Lux) Alcyon
Stage 6 Fri 22 Jun	Vannes to Les Sables- d'Olonne (TTT) 111 finishers	204 km 6h23'44" 31.9 kph	Nicolas Frantz (Lux) Alcyon	Nicolas Frantz (Lux) Alcyon
Stage 7 Sat 23 Jun	Les Sables-d'Olonne to Bordeaux (TTT) 103 finishers	285 km 9h21'33" 30.5 kph	Victor Fontan (Fra) Elvish	Nicolas Frantz (Lux) Alcyon
Stage 8 Sun 24 Jun	Bordeaux to Hendaye (TTT) 103 finishers	225 km 6h47'25" 33.1 kph	Maurice Dewaele (Bel) Alcyon	Nicolas Frantz (Lux) Alcyon
Mon 25 Jun	Rest day			
Stage 9 Tue 26 Jun	Hendaye to Luchon 77 finishers	387 km 16h13'10" 23.9 kph	Victor Fontan (Fra) Elvish	Nicolas Frantz (Lux) Alcyon
	Major climbs: Col d'Aubisque (1,709m) Camille van de Casteelle (Bel) JB Louvet; Col du Tourmalet (2,115m) Camille van de Casteele (Bel) JB Louvet			
Wed 27 Jun	Rest day			
Stage 10 Thu 28 Jun	Luchon to Perpignan 74 finishers	323 km 12h27'22" 25.9 kph	André Leducq (Fra) Alcyon	Nicolas Frantz (Lux) Alcyon
	Major climbs: Col de Portet d'Aspet (1,069m) Antonin Magne (Fra) Alléluia; Col de Port (1,249m) Antonin Magne (Fra) Alléluia; Col du Puymorens (1,915m) Nicolas Frantz (Lux) Alcyon			
Fri 29 Jun	Rest day			
Stage 11 Sat 30 Jun	Perpignan to Marseille 73 finishers	363 km 14h41'50" 24.7 kph	André Leducq (Fra) Alcyon	Nicolas Frantz (Lux) Alcyon
Sun 1 Jul	Rest day			

Stage-by-Stage Results for the 1928 Tour de France			Stage Winner	Maillot Jaune
Stage 12 Mon 2 Jul	Marseille to Nice 73 finishers	330 km 13h40'50" 24.1 kph	Nicolas Frantz (Lux) Alcyon	Nicolas Frantz (Lux) Alcyon
	Major climbs: Col de Braus (1,002m) André Leducq (Fra) Alcyon; Col de Castillon (706m) André Leducq (Fra) Alcyon			
Tue 3 Jul	Rest day			
Stage 13 Wed 4 Jul	Nice to Grenoble 73 finishers	333 km 14h00'36" 23.8 kph	Antonin Magne (Fra) Alléluia	Nicolas Frantz (Lux) Alcyon
	Major climbs: Col d'Allos (2,250m) Nicolas Frantz (Lux) Alcyon + Victor Fontan (Fra) Elvish; Col Bayard (1,246m) Antonin Magne (Fra) Alléluia			
Thu 5 Jul	Rest day			
Stage 14 Fri 6 Jul	Grenoble to Évian 71 finishers	329 km 12h35'32" 26.1 kph	Julien Moineau (Fra) Allelluia	Nicolas Frantz (Lux) Alcyon
	Major climbs: Col du Lautaret (2,058m) Antonin Magne (Fra) Alléluia; Col du Galibier (2,556m) August Verdyck (Bel) JB Louvet; Col du Télégraphe (1,566m) Camille van de Casteele (Bel) JB Louvet; Col des Aravis (1,498m) Julien Moineau (Fra) Alléluia			
Sat 7 Jul	Rest day			
Stage 15 Sun 8 Jul	Évian to Pontarlier (TTT) 66 finishers	213 km 6h43'37" 31.7 kph	Pierre Magne (Fra) Alléluia	Nicolas Frantz (Lux) Alcyon
	Major climbs: Col de la Faucille (1,323m) n/a			
Stage 16 Mon 9 Jul	Pontarlier to Belfort (TTT) 56 finishers	119 km 3h33'22" 33.5 kph	André Leducq (Fra) Alcyon	Nicolas Frantz (Lux) Alcyon
Stage 17 Tue 10 Jul	Belfort to Strasbourg (TTT) 55 finishers	145 km 4h24'30" 32.9 kph	Joseph Mauclair (Fra) Armor	Nicolas Frantz (Lux) Alcyon
Stage 18 Wed 11 Jul	Strasbourg to Metz (TTT) 54 finishers	165 km 4h59'19" 33.1 kph	Nicolas Frantz (Lux) Alcyon	Nicolas Frantz (Lux) Alcyon
Stage 19 Thu 12 Jul	Metz to Charleville (TTT) 53 finishers	159 km 4h36'15" 34.5 kph	Marcel Huot (Fra) Alléluia	Nicolas Frantz (Lux) Alcyon
Stage 20 Fri 13 Jul	Charleville to Malo-les-Bains (TTT) 41 finishers	271 km 8h47'31" 30.8 kph	Maurice Dewaele (Bel) Alcyon	Nicolas Frantz (Lux) Alcyon
Stage 21 Sat 14 Jul	Malo-les-Bains to Dieppe (TTT) 41 finishers	234 km 7h43'33" 30.3 kph	Antonin Magne (Fra) Alléluia	Nicolas Frantz (Lux) Alcyon
Stage 22 Sun 15 Jul	Dieppe to Paris (Parc des Princes) 41 finishers	331 km 13h35'02" 24.4 kph	Nicolas Frantz (Lux) Alcyon	Nicolas Frantz (Lux) Alcyon

Total Prize fund: 100,000 francs (12,000 francs first prize)

Final Classification

Place	Rider	Team	Time	Age
1	Nicolas Frantz (Lux)	Alcyon	5,476 km 192h48'58" 28.400 kph	28
2	André Leducq (Fra)	Alcyon	+ 50'07"	24
3	Maurice Dewaele (Bel)	Alcyon	+ 56'16"	31
4	Jan Mertens (Bel)	Thomann	+ 1h19'18"	24
5	Julien Vervaecke (Bel)	Armor	+ 1h53'32"	28
6	Antonin Magne (Fra)	Alléluia	+ 2h14'02"	24
7	Victor Fontan (Fra)	Elvish	+ 5h07'47"	36
8	Marcel Bidot (Fra)	Alléluia	+ 5h18'28"	25
9	Marcel Huot (Fra)	Alléluia	+ 5h37'33"	31
10	Pierre Magne (Fra)	Alléluia	+ 5h41'20"	24
Lanterne Rouge				
41	Edouard Persin (Fra)	Champagne	+ 26h56'19"	26
Meilleur Grimpeur				
	Victor Fontan (Fra)	Elvish		36

1929: Victory for a Corpse

Faced with the public dislike of the team time trial format, Henri Desgrange had no choice but to back down and return the Tour to its normal massed start format. But he did so somewhat gracelessly, threatening to impose separate starts on the riders if the average speed of a stage fell below thirty kilometres an hour.

The route for the twenty-third Tour again followed the one introduced in 1927, with more tweaks. Some stages were softened, some toughened up, but overall it was the same Tour as the previous two years. Having dominated those two races, Nicolas Frantz was clearly a favourite for victory, but now he would have to prove he had earned those wins, that they weren't just down to Alcyon being the strongest team in the race. He would also have to overcome another previous winner of the race, Lucien Buysse. His Automoto team had passed on participation in the previous two Tours – and, along with Peugeot, also sat out the 1929 race – and he was returning wearing a Génial Lucifer jersey. A show-down between the winners of the previous three Tours was expected. Neither rider lived up to their billing, though, and both barely featured in the race for overall honours.

Desgrange deemed his experiment with regional teams to have been a success and four five-man and five four-man regional squads joined the riders in trade teams on the start line. Those trade teams were each able to field eight men, and came from Alcyon (along with a subsidiary brand, La Française, which had been acquired in 1924), Alléluia (and a subsidiary De Dion), Dilecta, Elvish (and a subsidiary brand, Fontan), Génial Lucifer and La Rafale. JB Louvet was the last team to join the race and only fielded a squad of five riders.

From the second stage Desgrange showed he had no desire to let the teams manipulate his race. Forty-five riders arrived together in Cherbourg but rather than letting them sprint for the line, Desgrange made them fight it out over five laps in the vélodrome (he had done something similar on one stage the year before). JB Louvet's Aimé Dossche, who had won the first stage, took second, behind Alcyon's André Leducq and held on to his yellow jersey, with three riders behind him, all tied on the same time.

On the fourth stage, one of those riders, Alcyon's Maurice Dewaele, emerged top of the heap and took the yellow jersey. At the end of the seventh stage Dewaele slipped back a couple of minutes and three men emerged at the top of the rankings, all tied on the same time. The rules had no way of separating these three riders and so, at the start of the eighth stage, Leducq, his team-mate Frantz and Elvish's Victor Fontan all wore yellow jerseys. Alcyon's Gaston Rebry solved that problem as the race hit the edge of the Pyrenees by surprising all three and taking their yellow jerseys away from them.

In the high mountains Fontan reigned supreme, as he had done on this same stage the year before. Escaping with his team-mate Salvador Cardona they split the honours in Luchon, Cardona taking the stage and Fontan the *maillot jaune*.

For the 37-year-old Fontan, this was his last chance at Tour glory. His *palmarès* bulged with wins in minor races such as the Tour de Corrèze, Vuelta a Guipúzcoa, Tour du Sud-Ouest (all 1923), Bordeaux-Angoulême, Volta Ciclista a Catalunya (both 1926), Criterium du Midi, Circuit de Béarn and the Vuelta Ciclista al País Vasco (all 1927). Having finished the 1928 Tour in seventh, with two stage wins and the *meilleur grimpeur* award, Fontan came to the 1929 race ready to challenge for the overall victory. Being from the area around the Pyrenees he was a capable climber, even despite having been shot in the leg during the War, and that's where his overall victory should have been built. But, as with so many riders in so many Tours, mechanical misfortune destroyed his dreams. On the second Pyrenean stage Fontan's forks broke and by the time he had been able to source a replacement bike he was already three-quarters of an hour down on the leaders. At which point he decided there was nothing left to fight for and quit the race, only the third rider to leave the Tour while leading overall.

Maurice Dewaele – who had finished second and third at the previous two Tours – inherited Fontan's lead, with a fifteen minute advantage over Génial Lucifer's Jef Demuysère. By Grenoble that had become 18 minutes. But disaster struck and Dewaele came down with a stomach problem. He spent the whole of the rest day in his hotel room, and when he arrived at the start of the stage to Évian – which included the climbs of the Lautaret, Galibier and Aravis – Dewaele was pale as a ghost. Somehow, though, his Alcyon team-mates were able to hide this fact from their rivals and – with, it is alleged, more than a little help from others in the *peloton* – shepherded Dewaele to the finish, safe in his yellow jersey. His margin over Demuysère remained unchanged, but the third-placed rider, La Rafale's Giuesppe Pancera, leap-frogged Demuysère and closed to within 15 minutes of Dewaele.

Dewaele recovered a bit over the next rest day but was still off form when the riders set off for Belfort. But again his Alcyon team-mates were able to shepherd him safely to the finish, his overall lead unchallenged by Pancera, Demuysère or, for that matter, anyone else. And that's pretty much how the rest of the race remained, with Dewaele riding into Paris in yellow, the only change being that Pancera slipped back to third, behind Demuysère. It was a victory that displeased Desgrange greatly – he complained that his Tour had been won by a corpse.

Nothing Desgrange had tried in the final stages of the race was able to disrupt the control exerted by Alcyon, who had spent 200,000 francs on their Tour team and were determined to get a return on their investment. On the nineteenth stage, to Charleville, Desgrange once again decided to send the riders off in two *pelotons* – as he had on the twelfth stage – the independents and regionals leaving ten minutes ahead of the trade teams. The next day Desgrange mixed things up, sending off two mixed *pelotons* of sponsored and unsponsored riders. All this served to do was confuse the watching public, who thought they saw Benoît Faure (from the regional Sud Est squad) win in Chareleville and Frantz win in Malo-les-Bains, only to be told that the time differences between groups of riders meant that Bernard van Rysselberghe (Dilecta) and Dewaele – now back to good health – had been the actual stage winners.

One experiment Desgrange could be happy with was the regional teams format, which he had introduced the previous year. Local fans had something new to cheer for, riders riding for them, in their colours, not some faceless bicycle manufacturer. And in those regional teams lay the key to Desgrange's next great experiment.

Stage-by-Stage Results for the 1929 Tour de France			Stage Winner	Maillot Jaune
Stage 1 Sun 30 Jun	Paris (Le Vésinet) to Caen 155 starters, 134 finishers	206 km 5h55'21" 41.2 kph	Aimé Dossche (Bel) JB Louvet	Aimé Dossche (Bel) JB Louvet
Stage 2 Mon 1 Jul	Caen to Cherbourg 131 finishers	140 km 4h20'51" 35.0 kph	André Leducq (Fra) Alcyon	Aimé Dossche (Bel) JB Louvet
Stage 3 Tue 2 Jul	Cherbourg to Dinan 123 finishers	199 km 6h21'03" 33.2 kph	Omer Taverne (Bel) Unsponsored	Aimé Dossche (Bel) JB Louvet
Stage 4 Wed 3 Jul	Dinan to Brest 120 finishers	206 km 6h41'54" 34.3 kph	Louis Delannoy (Bel) La Française	Maurice Dewaele (Bel) Alcyon
Stage 5 Thu 4 Jul	Brest to Vannes 114 finishers	208 km 6h29'03" 34.7 kph	Gustaaf van Slembrouck (Bel) Génial Lucifer	Maurice Dewaele (Bel) Alcyon
Stage 6 Fri 5 Jul	Vannes to Les Sables-d'Olonne 112 finishers	206 km 6h23'14" 34.3 kph	Paul le Drogo (Fra) Dilecta	Maurice Dewaele (Bel) Alcyon
Stage 7 Sat 6 Jul	Les Sables-d'Olonne to Bordeaux 103 finishers	285 km 9h13'07" 31.7 kph	Nicolas Frantz (Lux) Alcyon	Nicolas Frantz (Lux) Alcyon
				André Leducq (Fra) Alcyon
				Victor Fontan (Fra) Elvish
Stage 8 Sun 7 Jul	Bordeaux to Bayonne 102 finishers	182 km 5h36'25" 36.4 kph	Julien Moineau (Fra) Alléluia	Gaston Rebry (Bel) Alcyon
Mon 8 Jul	Rest day			
Stage 9 Tue 9 Jul	Bayonne to Luchon 89 finishers	363 km 16h31'57" 22.7 kph	Salvador Cardona (Esp) Fontan	Victor Fontan (Fra) Elvish
	Major climbs: Col d'Aubisque (1,709m) Lucien Buysse (Bel) Génial Lucifer; Col du Tourmalet (2,115m) Victor Fontan (Fra) Elvish			

Stage-by-Stage Results for the 1929 Tour de France			Stage Winner	Maillot Jaune
Wed 10 Jul	Rest day			
Stage 10 Thu 11 Jul	Luchon to Perpignan 77 finishers	323 km 11h42'48" 29.4 kph	Jef Demuysère (Bel) Génial Lucifer	Maurice Dewaele (Bel) Alcyon
	Major climbs: Col de Portet d'Aspet (1,069m) Louis Delannoy (Bel) La Française; Col de Port (1,249m) André Leducq (Fra) Alcyon; Col du Puymorens (1,915m) Benoît Faure (Fra) Sud Est			
Fri 12 Jul	Rest day			
Stage 11 Sat 13 Jul	Perpignan to Marseille 75 finishers	366 km 13h37'29" 28.2 kph	André Leducq (Fra) Alcyon	Maurice Dewaele (Bel) Alcyon
Sun 14 Jul	Rest day			
Stage 12 Mon 15 Jul	Marseille to Cannes 73 finishers	191 km 5h57'45" 38.2 kph	Marcel Bidot (Fra) La Française	Maurice Dewaele (Bel) Alcyon
Stage 13 Tue 16 Jul	Cannes to Nice 71 finishers	133 km 4h52'18" 33.3 kph	Benoît Faure (Fra) Sud Est	Maurice Dewaele (Bel) Aclyon
	Major climbs: Col de Braus (1,002m) Benoît Faure (Fra) Sud Est; Col de Castillon (706m) Benoît Faure (Fra) Sud Est			
Wed 17 Jul	Rest day			
Stage 14 Thu 18 Jul	Nice to Grenoble 69 finishers	333 km 13h19'06" 25.6 kph	Gaston Rebry (Bel) Alcyon	Maurice Dewaele (Bel) Alcyon
	Major climbs: Col d'Allos (2,250m) Jef Demuysère (Bel) Génial Lucifer; Col Bayard (1,246m) Jef Demuysère (Bel) Génial Lucifer			
Fri 19 Jul	Rest day			
Stage 15 Sat 20 Jul	Grenoble to Évian 67 finishers	329 km 13h09'37" 25.3 kph	Julien Vervaecke (Bel) Alcyon	Maurice Dewaele (Bel) Alcyon
	Major climbs: Col du Lautaret (2,058m) Gaston Rebry (Bel) Alcyon; Col du Galibier (2,556m) Gaston Rebry (Bel) Alcyon; Col des Aravis (1,498m) Nicolas Frantz (Lux) Alcyon			
Sun 21 Jul	Rest day			
Stage 16 Mon 22 Jul	Évian to Belfort 66 finishers	283 km 9h34'05" 31.4 kph	Charles Pélissier (Fra) JB Louvet	Maurice Dewaele (Bel) Alcyon
	Major climbs: Col de la Faucille (1,323m) Benoît Faure (Fra) Sud Est			
Stage 17 Tue 23 Jul	Belfort to Strasbourg 63 finishers	145 km 4h27'24" 36.3 kph	André Leducq (Fra) Alcyon	Maurice Dewaele (Bel) Alcyon
Stage 18 Wed 24 Jul	Strasbourg to Metz 62 finishers	165 km 5h47'10" 33.0 kph	André Leducq (Fra) Alcyon	Maurice Dewaele (Bel) Alcyon

Stage-by-Stage Results for the 1929 Tour de France			Stage Winner	Maillot Jaune
Stage 19 Thu 25 Jul	Metz to Charleville 61 finishers	159 km 4h44'06" 39.8 kph	Bernard van Rysselberghe (Bel) Dilecta	Maurice Dewaele (Bel) Alcyon
Stage 20 Fri 26 Jul	Charleville to Malo-les-Bains 60 finishers	270 km 9h16'16" 30.0 kph	Maurice Dewaele (Bel) Alcyon	Maurice Dewaele (Bel) Alcyon
Stage 21 Sat 27 Jul	Malo-les-Bains to Dieppe 60 finishers	234 km 9h03'52" 26.0 kph	André Leducq (Fra) Alcyon	Maurice Dewaele (Bel) Alcyon
Stage 22 Sun 28 Jul	Dieppe to Paris (Parc des Princes) 60 finishers	332 km 12h19'19" 27.7 kph	Nicolas Frantz (Lux) Alcyon	Maurice Dewaele (Bel) Alcyon

Total Prize fund: 150,000 francs (10,000 francs first prize)

Final Classification					
Place		Rider	Team	Time	Age
	1	Maurice Dewaele (Bel)	Alcyon	5,286 km 186h39'15" 28.319 kph	32
3	2	Giuseppe Pancera (Ita)	La Rafale	+34'23" + 44'23" (1)	30
2	3	Jef Demuysère (Bel)	Génial Lucifer	+22'10" + 57'10" (1)	21
	4	Salvador Cardona (Esp)	Fontan	+ 57'46"	28
	5	Nicolas Frantz (Lux)	Alcyon	+ 58'00"	29
	6	Louis Delannoy (Bel)	La Française	+ 1h06'09"	27
	7	Antonin Magne (Fra)	Alléluia	+ 1h08'00"	25
	8	Julien Vervaecke (Bel)	Alcyon	+ 2h01'37"	29
	9	Pierre Magne (Fra)	Alléluia	+ 2h03'00"	25
	10	Gaston Rebry (Bel)	Alcyon	+ 2h17'49"	24
Lanterne Rouge					
	60	André Léger (Fra)	Champagne	+ 31h37'55"	33
Independents					
		Benoît Faure	Sud Est		30
Meilleur Grimpeur					
		Victor Fontan (Fra)	Elvish		37

(1) Four months after the Tour ended Jef Demuysère was handed a 25 minutes time penalty, and Giuseppe Pancera one of ten minutes, the Belgian for an illegal drink and the Italian for help received fixed a puncture.

1930: Twentieth Century Boy

Pretty much from the Tour's beginning, Henri Desgrange had been waging a personal battle against the control exerted by the manufacturer-run teams. Desgrange's personal vision of what cycling should be was at odds with the commercial reality of sponsored teams. When, in 1921, Alphonse Baugé had called the Pyrenean climbs – where the Tour was effectively won – *les juges de la paix* he was referencing the French commercial courts and acknowledging that the Tour was as much a commercial battle for the teams as it was for Desgrange and *L'Auto*. In 1929, when Alcyon's riders rallied around Odile Defraye, they weren't just protecting the yellow jersey, they were protecting the 200,000 francs spent by Alcyon on the team.

For Desgrange, he wanted to see the best rider winning his race, regardless of who that rider rode for. And that wasn't always true of the riders who won the Tour. Of course, that Desgrange's own rules sometimes contributed to the strongest rider losing through time penalties… well that was neither here nor there. The real problem was with the manufacturers, always. They held riders back from other races to focus solely on the Tour, they allowed some riders to build not just their year but their whole career on the Tour.

While, after Henri Pélissier's 1923 victory, the Tour had slipped back to providing a succession of foreign winners, other sports were providing French sports fans with a sense of national pride, not least among them tennis. Between Jean Borotra, Jacques Brugnon, Henri Cochet and René Lacoste, France had been winning all the major tennis championships since 1924. More importantly, collectively the four – known to fans as *Les Quatre Mousquetaires* – had been winning tennis's premier team-based event, the Davis Cup. This, added to the popularity of the Olympic Games and the launch by FIFA of the World Cup football tournament, meant that the mood of the moment was ripe for national teams at the Tour. And so Desgrange decided to build on the regional team format, and have the whole race be undertaken by riders grouped in national and regional teams.

Two major problems, though, had to be overcome: first, how to deal with manufacturers, who were an imortant source of advertising income for *L'Auto* and were now to be excluded from the Tour; and second, how could *L'Auto* fund the additional cost of a Tour raced by national teams? Desgrange had committed to not just providing accommodation and food for the teams, but also providing the bikes the riders would be racing on. If he was going to take the manufacturers out of the Tour he was going to do it properly, not even allowing them the advertising that would come with their name on the bikes used by the riders.

The first problem was relatively easily overcome. With Peugeot and Automoto having been backing out of cycling sponsorship over the previous few years – and, through 1930, being more concerned with planning the merger of their companies – the only major manufacturer in a position to challenge Desgrange's authority was Alcyon. They, it turned out, got the contract to provide the anonymous yellow bikes Tour riders would use. This wouldn't be publicly acknowledged, but was private knowledge within the cycling community, which was enough of a benefit for Alcyon to be willing to go along with it.

The other major cost – accommodation – could be reduced by careful negotiation with the towns which would be hosting the Tour's stage ends and departs. Even with that, though, *L'Auto* was still taking on additional expense, which included the bills for the riders' entourage and their expenses (although the rules made clear that anything beyond basic medical care – doping, in other words – was the rider's responsibility). The solution to this came from a maker of chocolate drinks, Menier, who had been giving out samples at the Tour after the race passed and was more than happy to spend

50,000 francs in order to travel ahead of the race. The *caravanne publicitaire* would prove to be an important source of income for *L'Auto* and the Tour.

All of which just left the race itself. The basic route was pretty much the same as it had been in recent years, with a couple of tweaks. Only four of the 21 stages were above 300 kilometres, another four were below 200. The Pyrenees were tamed a bit more so as to try and leave the four stages around the Alps as the key battleground for the *maillot jaune*.

The national teams – eight-man squads from five nations – were representing France, Belgium, Italy, Germany and Spain. In the latter two cycling was popular, although their riders had never featured much at the Tour. The Belgian squad would provide a true test for the nation which had been dominating the Tour for the previous decade and more, and show whether they could win the Tour on their own, without French team-mates subduing their own ambition for the greater glory of their trade team sponsor. Absent from the Belgian squad was the defending champion Maurice Dewaele. The French squad was packed with rising talent, including Antonin Magne, André Leducq, Marcel Bidot and Charles Pélissier, as well as the aging Victor Fontan, being given a chance to make up for the previous year, when he abandoned in yellow.

The most interesting team at the race, though, came from Italy. Italian cycling was suffering many of the same problems as French – the manufacturer-led teams were in control – but the Giro d'Italia organisers were more accommodating to them, especially as, so far, they had helped ensure only Italian riders did well at the Italian Grand Tour. But one manufacturer, Legnano, ruled the roost in Italy, and one Legnano rider had been ruling the Giro for the last three years, and had been taking away the lion's share of stage wins as well (12 in 1927, six the following year and eight the year after). That rider was Alfredo Binda.

The Giro bosses and the Legnano bosses – owner Emilio Bozzi and *directeur sportif* Eberado Pavesi – accepted that another win for Binda at the *corsa rosa* would be good for neither party and agreed to keep him out of the race. All they had to do was convince Binda of the wisdom of this decision. A meeting was called, the case against riding the Giro was presented and … Binda agreed. But with one condition: he would have to be compensated for his losses. Generously, Binda limited those losses to just the prize money he could win at the Giro, and excluded the appearance fees a Giro win brought. In 1924 the Giro organisers had held the line when the major manufacturers – principally Bianchi and Maino – had demanded appearance fees for their riders, even when that meant a boycott of the race. But in 1930 they were more than willing to accept Binda's demand for a non-appearance fee (although whether or not they ever actually paid up is disputed).

This left Binda free to ride the Tour de France. And so Desgrange approached him with the offer of an appearance fee to come across the border and ride the Tour. Binda accepted, but made clear that his real focus for the season was the World Championships, which he had won in 1927 and wanted to win again. He would come to the Tour if he could ride it as training for the Worlds. Desgrange had come down hard on Costante Girardengo in 1914 when he pulled out of the race – as he tended to with most big name riders – but with Binda (as with Francis Pélissier in 1927) the father of the Tour was willing to accept that even starting the race brought some benefit to the race, and to *L'Auto*.

Whether or not Binda was actually trying to win the Tour was, by the end of the race's seventh stage, a moot point: a crash on the road to Hendaye saw him losing more than an hour to the yellow jersey wearer, his Italian team-mate and rival Learco Guerra (who normally rode for Maino). Guerra had taken the lead on the race's second stage and held on to a 12-second advantage over Pélissier and 1'24" over Magne all the way down France's Atlantic coastline. Guerra had already raced the Giro d'Italia, ahead of the Tour, where he won two stages and finished ninth overall, and was now looking like a good bet for the Tour title.

But Binda wasn't finished yet. First he took the stage to Pau, in a bunch sprint. Then he shook the race up in the Pyrenees, taking the stage win and helping Leducq dislodge Guerra and don the yellow jersey, with a lead of just over five minutes on Magne, and Guerra

11 minutes in arrears. At which point Binda decided he'd had enough of the Tour and quit the race to prepare for the World Championships later in the year (which he went on to win).

Leducq held his lead through the stages taking the race to Grenoble, by which time Guerra had slipped to 16 minutes off yellow and Magne had dropped to third, at 18 minutes. On the stage to Évian, Leducq – Dédé to friends and fans – had a bad day: crashing on the descent of the Galibier he damaged a pedal and another crash at the base of the Télégraphe saw him in need of a replacement pedal. The time lost making repairs saw Guerra – who was in a break up the road – become the virtual leader of the Tour and left Leducq wanting to quit. But his French team-mates rallied round and promised him their full support to drag him back up to the Italian.

And that's just what they did, dragging Dédé back to the front of the race. Once there, they set about making a statement that would silence any doubters: Pélissier, who had already won four stages (it would have been five but for the commissaires stripping him of the win in Bordeaux after Binda accused him of tugging his jersey), led Dédé out in the sprint and the yellow jersey crossed the line to take an impressive victory.

The manner in which Leducq's team-mates rallied around him was, in many ways, similar to the way Alcyon had protected Dewaele the year before. But whereas then Desgrange was infuriated by team members helping one another, the effort put in by Marcel Bidot, Magne and Pélissier to protect Ledqucq's *maillot jaune* made them heroes. They were, if only briefly, the new four musketeers, one for all and all for one. Of course, the big difference between 1929 and 1930 was that the year before the win had been for the sky blue jersey of Alcyon, while in 1930 it was for the *tricolore* of France. National pride enabled Desgrange to put aside his distaste for team work and instead sing the praises of men who, in other years, he might have lambasted.

After Évian the Tour was as good as over, with Guerra accepting his fate as runner up and Leducq riding into Paris as the Tour's first French winner since Henri Pélissier in 1923. The youngest Pélissier

– Charles – was able to go on the rampage in the race's final stages, taking four stages in a row and equalling René Pottier's performance from 1906, which had only been bettered by François Faber in 1909. With the four he had already won – which included the opening stage, allowing him to join his brothers Henri and Francis in having worn the *maillot jaune* – Pélissier took the record for the most stage wins in a single Tour.

France could also celebrate a new generation of riders coming of age, with Leducq being the first Tour winner to have been born in the twentieth century and Magne, Bidot and Pélissier all showing that the future of French cycling was bright. There was also the performance of Benoît Faure who, like Pélissier, was a favourite of Desgrange's and, despite riding as one of the unsponsored *touristes-routiers*, finished a creditable eighth overall and took the *meilleur grimpeur* prize. If anything could make the French victory sweeter it was the poor performance of the perfidious Belgians: all they managed was three stage wins and fourth place overall.

Stage-by-Stage Results for the 1930 Tour de France			Stage Winner	Maillot Jaune
Stage 1 Wed 2 Jul	Paris (Le Vésinet) to Caen 100 starters – 99 finishers	206 km 6h36'01" 31.2 kph	Charles Pélissier (Fra) France	Charles Pélissier (Fra) France
Stage 2 Thu 3 Jul	Caen to Dinan 94 finishers	203 km 7h00'17" 29.0 kph	Learco Guerra (Ita) Italy	Learco Guerra (Ita) Italy
Stage 3 Fri 4 Jul	Dinan to Brest 92 finishers	206 km 6h39'18" 31.0 kph	Charles Pélissier (Fra) France	Learco Guerra (Ita) Italy
Stage 4 Sat 5 Jul	Brest to Vannes 91 finishers	210 km 6h56'03" 30.3 kph	Omer Taverne (Bel) Belgium	Learco Guerra (Ita) Italy
Stage 5 Sun 6 Jul	Vannes to Les Sables-d'Olonne 89 finishers	202 km 6h35'24" 30.7 kph	André Leducq (Fra) France	Learco Guerra (Ita) Italy
Stage 6 Mon 7 Jul	Les Sables-d'Olonne to Bordeaux 89 finishers	285 km 9h45'41" 29.2 kph	~~Charles Pélissier (Fra) France~~ (1) Jean Aerts (Bel) Belgium	Learco Guerra (Ita) Italy
Stage 7 Tue 8 Jul	Bordeaux to Hendaye 79 finishers	222 km 6h11'22" 35.9 kph	Jules Merviel (Fra) France	Learco Guerra (Ita) Italy

Stage-by-Stage Results for the 1930 Tour de France			Stage Winner	Maillot Jaune
Stage 8 Wed 9 Jul	Hendaye to Pau 79 finishers	146 km 5h02'27" 29.0 kph	Alfredo Binda (Ita) Italy	Learco Guerra (Ita) Italy
Stage 9 Thu 10 Jul	Pau to Luchon 69 finishers	231 km 9h21'31" 24.7 kph	Alfredo Binda (Ita) Italy	André Leducq (Fra) France
	Major climbs: Col d'Aubisque (1,709m) Benoît Faure (Fra) Sud Est; Col du Tourmalet (2,115m) Benoît Faure (Fra) Sud Est			
Fri 11 Jul	Rest day			
Stage 10 Sat 12 Jul	Luchon to Perpignan 66 finishers	322 km 11h57'18" 26.9 kph	Charles Pélissier (Fra) France	André Leducq (Fra) France
	Major climbs: Col de Portet-d'Aspet (1,069m) Alfredo Binda (Ita) Italy; Col de Port (1,249m) n/a; Col de Puymorens (1,915m) n/a			
Sun 13 Jul	Rest day			
Stage 11 Mon 14 Jul	Perpignan to Montpellier 66 finishers	164 km 4h55'19" 33.3 kph	Charles Pélissier (Fra) France	André Leducq (Fra) France
Stage 12 Tue 15 Jul	Montpellier to Marseille 66 finishers	209 km 6h41'42" 31.2 kph	Antonin Magne (Fra) France	André Leducq (Fra) France
Stage 13 Wed 16 Jul	Marseille to Cannes 65 finishers	181 km 6h21'47" 28.4 kph	Learco Guerra (Ita) Italy	André Leducq (Fra) France
Stage 14 Thu 17 Jul	Cannes to Nice 64 finishers	132 km 4h33'51" 28.9 kph	Louis Péglion (Fra) Unsponsored	André Leducq (Fra) France
	Major climbs: Col de Braus (1,002m) Benoît Faure (Fra) Sud Est; Col de Castillon (706m) Louis Péglion (Fra) Provence			
Fri 18 Jul	Rest day			
Stage 15 Sat 19 Jul	Nice to Grenoble 64 finishers	333 km 13h48'58" 24.1 kph	Learco Guerra (Ita) Italy	André Leducq (Fra) France
	Major climbs: Col d'Allos (2,250m) Benoît Faure (Fra) Sud Est; Col Bayard (1,246m) Benoît Faure (Fra) Sud Est			
Sun 20 Jul	Rest day			
Stage 16 Mon 21 Jul	Grenoble to Évian 63 finishers	331 km 13h39'23" 24.2 kph	André Leducq (Fra) France	André Leducq (Fra) France
	Major climbs: Col du Lautaret (2,058m) Fernand Robache (Fra) touriste-routier; Col de Galibier (2,556m) Pierre Magne (Fra) France; Col des Aravis (1,498m) Marcel Mazeyrat (Fra) Sud Est			
Tue 22 Jul	Rest day			

Stage-by-Stage Results for the 1930 Tour de France			Stage Winner	Maillot Jaune
Stage 17 Wed 23 Jul	Évian to Belfort 61 finishers	282 km 9h56'28" 28.4 kph	Frans Bonduel (Bel) Belgium	André Leducq (Fra) France
	Major climbs: Col de la Faucille (1,323m) Charles Pélissier (Fra) France; Ballon d'Alsace (1,178m) Antonin Magne (Fra) France			
Stage 18 Thu 24 Jul	Belfort to Metz 61 finishers	223 km 8h27'43" 26.4 kph	Charles Pélissier (Fra) France	André Leducq (Fra) France
Stage 19 Fri 25 Jul	Metz to Charleville 60 finishers	159 km 5h05'23" 31.2 kph	Charles Pélissier (Fra) France	André Leducq (Fra) France
Stage 20 Sat 26 Jul	Charleville to Malo-les-Bains 59 finishers	271 km 10h05'10" 26.9 kph	Charles Pélissier (Fra) France	André Leducq (Fra) France
Stage 21 Sun 27 Jul	Malo-les-Bains to Paris (Parc des Princes) 59 finishers	300 km 12h10'09" 24.7 kph	Charles Pélissier (Fra) France	André Leducq (Fra) France

(1) Charles Pélissier was stripped of the stage because of an irregular sprint.

Prize fund: 606,000 francs (first prize: 12,000 francs)

Final Classification				
Place	**Rider**	**Team**	**Time**	**Age**
1	André Leducq (Fra)	France	4,822 km 172h12'16" 28.000 kph	26
2	Learco Guerra (Ita)	Italy	+ 14'13"	27
3	Antonin Magne (Fra)	France	+ 16'03"	26
4	Jef Demuysère (Bel)	Belgium	+ 21'34"	22
5	Marcel Bidot (Fra)	France	+ 41'18"	27
6	Pierre Magne (Fra)	France	+ 45'42"	26
7	Frans Bonduel (Bel)	Belgium	+ 56'19"	22
8	Benoît Faure (Fra)	Unsponsored	+ 58'34"	31
9	Charles Pélissier (Fra)	France	+ 1h04'37"	27
10	Adolf Schön (Ger)	Germany	+ 1h21'39"	24
Lanterne Rouge				
59	Marcel Ilpide (Fra)	Unsponsored	+ 15h10'18"	26
Meilleur Grimpeur				
	Benoît Faure (Fra)	Unsponsored		31
Team				
		France		

1931: France, Again

At the end of the 1930 Tour Henri Desgrange promised no changes for the 1931 race. But the man just couldn't help tweaking things. The number of stages went back up to 24 by splitting three of the Alpine stages in two. This reduced the number of stages above 300 kilometres to just three, and increased the number of stages below 200 to seven. In most other respects, the route was the same as in previous years.

The rules, though, again changed, and Desgrange re-introduced the idea of separate starts (first used in the 1903 Tour), with the stars being sent off 10 minutes before the others. As it had been in previous years, this was a response to the number of stages which ended in mass sprints: in 1930, on the eve of the Pyrenees, in Pau, 75 of the 79 riders left in the race finished together. Stages Three through Six, down France's Atlantic coast, had each seen sprints of more than 50 riders. While Desgrange talked up the danger of bunch sprints, the real problem – again – was what preceded them: a *peloton* dawdling along with nothing happening worth reporting.

The 1930 race had seen two stages run with separate starts, the seventh stage, to Hendaye, and the nineteenth stage, to Charleville. For 1931, Desgrange decided to up that number. If this was meant to make the stars ride harder, it actually produced the first *touriste-routier* to wear the yellow jersey: Max Bulla, the first Austrian to ride the Tour. Bulla's group was set off 10 minutes after the stars in the second stage. At the stage end in Dinan, Charles Pélissier – narrowly beaten the day before – took the sprint. Seven minutes later a group of *touristes-routiers* hit the finish, with Bulla taking the sprint. And he took the stage win, having covered the distance three minutes quicker than the stars.

Those three minutes saw Bulla donning the *maillot jaune*. The separate start format, though, hampered Bulla in the next stage, and his 15 minutes of fame came to an end. Unable to get a group of other *touristes-routiers* to work with him, he lost half an hour on the day. In the sprint at the stage end Pélissier wasn't even in contention, and the man of the moment was the 19-year-old Fabio Battestini (Italy) who became the Tour's youngest stage winner. Léon le Calvez (France) donned the *maillot jaune*, the first of 15 riders all on the same time. In all, six of the first 12 stages used the separate start format, and three of them ended up being won by *touristes-routiers*.

Raffaele di Paco (Italy) managed to relieve Le Calvez of the *maillot jaune* on the fourth stage, even though there were still 12 riders – including Le Calvez – on the same time. Pélissier finally broke his duck the next stage and somehow joined di Paco in the *maillot jaune*, even though there were eight other riders all on the same time. And then Charlot slipped out of the jersey the next stage – even though he still held the same time as di Paco, as did eight others.

The log jam at the front of the race finally began to break on the eighth stage – the last before the Pyrenees – when Pélissier took the stage and the *maillot jaune*, with just one rider, Erich Metze (Germany) tied for time with him. Over the Aubisque and the Tourmalet Pélissier – a sprinter better suited to the flat lands – suffered on the climbs, losing half an hour. He was not the only one to suffer. Defending champion André Leducq dropped 28 minutes, as did his France team-mate and the previous year's *meilleur grimpeur*, Benoît Faure. The big winner on the day was their other France team-mate Antonin Magne, who took the stage win and a lead of just under 10 minutes in the general classification over Italy's Antonio Pesenti, who was a stage winner in the 1930 Giro d'Italia.

Things pretty much settled down then until the race's fourteenth stage, the opening step of the second round of climbing, when a fall on the descent of the Braus saw Magne drop four minutes to Pesenti, who closed to within six minutes of the yellow jersey. And then things settled down again until the pre-penultimate stage,

Charleville to Malo-les-Bains, with Magne arriving in Charleville with his lead unchanged, despite an onslaught of challenges and some foul weather in the mountains. Less happy in Charleville was Pélissier, who initially won the stage ahead of di Paco but then got bumped down to second for an irregular sprint (the two would end the race with five stage wins each and sharing a 4,000 Franc prize put up by Berko for the rider who won the most stages).

That evening in Charleville Magne read some of his fan-mail. One letter in particular was interesting, telling as it did that Belgium's Jef Demuysère – who was third overall, 13 minutes in arrears – had singled out the stage to Malo-les-Bains for a coup on the *maillot jaune*. Magne's correspondent wrote that Demuysère and his Belgium team-mate Gaston Rebry – winner of that year's Paris-Roubaix – had planned a major offensive over the *pavé* roads of northern France.

Lo and behold, the next morning Rebry attacked and Demuysère went with him. As did Magne, who was prepared for their attack. Across the rain-slicked cobbles the three raced hard, Magne letting the two Belgians do all the work at the front. Nothing the two Belgians could do could shake Magne. Even a crash on a level crossing didn't separate him from their back wheels for long. At the stage end, Rebry was able to break clear to take the stage win, Magne more interested in marking his *maillot jaune* rival. Demuysère's consolation prize was that he moved up into second, no one having bothered to warn Pesenti about the planned coup.

For Magne, the final victory was more about enduring mental anguish than physical pain. All through the race he had carried the fear of not winning and, at the end, told *L'Auto*'s readers that he wouldn't want to go through that again, even if it meant another Tour title.

Stage-by-Stage Results for the 1931 Tour de France			Stage Winner	Maillot Jaune
Stage 1 Tue 30 Jun	Paris (Le Vésinet) to Caen 81 starters, 81 finishers	208 km 6h17'12" 33.1 kph	Alfred Haemerlinck (Bel) Belgium	Alfred Haemerlinck (Bel) Belgium
Stage 2 Wed 1 Jul	Caen to Dinan 74 finishers	212 km 6h37'14" 32.0 kph	Max Bulla (Aut) Unsponsored	Max Bulla (Aut) Unsponsored
Stage 3 Thu 2 Jul	Dinan to Brest 70 finishers	206 km 6h17'29" 32.7 kph	Fabio Battesini (Ita) Italy	Léon le Calvez (Fra) France
Stage 4 Fri 3 Jul	Brest to Vannes 69 finishers	211 km 6h08'16" 34.4 kph	André Godinat (Fra) Unsponsored	Raffaele di Paco (Ita) Italy
Stage 5 Sat 4 Jul	Vannes to Les Sables-d'Olonne 68 Finishers	202 km 6h36'49" 30.5 kph	Charles Pélissier (Fra) France	Charles Pélissier (Fra) France
				Raffaele di Paco (Ita) Italy
Stage 6 Sun 5 Jul	Les Sables-d'Olonne to Bordeaux 65 finishers	338 km 10h46'20" 31.4 kph	Alfred Haemerlinck (Bel) Belgium	Raffaele di Paco (Ita) Italy
Stage 7 Mon 6 Jul	Bordeaux to Bayonne 65 finishers	180 km 5h37'45" 32.0 kph	Gérard Loncke (Bel) Unsponsored	Raffaele di Paco (Ita) Italy
Stage 8 Tue 7 Jul	Bayonne to Pau 65 finishers	106 km 3h24'20" 31.1 kph	Charles Pélissier (Fra) France	Charles Pélissier (Fra) France
Stage 9 Wed 8 Jul	Pau to Luchon 64 inishers	231 km 8h56'03" 25.9 kph	Antonin Magne (Fra) France	Antonin Magne (Fra) France
	Major climbs: Col d'Aubisque (1,709m) Alfons Schepers (Bel) Belgium; Col du Tourmalet (2,115m) Jef Demuysère (Bel) Belgium			
Thu 9 Jul	Rest day			
Stage 10 Fri 10 Jul	Luchon to Perpignan 61 finishers	322 km 12h33'57" 25.6 kph	Raffaele di Paco (Ita) Italy	Antonin Magne (Fra) France
	Major climbs: Col des Ares (797m) n/a ; Col de Portet d'Aspet (1,069m) Antonin Magne (Fra) France; Col de Port (1,249m) Antonio Pesenti (Ita) Italy; Col du Puymorens (1,915m) Benoît Faure (Fra) France			
Sat 11 Jul	Rest day			
Stage 11 Sun 12 Jul	Perpignan to Montpellier 61 finishers	164 km 5h50'36" 28.1 kph	Raffaele di Paco (Ita) Italy	Antonin Magne (Fra) France

Stage-by-Stage Results for the 1931 Tour de France			Stage Winner	Maillot Jaune
Stage 12 Mon 13 Jul	Montpellier to Marseille 52 finishers	207 km 6h22'07" 32.5 kph	Max Bulla (Aut) Unsponsored	Antonin Magne (Fra) France
Stage 13 Tue 14 Jul	Marseille to Cannes 52 finishers	181 km 6h41'20" 27.1 kph	Charles Pélissier (Fra) France	Antonin Magne (Fra) France
Stage 14 Wed 15 Jul	Cannes to Nice 48 finishers	132 km 4h47'01" 27.6 kph	Eugenio Gestri (Ita) Italy	Antonin Magne (Fra) France
	Major climbs: Col de Braus (1,002m) Rafaele di Paco (Ita) Italy; Col de Castillon (706m) Rafaele di Paco (Ita) Italy			
Thu 16 Jul	Rest day			
Stage 15 Fri 17 Jul	Nice to Gap 48 finishers	233 km 8h43'01" 26.7 kph	Jef Demuysère (Bel) Belgium	Antonin Magne (Fra) France
	Major climbs: Col d'Allos (2,250m) Jef Demuysère (Bel) Belgium			
Stage 16 Sat 18 Jul	Gap to Grenoble 45 finishers	102 km 3h31'43" 28.9 kph	Charles Pélissier (Fra) France	Antonin Magne (Fra) France
	Major climbs: Col Bayard (1,246m) Antonin Magne (Fra) France			
Stage 17 Sun 19 Jul	Grenoble to Aix-les-Bains 43 finishers	230 km 8h37'02" 26.7 kph	Max Bulla (Aut) Unsponsored	Antonin Magne (Fra) France
	Major climbs: Col du Lautaret (2,058m) Maurice Dewaele (Bel) Belgium; Col du Galibier (2,556m) Jef Demuysère (Bel) Belgium			
Stage 18 Mon 20 Jul	Aix-les-Bains to Évian 43 finishers	204 km 7h57'13" 25.6 kph	Jef Demuysère (Bel) Belgium	Antonin Magne (Fra) France
	Major climbs: Col des Aravis (1,498m) Antonin Magne (Fra) France			
Stage 19 Tue 21 Jul	Évian to Belfort 43 finishers	282 km 10h33'48" 26.7 kph	Raffaele di Paco (Ita) Italy	Antonin Magne (Fra) France
	Major climbs: Col de la Faucille (1,323m) Erich Metze (Ger) Germany			
Stage 20 Wed 22 Jul	Belfort to Colmar 41 finishers	209 km 7h05'53" 29.4 kph	André Leducq (Fra) France	Antonin Magne (Fra) France
	Major climbs: Col de la Schlucht (1,139m) n/a			
Stage 21 Thu 23 Jul	Colmar to Metz 41 finishers	192 km 6h20'00" 30.3 kph	Raffaele di Paco (Ita) Italy	Antonin Magne (Fra) France

Stage-by-Stage Results for the 1931 Tour de France			Stage Winner	Maillot Jaune
Stage 22 Fri 24 Jul	Metz to Charleville 40 finishers	159 km 5h01'44" 31.6 kph	Charles Pélissier (Fra) France (1)	Antonin Magne (Fra) France
			Raffaele di Paco (Ita) Italy	
Stage 23 Sat 25 Jul	Charleville to Malo-les-Bains 36 finishers	271 km 8h08'16" 33.3 kph	Gaston Rebry (Bel) Belgium	Antonin Magne (Fra) France
Stage 24 Sun 26 Jul	Malo-les-Bains to Paris (Parc des Princes) 35 finishers	313 km 15h15'38" 20.5 kph	Charles Pélissier (Fra) France	Antonin Magne (Fra) France

(1) Charles Pélissier was stripped of the stage win because of an irregular sprint

Prize fund: 650,000 francs (first prize: 25,000 francs)

Final Classification				
Place	**Rider**	**Team**	**Time**	**Age**
1	Antonin Magne (Fra)	France	5,091 km 177h10'03" 28.735 kph	27
2	Jef Demuysère (Bel)	Belgium	+ 12'56"	23
3	Antonio Pesenti (Ita)	Italy	+ 22'51"	23
4	Gaston Rebry (Bel)	Belgium	+ 46'40"	26
5	Maurice Dewaele (Bel)	Belgium	+ 49'46"	34
6	Julien Vervaecke (Bel)	Belgium	+ 1h10'11"	31
7	Louis Péglion (Fra)	Belgium	+ 1h18'33"	25
8	Erich Metze (Ger)	Germany	+ 1h20'59"	22
9	Albert Büchi (Sui)	Australia- Switzerland	+ 1h29'29"	24
10	André Leducq (Fra)	France	+ 1h30'08"	27
Lanterne Rouge				
35	Richard Lamb (Aus)	Australia- Switzerland	+ 6h27'06"	23
Meilleur Grimpeur				
	Jef Demuysère (Bel)	Belgium		23
Team				
		Belgium		

1932: Bonifications

Charles Pélissier was clearly in a class of his own when it came to winning stages at the Tour, having won eight in 1930 and five in 1931. Yet he had finished those two Tours ninth and fourteenth, more than an hour down on his team-mates André Leducq and Antonin Magne. But his consistency was such that, in the 1930 Tour, he finished in the top three on 18 stages and in 1931 on eight. The time gains in those stages, though, were usually minor, while the time lost by Pélissier in the mountains was major. Henri Desgrange and his team at *L'Auto* put their minds to solving the problem of how a rider like Pélissier could win the Tour and came up with a brilliant wheeze: time bonuses.

Bonifications had first been used in the 1923 and 1924 Tours, with two and three minutes being given to the stage winners as a deduction from their overall time. For the 1932 Tour bonuses would be given to the first three riders across the line on each stage: four minutes for first, two minutes for second and one for third. That alone wouldn't have enabled Pélissier to have won either of the previous two Tours, but it would have levelled the playing field somewhat between him and the climbers. Pélissier, though, would not be at the twenty-sixth Tour, missing out of the start because of an injury.

The time bonuses would also, hopefully, solve the problem of big bunch sprints – and the boredom that preceded them, which journalists at *L'Auto*'s rival publications had been complaining about – and negate the need to use the separate start format which made the stage end confusing for fans at the finish.

What the bonifications actually achieved in 1932 was making a very close race look like it must have been an easy win: at the Parc

Reporting the 1932 Tour.

des Princes in Paris at the end of the race André Leducq (France) won his second Tour, with a margin of 24'03" over Kurt Stöpel (Germany – Austria). But strip out the 31 minutes of bonuses won by Leducq (which included six stage wins) and the seven minutes accumulated by Stöpel (which included one stage win) and the actual difference between the two riders was just three seconds.

Throughout the race the two riders had finished close to one another, usually in the main bunch (on Stage Seven, 69 of the 71 riders left in the race finished together, on Stage 14 all 63 riders left racing finished together: if the bonifications were meant to stop bunch sprints, they failed abjectly). Only on four stages was there any sizeable daylight between the two riders, Stöpel shipping small amounts of time on Stages Three, Five and Thirteen, while Leducq only conceded time on Stage 10.

The real difference between the two was that Leducq contested the sprints – as well as having five more stage wins than his German rival he twice finished second and three times third, compared to just three third places for Stöpel. As the race progressed and his win became more assured all Leducq had to do was shadow Stöpel, play the defensive game, and pay attention to any challenge coming from other quarters. The Belgians, though, were too disunited to mount a serious challenge, while the Italians seemed more content to bag stage wins – seven in all – than racing for the *maillot jaune*.

Stage-by-Stage Results for the 1932 Tour de France			Stage Winner	Maillot Jaune
Stage 1 Wed 6 Jul	Paris (Le Vésinet) to Caen 80 starters, 78 finishers	208 km 6h06'14" 34.1 kph	Jean Aerts (Bel) Belgium	Jean Aerts (Bel) Belgium
Stage 2 Thu 7 Jul	Caen to Nantes 78 finishers	300 km 9h51'34" 30.4 kph	Kurt Stöpel (Ger) Germany/Austria	Kurt Stöpel (Ger) Germany/Austria
Fri 8 Jul	Rest day			
Stage 3 Sat 9 Jul	Nantes to Bordeaux 78 finishers	387 km 12h54'33" 30.0 kph	André Leducq (Fra) France	André Leducq (Fra) France
Sun 10 Jul	Rest day			

Stage-by-Stage Results for the 1932 Tour de France			Stage Winner	Maillot Jaune
Stage 4 Mon 11 Jul	Bordeaux to Pau 78 finishers	206 km 6h23'20" 32.2 kph	Georges Ronsse (Bel) Belgium	André Leducq (Fra) France
Stage 5 Tue 12 Jul	Pau to Luchon 75 finishers	229 km 9h00'33" 25.4 kph	Antonio Pesenti (Ita) Italy	André Leducq (Fra) France
	Major climbs: Col d'Aubisque (1,709m) Vicente Trueba (Esp) Unsponsored; Col du Tourmalet (2,115m) Benoît Faure (Fra) Unsponsored			
Wed 13 Jul	Rest day			
Stage 6 Thu 14 Jul	Luchon to Perpignan 72 finishers	322 km 11h50'31" 27.2 kph	Frans Bonduel (Bel) Belgium	André Leducq (Fra) France
	Major climbs: Col des Ares (797m) n/a; Col de Portet-d'Aspet (1,069m) Luigi Barral (Ita) Unsponsored; Col de Port (1,249m) Eugenio Gestri (Ita) Italy; Col de Puymorens (1,915m) Amerigo Cacioni (Ita) Unsponsored			
Fri 15 Jul	Rest day			
Stage 7 Sat 16 Jul	Perpignan to Montpellier 71 finishers	168 km 5h33'17" 30.2 kph	Frans Bonduel (Bel) Belgium	André Leducq (Fra) France
Stage 8 Sun 17 Jul	Montpellier to Marseille 69 finishers	206 km 6h31'10" 31.6 kph	Michele Orecchia (Ita) Italy	André Leducq (Fra) France
Stage 9 Mon 18 Jul	Marseille to Cannes 68 finishers	191 km 6h29'31" 29.4 kph	Raffaele di Paco (Ita) Italy	André Leducq (Fra) France
Stage 10 Tue 19 Jul	Cannes to Nice 64 finishers	132 km 4h36'40" 28.6 kph	Francesco Camusso (Ita) Italy	André Leducq (Fra) France
	Major climbs: Col de Braus (1,002m) Francesco Camusso (Ita) Italy; Col de Castillon (706m) Francesco Camusso (Ita) Italy			
Wed 20 Jul	Rest day			
Stage 11 Thu 21 Jul	Nice to Gap 63 finishers	233 km 8h41'33" 26.8 kph	André Leducq (Fra) France	André Leducq (Fra) France
	Major climbs: Col d'Allos (2,250m) Benoît Faure (Fra) Unsponsored			
Stage 12 Fri 22 Jul	Gap to Grenoble 63 finishers	102 km 3h21'52" 30.3 kph	Roger Lapébie (Fra) France	André Leducq (Fra) France
	Major climbs: Col Bayard (1,246m) Vicente Trueba (Esp) Unsponsored			

Stage-by-Stage Results for the 1932 Tour de France			Stage Winner	Maillot Jaune
Stage 13 Sat 23 Jul	Grenoble to Aix-les-Bains 63 finishers	230 km 8h11'35" 28.1 kph	André Leducq (Fra) France	André Leducq (Fra) France
	Major climbs: Col du Lautaret (2,058m) n/a; Col du Galibier (2,556m) Francesco Camusso (Ita) Italy; Cold du Télégraphe (1,566m) n/a			
Stage 14 Sun 24 Jul	Aix-les-Bains to Évian 63 finishers	204 km 7h59'25" 25.5 kph	Raffaele di Paco (Ita) Italy	André Leducq (Fra) France
	Major climbs: Col des Aravis (1,498m) Jef Demuysère (Bel) Belgium			
Stage 15 Mon 25 Jul	Évian to Belfort 62 finishers	291 km 9h56'19" 29.3 kph	André Leducq (Fra) France	André Leducq (Fra) France
	Major climbs: Col de la Faucille (1,323m) Francesco Camusso (Ita) Italy			
Stage 16 Tue 26 Jul	Belfort to Strasbourg 60 finishers	145 km 4h04'30" 35.6 kph	Gérard Loncke (Bel) Belgium	André Leducq (Fra) France
Stage 17 Wed 27 Jul	Strasbourg to Metz 60 finishers	165 km 5h38'35" 29.2 kph	Raffaele di Paco (Ita) Italy	André Leducq (Fra) France
Stage 18 Thu 28 Jul	Metz to Charleville 60 finishers	159 km 5h09'48" 30.8 kph	André Leducq (Fra) France (1)	André Leducq (Fra) France
			Raffaele di Paco (Ita) Italy	
Stage 19 Fri 29 Jul	Charleville to Malo-les-Bains 57 finishers	271 km 8h40'15" 31.3 kph	Gaston Rebry (Bel) Belgium	André Leducq (Fra) France
Stage 20 Sat 30 Jul	Malo-les-Bains to Amiens 57 finishers	212 km 8h16'49" 25.6 kph	André Leducq (Fra) France	André Leducq (Fra) France
Stage 21 Sun 31 Jul	Amiens to Paris (Parc des Princes) 57 finishers	159 km 4h52'38" 32.6 kph	André Leducq (Fra) France	André Leducq (Fra) France

(1) André Leducq was stripped of the stage win for having received a push from a team-mate, contrary to the race rules.

Prize fund: 700,000 francs (first prize: 30,000 francs)

Final Classification

Place	Rider	Team	Time	Age
1	André Leducq (Fra)	France	4,479 km 154h11'49" 29.047 kph	28
2	Kurt Stöpel (Ger)	Germany/Austria	+ 24'03"	24
3	Francesco Camusso (Ita)	Italy	+ 26'21"	24
4	Antonio Pesenti (Ita)	Italy	+ 37'08"	24
5	Georges Ronsse (Bel)	Belgium	+ 41'04"	26
6	Frans Bonduel (Bel)	Belgium	+ 45'13"	24
7	Oskar Thierbach (Ger)	Germany/Austria	+ 58'44"	22
8	Jef Demuysère (Bel)	Belgium	+ 1h03'24"	24
9	Luigi Barral (Ita)	Italy	+ 1h06'57"	25
10	Georges Speicher (Fra)	France	+ 1h08'37"	25

Lanterne Rouge

57	Rudolf Risch (Ger)	Germany/Austria	+ 5h05'14"	24

Meilleur Grimpeur

	Vicente Trueba (Esp)	Unsponsored		26

Team

		Italy		

1933: Backwards

It would have been difficult for even chauvinism to blind Henri Desgrange to the fact that André Leducq's win the previous year was more efficient than it was exciting. The national team format that was meant to usher in all-out racing had produced a Tour not unlike those of the trade team years. Something would have to be done to shake the *peloton* up and make them race harder and not just dawdle along waiting for the final sprint. The only time the riders really seemed to make an obvious effort was on the mountainous stages, though even some of them tended to produce bunch finishes.

Over the years, the race had been able to make use of the full range of mountains available on the race's eastern side, running all the way from the Chartreuse Massif, through the Alps and the Jura and up to the Vosges. But in the Pyrenees there had been stagnation, with the race crossing France's southern border in two hops. While the first of those two – over the Aubisque and Tourmalet – was often decisive, the second was more often a damp squib. For 1933 the Pyrenees would feature four separate stages. Added to the seven climbing stages in the east, this made a Tour which would ideally suit a *grimpeur*. And just in case it didn't *L'Auto* finally made the *meilleur grimpeur* prize – which had been being awarded unofficially since 1906 – a full part of the competition, rechristening it the *Prix de la Grand Montagne* (with sponsorship provided by Martini-Rossi). That the Giro d'Italia had, the same year, also introduced a king of the mountains award was, of course, entirely coincidental.

One other factor influencing the decision to award an official king of the mountains prize was the rise of new climbing talent, including

France's Benoît Faure and Spain's Vicente Trueba, who had raced the Tour both for their national squads and as independent *touristes-routiers*. The unofficial climbing prize had come in on the back on René Pottier's performance in 1905 – when he was first over the Ballon d'Alsace – and now the introduction of the official version of the competition was coming on the back of the rise of new climbing talent. And it was Trueba – the Torrelavega Flea – who succeeded in taking the first *grand Prix de la Montagne*.

While, even with added stages, the Tour still followed more or less the same route as in previous years – now with no stages exceeding 300 kilometres and 13 below 200 (including one that fell below 100 kilometres) – there was one other major change: for the first time since 1912 the Tour would take a clockwise turn around France, putting the Alps before the Pyrenees. As for the bonifications system, it was retained with minor adjustments: the stage winner got two minutes, the runner up one.

The riders were waved off from Le Vésinet in Paris by the American-born exotic dancer Josephine Baker. The French team – with Charles Pélissier back as their road captain – took control on the first stage, with Maurice Archambaud (who had won the inaugural Grand Prix des Nations and set an unofficial Hour record the year before) donning the *maillot jaune* and holding on to it until the first phase of climbing, in the Alps. This was despite strong challenges from the Italians, led by Luigi Ganna, and the Belgians, who had Georges Lemaire in second overall. It was also despite the loss, through a crash, of Pélissier.

On the penultimate stage in the race's first climbing phase Lemaire managed to lift the yellow jersey off Archambaud's shoulders, over the Vars and Allos, after Archambaud had an off day with an upset stomach. Two stages later, though, Archambaud was back in control, Lemaire having been left isolated by his Belgian team-mates, who couldn't seem to agree on who they should be riding for, and the Frenchman profiting from two minutes in time bonuses for winning the stage.

The next day, on the road to Marseille, on what should have been a relatively easy transition stage. Archambaud's team-mate, Georges

Speicher, along with two French team-mates, was up the road policing the day's break, Archambaud in the chasing pack. But a puncture saw Archambaud dropped and lose seven minutes, which, coupled with the two minutes in bonifications Speicher earned for winning the stage, saw him leap from third to first overall.

Some felt that Speicher had stabbed his team-mate in the back but even Archambaud defended him, saying it was more important for a French rider to be leading the race than it was for it to have been him who was leading the race. The spirit of *esprit de corps* in the French team in these early years of the national team format was truly impressive.

Speicher, though, had just a 15-second lead over Lemaire. With the help of his team-mates Lemaire might have been able to overcome that in the Pyrenees, but that help never materialised, especially when Jean Aerts decided that stage wins for himself – and the time bonuses that came with them – were more important. Exiting the mountains Lemaire was out of contention and Speicher's only rivals of any consequence were the Italians Giuseppe Martano (riding as a *touriste-routier*) and Learco Guerra (leading the national squad). Neither, though, was able to mount much of a challenge and the real fight was for second, which Guerra won on the final stage when he took the stage win and enough in time bonuses to overtake Martano.

In fact, the final stages of the race offered little by way of excitement. On the stage from La Rochelle to Rennes the pace was so sedentary that Desgrange decided to withhold prize money and threatened to ban the remaining riders from the following year's Tour if they didn't pick up the pace the next day. Not that Rennes was totally without excitement: two French riders, René le Grevès of the national team and Léon Louyet, a *touriste-routier*, challenged for the stage, with Le Grevès coming out on top, only for the commissaires to bounce both of them for irregular sprinting and award the stage to Aerts.

Despite the lack of excitement in the closing stages, the national team format was doing wonders for *L'Auto*'s circulation, with an average of 730,000 copies of the paper selling every day during the

Tour, with a peak at 845,000 (this compared to normal circulation of 364,000 the rest of the year).

At the end of the race, Speicher – who, a month after the Tour ended, also claimed the rainbow jersey of World Champion – had accumulated eight minutes in bonuses. Martano, who finished in third, 5'08" off the lead, gained only two. Without the bonuses he would have won by 52 seconds. But, of course, without the bonifications it would have been a different race.

* * * * *

The 1932 race is an interesting challenge to the claim that Desgrange favoured a Tour in which just one rider finished. Riders had always been required to complete each stage within a certain time. By 1932, that limit was set at 8% of the stage winner's time. On Stage Two, that would have been 24 minutes. Sixty-three riders were already home in that time, but still out on the road were a few riders, including Italy's Raffaele di Paco. Rather than eliminate them Desgrange increased the time limit to 10%, which saved six riders (but not one of his personal favourites, Benoît Faure, who was riding as an independent). On the eighth stage the time limit needed to be increased to 15% to save 20 riders.

The most fun came on the tenth stage, when only seven riders made it home inside the time limit. That would have been the perfect way to get just one rider back to Paris. Instead, the time limit was again widened, saving 36 riders (admittedly, this did include the yellow jersey, so not widening the time limit would have upset a lot of people).

Stage-by-Stage Results for the 1933 Tour de France			Stage Winner	Maillot Jaune
Stage 1 Mon 27 Jun	Paris (Le Vésinet) to Lille 80 starters 72 finishers	262 km 7h48'45" 33.5 kph	Maurice Archambaud (Fra) France	Maurice Archambaud (Fra) France
Stage 2 Tue 28 Jun	Lille to Charleville 69 finishers	192 km 5h33'52" 34.5 kph	Learco Guerra (Ita) Italy	Maurice Archambaud (Fra) France
Stage 3 Wed 29 Jun	Charleville to Metz 68 finishers	166 km 4h37'24" 35.9 kph	Alfons Schepers (Bel) Belgium	Maurice Archambaud (Fra) France
Stage 4 Thu 30 Jun	Metz to Belfort 67 finishers	220 km 7h14'15" 30.4 kph	Jean Aerts (Bel) Belgium	Maurice Archambaud (Fra) France
	Major climbs: Ballon d'Alsace (1,178m) Vicente Trueba (Esp) Unsponsored			
Stage 5 Fri 1 Jul	Belfort to Évian 67 finishers	293 km 9h59'58" 29.3 kph	Léon Louyet (Bel) Unsponsored	Maurice Archambaud (Fra) France
	Major climbs: Col de la Faucille (1,323m) Antonin Magne (Fra) France			
Sat 2 Jul	Rest day			
Stage 6 Sun 3 Jul	Évian to Aix-les-Bains 66 finishers	207 km 6h55'07" 29.9 kph	Learco Guerra (Ita) Italy	Maurice Archambaud (Fra) France
	Major climbs: Col des Aravis (1,498m) Alfons Schepers (Bel) Belgium; Col de Tamié (907m) Maurice Archambaud (Fra) France			
Stage 7 Mon 4 Jul	Aix-les-Bains to Grenoble 61 finishers	229 km 8h43'46" 26.2 kph	Learco Guerra (Ita) Italy	Maurice Archambaud (Fra) France
	Major climbs: Col du Télégraphe (1,566m) Vicente Trueba (Esp) Unsponsored; Col du Galibier (2,556m) Vicente Trueba (Esp) Unsponsored; Col du Lautaret (2,058m) Vicente Trueba (Esp) Unsponsored			
Stage 8 Tue 5 Jul	Grenoble to Gap 51 finishers	102 km 3h25'40" 29.8 kph	Georges Speicher (Fra) France	Maurice Archambaud (Fra) France
	Major climbs: Côte de Laffrey (900m) Francesco Camusso (Ita) Italy; Col Bayard (1,246m) Georges Lemaire (Bel) Belgium			
Stage 9 Wed 6 Jul	Gap to Digne 49 finishers	227 km 8h46'08" 25.9 kph	Georges Speicher (Fra) France	Georges Lemaire (Bel) Belgium
	Major climbs: Col de Vars (2,110m) Vicente Trueba (Esp) Unsponsored; Col d'Allos (2,250m) Fernand Fayolle (Fra) Unsponsored			
Stage 10 Thu 7 Jul	Digne to Nice 43 finishers	156 km 4h32'30" 34.3 kph	Fernand Cornez (Fra) Unsponsored	Georges Lemaire (Bel) Belgium

Stage-by-Stage Results for the 1933 Tour de France			Stage Winner	Maillot Jaune
Fri 8 Jul	Rest day			
Stage 11 Sat 9 Jul	Nice to Cannes 42 finishers	128 km 3h55'53" 32.6 kph	Maurice Archambaud (Fra) France	Maurice Archambaud (Fra) France
	Major climbs: Col de Castillon (706m) Maurice Archambaud (Fra) France; Col de Braus (1,002m) Vicente Trueba (Esp) Unsponsored			
Stage 12 Sun 10 Jul	Cannes to Marseille 41 finishers	208 km 7h01'15" 29.6 kph	Georges Speicher (Fra) France	Georges Speicher (Fra) France
Stage 13 Mon 11 Jul	Marseille to Montpellier 41 finishers	168 km 6h03'46" 27.7 kph	André Leducq (Fra) France	Georges Speicher (Fra) France
Stage 14 Tue 12 Jul	Montpellier to Perpignan 41 finishers	166 km 6h04'40" 27.3 kph	André Leducq (Fra) France	Georges Speicher (Fra) France
Wed 13 Jul	Rest day			
Stage 15 Thu 14 Jul	Perpignan to Ax-les-Thermes 41 finishers	158 km 5h58'55" 26.4 kph	Jean Aerts (Bel) Belgium	Georges Speicher (Fra) France
	Major climbs: Col de Puymorens (1,915m) Antonin Magne (Fra) France			
Stage 16 Fri 15 Jul	Ax-les-Thermes to Luchon 41 finishers	165 km 5h47'01" 28.5 kph	Léon Louyet (Bel) Unsponsored	Georges Speicher (Fra) France
	Major climbs: Col de Port (1,249m) Vicente Trueba (Esp) Unsponsored; Col de Portet-d'Aspet (1,069m) Alfons Schepers (Bel) Belgium; Col des Ares (797m) Ludwig Geyer (Ger) Germany/Austria			
Stage 17 Sat 16 Jul	Luchon to Tarbes 40 finishers	91 km 2h57'24" 30.8 kph	Jean Aerts (Bel) Belgium	Georges Speicher (Fra) France
	Major climbs: Col de Peyresourde (1,569m) Vicente Trueba (Esp) Unsponsored; Col d'Aspin (1,489m) Vicente Trueba (Esp) Unsponsored			
Stage 18 Sun 17 Jul	Tarbes to Pau 40 finishers	185 km 7h00'23" 26.4 kph	Learco Guerra (Ita) Italy	Georges Speicher (Fra) France
	Major climbs: Col du Tourmalet (2,115m) Vicente Trueba (Esp) Unsponsored; Col d'Aubisque (1,709m) Vicente Trueba (Esp) Unsponsored			
Mon 18 Jul	Rest day			
Stage 19 Tue 19 Jul	Pau to Bordeaux 40 finishers	233 km 7h54'01" 29.5 kph	Jean Aerts (Bel) Belgium	Georges Speicher (Fra) France
Stage 20 Wed 20 Jul	Bordeaux to La Rochelle 40 finishers	183 km 5h53'22" 31.1 kph	Jean Aerts (Bel) Belgium	Georges Speicher (Fra) France

Stage-by-Stage Results for the 1933 Tour de France			Stage Winner	Maillot Jaune
Stage 21 Thu 21 Jul	La Rochelle to Rennes 40 finishers	266 km 9h12'04" 28.9 kph	~~René le Grevès (Fra)~~ ~~France (1)~~	Georges Speicher (Fra) France
			Jean Aerts (Bel) Belgium	
Stage 22 Fri 22 Jul	Rennes to Caen 40 finishers	169 km 4h56'00" 34.3 kph	René le Grevès (Fra) France	Georges Speicher (Fra) France
Stage 23 Sat 23 Jul	Caen to Paris (Parc des Princes) 40 finishers	222 km 6h52'23" 32.3 kph	Learco Guerra (Ita) Italy	Georges Speicher (Fra) France

(1) René le Grevès beat the Belgian *touriste-routier* Léon Louyet in the sprint, but both were declassified for irregular sprinting.

Prize fund: 749,000 francs (first prize: 30,000 francs)

Final Classification				
Place	Rider	Team	Time	Age
1	Georges Speicher (Fra)	France	4,395 km 147h51'37" 29.818 kph	26
2	Learco Guerra (Ita)	Italy	+ 24'03"	30
3	Giuseppe Martano (Ita)	Unsponsored	+ 26'21"	22
4	Georges Lemaire (Bel)	Belgium	+ 15'45"	28
5	Maurice Archambaud (Fra)	France	+ 21'22"	24
6	Vicente Trueba (Esp)	Unsponsored	+ 27'27"	27
7	Léon Level (Fra)	Unsponsored	+ 35'19"	23
8	Antonin Magne (Fra)	France	+ 36'37"	29
9	Jean Aerts (Bel)	Belgium	+ 42'53"	25
10	Kurt Stöpel (Ger)	Germany/Austria	+ 45'28"	25
Lanterne Rouge				
	Ernest Neuhard (Fra)	Unsponsored	+ 3h57'44"	25
King of the Mountains				
	Vicente Trueba (Esp)	Unsponsored		27
Team				
		France		

1934: The Martyrdom of René Vietto

Henri Desgrange really believed that the time bonus system could help animate dull stages and so – inevitably – he tinkered with it. For the 1935 Tour the stage winner would get 1'30", with 45 seconds available for the second rider. But, to really shake things up, the winner would also get an extra bonus of the gap back to the second rider, up to a maximum of two minutes. Good news for the sprinters, but what about the *grimpeurs*?

The pure climbers – men like Spain's Vicente Trueba – could fly over the mountains at the front of the action but none of the mountains were particularly close to the stage finishes, meaning the *rouleurs* could make up their losses on the descent and then stick it to the climbers on the run in to the finish (in four Tours Trueba had yet to win a stage, even though he ruled in the mountains). Well, if the finish couldn't be brought closer to the mountains, how about finding a way of bringing the mountains closer to the finish? Applying the bonus system could achieve that: the first rider over designated climbs was allowed bank the time back to the next rider and deduct it off his general classification time at the finish, subject to a maximum of two minutes on each of the climbs.

One stage of the twenty-eighth Tour stands out for showing just how much damage this bonus system could produce in the hands of that breed of rider between the sprinters and the *grimpeurs*, the *rouleurs*. The race's ninth stage, Gap to Digne, over the Vars and the Allos. The man was René Vietto, a 20-year-old native of Cannes riding his first Tour.

Like Georges Speicher the year before, Vietto was something of an unknown quantity. While few may have noticed his sixth-place finish in Paris-Nice earlier in the season or his victory in the GP Wolber the year before, those performances certainly were noticed by the French selectors. But, for the first week of the Tour, hardly anyone had noticed him, Vietto rarely meriting a mention in dispatches. All that changed in the Alps.

Vietto stamped his name on the Tour by taking the victory into Grenoble, overtaking the new *grand Prix de la Montagne* leader Frederico Ezquerra of the combined Switzerland/Spain team on the descent off the Galibier. Eighty kilometres into the stage to Digne, just after the village of Guillestre on the early slopes of the Vars, Vietto took off and wasn't seen again for the next 150 kilometres. By the top of the Vars he was leading the Spanish mountain goats Ezquerra and Vicente Trueba by two and three minutes, the yellow jersey group another minute back. Down the descent and past Barcelonnette Vietto maintained his advantage and then up over the Allos he added more time, summiting the mountain six and seven minutes ahead of the Spaniards and 10 minutes up on the yellow jersey, worn by his France team leader Antonin Magne.

For winning the stage Vietto pocketed 1'30" in time bonuses. For finishing the stage 2'23" ahead of the next rider, he gained another 2'00" minutes in bonifications. For crossing the Vars first, the bonus was the time back to Ezquerra, 1'20". And for crossing the Allos 6'12" clear of anyone else, another 2'00 in bonifications. In all, the bonifications pushed Vietto 6'50" closer to the *maillot jaune*, on top of the 6'28" he'd earned on the road. But, despite the time gained, Vietto still finished the day 35'09" behind his team leader in the general classification.

But that stage to Dignes was not an isolated incident. Vietto's fightback from nearly an hour's worth of time losses in the race's opening stage had begun two stages earlier, when he pulled back 3'23" on Magne on the road, which was augmented by 3'30" in bonifications. And the Tour was now heading toward mountains he knew well, the climbs around Cannes. And there, in front of fans who had actually heard of him, Vietto again put 3'23" into the yellow jersey on the road and gained another 1'55" in bonifications. Across six stages, the kid from Cannes had won back more than half an hour of his deficit and was now within half an hour of the race lead. And, ahead, lay even more mountains.

Three years earlier, when Magne had won the Tour for the first time, he had described the mental pressure as having been the hardest part of the whole thing. The pressure was bad enough when it came from without, that year Magne having to fend off challenges from Italy's Antonio Pesenti and Belgium's Jef Demuysère. And the Italian pressure was there again, this time in the form of Martano. But now there was also the pressure from within, Vietto, a young Turk ready for a fight. And since Magne himself had taken the yellow jersey from his own team-mate and defending champion, Georges Speicher, on the Tour's second stage, he could hardly complain if someone did the same to him. (On a technicality, Magne didn't take the jersey from Speicher: having won the Worlds the year before Speicher was wearing the rainbow jersey, which International Cycling Union (UCI) rules of the time gave precedence over the *maillot jaune*, meaning Speicher got to lead the Tour without wearing the yellow jersey.)

Who knows what would have happened if Magne and Vietto had been able to fight it out and let the road decide the result? Maybe the Italians would have sat back and profited from a fight between team-mates and Martano would have won the Tour at a canter. Maybe Magne would have shown that all the work he had done reconnoitring the race route and training in the Pyrenees had been the real root of his victory. Or maybe Vietto could have become the comeback kid, famed for ever for over-turning an impossible deficit. But the road didn't decide. A broken wheel did. And in two stages in the Pyrenees René Vietto became the Tour's biggest martyr.

In the transition stages between France's two main mountain ranges, Magne managed to eke back some of the time he had surrendered to Vietto, opening the gap to 36 minutes, and also bring his advantage over second-placed Martano to just under four minutes. But on the first day in the Pyrenees Magne damaged a wheel in the descent of the Puymorens. His team-mate Roger Lapébie passed him without offering assistance. Next to pass was Vietto. Magne asked for his bike, Vietto gave him his wheel. Once

Magne was back under way Vietto sat down on a low stone wall, his bike beside him minus its front wheel, waiting for a service vehicle to come along so he could get on his way again. As the seconds ticked by and began to pile up as minutes, it wasn't a service vehicle that came, but tears.

Tears had fallen – or reportedly fallen – many time in many Tours as different riders had seen their dreams shattered by reality. But what was different about Vietto's was that there was a photographer on hand to capture them. Four years earlier photography at the Tour took a great leap forward when film was able to be developed on the road and its images transmitted back to Paris immediately. Perhaps it was the immediacy that this brought about, putting Vietto's tears in front or fans in something close to real time, that made the story a hit with the public. Or maybe it was that the guy was just photogenic and with a really good story. More likely it was that Vietto's misery was repeated the very next day.

Descending the Portet d'Aspet Magne shipped his chain. Rather than announce his problem he quietly slipped off the back of the group he was in, in order to remount it without his rivals realising he had a problem (Léon Scieur's etiquette lesson for Hector Heusghem in 1921 aside, riders attacked when their rivals suffered misfortune). Only Magne's chain had damaged his spokes and he was again in need of a fresh wheel. This time Vietto was up the road, in the group Magne had just exited. Noticing the absence of the yellow jersey he turned around and went back up the climb, until he came to Magne and this time surrendered his bike. Across the two stages, Vietto slipped back to 45 minutes off yellow, almost exactly where he was after his win in Grenoble.

Two stages later, with no mechanical problems to hamper him, Magne stormed over the roads he had trained on just months ahead of the Tour and won into Tarbes. And showed his own climbing prowess by putting seven minutes into Vietto. The next day it was a reverse: Vietto once more showing off his climbing ability and taking back the seven minutes he'd ceded to Magne the day before. Too little and too late, for the mountains were now over, and Magne was back on terrain he was more comfortable with. And, two days out from Paris, that included a double innovation in the Tour's format: two stages in one day, one of them an individual time trial, the Tour's first *contra-la-montre* stage. Which Magne won, comfortably, sealing his victory.

* * * * *

Absent from the 1934 Tour was two-time winner (1930 and 1932) André Leducq. He had spent most of his career riding for Alcyon, having started off with one of the team's feeder squads, Thomann, but had left in a dispute over money: he wanted more, Alcyon didn't want to pay it. Leducq then joined the Mercier team, where he was bossed by Francis Pélissier who, like many former riders, was now making a career as a *directeur sportif*. To say that Alcyon were displeased would be an understatement. Alcyon boss Edmond Gentil having a degree of leverage with Desgrange – Alcyon provided the anonymous yellow bikes Tour riders rode – the issue was taken to the Father of the Tour and he took against Leducq, constantly misspelling his and his team's name in race reports in *L'Auto*. And denying him entry to the 1934 Tour. Having thrown out the manufacturer teams who had effectively decided who won the Tour, Desgrange was not above helping one of those teams dictate who would not win the Tour.

Stage-by-Stage Results for the 1934 Tour de France			Stage Winner	Maillot Jaune
Stage 1 Tue 3 Jul	Paris (Le Vésinet) to Lille 60 starters 58 finishers	262 km 8h16'50" 31.6 kph	Georges Speicher (Fra) France	Georges Speicher (Fra) France
Stage 2 Wed 4 Jul	Lille to Charleville 54 finishers	192 km 5h49'30" 33.0 kph	René le Grevès (Fra) France	Antonin Magne (Fra) France
Stage 3 Thu 5 Jul	Charleville to Metz 53 finishers	161 km 5h01'55" 32.0 kph	Roger Lapébie (Fra) France	Antonin Magne (Fra) France
Stage 4 Fri 6 Jul	Metz to Belfort 53 finishers	220 km 7h16'27" 30.2 kph	Roger Lapébie (Fra) France	Antonin Magne (Fra) France
Major climbs: Ballon d'Alsace (1,178m) Félicien Vervaecke (Bel) Unsponsored				

Stage-by-Stage Results for the 1934 Tour de France			Stage Winner	Maillot Jaune
Stage 5 Sat 7 Jul	Belfort to Évian 52 finishers	293 km 9h47'16" 29.9 kph	René le Grevès (Fra) France	Antonin Magne (Fra) France
			Georges Speicher (Fra) France	
Major climbs: Col de la Faucille (1,323m) René le Grevès (Fra) France				
Sun 8 Jul	Rest day			
Stage 6 Mon 9 Jul	Évian to Aix-les-Bains 48 finishers	207 km 6h45'16" 30.6 kph	Georges Speicher (Fra) France	Antonin Magne (Fra) France
Major climbs: Col des Aravis (1,498m) Félicien Vervaecke (Bel) Unsponsored; Col de Tamié (907m) René Vietto (Fra) France				
Stage 7 Tue 10 Jul	Aix-les-Bains to Grenoble 47 finishers	229 km 8h40'27" 26.4 kph	René Vietto (Fra) France	Antonin Magne (Fra) France
Major climbs: Col du Télégraphe (1,566m) Federico Ezquerra (Esp) Switzerland/Spain; Col du Galibier (2,556m) Federico Ezquerra (Esp) Switzerland/Spain				
Stage 8 Wed 11 Jul	Grenoble to Gap 44 finishers	102 km 3h28'16" 29.4 kph	Giuseppe Martano (Ita) Italy	Antonin Magne (Fra) France
Major climbs: Côte de Laffrey (900m) Vicente Trueba (Esp) Switzerland/Spain; Col Bayard (1,246m) Giuseppe Martano (Ita) Italy				
Stage 9 Thu 12 Jul	Gap to Digne 44 finishers	227 km 8h08'44" 27.9 kph	René Vietto (Fra) France	Antonin Magne (Fra) France
Major climbs: Col de Vars (2,110m) René Vietto (Fra) France; Col d'Allos (2,250m) René Vietto (Fra) France				
Stage 10 Fri 13 Jul	Digne to Nice 43 finishers	156 km 4h58'26" 31.4 kph	René le Grevès (Fra) France	Antonin Magne (Fra) France
Sat 14 Jul	Rest day			
Stage 11 Sun 15 Jul	Nice to Cannes 43 finishers	126 km 4h09'07" 30.3 kph	René Vietto (Fra) France	Antonin Magne (Fra) France
Major climbs: Col de Braus (1,002m) René Vietto (Fra) France; Col de Castillon (706m) René Vietto (Fra) France; La Turbie (555m) René Vietto (Fra) France				
Stage 12 Mon 16 Jul	Cannes to Marseille 42 finishers	195 km 6h49'29" 28.6 kph	Roger Lapébie (Fra) France	Antonin Magne (Fra) France
Stage 13 Tue 17 Jul	Marseille to Montpellier 41 finishers	172 km 5h04'54" 33.8 kph	Georges Speicher (Fra) France	Antonin Magne (Fra) France

Stage-by-Stage Results for the 1934 Tour de France			Stage Winner	Maillot Jaune
Stage 14 Wed 18 Jul	Montpellier to Perpignan 41 finishers	177 km 6h33'13" 27.0 kph	Roger Lapébie (Fra) France	Antonin Magne (Fra) France
Thu 19 Jul	Rest day			
Stage 15 Fri 20 Jul	Perpignan to Ax-les-Thermes 41 finishers	158 km 5h47'03" 27.3 kph	Roger Lapébie (Fra) France	Antonin Magne (Fra) France
	Major climbs: Col de Puymorens (1,915m) René Vietto (Fra) France			
Stage 16 Sat 21 Jul	Ax-les-Thermes to Luchon 41 finishers	165 km 5h26'14" 30.3 kph	Adriano Vignoli (Ita) Italy	Antonin Magne (Fra) France
	Major climbs: Col de Port (1,249m) René Vietto (Fra) France; Col de Portet-d'Aspet (1,069m) Adriano Vignoli (Ita) Italy; Col des Ares (797m) Adriano Vignoli (Ita) Italy			
Stage 17 Sun 22 Jul	Luchon to Tarbes 41 finishers	91 km 2h51'46" 31.8 kph	Antonin Magne (Fra) France	Antonin Magne (Fra) France
	Major climbs: Col de Peyresourde (1,569m) René Vietto (Fra) France; Col d'Aspin (1,489m) Antonin Magne (Fra) France			
Stage 18 Mon 23 Jul	Tarbes to Pau 39 finishers	172 km 6h32'01" 26.3 kph	René Vietto (Fra) France	Antonin Magne (Fra) France
	Major climbs: Col du Tourmalet (2,115m) René Vietto (Fra) France; Col d'Aubisque (1,709m) René Vietto (Fra) France			
Tue 24 Jul	Rest day			
Stage 19 Wed 25 Jul	Pau to Bordeaux 39 finishers	215 km 7h07'58" 30.1 kph	Ettore Meini (Ita) Unsponsored	Antonin Magne (Fra) France
Stage 20 Thu 26 Jul	Bordeaux to La Rochelle 39 finishers	183 km 6h48'26" 26.9 kph	Georges Speicher (Fra) France	Antonin Magne (Fra) France
Stage 21a Fri 27 Jul	La Rochelle to La Roche-sur-Yon 39 finishers	81 km 3h00'06" 27.0 kph	René le Grevès (Fra) France	Antonin Magne (Fra) France
Stage 21b Fri 27 Jul	La Roche-sur-Yon to Nantes (ITT) 39 finishers	90 km 2h32'05" 35.5 kph	Antonin Magne (Fra) France	Antonin Magne (Fra) France
Stage 22 Sat 28 Jul	Nantes to Caen 39 finishers	275 km 8h47'55" 31.3 kph	Raymond Louviot (Fra) France	Antonin Magne (Fra) France
Stage 23 Sun 29 Jul	Caen to Paris (Parc des Princes) 39 finishers	221 km 7h11'41" 30.7 kph	Sylvère Maes (Bel) Belgium	Antonin Magne (Fra) France

Prize fund: 727,610 francs (first prize: 30,000 francs)

Final Classification

Place	Rider	Team	Time	Age
1	Antonin Magne (Fra)	France	4,470 km 147h13'58" 30,360 kph	30
2	Giuseppe Martano (Ita)	Italy	+ 27'31"	23
3	Roger Lapébie (Fra)	France	+ 52'15"	23
4	Félicien Vervaecke (Bel)	Unsponsored	+ 57'40"	27
5	René Vietto (Fra)	France	+ 59'02"	20
6	Ambrogio Morelli (Ita)	Unsponsored	+ 1h12'02"	28
7	Ludwig Geyer (Ger)	Germany	+ 1h12'51"	30
8	Sylvère Maes (Bel)	Unsponsored	+ 1h20'56"	24
9	Mariano Cañardo (Esp)	Switzerland/Spain	+ 1h29'39"	28
10	Vicente Trueba (Esp)	Switzerland/Spain	+ 1h40'39"	28

Lanterne Rouge

39	Antonio Folco (Ita)	Italy	7h15'36"	27

King of the Mountains

	René Vietto (Fra)	France		20

Team

		France		

1935: A Death in the Family

The typical Tour de France cyclist is often thought to be a farmer's son, a young man used to long hours of back-breaking work for whom the toil of the Tour was an escape from the farm. The hard labour required by cycling was bred into them as youths. Some fit the type. Many don't and instead came from middle-class backgrounds. Louis Trousselier was the son of a florist. Lucien Petit-Breton's father was a jeweller. Henri Pélissier's was in the dairy industry. For them, cycling may also have been an escape, but one that required harder work than they might otherwise have endured.

The Spaniard Francisco Cepeda was of this latter type, his father a banker. Cycling was something he was good at. Not good enough to be one of the stars of the sport, but good enough. Starting his career in the mid-twenties, he won a few races and placed well in others, enough to earn him selection for the Spanish team in 1930 when the Tour went international. Cepeda finished twenty-seventh overall and the following year was back for more, the sole representative of the Spanish "team" and one of the many who fell by the wayside as the Tour progressed, abandoning on the twentieth stage. Two years later he came back as one of the unsponsored *touristes-routiers* but didn't make it to the end of the first stage.

Come 1935, Spanish cycling was improving and on the last Monday in April 50 riders set out on the inaugural Vuelta a España, the Madrid newspaper *Informaciones*'s attempt to replicate the Tour in Spain. Cepeda was there that day, and was still there on 15 May when the Vuelta returned to Madrid, one of the 20 riders who managed to complete the race. From there Cepeda went on to the Tour, a member of the Spain Individuals squad. And on the seventh stage of the race, while descending the Galibier, the Spaniard crashed and fractured his skull. Three days later he died in a hospital in Grenoble, not having regained consciousness. Cepeda was the first racing fatality in the Tour's 29 year history, and only the second rider to die during the race, after Adolphe Hélière's death in 1910 following a rest-day incident.

Cycling was – and still is – a dangerous sport. Riders dying during races was relatively rare, but not unusual, particularly in track racing. But it also happened in road races: Georges Lemaire, who had worn the yellow jersey briefly in the 1933 Tour and finished fourth overall, died in a road race two months after that Tour ended. Through the 1930s the French cycling federation had been trying to improve rider safety in road races and tried to get riders to wear helmets, a move that met with considerable resistance from the riders. Perhaps a helmet would have protected Cepeda when he fell on the Galibier. Perhaps not. What's more interesting, though, is why he crashed in the first place.

At this stage in the bicycle's evolution wheels used wooden rims. But new alloy rims were beginning to appear and it was these that Henri Desgrange and his team at *L'Auto* equipped the riders in the 1935 Tour with. Quickly, though, it became apparent there was a problem with these wheels. The alloy rims over-heated under braking, and that heat softened the glue holding the tubulars to the rim, causing tyres to roll and riders to crash. Or it could even sometimes cause the tyres to explode. By the time the sixth stage came around Desgrange knew he had a problem and set about resolving it by ordering new wheels with wooden rims. These didn't arrive until the tenth stage, by which time Cepeda had crashed and, that night, died.

The Spain Individuals team Cepeda was riding for was part of a compromise between Desgrange and the major manufacturers. Excluded from the Tour under the national team format they were unhappy with the way Desgrange was dealing with the *touristes-routiers*. Though technically they were meant to be unsponsored individuals, some rode for smaller trade teams, and at the Tour they wore their sponsor's name on their jersey. In 1934 Desgrange placated the manufacturers by excluding the *touristes-routiers* and instead inviting 20 individuals, who – unlike the *touristes-routiers* – received a per diem of 100 francs per stage but couldn't sport their sponsor's name on their jerseys. For 1935 Desgrange organised those individual riders into B teams – which the main squad was able to draw on as substitutes, should the need arise – and was able to bring back the *touristes-routiers*, who were now also barred from carrying sponsors' names on their clothing.

On the same day that Cepeda crashed and was taken to hospital, two-time winner Antonin Magne also exited the race and with him went France's best chance of a victory. Magne was victim of a crash involving a number of riders and some of the race's following vehicles. He had been second overall, four minutes down on the yellow jersey, which was being sported by Belgium's Romain Maes.

Maes had taken the *maillot jaune* on the opening stage and was destined to not surrender it, wearing it from the first day to last. His Belgium national team *director sportif* Karel Steyaert had ordered his riders to bend their backs and bring home some bounty and, 60 kilometres from home on that first stage, Maes attacked alone and quickly opened a lead of more than a minute on a chasing group containing Magne and Charles Pélissier.

Forty kilometres later he nipped across a level crossing just before the gates closed and gained the thick end of another minute on his pursuers, who had to wait for a freight train to pass before resuming their chase. The 22-year-old native of Flanders surrendered half his lead approaching the finish, but held on to take the stage by 53 seconds over his pursuers. The bonifications system had by now been amended, with the extra bonus of the gap back to the next rider dropped and stage winner just getting the basic 1'30" time deduction. The net effect of this was to give Maes a lead of two and a half minutes over his team-mate Edgard de Caluwé and more than three minutes on Magne.

Magne ceded more time over the Ballon d'Alsace on the fourth stage and fell to more than five minutes behind Maes. The fifth stage was the first of six split stages the riders faced in the race, Desgrange having deemed his experiment of the year before a resounding success and expanded it for 1935. In the afternoon's individual time trial Magne clawed back some time from Maes, but was still four minutes off the race lead, which is where he stood before the start of the seventh stage and his exit from the race.

That time trial stage saw the Tour return to 1904 with accusations abounding that riders had been paced by vehicles and at least one rider accused of being towed along. Various fines, time penalties and reprimands were handed out and it was hoped that the remaining time trials would be raced fairly.

Having spent the first four years of the national team format at the Tour riding like a bunch of individuals, the Belgians finally seemed to have discovered team work in 1935 and rode hard to protect the Maes's yellow jersey, particularly after the Allos and Vars climbs when Maes showed signs of weakness. But attempts to exploit that weakness by the squads from Italy and France proved fruitless.

Fruitless though the attempts to overthrow Maes were, they did provide moments of levity, such as on the seventeenth stage, to Bordeaux, when the riders in the main *peloton* came across bottles of beer lined up alongside the road 40 kilometres out from the finish. Stopping to quench their thirst – alcohol was still believed to be good for riders and the drinks company Ricqlès even provided them with complementary drinks ahead of the race – they were surprised to see Jules Merviel ride straight past them. And were even more surprised when they didn't see him again until after he had won the stage. The beer had been part of a cunning plan put in place by Merviel, a member of the France team.

On the eighteenth stage – run as a split stage, a road race in the morning and an individual time trial in the afternoon – levity turned to farce when the winners of both portions of the stage ended up being relegated by the commissaires. In the morning's road race Jean Aerts (Belgium) had crossed the line first but was demoted and the stage awarded to René le Grevès (France).

Following the shenanigans in the first individual time trial Desgrange had re-arranged the second, on Stage 13, as a team time trial and then, for the third, on Stage 14, reverted to the individual format. But once again fines, time penalties and reprimands had to be handed out as riders exploited *L'Auto*'s inability to keep them all under surveillance with just a handful of official cars and couple of motorcycles. And the same inability was present come the individual time trial on the eighteenth stage. Jean Fontenay (France Individuals) won the stage but that evening got demoted and handed a five-minute time penalty for having paced behind a motor car when he thought no one was looking. In his place André Leducq (France) got the win, but, years later, in his autobiography he admitted that he too had been able to pace behind cars during the time trial.

For the final two scheduled time trials the next day and the day after Desgrange decided to use the team format, but this late in the race that was asking a lot of the riders. France – for all the team's inability to challenge the Belgians – was the best equipped, with five riders left on the main team and three in the Individuals. The Belgium and German squads were both down to three riders, with the same number again on their B teams. All of the main Italy squad had gone home and there were just two riders left on the B team. Spain was also reduced to just two riders, one on the main team, one on the other. So Desgrange decreed international alliances the order of the day, an unsavoury solution for all concerned. While the split stage format fitted perfectly with Desgrange's desire to see the riders being pushed to race hard, if it was going to work then the organisation of the time trials would need considerable improvements.

* * * * *

Francisco Cepeda was not the only rider the Tour mourned that year. Two months before the race Henri Pélissier had been shot and killed by his lover. Following the deaths of René Pottier in 1907, Lucien Petit-Breton, François Faber and Octave Lapize all during the War, and Ottavio Bottecchia in 1927 he was the sixth of the 20 former Tour champions to have died so far in the race's history.

Stage-by-Stage Results for the 1935 Tour de France			Stage Winner	Maillot Jaune
Stage 1 Thu 4 Jul	Paris (Le Vésinet) to Lille 93 starters 90 finishers	7h23'58" 262 km 35.4 kph	Romain Maes (Bel) Belgium	Romain Maes (Bel) Belgium
Stage 2 Fri 5 Jul	Lille to Charleville 85 finishers	5h32'18" 192 km 34.7 kph	Charles Pélissier (Fra) France Individuals	Romain Maes (Bel) Belgium
Stage 3 Sat 6 Jul	Charleville to Metz 84 finishers	4h29'07" 161 km 35.9 kph	Raffaele di Paco (Ita) Italy	Romain Maes (Bel) Belgium
Stage 4 Sun 7 Jul	Metz to Belfort 84 finishers	7h00'14" 220 km 31.4 kph	Jean Aerts (Bel) Belgium	Romain Maes (Bel) Belgium
	Major climbs: Ballon d'Alsace (1,178m) Félicien Vervaecke (Bel) Belgium			
Stage 5a Mon 8 Jul	Belfort to Geneva 84 finishers	8h21'22" 262 km 31.4 kph	Maurice Archambaud (Fra) France	Romain Maes (Bel) Belgium
	Major climbs: Col de la Faucille (1,323m) n/a			
Stage 5b Mon 8 Jul	Geneva to Évian (ITT) 78 finishers	1h37'24" 58 km 35.7 kph	Raffaele di Paco (Ita) Italy	Romain Maes (Bel) Belgium
Tue 9 Jul	Rest Day			
Stage 6 Wed 10 Jul	Évian to Aix-les-Bains 75 finishers	6h23'42" 207 km 32.4 kph	René Vietto (Fra) France	Romain Maes (Bel) Belgium
	Major climbs: Col des Aravis (1,498m) René Vietto (Fra) France; Col de Tamié (907m) René Vietto (Fra) France			
Stage 7 Thu 11 Jul	Aix-les-Bains to Grenoble 70 finishers	7h33'13" 229 km 30.3 kph	Francesco Camusso (Ita) Italy	Romain Maes (Bel) Belgium
	Major climbs: Col du Télégraphe (1,566m) Francesco Camusso (Ita) Italy; Col du Galibier (2,556m) Gabriel Ruozzi (Fra) Unsponsored; Col du Lautaret (2,058m) Gabriel Ruozzi (Fra) Unsponsored			
Stage 8 Fri 12 Jul	Grenoble to Gap 66 finishers	3h24'07" 102 km 30.0 kph	Jean Aerts (Bel) Belgium	Romain Maes (Bel) Belgium
	Major climbs: Côte de Laffrey (900m) Gabriel Ruozzi (Fra) Unsponsored; Col Bayard (1,246m) Gabriel Ruozzi (Fra) Unsponsored			
Stage 9 Sat 13 Jul	Gap to Digne 58 finishers	8h01'27" 227 km 28.3 kph	René Vietto (Fra) France	Romain Maes (Bel) Belgium
	Major climbs: Col de Vars (2,110m) Félicien Vervaecke (Bel) Belgium; Col d'Allos (2,250m) Félicien Vervaecke (Bel) Belgium			
Stage 10 Sun 14 Jul	Digne to Nice 58 finishers	4h22'35" 156 km 35.6 kph	Jean Aerts (Bel) Belgium	Romain Maes (Bel) Belgium
Mon 15 Jul	Rest Day			

Stage-by-Stage Results for the 1935 Tour de France			Stage Winner	Maillot Jaune
Stage 11 Tue 16 Jul	Nice to Cannes 58 finishers	4h24'53" 126 km 28.5 kph	Romain Maes (Bel) Belgium	Romain Maes (Bel) Belgium
Major climbs: Col de Braus (1,002m) Gabriel Ruozzi (Fra) Unsponsored; Col de Castillon (706m) Francesco Camusso (Ita) Italy; La Turbie (555m) Orlando Teani (Ita) Italy Individuals				
Stage 12 Wed 17 Jul	Cannes to Marseille 53 finishers	6h03'02" 195 km 32.2 kph	Charles Pélissier (Fra) France Individuals	Romain Maes (Bel) Belgium
Stage 13a Thu 18 Jul	Marseille to Nîmes 53 finishers	4h09'16" 112 km 27.0 kph	Vasco Bergamaschi (Ita) Italy	Romain Maes (Bel) Belgium
Stage 13b Thu 18 Jul	Nîmes to Montpellier (TTT) 53 finishers	1h16'04" 56 km 44.2 kph	Georges Speicher (Fra) France	Romain Maes (Bel) Belgium
Stage 14a Fri 19 Jul	Montpellier to Narbonne 53 finishers	3h55'12" 103 km 26.3 kph	René le Grevès (Fra) France	Romain Maes (Bel) Belgium
Stage 14b Fri 19 Jul	Narbonne to Perpignan (ITT) 53 finishers	1h39'08" 63 km 38.1 kph	Maurice Archambaud (Fra) France	Romain Maes (Bel) Belgium
Stage 15 Sat 20 Jul	Perpignan to Luchon 48 finishers	11h39'23" 325 km 27.9 kph	Sylvère Maes (Bel) Belgium Individuals	Romain Maes (Bel) Belgium
Major climbs: Col du Puymorens (1,915m) Félicien Vervaecke (Bel) Belgium; Col de Port (1,249m) Félicien Vervaecke (Bel) Belgium; Col de Portet d'Aspet (1,069m) Félicien Vervaecke (Bel) Belgium				
Sun 21 Jul	Rest Day			
Stage 16 Mon 22 Jul	Luchon to Pau 47 finishers	7h12'22" 194 km 26.9 kph	Ambrogio Morelli (Ita) Italy Individuals	Romain Maes (Bel) Belgium
Major climbs: Col de Peyresourde (1,569m) Félicien Vervaecke (Bel) Belgium; Col d'Aspin (1,489m) Félicien Vervaecke (Bel) Belgium; Col du Tourmalet (2,115m) Sylvère Maes (Bel) Belgium Individuals; Col d'Aubisque (1,709m) Ambrogio Morelli (Ita) Italy Individuals				
Tue 23 Jul	Rest Day			
Stage 17 Wed 24 Jul	Pau to Bordeaux 47 finishers	7h34'30" 224 km 29.6 kph	Julien Moineau (Fra) France Individuals	Romain Maes (Bel) Belgium
Stage 18a Thu 25 Jul	Bordeaux to Rochefort 47 finishers	4h17'51" 158 km 37.0 kph	~~Jean Aerts (Bel)~~ ~~Belgium~~ (1) René le Grevès (Fra) France	Romain Maes (Bel) Belgium
Stage 18b Thu 25 Jul	Rochefort to La Rochelle (ITT) 47 finishers	52'19" 33 km 37.8 kph	~~Jean Fontenay (Fra)~~ ~~France Individuals~~ (2) André Leducq (Fra) France	Romain Maes (Bel) Belgium

Stage-by-Stage Results for the 1935 Tour de France			Stage Winner	Maillot Jaune
Stage 19a Fri 26 Jul	La Rochelle to La Roche-sur-Yon 47 finishers	2h54'51" 81 km 27.8 kph	René le Grevès (Fra) France	Romain Maes (Bel) Belgium
Stage 19b Fri 26 Jul	La Roche-sur-Yon to Nantes (TTT) 47 finishers	2h45'47" 95 km 34.4 kph	Jean Aerts (Bel) Belgium	Romain Maes (Bel) Belgium
Stage 20a Sat 27 Jul	Nantes to Vire 47 finishers	8h33'13" 220 km 25.7 kph	René le Grevès (Fra) France	Romain Maes (Bel) Belgium
Stage 20b Sat 27 Jul	Vire to Caen (TTT) 47 finishers	1h25'19" 38.7 kph 55 km	Ambrogio Morelli (Ita) Italy Individuals	Romain Maes (Bel) Belgium
Stage 21 Sun 28 Jul	Caen to Paris (Parc des Princes) 46 finishers	6h57'45" 221 km 31.7 kph	Romain Maes (Bel) Belgium	Romain Maes (Bel) Belgium

(1) Jean Aerts was originally declared the stage winner in a confused finish and, when the commissaires reconsidered their decision, he was demoted to second on the stage and the victory given to René le Grèves
(2) Jean Fontenay was stripped of the stage win after it was found he had taken pace behind a motor vehicle

Prize fund: 1,092,050 francs (first prize: not known)

Final Classification				
Place	**Rider**	**Team**	**Time**	**Age**
1	Romain Maes (Bel)	Belgium	4,338 km 141h32'00" 30.650 kph	22
2	Ambrogio Morelli (Ita)	Italy Individuals	+ 17'52"	29
3	Félicien Vervaecke (Bel)	Belgium	+ 24'06"	28
4	Sylvère Maes (Bel)	Belgium Individuals	+ 35'24"	25
5	Jules Lowie (Bel)	Belgium Individuals	+ 51'26"	21
6	Georges Speicher (Fra)	France	+ 54'29"	28
7	Maurice Archambaud (Fra)	France	+ 1h09'28"	26
8	René Vietto (Fra)	France	+ 1h21'03"	21
9	Gabriel Ruozzi (Fra)	Unsponsored	+ 1h34'02"	21
10	Oskar Thierbach (Ger)	Germany	+ 2h00'04"	25
Lanterne Rouge				
46	Willi Kutschbach (Ger)	Germany	+ 7h40'39"	28
Independent				
	Gabriel Ruozzi (Fra)			21
King of the Mountains				
	Félicien Vervaecke (Bel)	Belgium		28
Team				
		France		

1936: The Other Maes

Before Henri Desgrange extended the hand of friendship across the Pyrenees and invited a Spanish national team to compete in the 1930 Tour, a dozen or so individual Spaniards had made the trek north to Paris to start the Tour. With the exception of Salvador Cardona's stage win for Fontan in 1929 they had left little mark on the main Tour. When it came to the mountains, though, in the years after the national team format was introduced the Spaniards showed they could be something special, with Vicente Trueba winning the climbing prizes in the 1932 and 1933 Tours. In the 1936 Tour the fight for the king of the mountains title was duked out between Federico Ezquerra and Julián Berrendero.

Ezquerra had led the rankings in the climbing competition during the 1934 Tour, only to be overtaken by René Vietto. Desgrange dubbed the Spaniard the Eagle of the Galibier after he set a new record for the ascent, and talked of him as a potential Tour winner, which was stretching things a bit, given the nature of the race. But Ezquerra's rival for the climber's title in the 1936 Tour, Berrendero, well he was a man who maybe could have gone the full distance.

The climbing competition in the thirtieth Tour opened on the fourth stage, through the Vosges from Metz to Belfort, with the ascent of the Ballon d'Alsace. Ezquerra and Berrendero were able to put daylight between themselves and the others and it was the more experienced Ezquerra who took the KOM points – and a time bonus of the gap back to Berrendero, three seconds – at the top of the climb. He was then able to hold onto his King of the Mountains lead through to stage nine, the last day in the Alps, when Berrendero rose up over the Allos and Vars and took the lead. That, though, was only temporary, Ezquerra striking back on the road to Cannes, Stage 11, and retaking the Mountains lead on the last climbs before the Pyrenees. There, one bad day ended Ezquerra's challenge and Berrendero rode into Paris as the third Spaniard to grab the Tour's Mountains title.

But it was a victory tinged with sadness, for as the Tour exited the Alps, at home in Spain Civil War erupted as a military-supported coup sought to overthrow the elected government. For the Spaniards it would be some time before it would be safe to return home.

One man who did not get to witness the battle between the two Spaniards in the mountains was Henri Desgrange. The Father of the Tour was by now a septuagenarian and showing the wear and tear of a life well lived. He was forced to leave the race after the second stage for health reasons and passed the reins to his deputy, Jacques Goddet, son of Desgrange's late business partner and *L'Auto*'s financial controller Victor Goddet.

For the Tour itself, 1936 was a good year, Léon Blum's short-lived Popular Front government granting the workers of France two weeks paid annual leave. For the Tour this would free up time for more crowds to come out and watch the race go by. But it would also create competition throughout France to attract those holidaymakers. Which, in turn, created an opportunity for *L'Auto* to capitalise on, the Tour offering towns and cities a platform to showcase their wares to potential tourists, at a price.

Interest in the Tour was also extended beyond France's borders, with teams from Romania and Yugoslavia invited along. And, somewhat surprising given their geographic proximity to France, this thirtieth Tour also saw the début of a team from the Netherlands. Missing, though, was a team from Italy, Benito Mussolini not yet sold on the idea of winning hearts and minds through sporting success and ordering the Italian cycling federation to skip the Tour.

Within the 1936 race itself, it was victory once more for the Black Squadron bossed again by Karel Steyaert (sometimes better known by the pen name he wrote under, Karel van Wijnendaele, and the man who had created the Ronde van Vlaanderen in 1913), whose admonition to his riders the previous year that they bend their backs

Sylvère Maes on the Col d'Izoard in the 1936 Tour.

had helped launch Romain Maes into the *maillot jaune*. This time round it was another Maes who took the win, Romain's namesake Sylvère.

Maes took control of the race in Briançon, on Stage Eight (the day after the other Maes abandoned), when the yellow jersey-wearing Maurice Archambaud (France) lost time with two punctures in the final 40 kilometres of the stage. The Belgian then cemented his victory by adding four stage wins (in the team time trials in Montpellier, Perpignan and La Rochelle, as well as one in the Pyrenees on the stage to Pau). So sure was he of his overall victory that as early as Stage 15 – a week after he took the lead and still a week away from Paris – he ordered a silk yellow jersey for his victory parade in the Parc des Princes.

The day after the last of Maes's four stage wins – in La Rochelle – came a day when the Tour really pushed things to their limit, squeezing three stages into one day: an 81-kilometre road race from La Rochelle to La Roche-sur-Yon, followed by a 65-kilometre team time trial to Cholet, and ending with a 67-kilometre road stage taking the riders to Angers. At 213 kilometres in all it was far from being the toughest day at the office, but three starts in the one day was in itself a trying – and tiring – experience for the riders. But a boon for the Tour, providing more opportunities to raise revenue from towns willing to pay for the privilege of hosting the race, even if only for an hour or two.

Stage-by-Stage Results for the 1936 Tour de France			Stage Winner	Maillot Jaune
Stage 1 Tue 7 Jul	Paris (Le Vésinet) to Lille 90 starters 90 finishers	7h06'18" 258 km 36.3 kph	Paul Egli (Sui) Switzerland	Paul Egli (Sui) Switzerland
Stage 2 Wed 8 Jul	Lille to Charleville 86 finishers	5h32'21" 192 km 34.7 kph	Robert Wierinckx (Bel) Belgium	Maurice Archambaud (Fra) France
Stage 3 Thu 9 Jul	Charleville to Metz 82 finishers	4h22'22" 161 km 36.8 kph	Mathias Clemens (Lux) Spain/Luxembourg	Arsène Mersch (Lux) Spain/Luxembourg
Stage 4 Fri 10 Jul	Metz to Belfort 81 finishers	6h50'26" 220 km 32.2 kph	Maurice Archambaud (Fra) France	Maurice Archambaud (Fra) France
	Major climbs: Ballon d'Alsace (1,178m) Federico Ezquerra (Esp) Spain/Luxembourg			

Stage-by-Stage Results for the 1936 Tour de France			Stage Winner	Maillot Jaune
Stage 5 Sat 11 Jul	Belfort to Évian-les-Bains 78 finishers	9h33'45" 298 km 31.2 kph	René le Grèves (Fra) France	Maurice Archambaud (Fra) France
	Major climbs: Col de la Faucille (1,323m) n/a			
Sun 12 Jul	Rest Day			
Stage 6 Mon 13 Jul	Évian-les-Bains to Aix-les-Bains 72 finishers	6h24'51" 212 km 33.1 kph	Éloi Meulenberg (Bel) Belgium	Maurice Archambaud (Fra) France
	Major climbs: Col des Aravis (1,498m) Federico Ezquerra (Esp) Spain/Luxembourg; Col de Tamié (907m) François Neuville (Bel) Belgium			
Stage 7 Tue 14 Jul	Aix-les-Bains to Grenoble 63 finishers	8h32'02" 230 km 27.0 kph	Theo Middelkamp (Ned) Netherlands	Maurice Archambaud (Fra) France
	Major climbs: Col du Télégraphe (1,566m) Romain Maes (Bel) Belgium; Col du Galibier (2,556m) Federico Ezquerra (Esp) Spain/Luxembourg; Col du Lautaret (2,058m) Federico Ezquerra (Esp) Spain/Luxembourg			
Stage 8 Wed 15 Jul	Grenoble to Briançon 62 finishers	6h15'32" 194 km 31.0 kph	Jean-Marie Goasmat (Fra) Unsponsored	Sylvère Maes (Bel) Belgium
	Major climbs: Côte de Laffrey (900m) Julián Berrendero (Esp) Spain/Luxembourg; Col Bayard (1,246m) Pierre Cloarec (Fra) France			
Stage 9 Thu 16 Jul	Briançon to Digne 59 finishers	8h06'15" 220 km 27.1 kph	Léon Level (Fra) Unsponsored	Sylvère Maes (Bel) Belgium
	Major climbs: Col d'Izoard (2,360m) Sylvère Maes (Bel) Belgium; Col de Vars (2,110m) Julián Berrendero (Esp) Spain/Luxembourg; Col d'Allos (2,250m) Julián Berrendero (Esp) Spain/Luxembourg			
Fri 17 Jul	Rest Day			
Stage 10 Sat 18 Jul	Digne to Nice 57 finishers	4h44'16" 156 km 32.9 kph	Paul Maye (Fra) France	Sylvère Maes (Bel) Belgium
Stage 11 Sun 19 Jul	Nice to Cannes 57 finishers	4h03'18" 126 km 31.1 kph	Federico Ezquerra (Esp) Spain/Luxembourg	Sylvère Maes (Bel) Belgium
	Major climbs: Col de Braus (1,002m) Félicien Vervaecke (Bel) Belgium; Col de Castillon (706m) Federico Ezquerra (Esp) Spain/Luxembourg			
Mon 20 Jul	Rest Day			
Stage 12 Tue 21 Jul	Cannes to Marseille 56 finishers	6h36'10" 195 km 29.5 kph	René le Grevès (Fra) France	Sylvère Maes (Bel) Belgium
Stage 13a Wed 22 Jul	Marseille to Nîmes 52 finishers	4h12'15" 112 km 26.6 kph	René le Grevès (Fra) France	Sylvère Maes (Bel) Belgium

Stage-by-Stage Results for the 1936 Tour de France			Stage Winner	Maillot Jaune
Stage 13b Wed 22 Jul	Nîmes to Montpellier (TTT) 52 finishers	1h09'31" 52 km 44.9 kph	Sylvère Maes (Bel) Belgium	Sylvère Maes (Bel) Belgium
Stage 14a Thu 23 Jul	Montpellier to Narbonne 46 finishers	3h25'40" 103 km 30.0 kph	René le Grevès (Fra) France	Sylvère Maes (Bel) Belgium
Stage 14b Thu 23 Jul	Narbonne to Perpignan (TTT) 45 finishers	1h35'18" 63 km 39.7 kph	Sylvère Maes (Bel) Belgium	Sylvère Maes (Bel) Belgium
Fri 24 Jul	Rest Day			
Stage 15 Sat 25 Jul	Perpignan to Luchon 43 finishers	11h57'32" 325 km 27.2 kph	Sauveur Ducazeaux (Fra) Unsponsored	Sylvère Maes (Bel) Belgium
	Major climbs: Col du Puymorens (1,915m) Federico Ezquerra (Esp) Spain/Luxembourg; Col de Port (1,249m) Félicien Vervaecke (Bel) Belgium; Col de Portet d'Aspet (1,069m) Sauveur Ducazeaux (Fra) Unsponsored; Col des Ares (797m) Sauveur Ducazeaux (Fra) Unsponsored			
Sun 26 Jul	Rest Day			
Stage 16 Mon 27 Jul	Luchon to Pau 43 finishers	7h12'52" 194 km 26.9 kph	Sylvère Maes (Bel) Belgium	Sylvère Maes (Bel) Belgium
	Major climbs: Col de Peyresourde (1,569m) Julián Berrendero (Esp) Spain/Luxembourg; Col d'Aspin (1,489m) Yvon Marie (Fra) Unsponsored; Col du Tourmalet (2,115m) Sylvère Maes (Bel) Belgium; Col d'Aubisque (1,709m) Sylvère Maes (Bel) Belgium			
Tue 28 Jul	Rest Day			
Stage 17 Wed 29 Jul	Pau to Bordeaux 43 finishers	7h20'25" 229 km 31.2 kph	René le Grevès (Fra) France	Sylvère Maes (Bel) Belgium
Stage 18a Thu 30 Jul	Bordeaux to Saintes 43 finishers	3h30'07" 117 km 33.4 kph	Éloi Meulenberg (Bel) Belgium	Sylvère Maes (Bel) Belgium
Stage 18b Thu 30 Jul	Saintes to La Rochelle (TTT) 43 finishers	1h46'53" 75 km 42.1 kph	Sylvère Maes (Bel) Belgium	Sylvère Maes (Bel) Belgium
Stage 19a Fri 31 Jul	La Rochelle to La Roche-sur-Yon 43 finishers	2h49'29" 81 km 28.7 kph	Marcel Kint (Bel) Belgium	Sylvère Maes (Bel) Belgium
Stage 19b Fri 31 Jul	La Roche-sur-Yon to Cholet (TTT) 43 finishers	1h33'06" 65 km 41.9 kph	Félicien Vervaecke (Bel) Belgium	Sylvère Maes (Bel) Belgium
Stage 19c Fri 31 Jul	Cholet to Angers 43 finishers	1h38'30" 67 km 40.8 kph	Paul Maye (Fra) France	Sylvère Maes (Bel) Belgium
Stage 20a Sat 1 Aug	Angers to Vire 43 finishers	7h38'20" 204 km 26.7 kph	René le Grevès (Fra) France	Sylvère Maes (Bel) Belgium

Stage-by-Stage Results for the 1936 Tour de France			Stage Winner	Maillot Jaune
Stage 20b Sat 1 Aug	Vire to Caen (TTT) 43 finishers	1h18'16" 55 km 42.2 kph	Antonin Magne (Fra) France	Sylvère Maes (Bel) Belgium
Stage 21 Sun 2 Aug	Caen to Paris (Parc des Princes) 43 finishers	7h07'50" 234 km 32.8 kph	Arsène Mersch (Lux) Spain/Luxembourg	Sylvère Maes (Bel) Belgium

Prize fund: 1,000,000 francs (first prize: 100,000 francs)

Final Classification

Place	Rider	Team	Time	Age
1	Sylvère Maes (Bel)	Belgium	4,442 km 142h47'32" 31.108 kph	26
2	Antonin Magne (Fra)	France	+ 26'55"	32
3	Félicien Vervaecke (Bel)	Belgium	+ 27'53"	29
4	Pierre Clemens (Lux)	Spain/Luxembourg	+ 42'42"	23
5	Arsène Mersch (Lux)	Spain/Luxembourg	+ 52'52"	22
6	Mariano Cañardo (Esp)	Spain/Luxembourg	+ 1h03'04"	30
7	Mathias Clemens (Lux)	Spain/Luxembourg	+ 1h10'44"	20
8	Léo Amberg (Sui)	Switzerland	+ 1h19'13"	24
9	Marcel Kint (Bel)	Belgium	+ 1h22'25"	21
10	Léon Level (Fra)	Unsponsored	+ 1h27'57"	26
Lanterne Rouge				
43	Aldo Bertocco (Fra)	Unsponsored	+ 4h49'07"	24
Independent				
	Léon Level (Fra)	Unsponsored		26
King of the Mountains				
	Julián Berrendero (Esp)	Spain/Luxembourg		24
Points				
	Sylvère Maes (Bel)	Belgium		26
Team				
		Belgium		

1937: Walkover

First it was the Tour that Gino Bartali should have won. Then it was the second Tour that Sylvère Maes should have won. Finally it was the race that Roger Lapébie did win.

For Bartali, this was a Tour that the Italian dictator Benito Mussolini wanted him to win, *il Duce* having been converted to the cause of national pride through sporting success after attending the Berlin Olympics the previous year. *Il Pio* – Bartali's nickname was a reference to his religious beliefs – came into the Tour on the back of a second success at the Giro d'Italia (he'd won in 1936 and backed that up with another win in 1937). He grabbed the Tour's lead a week in, on the stage to Grenoble, after the *maillot jaune* had already passed across the shoulders of Luxembourg's Jean Majérus, Belgium's Marcel Kint and Germany's Erich Bautz.

The Italian had attacked on the descent of the Télégraphe and was briefly joined by his team-mate Francesco Camuso who, once it was clear Bartali had the win in the bag, dropped back in order to maximise the time bonuses gained by his team leader (the bonification system still included the gap back to the next rider as an additional bonus). Between time gained on the road and bonuses picked up in the mountains and at the stage end Bartali turned a 12'03" deficit at the start of the day into a 19'08" lead at the day's end. Given Bartali's successes in Italy that looked like a lead that would carry him all the way to Paris in yellow. Fate, though, had other plans.

A day after donning the yellow jersey Bartali was descending toward Briançon when the reigning Paris-Roubaix champion Jules Rossi crashed in front of him. *Il Pio* tried to avoid his fallen team-mate and in so doing went over the low parapet of a bridge and tumbled into the river below. By the time he was pulled out of the river and put back on his bike Bartali's 19 minutes race lead was slipping away and, despite the Trojan work of his team-mates who dragged him to the stage end in Briançon, *il Pio*'s overall lead was slashed to just two minutes.

The next day, the effects of his crash hampering him, Bartali bled time over the Izoard, Vars and Allos and finished the stage 22'33" down on the day and, in the general classification, 10'20" behind the new yellow jersey, the defending champion Sylvère Maes. That yellow jersey had almost gone to another Italian, Mario Vicini, riding as one of the unsupported independent riders. He looked to have done enough on the day to take the race lead and was almost awarded it until a sharp-eyed bean-counter remembered a one-minute time penalty Vicini had been slapped with because of an illegal feed. That put the Italian 35 seconds off Maes's yellow jersey, with Roger Lapébie another 47 seconds back.

Bartali lasted another four days – two race days and two rest days – before abandoning, a chest infection having set in after his dip in the river. Vicini had no real likelihood of unseating Maes – he was, after all, just an unsupported rider while Maes had the might of Belgium's Black Squadron behind him – but still hung in there in the stages that followed, even after conceding five minutes during Stage 11b's team time trial. Vicini even pulled back a couple of minutes, bringing him to just over three minutes off the race lead when the race arrived in Bordeaux at the end of the sixteenth stage. And it was on that sixteenth stage that Maes's tilt at a second Tour win came to a very unsatisfactory end.

Maes's biggest challenger was not the unsupported Italian but Roger Lapébie, who came back at the Belgian in the Pyrenees. At the start of the Luchon-Pau stage Lapébie had a 2'18" deficit on Maes, and, shortly after the stage started, that looked set to balloon until the Frenchman's handlebars broke – the result of sabotage, someone having taken a saw to his bike. Seeing Lapébie's problems, Steyaert sent his Black Squadron on the attack. But, rather than hurting Lapébie, all he did was harm Maes, Lapébie coming back at the Belgians and taking second on the stage and 45 seconds in time bonuses. The commissaires, though, took a dim view of some of the assistance given to Lapébie during his fightback, fans, friends and family having pushed him on the climbs. So the Frenchman was slapped with a 1'30" time penalty, pushing Maes's lead out to just over three minutes.

The next stage – Pau to Bordeaux, after a rest day – Maes blew the time gained through the penalty given to Lapébie and ceded 1'38" on the road to his French rival and another 45 seconds in time bonuses, Lapébie again finishing second on the stage. The Frenchman was now just 40 seconds off Maes's lead. And then it was Maes's turn to get slapped with a time penalty, 15 seconds for having been supported during the stage by two Belgians riding as unsupported independents.

Steyaert, the Belgian boss, was furious. He complained that the fans had thrown pepper at his riders (this was Lapébie's home turf, and his local fans were far from happy with the time penalty he had received in the Pyrenees). He complained that level crossing gates had been closed in front of his riders. He complained that even the race organisers were against his riders (and they did seem to be, a scheduled time trial – a format in which the Belgians excelled – in Ax-les-Thermes was cancelled and turned into another road race). So, despite the fact that his rider was in the *maillot jaune*, Steyaert declared that enough was enough and pulled the Belgian team from the race. (And, in so doing, cannily left it an open question as to whether Maes had enough on Lapébie to hold him off until Paris.)

And so the race lead passed to Roger Lapébie, with Vicini, the unsupported Italian, still in there, three minutes behind the Frenchman. The covert support of the Italian team, though, saw Vicini slapped with a two-minute time penalty late in the race, as Lapébie protected his lead and ensured his overall victory. It wasn't the prettiest of France's six wins since the national team format was introduced – harking back as it did to the days of Firmin Lambot – but it was certainly effective.

Stage-by-Stage Results for the 1937 Tour de France			Stage Winner	Maillot Jaune
Stage 1 Wed 30 Jun	Paris (Le Vésinet) to Lille 98 starters 97 finishers	6h57'48" 263 km 37.8 kph	Jean Majérus (Lux) Luxembourg	Jean Majérus (Lux) Luxembourg
Stage 2 Thu 1 Jul	Lille to Charleville 91 finishers	5h18'31" 192 km 36.2 kph	Maurice Archambaud (Fra) France	Jean Majérus (Lux) Luxembourg
Stage 3 Fri 2 Jul	Charleville to Metz 91 finishers	4h13'02" 161 km 38.2 kph	Walter Generati (Ita) Italy	Marcel Kint (Bel) Belgium
Stage 4 Sat 3 Jul	Metz to Belfort 90 finishers	6h28'56" 220 km 33.9 kph	Erich Bautz (Ger) Germany	Erich Bautz (Ger) Germany
Major climbs: Ballon d'Alsace (1,178m) Erich Bautz (Ger) Germany				
Stage 5a Sun 4 Jul	Belfort to Lons-le-Saunier 86 finishers	5h36'15" 175 km 31.2 kph	Henri Puppo (Fra) Unsponsored	Erich Bautz (Ger) Germany
Stage 5b Sun 4 Jul	Lons-le-Saunier to Champagnole (TTT) 86 finishers	55'33" 34 km 36.7 kph	Sylvère Maes (Bel) Belgium	Erich Bautz (Ger) Germany
Stage 5c Sun 4 Jul	Champagnole to Geneva 78 finishers	2h28'29" 93 km 37.6 kph	Leo Amberg (Sui) Switzerland	Erich Bautz (Ger) Germany
Mon 5 Jul	Rest Day			
Stage 6 Tue 6 Jul	Geneva to Aix-les-Bains 76 finishers	5h26'25" 180 km 33.1 kph	Gustaaf Deloor (Bel) Unsponsored	Erich Bautz (Ger) Germany
Major climbs: Col des Aravis (1,498m) Gino Bartali (Ita) Italy; Col de Tamié (907m) Félicien Vervaecke (Bel) Belgium				
Stage 7 Wed 7 Jul	Aix-les-Bains to Grenoble 72 finishers	8h02'57" 228 km 28.3 kph	Gino Bartali (Ita) Italy	Gino Bartali (Ita) Italy
Major climbs: Col du Télégraphe (1,566m) Pierre Gallien (Fra) Unsponsored; Col du Galibier (2,556m) Gino Bartali (Ita) Italy				
Stage 8 Thu 8 Jul	Grenoble to Briançon 67 finishers	5h55'45" 194 km 32.7 kph	Otto Weckerling (Ger) Germany	Gino Bartali (Ita) Italy
Major climbs: Côte de Laffrey (900m) Gino Bartali (Ita) Italy; Col Bayard (1,246m) Otto Weckerling (Ger) Germany				
Stage 9 Fri 9 Jul	Briançon to Digne 62 finishers	7h27'43" 220 km 29.5 kph	Roger Lapébie (Fra) France	Sylvère Maes (Bel) Belgium
Major climbs: Col d'Izoard (2,360m) Julián Berrendero (Esp) Spain; Col de Vars (2,110m) Edouard Vissers (Bel) Unsponsored; Col d'Allos (2,250m) Mario Vicini (Ita) Unsponsored				

Stage-by-Stage Results for the 1937 Tour de France			Stage Winner	Maillot Jaune
Sat 10 Jul	Rest Day			
Stage 10 Sun 11 Jul	Digne to Nice 61 finishers	8h29'19" 251 km 29.6 kph	Félicien Vervaecke (Bel) Belgium	Sylvère Maes (Bel) Belgium
	Major climbs: Col de Braus (1,002m) Félicien Vervaecke (Bel) Belgium			
Mon 12 Jul	Rest Day			
Stage 11a Tue 13 Jul	Nice to Toulon 61 finishers	5h25'14" 169 km 31.2 kph	Éloi Meulenberg (Bel) Belgium	Sylvère Maes (Bel) Belgium
Stage 11b Tue 13 Jul	Toulon to Marseille (TTT) 59 finishers	1h41'09" 65 km 38.6 kph	Gustave Danneels (Bel) Belgium	Sylvère Maes (Bel) Belgium
Stage 12a Wed 14 Jul	Marseille to Nîmes 59 finishers	3h39'37" 112 km 30.6 kph	Alphonse Antoine (Fra) Unsponsored	Sylvère Maes (Bel) Belgium
Stage 12b Wed 14 Jul	Nîmes to Montpellier 58 finishers	1h16'49" 51 km 39.8 kph	René Pedroli (Sui) Switzerland	Sylvère Maes (Bel) Belgium
Stage 13a Thu 15 Jul	Montpellier to Narbonne 58 finishers	2h32'39" 103 km 40.5 kph	Francesco Camusso (Ita) Italy	Sylvère Maes (Bel) Belgium
Stage 13b Thu 15 Jul	Narbonne to Perpignan 58 finishers	1h31'08" 63 km 41.5 kph	Éloi Meulenberg (Bel) Belgium	Sylvère Maes (Bel) Belgium
Fri 16 Jul	Rest Day			
Stage 14a Sat 17 Jul	Perpignan to Bourg-Madame 58 finishers	3h55'15" 99 km 25.3 kph	Éloi Meulenberg (Bel) Belgium	Sylvère Maes (Bel) Belgium
Stage 14b Sat 17 Jul	Bourg-Madame to Ax-les-Thermes 58 finishers	2h00'05" 59 km 29.5 kph	Mariano Cañardo (Esp) Spain	Sylvère Maes (Bel) Belgium
	Major climbs: Col du Puymorens (1,915m) Julián Berrendero (Esp) Spain			
Stage 14c Sat 17 Jul	Ax-les-Thermes to Luchon 56 finishers	6h22'48" 167 km 26.2 kph	Éloi Meulenberg (Bel) Belgium	Sylvère Maes (Bel) Belgium
	Major climbs: Col de Port (1,249m) Julián Berrendero (Esp) Spain; Col de Portet d'Aspet (1,069m) Julián Berrendero (Esp) Spain; Col des Ares (797m) Sylvère Maes (Bel) Belgium			
Sun 18 Jul	Rest Day			

Stage-by-Stage Results for the 1937 Tour de France			Stage Winner	Maillot Jaune
Stage 15 Mon 19 Jul	Luchon to Pau 55 finishers	7h01'01" 194 km 27.7 kph	Julián Berrendero (Esp) Spain	Sylvère Maes (Bel) Belgium
	Major climbs: Col de Peyresourde (1,569m) Julián Berrendero (Esp) Spain; Col d'Aspin (1,489m) Julián Berrendero (Esp) Spain; Col du Tourmalet (2,115m) Julián Berrendero (Esp) Spain; Col d'Aubisque (1,709m) Mario Vicini (Ita) Unsponsored			
Tue 20 Jul	Rest Day			
Stage 16 Wed 21 Jul	Pau to Bordeaux 55 finishers	7h56'50" 235 km 29.6 kph	Paul Chocque (Fra) France	Sylvère Maes (Bel) Belgium
Stage 17a Thu 22 Jul	Bordeaux to Royan 55 finishers	3h05'12" 123 km 39.9 kph	Erich Bautz (Ger) Germany	Roger Lapébie (Fra) France
Stage 17b Thu 22 Jul	Royan to Saintes 46 finishers	1h06'27" 37 km 33.4 kph	Adolph Braeckeveldt (Bel) Unsponsored Heinz Wengler (Ger) Germany	Roger Lapébie (Fra) France
Stage 17c Thu 22 Jul	Saintes to La Rochelle 46 finishers	2h25'50" 67 km 27.6 kph	Roger Lapébie (Fra) France	Roger Lapébie (Fra) France
Stage 18a Fri 23 Jul	La Rochelle to La Roche-sur-Yon (ITT) 46 finishers	1h59'10" 82 km 41.3 kph	Roger Lapébie (Fra) France	Roger Lapébie (Fra) France
Stage 18b Fri 23 Jul	La Roche-sur-Yon to Rennes 46 finishers	6h06'14" 172 km 28.2 kph	Paul Chocque (Fra) France	Roger Lapébie (Fra) France
Stage 19a Sat 24 Jul	Rennes to Vire 46 finishers	3h21'56" 114 km 33.9 kph	Raymond Passat (Fra) Unsponsored	Roger Lapébie (Fra) France
Stage 19b Sat 24 Jul	Vire to Caen (ITT) 46 finishers	1h28'36" 59 km 39.9 kph	Leo Amberg (Sui) Switzerland	Roger Lapébie (Fra) France
Stage 20 Sun 25 Jul	Caen to Paris (Parc des Princes) 46 finishers	7h23'42" 234 km 31.6 kph	Edouard Vissers (Bel) Unsponsored	Roger Lapébie (Fra) France

Prize fund: 800,000 francs (first prize: 200,000 francs)

Final Classification

Place	Rider	Team	Time	Age
1	Roger Lapébie (Fra)	France	4,415 km 138h58'31" 31.768 kph	26
2	Mario Vicini (Ita)	Unsponsored	+ 7'17"	24
3	Léo Amberg (Sui)	Switzerland	+ 26'13"	25
4	Francesco Camusso (Ita)	Italy	+ 26'53"	29
5	Sylvain Marcaillou (Fra)	France	+ 35'36"	26
6	Edouard Vissers (Bel)	Unsponsored	+ 38'13"	25
7	Paul Chocque (Fra)	France	+ 1h05'19"	27
8	Pierre Gallien (Fra)	Unsponsored	+ 1h06'33"	25
9	Erich Bautz (Ger)	Germany	+ 1h06'41"	24
10	Jean Fréchaut (Fra)	Unsponsored	+ 1h24'34"	22

Lanterne Rouge

46	Aloïs Klensch (Lux)	Luxembourg	+ 6h39'25"	23

King of the Mountain

	Félicien Vervaecke (Bel)	Belgium		30

Team

		France		

1938: Gino

Il Duce, Benito Mussolini, really wanted the glory of a Tour de France win for Italy. His hopes dashed in 1937 as Bartali went for the Giro/Tour double, he issued an order for 1938: the Tour, and only the Tour. Bartali, the defending Giro d'Italia champion, was ordered to sit out the *corsa rosa* and concentrate solely on winning the Tour de France.

For most of the opening week of the race the big guns held fire, as was the norm, and lesser riders got their days in the sun. Germany's Willi Oberbeck took the opening stage and the first yellow jersey, but was relieved of the latter the next day when Luxembourg's Jean Majérus came out on top. The race then held steady through to the sixth stage, where André Leducq found himself taking the lead in the second part of the day's split stage. Three days later the Tour reached the Pyrenees and the real race began.

Bartali went on the attack in the mountains, keen to pick up as many time bonuses as he could – there was still a minute available to the first rider over the top of rated climbs, as well as stage end bonifications. The Italian led the race over the Aubisque, Tourmalet and Aspin, but descending the last – and with the Peyresourde still to come – *il Pio*'s wheel broke and he finished the stage 55 seconds down on the day's winner and the new yellow jersey, Belgium's Félicien Vervaecke. In the general classification Bartali was now 2'18" off the lead.

Vervaecke was able to hold on to the yellow jersey through to the next round of climbs, surviving the first day over the Col de Braus even when he was hit with a 30-second time penalty for having impeded Bartali at the top of the climb. But in the next stage, over the Allos, Vars and Izoard, Bartali put more than 17 minutes into the Belgian and took the stage win more than five minutes clear of the next rider, his team-mate Mario Vicini. *Il Pio* had stuck with the front runners on the early climbs, only nipping ahead at the summits to take the time bonuses, and it was only a few kilometres before the summit of the Izoard that the Italian spread his wings and rode away from his erstwhile companions. It was a devastating day of climbing and – barring a repeat of the accident that had shattered his dreams the year before – Bartali had the victory in the bag.

And the accident never came. There were minor setbacks, but nothing of any great consequence. Bartali added the Tour to his *palmarès* and Mussolini got the Italian victory he dreamed of. Job done.

* * * * *

It was another Tour of firsts and lasts. Two of the stars of French cycling, two-time winners Antonin Magne and André Leducq, called quits on their careers. Born 12 days apart in 1904 they had both debuted at the 1927 Tour and both won the race twice. And, on the last day on their Tour careers, they rode into Paris's Parc des Princes together, ahead of the *peloton*, and crossed the finish line to take a final joint stage win.

Among the firsts there was Émile Masson Jnr, who became the first son to follow in his father's wheeltracks by also winning a stage in the Tour (his father, Émile Masson Snr, had (jointly) led the 1920 Tour during the opening week and won two stages in 1922). In Belfort Masson – who had won Flèche Wallonne earlier in the season – was away with the day's break and looked set to be taking one of the minor places in the sprint when Germany's Otto Weckerling went for the win in the vélodrome finish. But instead of hearing the cheer of the crowds as he crossed the line the German heard the sound of the bell, signalling the last lap: he had sprinted too soon. Next time around Masson got the upper hand, and tasted victory as his father before him had.

Another first came courtesy of Gino Bartali: the first time the winner of the final yellow jersey was also the winner of the King of the Mountains competition. And there were more firsts for the Tour's burgeoning radio coverage, with the first high-altitude live transmission as the race crossed the 2,769 metre Col d'Iseran. With *L'Auto*'s circulation falling in the face of increased competition from other papers, other forms of media were becoming more and more important in telling the story of the Tour.

Stage-by-Stage Results for the 1938 Tour de France			Stage Winner	Maillot Jaune
Stage 1 Tue 5 Jul	Paris (Le Vésinet) to Lille 96 starters 94 finishers	6h38'25" 215 km 32.4 kph	Willi Oberbeck (Ger) Germany	Willi Oberbeck (Ger) Germany
Stage 2 Wed 6 Jul	Lille to Saint-Brieuc 91 finishers	7h01'07" 237 km 33.8 kph	Jean Majérus (Lux) Luxembourg	Jean Majérus (Lux) Luxembourg
Stage 3 Thu 7 Jul	Saint-Brieuc to Nantes 91 finishers	7h39'01" 238 km 31.1 kph	Gerrit Schulte (Ned) Netherlands	Jean Majérus (Lux) Luxembourg
Stage 4a Fri 8 Jul	Nantes to La Roche-sur-Yon 91 finishers	2h04'49" 62 km 29.8 kph	Éloi Meulenberg (Bel) Belgium	Jean Majérus (Lux) Luxembourg
Stage 4b Fri 8 Jul	La Roche-sur-Yon to La Rochelle 91 finishers	2h34'20" 83 km 32.3 kph	Éloi Meulenberg (Bel) Belgium	Jean Majérus (Lux) Luxembourg
Stage 4c Fri 8 Jul	La Rochelle to Royan 91 finishers	2h32'13" 83 km 32.7 kph	Félicien Vervaecke (Bel) Belgium	Jean Majérus (Lux) Luxembourg
Sat 9 Jul	Rest Day			
Stage 5 Sun 10 Jul	Royan to Bordeaux 91 finishers	5h12'42" 198 km 38.0 kph	Éloi Meulenberg (Bel) Belgium	Jean Majérus (Lux) Luxembourg
Stage 6a Mon 11 Jul	Bordeaux to Arcachon 90 finishers	1h16'20" 53 km 41.3 kph	Jules Rossi (Ita) Italy	Jean Majérus (Lux) Luxembourg
Stage 6b Mon 11 Jul	Arcachon to Bayonne 90 finishers	5h06'34" 171 km 33.5 kph	Glauco Servadei (Ita) Italy	André Leducq (Fra) France
Stage 7 Tue 12 Jul	Bayonne to Pau 90 finishers	2h51'22" 115 km 40.3 kph	Theo Middelkamp (Ned) Netherlands	André Leducq (Fra) France
Wed 13 Jul	Rest Day			

Stage-by-Stage Results for the 1938 Tour de France			Stage Winner	Maillot Jaune
Stage 8 Thu 14 Jul	Pau to Luchon 77 finishers	7h15'19" 193 km 26.6 kph	Félicien Vervaecke (Bel) Belgium	Félicien Vervaecke (Bel) Belgium
	Main climbs: Col d'Aubisque (1,709m) Gino Bartali (Ita) Italy; Col du Tourmalet (2,115m) Gino Bartali (Ita) Italy; Col d'Aspin (1,489m) Gino Bartali (Ita) Italy; Col de Peyresourde (1,569m) Félicien Vervaecke (Bel) Belgium			
Fri 15 Jul	Rest Day			
Stage 9 Sat 16 Jul	Luchon to Perpignan 72 finishers	7h08'15" 260 km 36.4 kph	Jean Fréchaut (Fra) France	Félicien Vervaecke (Bel) Belgium
	Main climbs: Col des Ares (797m) Pierre Gallien (Fra) France; Col de Portet d'Aspet (1,069m) Gino Bartali (Ita) Italy			
Stage 10a Sun 17 Jul	Perpignan to Narbonne 72 finishers	1h56'09" 63 km 32.5 kph	Antoon van Schendel (Ned) Netherlands	Félicien Vervaecke (Bel) Belgium
Stage 10b Sun 17 Jul	Narbonne to Béziers (ITT) 72 finishers	39'31" 27 km 41.0 kph	Félicien Vervaecke (Bel) Belgium	Félicien Vervaecke (Bel) Belgium
Stage 10c Sun 17 Jul	Béziers to Montpellier 72 finishers	2h06'23" 73 km 34.7 kph	Antonin Magne (Fra) France	Félicien Vervaecke (Bel) Belgium
Stage 11 Mon 18 Jul	Montpellier to Marseille 69 finishers	6h52'10" 223 km 32.5 kph	Gino Bartali (Ita) Italy	Félicien Vervaecke (Bel) Belgium
Stage 12 Tue 19 Jul	Marseille to Cannes 67 finishers	6h35'26" 199 km 30.2 kph	Jean Fréchaut (Fra) France	Félicien Vervaecke (Bel) Belgium
Wed 20 Jul	Rest Day			
Stage 13 Thu 21 Jul	Cannes to Digne 62 finishers	9h19'49" 284 km 30.4 kph	Dante Gianello (Fra) Bleuets	Félicien Vervaecke (Bel) Belgium
	Main climbs: Col de Braus (1,002m) Gino Bartali (Ita) Italy; Col de Castillon (706m) n/a			
Stage 14 Fri 22 Jul	Digne to Briançon 57 finishers	8h49'07" 219 km 24.8 kph	Gino Bartali (Ita) Italy	Gino Bartali (Ita) Italy
	Main climbs: Col d'Allos (2,250m) Gino Bartali (Ita) Italy; Col de Vars (2,110m) Gino Bartali (Ita) Italy; Col d'Izoard (2,360m) Gino Bartali (Ita) Italy			
Stage 15 Sat 23 Jul	Briançon to Aix-les-Bains 56 finishers	10h52'24" 311 km 28.6 kph	Marcel Kint (Bel) Belgium	Gino Bartali (Ita) Italy
	Main climbs: Col du Galibier (2,556m) Mario Vicini (Ita) Italy; Col de l'Iseran (2,770m) Félicien Vervaecke (Bel) Belgium			

Stage-by-Stage Results for the 1938 Tour de France			Stage Winner	Maillot Jaune
Sun 24 Jul	Rest Day			
Stage 16 Mon 25 Jul	Aix-les-Bains to Besançon 56 finishers	9h39'56" 284 km 29.4 kph	Marcel Kint (Bel) Belgium	Gino Bartali (Ita) Italy
	Main climbs: Col de la Faucille (1,323m) Gino Bartali (Ita) Italy			
Stage 17a Tue 26 Jul	Besançon to Belfort 56 finishers	2h27'48" 89 km 36.3 kph	Émile Masson Jr (Bel) Belgium	Gino Bartali (Ita) Italy
Stage 17b Tue 26 Jul	Belfort to Strasbourg 55 finishers	4h30'20" 143 km 31.7 kph	Jean Fréchaut (Fra) France	Gino Bartali (Ita) Italy
Stage 18 Wed 27 Jul	Strasbourg to Metz 55 finishers	5h43'27" 186 km 32.5 kph	Marcel Kint (Bel) Belgium	Gino Bartali (Ita) Italy
Stage 19 Thu 28 Jul	Metz to Reims 55 finishers	6h35'21" 196 km 29.7 kph	Fabien Galateau (Fra) Cadets	Gino Bartali (Ita) Italy
Fri 29 Jul	Rest Day			
Stage 20a Sat 30 Jul	Reims to Laon 55 finishers	1h03'17" 48 km 45.5 kph	Glauco Servadei (Ita) Italy	Gino Bartali (Ita) Italy
Stage 20b Sat 30 Jul	Laon to Saint-Quentin (ITT) 55 finishers	1h04'40" 42 km 39.0 kph	Félicien Vervaecke (Bel) Belgium	Gino Bartali (Ita) Italy
Stage 20c Sat 30 Jul	Saint-Quentin to Lille 55 finishers	3h07'12" 107 km 34.3 kph	François Neuville (Bel) Belgium	Gino Bartali (Ita) Italy
Stage 21 Sun 31 Jul	Lille to Paris (Parc des Princes) 55 finishers	8h54'50" 279 km 31.3 kph	Antonin Magne (Fra) France	Gino Bartali (Ita) Italy
			André Leducq (Fra) Cadets	

Prize fund: 900,000 francs (first prize: 100,000 francs)

Final Classification

Place	Rider	Team	Time	Age
1	Gino Bartali (Ita)	Italy	4,694 km 148h29'12" 31.565 kph	24
2	Félicien Vervaecke (Bel)	Belgium	+ 18'27"	31
3	Victor Cosson (Fra)	France	+ 29'26"	22
4	Edouard Vissers (Bel)	Belgium	+ 35'08"	26
5	Mathias Clemens (Lux)	Luxembourg	+ 42'08"	22
6	Mario Vicini (Ita)	Italy	+ 44'59"	25
7	Jules Lowie (Bel)	Belgium	+ 48'56"	24
8	Antonin Magne (Fra)	France	+ 49'00"	34
9	Marcel Kint (Bel)	Belgium	+ 59'49"	23
10	Dante Gianello (Fra)	Bleuets	+ 1h06'47"	26
Lanterne Rouge				
55	Janus Hellemons (Ned)	Netherlands	+ 5h02'34"	26
King of the Mountains				
	Gino Bartali (Ita)	Italy		24
Team				
		Belgium		

1939: Maes, Again

When René Vietto burst onto the scene in the 1934 Tour de France, many believed that the 20-year-old debutant could have won the race if he hadn't been held back in the mountains in order to work for his team leader, Antonin Magne. Wiser heads, of course, pointed to the time Vietto had lost early in the race, and the fact that, compared with Magne, he was the weaker performer in time trials and so would have lost anyway. Ideally, Vietto should have settled the matter the following year, by proving his value, but again he blew his chances early in the race and was out of the running before things really got going. As happened again in 1936. And 1937. And 1938. The longer it went on, the more Vietto seemed to be proving the doubters right.

In 1939 Vietto – now riding for the regional Sud-Est squad – finally set about proving the doubters wrong and, as early as the fourth stage of the Tour, was wearing the yellow jersey, albeit with just a slim safety margin (six seconds over Luxembourg's Mathias Clemens). Former winner Sylvère Maes, on the other hand, was already six minutes off the pace. Advantage Vietto.

By the time the Tour arrived in the Pyrenees, at the start of Stage Nine, Pau to Toulouse, Vietto was still in yellow (with a 58-second lead over Albertin Disseaux, of the Belgium B squad). Maes, though, had already cut his deficit in half and was just three minutes behind Vietto. Maes, though, wasn't interested in taking the jersey in the race's one stage in the Pyrenees. He had a plan, a plan that would see him biding his time until the Tour hit the Alps and putting everyone to the sword in the Casse Déserte.

In Digne, on the eve of the Maes's appointment with destiny, Vietto was still wearing the *maillot jaune*, his Belgian rival right behind him, 49 seconds back. For Vietto, it was the end of the dream. He had been living on borrowed time, riding through a chest infection and injured knee that required nightly injections. And when Maes launched his fatal attack 15 kilometres from the summit of the Izoard, riding away from Vietto, who had doggedly held his own over the early climbs, the Frenchman was simply powerless to react to the Belgian's assault. Maes put 17 minutes into Vietto, who, despite his bad day in the mountains, still managed to hold on to second overall. Another 10 minutes of misery were heaped upon Vietto in the Dijon time trial. The doubters seemed to have been right.

For Maes – a protégé of Edmond Gentil at the Alcyon squad – this was a more personal victory than his 1936 victory. That had been a win for the Black Squadron, a team effort all the way. This time, the win was less about the leadership of Belgian *directeur sportif* Karel Steyaert who, early in the race, was critical of the way his riders were riding for themselves, not the team. No, this win was all about Maes's own careful planning, his decision to hold fire until the Izoard and win the Tour with one attack. This was a win very much for the man, not the team.

* * * * *

Though passing the reigns of power to Jacques Goddet, Henri Desgrange stayed involved with his race, still the Father of the Tour. Goddet, though, was beginning to make the race his own. One innovation he tried to introduce was the daily elimination of the *lanterne rouge*, the last man in the Tour's general classification. This was to run from the second stage onwards. At the end of the sixth stage Jean Majérus (Luxembourg), who had worn the yellow jersey in 1937 and 1938 was eliminated, the highest profile rider to be culled by this new rule. When the race reached Pau the next day the *lanterne rouge* was Amédée Fournier, the man who had donned the *maillot jaune* on the race's opening day and then added a second stage win, in Nantes. Fournier was too big a fish to throw away. So Goddet dropped the elimination rule.

Stage-by-Stage Results for the 1939 Tour de France			Stage	Maillot Jaune
Stage 1 Mon 10 Jul	Paris (Le Vésinet) to Caen 79 starters 79 finishers	6h21'27" 215 km 33.8 kph	Amédée Fournier (Fra) Nord-Est/Île-de-France	Amédée Fournier (Fra) Nord-Est/Île-de-France
Stage 2a Tue 11 Jul	Caen to Vire 78 finishers (ITT)	1h40'13" 64 km 38.0 kph	Romain Maes (Bel) Belgium	Romain Maes (Bel) Belgium
Stage 2b Tue 11 Jul	Vire to Rennes 78 finishers	3h10'45" 119 km 37.6 kph	Éloi Tassin (Fra) Ouest	Jean Fontenay (Fra) Ouest
Stage 3 Wed 12 Jul	Rennes to Brest 77 finishers	6h52'50" 244 km 35.5 kph	Pierre Cloarec (Fra) Ouest	Jean Fontenay (Fra) Ouest
Stage 4 Thu 13 Jul	Brest to Lorient 73 finishers	4h38'56" 174 km 37.4 kph	Raymond Louviot (Fra) France	René Vietto (Fra) Sud-Est
Stage 5 Fri 14 Jul	Lorient to Nantes 69 finishers	5h40'13" 207 km 36.5 kph	Amédée Fournier (Fra) Nord-Est/Île-de-France	René Vietto (Fra) Sud-Est
Stage 6a Sat 15 Jul	Nantes to La Rochelle 69 finishers	4h23'05" 144 km 32.8 kph	Lucien Storme (Bel) Belgium	René Vietto (Fra) Sud-Est
Stage 6b Sat 15 Jul	La Rochelle to Royan 65 finishers	3h00'23" 107 km 35.6 kph	Edmond Pagès (Fra) Sud-Ouest	René Vietto (Fra) Sud-Est
Sun 16 Jul	Rest Day			
Stage 7 Mon 17 Jul	Royan to Bordeaux 64 finishers	5h47'16" 198 km 34.2 kph	Raymond Passat (Fra) Sud-Ouest	René Vietto (Fra) Sud-Est
Stage 8a Tue 18 Jul	Bordeaux to Salies-de-Béarn 64 finishers	6h35'43" 210 km 31.9 kph	Marcel Kint (Bel) Belgium	René Vietto (Fra) Sud-Est
Stage 8b Tue 18 Jul	Salies-de-Béarn to Pau (ITT) 61 finishers	1h52'05" 69 km 36.7 kph	Karl Litschi (Sui) Switzerland	René Vietto (Fra) Sud-Est
Stage 9 Wed 19 Jul	Pau to Toulouse 52 finishers	10h23'27" 311 km 29.9 kph	Edouard Vissers (Bel) Belgium	René Vietto (Fra) Sud-Est
	Major climbs: Col d'Aubisque (1,709m) Edouard Vissers (Bel) Belgium; Col du Tourmalet (2,115m) Edouard Vissers (Bel) Belgium; Col d'Aspin (1,489m) Edouard Vissers (Bel) Belgium			
Thu 20 Jul	Rest Day			
Stage 10a Fri 21 Jul	Toulouse to Narbonne 52 finishers	4h07'35" 149 km 36.0 kph	Pierre Jaminet (Fra) France	René Vietto (Fra) Sud-Est

Stage-by-Stage Results for the 1939 Tour de France			Stage	Maillot Jaune
Stage 10b Fri 21 Jul	Narbonne to Béziers (ITT) 52 finishers	37'30" 27 km 43.2 kph	Maurice Archambaud (Fra) Nord-Est/Île-de-France	René Vietto (Fra) Sud-Est
Stage 10c Fri 21 Jul	Béziers to Montpellier 52 finishers	1h50'09" 70 km 38.4 kph	Maurice Archambaud (Fra) Nord-Est/Île-de-France	René Vietto (Fra) Sud-Est
Stage 11 Sat 22 Jul	Montpellier to Marseille 51 finishers	6h30'55" 212 km 32.5 kph	Fabien Galateau (Fra) Sud-Est	René Vietto (Fra) Sud-Est
Stage 12a Sun 23 Jul	Marseille to Saint-Raphaël 51 finishers	5h11'15" 157 km 30.3 kph	François Neuens (Lux) Luxembourg	René Vietto (Fra) Sud-Est
Stage 12b Sun 23 Jul	Saint-Raphaël to Monaco 51 finishers	3h34'20" 122 km 34.0 kph	Maurice Archambaud (Fra) Nord-Est/Île-de-France	René Vietto (Fra) Sud-Est
Stage 13 Mon 24 Jul	Monaco to Monaco 51 finishers	3h17'56" 101 km 30.8 kph	Pierre Gallien (Fra) Nord-Est/Île-de-France	René Vietto (Fra) Sud-Est
Major climbs: Col de Braus (1,002m) Sylvère Maes (Bel) Belgium				
Stage 14 Tue 25 Jul	Monaco to Digne 51 finishers	6h15'58" 175 km 27.9 kph	Pierre Cloarec (Fra) Ouest	René Vietto (Fra) Sud-Est
Stage 15 Wed 26 Jul	Digne to Briançon 50 finishers	8h24'20" 219 km 26.1 kph	Sylvère Maes (Bel) Belgium	Sylvère Maes (Bel) Belgium
Major climbs: Col d'Allos (2,250m) Edouard Vissers (Bel) Belgium; Col de Vars (2,110m) Edouard Vissers (Bel) Belgium; Col d'Izoard (2,360m) Sylvère Maes (Bel) Belgium				
Stage 16a Thu 27 Jul	Briançon to Bonneval-sur-Arc 50 finishers	5h04'39" 126 km 24.8 kph	Pierre Jaminet (Fra) France	Sylvère Maes (Bel) Belgium
Major climbs: Col du Galibier (2,556m) Dante Gianello (Fra) France; Col du Télégraphe (1,566m) René Vietto (Fra) Sud-Est				
Stage 16b Thu 27 Jul	Bonneval-sur-Arc to Bourg-Saint-Maurice (ITT) 50 finishers	1h55'41" 64 km 33.5 kph	Sylvère Maes (Bel) Belgium	Sylvère Maes (Bel) Belgium
Major climbs: Col de l'Iseran (2,770m) Sylvère Maes (Bel) Belgium				
Stage 16c Thu 27 Jul	Bourg-Saint-Maurice to Annecy 50 finishers	3h44'17" 104 km 27.7 kph	Antoon van Schendel (Ned) Netherlands	Sylvère Maes (Bel) Belgium
Major climbs: Col de Tamié (907m) Antoon van Schendel (Bel) Belgium				
Fri 28 Jul	Rest Day			

Stage-by-Stage Results for the 1939 Tour de France			Stage	Maillot Jaune
Stage 17a Sat 29 Jul	Annecy to Dôle 50 finishers	7h17'58" 226 km 31.0 kph	François Neuens (Lux) Luxembourg	Sylvère Maes (Bel) Belgium
	Major climbs: Col de la Faucille (1,323m) Sylvère Maes (Bel) Belgium			
Stage 17b Sat 29 Jul	Dôle to Dijon (ITT) 50 finishers	1h24'28" 59 km 41.9 kph	Maurice Archambaud (Fra) Nord-Est/Île-de-France	Sylvère Maes (Bel) Belgium
Stage 18a Sun 30 Jul	Dijon to Troyes 50 finishers	5h02'10" 151 km 30.0 kph	René le Grevès (Fra) Ouest	Sylvère Maes (Bel) Belgium
Stage 18b Sun 30 Jul	Troyes to Paris (Parc des Princes) 49 finishers	6h30'49" 201 km 30.9 kph	Marcel Kint (Bel) Belgium	Sylvère Maes (Bel) Belgium

Prize fund: 900,000 francs (first prize: 100,000 francs)

Final Classification				
Place	**Rider**	**Team**	**Time**	**Age**
1	Sylvère Maes (Bel)	Belgium	4,224 km 132h03'16" 31.986 kph	29
2	René Vietto (Fra)	Sud-Est	+ 30'38"	25
3	Lucien Vlaemynck (Bel)	Belgium B	+ 32'07"	24
4	Mathias Clemens (Lux)	Luxembourg	+ 36'08"	23
5	Edouard Vissers (Bel)	Belgium	+ 38'05"	27
6	Sylvain Marcaillou (Fra)	France	+ 45'15"	28
7	Albertin Disseaux (Bel)	Belgium B	+ 46'53"	24
8	Jan Lambrichs (Ned)	Netherlands	+ 48'00"	24
9	Albert Ritserveldt (Bel)	Belgium B	+ 48'27"	23
10	Cyriel Vanoverberghe (Bel)	Belgium B	+ 49'44"	27
Lanterne Rouge				
49	Armand le Moal (Bel)	Ouest	+ 4h26'39"	25
King of the Mountains				
	Sylvère Maes (Bel)	Belgium		29
Team				
		Belgium		

1940-45: Life During Wartime

One month after the 1939 Tour ended, Germany invaded Poland. Two days later, France – along with Great Britain – declared war on Germany. Sport was put on the back burner as the Great War resumed. But the war that came turned out to be a phoney war and, for the next eight months life went on pretty much as it had always gone on. And on too went plans for the 1940 Tour, with Henri Desgrange – still very much involved with the Tour he had fathered – even considering inviting a team of Americans to the race.

Plans for the 1940 Tour proceeded through the winter and into spring but, a week before the Giro d'Italia set off from Milan in the middle of May, the phoney war became a shooting war when Germany invaded France, Belgium, the Netherlands and Luxembourg. The Tour was very much put on hold. The Germans blitzkrieged France into submission and on 14 June – six weeks after the invasion began – Paris fell. A week later an armistice was signed between France and Germany. The shooting war was over and France entered the years of the Occupation. The country was divided into two zones, the north occupied and ruled by the Germans with the Vichy government of Marshal Pétain, the hero of Verdun, governing the south.

In August, in his villa on the Côte d'Azur, old age and illness finally caught up with Desgrange and the Father of the Tour died. Jacques Goddet, the closest thing he had to a son, took full charge of the editorial side of L'Auto and the organisation of its stable of sporting events. The actual ownership of L'Auto, though, was not in Goddet's hands.

Over the years since Jules-Albert (the Comte) de Dion had brought together a group of like-minded businessmen to launch *L'Auto-Vélo* in 1900 the majority shareholding had passed into the hands of Victor Goddet – the man who held *L'Auto-Vélo*'s purse strings when Géo Lefèvre first punted the idea of the Tour de France in 1902 – and Raymond Patenôtre. When Victor Goddet had died in 1926 the majority of his shares in *L'Auto* passed to his eldest son Maurice. Along with Patenôtre, Maurice Goddet cashed in his investment and their shares had been sold to a group of German industrialists. And so it was Germans who now controlled *L'Auto*.

In an effort to show that all was normal the German authorities sought to convince Goddet and his team at *L'Auto* to hold the Tour in 1941. Initially Goddet argued that sport and politics should not mix and the Tour should go on but, on mature reflection, he decided against reviving the Tour while France was occupied.

The following year, after Goddet yet again declined an invitation to bring back the Tour, the Germans turned to a former *L'Auto* staffer and manager of the 1937 Tour-winning France team, Jean Leulliot, then in charge of the right-wing newspaper *La France Socialiste*. Leulliot and his paper organised a week-long ersatz Tour, the Circuit de France. Between 29 September and 4 October, 69 riders covered 1,650 kilometres over six stages, running from Paris to Le Mans (won by Guy Lapébie), Poitiers (Frans Bonduel), Limoges (Georges Guiller), Clermont-Ferrand (Louis Caput), Saint-Étienne (François Neuville), Lyon (a team time trial won by Génial Lucifer), Dijon (Albert Goutal) and finishing back in Paris (Raymond Louviot), with Francois Neuville taking the overall win, ahead of Louis Thiétard and Luis Caput, and Pierre Brambilla talking the climbers' competition.

Goddet and his team at *L'Auto* responded by inviting their readers to create a fantasy French team to ride a fantasy Tour de France.

In November 1942 the Occupation was extended to the Vichy zone governed by Pétain when German and Italian troops invaded the south of the country.

For 1943, *L'Auto* decided to organise a season-long Grand Prix du Tour de France, running from the end of April to early September across nine races still being organised by the paper. The races were Paris-Roubaix (won by Marcel Kint), the GP de Provence (Émile Ídee), Paris-Dijon (Lucien de Guével), Paris-Reims (Jules Rossi), Paris-Tours (Gaby Gaudin), the Course dans Paris (André Declerck), the GP d'Auvergne (Jean-Marie Goasmat), the GP des Alpes (Dante Gianello) and the GP de l'Industrie du Cycle (Edouard Fachtleiner), with the overall title going to Jo Goutrobe.

The GP du Tour de France was again organised in 1944 but had to be cancelled when, in June, the Liberation of France commenced with the D-Day landings. In July, Caen fell to British and Canadian troops, although not much was left of the city as it was bombed almost out of existence by both sides. In August US troops waded ashore along the Côte d'Azur and on 25 June Paris was liberated. On 2 May 1945 Berlin surrendered and on 8 May Germany's final, formal surrender agreement was signed. The war was over and normal life could soon resume.

* * * * *

Through the years of the First World War, upwards of 50 veterans of the Tour had been killed in action. The Second World War took a much lighter toll on *les géants de la route*.

Over the five years of the conflict only a handful of stars of the Tour died, few of them as a direct consequence of the war. The Belgian Marcel Buysse – fourth in 1912, third in 1913 and the winner of six stages – died just as war was declared, 3 October, 1939. He was quickly followed by his compatriot Aloïs Catteau – tenth in 1903, third in 1904, sixth in 1906 and ninth in 1907 – who died on 1 November.

Another Belgian, Julien Vervaecke – third in 1927, fifth in 1928, eighth in 1929, and sixth in 1931 – died on 1 May, 1940.

On 18 March of the following year the man who had inherited victory in the 1904 Tour, Henri Cornet, and then gone on to add Paris-Roubaix to his *palmarès*, became the eighth Tour champion to die. Belgium's Louis Coolsaet – seventh in 1904 – died on 12 May the same year. Three months later France's Paul Duboc – fourth in 1909, second and winner of the climbers' prize in 1911 – was also dead.

In 1942 Julien Lootens – the school teacher who had been a star of the Six Day circuit and raced the inaugural Tour under the *nom de guerre* Samson, finishing seventh – died on 6 August.

The following year Jean Alavoine – third in 1909, fifth in 1912, third in 1914, second in 1919, second again in 1920, along with the climbers' competition – died on 18 July. Hippolyte Aucouturier – veteran of the first Tour, disqualified after the second, and second in the third – died on 22 April.

There are others – stage winners such as the German Heinz Wengler or Italy's Eugenio Gestry or Belgium's Lucien Storme – but the point is that, compared to the deaths during the Great War, they were few, and few were actually killed in fighting. Whereas the First War wiped out a generation of riders, the professional *peloton* was, largely, untouched by the Second. Even so, when the Tour returned, it would be with a new *peloton*, the old guard left behind by the war.

1946: The Race to Win the Tour de France

With France liberated and the war over, life – epitomised by the return of the Tour to the roads of France – should have got back to normal quickly. But France had a major problem to cope with: how to deal with those who had collaborated with their occupiers? One of the first official measures to deal with this was to shut down every newspaper that had continued to print during the Occupation. *L'Auto* was no more.

New licences were issued and new papers rose from the ashes of old, but those initial licenses were only for general-interest papers. Newsprint was in too short supply to immediately justify the frivolity of the sporting press. That changed in early 1946, and a number of licences were handed out for sports papers. Jacques Goddet – heir to Henri Desgrange's throne – secured one such licence for his new paper, *L'Équipe* (the team). It was *L'Auto* of old in all but name and the yellow newsprint Desgrange's paper had printed on. But it didn't own any of *L'Auto*'s old assets. In particular, it didn't own the Tour de France.

Organising a Tour in 1946 wasn't possible. France had too much rebuilding to do. But it was possible to try and capture some of the spirit of the Tour and two ersatz Tours were organised. In early July, *Ce Soir* – one of the pre-war general-interest newspapers to survive, having been banned during the Occupation because of its Communist leanings – organised La Ronde de France, running from Bordeaux to Paris and open to trade teams. For this venture *Ce Soir* partnered with the newly launched *Sports* newspaper. The 1,321-kilometre Ronde de France ran from 1 to 14 July, travelling from Bordeaux to Pau (where Elio Bertocchi won the stage), Toulouse (Giulio Breschi), Montpellier

(Raymond Louviot), Gap (Giulio Breschi) and finished in Grenoble (Apo Lazaridès), with Giulio Breschi taking the overall honours ahead of Elio Bertocchi and Edouard Fachtleiner.

In late July, *Le Parisien Libéré* – a general-interest newspaper launched by Émilien Amaury on the eve of the liberation of Paris – promoted La Course du Tour de France, running from Monaco to Paris and open to national and regional teams. In this Amaury teamed up with La Société du Parc des Princes, the company which controlled Paris's vélodromes and which was co-owned – and controlled in all but name – by Jacques Goddet. The 1,316-kilometre La Course du Tour de France ran from Monaco to Digne (Aldo Baito took that stage), Briançon (René Vietto), Aix-les-Bains (Jean Robic), Dijon (Adolfo Leoni) before finishing in Paris (Adolfo Leoni), with Apo Lazaridès taking the overall honours ahead of René Vietto and Jean Robic.

What then followed was a struggle for the soul of the Tour de France between the organisers of those two races. And it was struggle which, in many ways, was a microcosm of the struggle that was then ongoing for the soul of France itself, a struggle between the right and the left. *Ce Soir* and *Sports* were firmly on the left, Amaury and Goddet very much on the right.

Amaury was a self-made man who, the story goes, left home before he was a teenager and, associating himself with men of influence, quickly rose through the ranks of power. At the outset of the war he fought against the invading Germans. During the Occupation, Pétain gave him a role in the new Vichy regime, putting Amaury in charge of propaganda for the well-being of the family. Amaury, though, was a *résistant* (codenamed Jupiter) and used his position to help the cause. *Résistance* was not just about blowing things up; there was also the clandestine publishing of news and propaganda. Amaury was able to use his position within the Vichy power structure to help here, procuring newsprint and access to printing presses. One of these was *L'Auto*'s.

With the end of the Occupation in sight, Amaury became one of France's post-Occupation oligarchs, deciding to get into the newspaper and magazine business. From the ashes of *Le Petit Parisien*

– the newspaper which had published Albert Londres' denunciation of the Tour de France in 1924 – he created *Le Parisien Libéré*, which was initially housed in *Le Petite Parisien*'s former offices. Amaury added other titles to his embryonic empire, including a weekly magazine, *Carrefour*, in which Goddet invested. But for Amaury to have any involvement in the Tour's future, he had a minor problem to resolve: Goddet's behaviour during the war.

As a part of France's post-Occupation purge, Henri Desgrange's protégé was charged with collaboration. The seriousness of these charges should not be underestimated: more than 26,000 collaborators were sentenced to terms of imprisonment; more than 13,000 were sentenced to hard labour; as many as 7,000 death sentences were handed down (although fewer than 800 of them were actually carried out). One man of the press who received the ultimate sanction was Albert Lejeune, publisher of the Paris-based *Le Petit Journal* and the Nice-based *Le Petit Niçois*. Lejeune was creator, in 1933, of Paris-Nice, and the man who was responsible for the sale of Raymond Patenôtre's shares in *L'Auto* to the Germans.

Two important issues arose with regard to Goddet's war record: the issue of whether Goddet had shown excessive zeal in following the orders of *L'Auto*'s new German owners when they required that the paper should have a pro-Vichy and pro-German stance; and Goddet's actions during what has come to be known as the Raffle du Vél d'Hiv. The latter was the 1942 round-up by French police in Paris of more than 10,000 non-national Jews – men, women and children – and their subsequent deportation to concentration camps. Many of them were held for nearly a week at the Vélodrome d'Hiver, originally built and owned by Henri Desgrange and Victor Goddet. Jacques Goddet was the man in charge of the stadium when the round-up commenced. When the authorities asked him to hand over the keys, he complied.

Amaury and others spoke in Goddet's defence during his trial and, set against the criticism levelled at him, was the fact that Amaury had had access to *L'Auto*'s presses for *résistance* purposes. Goddet was, eventually, cleared of the collaboration charges. (Jean Leulliot – who had organised the 1943 Circuit de France and would later go on to take control of Paris-Nice – also faced collaboration charges and was also cleared, having, Goddet among others, speaking in his favour.)

With two ersatz Tours having been run in the summer of 1946, the fight proper for the soul of the Tour de France commenced in the autumn when the French cycling federation and the UCI received two rival applications to run three-week stages races in France in 1947. *Ce Soir* put in an application for the Ronde de France, to run from 20 June to 14 July. La Société du Parc des Princes put in an application to run the Tour de France from 24 June to 20 July. Two rival national tours, running at the same time? Someone would have to lose. At its December 1946 congress the UCI granted the calendar slot to the Tour de France.

The new UCI-sanctioned Tour de France was to be run by the Goddet-controlled La Société du Parc des Princes, with Amaury's *Le Parisien Libéré* as financial partner. But, before the war, La Société du Parc des Princes was co-owned by *L'Auto* and the assets of *L'Auto* were now owned by the state, through the Société Nationale des Entreprises de Presse (SNEP). In collaboration with the Fédération Nationale de la Presse Française (FNPF) the SNEP therefore claimed title to the newly-sanctioned Tour through *L'Auto*'s 49.5% stake in La Société du Parc des Princes. Having been shunned by the UCI in their attempt to win the Tour's calendar slot, *Ce Soir* and *Sports* then publicly called on the FNPF to organise the 1947 Tour itself, with the FNPF's member journals underwriting some of the costs.

Émilien Amaury, though, was busy behind the scenes spiking the guns of *Ce Soir* and *Sports*. Using all the political clout he had available to him, he convinced the SNEP and the FNPF to ignore *Ce Soir* and *Sports* and grant full control of the Tour to La Société du Parc des Princes, leaving it up to them to decide how to finance the race.

La Société du Parc des Princes was not without suitors offering to come on board and shoulder the financial burden of running the Tour. In the end – just weeks before the 1947 Tour commenced – two were chosen: *L'Équipe* and *Le Parisien Libéré*. Jacques Goddet had finally and categorically won the battle to secure the rights of the Tour for *L'Auto*'s spiritual successor, *L'Équipe*. But the victory came at a cost: he had to cede 50% of the race to Émilien Amaury.

1947: A New Beginning

While the real fight for the soul of the Tour de France had been won privately, behind closed doors, Émilien Amaury using his clout in Gaullist circles to bring about the outcome that most favoured himself and Jacques Goddet, much of the French media had kept the rest of the struggle in public view. Unseemly as it may have been at times, right and left having at one and other, the public squabbling did at least serve to keep the race in the public's gaze even during its absence.

On the morning of Wednesday 25 June 1947, an estimated 300,000 people thronged the streets of Paris to watch the Tour end its seven-year absence and the 100 riders of the thirty-fourth Tour set out on their 4,642-kilometre loop of the country, set off on their way by the French boxing star Marcel Cerdan. All that was need now was a race worthy of the weight of expectation, a fight for the *maillot jaune* equal to the fight for the Tour itself.

The returned Tour was the same Tour as before, yet in many ways it was one that was quite different. *L'Auto* was gone, replaced by *L'Équipe*. Henri Desgrange was in his grave, leaving his protégé Jacques Goddet free to fully impose his own personality on the race. And Goddet's new business partner Émilien Amaury ordered that the race was to cease solely being a marketing stunt to sell more newspapers and, financially, should stand on its own two feet. Given the state of the post-war French economy, that would take time. The first casualty of this new financial imperative was the bikes the riders rode on: out went the Tour-provided anonymous yellow bikes of the pre-war years, and the manufacturers were allowed return to the race, even if the riders still rode for national and regional teams.

Perhaps the biggest difference, though, was in the make up of the *peloton*. When the race returned in 1919 after its Great War hiatus half the field – 34 of 67 riders – had already started at least one Tour. In all, more that 70 veterans of pre-Great War Tours returned to the race at least once. But of the 100 riders who assembled to set out in 1947 only 13 had already started at least one Tour. In subsequent years they would be joined by just six other veterans of pre-war Tours. A new generation was about to bring a new sensibility to the Tour, rebuild it in their image and show that they were the equal of *les géants de la route* of the past.

Leading that fight was a giant of the past, one of the Tour's great nearly men, René Vietto, *le Roi René*, the man whose noble sacrifice in 1934 had touched the hearts of a generation. Vietto was part of a mix of young and old stars making up the France squad and on the race's second stage he threw down his marker and claimed the leadership of the team with a 130 kilometre solo attack that won him the stage and allowed him relieve Ferdi Kübler (of the mixed Switzerland/Luxembourg squad) of the race lead.

In so many of the post-1934 Tours Vietto had squandered his chances of overall victory by losing time in the race's opening stages. But here he was, in 1947, attacking when an attack was least expected. This was a Vietto who looked like he had built on the form that had taken him to second overall in Amaury and Goddet's Le Course du Tour de France the year before. This was a Vietto who looked like he was finally set to win the Tour, make up for the hurt of 1939 and prove right those who believed he could have won in 1934.

Vietto, though, was not the only man with his eyes on the big prize and in the first part of the race his biggest rival was Aldo Ronconi, of the Italy squad. The Italians were without their two biggest stars of the moment – Gino Bartali and Fausto Coppi – who had declined invitations to take on the Tour, fearing that the French were not yet ready to greet their former foes (and invaders) warmly. Ronconi's Italian team was, instead, a ragbag of Italian and expatriate Italian riders, bossed not by Costante Giradengo, who had led Bartali to victory in 1938, but by a journalist from *La Gazzetta dello Sport*, Guido Giardini.

And it was a team in name only, with Ronconi expressing his belief that the expatriate riders – in particular Pierre Brambilla, who had won the climber's prize in Jean Leulliot's Circuit de France in 1943 and three years later finished eighth in *Ce Soir's* Ronde de France and seventh in La Course du Tour the France – were scared of how they would be greeted upon their return to their homes in France after the Tour if they were seen working for an Italian victory.

Ronconi himself was not going to be put off by what the French public thought and took on the fight alone. As Vietto had on the second stage, the Italian attacked alone on the third and after a 100-kilometre escape ended the day second overall, a minute and a half off Vietto in yellow. For the next three days, as the Tour rolled toward its first rest day, in Lyon, and the eve of the race's first appointment with the high hills, the French and Italian challengers held fire.

In the Alps, over relatively minor climbs like the Cucheron and Port, *le Roi René* crumbled, the youthful climber of 1934 overtaken by age (he was by now 33 years old) and Ronconi claimed yellow. But, though he might have been blessed with talent, the Italian was not blessed with team-mates willing to defend his lead. Two stages after losing the jersey, Vietto bounced back over the Col d'Allos and reclaimed the *maillot jaune*. And held on to it in the Pyrenees, even when faced with unexpected events such as one of *L'Équipe's* planes crashing onto the road ahead of him as he climbed the Tourmalet.

But Vietto still had one fatal weakness to overcome: he couldn't time-trial for toffee, and Goddet and his team had thrown a monster 139-kilometre race against the clock at the riders. The team time trial stages of the 1920s had been longer, sure, but this was the longest solo time trial the Tour had yet forced upon its riders. And Vietto suffered, ending the day fourth overall, more than five minutes off the new race leader, Pierre Brambilla.

Born in Switzerland of Italian parents, Brambilla was French in all but the passport he carried. A solid climber who was also a capable time trialist, the Tour now seemed to be his, with just two stages separating him from a lap of honour in the Parc des Princes. The first of those two stages went off as quietly as expected, but the final day's racing – which, by now, was already turning into a processional ride into Paris – saw fireworks. And the man lighting the blue touch paper was Jean Robic (Ouest).

Robic had had a solid Tour, the sort that would normally have hinted at good things to come in the years ahead. He'd won three stages, into Strasbourg after a solo breakaway and in Grenoble and Pau after two good days in the Alps and Pyrenees. But that good day in the Alps had been followed by a bad one: he gained six minutes on the yellow jersey in Grenoble, and then lost them the very next day. In the Pyrenees, though, Robic clawed himself back to just over eight minutes off yellow, and managed to hold on to that position. In the time trial he finished second, faster than Vietto, Brambilla or Ronconi. Robic was now within three minutes of Brambilla's yellow jersey, in third on General Classification(GC), with Ronconi just over two minutes ahead of him in second. And that was where he stood when he seized his opportunity on the final stage.

About 70 kilometres into the final stage, a group of seven riders went up the road, a couple of them regional riders, a couple from the Belgium squad, a couple from the Switzerland/Luxembourg team and one from the France squad. None were a threat to the yellow jersey, and so the *peloton* was happy to let them off the leash and, within 50 kilometres, they had a lead of more than 10 minutes built up. It was at this point, on a minor climb near Rennes, that Robic attacked. He immediately opened a gap on Brambilla, but then the Italian responded. At which point Edouard Fachleitner (France) made his move.

Fachleitner had started the stage fifth overall, seven minutes off yellow, four behind Robic. And he now had a team-mate more than 10 minutes up the road, who would be able to drop back and help him. Robic's podium place was being challenged. So he responded to the attack. And he and Fachleitner dropped Brambilla. Now it was a race for the yellow jersey. Robic, holding the better GC position, offered Fachleitner a deal: work with him and earn a podium place (and a nice pay off), work against him and get nothing.

Fachleitner decided that something was better than nothing and the two pushed on.

For Brambilla, this was a problem, but it shouldn't have been serious. He had Ronconi just behind him. But even with Ronconi's help, the Robic-Fachleitner tandem was opening up a sizeable gap. Within 25 kilometres, still more than 100 kilometres out from Paris, they had the thick end of two minutes. By Paris, that gap had grown to more than 13 minutes. Brambilla lost the Tour, Fachleitner climbed up to second overall and Robic – who hadn't worn the *maillot jaune* once during the Tour – took the final jersey. The fight to own the Tour was matched by a Tour just as exciting and just as full of intrigue.

Stage-by-Stage Results for the 1947 Tour de France			Stage Winner	Maillot Jaune
Stage 1 Wed 25 Jun	Paris (Pierrefitte) to Lille 100 starters 99 finishers	236 km 6h51'55" 34 kph	Ferdi Kübler (Sui) Switzerland/ Luxembourg	Ferdi Kübler (Sui) Switzerland/ Luxembourg
Stage 2 Thu 26 Jun	Lille to Brussels 89 finishers	182 km 5h05'52" 36 kph	René Vietto (Fra) France	René Vietto (Fra) France
Stage 3 Fri 27 Jun	Brussels to Luxembourg 73 finishers	314 km 10h59'13" 29 kph	Aldo Ronconi (Ita) Italy	René Vietto (Fra) France
Stage 4 Sat 28 Jun	Luxembourg to Strasbourg 72 finishers	223 km 8h14'29" 27 kph	Jean Robic (Fra) Ouest	René Vietto (Fra) France
Stage 5 Sun 29 Jun	Strasbourg to Besançon 71 finishers	248 km 8h10'45" 30 kph	Ferdi Kübler (Sui) Switzerland/ Luxembourg	René Vietto (Fra) France
Stage 6 Mon 30 Jun	Besançon to Lyon 69 finishers	249 km 6h55'37" 36 kph	Lucien Teisseire (Fra) France	René Vietto (Fra) France
Tue 1 Jul	Rest day			
Stage 7 Wed 2 Jul	Lyon to Grenoble 66 finishers	172 km 5h29'46" 31 kph	Jean Robic (Fra) Ouest	Aldo Ronconi (Ita) Italy
Major climbs: Col de l'Epine (987m) Apo Lazaridès (Fra) Sud-Est; Col du Granier (1,134m) Pierre Brambilla (Ita) Italy; Col du Cucheron (1,139m) Jean Robic (Fra) Ouest; Col de Porte (1,326m) Jean Robic (Fra) Ouest				

Stage-by-Stage Results for the 1947 Tour de France			Stage Winner	Maillot Jaune
Stage 8 Thu 3 Jul	Grenoble to Briançon 62 finishers	185 km 6h49'07" 27 kph	Fermo Camellini (Ita) Netherlands/Etrangers de France	Aldo Ronconi (Ita) Italy
	Major climbs: Col du Glandon (1,924m) Edouard Klabinski (Pol) Netherlands/Etrangers de France; Col de la Croix de Fer (2,067m) Fermo Camellini (Ned) Netherlands/Etrangers de France; Col du Télégraphe (1,566m) Fermo Camellini (Ned) Netherlands/Etrangers de France; Col du Galibier (2,556m) Fermo Camellini (Ned) Netherlands/Etrangers de France			
Fri 4 Jul	Rest day			
Stage 9 Sat 5 Jul	Briançon to Digne 60 finishers	217 km 7h23'15" 29 kph	René Vietto (Fra) France	René Vietto (Fra) France
	Major climbs: Col d'Izoard (2,360m) Jean Robic (Fra) Ouest; Col de Vars (2,110m) Jean Robic (Fra) Ouest; Col d'Allos (2,250m) René Vietto (Fra) France			
Stage 10 Sun 6 Jul	Digne to Nice 58 finishers	255 km 8h07'59" 31 kph	Fermo Camellini (Ita) Netherlands/Etrangers de France	René Vietto (Fra) France
	Major climbs: Col de Braus (1,002m) Apo Lazaridès (Fra) Sud-Est; Col de Castillon (706m) Fermo Camellini (Ned) Netherlands/Etrangers de France; La Turbie (555m) Fermo Camellini (Ned) Netherlands/Etrangers de France			
Stage 11 Mon 7 Jul	Nice to Marseille 58 finishers	230 km 6h31'00" 35 kph	Édouard Fachleitner (Fra) France	René Vietto (Fra) France
Stage 12 Tue 8 Jul	Marseille to Montpellier 58 finishers	165 km 4h57'40" 33 kph	Henri Massal (Fra) France	René Vietto (Fra) France
Wed 9 Jul	Rest day			
Stage 13 Thu 10 Jul	Montpellier to Carcassonne 57 finishers	172 km 5h18'35" 32 kph	Lucien Teisseire (Fra) France	René Vietto (Fra) France
Stage 14 Fri 11 Jul	Carcassonne to Luchon 57 finishers	253 km 8h10'11" 31 kph	Albert Bourlon (Fra) Centre/Sud-Ouest	René Vietto (Fra) France
	Major climbs: Col de Port (1,249m) Albert Bourlon (Fra) Centre/Sud-Ouest; Col de Portet d'Aspet (1,069m) Albert Bourlon (Fra) Centre/Sud-Ouest			
Sat 12 Jul	Rest day			
Stage 15 Sun 13 Jul	Luchon to Pau 55 finishers	195 km 6h46'11" 29 kph	Jean Robic (Fra) France	René Vietto (Fra) France
	Major climbs: Col de Peyresourde (1,569m) Jean Robic (Fra) Ouest; Col d'Aspin (1,489m) Jean Robic (Fra) Ouest; Col du Tourmalet (2,115m) Jean Robic (Fra) Ouest; Col d'Aubisque (1,709m) Jean Robic (Fra) Ouest			
Stage 16 Mon 14 Jul	Pau to Bordeaux 55 finishers	195 km 5h41'39" 34 kph	~~Pietro Tarchini (Sui)~~ ~~Switzerland/~~ ~~Luxembourg (1)~~ Giuseppe Tacca (Ita) Italy	René Vietto (Fra) France

Stage-by-Stage Results for the 1947 Tour de France			Stage Winner	Maillot Jaune
Stage 17￼Tue 15 Jul	Bordeaux to Les Sables-d'Olonne 54 finishers	272 km 8h59'05" 30 kph	Éloi Tassin (Fra) Ouest	René Vietto (Fra) France
Stage 18￼Wed 16 Jul	Les Sables-d'Olonne to Vannes 54 finishers	236 km 7h10'07" 33 kph	Pietro Tarchini (Sui) Switzerland/ Luxembourg	René Vietto (Fra) France
Stage 19￼Thu 17 Jul	Vannes to Saint-Brieuc (ITT) 54 finishers	139 km 3h49'36" 36 kph	Raymond Impanis (Bel) Belgium	Pierre Brambilla (Ita) Italy
Stage 20￼Fri 18 Jul	Saint-Brieuc to Caen 53 finishers	235 km 6h23'37" 37 kph	Maurice Diot (Fra) Île-de-France	Pierre Brambilla (Ita) Italy
Sat 19 Jul	Rest day			
Stage 21￼Sun 20 Jul	Caen to Paris (Parc des Princes) 53 finishers	257 km 7h16'13" 35 kph	Albéric Schotte (Bel) Belgium	Jean Robic (Fra) Ouest

(1) Pietro Tarchini was stripped of the stage win for an irregular sprint.

Prize fund: 4,580,000 francs (first prize: 500,000 francs)

Final Classification				
Place	**Rider**	**Team**	**Time**	**Age**
1	Jean Robic (Fra)	Ouest	4,642 km 148h11'25" 31.412 kph	26
2	Édouard Fachleitner (Fra)	France	+ 3'58"	26
3	Pierre Brambilla (Ita)	Italy	+ 10'07"	28
4	Aldo Ronconi (Ita)	Italy	+ 11'00"	28
5	René Vietto (Fra)	France	+ 15'23"	33
6	Raymond Impanis (Bel)	Belgium	+ 18'14"	21
7	Fermo Camellini (Ita)	Netherlands/ Etrangers de France	+ 24'08"	32
8	Giordano Cottur (Ita)	Italy	+ 1h06'03"	33
9	Jean-Marie Goasmat (Fra)	Ouest	+ 1h16'03"	34
10	Apo Lazaridès (Fra)	Sud-Est	+ 1h18'44"	21
Lanterne Rouge				
53	Pietro Tarchini	Switzerland/ Luxembourg	+ 7h48'18"	25
King of the Mountains				
	Pierre Brambilla (Ita)	Italy		28
Team				
		France		

1948: The Best Rider, The Best Race

The Tour was already, incontestably, the premier road race on the cycling calendar. But that calendar was far from perfect. For many years people had been arguing for its reform, some way of putting some shape on it and ensuring that the best riders rode the best races – and giving fans some way of identifying what really were the best races – but no one had made much of an effort to try and take control. In 1948 *L'Équipe* and *La Gazzetta dello Sport* stepped up to the plate and, along with the Belgian papers *Het Nieuwsblad-Sportwereld* and *Les Sports* set about linking key races they organised and creating a season-long league – the Challenge Desgrange-Colombo, named after Henri Desgrange and Emilio Colombo, fathers of the Tour de France and the Giro d'Italia.

The initial races included in the Challenge Desgrange-Colombo were Milan-Sanremo (*La Gazzetta* – 29/3/1948), Paris-Roubaix (*L'Équipe* – 4/4/1948), Paris-Brussels (*L'Équipe* – 11/4/1948), the Ronde van Vlaanderen (*Het Nieuwsblad* – 18/4/1948), the Flèche Wallonne (*Les Sports* – 21/4/1948), Paris-Tours (*L'Équipe* – 25/4/1948), the Giro d'Italia (*La Gazzetta* – 15/5/1948 to 6/6/1948), the Tour de France (*L'Équipe* – 30/6/1948 to 25/7/1948), and the Giro di Lombardia (*La Gazzetta* – 24/10/1948).

The one problem the *grande boucle* faced was that, for too many of its winners, the Tour was the only major mark on their *palmarès*. Jean Robic had been French cyclo-cross champion, Sylvère Maes had won Paris-Roubaix three years before the first of his two Tour victories, and Roger Lapébie's best wins before his Tour victory had come in Paris-Nice and the Critérium National, as well as a couple of Six Day races on the track. Romain Maes had no major wins on his *palmarès* before his Tour win, and Georges Speicher's *palmarès* was similarly sparse, though he did immediately back up his Tour win by winning the World Championships.

Even 'great' riders such as André Leducq and Antonin Magne had mostly built their reputations in the Tour (Leducq did win Paris-Roubaix before his first Tour win). In essence, the Tour had become somewhat divorced from the rest of the calendar, lost its links with races such as Paris-Roubaix and Bordeaux-Paris. By creating a new season-long challenge that encouraged the best riders to ride the same races, the prestige of those riders would rise and thus add further prestige to the races included in the calendar.

The Challenge Desgrange-Colombo also served another purpose: by protecting the included races it sought to limit the prestige of other races, particularly those organised by rival publishers. Some of those other races, such as Paris-Nice or the Grand Prix des Nations, prospered regardless. Others, such as the Tour de Suisse, Liège-Bastogne-Liège and the Vuelta a España, would eventually join the Challenge. Many others, though, simply fell by the wayside, unable to compete against the Challenge's cartel.

Most people, of course, didn't need something like the Challenge Desgrange-Colombo to identify the best riders of the moment. It was clear to everyone that they were the Italians Gino Bartali and Fausto Coppi. Between them they had won Milan-Sanremo (Bartali 1939, 1940 and 1947; Coppi 1946 and 1948), the Giro d'Italia (Bartali 1936, 1937 and 1946; Coppi 1940 and 1947), the Tour de France (Bartali 1938) and the Giro di Lombardia (Bartali 1939 and 1940, Coppi 1946 and 1947).

By the summer of 1948 both were in need of a win at the Tour as much as the Tour was in need of one of them winning it. At the Giro the two Italians had marked each other out of the race, enabling Fiorenzo Magni to earn victory. But putting the two Italian champions on the same national team at the Tour seemed like a recipe for disaster. In the end Coppi solved that problem by deciding to skip the Tour, leaving Bartali as the clear leader of an Italian squad, bossed by the great Alfredo Binda.

Bartali's win in 1948 has gone down in legend, not just for the fact that no one has ever won the Tour with a 10-year gap between victories (Philippe Thys went six years between his second and third wins, seven between first and last). Most of the win's fame, though, rests on the belief that it stopped a civil war breaking out in Italy.

Bartali opened his account at the 1948 Tour by claiming the *maillot jaune* on the opening stage. Far too early to defend all the way to Paris, but a solid statement of intent and the next day he surrendered the race lead to Jan Engels of the Aiglons Belges – Belgian Eaglets – squad, who was then superseded by one of the coming men of French cycling, Louison Bobet.

Bobet briefly lost the race lead but then scrambled his way back to the top with a stage win in Biarritz. Arriving in Cannes at the end of the twelfth stage – the Pyrenees behind him, the Alps ahead – Bobet took his second Tour stage win and held a narrow lead of 2'29" over the Belgian Roger Lambrecht, riding for the mixed Internationaux team. And away down in seventh place, more than 20 minutes off Bobet's time, was the Italian champion Bartali.

Bartali had ceded a quarter of an hour to Bobet on the third stage, where the Frenchman donned the *maillot jaune*, the Italians perhaps not considering the up-and-coming French star to be much of a threat so early in the race (in his first full season as professional Bobet had had to abandon the 1947 Tour in tears in the Alps). Bobet's win in Biarritz gave him a lead of 20'51" over Bartali. Winning both of the Pyrenean stages brought Bartali back to 18'18" off Bobet.

Then the Frenchman had a bad day on the road to Marseille, a boil on his foot hampering him and he only narrowly held on to his overall lead (reduced to just 29 seconds over Lambrecht). Bartali, taking advantage of his foe's distress, closed to 11'49" off yellow. On the road to Cannes Bobet launched a counter-offensive and it was Bartali's turn to have a bad day, punctures hampering him, and the yellow-jerseyed Frenchman widened the gap to the Italian to 21'28".

The Tour already seemed to be over for the 34-year-old Bartali, and the French were already dreaming of a new star winning the

Tour: the 23-year-old Bobet, who just had a few Belgians to put in their place in order to be assured of victory. And then came one of the Tour's most famous rest days, in Cannes.

It was Bastille Day, Wednesday 14 July 1948. As the morning drew to a close, across the Alps from Cannes, Palmiro Togliatti, leader of the Italian Communist Party, was leaving the parliament building when a would-be assassin put three bullets in his chest. When news of the assassination attempt was broadcast on radio workers around the country downed tools and took to the streets. Back in Cannes, Italian journalists broke the news to Bartali and told him they had been called back to Italy. That evening Bartali received a phone call from the Italian Prime Minister and leader of the Christian Democrats, Alcide de Gasperi, with whom he was friends. De Gasperi spoke to Bartali of what was happening in Italy. They also talked about the Tour and Bartali's prospects, with De Gasperi wishing his friend well and asking that he bring victory home to Italy.

The next day the Tour resumed, the stage taking the riders up to Briançon, via the Allos, Vars and Izoard. Bobet's team-mate and defending champion Jean Robic went on the attack and led over the first two climbs, his own dreams of yellow more important than Bobet's, who was nearly four minutes down the road by the top of the Vars.

Three minutes ahead of Bobet was Bartali, who launched an attack on the Izoard that saw him soloing to his third stage win of the Tour. Bobet was more than 18 minutes down on the day, having lost time on the Izoard with a broken pedal and problems with his replacement bike, and only held on to his yellow jersey by 1'06" over Bartali, who had taken two minutes in bonifications and had leaped up to second place overall. The news was well received in Italy, where order was already returning to the streets. (As for Vietto, who had attacked at the start of the day, he crumbled on the Izoard and finished the stage 10 minutes behind Bartali.)

The next day, on the road to Aix-les-Bains, Bartali again went on the offensive, and Bobet again crumbled in the mountains, losing seven minutes on the road, and the yellow jersey along with them.

With another two minutes in bonifications taken off his time, Bartali now held the *maillot jaune* by eight minutes.

And then Bartali did it for a third time, on the road to Lausanne, the Italian taking his third stage on the trot, his fifth of the Tour, and putting another four minutes into Bobet on the road and another minute in bonifications.

What followed was a victory parade for Bartali and more ignominy for Bobet, the great French hope tumbling to fourth overall, more than half an hour in arrears of his Italian rival.

Stage-by-Stage Results for the 1948 Tour de France			Stage Winner	Maillot Jaune
Stage 1 Wed 30 Jun	Paris (Saint-Cloud) to Trouville 120 starters 117 finishers	237 km 6h50'24" 34.6 kph	Gino Bartali (Ita) Italy	Gino Bartali (Ita) Italy
Stage 2 Thu 1 Jul	Trouville to Dinard 114 finishers	259 km 7h29'55" 34.5 kph	Vincenzo Rossello (Ita) Italy	Jan Engels (Bel) Aiglons Belges
Stage 3 Fri 2 Jul	Dinard to Nantes 110 finishers	251 km 6h48'31" 36.9 kph	Guy Lapébie (Fra) Centre/Sud-Ouest	Louison Bobet (Fra) France
Stage 4 Sat 3 Jul	Nantes to La Rochelle 106 finishers	166 km 4h01'42" 41.2 kph	Jacques Pras (Fra) Centre/Sud-Ouest	Roger Lambrecht (Bel) Internationaux
Stage 5 Sun 4 Jul	La Rochelle to Bordeaux 104 finishers	262 km 7h03'32" 37.1 kph	Raoul Remy (Fra) Sud-Est	Roger Lambrecht (Bel) Internationaux
Stage 6 Mon 5 Jul	Bordeaux to Biarritz 100 finishers	244 km 6h27'14" 37.8 kph	Louison Bobet (Fra) France	Louison Bobet (Fra) France
Stage 7 Tue 6 Jul	Biarritz to Lourdes 94 finishers	219 km 6h40'47" 32.8 kph	Gino Bartali (Ita) Italy	Louison Bobet (Fra) France
	Major climbs: Col d'Aubisque (1,709m) Bernard Gauthier (Fra) Sud-Ouest			
Wed 7 Jul	Rest day			
Stage 8 Thu 8 Jul	Lourdes to Toulouse 90 finishers	261 km 8h27'25" 30.9 kph	Gino Bartali (Ita) Italy	Louison Bobet (Fra) France
	Major climbs: Col du Tourmalet (2,115m) Jean Robic (Fra) France; Col d'Aspin (1,489m) Jean Robic (Fra) France; Col de Peyresourde (1,569m) Jean Robic (Fra) France; Col des Ares (797m) Jean Robic (Fra) France			
Fri 9 Jul	Rest day			

Stage-by-Stage Results for the 1948 Tour de France			Stage Winner	Maillot Jaune
Stage 9 Sat 10 Jul	Toulouse to Montpellier 85 finishers	246 km 6h03'01" 40.7 kph	Raymond Impanis (Bel) Belgium	Louison Bobet (Fra) France
Stage 10 Sun 11 Jul	Montpellier to Marseille 79 finishers	248 km 6h55'40" 35.8 kph	Raymond Impanis (Bel) Belgium	Louison Bobet (Fra) France
Stage 11 Mon 12 Jul	Marseille to Sanremo 77 finishers	245 km 7h23'53" 33.1 kph	Gino Sciardis (Ita) Internationaux	Louison Bobet (Fra) France
Stage 12 Tue 13 Jul	Sanremo to Cannes 70 finishers	170 km 5h22'56" 31.6 kph	Louison Bobet (Fra) France	Louison Bobet (Fra) France
	Major climbs: Col de Castillon (706m) Roger Lambrecht (Bel) Internationaux; Col de Turini (1,607m) Louison Bobet (Fra) France			
Wed 14 Jul	Rest day			
Stage 13 Thu 15 Jul	Cannes to Briançon 63 finishers	274 km 10h09'28" 27.0 kph	Gino Bartali (Ita) Italy	Louison Bobet (Fra) France
	Major climbs: Col d'Allos (2,250m) Jean Robic (Fra) France; Col de Vars (2,110m) Jean Robic (Fra) France; Col d'Izoard (2,360m) Gino Bartali (Ita) Italy			
Stage 14 Fri 16 Jul	Briançon to Aix-les-Bains 51 finishers	263 km 9h30'18" 27.7 kph	Gino Bartali (Ita) Italy	Gino Bartali (Ita) Italy
	Major climbs: Col du Galibier (2,556m) Lucien Teisseire (Fra) France; Col de la Croix de Fer (2,067m) Gino Bartali (Ita) Italy; Col de Porte (1,326m) Gino Bartali (Ita) Italy; Col du Cucheron (1,139m) Gino Bartali (Ita) Italy; Col du Granier (1,134m) Gino Bartali (Ita) Italy			
Sat 17 Jul	Rest day			
Stage 15 Sun 18 Jul	Aix-les-Bains to Lausanne 50 finishers	256 km 8h29'55" 30.1 kph	Gino Bartali (Ita) Italy	Gino Bartali (Ita) Italy
	Major climbs: Col des Aravis (1,498m) Gino Bartali (Ita) Italy; Col de la Forclaz (1,527m) Apo Lazaridès (Fra) France			
Stage 16 Mon 19 Jul	Lausanne to Mulhouse 47 finishers	243 km 6h44'07" 36.1 kph	Edward van Dijck (Bel) Belgium	Gino Bartali (Ita) Italy
	Major climbs: Vue des Alpes (1,283m) Gino Bartali (Ita) Italy			
Stage 17 Tue 20 Jul	Mulhouse to Strasbourg (ITT) 46 finishers	120 km 2h55'17" 41.1 kph	Roger Lambrecht (Bel) Internationaux	Gino Bartali (Ita) Italy
Stage 18 Wed 21 Jul	Strasbourg to Metz 45 finishers	195 km 5h54'37" 33.0 kph	Giovanni Corrieri (Ita) Italy	Gino Bartali (Ita) Italy

Stage-by-Stage Results for the 1948 Tour de France			Stage Winner	Maillot Jaune
Thu 22 Jul	Rest day			
Stage 19 Fri 23 Jul	Metz to Liège 44 finishers	249 km 7h18'55" 34.0 kph	Gino Bartali (Ita) Italy	Gino Bartali (Ita) Italy
Stage 20 Sat 24 Jul	Liège to Roubaix 44 finishers	228 km 6h31'36" 34.9 kph	Bernard Gauthier (Fra) Sud-Est	Gino Bartali (Ita) Italy
Stage 21 Sun 25 Jul	Roubaix to Paris (Parc des Princes) 44 finishers	286 km 9h01'51" 31.7 kph	Giovanni Corrieri (Ita) Italy	Gino Bartali (Ita) Italy

Prize fund: 7,000,000 francs (first prize: 600,000 francs)

Final Classification				
Place	Rider	Team	Time	Age
1	Gino Bartali (Ita)	Italy	4,922 km 147h10'36" 33.442 kph	34
2	Albéric Schotte (Bel)	Belgium	+ 26'16"	28
3	Guy Lapébie (Fra)	Centre/Sud-Ouest	+ 28'48"	31
4	Louison Bobet (Fra)	France	+ 32'59"	23
5	Jeng Kirchen (Lux)	Netherlands/ Luxembourg	+ 37'53"	28
6	Lucien Teisseire (Fra)	France	+ 40'17"	28
7	Roger Lambrecht (Bel)	Internationaux	+ 49'56"	32
8	Fermo Camellini (Ita)	Internationaux	+ 51'36"	33
9	Louis Thiétard (Fra)	Paris	+ 55'23"	38
10	Raymond Impanis (Bel)	Belgium	+ 1h00'03"	22
Lanterne Rouge				
44	Vittorio Seghezzi (Ita)	Italian Cadets	+ 4h26'43"	24
King of the Mountains				
	Gino Bartali (Ita)	Italy		34
Team				
		Belgium		

1949: Doing the Double

In the 40 years the Tour de France and Giro d'Italia had co-existed, no reigning Giro champion had immediately followed up his success at the *corsa rosa* with a win in the *grande boucle*. Across the 28 times the double had been possible, it had actually only been tried five times, starting with Luigi Ganna in 1909 who was followed by Giuseppe Enrici in 1924, Antonio Pesenti in 1932, Vasco Bergamaschi in 1935, and Gino Bartali in 1937. Only Enrici and Pesenti had actually managed to finish the Tour, both just off the podium in fourth place overall, the other three had each failed to finish, Bartali's withdrawal in 1937 probably the most well-known.

Doing the double was not without difficulties. The Giro averaged about 3,500 kilometres – compared to the Tour's 5,000 – and there were typically only three or four weeks between the two races (it had varied between 11 and 54 days). Recovering between the two races was obviously a problem to be overcome. But the bigger reason not to follow a Giro win with the Tour was money: the Giro winner received invitations to road and track races up and down Italy, each coming with generous appearance fees. Tackling the Tour meant taking a gamble and passing up guaranteed short-term wealth for the possibility of a larger medium term pay-off.

In 1949 though, for Fausto Coppi the lure of a tilt at the Tour after his win at the Giro was too enticing, for pulling off the double would firmly put clear blue water between him and his Italian rival, Gino Bartali, in terms of successes.

Coppi had burst on to the Italian cycling scene in 1940, when he'd been signed as a *gregario* – an Italian *domestique* – for Bartali at Legnano, the dominant Italian trade team. At that year's Giro

– which had a shorter war-time hiatus than its French cousin – Coppi was the surprise victor, and it was clear that Bartali, the champion of Italian cycling, had a real rival. Through the rest of the war years each won his share of races still being organised, but with Coppi adding the Hour record to his *palmarès* in 1942 he seemed to be edging ahead.

Through 1946 to 1947 the two seemed to be trading wins: Coppi took Milan-Sanremo while Bartali took the Giro; the following year Bartali took Milan-Sanremo while Coppi took the Giro. In 1948 they seemed set to follow the same script, Coppi opening the season with *la primavera*, but at the *corsa rosa* the two were so determined to stop each other winning that Fiorenzo Magni was able to steal the victory from out of their pockets. Bartali responded by adding a second Tour win to his *palmarès*, Coppi was left to lick his wounds.

Coppi struck back in 1949 by taking his third victory in Milan-Sanremo and then, at the Giro, pulling off the victory with an epic stage win in Pinerolo having soloed over the Vars, Izoard and Sestriere passes. Then came the lure of the Tour, starting just 19 days after the Giro ended. Not just a chance to do the double, but also a chance of the first win for a Tour debutant since the early days of the race.

For the 1949 Tour Jacques Goddet and his team at *L'Équipe* stuck with more or less the same route as the previous two editions, with the usual minor tweaks as different towns and cities outbid one and other to host the race. The riders headed west from Paris and then down France's Atlantic seaboard (all the way to San Sebastián, across the border in Spain), before turning east across the Pyrenees and (after a trip across the Italian border to Sanremo) up to Colmar by way of the Alps, before heading back to Paris by way of Nantes.

Financially, the new Tour was quickly attracting new sponsors. The wool company Les Laines Sofil had come on the year before as sponsors of the yellow jersey (which, since 1947, was now sporting the initials of Henri Desgrange, in memory of the late Father of the Tour). Vitteloise joined as sponsors of the King of the Mountains competition, while the bill for the team prize was being picked up by Martini. While the race was still important when it came to

Fausto Coppi rides to victory in the 1949 Tour.

selling newspapers – *L'Équipe* had average circulation of about 600,000 copies – the race was now very much entering the TV age, with live coverage of the finale in the Parc des Princes having started the year before. In 1949 came a five-times-a-week evening news programme covering the Tour. And the story they told was about Fausto Coppi.

Putting Coppi and Bartali on the same team could have been a recipe for disaster. The French and the Belgian national teams had both seen Tour dreams shattered by disunity in their ranks (the united front shown by the French in the first few years of the national team format had soon disappeared). But Alfredo Binda was in a different class. A former rider himself – one of Italy's champions of champions – he understood his riders. And so, before the Tour started, Coppi and Bartali and Binda sat down and thrashed out a deal. Each rider would get the same number of *domestiques* riding for him and each agreed the terms under which they could attack one another. All Binda had to worry about was getting them to stick to their deal.

For Coppi, the chance of Tour success almost ended on the fifth day of racing, Rouen to Saint-Malo. A group of regional riders – three Italians who had now taken out French citizenship, including Pierre Brambilla – went on the attack and Coppi decided to give chase, dragging along with him five other riders, including the yellow jersey of Jacques Marinelli (Île-de-France) and Switzerland's Ferdi Kübler. By Caen the breakaways had built up a nine-minute lead on the chasers behind. But in Caen Coppi crashed, damaging his bike. And Coppi cracked, mentally, thinking Binda, who was behind with Bartali, was favouring *Il Pio*. The Italian team tried to get Coppi going, but the fight seemed to have left him. Even Bartali, when he caught up, waited and tried to egg him on, until Binda ordered him to press on. Bartali finished the stage five and a half minutes down on stage winner Kübler, while Coppi shed more than 18 minutes.

The next major appointment came on stage seven, a 92-kilometre time trial from Les Sables-d'Olonne to La Rochelle. There Coppi – who was the holder of the Hour record – clawed back five of the 13 minutes he had ceded to Bartali.

The eleventh stage saw the riders tackle the Pyrenees, with just one day's climbing scheduled. Coppi went on the attack over the Aubisque and Tourmalet, but missed out on the stage win, punctures slowing him down. Even so, he gained time on the road and more time in bonifications and closed to with two minutes of Bartali and within 15 minutes of the yellow jersey – which Fiorenzo Magni, riding for the Italian Cadets squad, had taken over the previous stage.

And then on Stage 16 – 18 July, Bartali's thirty-fifth Birthday – Coppi and Bartali simply rode away from the rest of the Tour on the Izoard, climbing through the Casse Déserte together, more like friends out for a ride than two Italian champions trying to outdo one another. It being his birthday, Bartali got the stage, with Coppi even waiting for him on the descent into Briançon when his great rival punctured. Cannily, though, Coppi had picked up more time bonuses than Bartali and closed to within 1'22" of yellow.

That he donned after the next stage, to Aosta, across the border in Italy, in front of his adoring fans (who, it must be said, presented a poor image, hurling stones and insults at the race convoy). This time when Bartali punctured and fell there were no favours, Binda telling Coppi to push on alone. Coppi took the stage and, between bonifications and time gained on the road, now led the Tour by just shy of four minutes, his team-mate Bartali in second.

More time was added in the final time trial, 137 kilometres from Colmar to Nancy, and *Il Campionissimo* rode into Paris's Parc des Princes, the first man to double the Italian and French Grand Tours.

Stage-by-Stage Results for the 1949 Tour de France			Stage Winner	Maillot Jaune
Stage 1 Thu 30 Jun	Paris (Livry-Gargan) to Reims 120 starters 118 finishers	182 km 5h13'59" 34.8 kph	Marcel Dussault (Fra) Centre/Sud-Ouest	Marcel Dussault (Fra) Centre/Sud-Ouest
Stage 2 Fri 1 Jul	Reims to Brussels 114 finishers	273 km 8h37'58" 31.6 kph	Roger Lambrecht (Bel) Belgium	Roger Lambrecht (Bel) Belgium
Stage 3 Sat 2 Jul	Brussels to Boulogne-sur-Mer 114 finishers	211 km 6h05'50" 34.6 kph	Norbert Callens (Bel) Belgium	Norbert Callens (Bel) Belgium
Stage 4 Sun 3 Jul	Boulogne-sur-Mer to Rouen 103 finishers	185 km 5h10'04" 35.8 kph	Lucien Teisseire (Fra) France	Jacques Marinelli (Fra) Île-de-France
Stage 5 Mon 4 Jul	Rouen to St Malo 92 finishers	293 km 8h27'13" 34.7 kph	Ferdi Kübler (Sui) Switzerland	Jacques Marinelli (Fra) Île-de-France
Stage 6 Tue 5 Jul	St. Malo to Les Sables-d'Olonne 88 finishers	305 km 8h39'07" 35.3 kph	Adolphe Deledda (Fra) Sud-Est	Jacques Marinelli (Fra) Île-de-France
Wed 6 Jul	Rest day			
Stage 7 Thu 7 Jul	Les Sables-d'Olonne to La Rochelle (ITT) 88 finishers	92 km 2h18'10" 39.9 kph	Fausto Coppi (Ita) Italy	Jacques Marinelli (Fra) Île-de-France
Stage 8 Fri 8 Jul	La Rochelle to Bordeaux 86 finishers	262 km 7h27'22" 35.1 kph	Guy Lapébie (Fra) France	Jacques Marinelli (Fra) Île-de-France
Stage 9 Sat 9 Jul	Bordeaux to San Sebastián 86 finishers	228 km 6h30'49" 35.0 kph	Louis Caput (Fra) Île-de-France	Jacques Marinelli (Fra) Île-de-France
Stage 10 Sun 10 Jul	San Sebastián to Pau 75 finishers	192 km 5h53'04" 32.6 kph	Fiorenzo Magni (Ita) Italian Cadets	Fiorenzo Magni (Ita) Italian Cadets
Mon 11 Jul	Rest day			
Stage 11 Tue 12 Jul	Pau to Luchon 70 finishers	193 km 7h06'22" 27.2 kph	Jean Robic (Fra) Ouest/Nord	Fiorenzo Magni (Ita) Italian Cadets
	Major climbs: Col d'Aubisque (1,709m) Fausto Coppi (Ita) Italy; Col du Tourmalet (2,115m) Fausto Coppi (Ita) Italy; Col d'Aspin (1,489m) Apo Lazaridès (Fra) France; Col de Peyresourde (1,569m) Jean Robic (Fra) Ouest/Nord			
Stage 12 Wed 13 Jul	Luchon to Toulouse 69 finishers	134 km 3h32'11" 37.9 kph	Rik van Steenbergen (Bel) Belgium	Fiorenzo Magni (Ita) Italian Cadets

Stage-by-Stage Results for the 1949 Tour de France			Stage Winner	Maillot Jaune
Stage 13 Thu 14 Jul	Toulouse to Nîmes 68 finishers	289 km 8h29'04" 34.1 kph	Emile Idée (Fra) Île-de-France	Fiorenzo Magni (Ita) Italian Cadets
Stage 14 Fri 15 Jul	Nîmes to Marseille 68 finishers	199 km 6h17'08" 31.7 kph	Jean Goldschmidt (Lux) Luxembourg	Fiorenzo Magni (Ita) Italian Cadets
Stage 15 Sat 16 Jul	Marseille to Cannes 65 finishers	215 km 6h02'29" 35.6 kph	Désiré Keteleer (Bel) Belgium	Fiorenzo Magni (Ita) Italian Cadets
Sun 17 Jul	Rest day			
Stage 16 Mon 18 Jul	Cannes to Briançon 62 finishers	275 km 10h25'35" 26.4 kph	Gino Bartali (Ita) Italy	Gino Bartali (Ita) Italy
	Major climbs: Col d'Allos (2,250m) Fausto Coppi (Ita) Italy; Col de Vars (2,110m) Ferdi Kübler (Sui) Switzerland; Col d'Izoard (2,360m) Fausto Coppi (Ita) Italy			
Stage 17 Tue 19 Jul	Briançon to Aosta 59 finishers	257 km 9h08'48" 28.1 kph	Fausto Coppi (Ita) Italy	Fausto Coppi (Ita) Italy
	Major climbs: Col de Montgenèvre (1,860m) Gino Bartali (Ita) Italy; Mont Cenis (2,083m) Pierre Tacca (Fra) Île-de-France; Col de l'Iseran (2,770m) Pierre Tacca (Fra) Île-de-France; Col du Petit Saint-Bernard (2,188m) Gino Bartali (Ita) Italy			
Wed 20 Jul	Rest day			
Stage 18 Thu 21 Jul	Aosta to Lausanne 57 finishers	265 km 9h05'56" 29.1 kph	Vincenzo Rossello (Ita) Italy	Fausto Coppi (Ita) Italy
	Major climbs: Col du Grand Saint-Bernard (2,470m) Gino Bartali (Ita) Italy; Col des Mosses (1,448m) Jean Robic (Fra) Ouest/Nord			
Stage 19 Fri 22 Jul	Lausanne to Colmar 55 finishers	283 km 8h59'57" 31.5 kph	Raphaël Géminiani (Fra) France	Fausto Coppi (Ita) Italy
	Major climbs: Vue des Alpes (1,283m) Raphaël Géminiani (Fra) France			
Stage 20 Sat 23 Jul	Colmar to Nancy (ITT) 55 finishers	137 km 3h38'50" 37.6 kph	Fausto Coppi (Ita) Italy	Fausto Coppi (Ita) Italy
	Major climbs: Col du Bonhomme (950m) Fausto Coppi (Ita) Italy			
Stage 21 Sun 24 Jul	Nancy to Paris (Parc des Princes) 55 finishers	340 km 10h49'35" 31.4 kph	Rik van Steenbergen (Bel) Belgium	Fausto Coppi (Ita) Italy

Prize fund: 12,000,000 francs (first prize: 1,000,000 francs)

Final Classification

Place	Ride	Team	Team	Age
1	Fausto Coppi (Ita)	Italy	4,808 km 149h40'49" 32.121 kph	29
2	Gino Bartali (Ita)	Italy	+ 10'55"	35
3	Jacques Marinelli (Fra)	Île-de-France	+ 25'13"	23
4	Jean Robic (Fra)	Ouest/Nord	+ 34'28"	28
5	Marcel Dupont (Bel)	Aiglons Belges	+ 38'59"	31
6	Fiorenzo Magni (Ita)	Italian Cadets	+ 42'10"	28
7	Stan Ockers (Bel)	Belgium	+ 44'35"	29
8	Jean Goldschmit (Lux)	Luxembourg	+ 47'24"	25
9	Apo Lazaridès (Fra)	France	+ 52'28"	23
10	Pierre Cogan (Fra)	Ouest/Nord	+ 1h08'55"	35

Lanterne Rouge

55	Guido de Santi (Ita)	Italy	+ 6h07'21"	26

King of the Mountains

	Fausto Coppi (Ita)	Italy		29

Team

		Italy		

1950: The Year of the Swiss

In Carol Reed's 1949 film of Graham Greene's *The Third Man*, Orson Welles says that five hundred years of democracy and peace in Switzerland had produced nothing more than the cuckoo clock. Well they also produced Ferdi Kübler, who went on to win the 1950 Tour de France. Perhaps, then, it is fitting that the man who set the 116 riders of the thirty-seventh Tour de France off on their 26-day tour of the French countryside was none other than Welles himself. Even more appropriately, right up until the moment Kübler donned the *maillot jaune*, this Tour was actually about the third man of Italian cycling, Fiorenzo Magni.

Kübler had a string of Swiss pursuit and road titles to his name and had already won both of his country's home tours – the Tour de Suisse (1942 and 1948) and the Tour de Romandie (1948). On his Tour de France debut in 1947 he'd bagged a couple of stage wins and, briefly, worn the yellow jersey. He was clearly a rising talent and, along with his compatriot Hugo Koblet – who won the 1950 Giro d'Italia and followed that up with a win at the Tour de Suisse, which ended just six days before the Tour started – was at the forefront of a new wave of Swiss cycling talent. But, when it came to picking favourites for the 1950 Tour, he was not most people's first choice.

Most people figured that the 1950 Tour would go, for the third time in succession, to Italy. Not to Fausto Coppi though. He had won Paris-Roubaix and the Flèche Wallonne earlier in the season and looked fighting fit, but in a crash at the Giro he broke his pelvis and he was ruled out of the Tour. That still left Coppi's great rival Gino Bartali who, though he would turn 36 during the Tour, had already won Milan-Sanremo earlier in the season. And it also left that third man of Italian cycling, Fiorenzo Magni, winner of the 1948 Giro and already the Lion of Flanders, having won the Ronde van Vlaanderen twice (1949 and 1950). As in 1949 when the Italian team had to find some way to fit both Coppi and Bartali in the same team, an agreement was drawn up between Bartali and Magni, giving each of them half of the squad as 'their' *gregari*. One or other of them, it seemed sure, was set to win the Tour.

In the race's opening stages French fans began to get annoyed by the tactics of the Italian riders. When Italians got into a break, they refused to share the workload, making the argument that they were riding for Bartali, not themselves. This is a normal racing tactic, understandable, though not well liked, particularly when the non-working rider takes the stage win, as Giovanni Corrierri did in Bordeaux on the Tour's fifth stage. But it was really annoying the French fans when it was coming from riders on the Italian Cadets squad, who weren't supposed to be riding for Bartali. The Cadets had taken the laurels on the second and third stages, into Liège and Lille, with Adolfo Leoni and Alfredo Pasotti taking the honours, and it was Pasotti's riding into Lille in particular that upset French fans. And when Pasotti pulled the same stunt on the ninth stage, into Bordeaux, French fans really got upset and booed the Italian.

The race really began to wake up when it entered the Pyrenees on the eleventh stage, with Bartali taking the win into Saint-Gaudens – over the Aubisque, Tourmalet and Aspen – and Magni donning the *maillot jaune*. In the race's general classification Magni held a 2'31" lead over Kübler – who had won the sixth stage's individual time trial, despite being handed a 15-second time penalty for wearing a silk jersey (having a woollen company sponsor the yellow jersey came with consequences) – and 3'20" over French hope Louison Bobet, with Bartali down in sixth, 4'17" off the lead. But events on the road to Saint-Gaudens saw Magni's stint in yellow come to a very sudden and unexpected end.

On the summit of the Col d'Aspin Bartali, Bobet and Jean Robic (riding for the regional Ouest squad) had tangled when Bartali tried to avoid a press motorcycle and crashed. In his version of the story of what happened next he was assaulted by French fans as he attempted to regain his feet, with one of those fans wielding a knife. Jacques Goddet himself had to wade it with a stick to push the fans back (an incident that echoed Géo Lefèvre on the Col de la République in the 1904 Tour). Bartali was furious and, despite going on to take the stage win, decided unilaterally that the Italian riders would not take the start the next day.

Bartali's version of events, though, is disputed. Yes, it is generally accepted, the fans in the Pyrenees had hurled abuse at him and other Italian riders. But the melee on the Aspin was explained as fans simply trying to help a fallen rider get up, and themselves falling over one and other. As for the knife, yes, it is said, it was there. But in the hands of a fan who was using it to slice some food he was eating. There was no threat to Bartali's life, just a simple – perhaps even understandable – misunderstanding.

Goddet and Alfredo Binda – the Italian squad's *director sportif* – tried to get Bartali to calm down and agree to ride on, but the Italian champion was not for turning. The lives of Italian riders were in danger, he insisted, and the only thing to do was for everyone to go home. And when Bartali said everyone, he meant everyone: he and his half of the Italian squad, as well as Fiorenzo Magni – in his new yellow jersey – and his half of the team. And the Italian Cadets, whose behaviour earlier in the race had fuelled the fury of the French fans in the first place.

There were shades of the 1937 Belgian withdrawal about Bartali's actions. That year the Belgian DS, Karel Steyaert, had seen the writing on the wall and seized on the opportunity to pull his team out of the race even when Sylvère Maes was in yellow, figuring a noble retreat was better than an ignoble defeat. For Bartali, Magni taking the yellow jersey had all but wiped out his own chances. And a win for Magni would damage Bartali's standing in Italian cycling (and, along with it, his earnings).

Magni, for his part, showed admirable loyalty to the Italian *tricolore* and accepted the team's decision to withdraw, even though it meant he wouldn't get a chance to actually race in the *maillot jaune*. And so for the fifth time in the race's history – after Maes in

1937, Victor Fontan in 1929, Francis Pélissier in 1927 and René Pottier in 1905 – the leader of the Tour was forced to exit. As a mark of respect to the manner in which he had taken over the race's lead, Kübler refused to wear the yellow jersey when the Tour set off from Saint-Gaudens the next morning.

Peace fell on the race for the next few stages as the Tour worked its way west and on to the next round of mountains, some of the riders even taking time to have a dip in the sea as the race approached Nice. The peace also enabled the Tour's first African team – North Africa, a mix of Moroccan and Algerian riders, some of French and Portuguese descent – to enjoy back-to-back stage wins in Nîmes and Toulon. With Franco-Italian relations on a low – questions were being asked in parliament in both countries – a planned excursion into Italy on the fifteenth stage was cancelled and the stage finish shifted from Sanremo to Menton.

Those peaceful stages were the undoing of French hopes. With Magni out of the race and Kübler in yellow the French had Bobet and Raphaël Géminiani sitting pretty and ready to offer a serious challenge, just 49 and 54 seconds off the lead when the stage from Saint-Gaudens to Perpignan ended. One day later the French duo were 10'58" and 11'03" off yellow and out of contention. Their downfall? Mechanical problems on the road to Nîmes, with their rivals taking full advantage of their misfortune to stuff time into them.

Kübler's chief rival now was Belgium's Constant 'Stan' Ockers, just 1'06" behind him (Pierre Brambilla, now a French citizen and riding for the regional Sud-Est squad, was in third, 9'01" in arrears). A stage win in Nice gave the Swiss star an extra minute, courtesy of bonifications. Ockers shadowed Kübler as best he could in the following stages, but the cowboy-hat loving Eagle of Adliswil kept picking up time bonuses and widening his lead, having 3'26" on the on the eve of the Tour's second and final individual time trial. That was the pre-penultimate stage and a mountainous affair that took in the Col de la Croix de Chaubouret, suiting Kübler far more than it did Ockers. When it was over the Swiss's overall lead had been pushed out to a virtually unassailable 9'30", allowing him to treat the final two stages as a coronation parade.

Obviously, Magni's withdrawal meant that some saw Kübler as having inherited the win, a modern-day Firmin Lambot. How Magni would have done had he refused to withdraw can only be guessed at. But with Binda as his *directeur sportif* and even half the Italian team at his disposal, you'd have to bet on him making a fight of it.

Stage-by-Stage Results for the 1950 Tour de France			Stage Winner	Maillot Jaune
Stage 1 Thu 13 Jul	Paris (Nogent-sur-Marne) to Metz 116 starters 116 finishers	307 km 9h23'08" 32.7 kph	Jean Goldschmit (Lux) Luxembourg	Jean Goldschmit (Lux) Luxembourg
Stage 2 Fri 14 Jul	Metz to Liège 116 finishers	241 km 7h02'07" 34.3 kph	Adolfo Leoni (Ita) Italian Cadets	Jean Goldschmit (Lux) Luxembourg
Stage 3 Sat 15 Jul	Liège to Lille 115 finishers	232.5 km 6h52'37" 33.8 kph	Alfredo Pasotti (Ita) Italian Cadets	Bernard Gauthier (Fra) Sud-Est
Stage 4 Sun 16 Jul	Lille to Rouen 113 finishers	231 km 7h12'26" 32.1 kph	Stan Ockers (Bel) Belgium	Bernard Gauthier (Fra) Sud-Est
Stage 5 Mon 17 Jul	Rouen to Dinard 110 finishers	316 km 10h35'51" 29.8 kph	Giovanni Corrieri (Ita) Italy	Bernard Gauthier (Fra) Sud-Est
Tue 18 Jul	Rest day			
Stage 6 Wed 19 Jul	Dinard to Saint-Brieuc (ITT) 104 finishers	78 km 1h57'22" 39.9 kph	Ferdi Kübler (Sui) Switzerland	Jean Goldschmit (Lux) Luxembourg
Stage 7 Thu 20 Jul	Saint-Brieuc to Angers 101 finishers	248 km 6h43'05" 36.9 kph	Nello Lauredi (Fra) France	Bernard Gauthier (Fra) Sud-Est
Stage 8 Fri 21 Jul	Angers to Niort 98 finishers	181 km 4h36'30" 39.3 kph	Fiorenzo Magni (Ita) Italy	Bernard Gauthier (Fra) Sud-Est
Stage 9 Sat 22 Jul	Niort to Bordeaux 94 finishers	206 km 5h30'25" 37.4 kph	Alfredo Pasotti (Ita) Italian Cadets	Bernard Gauthier (Fra) Sud-Est
Stage 10 Sun 23 Jul	Bordeaux to Pau 93 finishers	202 km 5h28'59" 36.8 kph	Marcel Dussault (Fra) Centre/Sud-Ouest	Bernard Gauthier (Fra) Sud-Est
Mon 24 Jul	Rest day			

Stage-by-Stage Results for the 1950 Tour de France			Stage Winner	Maillot Jaune
Stage 11 Tue 25 Jul	Pau to Saint-Gaudens 87 finishers	230 km 7h28'17" 30.8 kph	Gino Bartali (Ita) Italy	Fiorenzo Magni (Ita) Italy
	Major climbs: Col d'Aubisque (1,709m) Jean Robic (Fra) Ouest; Col du Tourmalet (2,115m) Kléber Piot (Fra) Île-de-France/Nord-Est; Col d'Aspin (1,489m) Kléber Piot (Fra) Île-de-France/Nord-Est			
Stage 12 Wed 26 Jul	Saint-Gaudens to Perpignan 70 finishers	233 km 6h29'13" 35.9 kph	Maurice Blomme (Bel) Belgium	Ferdi Kübler (Sui) Switzerland
Stage 13 Thu 27 Jul	Perpignan to Nîmes 64 finishers	215 km 6h22'56" 33.7 kph	Marcel Molinès (Alg) North Africa	Ferdi Kübler (Sui) Switzerland
Stage 14 Fri 28 Jul	Nîmes to Toulon 62 finishers	222 km 6h49'54" 32.5 kph	Custadio dos Reis (Fra) North Africa	Ferdi Kübler (Sui) Switzerland
Stage 15 Sat 29 Jul	Toulon to Menton 61 finishers	205.5 km 6h45'23" 30.4 kph	Bim Diederich (Lux) Luxembourg	Ferdi Kübler (Sui) Switzerland
	Major climbs: Mont des Mules (465m) Bim Diederich (Lux) Luxembourg			
Stage 16 Sun 30 Jul	Menton to Nice 59 finishers	96 km 3h02'54" 31.5 kph	Ferdi Kübler (Sui) Switzerland	Ferdi Kübler (Sui) Switzerland
	Major climbs: Col de Castillon (706m) Louison Bobet (Fra) France; Col de Turini (1,607m) Jean Robic (Fra) Ouest			
Mon 31 Jul	Rest day			
Stage 17 Tue 1 Aug	Nice to Gap 58 finishers	229 km 7h58'31" 28.7 kph	Raphaël Géminiani (Fra) France	Ferdi Kübler (Sui) Switzerland
	Major climbs: Col du Vasson (1,700m) Armand Baeyens (Bel) Aiglons Belges; Col de la Cayolle (2,326m) Jean Robic (Fra) Ouest; Col de la Sentinelle (980m) Raphaël Géminiani (Fra) France			
Stage 18 Wed 2 Aug	Gap to Briançon 53 finishers	165 km 6h09'20" 26.8 kph	Louison Bobet (Fra) France	Ferdi Kübler (Sui) Switzerland
	Major climbs: Col de Vars (2,110m) Louison Bobet (Fra) France; Col d'Izoard (2,360m) Louison Bobet (Fra) France			
Stage 19 Thu 3 Aug	Briançon to Saint-Étienne 53 finishers	291 km 8h49'11" 33.0 kph	Raphaël Géminiani (Fra) France	Ferdi Kübler (Sui) Switzerland
	Major climbs: Col du Lautaret (2,058m) Apo Lazaridès (Fra) France; Saint-Nizier (1,180m) Apo Lazaridès (Fra) France; Col de la République (Col du Grand Bois) (1,161m) Raphaël Géminiani (Fra) France			
Fri 4 Aug	Rest day			

Stage-by-Stage Results for the 1950 Tour de France			Stage Winner	Maillot Jaune
Stage 20 Sat 5 Aug	Saint-Étienne to Lyon (ITT) 51 finishers	98 km 2h29'35" 39.3 kph	Ferdi Kübler (Sui) Switzerland	Ferdi Kübler (Sui) Switzerland
	Major climbs: Col de la Croix de Chaubouret (1,230m) Ferdi Kübler (Sui) Switzerland			
Stage 21 Sun 6 Aug	Lyon to Dijon 51 finishers	233 km 6h42'38" 34.7 kph	Gino Sciardis (Fra) Ouest	Ferdi Kübler (Sui) Switzerland
Stage 22 Mon 7 Aug	Dijon to Paris (Parc des Princes) 51 finishers	314 km 9h36'12" 32.7 kph	Emile Baffert (Fra) France	Ferdi Kübler (Sui) Switzerland

Prize fund: 14,000,000 francs (first prize: 1,000,000 francs)

Final Classification				
Place	**Rider**	**Team**	**Time**	**Age**
1	Ferdi Kübler (Sui)	Switzerland	4,773 km 145h36'56" 32.778 kph	31
2	Stan Ockers (Bel)	Belgium	+ 9'30"	30
3	Louison Bobet (Fra)	France	+ 22'19"	25
4	Raphaël Géminiani (Fra)	France	+ 31'14"	25
5	Jean Kirchen (Lux)	Luxembourg	+ 34'21"	30
6	Kléber Piot (Fra)	Île-de-France/ Nord-Est	+ 41'35"	29
7	Pierre Cogan (Fra)	Centre/Sud-Ouest	+ 52'22"	36
8	Raymond Impanis (Bel)	Belgium	+ 53'34"	24
9	Georges Meunier (Fra)	Centre/Sud-Ouest	+ 54'29"	25
10	Jean Goldschmit (Lux)	Luxembourg	+ 55'21"	26
Lanterne Rouge				
51	Fritz Zbinden (Sui)	Switzerland	+ 4h'06'47"	28
King of the Mountains				
	Louison Bobet (Fra)	France		25
Team				
		Belgium		

1951: This Charming Man

When Émilien Amaury had stepped up and helped Jacques Goddet secure the future of the Tour de France in 1947 he did so at a price, half of the race. He also insisted that the Tour should in future be run as a business in its own right and no longer merely be about selling more newspapers. To this end he installed his own man, Félix Lévitan, to look after the business side of the race.

From the re-birth of the race in 1947 finances became more and more important: the race no longer supplied the bikes the riders rode on and, without towns and cities willing to pay for the privilege of hosting them, out went split stages. If towns and cities outside of France were willing to bid more than French towns to host stages, then the Tour would go to them: Brussels and Luxembourg in 1947, Liège and Sanremo in 1948, Brussels again in 1949 along with San Sebastián and Aosta, Liège again in 1950, Ghent in 1951. The bidding for the privilege of hosting the Tour took the race into the Massif Central in 1951, which brought the Tour's first crossing of the Ventoux. And in 1951 the bidding saw the Tour return to an idea tried only once before, back in 1926: starting the race outside of Paris, with Metz getting the honour of setting the Tour riders on their way.

Throughout the pre-Second World War history of the Tour, in France, stars of the road had been playing second fiddle to stars of the track. Track stars were cycling's aristocracy; road stars were lower-class. Looking at the two – the stars of the track in their wonderful silk jerseys, stars of the road covered in mud, their jerseys often torn – it's not hard to see how this could be. To some extent, the class war between the two was partly stoked by the sporting press. Road riders were *domestiques* – though Henri Desgrange, who coined the term, fought (in vain) to stop riders helping one and other – and they were *ouvriers de la pédale* (workers of the pedal, manual labourers).

The portrayal of road racers as working-class, while it might have fitted the labour the riders were performing, wasn't always very accurate when it came to the riders themselves. Stars from Louis Trousselier (the son of a florist) to Lucien Petit-Breton (the son of a jeweller) to Henri Pélissier and his brothers (the sons of a dairy owner) could be said to have been middle-class. Even the Tour's quintessential working-class hero, Maurice Garin, had left behind his chimney-sweep roots and become the owner of a bike shop in Roubaix with two of his brothers by the time the Tour was born. But the words written – and the photographs printed of the riders – reinforced the notion of them as being firmly lower-class.

This had begun to change, slowly, in the 1930s, when riders like Charles Pélissier and André Leducq came along, handsome men who the housewives could fall in love with. It really began to change when Fausto Coppi arrived on the scene, with his dark glasses and white gloves and an understanding that you had to look the part. Other riders quickly followed Coppi's example, and one with a brilliant understanding of the image he presented was Switzerland's Hugo Koblet, winner of the 1950 Giro d'Italia and the man who followed his compatriot Ferdi Kübler into the Tour de France's Hall of Fame.

Koblet was, like Kübler and Coppi before him, a national pursuit champion as well as a successful road rider. Unlike others, he also rode – and won – Six Day races, on both sides of the Atlantic. He was a rider with his feet in both camps, track and road, but it is on the road that he achieved his most lasting successes. And the most lasting of these came en route to winning the 1951 Tour, a day that has gone down in Tour legend, the 177-kilometre eleventh stage, Brive to Agen.

Roger Lévêque, of the regional Ouest/Sud-Ouest squad, was wearing the yellow jersey, having taken control of the race on the sixth stage. Raphaël Géminiani and Louison Bobet were at 6'44" and 8'31", Coppi further back, at 9'06", with Koblet at a comfortable

7'02" off the lead. In the two days before Brive-Agen the *peloton* had been through the hills of the Massif Central around Clermont-Ferrand (Géminiani's home town), with the Pyrenees to come on Stages 12, 13 and 14 and the Alps after that. It should have been a relatively quiet day in the Tour, the big guns saving their powder for the challenges to come.

Early into the stage Roger Castellan of the Est/Sud-Est squad went up the road with Louis Déprez of the Île-de-France/Nord-Ouest team. These were stages for the regional riders to shine, and they were taking every opportunity to do just that. Déprez dropped Castellan and powered on alone until another rider came up behind him: Koblet. With still 135 kilometres to go Koblet dropped Déprez and, alone, began to widen his gap on the *peloton* behind him.

The art of the breakaway is not to ride hard all day fighting to hold off the chasing group. The real effort comes in two parts: at the start of the break, when you open the gap, and at the end of the stage when you try to profit from your labour. In between, the trick is to hold the gap steady, keep the *peloton* believing they can catch you when they finally begin their chase. And Koblet did just that, building his lead up to four minutes and then holding it there.

Behind, in the *peloton*, the riders were happy enough with the situation and rode along at a comfortable pace. Bobet was able to drop out of the back of the bunch with a puncture and get back on again without any major effort. At about 70 kilometres from the finish the chase began, the Italians (Coppi and his team-mates Gino Bartali and Fiorenzo Magni) and the French (Géminiani and Bobet) winding things up and trying to eat into Koblet's lead. But to no avail. They pulled back two minutes but were still 2'35" behind Koblet when they arrived in Agen.

In those two minutes at the finish in Agen Koblet had time to comb his hair and clean his face for the cameras. In Émilien Amaury's *Le Parisien Libéré* the singer Jacques Grello coined a new nickname for the Swiss star that has come to define the man: *le pédaleur de charme*.

Koblet didn't take the yellow jersey that day in Agen, Lévêque doing enough to get one more day in the *maillot jaune*. But one more day was all it proved to be, for the next day Wim van Est – of the Netherlands squad – got away in a break that allowed him to build up a huge lead, 18 minutes at the finish, and took the lead, the first Dutch rider to lead the Tour. He too, though, only lasted one day in yellow, and not even a full day at that. For in the Pyrenees the next day, while descending the Col d'Aubisque, Van Est went over the edge of the road and dropped down the mountain, freefalling until a tree arrested his descent. When his Dutch team car came to the spot where he fell they had to fashion a rope from their spare tyres and, attaching that to their car's tow rope, hauled Van Est up the 70 metres he had fallen.

The lead then fell to Gilbert Bauvin, from the Île-de-France/Nord-Ouest team, on a day that should have brought glory to Géminiani. He had crossed the finish line in Dax first and should have taken two minutes in bonifications, on top of the nine minutes his group had on the riders behind – who included Koblet, Coppi and Bobet – but got bumped down to fourth after the commissaires took a look at the way he had sprinted, which they didn't like. Even so, the advantage had swung to Gém, who now had a 6'38" lead over Koblet and 12'17" on Coppi and 14'19" on Bobet.

The Tour was decided on the next stage, the fourteenth, Tarbes to Luchon, taking in the Tourmalet, the Aspen and the Peyresourde. It may have been Bartali's birthday but there were to be no gifts for him, not this year. From the start it was Coppi on the offensive, but with him went Koblet. Over the summit of the Tourmalet the Italian had a slight advantage but the two went up the Aspin and Peyresourde together. Behind, the others chased, in vain. Gém had lost more than three minutes before the summit of the Peyresourde and lost another three on the run in to Luchon, where Koblet had narrowly beaten Coppi for the stage, and the greater share of the bonifications. Which finally put Koblet in yellow, 21 seconds up on Bauvin, 32 seconds on Géminiani, and 5'09" on Bobet.

The *pédaleur de charme* added to his lead two days later, taking his fourth stage of the race in Montpellier on a day when Coppi suffered a *défaillance* and lost more than half an hour, and any lingering hope of taking a second Tour win.

In the Alps, over the Vars and the Izoard, Coppi took some consolation by taking the stage win in Briançon, and Koblet put more time into Géminiani, stretching his lead out to a safe 9'02", which grew to 22'00" after the Swiss star took his second time trial victory of the race in Geneva, securing the victory and adding a second Grand Tour – on top of his 1950 Giro win – to his *palmarès*.

Stage-by-Stage Results for the 1951 Tour de France			Stage Winner	Maillot Jaune
Stage 1 Wed 4 Jul	Metz to Reims 123 starters 123 finishers	185 km 5h23'10" 34.3 kph	Giovanni Rossi (Sui) Switzerland	Giovanni Rossi (Sui) Switzerland
Stage 2 Thu 5 Jul	Reims to Ghent 118 finishers	228 km 6h28'54" 35.2 kph	Bim Diederich (Lux) Luxembourg	Bim Diederich (Lux) Luxembourg
Stage 3 Fri 6 Jul	Ghent to Le Tréport 117 finishers	219 km 7h04'14" 31.0 kph	Georges Meunier (Fra) Ouest/Sud-Ouest	Bim Diederich (Lux) Luxembourg
Stage 4 Sat 7 Jul	Le Tréport to Paris 115 finishers	188 km 4h42'15" 40.0 kph	Roger Lévêque (Fra) Ouest/Sud-Ouest	Bim Diederich (Lux) Luxembourg
Stage 5 Sun 8 Jul	Paris to Caen 115 finishers	215 km 6h09'34" 34.9 kph	Serafino Biagioni (Ita) Italy	Serafino Biagioni (Ita) Italy
Stage 6 Mon 9 Jul	Caen to Rennes 111 finishers	182 km 5h22'10" 33.9 kph	Édouard Muller (Fra) France	Roger Lévêque (Fra) Ouest/Sud-Ouest
Stage 7 Tue 10 Jul	La Guerche to Angers (ITT) 99 finishers	85 km 2h05'40" 40.6 kph	Hugo Koblet (Sui) Switzerland	Roger Lévêque (Fra) Ouest/Sud-Ouest
Stage 8 Wed 11 Jul	Angers to Limoges 98 finishers	241 km 7h08'20" 33.8 kph	André Rosseel (Bel) Belgium	Roger Lévêque (Fra) Ouest/Sud-Ouest
Thu 12 Jul	Rest day			
Stage 9 Fri 13 Jul	Limoges to Clermont Ferrand 97 finishers	236 km 6h59'40" 33.7 kph	Raphaël Géminiani (Fra) France	Roger Lévêque (Fra) Ouest/Sud-Ouest
	Major climbs: Col de la Moreno (1,065m) Raphaël Géminiani (Fra) France; Col de Ceyssat (1,076m) Raphaël Géminiani (Fra) France			
Stage 10 Sat 14 Jul	Clermont Ferrand to Brive 94 finishers	216 km 6h35'15" 32.8 kph	Bernardo Ruiz (Esp) Spain	Roger Lévêque (Fra) Ouest/Sud-Ouest
	Major climbs: Col de la Croix-Morand (1,401m) Bernardo Ruiz (Esp) Spain; La Roche Vendeix (1,139m) Bernardo Ruiz (Esp) Spain; Puy de Bort (840m) Bernardo Ruiz (Esp) Spain			

Stage-by-Stage Results for the 1951 Tour de France			Stage Winner	Maillot Jaune
Stage 11 Sun 15 Jul	Brive to Agen 92 finishers	177 km 4h32'41" 38.9 kph	Hugo Koblet (Sui) Switzerland	Roger Lévêque (Fra) Ouest/Sud-Ouest
Stage 12 Mon 16 Jul	Agen to Dax 92 finishers	185 km 5h00'25" 36.9 kph	Wim van Est (Ned) Netherlands	Wim van Est (Ned) Netherlands
Stage 13 Tue 17 Jul	Dax to Tarbes 89 finishers	201 km 5h47'57" 34.7 kph	~~Raphaël Géminiani (Fra)~~ ~~France (1)~~ Serafino Biagioni (Ita) Italy	Gilbert Bauvin (Fra) Île-de-France/ Nord-Ouest
Major climbs: Col d'Aubisque (1,709m) Raphaël Géminiani (Fra) France				
Stage 14 Wed 18 Jul	Tarbes to Luchon 85 finishers	142 km 4h41'41" 30.2 kph	Hugo Koblet (Sui) Switzerland	Hugo Koblet (Sui) Switzerland
Major climbs: Col du Tourmalet (2,115m) Bim Diederich (Lux) Luxembourg; Col d'Aspin (1,489m) Fausto Coppi (Ita) Italy; Col de Peyresourde (1,569m) Fausto Coppi (Ita) Italy				
Stage 15 Thu 19 Jul	Luchon to Carcassonne 77 finishers	213 km 6h22'01" 33.5 kph	André Rosseel (Bel) Belgium	Hugo Koblet (Sui) Switzerland
Major climbs: Col des Ares (797m) José Serra (Esp) Spain; Col de Portet d'Aspet (1,069m) Gino Bartali (Ita) Italy				
Stage 16 Fri 20 Jul	Carcassonne to Montpellier 75 finishers	192 km 5h27'14" 35.2 kph	Hugo Koblet (Sui) Switzerland	Hugo Koblet (Sui) Switzerland
Sat 21 Jul	Rest day			
Stage 17 Sun 22 Jul	Montpellier to Avignon 75 finishers	224 km 7h24'44" 30.2 kph	Louison Bobet (Fra) France	Hugo Koblet (Sui) Switzerland
Major climbs: Mont Ventoux (1,909m) Lucien Lazaridès (Fra) France				
Stage 18 Mon 23 Jul	Avignon to Marseille 73 finishers	173 km 4h56'46" 35.0 kph	Fiorenzo Magni (Ita) Italy	Hugo Koblet (Sui) Switzerland
Stage 19 Tue 24 Jul	Marseille to Gap 73 finishers	208 km 7h15'41" 28.6 kph	Armand Baeyens (Bel) Belgium	Hugo Koblet (Sui) Switzerland
Major climbs: Col de la Sentinelle (980m) Armand Baeyens (Bel) Belgium				
Stage 20 Wed 25 Jul	Gap to Briançon 71 finishers	165 km 5h34'04" 29.6 kph	Fausto Coppi (Ita) Italy	Hugo Koblet (Sui) Switzerland
Major climbs: Col de Vars (2,110m) Fausto Coppi (Ita) Italy; Col d'Izoard (2,360m) Fausto Coppi (Ita) Italy				

Stage-by-Stage Results for the 1951 Tour de France			Stage Winner	Maillot Jaune
Stage 21 Thu 26 Jul	Briançon to Aix-les-Bains 69 finishers	201 km 6h45'24" 29.7 kph	Bernardo Ruiz (Esp) Spain	Hugo Koblet (Sui) Switzerland
	Major climbs: Col du Lautaret (2,058m) Gino Sciardis (Fra) Île-de-France/Nord-Est; Côte de Laffrey (900m) Gino Bartali (Ita) Italy; Col de Porte (1,326m) Bernard Gauthier (Fra) France; Col du Cucheron (1,139m) Bernard Gauthier (Fra) France; Col du Granier (1,134m) Bernardo Ruiz (Esp) Spain			
Stage 22 Fri 27 Jul	Aix-les-Bains to Geneva (ITT) 66 finishers	97 km 2h39'45" 36.4 kph	Hugo Koblet (Sui) Switzerland	Hugo Koblet (Sui) Switzerland
Stage 23 Sat 28 Jul	Geneva to Dijon 66 finishers	197 km 6h11'32" 31.8 kph	Germain Derijcke (Bel) Belgium	Hugo Koblet (Sui) Switzerland
	Major climbs: Col de la Faucille (1,323m) Gino Bartali (Ita) Italy			
Stage 24 Sun 29 Jul	Dijon to Paris (Parc des Princes) 66 finishers	322 km 9h58'19" 32.3 kph	Adolphe Deledda (Fra) Île-de-France/ Nord-Ouest	Hugo Koblet (Sui) Switzerland

(1) Raphaël Géminiani was stripped of the stage win because of an irregular sprint

Prize fund: 18,278,000 francs (first prize: 1,000,000 francs)

Final Classification				
Place	Rider	Team	Time	Age
1	Hugo Koblet (Sui)	Switzerland	4,690 km 142h20'14" 32.949 kph	26
2	Raphaël Géminiani (Fra)	France	+ 22'00"	26
3	Lucien Lazaridès (Fra)	France	+ 24'16"	28
4	Gino Bartali (Ita)	Italy	+ 29'09"	37
5	Stan Ockers (Bel)	Belgium	+ 32'53"	31
6	Pierre Barbotin (Fra)	France	+ 36'40"	24
7	Fiorenzo Magni (Ita)	Italy	+ 39'14"	30
8	Gilbert Bauvin (Fra)	Est/Sud-Est	+ 45'53"	23
9	Bernardo Ruiz (Esp)	Spain	+ 45'55"	26
10	Fausto Coppi (Ita)	Italy	+ 46'51"	31
Lanterne Rouge				
66	Abd El Kader Zaaf (Alg)	North Africa	+ 4h58'18"	34
King of the Mountains				
	Raphaël Géminiani (Fra)	France		26
Team				
		France		

1952: Doubling the Double

The Metz *grand départ* in 1951 having been deemed a success, the 1952 Tour again followed the money and started outside the City of Lights, this time in Brest, on the western tip of Brittany. The Tour was more popular than ever, with TV serving up three daily news programmes covering the race – as well as radio providing increased coverage too – generating more publicity for the Tour, and increasing its value to host towns.

The major innovation of the 1952 Tour was summit finishes. Pretty much from the moment mountains first appeared in the Tour the organisers realised that, while they could be decisive, their impact was often diluted by the distance between the last major climb and the finish town, which allowed non-climbers to regain time lost to the true *grimpeurs*. Bonifications were brought in to help counter this, the first rider over designated summits getting a time bonus. But, short of moving the mountains closer to the stage finish, there was nothing much that could be done to really help the *grimpeurs*. Yes, of course, you could move the finish closer to the mountain, that was obvious. But who would pay for that? The towns and cities paying to host the Tour's stages wanted the Tour to finish in their town or city, not on some lonely mountain miles out of town.

Or at least that was the case until 1952. The first thing to change was that there were people who had a reason to pay for a stage to end on a mountain: the operators of ski resorts, and first up to the plate were operators of the resorts at l'Alpe d'Huez and Sestriere. They were joined by the good burghers of Clermont-Ferrand – home to the Michelin tyre company – who had hosted the Tour the previous year for the first time and in 1952 were happy to pay for a stage to finish on the slopes of an extinct volcano 10 kilometres west of the city, the Puy de Dôme. And on each of those three summit finishes, one man reigned supreme: *il Campionisimo*, Fausto Coppi, who came into the Tour on the back of his fourth success at the Giro d'Italia.

The first week of the Tour had seen Belgium's Rik van Steenbergen wear the yellow jersey for two stages before Nello Lauredi – Italian-born, but now a French citizen and a member of the national squad – took control of the race. Fiorenzo Magni, riding as part of the Italian national squad, took the jersey from Lauredi, who then took it back, only for Magni to take it again in the Vosges. The next day Magni's team-mate Andrea Carrea donned the jersey in the Jura, on the eve of the Tour's first summit finish at Alpe d'Huez. There the cream rose to the top, and Coppi donned the jersey.

At the end of that stage Coppi held the *maillot jaune* by five seconds over team-mate Carrea, 1'50" over Magni and 5'11" over Lauredi. Two Belgian riders, Alex Close and Stan Ockers, were at 7'06" and 13'25" with Bartali next at 13'57". Among Lauredi's team-mates on the French national squad, Jean Robic (winner in 1947) was just inside the top ten at 18'17" with Raphaël Géminiani some way behind him, at 19'12". Marcel Bidot, *directeur sportif* of the French squad, decided his riders would have to take the fight to the Italians on the next stage, another ski resort summit finish, this time at Sestriere.

The pass at Sestriere had been climbed by riders in the Giro d'Italia as early as 1911 – the first time the Giro had climbed above 2,000 metres – but had not previously been scaled by riders in the Tour. On the morning of Sunday, 6 July, the remaining 88 riders in the race (122 had left Brest 12 days earlier) set off from Bourg d'Oissans at the foot of l'Alpe d'Huez, the climbs of the Croix de Fer (2,067 metres), the Galibier (2,556 metres) and Montgenèvre (1,880 metres) ahead of them before they had to climb to the top of Sestriere (2,035 metres).

Lauredi and Géminiani, along with team-mates Jean Dotto and Lucien Lazaridès, set the pace over the Glandon and the Croix de Fer. The French attack sent many riders out the back and by the time they hit the Télégraphe there were just over a dozen riders at the front of the race, Coppi and his yellow jersey among them. They also included a 20-year-old Breton on the Ouest/Sud-Ouest squad, Jean le Guilly, who decided to take his shot at glory on the Télégraphe and rode off the front on his own. All of which got Coppi's goat, and on the Galibier he decided it was time to teach the French a lesson in cycling, powering off on his own, catching and dropping le Guilly, crossing the summit of the mountain 2'45" clear.

Over the next 74 kilometres – through Briançon and over the Montgenèvre before the final climb to Sestriere – Coppi stretched his lead until, at the finish, he was 7'09" clear of the Spanish climbing ace Bernardo Ruiz, 9'33" up on Ockers and 10'11" on Close. The best of the French was Robic, at 11'24" with Géminiani at 17'28" and poor Lauredi 23'40" down on the day. These were roads Coppi knew, roads on which he had cemented his 1949 Giro d'Italia victory with a similarly stunning day of riding.

With bonifications taken into account, Coppi now had a commanding lead – 19'57" clear of his nearest challenger, Close – and the race was as good as over. So much so, in fact, that Goddet and his team had to dip into the kitty and double the prize for second place in order to give the rest of the field something to race for over the remaining two weeks.

* * * * *

In a sport in which individuals shine, the efforts of the team behind are often overlooked and that is particularly true in an era of great champions, who stand head and shoulders above the rest of the *peloton*. But the team work involved should not be ignored.

Coppi's victories, as in Sestriere, often came on the back of long, solo efforts. But the Italian champion of champions was not a man alone, he had the support behind him of a team willing to dedicate themselves to him. Tour legend has it that when Carrea – one of Coppi's most loyal *gregari* – won the stage on Alpe d'Huez and donned the yellow jersey, he apologised to Coppi and promised it would only be temporary, that he wasn't out to challenge his boss. The Italians, particularly under the leadership of team boss Alfredo Binda, were very good at unity, even when disunited.

Hugo Koblet and Learco Guerra
at the 1952 Tour.

In 1949, when Coppi and Gino Bartali were joint leaders of the team, an agreement had been thrashed out between the riders before the race, detailing how the team would ride, and a similar agreement had been in force in 1950 when Bartali and Magni were leading the team the following year. OK, that one didn't work out so well, with Bartali throwing a strop and insisting that all the Italian riders leave the race, but Binda can perhaps be excused there, the circumstances being beyond his control.

And perhaps Binda had erred in 1951 in giving so much support to Coppi, not realising that the *Campionissimo* was unsettled by the death of his brother in a race shortly before the Tour started and therefore unable to perform at his best. But at least even there the team was united behind Coppi – and that was in a team that had all three Italian stars, Bartali, Coppi and Magni – and Binda's error there was more tactics than man-management. The 1952 Italian squad had again had the three Italian champions, and Binda's management of their individual egos was a major part of Coppi's success, a vital back-up to the effort he himself put in alone when he rode off the front of the race.

Unity in the national team era was not always easy to impose. The first French squads under the national team format had been perfect examples of team discipline, the riders – particularly Antonin Magne, André Leducq, Charles Pélissier and Marcel Bidot – willing to unite and work for a team victory, regardless of their own individual ambitions. That French unity didn't last long though and particularly after the Tour returned in 1947 French teams were riven by inter-team rivalry. In 1948, when Bartali beat Louison Bobet, Binda was quick to heap praise upon the Frenchman, claiming that had Bobet had him as his *directeur sportif*, he would have beaten Bartali: praise for the rider and a pretty clear criticism of his *directeur sportif* and team-mates.

Team unity could help a champion secure a win. Disunity could deny it. For the French, and Louison Bobet in particular, working out how to bring about that unity was as big a challenge as winning the Tour itself.

Stage-by-Stage Results for the 1952 Tour de France			Stage Winner	Maillot Jaune
Stage 1 Wed 25 Jun	Brest to Rennes 122 starters 121 finishers	246 km 6h27'31" 38.1 kph	Rik van Steenbergen (Bel) Belgium	Rik van Steenbergen (Bel) Belgium
Stage 2 Thu 26 Jun	Rennes to Le Mans 117 finishers	181 km 4h52'02" 37.2 kph	André Rosseel (Bel) Belgium	Rik van Steenbergen (Bel) Belgium
Stage 3 Fri 27 Jun	Le Mans to Rouen 114 finishers	189 km 5h12'31" 36.3 kph	Nello Lauredi (Fra) France	Nello Lauredi (Fra) France
Stage 4 Sat 28 Jun	Rouen to Roubaix 110 finishers	232 km 6h23'19" 36.3 kph	Pierre Molinéris (Fra) Sud-Est	Nello Lauredi (Fra) France
Stage 5 Sun 29 Jun	Roubaix to Namur 105 finishers	197 km 5h54'28" 33.3 kph	Bim Diederich (Lux) Luxembourg	Nello Lauredi (Fra) France
Stage 6 Mon 30 Jun	Namur to Metz 100 finishers	228 km 7h07'56" 32.0 kph	Fiorenzo Magni (Ita) Italy	Fiorenzo Magni (Ita) Italy
Stage 7 Tue 1 Jul	Metz to Nancy (ITT) 100 finishers	60 km 1h32'59" 38.7 kph	Fausto Coppi (Ita) Italy	Nello Lauredi (Fra) France
Stage 8 Wed 2 Jul	Nancy to Mulhouse 90 finishers	252 km 8h17'21" 30.4 kph	Raphaël Géminiani (Fra) France	Fiorenzo Magni (Ita) Italy
	Major climbs: Col de la Grosse Pierre (923m) José Perez (Esp) Spain; Col de Bussang (754m) Raphaël Géminiani (Fra) France; Ballon d'Alsace (1,178m) Raphaël Géminiani (Fra) France; Col du Hundsruck (752m) Raphaël Géminiani (Fra) France; Col Amic (825m) Raphaël Géminiani (Fra) France			
Stage 9 Thu 3 Jul	Mulhouse to Lausanne 89 finishers	238 km 7h23'16" 32.2 kph	Walter Diggelmann (Sui) Switzerland	Andrea Carrea (Ita) Italy
	Major climbs: Col du Mollendruz (1,185m) Raoul Rémy (Fra) France			
Stage 10 Fri 4 Jul	Lausanne to l'Alpe d'Huez 88 finishers	266 km 8h51'40" 30.0 kph	Fausto Coppi (Ita) Italy	Fausto Coppi (Ita) Italy
	Major climbs: L'Alpe d'Huez (1,860m) Fausto Coppi (Ita) Italy			
Sat 5 Jul	Rest day			
Stage 11 Sun 6 Jul	Le Bourg-d'Oisans to Sestriere 82 finishers	182 km 6h36'59" 27.5 kph	Fausto Coppi (Ita) Italy	Fausto Coppi (Ita) Italy
	Major climbs: Col de la Croix de Fer (2,067m) Fausto Coppi (Ita) Italy; Col du Galibier (2,556m) Fausto Coppi (Ita) Italy; Col de Montgenèvre (1,860m) Fausto Coppi (Ita) Italy; Colle del Sestriere (2,035m) Fausto Coppi (Ita) Italy			

Stage-by-Stage Results for the 1952 Tour de France			Stage Winner	Maillot Jaune
Stage 12 Mon 7 Jul	Sestriere to Monaco 82 finishers	251 km 8h13'19" 30.5 kph	Jan Nolten (Ned) Netherlands	Fausto Coppi (Ita) Italy
	Major climbs: Col de Tende (1,321m) Jean Robic (Fra) France; Col de Brouis (880m) Jean Dotto (Fra) France; Col de Castillon (706m) Jan Nolten (Ned) Netherlands; La Turbie (480m) Jan Nolten (Ned) Netherlands			
Stage 13 Tue 8 Jul	Monaco to Aix-en-Provence 82 finishers	214 km 7h06'39" 30.1 kph	Raoul Rémy (Fra) France	Fausto Coppi (Ita) Italy
Stage 14 Wed 9 Jul	Aix-en-Provence to Avignon 81 finishers	178 km 6h16'49" 28.3 kph	Jean Robic (Fra) France	Fausto Coppi (Ita) Italy
	Major climbs: Mont Ventoux (1,909m) Jean Robic (Fra) France			
Stage 15 Thu 10 Jul	Avignon to Perpignan 81 finishers	275 km 7h07'16" 38.6 kph	Georges Decaux (Fra) Paris	Fausto Coppi (Ita) Italy
Stage 16 Fri 11 Jul	Perpignan to Toulouse 81 finishers	200 km 6h53'52" 29.0 kph	André Rosseel (Bel) Belgium	Fausto Coppi (Ita) Italy
Sat 12 Jul	Rest day			
Stage 17 Sun 13 Jul	Toulouse to Bagnères-de-Bigorre 81 finishers	204 km 6h43'16" 30.4 kph	Raphaël Géminiani (Fra) France	Fausto Coppi (Ita) Italy
	Major climbs: Col des Ares (797m) n/a; Col de Peyresourde (1,569m) Antonio Gelabert (Esp) Spain; Col d'Aspin (1,489m) Raphaël Géminiani (Fra) France			
Stage 18 Mon 14 Jul	Bagnères-de-Bigorre to Pau 78 finishers	149 km 4h42'04" 31.7 kph	Fausto Coppi (Ita) Italy	Fausto Coppi (Ita) Italy
	Major climbs: Col du Tourmalet (2,115m) Fausto Coppi (Ita) Italy; Col d'Aubisque (1,709m) Fausto Coppi (Ita) Italy			
Stage 19 Tue 15 Jul	Pau to Bordeaux 78 finishers	195 km 5h15'16" 37.1 kph	Hans Dekkers (Ned) Netherlands	Fausto Coppi (Ita) Italy
Stage 20 Wed 16 Jul	Bordeaux to Limoges 78 finishers	228 km 6h32'48" 34.8 kph	Jacques Vivier (Fra) Ouest/Sud-Ouest	Fausto Coppi (Ita) Italy
Stage 21 Thu 17 Jul	Limoges to Puy-de-Dôme 78 finishers	245 km 9h40'51" 25.3 kph	Fausto Coppi (Ita) Italy	Fausto Coppi (Ita) Italy
	Major climbs: La Roche Vendeix (1,139m) Fausto Coppi (Ita) Italy; Col de la Croix-Morand (1,401m) Gino Bartali (Ita) Italy; Puy-de-Dôme (1,415m) Fausto Coppi (Ita) Italy			

Stage-by-Stage Results for the 1952 Tour de France			Stage Winner	Maillot Jaune
Stage 22 Fri 18 Jul	Clermont Ferrand to Vichy (ITT) 78 finishers	63 km 1h33'11" 40.6 kph	Fiorenzo Magni (Ita) Italy	Fausto Coppi (Ita) Italy
Stage 23 Sat 19 Jul	Vichy to Paris (Parc des Princes) 78 finishers	354 km 11h28'55" 30.8 kph	Antonin Rolland (Fra) France	Fausto Coppi (Ita) Italy

Prize fund: 28,000,000 francs (first prize: 1,000,000 francs)

Final Classification

Place	Rider	Team	Time	Age
1	Fausto Coppi (Ita)	Italy	4,898 km 151h57'20" 32.233 kph	32
2	Stan Ockers (Bel)	Belgium	+ 28'17"	32
3	Bernardo Ruiz (Esp)	Spain	+ 34'38"	27
4	Gino Bartali (Ita)	Italy	+ 35'25"	38
5	Jean Robic (Fra)	France	+ 35'36"	31
6	Fiorenzo Magni (Ita)	Italy	+ 38'25"	31
7	Alex Close (Bel)	Belgium	+ 38'32"	30
8	Jean Dotto (Fra)	France	+ 48'01"	24
9	Andrea Carrea (Ita)	Italy	+ 50'20"	27
10	Antonio Gelabert (Esp)	Spain	+ 58'16"	30
Lanterne Rouge				
78	Henri Paret (Mor)	North Africa	+ 7h15'09"	22
King of the Mountains				
	Fausto Coppi (Ita)	Italy		32
Team				
		Italy		

1953: Bobet, At Last

The Tour was now into its fiftieth year – though only its fortieth race – and Jacques Goddet and his team at *L'Équipe* and *Le Parisien Libéré* celebrated the race's first half century. Five of the six stage towns from the first Tour were on the route, Nantes, Bordeaux, Marseille, Lyon and Paris, with only Toulouse missing out on the celebrations.

Of the 28 men who had so far won the race nine were dead: René Pottier (winner in 1906) died in 1907; François Faber (1909) in 1915; Octave Lapize (1910) in 1917; Lucien Petit-Breton (1907 and 1908) in 1917; Ottavio Bottecchia (1924 and 1925) in 1927; Henri Pélissier (1923) in 1935; Louis Trousselier (1905) in 1939; Henri Cornet (1904) in 1941; and Maurice Dewaele (1929), the most recent to die, in February 1952.

Of the surviving winners, 15 were in attendance at the Parc the Princes for the race's final lap: Maurice Garin (winner in 1903); Gustave Garrigou (1911); Philippe Thys (1913, 1914 and 1920); Lucien Buysse (1926); André Leducq (1930 and 1932); Antonin Magne (1931 and 1934); Georges Speicher (1933); Romain Maes (1935); Sylvère Maes (1936 and 1939); Roger Lapébie (1937); Gino Bartali (1938 and 1948); Jean Robic (1947); Fausto Coppi (1949 and 1952); Ferdi Kübler (1950); and Hugo Koblet (1951). The absentees were Odile Defraye (1912), Firmin Lambot (winner in 1919 and 1922), Léon Scieur (1921) and Nicolas Frantz (1927 and 1928). That the 82-year-old Garin – who had had his victory in the 1904 Tour taken away from him – was in attendance was a lesson in how the Tour was able to forgive and forget, no matter how large the crime.

A new jersey was added to the Tour's wardrobe, green for the winner of the points competition (the Giro had just done the same), based – like the Tours between 1905 and 1912 – on the position riders finished in on each stage, and for its inaugural year was called the *Grand Prix du Cinquantenaire* and sponsored by La Belle Jardinière. A prize of 1,000,000 francs – half what the final *maillot jaune* received – was on offer to the winner (with 500,000 francs for second, down to 100,000 for fifth).

Down to the Pyrenees over the race's opening phase the yellow jersey was shared by Fritz Schär (Switzerland) and Roger Hassenforder (Nord-Es/Centre), with Schär wearing it first and then taking it back from Hassenforder. On the second day in the Pyrenees, Jean Robic rose to the top and took the lead, finally getting a chance to race in the jersey he had won on the very last day of the 1949 Tour. The next day he surrendered it as his Ouest squad turned the Tour on its head, with a breakaway group that contained Robic's team-mates François Mahé and Jean Malléjac putting more than 20 minutes into the *peloton*. The yellow jersey passed to Mahé, who'd started the stage seventh overall, nearly 12 minutes behind Robic.

On the next stage, Albi to Béziers, the French team decided it was time to take control of the race and break up the party the regional Ouest riders were having. Showing the unity they had when they launched an attack on to the road to Sestriere the year before, they went on the attack. At the end of the stage, Robic had lost more than half an hour and any hope of success and Mahé had lost the yellow jersey. But the man in yellow was still from the Ouest squad: Malléjac. And the French unity that had started the attack evaporated at the stage finish.

Nine riders had arrived in Béziers together, four of them from the French squad. And those four French riders pulled off a clean sweep. Of the quartet – Nello Lauredi, Raphaël Géminiani, Louison Bobet and Antonin Rolland – Bobet had been best positioned in the general classification at the start of the stage. But in the sprint against his team-mates he finished third. He had gained time on the road, but missed out on the extra time bonuses that would have lifted him closer to yellow. That evening in the team hotel an argument erupted, with Bobet claiming the others should have supported him, let him gain the time bonus. The others didn't quite agree – they were all within five minutes of one and other – and things started to get a bit physical before peace was restored.

The next morning team boss Marcel Bidot decided it was time to sort this mess out. Sitting his riders down he went around the room, asking each in turn if they thought they could win the race. Each said they could bring home a good showing for the team but that they couldn't be sure of victory. Each, that is, until it came to Bobet. He stuck his neck on the line and said that yes, he thought he could win the race. But only if his team-mates helped him. And for that help he was willing to pay them, offering to split the winnings he would receive among them. (Other riders – particularly Fausto Coppi – shared their race winnings with their team-mates, that money being relatively insignificant when compared to the appearance fees a major win would guarantee.)

For the next five stages Bobet waited for his time to come; like Sylvère Maes in 1939, he knew where and when he was going to win this Tour and was willing to be patient. And, like Maes in 1939, Bobet picked the stage up through the Casse Déserte – Stage 18, Gap to Briançon – as the moment he would win the Tour.

On the Col de Vars – with a team-mate (Adolphe Deledda) up the road in a break alongside two regional riders – Bobet launched his attack, taking with him the Spaniard Jesús Loroño. At the top of the Vars the pair were 45 seconds clear of the *peloton*, more than a minute up on Malléjac, and 1'45" behind the break. That gap to the break evaporated on the descent and, with team-mate Deledda now helping with the pace, Bobet widened his gap to the chasers behind. On the Izoard and up through the Casse Déserte he soloed to victory, having a five-minute lead at the stage's end and more than 10 minutes on Malléjac. With a lead of more than eight minutes over Malléjac – now in second place – Bobet had at last won the Tour.

Stage-by-Stage Results for the 1953 Tour de France			Stage Winner	Maillot Jaune
Stage 1 Fri 3 Jul	Strasbourg to Metz 119 starters 118 finishers	195 km 4h55'00" 39.7 kph	Fritz Schär (Sui) Switzerland	Fritz Schär (Sui) Switzerland
Stage 2 Sat 4 Jul	Metz to Liège 115 finishers	227 km 6h20'52" 35.8 kph	Fritz Schär (Sui) Switzerland	Fritz Schär (Sui) Switzerland
Stage 3 Sun 5 Jul	Liège to Lille 114 finishers	221 km 6h06'21" 36.2 kph	Louison Bobet (Fra) France	Fritz Schär (Sui) Switzerland
Stage 4 Mon 6 Jul	Lille to Dieppe 112 finishers	188 km 5h20'19" 35.2 kph	Gerrit Voorting (Ned) Netherlands	Fritz Schär (Sui) Switzerland
Stage 5 Tue 7 Jul	Dieppe to Caen 109 finishers	200 km 5h38'35" 35.4 kph	Jean Malléjac (Fra) Ouest	Roger Hassenforder (Fra) Nord-Est/Centre
Stage 6 Wed 8 Jul	Caen to Le Mans 104 finishers	206 km 5h10'53" 39.8 kph	Martin van Geneugden (Bel) Belgium	Roger Hassenforder (Fra) Nord-Est/Centre
Stage 7 Thu 9 Jul	Le Mans to Nantes 100 finishers	181 km 4h46'08" 38.0 kph	Livio Isotti (Ita) Italy	Roger Hassenforder (Fra) Nord-Est/Centre
Stage 8 Fri 10 Jul	Nantes to Bordeaux 100 finishers	345 km 9h56'40" 34.7 kph	Jan Nolten (Ned) Netherlands	Roger Hassenforder (Fra) Nord-Est/Centre
Sat 11 Jul	Rest day			
Stage 9 Sun 12 Jul	Bordeaux to Pau 100 finishers	197 km 5h09'58" 38.1 kph	Fiorenzo Magni (Ita) Italy	Fritz Schär (Sui) Switzerland
Stage 10 Mon 13 Jul	Pau to Cauterets 97 finishers	103 km 3h14'30" 31.8 kph	Jesús Loroño (Esp) Spain	Fritz Schär (Sui) Switzerland
	Major climbs: Col d'Aubisque (1,709m) Jesús Loroño (Esp) Spain; Cauterets (934m) Jesús Loroño (Esp) Spain			
Stage 11 Tue 14 Jul	Cauterets to Luchon 94 finishers	115 km 3h50'06" 30.0 kph	Jean Robic (Fra) Ouest	Jean Robic (Fra) Ouest
	Major climbs: Col du Tourmalet (2,115m) Jean Robic (Fra) Ouest; Col d'Aspin (1,489m) Jean Robic (Fra) Ouest; Col de Peyresourde (1,569m) Jean Robic (Fra) Ouest			
Stage 12 Wed 15 Jul	Luchon to Albi 91 finishers	228 km 5h40'40" 40.2 kph	André Darrigade (Fra) Sud-Ouest	François Mahé (Fra) Ouest

Stage-by-Stage Results for the 1953 Tour de France			Stage Winner	Maillot Jaune
Stage 13 Thu 16 Jul	Albi to Béziers 89 finishers	189 km 5h18'41" 35.6 kph	Nello Lauredi (Fra) France	Jean Malléjac (Fra) Ouest
Major climbs: Col des Treize Vents (600m) Joseph Mirando (Fra) Sud-Est				
Stage 14 Fri 17 Jul	Béziers to Nîmes 83 finishers	214 km 6h21'23" 33.7 kph	Bernard Quennehen (Fra) Nord-Est/Centre	Jean Malléjac (Fra) Ouest
Stage 15 Sat 18 Jul	Nîmes to Marseille 83 finishers	173 km 4h32'33" 38.1 kph	Maurice Quentin (Fra) Île-de-France	Jean Malléjac (Fra) Ouest
Stage 16 Sun 19 Jul	Marseille to Monaco 82 finishers	236 km 7h20'53" 32.1 kph	Wim van Est (Ned) Netherlands	Jean Malléjac (Fra) Ouest
Major climbs: Col d'Éze (512m) Joseph Mirando (Fra) Sud-Est				
Mon 20 Jul	Rest day			
Stage 17 Tue 21 Jul	Monaco to Gap 82 finishers	261 km 8h18'34" 31.4 kph	Wout Wagtmans (Ned) Netherlands	Jean Malléjac (Fra) Ouest
Major climbs: Col du Pilon (795m) Joseph Mirando (Fra) Sud-Est; Col des Léques (1,146m) Joseph Mirando (Fra) Sud-Est; Col du Labouret (1,240m) José Serra (Esp) Spain; Col de la Sentinelle (980m) Wout Wagtmans (Ned) Netherlands				
Stage 18 Wed 22 Jul	Gap to Briançon 77 finishers	165 km 5h11'17" 31.8 kph	Louison Bobet (Fra) France	Louison Bobet (Fra) France
Major climbs: Col de Vars (2,110m) Adolphe Deledda (Fra) France; Col d'Izoard (2,360m) Louison Bobet (Fra) France				
Stage 19 Thu 23 Jul	Briançon to Lyon 76 finishers	227 km 6h18'15" 36.0 kph	Georges Meunier (Fra) Nord-Est/Centre	Louison Bobet (Fra) France
Major climbs: Col du Lautaret (2,058m) Jean Le Guilly (Fra) France				
Stage 20 Fri 24 Jul	Lyon to Saint-Étienne (ITT) 76 finishers	70 km 1h49'00" 38.5 kph	Louison Bobet (Fra) France	Louison Bobet (Fra) France
Stage 21 Sat 25 Jul	Saint-Étienne to Montluçon 76 finishers	210 km 6h20'08" 33.1 kph	Wout Wagtmans (Ned) Netherlands	Louison Bobet (Fra) France
Stage 22 Sun 26 Jul	Montluçon to Paris (Parc des Princes) 76 finishers	328 km 9h42'53" 33.8 kph	Fiorenzo Magni (Ita) Italy	Louison Bobet (Fra) France

Prize fund: 35,000,000 francs (first prize: 2,000,000 francs)

Final Classification

Place	Rider	Team	Time	Age
1	Louison Bobet (Fra)	France	4,476 km 129h23'25" 34.593 kph	28
2	Jean Malléjac (Fra)	Ouest	+ 14'18"	24
3	Giancarlo Astrua (Ita)	Italy	+ 15'02"	25
4	Alex Close (Bel)	Belgium	+ 17'35"	31
5	Wout Wagtmans (Ned)	Netherlands	+ 18'05"	23
6	Fritz Schär (Sui)	Switzerland	+ 18'44"	27
7	Antonin Rolland (Fra)	France	+ 23'03"	28
8	Nello Lauredi (Fra)	France	+ 26'03"	27
9	Raphaël Géminiani (Fra)	France	+ 27'18"	28
10	François Mahé (Fra)	Ouest	+ 28'26"	22
Lanterne Rouge				
76	Claude Rouer (Fra)	Île-de-France	+ 4h09'10"	23
Points				
	Fritz Schär (Sui)	Switzerland		27
King of the Mountains				
	Jesús Loroño (Esp)	Spain		27
Team				
		Netherlands		

1954: Bobet, Again

By 1954, the French economy was doing well as austerity gave way to prosperity, and the impact of this was clear at the Tour de France, where Jacques Goddet was able to resurrect one of Henri Desgrange's more cruel innovations in the Tour: split stages. Two days' racing – sometimes even three in Desgrange's time – for the price of one, host towns happy to pay for the privilege of hosting the Tour even for only a few hours. The strength of the economy also enabled Félix Lévitan to get rid of the army-surplus jeeps Tour officials had been driving the past few years and replace them with cars supplied – for a fee – by Peugeot.

But, well as the country's economy was doing, the cycling industry itself was in trouble as mopeds replaced bicycles. There was less and less money available to sponsor cycling teams. So teams were having to look outside of the cycling industry in order to raise the revenue to keep themselves afloat.

While small teams in Britain and Spain had been getting away with this *extra-sportif* sponsorship for several years without anyone complaining – it was, technically, against the UCI's rules – it became an issue when a major team in the professional *peloton* did the same. One of the reasons this was considered a problem was that it raised the possibility of teams approaching some of the same firms race organisers needed in order to keep their events going. And, especially for Félix Lévitan, who was trying to make the Tour pay its way, this was not on.

That first major team to break the *extra-sportif* embargo was the squad Fiorenzo Magni raced for. When the bike maker Ganna, who had been the team's main sponsor, informed Magni they would no longer be able to fund the team, he went in search of fresh finance and approached the Nivea face cream company. (Others followed his example, including Gino Bartali, who brought the rubber-raincoats-to-chewing-gum maker Brooklyn on board for the team his bike company sponsored.)

From the first major race of the season, Milan-Sanremo in March, there were problems for Magni's new Nivea-sponsored team. Sometimes Magni got to ride and simply got fined for having Nivea's name on his jersey, sometimes – particularly in France and especially at races run by *L'Équipe* – organisers or race *commissaires* stopped him from riding. At Paris-Roubaix in April Fausto Coppi – who was riding for the relatively wealthy Bianchi squad – showed his support for his compatriot by refusing to ride unless Magni was allowed start. Not that that helped much, Goddet and Lévitan were determined to stop the teams accessing *extra-sportive* sponsorship.

At the Giro d'Italia in May and June the riders made their feelings known, sufficiently clearly for the Italian federation to decide that sending a team to the Tour de France would be a bad idea. And so the Italian riders were kept at home for the 1954 Tour. Goddet and Lévitan had won the *extra-sportif* battle, but at a cost.

The *extra-sportif* battle may have taken Coppi, Magni and Bartali out of the race but there was still an impressive field. The Swiss fielded a squad that contained previous winners Ferdi Kübler and Hugo Koblet, as well as Fritz Schär, who had worn the yellow jersey the previous year and was the winner of the Tour's first green jersey. Stan Ockers – second overall in 1950 – was back for Belgium. And the French were once again fielding a team with a surfeit of talent: Louison Bobet, the defending champion, along with Raphaël Géminiani, Nello Lauredi and Antonin Rolland. But no Jean Robic. He was again reduced to riding for the regional Ouest squad.

The race had begun in Amsterdam, capital of the Netherlands – more money for the Tour's coffers and the first international *grand départ* – and the *maillot jaune* went Dutch, Wout Wagtmans taking the opening stage and holding the jersey for the next two days. On the second stage, Bobet showed his willingness to lead from the front and took the stage win and, two days later, dislodged Wagtmans

Ferdi Kübler (second from left) wins the Toulouse to Millau stage in the 1954 Tour, beating Louison Bobet (right), Stan Ockers (hidden) and Raphaël Géminiani (left).

from yellow during the morning's team time trial. The race was only a few days old and the defending champion was already wearing the *maillot jaune*

On the eighth stage Bobet surrendered the lead, rather than running the risk of wearing his team out trying to defend it all the way to Paris. And the man who inherited it was Wagtmans again, back in yellow.

The first day in the Pyrenees failed to shake things up too much but on the second Wagtmans lost the lead to Gilbert Bauvin of the Nord-Est – Centre regional squad. Two days later, on the rolling roads of the Cévennes up to Millau, Bobet was back in the lead and Bauvin reduced to second, 4'33" in arrears. Another five minutes or so back were two of the Swiss trio who looked like they might be able to make a race of it, Schär and Kübler (the third, Koblet, had been forced out of the race the day before). Their challenge, though, just never came.

Schär pulled back a few seconds on the road to Grenoble, over the Col de la Romeyère when Bobet found himself isolated, but once more Bobet had an appointment with greatness on the Izoard, where he again sealed his victory.

Four kilometres into the climb of the Izoard, only Kübler and Jean Malléjac were left with Bobet as they chased the day's early breakaways. One kilometre later Bobet was chasing alone, distancing his companions. With the breakaways swept up, Bobet soloed to the stage win, nearly two minutes up on Kübler, who leap-frogged his compatriot Schär to claim second place.

Bobet added more time – and another stage win – in the 72-kilometre time trial from Épinal to Nancy and two days later rode into the Parc des Princes, the first back-to-back Tour winner since Nicolas Frantz in 1928, and the first Frenchman to achieve that feat since Lucien Petit-Breton two decades before that.

Stage-by-Stage Results for the 1954 Tour de France			Stage Winners	Maillot Jaune
Stage 1 Thu 8 Jul	Amsterdam to Brasschaat 110 starters 108 finishers	216 km 5h23'27" 40.1 kph	Wout Wagtmans (Ned) Netherlands	Wout Wagtmans (Ned) Netherlands
Stage 2 Fri 9 Jul	Beveren to Lille 108 finishers	255 km 6h51'52" 37.1 kph	Louison Bobet (Fra) France	Wout Wagtmans (Ned) Netherlands
Stage 3 Sat 10 Jul	Lille to Rouen 107 finishers	219 km 6h19'52" 34.6 kph	Marcel Dussault (Fra) Sud-Ouest	Wout Wagtmans (Ned) Netherlands
Stage 4a Sun 11 Jul	Rouen to Circuit des Essarts (TTT) 107 finishers	10.4 km 15'04" 41.4 kph	Switzerland	Louison Bobet (Fra) France
Stage 4b Sun 11 Jul	Rouen to Caen 103 finishers	131 km 3h16'03" 40.1 kph	Wim van Est (Ned) Netherlands	Louison Bobet (Fra) France
Stage 5 Mon 12 Jul	Caen to Saint-Brieuc 97 finishers	224 km 6h04'06" 36.9 kph	Ferdi Kübler (Sui) Switzerland	Louison Bobet (Fra) France
Stage 6 Tue 13 Jul	Saint-Brieuc to Brest 96 finishers	179 km 4h55'09" 36.4 kph	Dominique Forlini (Fra) Île-de-France	Louison Bobet (Fra) France
Stage 7 Wed 14 Jul	Brest to Vannes 93 finishers	211 km 5h24'22" 39.0 kph	Jacques Vivier (Fra) Sud-Ouest	Louison Bobet (Fra) France
Stage 8 Thu 15 Jul	Vannes to Angers 92 finishers	190 km 4h27'04" 42.7 kph	Fred de Bruyne (Bel) Belgium	Wout Wagtmans (Ned) Netherlands
Stage 9 Fri 16 Jul	Angers to Bordeaux 92 finishers	343 km 10h03'25" 34.1 kph	Henk Faanhof (Ned) Netherlands	Wout Wagtmans (Ned) Netherlands
Sat 17 Jul	Rest day			
Stage 10 Sun 18 Jul	Bordeaux to Bayonne 90 finishers	202 km 4h56'45" 40.8 kph	Gilbert Bauvin (Fra) Nord-Est/Centre	Wout Wagtmans (Ned) Netherlands
Stage 11 Mon 19 Jul	Bayonne to Pau 88 finishers	241 km 6h54'24" 34.9 kph	Stan Ockers (Bel) Belgium	Wout Wagtmans (Ned) Netherlands
	Major climbs: Col d'Aubisque (1,709m) Federico Bahamontes (Esp) Spain			
Stage 12 Tue 20 Jul	Pau to Luchon 86 finishers	161 km 5h27'27" 29.5 kph	Gilbert Bauvin (Fra) Nord-Est/Centre	Gilbert Bauvin (Fra) Nord-Est/Centre
	Major climbs: Col du Tourmalet (2,115m) Federico Bahamontes (Esp) Spain; Col d'Aspin (1,489m) Louison Bobet (Fra) France; Col de Peyresourde (1,569m) Federico Bahamontes (Esp) Spain			

Stage-by-Stage Results for the 1954 Tour de France			Stage Winners	Maillot Jaune
Stage 13 Wed 21 Jul	Luchon to Toulouse 82 finishers	203 km 5h19'13" 38.2 kph	Fred de Bruyne (Bel) Belgium	Gilbert Bauvin (Fra) Nord-Est/Centre
Stage 14 Thu 22 Jul	Toulouse to Millau 78 finishers	225 km 6h32'34" 34.4 kph	Ferdi Kübler (Sui) Switzerland	Louison Bobet (Fra) France
	Major climbs: Col de la Fontasse (537m) Lucien Lazaridès (Fra) Sud-Est; Montiaux (1,030m) Federico Bahamontes (Esp) Spain; Col de la Bassine (885m) Federico Bahamontes (Esp) Spain; Côte de Tiergues (594m) Federico Bahamontes (Esp) Spain			
Stage 15 Fri 23 Jul	Millau to Le Puy 77 finishers	197 km 6h18'13" 31.3 kph	Dominique Forlini (Fra) Île-de-France	Louison Bobet (Fra) France
	Major climbs: Le Causse du Sauveterre (1,020m) Robert Varnajo (Fra) Ouest; Col de la Pierre Plantée (1,264m) André Darrigade (Fra) France; Côte de Pradelles (1,167m) Gerrit Voorting (Ned) Netherlands			
Stage 16 Sat 24 Jul	Le Puy to Lyon 74 finishers	194 km 5h28'58" 35.4 kph	Jean Forestier (Fra) France	Louison Bobet (Fra) France
	Major climbs: Col de la République (Col du Grand Bois) (1,161m) Robert Varnajo (Fra) Ouest; Pertuis (1,026m) Robert Varnajo (Fra) Ouest			
Sun 25 Jul	Rest day			
Stage 17 Mon 26 Jul	Lyon to Grenoble 74 finishers	182 km 5h40'43" 32.1 kph	Lucien Lazaridès (Fra) Sud-Est	Louison Bobet (Fra) France
	Major climbs: Col de la Romeyère (1,074m) Federico Bahamontes (Esp) Spain; Saint-Nizier (1,180m) Jean Le Guilly (Fra) Île-de-France			
Stage 18 Tue 27 Jul	Grenoble to Briançon 73 finishers	216 km 7h26'42" 29.0 kph	Louison Bobet (Fra) France	Louison Bobet (Fra) France
	Major climbs: Côte de Laffrey (900m) Federico Bahamontes (Esp) Spain; Col Bayard (1,246m) Federico Bahamontes (Esp) Spain; Col d'Izoard (2,360m) Louison Bobet (Fra) France			
Stage 19 Wed 28 Jul	Briançon to Aix-les-Bains 73 finishers	221 km 7h19'02" 30.2 kph	Jean Dotto (Fra) Sud-Est	Louison Bobet (Fra) France
	Major climbs: Col du Galibier (2,556m) Federico Bahamontes (Esp) Spain; Marcocaz (960m) Jean Dotto (Fra) Sud-Est; Les Prés (1,142m) Jean Dotto (Fra) Sud-Est; Col de Plainpalais (1,173m) Jean Dotto (Fra) Sud-Est			
Stage 20 Thu 29 Jul	Aix Les Bains to Besançon 71 finishers	243 km 7h05'31" 34.3 kph	Lucien Teisseire (Fra) France	Louison Bobet (Fra) France
	Major climbs: Col de la Faucille (1,323m) Federico Bahamontes (Esp) Spain			

Stage-by-Stage Results for the 1954 Tour de France			Stage Winners	Maillot Jaune
Stage 21a Fri 30 Jul	Besançon to Épinal 70 finishers	134 km 3h45'48" 35.6 kph	François Mahé (Fra) Ouest	Louison Bobet (Fra) France
Stage 21b Fri 30 Jul	Épinal to Nancy (ITT) 70 finishers	72 km 1h47'10" 40.3 kph	Louison Bobet (Fra) France	Louison Bobet (Fra) France
Stage 22 Sat 31 Jul	Nancy to Troyes 69 finishers	216 km 6h35'03" 32.8 kph	Fred de Bruyne (Bel) Belgium	Louison Bobet (Fra) France
Stage 23 Sun 1 Aug	Troyes to Paris (Parc des Princes) 69 finishers	180 km 5h09'23" 34.9 kph	Robert Varnajo (Fra) Ouest	Louison Bobet (Fra) France

Prize fund: 38,445,000 francs (first prize: 2,000,000 francs)

Final Classification				
Place	Rider	Team	Time	Age
1	Louison Bobet (Fra)	France	4,656 km 140h06'05" 33.229 kph	29
2	Ferdi Kübler (Sui)	Switzerland	+ 15'49"	35
3	Fritz Schär (Sui)	Switzerland	+ 21'46"	28
4	Jean Dotto (Fra)	Sud-Est	+ 28'21"	26
5	Jean Malléjac (Fra)	Ouest	+ 31'38"	25
6	Stan Ockers (Bel)	Belgium	+ 36'02"	34
7	Louis Bergaud (Fra)	Sud-Ouest	+ 37'55"	25
8	Vincent Vitetta (Fra)	Sud-Est	+ 41'14"	28
9	Jean Brankart (Bel)	Belgium	+ 42'08"	24
10	Gilbert Bauvin (Fra)	Centre – Nord-Est	+ 42'21"	26
Lanterne Rouge				
69	Marcel Dierkens (Lux)	Luxembourg – Austria	+ 6h07'29"	28
Points				
	Ferdi Kübler (Sui)	Switzerland		35
King of the Mountains				
	Federico Bahamontes (Esp)	Spain		26
Team				
		Switzerland		

1955: Angels with Dirty Faces

It would be wrong to say that it all began on the Ventoux – it all began a long, long time before that – but, on a hot Monday in July of 1955, that bald mountain in the heart of Provence marked the turning of a page. Cycling's doping problem was laid bare for all to see.

No one knows when the doping began. Away back at the start doping wasn't doping, it was just medical care. Authorities were only interested when medical care became careless. In 1897 the British cycling authorities had banned the trainer Choppy Warburton – whose techniques were beloved by Alphonse Baugé – from their events after he was accused of poisoning one of his riders, Jimmy Michael. Six Day races in particular became associated with the use of products such as cocaine (which acted as a stimulant), strychnine (to dull pain) and nitroglycerine (to ease breathing). On the track there had always been a degree of openness about the use of such products, though never to the extent that such openness could detract from the effort and skill required of a rider in order to attain victory.

Henri Desgrange himself had had to confront the problem of doping at the 1920 Tour, writing that some of the riders thought nothing of doping. Desgrange, though, aimed his ire not at the riders but at their entourage: the doctors who provided the products and the managers who he believed encouraged doping. Albert Londres had caused a scandal at the 1924 Tour when, in criticising the conditions endured by the riders on the race, he quoted the Pélissier brothers telling him that they rode on dynamite. In 1930, when the Tour switched to the national team format, the rule book made clear that the medical care of riders was the responsibility of the teams, *L'Auto* would not be picking up that tab for that. The following year Jacques Goddet – then still just a journalist with *L'Auto* – complained that riders were addicted to poison.

After the Second World War things took a turn for the worse when amphetamines – widely used by the military on all sides of the conflict to keep their men alert and ready for action – became readily available to the general public. Interviewed in 1949, Fausto Coppi was asked about his use of such drugs. He didn't try to hide behind equivocation or games of semantics and openly admitted that he used stimulants.

This he was able to do because doping was not against the rules. Some sports bodies had banned the use of stimulants: the Jockey Club in the US as early as 1897 with other Jockey Clubs following their lead, the British in 1902; the IAAF as early as 1928. But cycling had no such prohibitions. The issue was very much down to the ethics of the riders and those responsible for their care. Some were downright puritanical in their attitudes and believed even alcohol should not be used, that riders should ride *à l'eau* (on water). Others believed riders should have access to the best that medical science could offer in order to help them attain their full potential.

That some doping products are dangerous is clear, particularly with products such as cocaine, strychnine and nitroglycerine. But those products had been used for such a long time that their dangers were understood and care was taken in their administration. Amphetamines, though, were still relatively new, and not all of their dangers were fully grasped, particularly the problem of dehydration. Which, at a time when riders thought imitating camels was a good idea and drank as little as possible during a race, was actually a major problem. Especially when you had to climb a mountain on a hot summer's day.

Mont Ventoux had been added to the Tour's itinerary in 1951, falling part way between Montpellier and Avignon, and was traversed again the following year when the riders went from Aix-en-Provence to Avignon, on neither occasion having much of an impact on the overall race. After that it took a break before returning in 1955, on the stage from Marseille to Avignon. And it was on that stage that things took a turn for the worse.

Coming into the eleventh stage France had the *maillot jaune*, with Antonin Rolland having been wearing it since the first day in the Alps on Stage Eight. He had a lead of just over 11 minutes on Pasquale Fornara of Italy. This was an Italian team of lesser riders, the *extra-sportif* war still waging and Italy effectively sending a B team to the race. Thirty seconds behind Fornara, in third overall, was the defending champion, Louison Bobet, sporting the rainbow jersey of World Champion, which he had won the previous year. Charly Gaul (riding for the Luxembourg/Mixte team) was another 20 seconds back in fourth. Two other French riders were inside the top ten, Raphaël Géminiani in eighth and 19 minutes off the lead and Jean Malléjac in ninth, another six minutes back.

When the race hit the Ventoux, in the scorching heat of the early afternoon, riders began behaving oddly, suffering in the heat. Ten kilometres before the summit Malléjac collapsed, after zigzagging along the road. Only the intervention of the Tour's doctor, Pierre Dumas, saved his life. The Frenchman was unconscious for 15-minutes and Dumas had to inject him with solucamphre in order to restart his heart. When Malléjac regained consciousness, Dumas described him as being in a state of delirium tremens and in the ambulance that ferried him off the Ventoux he had to be forcibly pacified as he yelled and tried to get out and back into the race.

Malléjac was not the only rider to suffer. Kübler covered the final kilometre in a 20 minute zigzag. Mahé too was in trouble, as was Richard van Genechten of the Belgium squad. Gaul – the Angel of the Mountains – had to be given oxygen and his *directeur sportif*, two-time Tour winner Nicolas Frantz, claimed his rider was the victim of attempted murder. 'Whoever convinced him to dope,' Frantz said, 'has committed a crime.'

Tour director Jacques Goddet summed up the day's events on the Ventoux thus: 'On this condemned spot the battle raged, while men fell by the side of the road on the glowing hot mountain. Bundles of men, who've previously shown themselves so enduring and capable of acting. But nothing breaks the rhythm of the 1955 Tour de France.'

Nothing broke the rhythm of the race, but the Ventoux was a turning point, the sport's doping problems laid bare. Roland Barthes, the French semiotician, made reference to the incident in one of his *Mythologies* essays, *The Tour de France As Epic*, describing the mountain as 'a God of Evil, to which sacrifice must be made. A veritable Moloch, despot of the cyclists, it never forgives the weak and exacts an unjust tribute of sufferings.' Of the doping culture which was laid bare that day, Barthes had this say: 'to dope the racer is as criminal, as sacrilegious as trying to imitate God; it is stealing from God the privilege of the spark. God, moreover, knows how to take revenge on such occasions: as the wretched Malléjac knows, a provocative doping leads to the gates of madness (punishment of the theft of fire).' It would take more than the intervention of God, though, to solve cycling's doping problem.

The stage itself fell to Bobet, who climbed up to second overall, just under five minutes behind team-mate Rolland in yellow. Things more or less stayed the same as the race moved to the Pyrenees on Stages 17 and 18, where Bobet went in pursuit of Gaul on the Peyresourde as Rolland struggled. Gaul took the stage, Bobet the *maillot jaune*, Rolland dropping to second, 3'08" in arrears.

Bobet added another three minutes on the next Pyrenean stage, exiting the mountains with a six-minute lead and the knowledge that he could extend that in the penultimate day's time trial. Boils prevented him putting in a stage-winning performance there, but nothing could stop his march to the first three-in-a-row in Tour history.

* * * * *

The *extra-sportif* war, which had started in Italy, had by now reached France. Good riders like Jean Dotto and Nello Lauredi struggled to find teams with the budget to afford them. Raphaël Géminiani took a lead and signed the drinks company Saint-Raphaël as a sponsor for his trade team, Saint-Raphaël/Géminiani. The French federation reprimanded him. But they didn't ban him. The fight against non-cycling sponsors was being lost as the reality of cycling's precarious economic position became clear. It would end the following year, when the UCI – with the Frenchman Achille Joinard as its president – forced through a change in regulations which would allow limited entry to non-cycling sponsors.

Stage-by-Stage Results for the 1955 Tour de France			Stage Winner	Maillot Jaune
Stage 1a Thu 7 Jul	Le Havre to Dieppe 130 starters 130 finishers	102 km 2h39'31" 38.4 kph	Miguel Poblet (Esp) Spain	Miguel Poblet (Esp) Spain
Stage 1b Thu 7 Jul	Dieppe to Dieppe (TTT) 130 finishers	12.5 km 16'25" 45.7 kph	Netherlands	Wout Wagtmans (Ned) Netherlands
Stage 2 Fri 8 Jul	Dieppe to Roubaix 127 finishers	204 km 5h54'00" 34.6 kph	Antonin Rolland (Fra) France	Wout Wagtmans (Ned) Netherlands
Stage 3 Sat 9 Jul	Roubaix to Namur 121 finishers	210 km 6h37'39" 31.7 kph	Louison Bobet (Fra) France	Wout Wagtmans (Ned) Netherlands
Stage 4 Sun 10 Jul	Namur to Metz 119 finishers	225 km 6h41'07" 33.7 kph	Willy Kemp (Lux) Luxembourg/Mixte	Antonin Rolland (Fra) France
Stage 5 Mon 11 Jul	Metz to Colmar 116 finishers	229 km 5h57'54" 38.4 kph	Roger Hassenforder (Fra) Nord-Est/Centre	Antonin Rolland (Fra) France
Stage 6 Tue 12 Jul	Colmar to Zürich 113 finishers	195 km 4h32'14" 43.0 kph	André Darrigade (Fra) France	Antonin Rolland (Fra) France
Stage 7 Wed 13 Jul	Zürich to Thonon-les-Bains 108 finishers	267 km 7h22'01" 36.2 kph	Jos Hinsen (Ned) Netherlands	Wim van Est (Ned) Netherlands
Stage 8 Thu 14 Jul	Thonon-les-Bains to Briançon 101 finishers	253 km 7h42'55" 32.8 kph	Charly Gaul (Lux) Luxembourg/Mixte	Antonin Rolland (Fra) France
	Major climbs: Col des Aravis (1,498m) Charly Gaul (Lux) Luxembourg/Mixte; Col du Télégraphe (1,566m) Charly Gaul (Lux) Luxembourg/Mixte; Col du Galibier (2,556m) Charly Gaul (Lux) Luxembourg/Mixte			
Stage 9 Fri 15 Jul	Briançon to Monaco 92 finishers	275 km 8h15'50" 33.3 kph	Raphaël Géminiani (Fra) France	Antonin Rolland (Fra) France
	Major climbs: Col de Vars (2,110m) Charly Gaul (Lux) Luxembourg/Mixte; Col de la Cayolle (2,326m) Charly Gaul (Lux) Luxembourg/Mixte; Col du Vasson (1,700m) Charly Gaul (Lux) Luxembourg/Mixte; La Turbie (555m) Raphaël Géminiani (Fra) France			
Stage 10 Sat 16 Jul	Monaco to Marseille 87 finishers	240 km 6h45'12" 35.5 kph	Lucien Lazaridès (Fra) Sud-Est	Antonin Rolland (Fra) France
Sun 17 Jul	Rest day			
Stage 11 Mon 18 Jul	Marseille to Avignon 79 finishers	198 km 5h42'32" 34.7 kph	Louison Bobet (Fra) France	Antonin Rolland (Fra) France
	Major climbs: Mont Ventoux (1,909m) Louison Bobet (Fra) France			

Stage-by-Stage Results for the 1955 Tour de France			Stage Winner	Maillot Jaune
Stage 12 Tue 19 Jul	Avignon to Millau 76 finishers	240 km 6h53'50" 34.8 kph	Alessandro Fantini (Ita) Italy	Antonin Rolland (Fra) France
	Major climbs: Col du Minier (1,270m) Louis Caput (Fra) Île-de-France			
Stage 13 Wed 20 Jul	Millau to Albi 75 finishers	205 km 5h25'41" 37.8 kph	Daan de Groot (Ned) Netherlands	Antonin Rolland (Fra) France
Stage 14 Thu 21 Jul	Albi to Narbonne 75 finishers	156 km 4h12'05" 37.1 kph	Louis Caput (Fra) Île-de-France	Antonin Rolland (Fra) France
	Major climbs: Col de la Fontasse (537m) François Mahé (Fra) France			
Stage 15 Fri 22 Jul	Narbonne to Ax-les-Thermes 74 finishers	151 km 4h32'53" 33.2 kph	Luciano Pezzi (Ita) Italy	Antonin Rolland (Fra) France
Sat 23 Jul	Rest day			
Stage 16 Sun 24 Jul	Ax-les-Thermes to Toulouse 72 finishers	123 km 2h57'09" 41.7 kph	Rik van Steenbergen (Bel)	Antonin Rolland (Fra) France
Stage 17 Mon 25 Jul	Toulouse to Saint-Gaudens 70 finishers	249 km 7h31'31" 33.1 kph	Charly Gaul (Lux) Luxembourg/Mixte	Louison Bobet (Fra) France
	Major climbs: Col d'Aspin (1,489m) Charly Gaul (Lux) Luxembourg/Mixte; Col de Peyresourde (1,569m) Charly Gaul (Lux) Luxembourg/Mixte			
Stage 18 Tue 26 Jul	Saint-Gaudens to Pau 70 finishers	206 km 6h39'39" 30.9 kph	Jean Brankart (Bel) Belgium	Louison Bobet (Fra) France
	Major climbs: Col du Tourmalet (2,115m) Miguel Poblet (Esp) Spain; Col d'Aubisque (1,709m) Charly Gaul (Lux) Luxembourg/Mixte			
Stage 19 Wed 27 Jul	Pau to Bordeaux 70 finishers	195 km 5h15'38" 37.1 kph	Wout Wagtmans (Ned) Netherlands	Louison Bobet (Fra) France
Stage 20 Thu 28 Jul	Bordeaux to Poitiers 70 finishers	243 km 7h24'12" 32.8 kph	Jean Forestier (Fra) France	Louison Bobet (Fra) France
Stage 21 Fri 29 Jul	Châtellerault to Tours (ITT) 69 finishers	68.6 km 1h39'51" 41.2 kph	Jean Brankart (Bel) Belgium	Louison Bobet (Fra) France
Stage 22 Sat 30 Jul	Tours to Paris (Parc des Princes) 69 finishers	229 km 6h38'25" 34.5 kph	Miguel Poblet (Esp) Spain	Louison Bobet (Fra) France

Prize fund: 36,685,000 francs (first prize: 2,000,000 francs)

Final Classification

Place	Rider	Team	Time	Age
1	Louison Bobet (Fra)	France	4,495 km 130h29' 26" 34.446 kph	30
2	Jean Brankart (Bel)	Belgium	+ 4'53"	25
3	Charly Gaul (Lux)	Luxembourg/Mixte	+ 11'30"	23
4	Pasquale Fornara (Ita)	Italy	+ 12'44"	30
5	Antonin Rolland (Fra)	France	+ 13'18"	30
6	Raphaël Géminiani (Fra)	France	+ 15'01"	30
7	Giancarlo Astrua (Ita)	Italy	+ 18'13"	27
8	Stan Ockers (Bel)	Belgium	+ 27'13"	35
9	Alex Close (Bel)	Belgium	+ 31'10"	33
10	François Mahé (Fra)	France	+ 36'27"	24

Lanterne Rouge

69	Tony Hoar (GBr)	Great Britain	+ 6h06'01"	23

Points

	Stan Ockers (Bel)	Belgium		35

King of the Mountains

	Charly Gaul (Lux)	Luxembourg/Mixte		23

Team

		France		

1956: Roger Who?

Henri Desgrange's ideal Tour would have seen all the riders riding flat out, all day every day. To some extent Jacques Goddet shared this view and he had even on occasion threatened to withhold prize money when he felt the *peloton* had taken things too easy. For the riders, though, that was not the way they wanted to race. For the stars of the Tour, the race could be broken down into a number of key stages where they had to perform and a number of stages where they would have to defend their position. The rest of the race was primarily about conserving their strength. And so, on those last days, the stars tended to let a break go without gaining too much time.

Sometimes, though, the amount of rope given to the day's break would be misjudged and a group of riders would hold a sizeable lead at the end of the stage, turning the general classification on its head. Normally, though, when that happened the natural order reasserted itself within a few days, and the breakaways faded away down the general classification as the stars came out and came back to the top. But the day was bound to come when the breakaways didn't roll over and play dead, when the breakaways showed some bite. For the Tour that day came in 1956 when a little heralded rider from the regional Nord-Est/Centre squad showed the aces that he deserved a bit more respect than they had shown him.

Roger Walkowiak had been a late sign-up for the Nord-Est/Centre squad, drafted in as a replacement for Gilbert Bauvin, who had been bumped up to the national team. Walko had ridden for the team on two of his previous Tours, in 1955 and 1953, having debuted in 1951 for the Ouest/Sud-Ouest squad. His Tour record didn't suggest he would ever win the Tour, but it did mark him out as a rider capable of getting into a break and putting in the effort to stay away. And he did just that in the 1956 Tour. Not just once, but three times, on three successive stages.

Coming into stage four – a split stage with a 15-kilometre time trial followed by a 125-kilometre road stage – Walkowiak was 17'34" off the yellow jersey being worn by Belgium's Gilbert Desmet. To put some perspective on that, among the pre-race favourites Charly Gaul (Luxembourg/Mixte) and Stan Ockers (Belgium) were both 16'02" off Desmet's pace. After the morning's time trial (won by Gaul) Walkowiak fell to 18'16" off the yellow jersey, still being sported by Desmet. Gaul was at 15'04", Ockers 15'37". This was a Tour lacking in any former winners, with both Louison Bobet and Fausto Coppi recovering from injury, while Hugo Koblet and Ferdi Kübler weren't available. It was a race that ideally suited riders like Gaul and Ockers.

In the road stage that followed the race fractured. A break went away early, and then another group gave chase, while the main *peloton* ambled on. Ockers made the chase group while Gaul missed the bus and got stuck in the *peloton*, losing about 14 minutes to his Belgian rival at the end of the day. One man who didn't miss the bus and did make it into the chase group was Walkowiak, who even actually managed to gain a couple of seconds on Ockers at the end of the stage. (André Darrigade, who had won the opening stage, also made the chase group and finished the stage back in yellow.)

The next day, on the road to Saint-Malo, a break was allowed go clear, and it took three minutes out of the *peloton* at the finish. In the break was that man Walkowiak. The day after that, the same story, only this time the break gained 11 minutes. And Walko was again in it, and now 7'18" off Darrigade's yellow jersey, while Ockers was at 19'34" and Gaul 33'09". And then it happened for a third time, on the road to Angers. Only this time the break that went clear – 30 odd riders – really put some time into the *peloton*: nearly 19 minutes of it. And Walkowiak, who for three days in a row had been in the winning break, he found himself in yellow with a 31'02" advantage over Ockers, 44'37" over Gaul.

At this stage, Walkowiak was clearly just keeping the jersey warm for someone like Gilbert Bauvin (France) or Nello Lauredi (Sud-Est), who made the Angers break. And keep it warm he did, through to the first rest day, 14 July, Bastille Day. And when the race resumed Walkowiak lost the jersey. Or, actually, he surrendered it, he and his *directeur sportif* Sauveur Ducazeaux having decided it would be wiser to let someone else worry about chasing down attacks every day while Walkowiak, without the *maillot jaune*, could ride along in the *peloton* somewhat anonymously, conserving his strength for the latter part of the race.

And that's just what Walko did: a break was allowed go clear, Gerrit Voorting (Netherlands) took the race lead, and Walkowiak became just another regional rider who had kept the yellow jersey warm for others. Through the Pyrenees he held his own and did the same across the transition stages taking the race into the Alps. Riding anonymously. Until the eighteenth stage, Turin to Grenoble, when he popped out of the *peloton* and took back the yellow jersey.

Going into that stage Walkowiak was 4'27" off the race lead, held by Wout Wagtmans (Netherlands). Over the Croix de Fer, where Wagtmans fell away, Walkowiak held his own in a chase group that tried to close down on Gaul and Ockers, who were riding for the stage win. Seven minutes after Gaul took the stage win, Walkowiak rolled home with Gastone Nencini (Italy) and Federico Bahamontes (Spain). Once again leading the Tour, the rider from the regional team now held a 3'56" lead over his more famous national squad rival, Bauvin (whose promotion to the national team had created a vacancy for Walkowiak on the Nord-Est/Centre squad and who, the rest of the year round, was Walkowiak's team-mate at Saint-Raphaël/Géminiani). Four stages remained. Walkowiak's win was far from secure.

That was made clear the very next day. Crossing the Oeillon Walkowiak was on the back foot, the yellow jersey crashing and Bauvin riding away from him, with Gaul, Ockers, Bahamontes and others along to help. But now Walko's Nord-Est/Centre team-mates rallied around. Rested during the middle phase of the race by not having to defend the jersey, they still had something left in the tank when it was most needed. Enough to bring Walko back up to Bauvin and save his lead.

In the following day's time trial – 73 kilometres from Saint-Étienne to Lyon – Walkowiak surrendered two minutes to Bauvin, cutting his lead to a narrow 1'25", but for Bauvin it was now too big a gap to close; Walkowiak on his home turf and with the crowd behind him and the yellow jersey on his back, was riding with all the authority of one of the greats. Walkowiak rode into Paris and added his name to the Tour's role of honour. And, as Firmin Lambot had in 1922, he did it without winning a single stage en route to that victory.

* * * * *

A year after the events on the Ventoux, the Tour had another interesting experience in 1956 when, on the fifteenth stage, the entire Belgian squad went down with a mysterious illness. Bad fish at the team hotel was blamed, but few believed it to be as simple as that and suspected a bad batch of drugs had been administered the night before.

Stage-by-Stage Results for the 1956 Tour de France			Stage Winner	Maillot Jaune
Stage 1 Thu 5 Jul	Reims to Liège 120 starters 118 finishers	223 km 5h19'15" 41.9 kph	André Darrigade (Fra) France	André Darrigade (Fra) France
Stage 2 Fri 6 Jul	Liège to Lille 115 finishers	217 km 6h35'31" 32.9 kph	Fred de Bruyne (Bel) Belgium	André Darrigade (Fra) France
Stage 3 Sat 7 Jul	Lille to Rouen 113 finishers	225 km 6h34'31" 34.2 kph	Arrigo Padovan (Ita) Italy	Gilbert Desmet (Bel) Belgium
Stage 4a Sun 8 Jul	Rouen to Circuit des Essarts (ITT) 113 finishers	15.1 km 22'19" 40.6 kph	Charly Gaul (Lux) Luxembourg/Mixte	Gilbert Desmet (Bel) Belgium
Stage 4b Sun 8 Jul	Rouen to Caen 109 finishers	125 km 2h56'44" 42.4 kph	Roger Hassenforder (Fra) Ouest	André Darrigade (Fra) France
Stage 5 Mon 9 Jul	Caen to Saint-Malo 108 finishers	189 km 4h51'49" 38.9 kph	Joseph Morvan (Fra) Ouest	André Darrigade (Fra) France

Stage-by-Stage Results for the 1956 Tour de France			Stage Winner	Maillot Jaune
Stage 6 Tue 10 Jul	Saint-Malo to Lorient 108 finishers	192 km 4h39'19" 41.2 kph	Fred de Bruyne (Bel) Belgium	André Darrigade (Fra) France
Stage 7 Wed 11 Jul	Lorient to Angers 108 finishers	244 km 5h59'20" 40.7 kph	Alessandro Fantini (Ita) Italy	Roger Walkowiak (Fra) Nord-Est/Centre
Stage 8 Thu 12 Jul	Angers to La Rochelle 107 finishers	180 km 4h14'56" 42.4 kph	Miguel Poblet (Esp) Spain	Roger Walkowiak (Fra) Nord-Est/Centre
Stage 9 Fri 13 Jul	La Rochelle to Bordeaux 106 finishers	219 km 5h31'00" 39.7 kph	Roger Hassenforder (Fra) Ouest	Roger Walkowiak (Fra) Nord-Est/Centre
Sat 14 Jul	Rest day			
Stage 10 Sun 15 Jul	Bordeaux to Bayonne 105 finishers	201 km 4h59'39" 40.2 kph	Fred de Bruyne (Bel) Belgium	Gerrit Voorting (Ned) Netherlands
Stage 11 Mon 16 Jul	Bayonne to Pau 100 finishers	255 km 6h35'57" 38.6 kph	Nino Defilippis (Ita) Italy	André Darrigade (Fra) France
	Major climbs: Col d'Aubisque (1,709m) Valentin Huot (Fra) Sud-Ouest			
Stage 12 Tue 17 Jul	Pau to Luchon 99 finishers	130 km 3h54'40" 33.2 kph	Jean-Pierre Schmitz (Lux) Luxembourg/Mixte	Jan Adriaenssens (Bel) Belgium
	Major climbs: Col d'Aspin (1,489m) Nino Defilippis (Ita) Italy; Col de Peyresourde (1,569m) Jean Schmitz (Lux) Luxembourg/Mixte			
Stage 13 Wed 18 Jul	Luchon to Toulouse 99 finishers	176 km 4h49'46" 36.4 kph	Nino Defilippis (Ita) Italy	Jan Adriaenssens (Bel) Belgium
	Major climbs: Col des Ares (797m) Bruni Monti (Ita) Italy; Col de Portet d'Aspet (1,069m) Charly Gaul (Lux) Luxembourg/Mixte; Col de Latrape (1,100m) Charly Gaul (Lux) Luxembourg/Mixte			
Stage 14 Thu 19 Jul	Toulouse to Montpellier 97 finishers	231 km 5h26'05" 42.5 kph	Roger Hassenforder (Fra) Ouest	Jan Adriaenssens (Bel) Belgium
Stage 15 Fri 20 Jul	Montpellier to Aix-en-Provence 95 finishers	204 km 5h01'10" 40.6 kph	Joseph Thomin (Fra) Ouest	Wout Wagtmans (Ned) Netherlands
Sat 21 Jul	Rest day			
Stage 16 Sun 22 Jul	Aix-en-Provence to Gap 94 finishers	203 km 5h30'15" 36.9 kph	Jean Forestier (Fra) France	Wout Wagtmans (Ned) Netherlands
	Major climbs: Col du Pointu (499m) Jean Forestier (Fra) France; Col de la Croix de l'Homme Mort (1,163m) Jean Forestier (Fra) France; Col de la Sentinelle (980m) Jean Forestier (Fra) France			

Stage-by-Stage Results for the 1956 Tour de France			Stage Winner	Maillot Jaune
Stage 17 Mon 23 Jul	Gap to Turin 94 finishers	234 km 6h42'09" 34.9 kph	Nino Defilippis (Ita) Italy	Wout Wagtmans (Ned) Netherlands
	Major climbs: Col d'Izoard (2,360m) Valentin Huot (Fra) Sud-Ouest; Col de Montgenèvre (1,860m) Valentin Huot (Fra) Sud-Ouest; Colle del Sestriere (2,035m) Charly Gaul (Lux) Luxembourg/Mixte			
Stage 18 Tue 24 Jul	Turin to Grenoble 92 finishers	250 km 8h14'11" 30.4 kph	Charly Gaul (Lux) Luxembourg/Mixte	Roger Walkowiak (Fra) Nord-Est/Centre
	Major climbs: Col du Mont Cenis (2,083m) Federico Bahamontes (Esp) Spain; Col de la Croix de Fer (2,067m) René Marigil (Esp) Spain; Col du Luitel (1,262m) Charly Gaul (Lux) Luxembourg/Mixte			
Stage 19 Wed 25 Jul	Grenoble to Saint-Étienne 92 finishers	173 km 5h32'08" 31.3 kph	Stan Ockers (Bel) Belgium	Roger Walkowiak (Fra) Nord-Est/Centre
	Major climbs: Crêt de l'Oeillon (1,210m) Federico Bahamontes (Esp) Spain; Col de la République (Col du Grand Bois) (1,161m) Stan Ockers (Bel) Belgium			
Stage 20 Thu 26 Jul	Saint-Étienne to Lyon (ITT) 90 finishers	73 km 1h46'47" 41.0 kph	Miguel Bover (Esp) Spain	Roger Walkowiak (Fra) Nord-Est/Centre
Stage 21 Fri 27 Jul	Lyon to Montluçon 89 finishers	237 km 7h04'02" 33.5 kph	Roger Hassenforder (Fra) Ouest	Roger Walkowiak (Fra) Nord-Est/Centre
	Major climbs: Col de la Luère (715m) Jean Dotto (Fra) Sud-Est; Col de Beau Louis (840m) Roger Hassenforder (Fra) Ouest			
Stage 22 Sat 28 Jul	Montluçon to Paris (Parc des Princes) 88 finishers	331 km 9h28'05" 35.0 kph	Gastone Nencini (Ita) Italy	Roger Walkowiak (Fra) Nord-Est/Centre

Prize fund: 38,000,000 francs (first prize: 2,000,000 francs)

Final Classification

Place	Rider	Team	Time	Age
1	Roger Walkowiak (Fra)	Nord-Est/Centre	4,498 km 124h01'16" 36.268 kph	29
2	Gilbert Bauvin (Fra)	France	+ 1'25"	29
3	Jan Adriaensens (Bel)	Belgium	+ 3'44"	24
4	Federico Bahamontes (Esp)	Spain	+ 10'14"	28
5	Nino Defilippis (Ita)	Italy	+ 10'25"	24
6	Wout Wagtmans (Ned)	Netherlands	+ 10'59"	27
7	Nello Lauredi (Fra)	Sud-Est	+ 14'01"	31
8	Stan Ockers (Bel)	Belgium	+ 16'52"	36
9	René Privat (Fra)	France	+ 22'59"	26
10	Antonio Barbosa (Por)	Luxembourg/Mixte	+ 26'03"	25

Lanterne Rouge

88	Roger Chaussabel (Fra)	Sud-Est	+ 4h10'18"	24

Points

	Stan Ockers (Bel)	Belgium		36

King of the Mountains

	Charly Gaul (Lux)	Luxembourg/Mixte		24

Super Combativité

	André Darrigade (Fra)	France		27

Team

		Belgium		

1957: New Kid on the Block

In the decade since the Tour's return from it's wartime hiatus a new generation of riders, distant from their pre-war ancestors, had remade the Tour in their own image. The race had been won by major and (somewhat) minor riders: Jean Robic, Gino Bartali, Fausto Coppi, Ferdi Kübler, Hugo Koblet, Louison Bobet and Roger Walkowiak. Each had added something, some new myth or legend to the race's never ending story. But even though it was only a decade, it was already time to ring in the changes, to bring forth a new generation. It was already time for climbers like Charly Gaul and Federico Bahamontes to show they weren't just men of the mountains. And time for the greatest time trialist the race had yet seen to make his debut, Jacques Anquetil.

The Norman's entry to the Tour was eased by Bobet's decision to sit the race out and, as the 32-year-old three-time winner put it, let the youngsters take the responsibility of winning. That opened the door for team boss Marcel Bidot to bring the 23-year-old Anquetil into the squad. Already a prodigious time trial talent – he had won the GP des Nations every year since 1954 and set a new Hour record in 1956 – Anquetil already had already added a victory in Paris-Nice to his *palmarès* before Bidot selected him.

The French still had the usual problem of a surfeit of talent: Roger Walkowiak, as the defending champion, obviously had to be on the national team. As did the man who ran him a close second, Gilbert Bauvin. And then there was André Darrigade, a man who could win stages with ease. Would they – and Anquetil – all be able to work together, for the one goal, a victory for France? It was Darrigade (Anquetil's team-mate at Helyett/Potin) who helped answer that question, declaring that he would be riding for his friend Anquetil.

Darrigade, as he had the year before, took the opening stage and the first yellow and green jerseys of the race (with runner up Miguel Poblet of Spain getting to wear the green one). Anquetil finished safely in the main *peloton*, a minute or so behind his team-mate, but was already having to learn about riding the Tour the hard way. A little over half way through the stage he'd tumbled and picked up some road rash after having been dawdling at the back of the *peloton*. The back was no place for champions.

The opening stage was run off in sweltering heat, as was the next, and on the road from Granville to Caen, Charly Gaul (Luxembourg/ Mixte) climbed off and went home. He was not the only rider to make an early exit. Of the 120 riders who started the Tour, 31 had already gone home by the time the race reached the end of its fourth stage. *L'Équipe* likened these opening stages to a death march and compared the race to a crematorium on wheels. With all that was now known about the *peloton*'s abuse of amphetamines – and the way riders who used them rode in the heat – some suspected doping as being behind the exit of so many.

Stage three saw the *peloton* riding two stages in one, a team time trial followed by a road race, and it was in the latter that Anquetil took his first stage win. Somewhat appropriately, this was in his home town of Rouen (he was born and grew up in the hills above the city). Two days later he was wearing his first *maillot jaune*, which he held for another two days before surrendering it, letting someone else – Nicolas Barone of the Île-de-France squad in this case – worry about defending it.

A day later, on the road to Besançon, and Anquetil was in trouble when his team-mate Jean Forestier got away in a break that put the thick end of 18 minutes into the *peloton*. Shades of 1956? Even worse, actually. Forestier had some hard races on his *palmarès*, including two victories in the Tour de Romandie and the one-day classics Paris-Roubaix and the Ronde van Vlaanderen. Now, 14'28" off yellow and the mountains about to begin, Anquetil's chances of victory looked like they might already be gone.

Darrigade made clear to Anquetil that a 14 minutes deficit would be too much to take into the mountains and he was going to have to do something about it. In the next stage Anquetil did, attacking in the feedzone on the road to Thonon-les-Baines. As well as taking his second stage win, the attack allowed him to close the gap to yellow to just 2'39".

Anquetil took the race lead again on the first day in the Alps, holding his own with the climbers while Forestier faded and fell away. Things stayed much the same as the race went down through the Alps and across the transition stages toward to Pyrenees. But before the mountains came a brief excursion into Spain and a short time trial up Montjuich – which, naturally, Anquetil won.

Anquetil and his French team-mates had a torrid time of it in the mountains, and, while Anquetil managed to come out with the jersey still on his back, his team-mates slid down the general classification, with Belgium's Marcel Janssens rising up to second, 9'14" off yellow. Too much to overcome, especially when Anquetil put another five minutes into him in the last time trial, on the pre-penultimate day of the race. The debutant Norman's first Tour win was in the bag.

* * * * *

Nineteen fifty seven saw the usual round of births, deaths and marriages and among the buried was Maurice Garin, the little chimney sweep who had won the first Tour. Also among the dead were a couple of journalists, radio reporters Alex Virot and Roger Wagner. They had helped revolutionise radio's coverage of the Tour and both died when the motorbike they were riding on went off the road as they followed the Tour through the Pyrenees.

But even as radio coverage of the Tour improved, it was hard to ignore to the box in the corner, TV, which was assuming more and more importance. Unfortunately, for 1957, the increased coverage – more reports from the race route – was somewhat delayed, Félix

Lévitan seeking to capitalise on TV broadcasts and demanding revenue in return for broadcast rights. The national TV company didn't feel a fee should be paid and a stand-off ensued, which meant that coverage of the race was by delayed transmission, each stage being shown the following day. The fight over who should gain the most from the Tour's broadcast rights had begun.

Stage-by-Stage Results for the 1957 Tour de France			Stage Winner	Maillot Jaune
Stage 1 Thu 27 Jun	Nantes to Granville 120 starters 117 finishers	204 km 4h56'18" 41.3 kph	André Darrigade (Fra) France	André Darrigade (Fra) France
Stage 2 Fri 28 Jun	Granville to Caen 106 finishers	226 km 6h09'22" 36.7 kph	René Privat (Fra) France	René Privat (Fra) France
Stage 3a Sat 29 Jun	Circuit de La Prairie (TTT) 106 finishers	15 km 19'18" 46.6 kph	France	René Privat (Fra) France
Stage 3b Sat 29 Jun	Caen to Rouen 101 finishers	134 km 3h23'44" 39.5 kph	Jacques Anquetil (Fra) France	René Privat (Fra) France
Stage 4 Sun 30 Jun	Rouen to Roubaix 89 finishers	232 km 6h23'34" 36.3 kph	Marcel Janssens (Bel) Belgium	René Privat (Fra) France
Stage 5 Mon 1 Jul	Roubaix to Charleroi 87 finishers	170 km 4h25'26" 38.4 kph	Gilbert Bauvin (Fra) France	Jacques Anquetil (Fra) France
Stage 6 Tue 2 Jul	Charleroi to Metz 83 finishers	248 km 6h29'54" 38.2 kph	André Trochut (Fra) Sud-Ouest	Jacques Anquetil (Fra) France
Stage 7 Wed 3 Jul	Metz to Colmar 82 finishers	223 km 6h21'13" 35.1 kph	Roger Hassenforder (Fra) Nord-Est/Centre	Nicolas Barone (Fra) Île-de-France
	Major climbs: Collet du Linge (983m) Louis Bergaud (Fra) France			
Stage 8 Thu 4 Jul	Colmar to Besançon 80 finishers	192 km 5h18'59" 36.1 kph	Pierino Baffi (Ita) Italy	Jean Forestier (Fra) France
Stage 9 Fri 5 Jul	Besançon to Thonon-les-Bains 77 finishers	188 km 5h04'38" 37.0 kph	Jacques Anquetil (Fra) France	Jean Forestier (Fra) France
Sat 6 Jul	Rest day			
Stage 10 Sun 7 Jul	Thonon-les-Bains to Briançon 75 finishers	247 km 7h48'26" 31.6 kph	Gastone Nencini (Ita) Italy	Jacques Anquetil (Fra) France
	Major climbs: Col de Tamié (907m) Louis Bergaud (Fra) France; Col du Télégraphe (1,566m) Gastone Nencini (Ita) Italy; Col du Galibier (2,556m) Marcel Janssens (Bel) Belgium			

Stage-by-Stage Results for the 1957 Tour de France			Stage Winner	Maillot Jaune
Stage 11 Mon 8 Jul	Briançon to Cannes 73 finishers	286 km 9h18'59" 30.7 kph	René Privat (Fra) France	Jacques Anquetil (Fra) France
	Major climbs: Col d'Allos (2,250m) Louis Bergaud (Fra) France; Col de Luens (1,054m) Louis Bergaud (Fra) France; Saint-Cézaire (500m) Marcel Janssens (Bel) Belgium			
Stage 12 Tue 9 Jul	Cannes to Marseille 70 finishers	239 km 7h42'52" 31.0 kph	Jean Stablinski (Fra) France	Jacques Anquetil (Fra) France
	Major climbs: Mont Faron (665m) Jean Stablinski (Fra) France; Col de l'Espigoulier (728m) Jean Stablinski (Fra) France			
Stage 13 Wed 10 Jul	Marseille to Alès 67 finishers	160 km 5h02'54" 31.7 kph	Nino Defilippis (Ita) Italy	Jacques Anquetil (Fra) France
Stage 14 Thu 11 Jul	Alès to Perpignan 67 finishers	246 km 6h17'23" 39.1 kph	Roger Hassenforder (Fra) Nord-Est/Centre	Jacques Anquetil (Fra) France
Stage 15a Fri 12 Jul	Perpignan to Barcelona 66 finishers	197 km 5h24'47" 36.4 kph	René Privat (Fra) France	Jacques Anquetil (Fra) France
Stage 15b Fri 13 Jul	Barcelona to Montjuich (ITT) 66 finishers	9.8 km 14'29" 40.6 kph	Jacques Anquetil (Fra) France	Jacques Anquetil (Fra) France
Sat 14 Jul	Rest day			
Stage 16 Sun 14 Jul	Barcelona to Ax-les-Thermes 63 finishers	220 km 6h13'34" 35.3 kph	Jean Bourlès (Fra) Ouest	Jacques Anquetil (Fra) France
	Major climbs: Col de Tosas (1,865m) Jean Bourles (Fra) Ouest; Col du Puymorens (1,915m) Jean Bourles (Fra) Ouest			
Stage 17 Mon 15 Jul	Ax-les-Thermes to Saint-Gaudens 60 finishers	236 km 7h00'06" 33.7 kph	Nino Defilippis (Ita) Italy	Jacques Anquetil (Fra) France
	Major climbs: Col de Portet d'Aspet (1,069m) Mies Stolker (Ned) Netherlands; Col du Portillon (1,298m) Désiré Keteleer (Bel) Belgium; Col de Port (1,249m) Désiré Keteleer (Bel) Belgium			
Stage 18 Tue 16 Jul	Saint-Gaudens to Pau 58 finishers	207 km 6h37'31" 31.2 kph	Gastone Nencini (Ita) Italy	Jacques Anquetil (Fra) France
	Major climbs: Col du Tourmalet (2,115m) José Da Silva (Por) Luxembourg/Mixte; Col d'Aubisque (1,709m) Jean Dotto (Fra) Sud-Est			
Stage 19 Wed 17 Jul	Pau to Bordeaux 58 finishers	194 km 5h04'22" 38.2 kph	Pierino Baffi (Ita) Italy	Jacques Anquetil (Fra) France
Stage 20 Thu 18 Jul	Bordeaux to Libourne (ITT) 58 finishers	66 km 1h32'17" 42.9 kph	Jacques Anquetil (Fra) France	Jacques Anquetil (Fra) France

Stage-by-Stage Results for the 1957 Tour de France			Stage Winner	Maillot Jaune
Stage 21 Fri 19 Jul	Libourne to Tours 56 finishers	317 km 9h55'53" 31.9 kph	André Darrigade (Fra) France	Jacques Anquetil (Fra) France
Stage 22 Sat 20 Jul	Tours to Paris (Parc des Princes) 56 finishers	227 km 5h58'31" 38.0 kph	André Darrigade (Fra) France	Jacques Anquetil (Fra) France

Prize fund: 40,000,000 francs (first prize: 2,000,000 francs)

Final Classification				
Place	**Rider**	**Team**	**Time**	**Age**
1	Jacques Anquetil (Fra)	France	4,669 km 135h44'42" 34.520 kph	24
2	Marcel Janssens (Bel)	Belgium	+ 14'56"	26
3	Adolf Christian (Aut)	Switzerland	+ 17'20"	23
4	Jean Forestier (Fra)	France	+ 18'02"	27
5	Jesus Loroño (Esp)	Spain	+ 20'17"	32
6	Gastone Nencini (Ita)	Italy	+ 26'03"	27
7	Nino Defilippis (Ita)	Italy	+ 27'57"	25
8	Wim van Est (Ned)	Netherlands	+ 28'10"	34
9	Jan Adriaenssens (Bel)	Belgium	+ 34'07"	25
10	Jean Dotto (Fra)	Sud-Est	+ 36'31"	29
Lanterne Rouge				
56	Guy Million (Fra)	Île-de-France	+ 4h41'11"	25
Points				
	Jean Forestier (Fra)	France		27
King of the Mountains				
	Gastone Nencini (Ita)	Italy		27
Super Combativité				
	Nicolas Barone (Fra)	Île-de-France		26
Team				
		France		

1958: The Angel of the Mountains

The 1958 Tour featured three time trials, including the first up to the summit of the Ventoux. Jacques Anquetil – already a five-time winner of the GP des Nations (the unofficial time trial world championships) and a former holder of the Hour record – should have been expected to win the two flat races against the clock but, surprisingly, Luxembourg's Charly Gaul came out on top in all three.

Gaul was already a champion and, arguably, should have already won the Tour. After failing to finish his first two Tours, he'd claimed the bottom step of the podium in the 1955 race, despite his problems in the heat of the Ventoux. A year later came the race he was favourite to win – with a victory in the Giro d'Italia still fresh in his legs – but somehow he contrived to let the opportunity fall between his fingers. A year after that he quit the race just two days into the Tour and so got to read about Jacques Anquetil's victorious début rather than have to witness it firsthand.

Even in the 1958 Tour – though one of the pre-race favourites, alongside Anquetil and Louison Bobet – Gaul did not look like he was quite ready to live up to his reputation, leaving it until the last of the trio of time trials (to Dijon, on the penultimate day of the race) to finally don the *maillot jaune*. No, rather than the race looking like it would deliver a victory to Luxembourg (or even to Anquetil or Bobet), the real race seemed to be between Italy and France, in the forms of Vito Favero (riding for the Italian national squad) and Raphaël Géminiani (riding for the regional Centre/Midi team).

Géminiani – who had finished second in 1951 and was generally good for a top ten finish in any of the Grand Tours – had missed out on selection for the French national squad when Anquetil insisted he couldn't be on the team, not with Louison Bobet back in the squad and Gém and Bobet being close friends. While Anquetil was only too happy to have a team-mate like Darrigade declare his loyalty to him, he wasn't willing to grant a potential rival such as Bobet a similar honour. Gém took his relegation to one of the regional squads badly, publicly insulting team-boss Marcel Bidot and threatening to make things tough at the Tour by going on the attack. And go on the attack is just what the man from Clermont-Ferrand did.

On the road to Saint-Brieuc – the sixth stage – the French team found itself in trouble when a break got away and a crash saw them having to chase hard for more than 60 kilometres to bring it back. Only, just when they had done that, Géminiani threw a new attack at them, he and his Centre/Midi team-mates launching a fresh assault which the French squad was too exhausted to bring back. Among the riders to spot their opportunity and go with Géminiani was Favero. At the end of the stage Gém's break had gained more than 10 minutes on the *peloton* and he was up to third overall, 2'32" behind the yellow jersey. That was now being sported by Gerrit Voorting (Netherlands/Luxembourg) after having passed across the shoulders of André Darrigade (France), Jos Hoevenaers (Belgium), Wim van Est (Netherlands/Luxembourg) and Gilbert Bauvin (France) since the race's start in Brussels. Favero, he was up to ninth, 9'28" off yellow. Bobet fell to 12'53", Anquetil 13'23" and Gaul 15'25". With 141.5 kilometres of time trials across Stages Eight, 18 and 23 all to come these weren't insurmountable time gaps, but they were worrying.

The first of the races against the clock came in Châteaulin and produced a surprise, with Gaul getting the better of Anquetil – Monsieur Contre-la-Montre, now being beaten in his own discipline – and gaining seven seconds on the road, along with another minute in bonifications. Bobet and Gém both lost two minutes, while Favero ceded four.

The next day Favero – who no one was treating as a threat – got away in a break with Darrigade and others and put nine minutes

Crossing a bridge on the road from Royan to Bordeaux in the 1958 Tour.

into the *peloton* and saw Darrigade back in yellow. The Italian was now up to second overall, 23 seconds off yellow, Géminiani a few places further back at 1'47", Anquetil at 9'47", Gaul at 11'31" and Bobet at 12'12". In the Pyrenees four days later Gém found himself inheriting Darrigade's yellow jersey, the early leaders falling away as the mountains rose up, with Favero holding on to his second place, just three seconds back.

The day after, with the help of 30 seconds in time bonuses for finishing second on the stage – in a big bunch gallop, more than a minute after Spain's Federico Bahamontes had taken the victory salute – Favero took the race lead from Gém. Another 30 seconds in bonifications the next day pushed the Italian's lead out to just shy of a minute.

There then followed two eventless transition stages, through Béziers and Nîmes, before the Tour tackled the Ventoux, with live TV coverage beaming the race into homes, cafés and bars around France. In the *contre-la-montre* up the bald mountain Gém got the better of Favero coming out of it with a 2'01" lead on the Italian and the yellow jersey back in his possession. But the big winner on the day was Gaul, who – despite the scorching heat and needing to be given oxygen at the end of the stage – won the day ahead of Federico Bahamontes and closed to just 3'43" off yellow, with Anquetil now at 7'27" and Bobet (who once knew how to tame this mountain) at 10'18". For the two French Tour champions their chances of final victory looked over, with the real question being whether either the unfancied Géminiani or Favero could hold off Gaul.

That question seemed to be answered in the affirmative the very next day when the Angel of the Mountains went and blew his gains over the bumpy roads to Gap, his rivals attacking when he had to change bikes and his mixed Netherlands/Luxembourg team simply not having the strength to help him mount a pursuit. The little climber from Luxembourg ended up shedding more than 11 minutes and – with Gém adding 30 seconds in bonifications to his lead – falling to eighth, 15'12" off yellow. Gaul was not the only one to lose time: Bobet slipped six minutes and fell to 16'55", while Favero lost a minute and a bit, falling to 3'17". Anquetil held his own against Géminiani, finishing the stage 7'57" off yellow, now up to third place overall.

Two days later, as the *peloton* raced over the mountainous roads between Briançon and Aix-les-Bains, Gaul served up an epic day's riding which changed everything. It was a day far removed from the heat wave the riders had started the Tour under, the rain and the temperature falling as the riders rode through the mountains of the Chartreuse. Perfect weather for the Angel of the Mountains, who spread his wings on the second of the day's five mountains, the Col du Luitel, and soared away from the chasers behind. By the summit of the Col de Porte Gaul had swept up the day's early break and was soloing to victory. And as he soared over the final two mountains – the Cucheron and the Granier – behind him Géminiani, Favero, Anquetil and Bobet were suffering their own personal hells. Of those four though, Favero found something still in the tank and mounted a comeback. Not nearly enough to challenge Gaul, but more than enough to put Géminiani under the cosh. In Aix-les-Bains the Italian finished 10 minutes down on Gaul, Gém another four minutes back. Bobet lost 19 minutes, Anquetil 23.

Favero was now in yellow, with Géminiani in second 39 seconds back, and Gaul up to third, 1'07" off yellow. With a time trial to come, that was no time at all. There Gaul – who had put more than two minutes into both Géminiani and Favero on the race's first flat time trial earlier in the race – took his fourth stage win, gaining more than three minutes on his French and Italian rivals, and winning the Tour.

Stage-by-Stage Results for the 1958 Tour de France			Stage Winner	Maillot Jaune
Stage 1 Thu 26 Jun	Brussels to Ghent 120 starters 118 finishers	184 km 4h33'12" 40.4 kph	André Darrigade (Fra) France	André Darrigade (Fra) France
Stage 2 Fri 27 Jun	Ghent to Dunkerque 116 finishers	198 km 5h12'02" 38.1 kph	Gerrit Voorting (Ned) Netherlands/ Luxembourg	Jos Hoevenaers (Bel) Belgium
Stage 3 Sat 28 Jun	Dunkerque to Mers-les-Bains 116 finishers	177 km 4h44'13" 37.4 kph	Gilbert Bauvin (Fra) France	Wim van Est (Ned) Netherlands/ Luxembourg

Stage-by-Stage Results for the 1958 Tour de France			Stage Winner	Maillot Jaune
Stage 4 Sun 29 Jun	Le Tréport to Versailles 115 finishers	205 km 5h04'04" 40.5 kph	Jean Gainche (Fra) Ouest/Sud-Ouest	Wim van Est (Ned) Netherlands/ Luxembourg
Stage 5 Mon 30 Jun	Versailles to Caen 113 finishers	232 km 5h29'44" 42.2 kph	Tino Sabbadini (Fra) Ouest/Sud-Ouest	Gilbert Bauvin (Fra) France
Stage 6 Tue 1 Jul	Caen to Saint-Brieuc 110 finishers	223 km 5h21'45" 41.6 kph	Martin van Geneugden (Bel) Belgium	Gerrit Voorting (Ned) Netherlands/ Luxembourg
Stage 7 Wed 2 Jul	Saint-Brieuc to Brest 108 finishers	170 km 4h03'31" 41.9 kph	~~Arrigo Padovan (Ita)~~ ~~Italy~~ (1) Brian Robinson (GBr) Internations	Gerrit Voorting (Ned) Netherlands/ Luxembourg
Stage 8 Thu 3 Jul	Châteaulin (ITT) 108 finishers	46 km 1h07'12" 41.1 kph	Charly Gaul (Lux) Netherlands/ Luxembourg	Gerrit Voorting (Ned) Netherlands/ Luxembourg
Stage 9 Fri 4 Jul	Quimper to Saint-Nazaire 108 finishers	206 km 4h48'27" 42.8 kph	André Darrigade (Fra) France	André Darrigade (Fra) France
Stage 10 Sat 5 Jul	Saint-Nazaire to Royan 106 finishers	255 km 6h04'57" 41.9 kph	Pierino Baffi (Ita) Italy	André Darrigade (Fra) France
Stage 11 Sun 6 Jul	Royan to Bordeaux 105 finishers	137 km 3h12'22" 42.7 kph	Arrigo Padovan (Ita) Italy	André Darrigade (Fra) France
Stage 12 Mon 7 Jul	Bordeaux to Dax 105 finishers	161 km 4h11'19" 38.4 kph	Martin van Geneugden (Bel) Belgium	André Darrigade (Fra) France
Stage 13 Tue 8 Jul	Dax to Pau 104 finishers	230 km 6h15'48" 36.7 kph	Louis Bergaud (Fra) France	Raphaël Géminiani (Fra) Centre/Midi
Major climbs: Col d'Aubisque (1,709m) Federico Bahamontes (Esp) Spain				
Stage 14 Wed 9 Jul	Pau to Luchon 104 finishers	129 km 3h35'22" 35.9 kph	Federico Bahamontes (Esp) Spain	Vito Favero (Ita) Italy
Major climbs: Col d'Aspin (1,489m) Federico Bahamontes (Esp) Spain; Col de Peyresourde (1,569m) Federico Bahamontes (Esp) Spain				
Stage 15 Thu 10 Jul	Luchon to Toulouse 96 finishers	176 km 4h40'41" 37.6 kph	André Darrigade (Fra) France	Vito Favero (Ita) Italy
Major climbs: Col de Portet d'Aspet (1,069m) Federico Bahamontes (Esp) Spain				

Stage-by-Stage Results for the 1958 Tour de France			Stage Winner	Maillot Jaune
Stage 16 Fri 11 Jul	Toulouse to Béziers 96 finishers	187 km 5h27'34" 34.3 kph	Pierino Baffi (Ita) Italy	Vito Favero (Ita) Italy
Stage 17 Sat 12 Jul	Béziers to Nîmes 95 finishers	189 km 5h10'15" 36.6 kph	André Darrigade (Fra) France	Vito Favero (Ita) Italy
Stage 18 Sun 13 Jul	Bédoin to Mont Ventoux (ITT) 94 finishers	21.5 km 1h02'09" 20.8 kph	Charly Gaul (Lux) Netherlands/ Luxembourg	Raphaël Géminiani (Fra) Centre/Midi
	Major climbs: Mont Ventoux (1,909m) Charly Gaul (Lux) Netherlands/Luxembourg			
Stage 19 Mon 14 Jul	Carpentras to Gap 92 finishers	178 km 4h53'18" 36.4 kph	Gastone Nencini (Ita) Italy	Raphaël Géminiani (Fra) Centre/Midi
	Major climbs: Col de la Sentinelle (980m) Gastone Nencini (Ita) Italy; Col de Perty (1,303m) Jean Dotto (Fra) Centre/Midi; Col de Foreyssasse (1,040m) Gastone Nencini (Ita) Italy			
Stage 20 Tue 15 Jul	Gap to Briançon 88 finishers	165 km 5h18'35" 31.1 kph	Federico Bahamontes (Esp) Spain	Raphaël Géminiani (Fra) Centre/Midi
	Major climbs: Col de Vars (2,110m) Nino Catalano (Ita) Italy; Col d'Izoard (2,360m) Federico Bahamontes (Esp) Spain			
Stage 21 Wed 16 Jul	Briançon to Aix-les-Bains 80 finishers	219 km 6h59'10" 31.3 kph	Charly Gaul (Lux) Netherlands/ Luxembourg	Vito Favero (Ita) Italy
	Major climbs: Col du Lautaret (2,058m) Piet van Est (Ned) Netherlands/Luxembourg; Col du Luitel (1,262m) Gianni Ferlenghi (Ita) Italy; Chamrousse (1,720m) Gianni Ferlenghi (Ita) Italy; Col de Porte (1,326m) Charly Gaul (Lux) Netherlands/Luxembourg; Col du Cucheron (1,139m) Charly Gaul (Lux) Netherlands/Luxembourg; Col du Granier (1,134m) Charly Gaul (Lux) Netherlands/Luxembourg			
Stage 22 Thu 17 Jul	Aix-les-Bains to Besançon 80 finishers	237 km 7h15'01" 32.7 kph	André Darrigade (Fra) France	Vito Favero (Ita) Italy
	Major climbs: Col de la Faucille (Côte des Rousses) (1,140m) Federico Bahamontes (Esp) Spain			
Stage 23 Fri 18 Jul	Besançon to Dijon (ITT) 78 finishers	74 km 1h40'27" 44.2 kph	Charly Gaul (Lux) Netherlands/ Luxembourg	Charly Gaul (Lux) Netherlands/ Luxembourg
Stage 24 Sat 19 Jul	Dijon to Paris (Parc des Princes) 78 finishers	320 km 9h25'46" 33.9 kph	Pierino Baffi (Ita) Italy	Charly Gaul (Lux) Netherlands/ Luxembourg

(1) Arrigo Padovan was stripped of the stage win following an irregular sprint.

Prize fund: 40,000,000 francs (first prize: 2,000,000 francs)

Final Classification

Place	Rider	Team	Time	Age
1	Charly Gaul (Lux)	Netherlands/ Luxembourg	4,319 km 116h59'05" 36.919 kph	26
2	Vito Favero (Ita)	Italy	+ 3'10"	26
3	Raphaël Géminiani (Fra)	Centre/Midi	+ 3'41"	33
4	Jan Adriaensens (Bel)	Belgium	+ 7'16"	26
5	Gastone Nencini (Ita)	Italy	+ 13'33"	28
6	Jozef Planckaert (Bel)	Belgium	+ 28'01"	24
7	Louison Bobet (Fra)	France	+ 31'39"	33
8	Federico Bahamontes (Esp)	Spain	+ 40'44"	30
9	Louis Bergaud (Fra)	France	+ 48'33"	30
10	Jos Hoevenaers (Bel)	Belgium	+ 58'26"	26
Lanterne Rouge				
78	Walter Favre (Sui)	Switzerland/Germany	+ 3h49'28"	27
Points				
	Jean Graczyk (Fra)	Centre/Midi		25
King of the Mountains				
	Federico Bahamontes (Esp)	Spain		30
Super Combativité				
	Federico Bahamontes (Esp)	Spain		30
Team				
		Belgium		

1959: Baha-mania

One of the most enduring legends about Federico Bahamontes is that, on his début at the Tour de France in 1954, he escaped the *peloton* and scaled the Col de la Romeyère alone. The race had already been through the Pyrenees and the Massif Central and was entering its final phase of mountains, the Alps. Baha was well out of contention for the overall honours but already more or less had the King of the Mountains title sewn up and had earned himself the nickname the Eagle of Toledo. While Bahamontes could get up the mountains with an ease lesser mortals gawped at, the Spaniard seemed to have more than a little difficulty coping with the descents. And so, having sealed the climbing points and realised at the summit that he had a couple of broken spokes, Bahamontes stopped that day on the Romeyère and waited for the race to catch up to him, and his team-car to arrive with a replacement wheel. And he ate an ice-cream while he did so.

Two years later Baha returned to the *grande boucle* – a knee injury having caused him to sit out the previous Tour – and ended the race an impressive fourth place overall, ten minutes behind Roger Walkowiak, having already started both the Vuelta a España and the Giro d'Italia that season. In 1957 he was one of the favourites for victory, but was forced out in circumstances that saw his *directeur sportif*, Luis Puig, banned from the race for having given his rider an injection at a time when the Tour's rules – in a reaction to the problems revealed in 1955 – required that all injections be administered by their own doctor, Pierre Dumas. A year later Baha won his first stages in the race and added a second climbing title.

By 1959, things seem to be finally clicking into place for the Spaniard: Fausto Coppi was his *directeur sportif* at Tricofilina/Coppi, and while the two had their fallings out (such as the Vuelta, which Baha rode for KAS), *il Campionissimo* seemed to give his charge the confidence to believe he could win the Tour outright, if he just played his cards right. And at the Spanish national team, Baha was fortunate to have Dalmacio Langarica as the team's *directeur sportif* and backing him for an all-or-nothing assault on the Tour.

And so the Eagle of Toledo started the forty-sixth Tour with a new-found confidence. And, from the off, that confidence was clear, the Spaniard attacking on the opening stage and putting time into his three key rivals – Charly Gaul on the combined Netherlands/Luxembourg squad and Jacques Anquetil and Roger Rivière on the French squad. (There were others to keep a watch on too – Italy's Ercole Baldini and Vito Favero, France's aging stars Louison Bobet and Raphaël Géminiani – but the chief rivals were those three: Gaul, Anquetil and Rivière.)

That time gained by Bahamontes early in the race – 1'29" – was a wise investment, for come the Tour's sixth stage, the first of three time trials, the Spaniard lost time: 2'58" to Rivière, 2'00" to Anquetil and 1'22" to Gaul.

Through the Pyrenees Baha was able to put the French duo on the back foot, reclaiming a small amount of time on both of them, while Gaul shadowed his every move and held his position relative to the Spaniard.

On a hot day along the rolling roads between Albi and Aurillac on Stage 13 any hope Gaul had of defending his Tour title more or less evaporated. Anquetil and Bahamontes got into a break at the feedzone in Rodez, a break which both Gaul and Rivière missed. On the climb at Montsalvy, Bahamontes was in top form, leading the escapees. But when Gaul hit the climb he just died a thousand deaths, losing 20 minutes on the day (and another 30 seconds in time penalties for accepting pushes from the crowds). Rivière, who had also missed the break going away, fared a little bit better than the Angel of the Mountains, losing just 3'52" on the day.

Two stages later came the showdown at the Puy de Dôme, a 12.5-kilometre time trial from bottom to top. On the Ventoux the previous year the Eagle had lost 31 seconds to the Angel, but on the much shorter Puy it was Baha who came out on top, putting 1'26" into Gaul and 3'37" and 3'41" into Rivière and Anquetil. The Spaniard was now just four seconds off yellow, with Anquetil 5'04" behind him, Rivière 7'24" and Gaul out of it at 23'43".

It was another two stages before Bahamontes finally donned the *maillot jaune* and – appropriately enough – it was on a day which saw the Tour once more cross the Romeyère, the mountain he had stopped on and eaten an ice cream all those years before. And it was on that col that the Spaniard launched the attack that won him that jersey. On the descent he was joined by Gaul and the two sped on through Villard-de-Lans and Saint-Nizier-du-Moucherotte before reaching Grenoble, where the Angel won the stage and the Eagle the jersey (while Anquetil and Rivière were pushed back another four minutes).

The Tour was not yet won, though. There were still five stages to ride. And on the very next of them Henry Anglade (of the regional Centre/Midi squad) figured that, at fourth overall and just 4'51" off yellow, he still had a chance, could do as Gaul had done the year before and upset the apple cart with one day in the mountains. And that chance came on the descent of the Petit-Bernard, with Bahamontes having problems, while Gaul pressed on, Anglade with him. The race was in the balance.

But also suffering with problems were Anquetil and Rivière. And, now in company with Bahamontes, they had a choice: sit back and watch as Anglade rode away with the Tour, or chase and help save Bahamontes's jersey? The year before, when Gaul attacked Géminiani and won the Tour, Gém was upset by the lack of support given to him by other French riders, particularly his friend Louison Bobet, who had instead tried to support his national squad team-mate Anquetil. Judas, Gém called Bobet. Yes, they were on rival teams (Bobet and Anquetil on the national team, Géminiani on the regional Centre/Midi squad) but on that day Gém felt they should have all raced for France and stopped a foreigner, Gaul, from winning the Tour. And now, a year on, a similar scenario was unfolding: Anquetil and Rivière could have blocked Bahamontes and let Anglade win the Tour for France. Instead, they chose to help the Spaniard. Anglade ended the day taking just a handful of seconds from Bahamontes and the Spaniard's yellow jersey was saved.

And that, more or less, was it. The penultimate day's time trial allowed Anquetil and Rivière – both specialists at the discipline – to pull back some time, but nothing that even came close to challenging Bahamontes's grasp on the *maillot jaune*. That this and the previous flat time trial were the only two stages on which the two French stars were able to put time into the Spaniard speaks volumes about the form Bahamontes was in that year and the control he exerted over the race from the first stage.

* * * * *

Exiting the Tour on the day that Bahamontes's jersey was saved was Bobet. Dropped on the Galibier the fight was gone from him. But, before he climbed off, Bobet climbed the Iseran one last time, one last ride through the Casse Déserte before abandoning the Tour. Fittingly for a champion, waiting for him atop the Iseran was Gino Bartali, there to usher him out of the Tour.

Two days later another former champion went home, but his end was less noble than that chosen by Bobet: Jean Robic was eliminated from the race having failed to make the time cut-off. And the man most responsible for his demise was Great Britain's Brian Robinson.

A Briton, Reginald Shirley, had entered to ride the 1908 Tour but never made the start and for the first few decades of the race's existence the closest the British got to the race was the London-born Georges Passerieu. That ended in 1937 when a combined Great Britain/Canada squad entered the race, made up of three men (Charlie Holland and Bill Burl, along with Pierre Gachon), none of whom made it back to Paris.

In 1955 the British tried again, this time with a 10-man team flying the flag for Queen and country. As well as taking home the experience of actually riding the Tour, they also brought home the *lanterne rouge*, Tony Hoar arriving in Paris in last place. The following year Robinson, a veteran of that 1955 effort, returned as a member of the Luxembourg/Mixte team, with whom he was again the sole British entrant the following year. A year after that, riding on the mixed Internations squad alongside riders from Austria, Denmark, Ireland, Portugal and two other Britons, Robinson took a stage win, after having been impeded in a sprint by Arrigo Padovan.

Again riding on the mixed Internations squad in 1959 Robinson had almost been turfed off the race at the end of fourteenth stage, to Clermont-Ferrand, until his *directeur sportif* – Sauveur Ducazeaux, Roger Walkowiak's DS in 1956 – remembered a recent change to the cut-off rule which protected any rider who started the day inside the top 10, as Robinson had. Ducazeaux was unable to save Robinson's team-mate Shay Elliott that day, the Irishman having tried to nurse Robinson through a *jour sans* and sacrificed his own Tour in doing so. Before he left the race, Robinson promised to win a stage in Elliott's honour.

The stage Robinson and Ducazeaux chose for victory was the twentieth, 202 kilometres to Chalon-sur-Soâne, which they turned into a time trial, Robinson setting out with lightweight wheels and tyres and soloing to victory. The problem was, he took that victory with a 20-minute lead. And, behind him, Robic was suffering. One journalist implored Robinson to slow down, even to stop for five or ten minutes, to save Robic, but the Briton wasn't having any of it. And so he pressed on, took the stage as he had promised he would, and achieved a form of vengeance for the axing of Elliott.

Stage-by-Stage Results for the 1959 Tour de France			Stage Winner	Maillot Jaune
Stage 1 Thu 25 Jun	Mulhouse to Metz 120 starters 120 finishers	238 km 5h33'45" 42.8 kph	André Darrigade (Fra) France	André Darrigade (Fra) France
	Major climbs: Col de Bussang (731m) Louis Bergaud (Fra) Centre/Midi			
Stage 2 Fri 26 Jun	Metz to Namur 120 finishers	240 km 6h25'02" 37.4 kph	Vito Favero (Ita) Italy	André Darrigade (Fra) France
Stage 3 Sat 27 Jun	Namur to Roubaix 119 finishers	217 km 6h11'04" 35.1 kph	Robert Cazala (Fra) France	Robert Cazala (Fra) France

Stage-by-Stage Results for the 1959 Tour de France			Stage Winner	Maillot Jaune
Stage 4 Sun 28 Jun	Roubaix to Rouen 118 finishers	230 km 6h40'36" 34.4 kph	Dino Bruni (Ita) Italy	Robert Cazala (Fra) France
Stage 5 Mon 29 Jun	Rouen to Rennes 118 finishers	286 km 8h06'36" 35.3 kph	Jean Graczyk (Fra) France	Robert Cazala (Fra) France
Stage 6 Tue 30 Jun	Blain to Nantes (ITT) 118 finishers	45.3 km 56'46" 47.9 kph	Roger Rivière (Fra) France	Robert Cazala (Fra) France
Stage 7 Wed 1 Jul	Nantes to La Rochelle 115 finishers	190 km 4h22'44" 43.4 kph	Roger Hassenforder (Fra) France	Robert Cazala (Fra) France
Stage 8 Thu 2 Jul	La Rochelle to Bordeaux 112 finishers	201 km 4h53'16" 41.1 kph	Michel Dejouhannet (Fra) Centre/Midi	Robert Cazala (Fra) France
Stage 9 Fri 3 Jul	Bordeaux to Bayonne 111 finishers	207 km 5h19'17" 38.9 kph	Marcel Queheille (Fra) Ouest/Sud-Ouest	Eddy Pauwels (Bel) Belgium
Sat 4 Jul	Rest day			
Stage 10 Sun 5 Jul	Bayonne to Bagnères-de-Bigorre 107 finishers	235 km 6h23'33" 36.8 kph	Marcel Janssens (Bel) Belgium	Michel Vermeulin (Fra) Paris/Nord-Est
	Major climbs: Col du Tourmalet (2,115m) Armand Desmet (Bel) Belgium			
Stage 11 Mon 6 Jul	Bagnères-de-Bigorre to Saint-Gaudens 106 finishers	119 km 3h19'30" 35.8 kph	André Darrigade (Fra) France	Michel Vermeulin (Fra) Paris/Nord-Est
	Major climbs: Col d'Aspin (1,489m) Jean Dotto (Fra) Centre/Midi; Col de Peyresourde (1,569m) Valentin Huot (Fra) Centre/Midi			
Stage 12 Tue 7 Jul	Saint-Gaudens to Albi 105 finishers	184 km 4h25'36" 41.6 kph	Rolf Graf (Sui) Switzerland/Germany	Michel Vermeulin (Fra) Paris/Nord-Est
Stage 13 Wed 8 Jul	Albi to Aurillac 90 finishers	219 km 6h12'19" 35.3 kph	Henry Anglade (Fra) Centre/Midi	Jos Hoevenaers (Bel) Belgium
	Major climbs: La Côte de Montsalvy (780m) Federico Bahamontes (Esp) Spain			
Stage 14 Thu 9 Jul	Aurillac to Clermont Ferrand 83 finishers	231 km 7h03'31" 32.7 kph	André Le Dissez (Fra) Paris/Nord-Est	Jos Hoevenaers (Bel) Belgium
	Major climbs: Le Pas de Peyrol (1,582m) Louis Bergaud (Fra) Centre/Midi; La Roche Vendeix (1,139m) Gérard Saint (Fra) Ouest/Sud-Ouest; Col de la Croix-Morand (1,401m) André Le Dissez (Fra) Paris/Nord-Est			
Stage 15 Fri 10 Jul	Puy de Dôme (ITT) 79 finishers	12.5 km 36'15" 20.7 kph	Federico Bahamontes (Esp) Spain	Jos Hoevenaers (Bel) Belgium
	Major climbs: Puy de Dôme (1,415m) Federico Bahamontes (Esp) Spain			

Stage-by-Stage Results for the 1959 Tour de France			Stage Winner	Maillot Jaune
Stage 16 Sat 11 Jul	Clermont Ferrand to Saint-Étienne 77 finishers	210 km 6h25'29" 32.7 kph	Dino Bruni (Ita) Italy	Eddy Pauwels (Bel) Belgium
	Major climbs: Col de la République (Col du Grand Bois) (1,161m) Federico Bahamontes (Esp) Spain			
Sun 12 Jul	Rest day			
Stage 17 Mon 13 Jul	Saint-Étienne to Grenoble 76 finishers	197 km 5h37'16" 35.0 kph	Charly Gaul (Lux) Netherlands/ Luxembourg	Federico Bahamontes (Esp) Spain
	Major climbs: Col de la Romeyère (1,074m) Federico Bahamontes (Esp) Spain			
Stage 18 Tue 14 Jul	Le Lautaret to Saint-Vincent 72 finishers	243 km 7h48'43" 31.1 kph	Ercole Baldini (Ita) Italy	Federico Bahamontes (Esp) Spain
	Major climbs: Col du Galibier (2,556m) Charly Gaul (Lux) Netherlands/Luxembourg; Col de l'Iseran (2,770m) Adolf Christian (Aut) Internations; Col du Petit Saint-Bernard (2,188m) Michele Gismondi (Ita) Italy			
Stage 19 Wed 15 Jul	Saint-Vincent to Annecy 68 finishers	251 km 8h33'31" 29.3 kph	Rolf Graf (Sui) Switzerland/Germany	Federico Bahamontes (Esp) Spain
	Major climbs: Col du Grand Saint-Bernard (2,470m) Carmelo Morales (Esp) Spain; Col de la Forclaz (1,527m) Gérard Saint (Fra) Ouest/Sud-Ouest; Les Montets (1,461m) Gérard Saint (Fra) Ouest/Sud-Ouest; Col de la Forclaz de Montmin (1,150m) Rolf Graf (Sui) Switzerland/Germany			
Stage 20 Thu 16 Jul	Annecy to Chalon-sur-Saône 66 finishers	202 km 5h52'21" 34.4 kph	Brian Robinson (GBr) Internations	Federico Bahamontes (Esp) Spain
Stage 21 Fri 17 Jul	Seurre to Dijon (ITT) 66 finishers	69.2 km 1h39'38" 41.7 kph	Roger Rivière (Fra) France	Federico Bahamontes (Esp) Spain
Stage 22 Sat 18 Jul	Dijon to Paris (Parc des Princes) 65 finishers	331 km 9h55'52" 33.3 kph	Joseph Groussard (Fra) Ouest/Sud-Ouest	Federico Bahamontes (Esp) Spain

Prize fund: 41,700,000 francs (first prize: 2,000,000 francs)

Final Classification

Place	Rider	Team	Time	Age
1	Federico Bahamontes (Esp)	Spain	4,358 km 123h46'45" 35.474 kph	31
2	Henry Anglade (Fra)	Centre/Midi	+ 4'01"	26
3	Jacques Anquetil (Fra)	France	+ 5'05"	26
4	Roger Rivière (Fra)	France	+ 5'17"	23
5	François Mahé (Fra)	Ouest/Sud-Ouest	+ 8'22"	29
6	Ercole Baldini (Ita)	Italy	+ 10'18"	26
6	Jan Adriaensens (Bel)	Belgium	+ 10'18"	27
8	Jos Hoevenaers (Bel)	Belgium	+ 11'02"	27
9	Gérard Saint (Fra)	Ouest/Sud-Ouest	+ 17'40"	24
10	Jean Brankart (Bel)	Belgium	+ 20'38"	29

Lanterne Rouge

65	Louis Bisilliat (Fra)	Centre/Midi	+ 3h12'35"	28

Points

	André Darrigade (Fra)	France		30

King of the Mountains

	Federico Bahamontes (Esp)	Spain		31

Super Combativité

	Gérard Saint (Fra)	Ouest/Sud-Ouest		24

Team

		Belgium		

1960: Agents' Secrets

For the fourth time in five years, the Tour got a new winner as Italy's Gastone Nencini wrote his name into the race's record books. For the French, it was another Tour that got away and will always be the race Roger Rivière should have won.

On paper the French had the race sewn up even before it began. Jacques Anquetil – then just a one-time winner and two-time loser of the Tour – was sitting the race out, having just added the Giro d'Italia to his *palmarès*. This left Rivière as the clear favourite and the sole leader of the French team, ably supported by talented riders such as Robert Cazala, François Mahé, Henry Anglade and Jean Dotto. This was a team that – individual ambitions not withstanding – should have been able to unite around Rivière to work together.

That things were not going to go in favour of France should have been clear from the first day when André Darrigade's five-year run of victories in the opening stage was brought to an end by Belgium's Julien Schepens. But that was soon forgotten, the opening day being two split stages, a road race in the morning and a 27.8-kilometre individual time trial in the afternoon. There Rivière triumphed. But the man wearing the *maillot jaune* was the Italian Nencini. He had been in the break in the morning – finishing third in the sprint – and earned a more than respectable second place to Rivière in the afternoon. While Rivière already had a 91-second gap to the Italian to overcome, the Frenchman could take comfort in the knowledge that there was another time trial to come three days out from Paris, this time over 83 kilometres. All Rivière had to do was stay close to Nencini for the rest of the race and then pass him in the time trial.

Things began to get complicated on the fourth stage, when a break got away containing a number of Rivière's team-mates. Jean Graczyk took the stage, but the real problems began when Henry Anglade donned the *maillot jaune*. Having finished second the previous year – partly, many believed, because Anquetil and Rivière had worked against him – he was now in a position to claim leadership of the French squad. But Marcel Bidot, still the French *directeur sportif*, was willing to put his faith in Rivière who, on the sixth stage, got away in a four-man break that also contained Nencini and ended up taking the stage win and putting 14 minutes into the *maillot jaune*. Belgium's Jan Adriaensens – who had seen the break go away and quickly joined in – was the new race leader, with Nencini at 1'12" and Rivière at 2'14".

Anglade was, quite naturally, furious, with both Rivière and team boss Marcel Bidot. But, at the same time, he knew there was little they could do: Rivière had not contributed to driving the break and was merely shadowing Nencini. No, the real object of Anglade's ire was the riders' agent Daniel Dousset.

At this point in cycling's history riders earned most of their income from appearance fees at small, local races: critériums. For the month of August in particular the riders went from critérium to critérium, pocketing appearance fees. Dousset – a former rider with a few successes on the track to his credit – was a key player in the critérium circuit, one of the men who decided which riders got invitations and which got to stay at home. One of the men, in other words, who could decide how much you earned in a year.

Anglade wasn't one of Dousset's clients – he was with Roger Piel, the other main riders' agent in France at the time – and he felt that the agent was manipulating the race so that one of his own riders came out on top. As he felt had happened the year before: Anquetil and Rivière were both clients of Dousset, as was Federico Bahamontes. For Dousset, if neither of his French stars could take the victory it was better it went to the Spaniard than a rider, French or not, signed to another agent.

Nencini grabbed the yellow jersey on the first day in the Pyrenees, but Rivière had been able to stick with him all day – uphill and down – and got the better of his rival in the sprint for the stage win and claimed the larger share of the bonifications, thus cutting his overall deficit to just 32 seconds. An upset stomach the next day, though, saw that slip out to 1'38", where Rivière was able to hold it at until the race reached Millau. And it was on the roads between Millau and Avignon that all of Rivière's hopes of winning the Tour – all his hopes of ever winning the Tour – came crashing down.

The accident happened on the seemingly harmless descent of the Col de Perjuret in the Causse Noir. The 24-year-old French star was once more shadowing his Italian rival when he ran out of road and flew off and down into a ravine, breaking his back. Out of the Tour, out of cycling.

That the crash was a racing accident is hard to dispute. Wim van Est had run out of road on the Aubisque trying to save his *maillot jaune* in 1951; this was only a little different to that. Nencini was simply a better descender and Rivière had been warned that he would come a cropper if he tried to keep up with the Italian. The Frenchman, though, was willing to ride his luck. And on the descent of the Perjuret he ran out of luck. And ran out of road. But there was more to it than that.

When they hauled him out of the ravine and got him to hospital, drugs were found in the pockets of Rivière's jersey. More drugs were found in his luggage at the team hotel. Some believe that these drugs had caused Rivière to crash, that either the Palfium (a painkiller) found in his jersey had dulled his nerves or he had somehow mis-injected himself, numbing his hand and restricting his ability to brake. Rivière did admit to having taken solucamphre and amphetamines before the stage start, but not to having tried to inject Palfium during the stage itself.

Whether the racing accident or the doping explanations were true hardly mattered, for once more the Tour found itself having to confront its doping problem. The pages of *L'Équipe* were filled with condemnation of the needle and the damage it was doing. But then things moved on and the story was quickly forgotten. Nothing stops the rhythm of the Tour. There was a race being won, by Nenicni, and that was more interesting than cycling's doping problem.

With Rivière out Nencini's closest challenger was now Belgium's Jan Adriaensens, one of the breakaways on stage six, who was 2'25" off the pace. But the Belgian failed to mount much of a challenge and Nencini was more or less without a rival as he raced on to Paris and the applause of the crowds in the Parc des Princes.

Stage-by-Stage Results for the 1960 Tour de France			Stage Winner	Maillot Jaune
Stage 1a Sun 26 Jun	Lille to Brussels 128 starters 126 finishers	108 km 2h46'21" 39.0 kph	Julien Schepens (Bel) Belgium	Julien Schepens (Bel) Belgium
Stage 1b Sun 26 Jun	Brussels to Brussels (ITT) 126 finishers	27.8 km 41'21" 40.3 kph	Roger Rivière (Fra) France	Gastone Nencini (Ita) Italy
Stage 2 Mon 27 Jun	Brussels to Malo-les-Bains 124 finishers	206 km 5h12'08" 39.6 kph	René Privat (Fra) France	Gastone Nencini (Ita) Italy
Stage 3 Tue 28 Jun	Malo-les-Bains to Dieppe 122 finishers	209 km 5h01'35" 41.6 kph	Nino Defilippis (Ita) Italy	Joseph Groussard (Fra) Ouest
Stage 4 Wed 29 Jun	Dieppe to Caen 121 finishers	211 km 5h14'42" 40.2 kph	Jean Graczyk (Fra) France	Henri Anglade (Fra) France
Stage 5 Thu 30 Jun	Caen to Saint-Malo 120 finishers	189 km 4h21'31" 43.4 kph	André Darrigade (Fra) France	Henri Anglade (Fra) France
Stage 6 Fri 1 Jul	Saint-Malo to Lorient 117 finishers	191 km 4h20'10" 44.0 kph	Roger Rivière (Fra) France	Jan Adriaensens (Bel) Belgium
Stage 7 Sat 2 Jul	Lorient to Angers 115 finishers	244 km 6h00'24" 40.6 kph	Graziano Battistini (Ita) Italy	Jan Adriaensens (Bel) Belgium
Stage 8 Sun 3 Jul	Angers to Limoges 114 finishers	240 km 5h50'59" 41.0 kph	Nino Defilippis (Ita) Italy	Jan Adriaensens (Bel) Belgium
Stage 9 Mon 4 Jul	Limoges to Bordeaux 111 finishers	225 km 5h38'35" 39.9 kph	Martin van Geneugden (Bel) Belgium	Jan Adriaensens (Bel) Belgium
Stage 10 Tue 5 Jul	Mont de Marsan to Pau 111 finishers	228 km 6h38'48" 34.3 kph	Roger Rivière (Fra) France	Gastone Nencini (Ita) Italy
Major climbs: Col du Soulor (1,474m) Graziano Battistini (Ita) Italy; Col d'Aubisque (1,709m) Graziano Battistini (Ita) Italy				

Stage-by-Stage Results for the 1960 Tour de France			Stage Winner	Maillot Jaune
Stage 11 Wed 6 Jul	Pau to Luchon 103 finishers	161 km 5h04'10" 31.8 kph	Kurt Gimmi (Sui) Switzerland/ Luxembourg	Gastone Nencini (Ita) Italy
	Major climbs: Col du Tourmalet (2,115m) Kurt Gimmi (Sui) Switzerland/Luxembourg; Col d'Aspin (1,489m) Kurt Gimmi (Sui) Switzerland/Luxembourg; Col de Peyresourde (1,569m) Kurt Gimmi (Sui) Switzerland/Luxembourg			
Stage 12 Thu 7 Jul	Luchon to Toulouse 98 finishers	176 km 4h37'52" 38.0 kph	Jean Graczyk (Fra) France	Gastone Nencini (Ita) Italy
	Major climbs: Col de Portet d'Aspet (1,069m) Jozef Planckaert (Bel) Belgium			
Stage 13 Fri 8 Jul	Toulouse to Millau 94 finishers	224 km 5h58'31" 37.5 kph	Louis Proost (Bel) Belgium	Gastone Nencini (Ita) Italy
Sat 9 Jul	Rest day			
Stage 14 Sun 10 Jul	Millau to Avignon 85 finishers	217 km 5h50'35" 37.1 kph	Martin van Geneugden (Bel) Belgium	Gastone Nencini (Ita) Italy
	Major climbs: Col d'Uglas (530m) Pierre Beuffeuil (Fra) Centre/Midi			
Stage 15 Mon 11 Jul	Avignon to Gap 85 finishers	187 km 5h15'15" 35.6 kph	Michel van Aerde (Bel) Belgium	Gastone Nencini (Ita) Italy
	Major climbs: Col de la Sentinelle (980m) Louis Rostollan (Fra) France			
Stage 16 Tue 12 Jul	Gap to Briançon 85 finishers	172 km 5h29'09" 31.4 kph	Graziano Battistini (Ita) Italy	Gastone Nencini (Ita) Italy
	Major climbs: Col de Vars (2,110m) Imerio Massignan (Ita) Italy; Col d'Izoard (2,360m) Imerio Massignan (Ita) Italy			
Stage 17 Wed 13 Jul	Briançon to Aix-les-Bains 84 finishers	229 km 7h30'20" 30.5 kph	Jean Graczyk (Fra) France	Gastone Nencini (Ita) Italy
	Major climbs: Col du Lautaret (2,058m) Jean Graczyk (Fra) France; Col du Luitel (1,262m) René Marigil (Esp) Spain; Col du Granier (1,134m) René Marigil (Esp) Spain			
Stage 18 Thu 14 Jul	Aix-les-Bains to Thonon-les-Bains 82 finishers	215 km 6h29'10" 33.1 kph	Fernando Manzaneque Sánchez (Esp) Spain	Gastone Nencini (Ita) Italy
	Major climbs: Col des Aravis (1,498m) Fernando Manzaneque (Esp) Spain; Col de la Colombière (1,618m) Fernando Manzaneque (Esp) Spain			
Stage 19 Fri 15 Jul	Pontarlier to Besançon (ITT) 81 finishers	83 km 1h59'28" 41.7 kph	Rolf Graf (Sui) Switzerland/ Luxembourg	Gastone Nencini (Ita) Italy

Stage-by-Stage Results for the 1960 Tour de France			Stage Winner	Maillot Jaune
Stage 20 Sat 16 Jul	Besançon to Troyes 81 finishers	229 km 5h52'25" 39.0 kph	Pierre Beuffeuil (Fra) Centre/Midi	Gastone Nencini (Ita) Italy
Stage 21 Sun 17 Jul	Troyes to Paris (Parc des Princes) 81 finishers	200 km 5h19'30" 37.6 kph	Jean Graczyk (Fra) France	Gastone Nencini (Ita) Italy

Prize fund: 400,000 francs (first prize: 20,000 francs) (1)

Final Classification				
Place	**Rider**	**Team**	**Time**	**Age**
1	Gastone Nencini (Ita)	Italy	4,173 km 112h08'42" 37.210 kph	30
2	Graziano Battistini (Ita)	Italy	+ 5'02"	24
3	Jan Adriaensens (Bel)	Belgium	+ 10'24"	28
4	Hans Jünkermann (DDR)	Germany	+ 11'21"	26
5	Jozef Planckaert (Bel)	Belgium	+ 13'02"	26
6	Raymond Mastrotto (Fra)	France	+ 16'12"	26
7	Arnaldo Pambianco (Ita)	Italy	+ 17'58"	25
8	Henry Anglade (Fra)	France	+ 19'17"	27
9	Marcel Rohrbach (Fra)	Centre/Midi	+ 20'02"	27
10	Imerio Massignan (Ita)	Italy	+ 23'28"	24
Lanterne Rouge				
81	José Berrendero (Esp)	Spain	+ 4h58'59"	27
Points				
	Jean Graczyk (Fra)	France		27
King of the Mountains				
	Imerio Massignan (Ita)	Italy		24
Super Combativité				
	Jean Graczyk (Fra)	France		27
Team				
		France		

(1) In 1960 the French Franc was revalued, 100 old Francs becoming 1 Franc

1961: On the Shoulders of Dwarves

A decade since the Tour turned its back on the City of Lights for its Grand Départ, the 1961 race saw the riders departing Rouen and racing toward Versailles, on the outskirts of Paris, in an opening stage that saw the riders having to race twice in the one day: a road race in the morning, followed by a time trial in the afternoon. And for the fifth time in six years, the man wearing the yellow jersey after the first stage was André Darrigade. One of the keys to the French sprinter's run of successes was his ability to identify the break that would stay away and get into it, he wasn't just winning by being fastest in a field sprint. Out of the break that stayed away in 1961, 11 riders arrived in Versailles together, nearly five minutes up on the main *peloton*, with Dédé the best of the bunch.

That should have ensured that Darrigade would hold the yellow jersey for most of the race's first week. Except that also in the winning break was his national squad team-mate Jacques Anquetil. And in the afternoon's 28.5-kilometre time trial around the Sun King's palace Monsieur Contra-la-Montre put so much time into his rivals that you probably could have timed him with a sun dial.

At the end of the first day's racing Anquetil held the *maillot jaune* with a near five-minute lead, and his key rivals were already seven minutes and more back. Three weeks later, when the Tour arrived in Paris at the end of its 4,397-kilometre odyssey around France, Anquetil was still wearing the same yellow jersey, no one having been able to take it away (technically, it was a different yellow jersey, Félix Lévitan's budget stretching to letting the leader have a new jersey every other day).

Anquetil's feat of leading the race from the first day to last – though not from the first stage to last – had only been pulled off three times previously in the Tour's history. In 1935 Romain Maes had donned the *maillot jaune* on the first day and never relinquished it, as had Nicolas Frantz in 1928 (as the defending winner, Frantz actually held the *maillot jaune* from the beginning of the first stage to the end of the last). And, of course, as had Maurice Garin, away back in that first Tour in 1903. (Philippe Thys in 1914 and Ottavio Bottecchia in 1924 had come close to pulling off the same feat, taking the lead on the opening stage and never quite relinquishing it, but each had to share that lead during the race, the Belgian with Jean Rossius, the Italian with Théophile Beeckman.)

Taking such an early lead in the race was not just down to Anquetil; his team-mates had a major role to play. And in that regard Anquetil had followed the recent lead of riders such as Fausto Coppi and Louison Bobet by agreeing to share his race winnings among them. But it was not just his team-mates on the national squad that Anquetil could count on. In that opening morning's break, as well as national-squad team-mates Darrigade and Joseph Groussard, Anquetil could also count on the support of Shay Elliott, one of two Irishmen riding on the Great Britain squad. But the rest of the year round Elliott was one of Anquetil's *domestiques* at Helyett. The national team format, at times, struggled to overcome loyalties built in the trade teams. And those trade teams were getting more and more vociferous in their calls to be allowed back into the Tour

For the French national team, it was a wonderful Tour. The yellow jersey, the green jersey (for Darrigade), the team classification and nine stage wins (four for Darrigade, two for Anquetil and one each for Jean Stablinski, Jean Forestier and Robert Cazala). For Jacques Goddet, though, while he had nothing but praise for Anquetil – who he saw as a true *géant de la route* – all he had was condemnation for the men who failed to challenge Maître Jacques. Dwarves, Goddet called them, terrible dwarves satisfied with mediocrity, happy just to get their name mentioned. They were, Goddet said, too conservative, seeing the sport as a business and thus unwilling to take risks.

* * * * *

Goddet criticising others for seeing the sport as a business was a bit rich, given that the Tour was just that and Félix Lévitan was doing his best to make it a profitable one. And Lévitan was a man with his eyes on the future, and one part of that was looking well beyond not just France's borders, but those of cycling's traditional heartlands. To the east, across the Iron Curtain, the Soviets had their own version of the Tour de France, the Peace Race, the success of which showed an appetite for cycling in territories heretofore ignored by the Tour. But the problem Lévitan faced was that the Peace Race was limited to amateurs. In many of the developing cycling nations, in fact, most of the sport was amateur.

What Lévitan wanted to do was to invite amateur teams to the Tour, but there was a problem to be overcome: the professional riders didn't agree. Rather than try to force the issue, Lévitan decided the Tour should create a new race, for amateurs. And it would be run off during the Tour, on some of the same roads raced by the professionals. And so, on 2 July, as the Tour riders raced from Chalon-sur-Saône to Saint-Étienne, riders in the inaugural Tour de l'Avenir – Tour of the Future – set out on a 145.5-kilometre loop of Saint-Étienne and, for the next two weeks, followed much of the Tour's route, the two races ending up in Paris on 16 July.

In time, Lévitan hoped, it would be possible to bring some of those amateur riders into the *grande boucle*, with the Tour de l'Avenir having convinced the professionals that they were worthy of the race. In the meanwhile, the Tour de l'Avenir would give the amateurs a chance to test themselves on the roads of the Tour and maybe ease their passage into the professional ranks. And, perhaps, also pushing news of the Tour into countries that had yet to fully embrace it.

Stage-by-Stage Results for the 1961 Tour de France			Stage Winner	Maillot Jaune
Stage 1a Sun 25 Jun	Rouen to Versailles 132 finishers	136.5 km 3h15'16" 41.9 kph	André Darrigade (Fra) France	André Darrigade (Fra) France
Stage 1b Sun 25 Jun	Versailles (ITT) 132 finishers	28.5 km 39'43" 43.1 kph	Jacques Anquetil (Fra) France	Jacques Anquetil (Fra) France
Stage 2 Mon 26 Jun	Pontoise to Roubaix 118 finishers	230.5 km 5h31'26" 41.7 kph	André Darrigade (Fra) France	Jacques Anquetil (Fra) France
Stage 3 Tue 27 Jun	Roubaix to Charleroi 114 finishers	197.5 km 5h00'51" 39.4 kph	Emile Daems (Bel) Belgium	Jacques Anquetil (Fra) France
Stage 4 Wed 28 Jun	Charleroi to Metz 112 finishers	237.5 km 6h23'31" 37.2 kph	Anatole Novak (Fra) Centre/Midi	Jacques Anquetil (Fra) France
Stage 5 Thu 29 Jun	Metz to Strasbourg 111 finishers	221 km 5h48'05" 38.1 kph	Louis Bergaud (Fra) Centre/Midi	Jacques Anquetil (Fra) France
	Major climbs: Mont Donon (727m) Louis Bergaud (Fra) Centre/Midi; Champ du Messin (1,010m) Stéphane Lach (Fra) Paris/Nord-Est			
Stage 6 Fri 30 Jun	Strasbourg to Belfort 102 finishers	180.5 km 4h35'39" 39.3 kph	Jef Planckaert (Bel) Belgium	Jacques Anquetil (Fra) France
	Major climbs: Col de la Schlucht (1,139m) Jef Planckaert (Bel) Belgium; Ballon d'Alsace (1,178m) Jef Planckaert (Bel) Belgium			
Stage 7 Sat 1 Jul	Belfort to Chalon-sur-Saône 97 finishers	214.5 km 5h21'11" 40.1 kph	Jean Stablinski (Fra) France	Jacques Anquetil (Fra) France
Stage 8 Sun 2 Jul	Chalon-sur-Saône to Saint-Étienne 95 finishers	240.5 km 7h05'10" 33.9 kph	Jean Forestier (Fra) France	Jacques Anquetil (Fra) France
	Major climbs: Sauvages (1,159m) Imerio Massignan (Ita) Italy			
Stage 9 Mon 3 Jul	Saint-Étienne to Grenoble 90 finishers	230 km 7h05'04" 32.5 kph	Charly Gaul (Lux) Switzerland/Luxembourg	Jacques Anquetil (Fra) France
	Major climbs: Col de la République (Col du Grand Bois) (1,161m) Guy Ignolin (Fra) Ouest/Sud-Ouest; Col du Granier (1,134m) Charly Gaul (Lux) Switzerland/Luxembourg; Col du Cucheron (1,139m) Charly Gaul (Lux) Switzerland/Luxembourg; Col de Porte (1,326m) Charly Gaul (Lux) Switzerland/Luxembourg			
Stage 10 Tue 4 Jul	Grenoble to Turin 85 finishers	250.5 km 7h30'59" 33.3 kph	Guy Ignolin (Fra) Ouest/Sud-Ouest	Jacques Anquetil (Fra) France
	Major climbs: Col de la Croix de Fer (2,067m) Guy Ignolin (Fra) Ouest/Sud-Ouest; Col du Mont Cenis (2,083m) Emmanuel Busto (Fra) Centre/Midi			

Stage-by-Stage Results for the 1961 Tour de France			Stage Winner	Maillot Jaune
Stage 11 Wed 5 Jul	Turin to Juan-les-Pins 83 finishers	225 km 6h42'01" 33.6 kph	Guido Carlesi (Ita) Italy	Jacques Anquetil (Fra) France
	Major climbs: Col de Tende (1,320m) Imerio Massignan (Ita) Italy; Col de Brouis (880m) Imerio Massignan (Ita) Italy; Col de Braus (1,002m) Imerio Massignan (Ita) Italy			
Stage 12 Thu 6 Jul	Juan-les-Pins to Aix-en-Provence 77 finishers	199 km 5h43'08" 34.8 kph	Michel van Aerde (Bel) Belgium	Jacques Anquetil (Fra) France
	Major climbs: Le Petit Galibier (535m) Renzo Accordi (Ita) Italy; Le Cengle (461m) Edouard Bihouée (Fra) Ouest/Sud-Ouest			
Stage 13 Fri 7 Jul	Aix-en-Provence to Montpellier 77 finishers	177.5 km 4h38'37" 38.2 kph	André Darrigade (Fra) France	Jacques Anquetil (Fra) France
Sat 8 Jul	Rest day			
Stage 14 Sun 9 Jul	Montpellier to Perpignan 75 finishers	174 km 4h21'42" 39.9 kph	Eddy Pauwels (Bel) Belgium	Jacques Anquetil (Fra) France
Stage 15 Mon 10 Jul	Perpignan to Toulouse 75 finishers	206 km 5h33'58" 37 kph	Guido Carlesi (Ita) Italy	Jacques Anquetil (Fra) France
Stage 16 Tue 11 Jul	Toulouse to Luchon (Superbagnères) 75 finishers	208 km 6h58'17" 29.8 kph	Imerio Massignan (Ita) Italy	Jacques Anquetil (Fra) France
	Major climbs: Col des Ares (797m) Imerio Massignan (Ita) Italy; Col du Portillon (1,298m) Imerio Massignan (Ita) Italy; Superbagnères (1,804m) Imerio Massignan (Ita) Italy			
Stage 17 Wed 12 Jul	Luchon to Pau 72 finishers	197 km 6h29'57" 30.3 kph	Eddy Pauwels (Bel) Belgium	Jacques Anquetil (Fra) France
	Major climbs: Col de Peyresourde (1,569m) Imerio Massignan (Ita) Italy; Col d'Aspin (1,489m) Marcel Queheille (Fra) Ouest/Sud-Ouest; Col du Tourmalet (2,115m) Marcel Queheille (Fra) Ouest/Sud-Ouest; Col d'Aubisque (1,709m) Eddy Pauwels (Bel) Belgium			
Stage 18 Thu 13 Jul	Pau to Bordeaux 72 finishers	207 km 5h37'18" 36.8 kph	Martin van Geneugden (Bel) Belgium	Jacques Anquetil (Fra) France
Stage 19 Fri 14 Jul	Bergerac to Périgueux (ITT) 72 finishers	74.5 km 1h42'32" 43.6 kph	Jacques Anquetil (Fra) France	Jacques Anquetil (Fra) France
Stage 20 Sat 15 Jul	Périgueux to Tours 72 finishers	309.5 km 8h35'59" 36 kph	André Darrigade (Fra) France	Jacques Anquetil (Fra) France
Stage 21 Sun 16 Jul	Tours to Paris (Parc des Princes) 72 finishers	252.5 km 6h31'17" 38.7 kph	Robert Cazala (Fra) France	Jacques Anquetil (Fra) France

Prize fund: 500,000 francs (first prize: 20,000 francs)

Final Classification

Place	Rider	Team	Time	Age
1	Jacques Anquetil (Fra)	France	4,397 km 122h01'33" 36.033 kph	28
2	Guido Carlesi (Ita)	Italy	+ 12'14"	25
3	Charly Gaul (Lux)	Switzerland/ Luxembourg	+ 12'16"	29
4	Imerio Massignan (Ita)	Italy	+ 15'59"	25
5	Hans Jünkermann (FRG)	Germany	+ 16'09"	27
6	Fernando Manzaneque (Esp)	Spain	+ 16'27"	27
7	José Pérez Francés (Esp)	Spain	+ 20'41"	25
8	Jean Dotto (Fra)	Centre/Midi	+ 21'44"	33
9	Eddy Pauwels (Bel)	Belgium	+ 26'57"	26
10	Jan Adriaensens (Bel)	Belgium	+ 28'05"	29

Lanterne Rouge

72	André Geneste (Fra)	Paris/Nord-Est	4h12'56"	31

Points

	André Darrigade (Fra)	France		32

King of the Mountains

	Imerio Massignan (Ita)	Italy		25

Super Combativité

		Ouest/Sud-Ouest		

Team

		France		

1962: A Victory for the Trade Teams

After 25 Tours de France run under the national and regional team format, trade teams were re-admitted to the race in 1962. Jacques Goddet and Félix Lévitan had been put under considerable pressure by the sponsors of those teams – who now included many companies from outside the cycling industry and had their own industry body, the *Association Française des Constructeurs et Associés Sportif* – but it was not just that pressure which swayed their minds. Of more importance than the financial needs of the teams were the financial needs of the Tour itself. And – in terms of sporting competition at least – the Tour was being challenged by the Giro d'Italia, which from its beginning had embraced trade teams. And, in the post-Coppi/Bartali era, the Giro was arguably attracting a better field, and maybe even serving up better racing. The trade teams – once banished for nearly killing the Tour – were now welcomed back as its new saviours.

The names of the 15 10-man trade teams who raced the 1962 Tour are, perhaps, of no great significance, but they are worth considering even if only to see the number of sponsors involved. They were, then, the following: ACBB/Saint-Raphaël/Helyett/ Hutchinson (Jacques Anquetil); Moschettieri/Ignis (Gastone Nencini); GS Gighi (Antonio Suárez); Liberia/Grammont/Clement (Henry Anglade); GS Gazzola/Fiorelli/Hutchinson (Charly Gaul); Pelforth/Sauvage/Lejeune (Joseph Groussard); Carpano (Nino Defilippis); VC XII/Leroux/Gitane/Dunlop (André Darrigade); Wiel's/Groene Loew (Eddy Pauwels); Margnat/Paloma/d'Alessandro (Federico Bahamontes); Peugeot/BP/Dunlop (Pino Cerami); Legnano/Pirelli (Imerio Massignan); GS Philco (Vittoria Adorni);

Faema/Flandria/Clement (Rik van Looy); Mercier/BP/Hutchinson (Robert Cazala).

Switching back to trade teams also altered the make up of the nationalities contesting the Tour. Of the 149 starters in 1962 (Legnano had lost a rider before the race began) one was Swiss, two were from Luxembourg, two were British, four German, six Spanish, six Dutch and 28 Belgian, with the rest coming from France and Italy (50 each). The return to the trade team format strengthened the representation from Belgium and Italy, but restricted the opportunities for riders from lesser cycling nations. At the same time, it was at the 1962 Tour that the first rider from beyond mainland Europe got to wear the *maillot jaune*, when Great Britain's Tom Simpson (riding with Darrigade's VC XII/Leroux squad) took the race lead, on Stage 12, from Pau to Saint-Gaudens.

The overall win once again went to Jacques Anquetil, his third in six years, putting him equal with Philippe Thys and Louison Bobet in the Tour's record books as a three-time winner. With his Saint-Raphaël squad bossed by Raphaël Géminiani (who, perhaps, could be accused of having helped deny Anquetil a victory in 1958) Maître Jacques was a clear favourite from the start, with his main challenges expected to come from former winners Gaul, Bahamontes and Nencini. But Anquetil also had to be wary of the enemy within: at the Vuelta a España earlier in the year team-mate Rudi Altig – the reigning pursuit World Champion – took the honours and Anquetil abandoned on the eve of the final stage rather than accept defeat at the hands his German team-mate. And it was the German who donned the first *maillot jaune* of the race, narrowly beating the man for whom winning the opening stage had become a habit, Darrigade.

For Anquetil, the Tour was about the two flat individual time trials: Stage Eight, 43 kilometres from Luchon to La Rochelle; and the more difficult Stage 20, 68 kilometres from Bourgoin to Lyon (there were two other time trials in the race, a 23-kilometre team time trial in Herentals, won by home-town boy and reigning World Champion Rik van Looy's Faema squad, and an 18.5-kilometre mountain time trial from Luchon to Superbagnères, won by

On the road from Briançon to Aix-les-Bains in the 1962 Tour.

Bahamontes). Having led from the first day to the last the year before, this time Anquetil chose to let others bear the pressure of protecting the yellow jersey. Using a plan similar to the one Roger Rivière had opted for in 1960, Anquetil's aim was to hold his own against his chief rivals up to that final time trial two days out from Paris and only take the race lead there. The job of his team-mates was to police breaks and protect their leader.

As expected, Anquetil won the time trial on Stage Eight, without donning the *maillot jaune*, which was passing from one rider to another: after Altig passed it to Darrigade on the second day it passed back to Altig, then to Ab Geldermans (a Saint-Raphaël team-mate of Altig and Anquetil), back to Darrigade, on to Willy Schroeders (of Rik Van Looy's famed Faema Red Guard) before Tom Simpson donned it on the first day in the Pyrenees. On that day Anquetil saw key rivals fall away, as Nencini and Baldini (both Moschettieri), Henry Anglade (Liberia) and team-mate Altig all lost big, while Anquetil – ably supported by his team-mates – held his own.

In the mountain time trial to Superbagnères, Bahamontes – who had more or less given up any GC ambitions – came out tops, effectively securing his fourth King of the Mountains title. Anquetil finished third, distancing further anyone who still thought they had a chance of beating him. The jersey passed off the shoulders of Simpson and back to Faema, this time in the shape of Jef Planckaert.

Then came another minor doping scandal for the Tour when, at the start of the next stage, from Luchon to Carcassonne, Nencini and a team-mate took ill. They were joined over the course of the day by four riders from the Wiel's/Groene Leeuw squad and, in all, 12 riders from eight teams left the race that day. Bad fish in the team hotel was blamed – as it had been by the Belgians in 1956 – but Jacques Goddet didn't believe this and suspected doping, a bad batch of drugs shared among the teams by a single *soigneur* as riders sought to regain time lost in the previous day's time trial. And Goddet let the readers of *L'Équipe* know that he suspected doping.

Planckaert – who had won Paris-Nice earlier in the season – held his own for the next week, until Anquetil took charge in the

68-kilometre time trial to Lyon and turned the final two stages into a victory parade. It was a somewhat cold and calculating victory, and the fans didn't really appreciate it. Anquetil had been booed in the Parc des Princes in 1959, after he and Roger Rivière had helped deny Henry Anglade the win, and the applause had been less than warm two years later when Anquetil took his second Tour victory. And when Anquetil made it three wins, it wasn't him they cheered for, but a plucky little rider from Limoges who had started the Tour with his arm in a plaster cast, claimed a stage win and finished on the bottom step of the podium: Raymond Poulidor.

Stage-by-Stage Results for the 1962 Tour de France			Stage Winner	Maillot Jaune
Stage 1 Sun 24 Jun	Nancy to Spa 147 finishers	253 km 6h36'33" 38.3 kph	Rudi Altig (FRG) ACBB/Saint-Raphaël	Rudi Altig (FRG) ACBB/Saint-Raphaël
Stage 2a Mon 25 Jun	Spa to Herentals 145 finishers	147 km 3h40'48" 39.9 kph	André Darrigade (Fra) VC XII/Leroux	André Darrigade (Fra) VC XII/Leroux
Stage 2b Mon 25 Jun	Herentals to Herentals (TTT) 145 finishers	23 km 29'01" 47.6 kph	Faema	André Darrigade (Fra) VC XII/Leroux
Stage 3 Tue 26 Jun	Brussels to Amiens 144 finishers	210 km 5h32'20" 37.9 kph	Rudi Altig (FRG) ACBB/Saint-Raphaël	Rudi Altig (FRG) ACBB/Saint-Raphaël
Stage 4 Wed 27 Jun	Amiens to Le Havre 143 finishers	196.5 km 4h51'17" 40.5 kph	Willy van den Berghen (Bel) Mercier	Rudi Altig (FRG) ACBB/Saint-Raphaël
Stage 5 Thu 28 Jun	Pont-l'Evêque to Saint-Malo 141 finishers	215 km 5h21'48" 40.1 kph	Emile Daems (Bel) GS Philco	Rudi Altig (FRG) ACBB/Saint-Raphaël
Stage 6 Fri 29 Jun	Dinard to Brest 138 finishers	235.5 km 5h41'21" 41.4 kph	Robert Cazala (Fra) Mercier	Ab Geldermans (Ned) ACBB/Saint-Raphaël
Stage 7 Sat 30 Jun	Quimper to Saint-Nazaire 130 finishers	201 km 4h30'55" 44.5 kph	Hubert Zilverberg (Ned) Faema	Ab Geldermans (Ned) ACBB/Saint-Raphaël
Stage 8a Sun 1 Jul	Saint-Nazaire to Luçon 129 finishers	155 km 3h29'01" 44.5 kph	Mario Minieri (Ita) GS Gighi	André Darrigade (Fra) VC XII/Leroux
Stage 8b Sun 1 Jul	Luçon to La Rochelle (ITT) 129 finishers	43 km 54'04" 47.7 kph	Jacques Anquetil (Fra) ACBB/Saint-Raphaël	André Darrigade (Fra) VC XII/Leroux
Stage 9 Mon 2 Jul	La Rochelle to Bordeaux 127 finishers	214 km 5h11'17" 41.2 kph	Antonio Bailetti (Ita) Carpano	Willy Schroeders (Bel) Faema

Stage-by-Stage Results for the 1962 Tour de France			Stage Winner	Maillot Jaune
Stage 10 Tue 3 Jul	Bordeaux to Bayonne 127 finishers	184.5 km 4h54'02" 37.6 kph	Willy Vannitsen (Bel) Wiel's	Willy Schroeders (Bel) Faema
Stage 11 Wed 4 Jul	Bayonne to Pau 125 finishers	155.5 km 3h54'36" 39.8 kph	Eddy Pauwels (Bel) Wiel's	Willy Schroeders (Bel) Faema
	Major climbs: Col d'Osquich (390m) Eddy Pauwels (Bel) Wiel's			
Stage 12 Thu 5 Jul	Pau to Saint-Gaudens 116 finishers	207.5 km 5h59'27" 34.6 kph	Robert Cazala (Fra) Mercier	Tom Simpson (GBr) VC XII/Leroux
	Major climbs: Col du Tourmalet (2,115m) Federico Bahamontes (Esp) Margnat; Col d'Aspin (1,489m) Federico Bahamontes (Esp) Margnat; Col de Peyresourde (1,569m) Federico Bahamontes (Esp) Margnat			
Stage 13 Fri 6 Jul	Luchon to Superbagnères (ITT) 116 finishers	18.5 km 47'23" 23.4 kph	Federico Bahamontes (Esp) Margnat	Jef Planckaert (Bel) Faema
	Major climbs: Superbagnères (1,804m) Federico Bahamontes (Esp) Margnat			
Stage 14 Sat 7 Jul	Luchon to Carcassonne 102 finishers	215 km 6h01'50" 35.7 kph	Jean Stablinski (Fra) ACBB/Saint-Raphaël	Jef Planckaert (Bel) Faema
	Major climbs: Col des Ares (797m) André Darrigade (Fra) VC XII/Leroux; Col de Portet d'Aspet (1069m) Federico Bahamontes (Esp) Margnat + Raymond Poulidor (Fra) Mercier			
Stage 15 Sun 8 Jul	Carcassonne to Montpellier 101 finishers	196.5 km 5h12'44" 37.7 kph	Willy Vannitsen (Bel) Wiel's	Jef Planckaert (Bel) Faema
Stage 16 Mon 9 Jul	Montpellier to Aix-en-Provence 100 finishers	185 km 4h33'13" 40.6 kph	Emile Daems (Bel) GS Philco	Jef Planckaert (Bel) Faema
Stage 17 Tue 10 Jul	Aix-en-Provence to Juan-les-Pins 99 finishers	201 km 5h27'36" 36.8 kph	Rudi Altig (FRG) ACBB/Saint-Raphaël	Jef Planckaert (Bel) Faema
Stage 18 Wed 11 Jul	Juan-les-Pins to Briançon 96 finishers	241.5 km 9h20'06" 25.9 kph	Emile Daems (Bel) GS Philco	Jef Planckaert (Bel) Faema
	Major climbs: Col de la Restefond (2,802m) Federico Bahamontes (Esp) Margnat; Col de Vars (2,110m) Eddy Pauwels (Bel) Wiel's; Col d'Izoard (2,360m) Federico Bahamontes (Esp) Margnat			
Stage 19 Thu 12 Jul	Briançon to Aix-les-Bains 94 finishers	204.5 km 6h25'32" 31.8 kph	Raymond Poulidor (Fra) Mercier	Jef Planckaert (Bel) Faema
	Major climbs: Col du Lautaret (2,058m) Juan Campillo (Esp) Margnat; Col du Luitel (1,262m) Juan Campillo (Esp) Margnat; Col de Porte (1,326m) Raymond Poulidor (Fra) Mercier; Col du Cucheron (1,139m) Raymond Poulidor (Fra) Mercier; Col du Granier (1,134m) Raymond Poulidor (Fra) Mercier			
Stage 20 Fri 13 Jul	Bourgoin to Lyon (ITT) 94 finishers	68 km 1h33'35" 43.6 kph	Jacques Anquetil (Fra) ACBB/Saint-Raphaël	Jacques Anquetil (Fra) ACBB/Saint-Raphaël

Stage-by-Stage Results for the 1962 Tour de France			Stage Winner	Maillot Jaune
Stage 21 Sat 14 Jul	Lyon to Pougues-les-Eaux 94 finishers	232 km 6h27'02" 36 kph	Dino Bruni (Ita) GS Gazzola	Jacques Anquetil (Fra) ACBB/Saint-Raphaël
Stage 22 Sun 15 Jul	Pougues-les-Eaux to Paris (Parc des Princes) 94 finishers	271 km 6h50'40" 39.6 kph	Rino Benedetti (Ita) Ignis	Jacques Anquetil (Fra) ACBB/Saint-Raphaël

Prize fund: 583,425 francs (first prize: 20,000 francs)

Final Classification				
Place	**Rider**	**Team**	**Time**	**Age**
1	Jacques Anquetil (Fra)	ACBB/Saint-Raphaël	4,274 km 114h31'54" 37.317 kph	29
2	Jef Planckaert (Bel)	Faema	+ 4'59"	28
3	Raymond Poulidor (Fra)	Mercier	+ 10'24"	26
4	Gilbert Desmet (Bel)	Wiel's	+ 13'01"	31
5	Ab Geldermans (Ned)	ACBB/Saint-Raphaël	+ 14'04"	27
6	Tom Simpson (GBr)	VC XII/Leroux	+ 17'09"	25
7	Imerio Massignan (Ita)	Legnano	+ 17'50"	26
8	Ercole Baldini (Ita)	Ignis	+ 19'00"	29
9	Charly Gaul (Lux)	GS Gazzola	+ 19'11"	30
10	Eddy Pauwels (Bel)	Wiel's	+ 23'04"	27
Lanterne Rouge				
94	Augusto Marcaletti (Ita)	Ignis	+ 4h29'28"	28
Points				
1	Rudi Altig (FRG)	ACBB/Saint-Raphaël		25
King of the Mountains				
1	Federico Bahamontes (Esp)	Margnat		34
Super Combativité				
	Eddy Pauwels (Bel)	Wiel's		27
Team				
		ACBB/Saint-Raphaël		

1963: Fifty Not Out

A decade after the Tour de France celebrated its Golden Jubilee it was time to mark the fiftieth edition of the race, and for this occasion the *grand départ* was returned to *la Ville-Lumière*, the riders setting out from Nogent-sur-Marne and heading east, before turning north and starting an anti-clockwise circuit of France.

With only 79 kilometres of individual time trials – as well as a 21.6-kilometre team effort – the organisers seemed to be sending out a signal that they wanted someone other than Jacques Anquetil, who was gunning for title number four and the chance to be the first man to double the French tour and its Spanish cousin, to win the race. Apart from the opening week and a half and the final three days, the rest of the race would see the riders facing major or minor climbs every day: two big days in the Pyrenees followed by three lumpy transition stages taking the riders into the four days of Alpine climbing, with the final individual time trial coming as soon as the Alps were exited. For Anquetil, at least, there would be very little time to rest.

Such a bumpy Tour suggested that the man most likely to succeed would be the 1959 winner, Federico Bahamontes (Margnat). And, as he had in his winning year, Baha was poking his nose out in front of the *peloton* from the opening stage, getting away in a break of four that stayed away and put a minute and a half into the riders behind. Baha was happy to roll home with the group and Eddy Pauwels (Wiel's) took the stage honours and the opening *maillot jaune*.

Two days later, in Roubaix, that passed to Ireland's Shay Elliott, riding for Anquetil's Saint-Raphaël squad. He had been away in a break that included team-mate and reigning World Champion Jean Stablisnki and – with a little help from Stab – got the drop on his fellow breakaways and took the stage win and the yellow jersey. That help Stab gave was not just one team-mate looking out for another, Stab owed Elliott for the previous year's World Championships, where he had chased the Irishman down in the closing laps and denied him the rainbow jersey. The Tour can be like that, a place to repay debts.

Anquetil, carrying the form that had helped him win the Vuelta a España earlier in the season, came out tops in the first of the two individual time trials, in Angers, with Raymond Poulidor an impressive second. Taking the *maillot jaune* from Elliott was one of two riders with the same name – Gilbert Desmet – both of whom had found homes with the Wiel's squad. Bahamontes saw his 1'19" advantage over Maître Jacques going into the time trial turn into a 1'19" deficit coming out of it. A blow, but with the mountains to come, not a fatal one.

On the first day in the Pyrenees, Pau to Bagnères-de-Bigorre by way of the Aubisque and Tourmalet, Bahamontes went on the attack and was joined by Poulidor, but Anquetil was able to cover their moves and win a four-up sprint at the end of the stage, gaining a minute in time bonuses on his Spanish rival. Exiting the Pyrenees, the overall positions more or less unchanged, Maître Jacques added another half minute in time bonuses, pushing his lead over Baha out to 2'59". The Spaniard had failed to take opportunities presented to him in the Pryénées, his *directeur sportif*, Raoul Rémy, advising him to hold back when others felt he should have attacked

Over the Col de la République and the Col de Porte on stage 15, Bahamontes went on the attack and gained two minutes on Anquetil on the road and another minute in bonuses and was now three seconds ahead of his French rival. Desmet's run in yellow finally ended the next day, the effort of defending the jersey for so long finally catching up with him. Bahamontes – celebrating his thirty-fifth birthday – was now in yellow with the thinnest of margins over Anquetil (three seconds). But – with just one day of tough climbing left, followed by a day of moderate climbs before Anquetil would be off the leash in the last individual time trial – a big effort was called for: an effort that would put minutes, not just seconds, into his French rival.

A last-minute route change, because of an avalanche on the main road over the Forclaz, saw the riders redirected over the Forclaz on a steeper than expected old road. That was where Bahamontes would be able to stretch his lead, maybe even earn enough time to still hold the lead after the time trial. Anquetil's *directeur sportif*, Raphaël Géminiani, knew the road from Tours past and figured that a bike change, to a lighter model with a lower gear, would allow his rider to turn the final kilometres of the stage into a time trial and claw back time Bahamontes would gain on the climb. Bike changes, though, were prohibited, except in the case of a mechanical malfunction. So Gém and Anquetil manufactured such a malfunction.

With Bahamontes attacking as expected on the climb, Anquetil signalled he needed a new bike on the climb. Gém was out of the team car, pliers hidden in his hand, and had his rider's rear brake cable cut before a commissaire arrived. The (manufactured) malfunction clear, the bike change was authorised and Anquetil was able to catch Bahamontes before the finish in Chamonix, the two arriving together. But with Anquetil taking the sprint he gained 30 seconds on Bahamontes through time bonuses and was in yellow ahead of the stage he was expected to win the race on.

Come that final time trial Anquetil put two minutes into Bahamontes and put a ribbon round his fourth Tour de France title. He was now equal with Louison Bobet with three wins in a row, and on a step above the former French favourite and the other three-time winner, the Belgian Philippe Thys. And he had pulled off the first Vuelta/Tour double.

Sixty years, 50 Tours, 34 different winners – Géo Lefèvre's little marketing stunt for an ailing newspaper had come a long, long way. Henri Desgrange had grown it into more than just a race, into something that was part of French culture. Under Émilien Amaury's co-ownership Jacques Goddet and Félix Lévitan were turning it into more than just a marketing stunt, making it a business in its own right. The race had seen cheating and death and still survived. Doping had, particularly in the past decade, become an ever more present problem confronting the race, but that was just another challenge to be overcome. The Tour had survived its first 50 editions. It would surely survive another fifty.

Stage-by-Stage Results for the 1963 Tour de France			Stage Winner	Maillot Jaune
Stage 1 Sun 23 Jun	Paris (Nogent-sur-Marne) to Épernay 130 finishers	152.5 km 3h30'03" 43.6 kph	Eddy Pauwels (Bel) Wiel's	Eddy Pauwels (Bel) Wiel's
Stage 2a Mon 24 Jun	Reims to Jambes 129 finishers	185.5 km 4h25'24" 41.9 kph	Rik van Looy (Bel) GBC	Eddy Pauwels (Bel) Wiel's
Stage 2b Mon 24 Jun	Jambes to Jambes (TTT) 129 finishers	21.6 km 1h23'54" 15.4 kph	Pelforth	Eddy Pauwels (Bel) Wiel's
Stage 3 Tue 25 Jun	Jambes to Roubaix 121 finishers	223.5 km 6h10'38" 36.2 kph	Shay Elliott (Irl) Saint-Raphaël	Shay Elliott (Irl) Saint-Raphaël
Stage 4 Wed 26 Jun	Roubaix to Rouen 120 finishers	235.5 km 6h41'04" 35.2 kph	Frans Melckenbeeck (Bel) Mercier	Shay Elliott (Irl) Saint-Raphaël
Stage 5 Thu 27 Jun	Rouen to Rennes 120 finishers	285 km 7h15'34" 39.3 kph	Antonio Bailetti (Ita) Carpano	Shay Elliott (Irl) Saint-Raphaël
Stage 6a Fri 28 Jun	Rennes to Angers 119 finishers	118.5 km 2h44'05" 43.3 kph	Roger de Breucker (Bel) Solo	Shay Elliott (Irl) Saint-Raphaël
Stage 6b Fri 28 Jun	Angers to Angers (ITT) 119 finishers	24.5 km 31'58" 46 kph	Jacques Anquetil (Fra) Saint-Raphaël	Gilbert Desmet (Bel) Wiel's
Stage 7 Sat 29 Jun	Angers to Limoges 119 finishers	236 km 6h01'59" 39.1 kph	Jan Janssen (Ned) Pelforth	Gilbert Desmet (Bel) Wiel's
Stage 8 Sun 30 Jun	Limoges to Bordeaux 114 finishers	231.5 km 5h34'20" 41.5 kph	Rik van Looy (Bel) GBC	Gilbert Desmet (Bel) Wiel's
Stage 9 Mon 1 Jul	Bordeaux to Pau 112 finishers	202 km 4h41'57" 43 kph	Pino Cerami (Bel) Peugeot	Gilbert Desmet (Bel) Wiel's
Stage 10 Tue 2 Jul	Pau to Bagnères-de-Bigorre 106 finishers	148.5 km 4h37'18" 32.1 kph	Jacques Anquetil (Fra) Saint-Raphaël	Gilbert Desmet (Bel) Wiel's
Major climbs: Col d'Aubisque (1,709m) Federico Bahamontes (Esp) Margnat; Col du Tourmalet (2,115m) Federico Bahamontes (Esp) Margnat + Raymond Poulidor (Fra) Mercier				
Stage 11 Wed 3 Jul	Bagnères-de-Bigorre to Luchon 101 finishers	131 km 3h47'34" 34.5 kph	Guy Ignolin (Fra) Saint-Raphaël	Gilbert Desmet (Bel) Wiel's
Major climbs: Col d'Aspin (1,489m) Guy Ignolin (Fra) Saint-Raphaël; Col de Peyresourde (1,569m) Federico Bahamontes (Esp) Margnat; Col du Portillon (1,298m) Guy Ignolin (Fra) Saint-Raphaël				

Stage-by-Stage Results for the 1963 Tour de France			Stage Winner	Maillot Jaune
Stage 12 Thu 4 Jul	Luchon to Toulouse 99 finishers	172.5 km 4h33'49" 37.8 kph	André Darrigade (Fra) Margnat	Gilbert Desmet (Bel) Wiel's
	Major climbs: Col des Ares (797m) Rik van Looy (Bel) GBC; Col de Portet d'Aspet (1,069m) Federico Bahamontes (Esp) Margnat			
Stage 13 Fri 5 Jul	Toulouse to Aurillac 99 finishers	234 km 6h58'05" 33.6 kph	Rik van Looy (Bel) GBC	Gilbert Desmet (Bel) Wiel's
	Major climbs: Estresses (498m) Rik van Looy (Bel) GBC			
Sat 6 Jul	Rest Day			
Stage 14 Sun 7 Jul	Aurillac to Saint-Étienne 95 finishers	236.5 km 6h46'34" 34.9 kph	Guy Ignolin (Fra) Saint-Raphaël	Gilbert Desmet (Bel) Wiel's
	Major climbs: Le Pas de Peyrol (1,589m) Federico Bahamontes (Esp) Margnat; Côte de Collat (1,008m) Guy Ignolin (Fra) Saint-Raphaël			
Stage 15 Mon 8 Jul	Saint-Étienne to Grenoble 94 finishers	174 km 4h59'13" 34.9 kph	Federico Bahamontes (Esp) Margnat	Gilbert Desmet (Bel) Wiel's
	Major climbs: Col de la République (Col du Grand Bois) (1,161m) Federico Bahamontes (Esp) Margnat; Col de Porte (1,326m) Federico Bahamontes (Esp) Margnat			
Stage 16 Tue 9 Jul	Grenoble to Val d'Isère 82 finishers	202 km 6h20'48" 31.8 kph	Fernando Manzaneque (Esp) Ferrys	Federico Bahamontes (Esp) Margnat
	Major climbs: Col de la Croix de Fer (2,067m) Claude Mattio (Fra) Margnat; Col de l'Iseran (2,770m) Fernando Manzaneque (Esp) Ferrys			
Stage 17 Wed 10 Jul	Val d'Isère to Chamonix 76 finishers	227.5 km 7h25'05" 30.7 kph	Jacques Anquetil (Fra) Saint-Raphaël	Jacques Anquetil (Fra) Saint-Raphaël
	Major climbs: Col du Petit Saint-Bernard (2,188m) Federico Bahamontes (Esp) Margnat; Col du Grand Saint-Bernard (2,470m) Federico Bahamontes (Esp) Margnat; Col de la Forclaz (1,527m) Federico Bahamontes (Esp) Margnat; Col des Montets (1,461m) Federico Bahamontes (Esp) Margnat			
Stage 18 Thu 11 Jul	Chamonix to Lons-le-Saunier 76 finishers	225 km 6h43'47" 33.4 kph	Frans Brands (Bel) Faema	Jacques Anquetil (Fra) Saint-Raphaël
	Major climbs: Col de la Faucille (1,323m) Guy Ignolin (Fra) Saint-Raphaël			
Stage 19 Fri 12 Jul	Arbois to Besançon (ITT) 76 finishers	54.5 km 1h12'20" 45.2 kph	Jacques Anquetil (Fra) Saint-Raphaël	Jacques Anquetil (Fra) Saint-Raphaël
Stage 20 Sat 13 Jul	Besançon to Troyes 76 finishers	233.5 km 6h20'06" 36.9 kph	Roger de Breucker (Bel) Solo	Jacques Anquetil (Fra) Saint-Raphaël
Stage 21 Sun 14 Jul	Troyes to Paris (Parc des Princes) 76 finishers	185.5 km 5h06'21" 36.3 kph	Rik van Looy (Bel) GBC	Jacques Anquetil (Fra) Saint-Raphaël

Prize fund: 550,000 francs (first prize: 20,000 francs)

Final Classification

Place	Rider	Team	Time	Age
1	Jacques Anquetil (Fra)	Saint-Raphaël	4,138 km 113h30'05" 37.092 kph	30
2	Federico Bahamontes (Esp)	Margnat	+ 3'35"	35
3	José Pérez Francés (Esp)	Ferrys	+ 10'14"	27
4	Jean-Claude Lebaube (Fra)	Saint-Raphaël	+ 11'55"	26
5	Armand Desmet (Bel)	Faema	+ 15'00"	32
6	Angelino Soler (Esp)	Faema	+ 15'04"	24
7	Renzo Fontona (Ita)	IBAC/Molteni	+ 15'27"	24
8	Raymond Poulidor (Fra)	Mercier	+ 16'46"	27
9	Hans Jünkermann (FRG)	Wiel's	+ 18'53"	29
10	Rik van Looy (Bel)	GBC/Libertas	+ 19'24"	30
Lanterne Rouge				
76	Willy Derboven (Bel)	GBC/Libertas	+ 2h45'10"	24
Points				
	Rik van Looy (Bel)	GBC/Libertas		30
King of the Mountains				
	Federico Bahamontes (Esp)	Margnat		35
Super Combativité				
	Rik van Looy (Bel)	GBC/Libertas		30
Team				
		Saint-Raphaël		

1964: Anquetil vs Poulidor

Federico Bahamontes had presented Jacques Anquetil with a formidable challenge at the 1963 Tour but at the following year's race the four-time Tour champion faced his stiffest challenge yet, when Raymond Poulidor finally rose to the occasion and gave the French a race they would never forget.

Coming into the 1964 Tour, both Anquetil and Poulidor were gunning for a Grand Tour double: the 28-year-old Poulidor (riding for the Mercier squad) had won the Vuelta a España, while the 30-year-old Anquetil (riding for Saint-Raphaël) had bagged the Giro d'Italia (his second victory at the *corsa rosa*). Throughout the race, the two held their own against each other. There were days when they would lose time, then days when they would make up their losses. Anquetil gained only a handful of seconds over Poulidor in the first of the race's three individual time trials – 20.8 kilometres on Stage 10b – and it looked like Poulidor, a capable time trialist and just 30 seconds behind Anquetil on general classification, might actually get the better of the reigning champion.

By the time the race exited the Alps, Poulidor was within nine seconds of Anquetil. In the time trial that followed Anquetil donned the yellow jersey, but Poulidor again lost less than half a minute, and this despite suffering a puncture, a poor bike change and a crash. Ahead lay one last climbing stage, to the Puy de Dôme, and a time trial on the final day. One or other of the two seemed set to win the Tour on one of those days.

Starting the stage from Brive to the Puy de Dôme Poulidor trailed Anquetil by 56 seconds. Maître Jacques could afford to cede time, but not much; putting time into Poulidor in the final time trial was not guaranteed. The climb of the Puy de Dôme comes in two parts, the opening nine kilometres or so having a gentle gradient of five or six per cent, with the final five kilometres kicking upward at more than 10 per cent (in those five kilometres the road climbs 568 metres).

Anquetil's hopes of holding an advantage going into the final time trial were boosted when two of the best climbers in the race, Spain's Julio Jiménez (Ferrys) and Federico Bahamontes (Margnat), got away in those final five kilometres and went in search of the stage win and more points in the King of the Mountains competition. Between them they would mop up the time bonuses available for the first and second rider on the stage (Jiménez took the stage and Bahamontes sealed his sixth climbing title in the Tour). Behind them, and obscuring their performances, was a battle royal between Poulidor and Anquetil.

Of the two, Poulidor was the better climber, more able to change his pace on the climb and put in accelerations that would drop non-climbers and make them tire themselves out chasing him down. Knowing this, Anquetil bluffed as best he could, riding alongside Poulidor, elbow to elbow, trying to make him believe he was stronger than he seemed. Maître Jacques also had the advantage of knowing the climb, while Poulidor would later admit that he had made the mistake of not reconnoitring it in advance.

In the final kilometre, as the gradient eased a little, Poulidor finally put in an attack that Anquetil couldn't respond to, riding away from the Tour champion. In that one kilometre of climbing Poulidor put more than 40 seconds into Anquetil. At the summit, Maître Jacques collapsed into the arms of his *directeur sportif* Raphaël Géminiani and asked one question: 'How much?' Gém understood the question referred to the general classification, what advantage Anquetil still held, and told him: 14 seconds. To which, Tour legend has it, Anquetil replied: 'That's 13 more than I need.' After the stage, Anquetil told the waiting press corps that, had he lost the jersey on the Puy de Dôme, he would have quit the race – as he had the Vuelta a España in 1962 when team-mate Rudi Altig got the better of him – and gone home that night.

Come the final time trial, 27.5 kilometres from Versailles to the Parc des Princes, taking place on Bastille Day, an estimated half a million fans came out and lined the road to watch the race pass. Poulidor needed just 15 seconds to win the Tour. Anything could happen. At all the intermediate time checks, the two were pretty much level pegging, Anquetil having the advantage, a slim one of just five seconds, with five kilometres to go. Then Anquetil began to open up the throttle, adding another four seconds in each of those kilometres to win the stage with an advantage of 21 seconds over Poulidor, and another 20 seconds in time bonuses, giving him a final margin of 55 seconds (up to then, the narrowest winning margin). Poulidor could have cut that to 45 had he taken second on the stage and 10 seconds in time bonuses, but even in that he was denied, with Anquetil's team-mate Rudi Altig beating him to that.

With five Tours to his name Anquetil was in a league of his own, two titles ahead of the next best. He had equalled Coppi's feat of doubling the Giro and the Tour (and, the year before, had doubled the Vuelta and the Tour). But, once again, it was his rival who received the applause of the crowds, French fans preferring the plucky looser Poulidor over their cold, calculating champion.

Stage-by-Stage Results for the 1964 Tour de France			Stage Winner	Maillot Jaune
Stage 1 Mon 22 Jun	Rennes to Lisieux 131 finishers	215 km 5h14'57" 41 kph	Edward Sels (Bel) Solo	Edward Sels (Bel) Solo
Stage 2 Tue 23 Jun	Lisieux to Amiens 131 finishers	208 km 5h07'47" 40.5 kph	André Darrigade (Fra) Margnat	Edward Sels (Bel) Solo
Stage 3a Wed 24 Jun	Amiens to Forest 129 finishers	196.5 km 5h07'32" 38.3 kph	Bernard van de Kerckhove (Bel) Solo	Bernard van de Kerckhove (Bel) Solo
Stage 3b Wed 24 Jun	Forest (TTT) 129 finishers	21.3 km 1h34'05" 13.6 kph	KAS	Bernard van de Kerckhove (Bel) Solo
Stage 4 Thu 25 Jun	Forest to Metz 128 finishers	291.5 km 8h26'00" 34.6 kph	Rudi Altig (FRG) Saint-Raphaël	Bernard van de Kerckhove (Bel) Solo
Stage 5 Fri 26 Jun	Metz to Fribourg 123 finishers	161.5 km 4h02'51" 39.9 kph	Willy Derboven (Bel) Solo	Rudi Altig (FRG) Saint-Raphaël
Major climbs: Col de Sainte-Marie (772m) Rudi Altig (FRG) Saint-Raphaël; Col du Haut de Ribeauvillé (742m) Georges Groussard (Fra) Pelforth				

Stage-by-Stage Results for the 1964 Tour de France			Stage Winner	Maillot Jaune
Stage 6 Sat 27 Jun	Fribourg to Besançon 120 finishers	200 km 5h05'18" 39.3 kph	Henk Nijdam (Ned) Televizier	Rudi Altig (FRG) Saint-Raphaël
Stage 7 Sun 28 Jun	Champagnole to Thonon-les-Bains 105 finishers	195 km 5h02'14" 38.7 kph	Jan Janssen (Ned) Pelforth	Rudi Altig (FRG) Saint-Raphaël
	Major climbs: Les Lacets de Septmoncel (910m) Vittorio Adorni (Ita) Salvarani; Col de la Faucille (1,323m) Julio Jiménez (Esp) Ferrys			
Stage 8 Mon 29 Jun	Thonon-les-Bains to Briançon 104 finishers	248.5 km 7h20'52" 33.8 kph	Federico Bahamontes (Esp) Margnat	Georges Groussard (Fra) Pelforth
	Major climbs: Col du Télégraphe (1,566m) Federico Bahamontes (Esp) Margnat; Col du Galibier (2,556m) Federico Bahamontes (Esp) Margnat			
Stage 9 Tue 30 Jun	Briançon to Monaco 98 finishers	239 km 7h26'59" 32.1 kph	Jacques Anquetil (Fra) Saint-Raphaël	Georges Groussard (Fra) Pelforth
	Major climbs: Col de Vars (2,110m) Julio Jiménez (Esp) Ferrys; Col de la Restefond (2,802m) Federico Bahamontes (Esp) Margnat; Levens (600m) Federico Bahamontes (Esp) Margnat			
Stage 10a Wed 1 Jul	Monaco to Hyères 96 finishers	187.5 km 5h30'58" 34 kph	Jan Janssen (Ned) Pelforth	Georges Groussard (Fra) Pelforth
Stage 10b Wed 1 Jul	Hyères to Toulon (ITT) 96 finishers	20.8 km 27'52" 44.8 kph	Jacques Anquetil (Fra) Saint-Raphaël	Georges Groussard (Fra) Pelforth
Stage 11 Thu 2 Jul	Toulon to Montpellier 96 finishers	250 km 7h49'28" 32 kph	Edward Sels (Bel) Solo	Georges Groussard (Fra) Pelforth
Stage 12 Fri 3 Jul	Montpellier to Perpignan 95 finishers	174 km 4h44'20" 36.7 kph	Jo de Roo (Ned) Saint-Raphaël	Georges Groussard (Fra) Pelforth
Stage 13 Sat 4 Jul	Perpignan to Andorra 86 finishers	170 km 4h54'53" 34.6 kph	Julio Jiménez (Esp) Ferrys	Georges Groussard (Fra) Pelforth
	Major climbs: Col de la Perche (1,610m) Julio Jiménez (Esp) Ferrys; Col du Puymorens (1,915m) Julio Jiménez (Esp) Ferrys			
Sun 5 July	Rest day			
Stage 14 Mon 6 Jul	Andorra to Toulouse 83 finishers	186 km 4h36'56" 40.3 kph	Edward Sels (Bel) Solo	Georges Groussard (Fra) Pelforth
	Major climbs: Port d'Envalira (2,407m) Julio Jiménez (Esp) Ferrys + Federico Bahamontes (Esp) Margnat			
Stage 15 Tue 7 Jul	Toulouse to Luchon 83 finishers	203 km 6h07'55" 33.1 kph	Raymond Poulidor (Fra) Mercier	Georges Groussard (Fra) Pelforth
	Major climbs: Col de Portet d'Aspet (1,069m) Julio Jiménez (Esp) Ferrys; Col des Ares (797m) Joaquim Galera (Esp) Ferrys; Col du Portillon (1,298m) Raymond Poulidor (Fra) Mercier			

Stage-by-Stage Results for the 1964 Tour de France			Stage Winner	Maillot Jaune
Stage 16 Wed 8 Jul	Luchon to Pau 81 finishers	197 km 6h18'47" 31.2 kph	Federico Bahamontes (Esp) Margnat	Georges Groussard (Fra) Pelforth
	Major climbs: Col de Peyresourde (1,569m) Julio Jiménez (Esp) Ferrys; Col d'Aspin (1,489m) Julio Jiménez (Esp) Ferrys; Col du Tourmalet (2,115m) Julio Jiménez (Esp) Ferrys; Col d'Aubisque (1,709m) Federico Bahamontes (Esp) Margnat			
Stage 17 Thu 9 Jul	Peyrehorade to Bayonne (ITT) 81 finishers	42.6 km 1h01'53" 41.3 kph	Jacques Anquetil (Fra) Saint-Raphaël	Jacques Anquetil (Fra) Saint-Raphaël
Stage 18 Fri 10 Jul	Bayonne to Bordeaux 81 finishers	187 km 5h05'12" 36.8 kph	André Darrigade (Fra) Margnat	Jacques Anquetil (Fra) Saint-Raphaël
Stage 19 Sat 11 Jul	Bordeaux to Brive 81 finishers	215.5 km 5h50'30" 36.9 kph	Edward Sels (Bel) Solo	Jacques Anquetil (Fra) Saint-Raphaël
Stage 20 Sun 12 Jul	Brive to Clermont-Ferrand (Le Puy de Dôme) 81 finishers	237.5 km 7h09'33" 33.2 kph	Julio Jiménez (Esp) Ferrys	Jacques Anquetil (Fra) Saint-Raphaël
	Major climbs: Saint-Privat (421m) Julio Jiménez (Esp) Ferrys; Puy de Dôme (1,415m) Julio Jiménez (Esp) Ferrys			
Stage 21 Mon 13 Jul	Clermont-Ferrand to Orléans 81 finishers	311 km 9h29'33" 32.8 kph	Jean Stablinski (Fra) Saint-Raphaël	Jacques Anquetil (Fra) Saint-Raphaël
Stage 22a Tue 14 Jul	Orléans to Versailles 81 finishers	118.5 km 3h25'24" 34.6 kph	Benoni Beheyt (Bel) Wiel's	Jacques Anquetil (Fra) Saint-Raphaël
Stage 22b Tue 14 Jul	Versailles to Paris (Parc des Princes) (ITT) 81 finishers	27.5 km 37'10" 44.4 kph	Jacques Anquetil (Fra) Saint-Raphaël	Jacques Anquetil (Fra) Saint-Raphaël

Prize fund: 543,200 francs (first prize: 20,000 francs)

Final Classification

Place	Rider	Team	Time	Age
1	Jacques Anquetil (Fra)	Saint-Raphaël	4,504 km 127h09'44" 35.419 kph	30
2	Raymond Poulidor (Fra)	Mercier	+ 0'55"	28
3	Federico Bahamontes (Esp)	Margnat	+ 4'44"	36
4	Henry Anglade (Fra)	Pelforth	+ 6'42"	31
5	Georges Groussard (Fra)	Pelforth	+ 10'34"	27
6	André Foucher (Fra)	Pelforth	+ 10'36"	30
7	Julio Jiménez (Esp)	Ferrys	+ 12'13"	29
8	Gilbert Desmet (Bel)	Wiel's	+ 12'17"	33
9	Hans Jünkermann (FRG)	Wiel's	+ 14'02"	30
10	Vittorio Adorni (Ita)	Salvarani	+ 14'19"	26
Lanterne Rouge				
81	Anatole Novak (Fra)	Saint-Raphaël	+ 3h19'02"	27
Points				
	Jan Janssen (Ned)	Pelforth		24
King of the Mountains				
	Federico Bahamontes (Esp)	Margnat		36
Super Combativité				
	Henry Anglade (Fra)	Pelforth		31
Team				
		Pelforth		

1965: An Unexpected Victor

Having launched *L'Équipe* in 1946, Jacques Goddet had led the paper to a dominant position as France's number one sports newspaper. Financially, though, Goddet was less successful and, by the mid-sixties, was forced to sell the paper to the man who had helped him save the Tour after the Second World War, Émilien Amaury. And with the paper came the Tour de France, now fully a part of the Amaury empire.

The Tour itself was going from strength to strength with TV now covering every stage and it and its shadow race, the Tour de l'Avenir, drawing crowds throughout the country. That shadow race also gave the Tour its next Italian champion, with Felice Gimondi winning the Tour de l'Avenir in 1964 and then, at his first attempt, taking the Tour crown the following year. And that might not have happened had his team, Salvarani, not needed to call the 22-year-old neophyte in as a last minute substitute when Bruno Fantinato had to be replaced.

With Rudi Altig's successes in the sport – he won the Vuelta a España and the Tour's green jersey in 1962, the Ronde van Vlaanderen in 1964 – German interest in cycling was on a high and the people of Köln were the paid the honour (after paying a fee) of hosting the race's *grand départ*.

When five-time winner Jacques Anquetil (now riding for Ford France) ruled himself out of the race, all eyes immediately fell on the man who had finished third on his début in 1962 and second two years after that, Raymond Poulidor (still with Mercier). A win for Poupou was what everyone wanted, not least Poulidor's agent, Roger Piel, who had approached Maître Jacques – whose affairs were managed by Daniel Dousset – with a tempting offer: stay at home and earn the easiest 50,000 francs of his career and Piel would even guarantee appearance fees at 50 critériums to sweeten the deal. Anquetil is said to have turned down Piel's offer, only to decide himself that a tilt at his sixth Tour title wouldn't be wise and only then decided to sit the race out.

The French riders' agents may have had the power to rule riders out of contention for victory – as Dousset was alleged to have done to Henry Anglade in 1959 and 1960 – but that was not always enough to guarantee victory for their preferred candidate. As Poulidor quickly discovered in the Tour.

With a second place on the second stage, from Liège to Roubaix, and the stage win in Rouen the next day – his first professional win – Gimondi donned the *maillot jaune*. These were the early days of the race, the phoney war. The first real shots weren't fired until Stage Five's individual time trial, 26.7 kilometres around Châteaulin, where Poulidor showed he was the man to beat in races against the clock. But Poupou only put seven seconds into Gimondi, and finished the stage still more than three minutes back on general classification. Gimondi, though, was not Poulidor's worry; he was more concerned with Vittorio Adorni, Gimondi's team leader at Salvarani and the man who had just won the Giro d'Italia. Relative to him, Poupou only had 17 seconds to make up.

As expected, Gimondi's stay in yellow didn't last long, Solo's Bernard Van de Kerckhove re-taking the race lead (he had led at the end of Stage Two and was the man Gimondi took the jersey from).

Come the Pyrenees, and the Tour found itself facing yet another doping controversy, with the heat up on the ninth stage (Dax to Bagnères-de-Bigorre) and riders dropping like flies. Among the dead flies complaining of upset stomachs were the yellow jersey, Van de Kerckhove, and the recent winner of the Giro, Adorni. Eleven riders in all left the race that day. But they were not the only ones in trouble. Earlier in the day riders in the Tour de l'Avenir had suffered similar problems and when their hotel rooms were searched, doping products were found. The Tour's doping problem – cycling's doping problem, sport's doping problem – was not just going to go away of its own accord, no matter how much journalists railed against it in newspapers and magazines whenever a new controversy arose.

With Van de Kerckhove having to abandon, and after putting in a good ride despite a puncture late in the stage that saw him having to chase Poulidor and the other GC contenders, Gimondi was back in yellow, with a 3'12" lead over the Frenchman, who was in second.

Things then settled down until the race's fourteenth stage, which finished atop Mont Ventoux. When the Spanish climbing ace Julio Jiménez (KAS) set off – en route to collecting the King of the Mountains title – Poulidor gave chase. Gimondi was unable to follow and the best he could do was to ride intelligently and limit his losses, ceding 90 seconds to his French rival on the stage – which Poulidor was able to win, after Jiménez punctured. Between the time on the road and time bonuses, Poupou was now within 34 seconds of wearing the *maillot jaune*.

Gimondi added another five seconds to his lead in Briançon, with Poulidor apparently willing to win *à l'Anquetil*, putting his rival to the sword in the time trial at Mont Revard two days later, which would see the riders racing 26.9 kilometres uphill. Except it wasn't all uphill, with the first 10 kilometres being on the flat before the climb began. And at the time check before the climb began Gimondi was the surprising leader, taking 20 seconds out of Poulidor. At the top that was 23 seconds. With time bonuses taken into account (20 seconds to Gimondi for winning the stage, 10 to Poulidor for coming second), the Italian neophyte now had a lead of 1'12". And Poulidor had just three stages left to in which win the Tour. Which, as the year before, ended with a time trial from Versailles to the Parc des Princes.

Raced over 37.8 kilometres, it should have been an exciting finale for a race that had, in fairness, lacked much in excitement, despite having been a close-run affair. Gimondi had defended his position intelligently, while Poulidor, perhaps scarred by the Puy de Dôme the year before, had failed to challenge him and instead left it all to the time trials. In the last of these Poulidor, who had held his own against Anquetil in the final time trial the year before until the closing kilometres, should have been able to at least challenge the Italian. But no challenge emerged and Poupou bled time at every intermediate check. The Frenchman lost 30 seconds on the road, and another 10 seconds in time bonuses and had to be content with his third visit to the Tour's podium in four years, and another race in which he had failed to even wear the *maillot jaune*.

For Gimondi, it was a phenomenal victory. His Salvarani *directeur sportif* Luciano Pezzi likened his final time trial performance to Coppi, and Italy, pining for the days of Coppi and Bartali, had a new star in the making. As for the Tour, it had seen a new debutant victor. Maurice Garin, Henri Cornet and Louis Trousselier each having won the Tour at the first attempt in the race's first three years, and Jean Robic had done the same when a new *peloton* took on the race immediately after World War Two. He was followed by Fausto Coppi, Hugo Koblet and Jacques Anquetil, seven riders in all who had achieved debutant victories. The *grande boucle* could surely look forward to the 22-year-old Italian returning in the years to come and joining the pantheon of greats who had more than one Tour success on their *palmarès*?

Stage-by-Stage Results for the 1965 Tour de France			Stage Winner	Maillot Jaune
Stage 1a Tue 22 Jun	Köln to Liège 129 finishers	149 km 4h06'49" 36.2 kph	Rik Van Looy (Bel) Solo	Rik Van Looy (Bel) Solo
Stage 1b Tue 22 Jun	Liège (TTT) 129 finishers	22.5 km 29'24 44.1 kph	Ford France	Rik Van Looy (Bel) Solo
Stage 2 Wed 23 Jun	Liège to Roubaix 129 finishers	200.5 km 5h27'45" 36.7 kph	Bernard Van de Kerckhove (Bel) Solo	Bernard Van de Kerckhove (Bel) Solo
Stage 3 Thu 24 Jun	Roubaix to Rouen 129 finishers	240 km 7h06'18" 33.8 kph	Felice Gimondi (Ita) Salvarani	Felice Gimondi (Ita) Salvarani
Stage 4 Fri 25 Jun	Caen to Saint-Brieuc 129 finishers	227 km 6h24'33" 35.4 kph	Edgard Sorgeloos (Bel) Solo	Felice Gimondi (Ita) Salvarani
Stage 5a Sat 26 Jun	Saint-Brieuc to Châteaulin 129 finishers	147 km 3h35'39" 40.9 kph	Cees van Espen (Ned) Televizier	Felice Gimondi (Ita) Salvarani

Stage-by-Stage Results for the 1965 Tour de France			Stage Winner	Maillot Jaune
Stage 5b Sat 26 Jun	Châteaulin (ITT) 129 finishers	26.7 km 37'43" 42.5 kph	Raymond Poulidor (Fra) Mercier	Felice Gimondi (Ita) Salvarani
Stage 6 Sun 27 Jun	Quimper to La Baule Pornichet 128 finishers	210.5 km 4h51'19" 43.4 kph	Guido Reybrouck (Bel) Flandria	Felice Gimondi (Ita) Salvarani
Stage 7 Mon 28 Jun	La Baule Pornichet to La Rochelle 128 finishers	219 km 5h04'47" 43.1 kph	Edward Sels (Bel) Solo	Bernard Van de Kerckhove (Bel) Solo
Stage 8 Tue 29 Jun	La Rochelle to Bordeaux 128 finishers	197.5 km 4h56'14" 40 kph	Jo de Roo (Ned) Televizier	Bernard van de Kerckhove (Bel) Solo
Stage 9 Wed 30 Jun	Dax to Bagnères-de-Bigorre 117 finishers	226.5 km 6h49'19" 33.2 kph	Julio Jiménez (Esp) KAS	Felice Gimondi (Ita) Salvarani
Major climbs: Col d'Aubisque (1,709m) Julio Jiménez (Esp) KAS; Col du Tourmalet (2,115m) Julio Jiménez (Esp) KAS				
Stage 10 Thu 1 Jul	Bagnères-de-Bigorre to Ax-les-Thermes 109 finishers	222.5 km 6h44'18" 33 kph	Guido Reybrouck (Bel) Flandria	Felice Gimondi (Ita) Salvarani
Major climbs: Col de Portet d'Aspet (1,069m) Julio Jiménez (Esp) KAS; Col de Port (1,249m) Rik van Looy (Bel) Solo; Col du Chioula (1,450m) Rik van Looy (Bel) Solo				
Stage 11 Fri 2 Jul	Ax-les-Thermes to Barcelona 105 finishers	240.5 km 6h55'59" 34.7 kph	José Pérez Francés (Esp) Ferrys	Felice Gimondi (Ita) Salvarani
Major climbs: Col du Puymorens (1,915m) José Pérez Francés (Fra) Ferrys; Col de Tosas (1,865m) José Pérez Francés (Fra) Ferrys				
Sat 3 July	Rest day			
Stage 12 Sun 4 Jul	Barcelona to Perpignan 105 finishers	219 km 6h07'52" 35.7 kph	Jan Janssen (Ned) Pelforth	Felice Gimondi (Ita) Salvarani
Stage 13 Mon 5 Jul	Perpignan to Montpellier 103 finishers	164 km 4h04'34" 40.2 kph	Adriano Durante (Ita) Molteni	Felice Gimondi (Ita) Salvarani
Stage 14 Tue 6 Jul	Montpellier to Mont Ventoux 103 finishers	173 km 5h47'31" 29.9 kph	Raymond Poulidor (Fra) Mercier	Felice Gimondi (Ita) Salvarani
Major climbs: Mont Ventoux (1,909m) Raymond Poulidor (Fra) Mercier				
Stage 15 Wed 7 Jul	Carpentras to Gap 100 finishers	167.5 km 4h37'57" 36.2 kph	Giuseppe Fezzardi (Ita) Molteni	Felice Gimondi (Ita) Salvarani
Major climbs: Col de Perty (1,303m) José-Antonio Momene (Esp) KAS; Col de la Sentinelle (980m) Giuseppe Fezzardi (Ita) Molteni				

Stage-by-Stage Results for the 1965 Tour de France			Stage Winner	Maillot Jaune
Stage 16 Thu 8 Jul	Gap to Briançon 100 finishers	177 km 5h46'32" 30.6 kph	Joaquín Galera (Esp) Fagor	Felice Gimondi (Ita) Salvarani
	Major climbs: Col de Vars (2,110m) Cees Haast (Ned) Televizier; Col d'Izoard (2,360m) Joaquín Galera (Esp) KAS			
Stage 17 Fri 9 Jul	Briançon to Aix-les-Bains 99 finishers	193.5 km 5h43'13" 33.8 kph	Julio Jiménez (Esp) KAS	Felice Gimondi (Ita) Salvarani
	Major climbs: Col du Lautaret (2,058m) Francisco Gabica (Esp) KAS; Col de Porte (1,326m) Julio Jiménez (Esp) KAS; Col du Cucheron (1,139m) Julio Jiménez (Esp) KAS; Col du Granier (1,134m) Julio Jiménez (Esp) KAS			
Stage 18 Sat 10 Jul	Aix-les-Bains to Le Revard (ITT) 99 finishers	26.9 km 59'50" 27 kph	Felice Gimondi (Ita) Salvarani	Felice Gimondi (Ita) Salvarani
	Major climbs: Mont Revard (1,537m) Felice Gimondi (Ita) Salvarani			
Stage 19 Sun 11 Jul	Aix-les-Bains to Lyon 98 finishers	165 km 4h01'37" 41 kph	Rik Van Looy (Bel) Solo	Felice Gimondi (Ita) Salvarani
	Major climbs: Col de l'Épine (987m) Gianni Motta (Ita) Molteni			
Stage 20 Mon 12 Jul	Lyon to Auxerre 97 finishers	298.5 km 8h42'03" 34.3 kph	Michael Wright (GBr) Wiel's	Felice Gimondi (Ita) Salvarani
Stage 21 Tue 13 Jul	Auxerre to Versailles 96 finishers	225.5 km 6h12'42" 36.3 kph	Gerben Karstens (Ned) Televizier	Felice Gimondi (Ita) Salvarani
Stage 22 Wed 14 Jul	Versailles to Paris (Parc des Princes) (ITT) 96 finishers	37.8 km 50'57" 44.5 kph	Felice Gimondi (Ita) Salvarani	Felice Gimondi (Ita) Salvarani

Prize fund: 414,275 francs (first prize: 20,000 francs)

Final Classification

Place	Rider	Team	Time	Age
1	Felice Gimondi (Ita)	Salvarani	4,188 km 116h42'06" 35.886 kph	22
2	Raymond Poulidor (Fra)	Mercier	+ 2'40"	29
3	Gianni Motta (Ita)	Molteni	+ 9'18"	22
4	Henry Anglade (Fra)	Pelforth	+ 12'43"	32
5	Jean-Claude Lebaube (Fra)	Ford France	+ 12'56"	27
6	José Pérez Francés (Esp)	Ferrys	+ 13'15"	28
7	Guido de Rosso (Ita)	Molteni	+ 14'48"	24
8	Frans Brands (Bel)	Flandria	+ 17'36"	25
9	Jan Janssen (Ned)	Pelforth	+ 17'52"	25
10	Francisco Gabica (Esp)	KAS	+ 19'11"	27

Lanterne Rouge

96	Joseph Groussard (Fra)	Pelforth	+ 2h37'38"	31

Points

	Jan Janssen (Ned)	Pelforth		25

King of the Mountains

	Julio Jiménez (Esp)	KAS		30

Super Combativité

	Felice Gimondi (Ita)	Salvarani		22

Team

		KAS		

1966: Revenge

The public attitude to doping had been undergoing major changes in the previous few years. As well as events at the Tour such as the Ventoux in 1955 and Roger Rivière's crash in 1960, the sport had seen the death of a Danish cyclist, the 23-year-old Knud Enemark Jensen, during the 100 kilometre time trial at the Rome Olympics in August. He died after fracturing his skull in a fall during the race. Despite the autopsy blaming heatstroke for Jensen's fall it became linked to doping, with a member of his entourage claiming he administered Roniacol to a number of the riders before the race. Regardless of the truth, Jensen's death became a *cause célèbre* among those who wanted to tackle the problem of doping in sport, helped focus minds and bring bodies to the table.

In 1963 members of various European sports governing bodies met to discuss the problem – at the instigation of the Tour's doctor, Pierre Dumas, who was aided by the French sports ministry – and came up with a simple definition of doping, which the IOC was able to adopt the following year in Tokyo. The same year, the governments of France and Belgium began to formulate anti-doping legislation, which finally came into force in 1965, with other countries promising to follow suit. This spurred sports governing bodies to at least look like they were taking charge of the problem. Having defeated a motion proposing that the UCI take responsibility for anti-doping in 1962, in 1966 the governing body added to its rules a number of regulations against the use of drugs.

All of this led to the first anti-doping tests at the Tour being carried out in 1966. Following the end of the eighth stage, riders' hotel rooms in Bordeaux were searched and a number of riders asked to provide urine samples, Raymond Poulidor among them. In response, the next morning the riders protested, climbing off their bikes shortly after the stage began and walking part of the route before getting underway again. The protest seems to have worked, for there were no more visits from the anti-doping authorities during the rest of the race.

That protest highlights one of the major problems of the early fight against doping: no one had sought to get the riders buy-in, get them to agree that there was a problem and that it was a problem that needed dealing with. Given that the sport had developed a culture of medical care dating back to the nineteenth century, simply banning such practices and expecting everyone to comply was senseless.

Making matters worse, though, was the attitude of the authorities, who seemed to be saying one thing while doing another. The tough talking against doping was rarely followed up by tough action. When Jacques Anquetil, Rudy Altig, Gianni Motta, Italo Zilioli and Jean Stablinski all failed to provide samples for testing at the 1966 World Championships in August – Altig, Anquetil and Poulidor having been the first three home in the road race – they were initially suspended but then cleared by the UCI. At a time when tough action was most needed, the UCI seemed to be saying to riders to carry on as normal.

The Tour itself, outside of that one visit from the anti-doping authorities and the protest it generated, saw Jacques Anquetil return to the race. Already with five wins to his name – two more than anyone else had managed – Maître Jacques wanted more. Maybe there were thoughts of the five wins Alfredo Binda and Fausto Coppi each had at the Giro d'Italia, and a desire to rise above even that at the Tour. Certainly Anquetil's career was not yet over: in the spring, he finally added a victory in one of the most important one day races to his *palmarès*, with a win in May at Liège-Bastogne-Liège. That was a victory which, as well as adding to the list of races Maître Jacques had won, put the reigning Tour champion Felice Gimondi in his place. He had followed up his Tour success by winning Paris-Roubaix and Paris-Brussels in April, and it was important than Anquetil show him he was still the boss.

Whatever the reason, Anquetil took one more tilt at the Tour. And with Gimondi opting out (his whole Salavarni team had opted out, some claiming they were concerned by France's new anti-doping law) the Tour – almost inevitably – became a race between two men: Anquetil (Ford France) and Raymond Poulidor (Mercier). And that is how Poulidor managed to lose the Tour one more time, by seeing Anquetil as his rival, the man he had to beat.

Things started to go wrong for Poulidor in the Pyrenees, when a large group of riders put seven minutes into him, Anquetil and the man then in yellow Rudi Altig (Molteni). Altig had a team-mate, Tommaso de Pra, in the break and it was he who took the stage and the *maillot jaune*. Anquetil had one of his team-mates in the break, Lucien Aimar (who ended the day 2'14" off yellow). Poulidor's Mercier squad, they had no one, and so responsibility for chasing the break fell to them. And they failed to bring it back.

De Pra's stay in yellow was brief; he lost the jersey the next day on the second Pyrenean stage, with Jean-Claude Lebaube (Kamome) donning yellow, only to lose it again on the third and final day in the Pyrenees, with Karl-Heinz Künde (Peugeot) exiting the first phase of mountains in yellow. And keeping up with him was Aimar, who was now up to 1'56" off yellow.

Künde held on to his lead through to and after the Stage 14b individual time trial, 20 kilometres around Vals-les-Bains, in which Poulidor got the better of Anquetil, but only reclaimed 47 seconds of his deficit to Aimar. Künde finally surrendered the jersey the next day, in Bourg d'Oisans, with Jan Janssen (Pelforth) briefly taking the race lead before Aimar finally donned yellow the day after that, across the Franco-Italian border in Turin.

Aimar had attacked Poulidor on the Col d'Ornon, with both Anquetil (nominally his team leader) and Altig (Molteni) apparently happy to let him go. Poulidor tried to chase but, on the descent in to Turin lost two minutes. A day later, Anquetil – who'd given up hopes of winning the Tour himself – worked as Aimar's *domestique* when Poulidor attacked on the road to Chamonix, Maître Jacques helping Aimar limit his losses to Poulidor to just 49 seconds. A day later Anquetil, suffering with a chest infection, climbed off and quit the race. He'd done as much as he could to stop Poulidor winning, now it was up to Aimar to seal the deal. All he had to do was stay upright for three days and then hold on to as much of his lead as he could in the race's finale, a 51.3-kilometre time trial from Rambouillet to the Parc des Princes.

Poulidor went into that time trial needing to make up a 4'22" deficit on Aimar. In the first 17 kilometres he pulled back 55 seconds. At kilometre 30 it was 2'10. But then Aimar started coming back. With 15 kilometres to go he'd pegged Poulidor's gains back to 2'03". In those final 15 kilometres Poulidor did manage to gain some time, but only widened his lead to 2'40". Too little. Lucien Aimar's Tour was won. And he had done it without winning a single stage.

Stage-by-Stage Results for the 1966 Tour de France			Stage Winner	Maillot Jaune
Stage 1 Tue 21 Jun	Nancy to Charleville 129 finishers	208.5 km 4h52'56" 42.7 kph	Rudi Altig (FRG) Molteni	Rudi Altig (FRG) Molteni
Stage 2 Wed 22 Jun	Charleville to Tournai 123 finishers	198 km 4h46'21" 41.5 kph	Guido Reybrouck (Bel) Smith's	Rudi Altig (FRG) Molteni
Stage 3a Thu 23 Jun	Tournai (TTT) 123 finishers	20.8 km 2h19'30" 8.9 kph	Televizier	Rudi Altig (FRG) Molteni
Stage 3b Thu 23 Jun	Tournai to Dunkerque 123 finishers	131.5 km 3h26'46" 38.2 kph	Gerben Karstens (Ned) Televizier	Rudi Altig (FRG) Molteni
Stage 4 Fri 24 Jun	Dunkerque to Dieppe 123 finishers	205 km 5h58'45" 34.3 kph	Willy Planckaert (Bel) Smith's	Rudi Altig (FRG) Molteni
Stage 5 Sat 25 Jun	Dieppe to Caen 122 finishers	178.5 km 4h55'50" 36.2 kph	Franco Bitossi (Ita) Filotex	Rudi Altig (FRG) Molteni
Stage 6 Sun 26 Jun	Caen to Angers 122 finishers	216.5 km 5h21'43" 40.4 kph	Edward Sels (Bel) Solo	Rudi Altig (FRG) Molteni
Stage 7 Mon 27 Jun	Angers to Royan 122 finishers	252.5 km 7h11'21" 35.1 kph	Albert van Vlierberghe (Bel) Smith's	Rudi Altig (FRG) Molteni
Stage 8 Tue 28 Jun	Royan to Bordeaux 122 finishers	137.5 km 2h58'26" 46.2 kph	Willy Planckaert (Bel) Smith's	Rudi Altig (FRG) Molteni
Stage 9 Wed 29 Jun	Bordeaux to Bayonne 122 finishers	201 km 5h15'58" 38.2 kph	Gerben Karstens (Ned) Televizier	Rudi Altig (FRG) Molteni

Stage-by-Stage Results for the 1966 Tour de France			Stage Winner	Maillot Jaune
Stage 10 Thu 30 Jun	Bayonne to Pau 121 finishers	234.5 km 6h37'00" 35.4 kph	Tommaso de Pra (Ita) Molteni	Tommaso de Pra (Ita) Molteni
	Major climbs: Col d'Aubisque (1,709m) Tommaso de Pra (Ita) Molteni			
Stage 11 Fri 1 Jul	Pau to Luchon 119 finishers	188 km 5h54'42" 31.8 kph	Marcello Mugnaini (Ita) Filotex	Jean-Claude Lebaube (Fra) Kamomé
	Major climbs: Col des Ares (797m) Joaquín Galera (Esp) KAS; Col de Menté (1,349m) Joaquín Galera (Esp) KAS; Col du Portillon (1,298m) Marcello Mugnaini (Ita) Filotex			
Sat 2 July	Rest day			
Stage 12 Sun 3 Jul	Luchon to Revel 119 finishers	218.5 km 6h32'15" 33.4 kph	Rudi Altig (FRG) Molteni	Karl-Heinz Künde (FRG) Peugeot
	Major climbs: Col des Ares (797m) Franco Bitossi (Ita) Filotex; Col de Portet d'Aspet (1,069m) Julio Jiménez (Esp) Ford France			
Stage 13 Mon 4 Jul	Revel to Sète 119 finishers	191.5 km 5h46'20" 33.2 kph	Georges Vandenberghe (Bel) Smith's	Karl-Heinz Künde (FRG) Peugeot
Stage 14a Tue 5 Jul	Montpellier to Vals-les-Bains 119 finishers	144 km 3h23'54" 42.4 kph	Jo de Roo (Ned) Televizier	Karl-Heinz Künde (FRG) Peugeot
Stage 14b Tue 5 Jul	Vals-les-Bains (ITT) 119 finishers	20 km 28'26" 42.2 kph	Raymond Poulidor (Fra) Mercier	Karl-Heinz Künde (FRG) Peugeot
Stage 15 Wed 6 Jul	Privas to Le Bourg-d'Oisans 116 finishers	203.5 km 5h46'50" 35.2 kph	Luis Otaño (Esp) Fagor	Karl-Heinz Künde (FRG) Peugeot
	Major climbs: Col d'Ornon (1,367m) Luis Otaño (Esp) Fagor			
Stage 16 Thu 7 Jul	Le Bourg-d'Oisans to Briançon 88 finishers	148.5 km 4h41'59" 31.6 kph	Julio Jiménez (Esp) Ford France	Jan Janssen (Ned) Pelforth
	Major climbs: Col de la Croix de Fer (2,067m) Joaquín Galera (Esp) KAS; Col du Télégraphe (1,566m) Julio Jiménez (Esp) Ford France; Col du Galibier (2,556m) Julio Jiménez (Esp) Ford France			
Stage 17 Fri 8 Jul	Briançon to Turin 84 finishers	160 km 4h03'00" 39.5 kph	Franco Bitossi (Ita) Filotex	Lucien Aimar (Fra) Ford France
	Major climbs: Col de Montgenèvre (1,860m) Julio Jiménez (Esp) Ford France; Colle del Sestriere (2,035m) Julio Jiménez (Esp) Ford France			
Sat 9 July	Rest day			
Stage 18 Sun 10 Jul	Ivrea to Chamonix 83 finishers	188 km 5h55'46" 31.7 kph	Edy Schutz (Lux) Smith's	Lucien Aimar (Fra) Ford France
	Major climbs: Col du Grand Saint-Bernard (2,470m) Martin van den Bossche (Bel) Smith's; Col de la Forclaz (1,527m) Edy Schutz (Lux) Smith's; Col des Montets (1,461m) Edy Schutz (Lux) Smith's			
Stage 19 Mon 11 Jul	Chamonix to Saint-Étienne 82 finishers	264.5 km 7h07'50" 37.1 kph	Ferdinand Bracke (Bel) Peugeot	Lucien Aimar (Fra) Ford France
	Major climbs: Col de la République (Col du Grand Bois) (1,161m) Ferdinand Bracke (Bel) Peugeot			

Stage-by-Stage Results for the 1966 Tour de France			Stage Winner	Maillot Jaune
Stage 20 Tue 12 Jul	Saint-Étienne to Montluçon 82 finishers	223.5 km 5h57'44" 37.5 kph	Henk Nijdam (Ned) Televizier	Lucien Aimar (Fra) Ford France
Stage 21 Wed 13 Jul	Montluçon to Orléans 82 finishers	232.5 km 6h06'09" 38.1 kph	Pierre Beuffeuil (Fra) Kamome	Lucien Aimar (Fra) Ford France
Stage 22a Thu 14 Jul	Orléans to Rambouillet 82 finishers	111 km 2h50'58" 39 kph	Edward Sels (Bel) Solo	Lucien Aimar (Fra) Ford France
Stage 22b Thu 14 Jul	Rambouillet to Paris (Parc des Princes) (ITT) 82 finishers	51.3 km 1h06'48" 46.1 kph	Rudi Altig (FRG) Molteni	Lucien Aimar (Fra) Ford France

Prize fund: 424,700 francs (first prize: 20,000 francs)

Final Classification				
Place	Rider	Team	Time	Age
1	Lucien Aimar (Fra)	Ford France	4,329 km 117h34'21" 36.760 kph	25
2	Jan Janssen (Ned)	Pelforth	+ 01'07"	26
3	Raymond Poulidor (Fra)	Mercier	+ 02'02"	30
4	José-Antonio Momene (Esp)	KAS	+ 05'19"	25
5	Marcello Mugnaini (Ita)	Filotex	+ 05'27"	25
6	Herman Van Springel (Bel)	Mann	+ 05'44"	22
7	Francisco Gabica (Esp)	KAS	+ 06'25"	28
8	Roger Pingeon (Fra)	Peugeot	+ 08'22"	25
9	Karl-Heinz Künde (FRG)	Peugeot	+ 09'06"	27
10	Martin Van Den Bossche (Bel)	Smith's	+ 09'57"	25
Lanterne Rouge				
82	Paolo Mannucci (Ita)	Filotex	+ 2h05'26"	24
Points				
	Willy Planckaert (Bel)	Smith's		22
King of the Mountains				
	Julio Jiménez (Esp)	Ford France		31
Super Combativité				
	Rudi Altig (FRG)	Molteni		29
Team				
		KAS		

1967: Death on the Mountain

Tour de France legend has it that, in 1910, when the *grande boucle* first threw the Pyrenees in front of the riders, Octave Lapize cried out 'Murderers!' at Henri Desgrange as he crossed the Tourmalet. Or it might have been the Aubisque. And it might have been to Victor Breyer that the word was said. And it might actually have been 'You're assassins!'

Journalists have long put words in the mouths of cyclists. It is often the job of the journalist to tidy up quotes, make them more pretty. Some, though, take that to extremes and create quotes from nothing. And one of the most famous cases of this are the words supposed to have been uttered by Tom Simpson as be rode to his death on the Ventoux during the 1967 Tour: "Put me back on my bike."

Simpson was 22-years-old when he rode his first Tour, in 1960. By the time he was 29 his *palmarès* already included the Ronde van Vlaanderen (1961), Bordeaux-Paris (1963), Milan-Sanremo (1964), the World Championships (1965) and the Giro di Lombardia (1965). At the Tour, his best performance came in 1962, when he donned the yellow jersey for one stage and finished sixth overall. Of the other five times he rode the race, three he failed to finish, and in the other two finished outside the top 10.

That Simpson was better suited to the one day races is self-evident. But riders like Simpson needed the Tour, for it was at the *grande boucle* that they forged reputations which helped earn them critérium appearances, the fees for which accounted for most of their earnings in a good year. In 1960, after finishing his first Tour, Simpson rode himself into a hospital bed chasing critériums, exhaustion getting the better of him after he'd packed in races in

Milan, Turin, Sallanches, Lyon, Belgium and Nice. These local races – almost always orchestrated, if not downright fixed, the fans coming to see their heroes win and generally getting what they wanted – were vital to all the riders, and if they wanted to put money in the bank, they had no choice but to ride them. In 1966, with the rainbow jersey of World Champion on his back, Simpson packed 40 critériums into 40 days. After a lean year results-wise in 1966 and after having failed to finish the previous two Tours, Simpson was in need of a performance at the *grande boucle* in 1967 in order to guarantee his critérium contracts. A top 10 finish, maybe even a stage win.

Having started his Tour career riding in Great Britain's colours Simpson was once again flying the flag in 1967. After just six Tours raced under the trade team format, the race had once more turned its back on the sport's key sponsors and reverted to the national and regional team format. This had been done in an attempt to break the link between the Tour and stories about doping, Félix Lévitan and Jacques Goddet believing that it was the sponsors who were most responsible for the sport's doping problem and that, by removing them from the race, the Tour at least would be freed of its links to doping. That the Tour had suffered doping scandals during the previous national team era – the Ventoux in 1955, the Belgians' bad fish in 1956, the high attrition rate in the early stages of the 1957 race, Roger Rivière's crash in 1960 – seemed to be lost on the Tour's bosses.

Coming into the thirteenth stage from Marseille to Carpentras, in which the riders crossed the Ventoux, Simpson was inside the top 10, in seventh place overall, 8'20" off the yellow jersey being worn by Roger Pingeon (riding for France in the Tour, Simpson's team-mate at Peugeot the rest of the year round). Two days in the Pyrenees were still to come, and a visit to the Puy de Dôme two days before Paris. This day on the Ventoux was a day Simpson needed to keep up with the front-runners, maybe even put some time into other riders in the top 10 and improve his overall position.

The day was hot, very hot, and at the start of it the Tour's doctor, Pierre Dumas, knew he would be busy if the riders did not take care,

Crossing a viaduct on the Col d'Allos
in the 1967 Tour.

measure their amphetamine intake and keep themselves hydrated. The trouble that came was worse than he imagined. As Jean Malléjac had a dozen years before, Simpson got into trouble on the Ventoux. He had held his own with the main *peloton* going up the mountain but, as the summit approached, the attacks began and the *peloton* fractured, Simpson fading to the second group. Then he began to zigzag across the road. Then he fell. His Great Britain team's *directeur sportif*, Alec Taylor, and team mechanic Harry Hall, put him back on his bike. Five hundred metres later he was once again on the ground. This time he didn't get up. Dumas quickly arrived and took over. Simpson was helicoptered off the mountain, to a hospital in Avignon, where he was pronounced dead.

That drugs – amphetamines – played a role in Simpson's death was confirmed by the autopsy on his body. Drugs had been found in his pockets, and in his luggage at the team hotel. Heart failure due to dehydration and exhaustion was the official cause of his death. Some denied the role played by amphetamines in this. Jacques Anquetil and Raphaël Géminiani are among those who blamed Dumas, saying he had not done enough to save the fallen rider. Pingeon, his Peugeot team-mate, blamed the national team format, saying Simpson would never have been put back on his bike if he was riding in Peugeot's colours. Most, even while blaming others, acknowledged that Simpson had doped. Some, though, denied even this.

Did Simpson dope? In 1960 the young Briton had told the *Observer*'s Chris Basher that he knew other riders were doping, but that he himself had so far refrained from the practice. However, he added, if he didn't get some results soon, he would have to follow their lead. Five years later, his *palmarès* bulging, Simpson spoke to a journalist from *People* and said that doping "in the worst sense of the word" was not a big feature in the sport, and questioned where the line should be drawn between medical care and performance enhancement.

Where the line should be drawn is always the problem. But by 1967 that line had been drawn, by national governments and the sporting authorities. Doping – amphetamines – was over the line.

And, as the contents of his luggage showed, Simpson had used amphetamines, hadn't simply given up their use just because the rules had changed. And Simpson was not alone in this. It was part of the culture of the sport, there from the beginning. But Simpson was the one to die.

He wasn't actually the only one to die. There were other riders, in other races, dead bodies whose autopsies showed the use of amphetamines. But they were minor riders in minor races, this was a death in front of cameras, on the biggest race there is. It mattered. How the authorities would respond to it, that was the big question.

* * * * *

The Tour itself was won comfortably by Pingeon. The race had begun with an innovation, a short prologue time trial the evening before the first stage. Felice Gimondi (Italy) was back after a year's absence, and Lucien Aimar (France) was there to defend his title. Aimar had to share space on the national team with Raymond Poulidor, riding his sixth Tour. But it was Pingeon who won out, getting away in a break on the first part of the fifth stage and taking the *maillot jaune*. Thereafter the French team rallied round him and helped protect his lead, Pingeon riding to an easy – but death-tainted – victory.

Stage-by-Stage Results for the 1967 Tour de France			Stage Winner	Maillot Jaune
Stage 1a Thu 29 Jun	Angers (ITT) 130 finishers	5.775 km 07'43" 44.9 kph	José-Maria Errandonea (Esp) Spain	José-Maria Errandonea (Esp) Spain
Stage 1b Fri 30 Jun	Angers to Saint-Malo 130 finishers	185.5 km 4h34'49" 40.5 kph	Walter Godefroot (Bel) Diables Rouges	José-Maria Errandonea (Esp) Spain
Stage 2 Sat 1 Jul	Saint-Malo to Caen 125 finishers	180 km 4h18'33" 41.8 kph	Willy Van Neste (Bel) Belgium	Willy van Neste (Bel) Belgium
Stage 3 Sun 2 Jul	Caen to Amiens 124 finishers	248 km 6h01'37" 41.1 kph	Marino Basso (Ita) Primavera	Giancarlo Polidori (Ita) Primavera
Stage 4 Mon 3 Jul	Amiens to Roubaix 124 finishers	191 km 4h46'44" 40 kph	Guido Reybrouck (Bel) Diables Rouges	Joseph Spruyt (Bel) Belgium

Stage-by-Stage Results for the 1967 Tour de France			Stage Winner	Maillot Jaune
Stage 5a Tue 4 Jul	Roubaix to Jambes 123 finishers	172 km 3h59'16" 43.1 kph	Roger Pingeon (Fra) France	Roger Pingeon (Fra) France
Stage 5b Tue 4 Jul	Jambes (TTT) 123 finishers	17 km 1h48'32" 9.4 kph	Belgium	Roger Pingeon (Fra) France
Stage 6 Wed 5 Jul	Jambes to Metz 121 finishers	238 km 6h13'28" 38.2 kph	Herman Van Springel (Bel) Belgium	Roger Pingeon (Fra) France
Stage 7 Thu 6 Jul	Metz to Strasbourg 119 finishers	205.5 km 5h46'23" 35.6 kph	Michael Wright (GBr) Great Britain	Raymond Riotte (Fra) France
	Major climbs: Mont Donon (727m) Guy Ignolin (Fra) Bleuets de France; Champ du Messin (1,010m) Marcello Mugnaini (Ita) Italy			
Stage 8 Fri 7 Jul	Strasbourg to Belfort (Ballon d'Alsace) 110 finishers	215 km 6h43'43" 32 kph	Lucien Aimar (Fra) France	Roger Pingeon (Fra) France
	Major climbs: Col du Kreuzweg (768m) Guerrino Tosello (Ita) Primavera; Col du Linge (983m) Jesús Aranzabal (Esp) Esperanza; Col de Platzerwasel (1,155m) Jesús Aranzabal (Esp) Esperanza; Ballon d'Alsace (1,178m) Lucien Aimar (Fra) France			
Stage 9 Sun 9 Jul	Belfort to Divonne-les-Bains 110 finishers	238.5 km 6h26'22" 37 kph	Guido Reybrouck (Bel) Diables Rouges	Roger Pingeon (Fra) France
	Major climbs: Col de la Faucille (Côte des Rousses) (1,140m) Mariano Díaz (Esp) Spain			
Stage 10 Mon 10 Jul	Divonne-les-Bains to Briançon 110 finishers	243 km 7h26'52" 32.6 kph	Felice Gimondi (Ita) Italy	Roger Pingeon (Fra) France
	Major climbs: Col de Tamié (907m) Guerrino Tosello (Ita) Primavera; Col du Télégraphe (1,566m) Julio Jiménez (Esp) Spain; Col du Galibier (2,556m) Julio Jiménez (Esp) Spain			
Stage 11 Tue 11 Jul	Briançon to Digne 106 finishers	197 km 6h05'04" 32.4 kph	José Samyn (Fra) Bleuets de France	Roger Pingeon (Fra) France
	Major climbs: Col de Vars (2,110m) Georges Chappe (Fra) Bleuets de France; Col d'Allos (2,250m) Georges Chappe (Fra) Bleuets de France			
Stage 12 Wed 12 Jul	Digne to Marseille 104 finishers	207.5 km 6h16'08" 33.1 kph	Raymond Riotte (Fra) France	Roger Pingeon (Fra) France
Stage 13 Thu 13 Jul	Marseille to Carpentras 98 finishers	211.5 km 6h58'15" 30.3 kph	Jan Janssen (Ned) Netherlands	Roger Pingeon (Fra) France
	Major climbs: Mont Ventoux (1,909m) Julio Jiménez (Esp) Spain			

Stage-by-Stage Results for the 1967 Tour de France			Stage Winner	Maillot Jaune
Stage 14 Fri 14 Jul	Carpentras to Sète 98 finishers	201.5 km 6h13'58" 32.3 kph	Barry Hoban (GBr) Great Britain	Roger Pingeon (Fra) France
Sat 15 July	Rest day			
Stage 15 Sun 16 Jul	Sète to Toulouse 98 finishers	230.5 km 6h28'23" 35.6 kph	Rolf Wolfshohl (FRG) Germany	Roger Pingeon (Fra) France
Stage 16 Mon 17 Jul	Toulouse to Luchon 94 finishers	188 km 5h38'19" 33.3 kph	Fernando Manzaneque (Esp) Esperanza	Roger Pingeon (Fra) France
	Major climbs: Col de Portet d'Aspet (1,069m) Fernando Manzaneque (Esp) Esperanza; Col de Menté (1,349m) Fernando Manzaneque (Esp) Esperanza; Col du Portillon (1,298m) Fernando Manzaneque (Esp) Esperanza			
Stage 17 Tue 18 Jul	Luchon to Pau 89 finishers	250 km 8h00'27" 31.2 kph	Raymond Mastrotto (Fra) Coqs de France	Roger Pingeon (Fra) France
	Major climbs: Col du Tourmalet (2,115m) Julio Jiménez (Esp) Spain; Col d'Aubisque (1,709m) Jean-Claude Theilliere (Fra) Coqs de France			
Stage 18 Wed 19 Jul	Pau to Bordeaux 88 finishers	206.5 km 5h52'45" 35.1 kph	Marino Basso (Ita) Primavera	Roger Pingeon (Fra) France
Stage 19 Thu 20 Jul	Bordeaux to Limoges 88 finishers	217 km 5h50'20" 37.2 kph	Jean Stablinski (Fra) France	Roger Pingeon (Fra) France
Stage 20 Fri 21 Jul	Limoges to Clermont- Ferrand (Le Puy de Dôme) 88 finishers	222 km 7h08'21" 31.1 kph	Felice Gimondi (Ita) Italy	Roger Pingeon (Fra) France
	Major climbs: Puy de Dôme (1,415m) Felice Gimondi (Ita) Italy			
Stage 21 Sat 22 Jul	Clermont-Ferrand to Fontainebleau 88 finishers	359 km 11h12'47" 32 kph	Paul Lemeteyer (Fra) France	Roger Pingeon (Fra) France
Stage 22a Sun 23 Jul	Fontainebleau to Versailles 88 finishers	104 km 2h45'44" 37.7 kph	René Binggeli (Sui) Switzerland/ Luxembourg	Roger Pingeon (Fra) France
Stage 22b Sun 23 Jul	Versailles to Paris (Parc des Princes) (ITT) 88 finishers	46.6 km 1h02'52" 44.5 kph	Raymond Poulidor (Fra) France	Roger Pingeon (Fra) France

Prize fund: 541,300 francs (first prize: 20,000 francs)

Final Classification

Place	Rider	Team	Time	Age
1	Roger Pingeon (Fra)	France	4,779 km 136h53'50" 34.756 kph	26
2	Julio Jiménez (Esp)	Spain	+ 03'40"	32
3	Franco Balmamion (Ita)	Primavera	+ 07'23"	27
4	Désiré Letort (Fra)	Bleuets de France	+ 08'18"	24
5	Jan Janssen (Ned)	Netherlands	+ 09'47"	27
6	Lucien Aimar (Fra)	France	+ 09'47"	26
7	Felice Gimondi (Ita)	Italy	+ 10'14"	24
8	Jozef Huysmans (Bel)	Belgium	+ 16'45"	25
9	Raymond Poulidor (Fra)	France	+ 18'18"	31
10	Fernando Manzaneque (Esp)	Esperanza	+ 19'22"	33

Lanterne Rouge

88	Jean-Pierre Genêt (Fra)	France	+ 2h21'01"	26

Points

	Jan Janssen (Ned)	Netherlands		27

King of the Mountains

	Julio Jiménez (Esp)	Spain		32

Super Combativité

	Désiré Letort (Fra)	Bleuets de France		24

Team

		France		

1968: Thirty-Eight Seconds

The day after the 1967 Tour ended, the builders moved into the Parc des Princes and began to tear it down, to make way for a new motorway, Paris's Périphérique. The Parc had hosted the finish of every Tour since the beginning (the first Tour had officially finished in Ville-d'Avray, with the riders then going on to the Parc des Princes for a victory lap). All the heroes of the Tour had been cheered there, some of them (as in the case of Jacques Anquetil) were even booed. The Parc was even more a part of the Tour than the *maillot jaune*. Jacques Goddet was less than pleased to see the place go and complained bitterly about the Parc's closure and the manner in which cycling was evicted from it to make way for a new road. But nothing stands in the way of progress, and down the Parc des Princes came.

So some changes were in order. The finish moved to the Piste Municipale in the Bois de Vincennes, better known as La Cipale. And from the off La Cipale saw magic: the second Tour to be won on the last day, and the Tour with the closest winning margin.

The man beaten was Herman Van Springel, riding for the Belgium A squad. Goddet and his partner, Félix Lévitan, were not yet willing to give up on the national team format re-introduced the previous year, and Belgium was fielding two squads, an A and a B team (France had three, A, B and C). Twenty-four-years-old, Van Springel was at the start of his career and an accomplished time trial rider, but it was in this discipline that he suffered defeat on the final day of the Tour, Jan Janssen (Netherlands) overturning a 16-second deficit at the start of the stage and leaping from third to first, with a winning margin of 38 seconds.

The 28-year-old Janssen was riding his sixth Tour, and had already finished second (in 1966) and fifth (1969) as well as bagging the green jersey three times (1964, 1965 and 1967). He was a rider known for his consistency, but was also a winner of important one-day races, including the Ronde van Vlaanderen (1965) and Paris-Roubaix (1967). He was also a former World Champion, having won the rainbow jersey in 1964. And, like many of the great riders coming through, he was a graduate of the Tour de l'Avenir, having won stages there in 1961 and 1962.

The Tour de l'Avenir, after seven years of having been a part of the Tour de France's rolling road-show, was now no longer being run alongside the Tour de France. For 1968, it was spun off as a separate race, run in September. Lévitan hadn't given up on his desire to bring amateurs into the Tour, but in the face of resistance from the professionals, who didn't want to share the road, the plan was temporarily parked.

Lévitan was also busy with other projects, still trying to make the Tour turn a profit. One of these was the introduction of a new jersey, white, for the leader of a combined category, a combination of scores in the points and king of the mountains competition. And the Tour itself was fighting to rebuild its image after Tom Simpson's death the year before. With the French government having exerted pressure on the UCI – effectively telling the sport's governing body to take control of the situation, or they would – drug tests were now firmly a part of cycling. At the Tour, they were to be carried out after the end of every stage, with the stage winner and others being required to provide samples for testing. José Samyn and Jean Stablinski (both riding for the France A squad) fell foul of the testers over the course of the Tour and were politely asked to leave the race.

Not everyone was happy with this new testing regime but there was little the riders could do to stop it. In 1967, two months after the Tour ended, Jacques Anquetil – who was vocal in calling for riders to have the right to dope – set a new record for the Hour, but because he refused to submit to a drug test, the UCI refused to ratify the record. Anquetil had been lucky in the past. At the 1966 edition

Keeping cool in the 1968 Tour.

of Liège-Bastogne-Liège (which he won) he had refused to undergo a drug test and was initially disqualified, but then reinstated. Similarly, he got away without punishment when he refused to be tested after the World Championships in 1966. He'd also escaped without punishment after admitting having doped to win the GP des Nations that same year. But by the time he rode that Hour in 1967, the anti-doping landscape had changed and the authorities had to be seen to be doing their job.

In the race itself, Van Springel (who had provided a sample that tested positive during the Tour's first anti-doping tests in the 1966) took control of the race on the third stage, relieving Charly Grosskost (France B) of the *maillot jaune* (Grosskost was one of the riders in the 1965 Tour de l'Avenir who was accused of doping on the day the Tour riders fell like flies on the Aubisque). Van Springel's stay in yellow was brief: he lost it the next day to Jean-Pierre Genêt (France A), and a day later it then passed to Georges Vandenberghe (Belgium B). He held the jersey through the Pyrenees and up to the start of the second phase of mountains, where it passed to Rolf Wolfshohl (Germany) and then Gregorio San Miguel (Spain) before finally returning to Van Springel on Stage 19, Grenoble to Sallanches.

As early as the ninth stage, journalists covering the race were complaining that it was too tame, there were too many sprint finishes, nothing was happening for them to report. They called for better riders. Goddet called for better journalists and accused them of having tired eyes. When Jean Leulliot – a former *l'Auto* writer, Roger Lapébie's *directeur sportif* when he won 1937, and now the organiser of Paris-Nice – dared to criticise Goddet on TV, the director of the Tour told him to shut up, that the Tour was "a God and should be worshipped as such." The next day, Stage 10, the Tour's press corps decided to mount a protest, partly blocking the race as it passed through Labouheyre, en route from Bordeaux to Bayonne.

Somewhat ironically, then, it was a press motorcycle that ended Raymond Poulidor's hopes of winning the Tour, riding into his rear wheel on Stage 15 just after the race had exited the Pyrenees and was travelling from Font-Romeu to Albi. Poulidor had been within 4'13" of the yellow jersey at the start of the stage and the *peloton* had attacked just as he went down. He ended the stage with a bloodied nose and 4'03" lost on the road. Two days later, not recovered from injuries sustained in the crash, Poulidor abandoned the Tour.

It was two days after that when Van Springel re-took the yellow jersey. Van Springel's lead at the end of that nineteenth stage was narrow – as far back as ninth in general classification, Roger Pingeon was within two and a half minutes of winning the Tour. Ferdinand Bracke (Belgium B) was seventh, just under two minutes behind his compatriot Van Springel. Lucien Aimar (France B) was in sixth, a minute and a half off the lead. And Janssen was in third, 16 seconds down on Van Springel. With three days of racing left, it was clear that the final time trial to La Cipale would decide the eventual winner.

Starting the final time trial, three riders were expected to put in performances: Bracke, the reigning holder of the Hour record (he had set a new distance in October the previous year); Van Springel, riding with the weight of the yellow jersey on his shoulders; and Janssen. Bracke got off to a quick start but faded on the undulating course, his effort in the Hour not having needed to go up any hills. At 25 kilometres Van Springel held a two-second advantage over Janssen, and his Tour victory seemed to be in the bag. But in the second half of the ride Dutchman pulled out all the stops and put 54 seconds into his Belgian rival. For the first time since Jean Robic's win in 1947, and for only the second time in the Tour's history, the Tour was won on the last stage. And Janssen had done it as Robic had, without once wearing the yellow jersey.

Stage-by-Stage Results for the 1968 Tour de France			Stage Winner	Maillot Jaune
Stage 1a Thu 27 Jun	Vittel (ITT) 110 finishers	6.1 km 8h27'17" 0.7 kph	Charly Grosskost (Fra) France B	Charly Grosskost (Fra) France B
Stage 1b Fri 28 Jun	Vittel to Esch-sur-Alzette 109 finishers	189 km 4h34'51" 41.3 kph	Charly Grosskost (Fra) France B	Charly Grosskost (Fra) France B
Stage 2 Sat 29 Jun	Arlon to Forest 106 finishers	210.5 km 5h31'41" 38.1 kph	Eric de Vlaeminck (Bel) Belgium B	Charly Grosskost (Fra) France B
Stage 3a Sun 30 Jun	Forest to Vorst (TTT) 106 finishers	22 km 29'28" 44.8 kph	Belgium A	Herman Van Springel (Bel) Belgium A
Stage 3b Sun 30 Jun	Forest to Roubaix 99 finishers	112 km 2h37'52" 42.6 kph	Walter Godefroot (Bel) Belgium B	Herman Van Springel (Bel) Belgium A
Stage 4 Mon 1 Jul	Roubaix to Rouen 96 finishers	238 km 6h23'30" 37.2 kph	Georges Chappe (Fra) France B	Jean-Pierre Genêt (Fra) France A
Stage 5a Tue 2 Jul	Rouen to Bagnoles-de-l'Orne 93 finishers	165 km 4h50'07" 34.1 kph	André Desvages (Fra) France C	Georges Vandenberghe (Bel) Belgium B
Stage 5b Tue 2 Jul	Bagnoles-de-l'Orne to Dinard 93 finishers	154.5 km 4h32'21" 34 kph	Jean Dumont (Fra) France C	Georges Vandenberghe (Bel) Belgium B
Stage 6 Wed 3 Jul	Dinard to Lorient 92 finishers	188 km 4h40'34" 40.2 kph	Aurelio González (Esp) Spain	Georges Vandenberghe (Bel) Belgium B
Stage 7 Thu 4 Jul	Lorient to Nantes 91 finishers	190 km 4h58'23" 38.2 kph	Franco Bitossi (Ita) Italy	Georges Vandenberghe (Bel) Belgium B
Stage 8 Fri 5 Jul	Nantes to Royan 90 finishers	223 km 5h25'26" 41.1 kph	Daniel van Rijckeghem (Bel) Belgium A	Georges Vandenberghe (Bel) Belgium B
Sat 6 July	Rest day			
Stage 9 Sun 7 Jul	Royan to Bordeaux 90 finishers	137.5 km 3h19'16" 41.4 kph	Walter Godefroot (Bel) Belgium B	Georges Vandenberghe (Bel) Belgium B
Stage 10 Mon 8 Jul	Bordeaux to Bayonne 90 finishers	202.5 km 5h23'39" 37.5 kph	Gilbert Bellone (Fra) France B	Georges Vandenberghe (Bel) Belgium B
Stage 11 Tue 9 Jul	Bayonne to Pau 86 finishers	183.5 km 5h28'47" 33.5 kph	Daniel van Rijckeghem (Bel) Belgium A	Georges Vandenberghe (Bel) Belgium B
Stage 12 Wed 10 Jul	Pau to Saint-Gaudens 71 finishers	226.5 km 7h33'34" 30 kph	Georges Pintens (Bel) Belgium A	Georges Vandenberghe (Bel) Belgium B
	Major climbs: Col d'Aubisque (1,709m) Julio Jiménez (Esp) Spain; Col du Tourmalet (2,115m) Jean-Pierre Ducasse (Fra) France B			

Stage-by-Stage Results for the 1968 Tour de France			Stage Winner	Maillot Jaune
Stage 13 Thu 11 Jul	Saint-Gaudens to Seo de Urgel 71 finishers	208.5 km 6h59'55" 29.8 kph	Herman Van Springel (Bel) Belgium A	Georges Vandenberghe (Bel) Belgium B
	Major climbs: Col de Port (1,249m) Andrés Gandarias (Esp) Spain; Port d'Envalira (2,407m) Aurelio González (Esp) Spain			
Stage 14 Fri 12 Jul	Seo de Urgel to Perpignan (Canet-Plage) 71 finishers	231.5 km 7h28'43" 31 kph	Jan Janssen (Ned) Netherlands	Georges Vandenberghe (Bel) Belgium B
	Major climbs: Col des Ares (797m) Franco Bitossi (Ita) Italy			
Sat 13 July	Rest day			
Stage 15 Sun 14 Jul	Font-Romeu to Albi 68 finishers	250.5 km 6h20'36" 39.5 kph	Roger Pingeon (Fra) France A	Georges Vandenberghe (Bel) Belgium B
Stage 16 Mon 15 Jul	Albi to Aurillac 68 finishers	199 km 5h39'09" 35.2 kph	Franco Bitossi (Ita) Italy	Rolf Wolfshohl (FRG) Germany
Stage 17 Tue 16 Jul	Aurillac to Saint-Étienne 66 finishers	236.5 km 7h02'33" 33.6 kph	Jean-Pierre Genêt (Fra) France A	Rolf Wolfshohl (FRG) Germany
	Major climbs: Le Pas de Peyrol (1,582m) Aurelio González (Esp) Spain; Côte de Collat (1,008m) Georges Chappe (Fra) France B			
Stage 18 Wed 17 Jul	Saint-Étienne to Grenoble 65 finishers	235 km 7h47'13" 30.2 kph	Roger Pingeon (Fra) France A	Gregorio San Miguel (Esp) Spain
	Major climbs: Col de la République (Col du Grand Bois) (1,161m) Aurelio González (Esp) Spain; Col de l'Épine (987m) Aurelio González (Esp) Spain; Col du Granier (1,134m) Roger Pingeon (Fra) France A; Col du Cucheron (1,139m) Roger Pingeon (Fra) France A; Col de Porte (1,326m) Roger Pingeon (Fra) France A			
Stage 19 Thu 18 Jul	Grenoble to Sallanches (Cordon) 64 finishers	200 km 7h06'23" 28.1 kph	Barry Hoban (GBr) Great Britain	Herman Van Springel (Bel) Belgium A
	Major climbs: Col des Aravis (1,498m) Barry Hoban (GBr) Great Britain; Col de la Colombière (1,618m) Barry Hoban (GBr) Great Britain; Col de Cordon (975m) Barry Hoban (GBr) Great Britain			
Stage 20 Fri 19 Jul	Sallanches to Besançon 63 finishers	242.5 km 6h56'02" 35 kph	Jozef Huysmans (Bel) Belgium A	Herman Van Springel (Bel) Belgium A
	Major climbs: Col de la Faucille (1,323m) Aurelio González (Esp) Spain			
Stage 21 Sat 20 Jul	Besançon to Auxerre 63 finishers	242 km 6h50'42" 35.4 kph	Eric Leman (Bel) Belgium B	Herman Van Springel (Bel) Belgium A
Stage 22a Sun 21 Jul	Auxerre to Melun 63 finishers	136 km 3h43'56" 36.4 kph	Maurice Izier (Fra) France C	Herman Van Springel (Bel) Belgium A
Stage 22b Sun 21 Jul	Melun to Paris (Piste Municipale de Vincennes) (ITT) 63 finishers	55.2 km 1h20'09" 41.3 kph	Jan Janssen (Ned) Netherlands	Jan Janssen (Ned) Netherlands

Prize fund: 574.850 francs (first prize: 20,000 francs)

Final Classification

Place	Rider	Team	Time	Age
1	Jan Janssen (Ned)	Netherlands	4,492 km 133h49'42" 33.556 kph	28
2	Herman Van Springel (Bel)	Belgium A	+ 0'38"	23
3	Ferdinand Bracke (Bel)	Belgium B	+ 3'03"	29
4	Gregorio San Miguel (Esp)	Spain	+ 3'17"	27
5	Roger Pingeon (Fra)	France A	+ 3'29"	27
6	Rolf Wolfshohl (FRG)	Germany	+ 3'46"	29
7	Lucien Aimar (Fra)	France B	+ 4'44"	27
8	Franco Bitossi (Ita)	Italy	+ 4'59"	27
9	Andrés Gandarias (Esp)	Spain	+ 5'05"	25
10	Ugo Colombo (Ita)	Italy	+ 7'55"	28

Lanterne Rouge

63	John Clarey (GBr)	Great Britain	+ 2h43'28"	27

Points

	Franco Bitossi (Ita)	Italy		27

King of the Mountains

	Aurelio González (Esp)	Spain		27

Combined

	Franco Bitossi (Ita)	Italy		27

Super Combativité

	Roger Pingeon (Fra)	France A		27

Team

		Spain		

1969: The Birth of the Cannibal

By the time the 1969 season opened Eddy Merckx (Faema) was already a two-time world champion (amateur and professional road races in 1964 and 1967) and had won the Giro d'Italia (1968), along with Milan-Sanremo (1966 and 1967) and Paris-Roubaix (1968). Add in a couple of Belgian Classics (Ghent-Wevelgem and the Flèche Wallonne in 1967) and a couple of Italian semi-Classics (the Tre Valli Varesine and the GP di Lugano in 1968), and he was clearly the man to watch for the coming season.

In the early season, the Belgian came out of Paris-Nice with three stage wins and overall victory, as well as the scalp of the declining champion, Jacques Anquetil. One of the innovations of that year's *course au soleil* was the introduction of the final day Col d'Èze time trial. Maître Jacques started the climb a minute and a half ahead of Merckx. Inside the final kilometre of the climb, with an estimated 50,000 fans lining the 10 kilometres of road from Nice to the summit of the climb, Merckx passed the fading star to seal his victory with a touch of panache and the symbolic passing of the baton from one era to the next.

Merckx followed Paris-Nice with monumental victories in *la primavera*, the Ronde and *la doyenne*. In Milan-Sanremo he turned a 10-metre advantage at the top of the Poggio into a 30-second lead as he crossed the finish line on the Via Roma, sprinting through the corners of the Poggio's descent at such speed that even the TV motorbike couldn't keep up. In the Ronde van Vlaanderen he simply rode away from the *peloton* in proper Flanders weather – rain and wind – with still 70 kilometres to race and all the major climbing done. By the time he reached the finish in Gentbrugge he was five and a half minutes clear of his closest rival, Felice Gimondi (Salvarani). In Liège-Bastogne-Liège Merckx sent a couple of Faema team-mates up the road after the turn at Bastogne and then, with 100 kilometres to go, himself popped off the front of the *peloton* on the Stockeau and joined them. Only Vic van Schil could hold Merckx's pace and the pair of Faema riders did a two-up time trial back to the Rocourt vélodrome in Liège, the third rider home – Barry Hoban (Mercier) – more than eight minutes adrift.

The Belgian then went into the Giro d'Italia, the defending champion and favourite for victory but was turfed off the race a week out from home, with four stage wins under his wheels and the *maglia rosa* on his back. Cycling's attempts to clean itself up brought him low and he was found to be a doping cheat. Then he was given the benefit of the doubt: not declared innocent, merely let off the last two weeks of the suspension he should have served for having tested positive at the Giro. That benefit of the doubt – aided more than somewhat by Félix Lévitan's role as co-director of the Tour and chairman of the UCI's professional arm, the FICP – enabled Merckx to finally make his début at the Tour de France.

The Tour organisers – Jacques Goddet and Félix Lévitan – had wanted Merckx to make his Tour debut the previous year. As had others. But Merckx – who would have been barely a week past his twenty-third birthday at the start of the 1968 race – demurred. To help guarantee his appearance in 1969 the Tour route visited the Brussels suburb of Woluwe-Saint-Pierre, a morning road race and an afternoon time trial that would give the Belgian ample opportunity to don the *maillot jaune* in front of his friends and family.

By the time the Tour had left Brussels Merckx was wearing the yellow jersey. He quickly surrendered it to a Faema team-mate (trade teams once more having replaced national squads), Julien Stevens, who held on to it for a few days before losing it in the Vosges. Then, on the Ballon d'Alsace, Merckx seized it back with an early show of force, catching his rivals napping and putting time into them when they least expected it. Through the Alps the Belgian only added insult to injury and by the time the race reached the Pyrenees it was all over bar the celebrating: Merckx was leading by more than eight minutes over Roger Pingeon (Peugeot), the 1967 winner, and more than nine over Felice Gimondi (Salvarani), the 1965 winner and the man who had added a second Giro d'Italia to his *palmarès* following Merckx's dismissal from the recent *corsa rosa*.

And then came a legendary stage, out of Luchon and over the Peyresourde, the Aspin, the Tourmalet, the Soulor and the Aubisque before tootling into the newly built town of Mourenx. On that July Tuesday in 1969, the day after Bastille Day when the French added an Aspirin to their morning espressos, Merckx was just four weeks past his twenty-fourth birthday. The impetuosity of youth had been tempered somewhat by the wisdom caringly passed to him by his elders – most notably Vittorio Adorni who, in Merckx's first season at Faema, had tried to teach him to be *tranquillo* – but he was still a callow youth, was still a kid who could park practical thinking in the pursuit of happiness on his bike. And on that legendary stage in the Pyrenees in the 1969 Tour Merckx was – he himself insists – just a boy wanting to have fun.

The race was already blowing apart early into the stage on the Peyresourde, riders attacking all over the place. As they closed on the summit of the Tourmalet the *maillot jaune* was in a select group of nine riders. And then, just metres from the summit, Merckx exploded past his Faema team-mate Martin Van den Bossche, pinched the king of the mountain points and barrelled down the descent, putting 45 seconds into the rest by the bottom of the Tourmalet.

That should have been the end of it, and Merckx did settle in to the wait for the rest to come back up to him. This was, after all, the time to be cautious, to think tactically, to control his own impetuosity. He had won two of the race's time trials, showed his strength on the Tour's first mountain and won a stage in the Alps. All Merckx now had to do was to stay upright for six more days, his eight-minute lead over Roger Pingeon (Peugeot) more than cushion enough. So Merckx waited, rolled on at a casual pace, refilled the tank with fuel taken on at the feed zone in Argelès-Gazost. But still the pursuers hadn't closed on him. The gap had actually opened a little. By the time Merckx hit the foot of the Soulor he was a minute clear of the men who were supposed to be pursuing him.

At which point Merckx thought to himself: the day was too beautiful; the stage was too large; the opportunity too much to turn down. This was a day for an exploit. A day for the fans. A day for the record books. You also have to wonder, though, if maybe Merckx hadn't also thought of that day just six weeks earlier on the Ligurian coast. That day when he'd collapsed on his bed in the Hotel Excelsior in Savona and cried. That day when he was expelled from the Giro d'Italia having failed a doping test.

Whatever Merckx was thinking about, thought quickly became deed. By the summit of the Soulor he'd added four minutes to his lead. By the summit of the Aubisque, 60 kilometres after jumping clear on the Tourmalet, Merckx's lead over his pursuers was eight minutes. He had still more than 70 kilometres to go. And Merckx just kept on going, grinding out the miles. By the time he rolled into Mourenx he was eight minutes up on the next rider home, Michele Dancelli (Molteni), his lead over Pingeon doubled to a shocking 16 minutes.

As the Tour had grown in importance – as other races had surrendered their own significance – fans had already grown used to tactical, defensive riding, a three week race boiling down to the final 10 kilometres of sprint stages, the last men to leave in a couple of time trials and one or two key days in the mountains when the race came come alive. Exploits were the domain of riders out of contention, usually reserved for transition stages. Fans had already grown used to seeing the yellow jersey surrounded by his key rivals, only ever pulling clear when it was time for the *mise à mort*. What Merckx gave the Tour that day in the Pyrenees wasn't just a mammoth solo ride, it was a mammoth solo ride by the man wearing the *maillot jaune*, a mammoth solo ride that threw all caution to the wind, a mammoth solo ride that gambled an existing eight-minute advantage on a spin of the wheel.

What is even better about Merckx's exploit that day in the Pyrenees is that it wasn't all plain sailing, wasn't as easy as the telling of it makes it seem. Things had gone wrong for Merckx. The Faema team car broke down, and Merck's *directeur sportif*, Lomme Driessens, had to hitch a lift in a press car, taking with him spare wheels in case

Merckx needed them. Fifty kilometres out from home Merckx fell victim to the dreaded *fringale*, bonked badly: in 16 kilometres he shed two minutes of his advantage over the riders behind. Somehow Merckx clung on, took on food, regained his composure. Finally, four hours and 130 kilometres after soloing clear on the Tourmalet, a ragged and pain-racked Merckx rode into Mourenx, an industrialised new town in the Pyrenees that had paid handsomely for its slot on the Tour's itinerary and been rewarded with an epic victory.

If the good burghers of Mourenx were smiling at the manner in which their investment in the Tour had been repaid, then Félix Lévitan's smile must have lit up a darkened room: Heaven and Earth had been moved to get Merckx into the Tour, and by God had it been worth the effort! This man Merckx was a godsend to a race that was going through a period of transition in the quest to balance the books financially. A couple of years of this sort of racing was just what the Tour needed. But, hopefully, not too many of them.

Over the following days Merckx further padded his advantage over Pingeon, but the real racing was by now over, his rivals had accepted their fates. On the final day, as the *grande boucle* raced into Paris, the Cipale vélodrome in Vincennes was filled out with 25,000 fans cheering the riders home as they rolled in one by one, time trialling to the end of the Tour. Fittingly, the last home was the first to leave from Roubaix 4,117 kilometres earlier, this time with the *maillot jaune* on his back.

As well as winning the last stage and the yellow jersey at that Tour Merckx also left the *grande boucle* with five other stage wins, and victory in the points, climbing and combination competitions, and also pocketed the Super Combativité prize. In all it was 10 new notches on his *palmarès* in just 23 days of racing (and it *was* 23 days of racing that year, the riders not given even a single *jour de répos*). Merckx also left the 1969 Tour de France with a new nickname: the Cannibal.

Merckx's victory in that Tour will forever be associated with the solo ride through the Pyrenees but his overall win was no solo victory: this was truly a team effort. In all, Merckx's Faema squad went home with 10 stage wins and the overall team prize. A Faema rider wore the *maillot jaune* on all bar three days of racing, the team collecting 23 of the race's 25 yellow jerseys. At the end of the race the Faema petty-cash tin was bulging with IOUs for the lion's share of the Tour's 600,000 francs prize fund. If all that's not enough of a show of team strength for you, then consider this: not a single Faema rider – Italian-sponsored but Belgians to a man – was among the 46 who failed to finish that Tour.

Stage-by-Stage Results for the 1969 Tour de France			Stage Winner	Maillot Jaune
Prologue Sat 28 Jun	Roubaix (ITT) 130 finishers	10.4 km 13'00" 48 kph	Rudi Altig (FRG) Salvarani	Rudi Altig (FRG) Salvarani
Stage 1a Sun 29 Jun	Roubaix to Woluwe-Saint-Pierre 130 finishers	147 km 3h18'29" 44.4 kph	Marino Basso (Ita) Molteni	Rudi Altig (FRG) Salvarani
Stage 1b Sun 29 Jun	Woluwe-Saint-Pierre (TTT) 130 finishers	15.6 km 1h37'45" 9.6 kph	Faema	Eddy Merckx (Bel) Faema
Stage 2 Mon 30 Jun	Woluwe-Saint-Pierre to Maastricht 127 finishers	181.5 km 4h35'42" 39.5 kph	Julien Stevens (Bel) Faema	Julien Stevens (Bel) Faema
Stage 3 Tue 1 Jul	Maastricht to Charleville-Mézières 127 finishers	213.5 km 5h56'15" 36 kph	Eric Leman (Bel) Flandria	Julien Stevens (Bel) Faema
Stage 4 Wed 2 Jul	Charleville-Mézières to Nancy 127 finishers	214 km 5h18'02" 40.4 kph	Rik Van Looy (Bel) Willem II	Julien Stevens (Bel) Faema
Stage 5 Thu 3 Jul	Nancy to Mulhouse 125 finishers	193.5 km 5h03'33" 38.2 kph	Joaquim Agostinho (Por) Frimatic	Désiré Letort (Fra) Peugeot
	Major climbs: Col de la Schlucht (1,139m) Mariano Díaz (Esp) Fagor; Col de Firstplan (722m) Joaquim Agostinho (Por) Frimatic			
Stage 6 Fri 4 Jul	Mulhouse to Ballon d'Alsace 114 finishers	133.5 km 3h37'25" 36.8 kph	Eddy Merckx (Bel) Faema	Eddy Merckx (Bel) Faema
	Major climbs: Col du Grand Ballon (1,343m) Lucien Van Impe (Bel) Sonolor; Col de la Grosse Pierre (923m) Rudi Altig (FRG) Salvarani; Ballon d'Alsace (1,178m) Eddy Merckx (Bel) Faema			
Stage 7 Sat 5 Jul	Belfort to Divonne-les-Bains 113 finishers	241 km 6h13'07" 38.8 kph	Mariano Diaz (Esp) Fagor	Eddy Merckx (Bel) Faema
	Major climbs: Col de la Faucille (Côte des Rousses) (1,140m) Mariano Díaz (Esp) Fagor			
Stage 8a Sun 6 Jul	Divonne-les-Bains (ITT) 113 finishers	8.8 km 10'38" 49.7 kph	Eddy Merckx (Bel) Faema	Eddy Merckx (Bel) Faema
Stage 8b Sun 6 Jul	Divonne-les-Bains to Thonon-les-Bains 112 finishers	136.5 km 3h30'46" 38.9 kph	Michele Dancelli (Ita) Molteni	Eddy Merckx (Bel) Faema

Stage-by-Stage Results for the 1969 Tour de France			Stage Winner	Maillot Jaune
Stage 9 Mon 7 Jul	Thonon-les-Bains to Chamonix 111 finishers	111 km 2h48'23" 39.6 kph	Roger Pingeon (Fra) Peugeot	Eddy Merckx (Bel) Faema
	Major climbs: Col de la Forclaz (1,527m) Roger Pingeon (Fra) Peugeot; Col des Montets (1,461m) Roger Pingeon (Fra) Peugeot			
Stage 10 Tue 8 Jul	Chamonix to Briançon 97 finishers	220.5 km 6h41'43" 32.9 kph	Herman Van Springel (Bel) Mann	Eddy Merckx (Bel) Faema
	Major climbs: Col de la Madeleine (2,000m) Andrés Gandarias (Esp) KAS; Col du Télégraphe (1,566m) Manuel Galera (Esp) Fagor; Col du Galibier (2,556m) Eddy Merckx (Bel) Faema			
Stage 11 Wed 9 Jul	Briançon to Digne 95 finishers	198 km 5h58'55" 33.1 kph	Eddy Merckx (Bel) Faema	Eddy Merckx (Bel) Faema
	Major climbs: Col de Vars (2,110m) Gabriel Mascaro (Esp) KAS; Col d'Allos (2,250m) Luis-Pedro Santamarina (Esp) Fagor; Coronbin (1,261m) Gabriel Mascaro (Esp) KAS			
Stage 12 Thu 10 Jul	Digne to Aubagne 95 finishers	161.5 km 4h23'15" 36.8 kph	Felice Gimondi (Ita) Salvarani	Eddy Merckx (Bel) Faema
	Major climbs: Col de l'Espigoulier (728m) Felice Gimondi (Ita) Salvarani			
Stage 13 Fri 11 Jul	Aubagne to La Grande-Motte 95 finishers	195.5 km 5h48'54" 33.6 kph	Guido Reybrouck (Bel) Faema	Eddy Merckx (Bel) Faema
Stage 14 Sat 12 Jul	La Grande-Motte to Revel 95 finishers	234.5 km 6h59'53" 33.5 kph	Joaquim Agostinho (Por) Frimatic	Eddy Merckx (Bel) Faema
Stage 15 Sun 13 Jul	Revel (ITT) 95 finishers	18.5 km 24'08" 46 kph	Eddy Merckx (Bel) Faema	Eddy Merckx (Bel) Faema
Stage 16 Mon 14 Jul	Revel (Castelnaudary) to Luchon 93 finishers	199 km 6h13'21" 32 kph	Raymond Delisle (Fra) Peugeot	Eddy Merckx (Bel) Faema
	Major climbs: Col de Portet d'Aspet (1,069m) Raymond Delisle (Fra) Peugeot; Col de Menté (1,349m) Raymond Delisle (Fra) Peugeot; Col du Portillon (1,298m) Raymond Delisle (Fra) Peugeot			
Stage 17 Tue 15 Jul	Luchon to Mourenx 87 finishers	214.5 km 7h04'28" 30.3 kph	Eddy Merckx (Bel) Faema	Eddy Merckx (Bel) Faema
	Major climbs: Col de Peyresourde (1,569m) Manuel Galera (Esp) Fagor; Col d'Aspin (1,489m) Manuel Galera (Esp) Fagor; Col du Tourmalet (2,115m) Eddy Merckx (Bel) Faema; Col d'Aubisque (1,709m) Eddy Merckx (Bel) Faema			
Stage 18 Wed 16 Jul	Mourenx to Bordeaux 86 finishers	201 km 5h44'43" 35 kph	Barry Hoban (GBr) Mercier	Eddy Merckx (Bel) Faema
Stage 19 Thu 17 Jul	Bordeaux to Brive 86 finishers	192.5 km 5h30'57" 34.9 kph	Barry Hoban (GBr) Mercier	Eddy Merckx (Bel) Faema

Stage-by-Stage Results for the 1969 Tour de France			Stage Winner	Maillot Jaune
Stage 20 Fri 18 Jul	Brive to Le Puy de Dôme 86 finishers	198 km 6h49'54" 29 kph	Pierre Matignon (Fra) Frimatic	Eddy Merckx (Bel) Faema
	Major climbs: Puy de Dôme (1,415m) Pierre Matignon (Fra) Frimatic			
Stage 21 Sat 19 Jul	Clermont-Ferrand to Montargis 86 finishers	329.5 km 9h37'47" 34.2 kph	Herman Van Springel (Bel) Mann	Eddy Merckx (Bel) Faema
Stage 22a Sun 20 Jul	Montargis to Créteil 86 finishers	111.5 km 2h56'18" 37.9 kph	Jozef Spruyt (Bel) Faema	Eddy Merckx (Bel) Faema
Stage 22b Sun 20 Jul	Créteil to Paris (Piste Municipale de Vincennes) (ITT) 86 finishers	36.8 km 47'38" 46.4 kph	Eddy Merckx (Bel) Faema	Eddy Merckx (Bel) Faema

Prize fund: 600,000 francs (first prize: 20,000 francs)

Final Classification				
Place	**Rider**	**Team**	**Time**	**Age**
1	Eddy Merckx (Bel)	Faema	4,117 km 116h16'02" 35.409 kph	24
2	Roger Pingeon (Fra)	Peugeot	17'54"	28
3	Raymond Poulidor (Fra)	Mercier	22'13"	33
4	Felice Gimondi (Ita)	Salvarani	29'24"	26
5	Andrés Gandarias (Esp)	KAS	33'04"	26
6	Marinus Wagtmans (Ned)	Willem II	33'57"	22
7	Pier-Franco Vianelli (Ita)	Molteni	42'40"	22
8	Joaquim Agostinho (Por)	Frimatic	51'24"	26
9	Désiré Letort (Fra)	Peugot	51'41"	26
10	Jan Janssen (Ned)	Bic	52'56"	29
Lanterne Rouge				
86	André Wilhelm (Fra)	Sonolor	3h51'53"	26
Points				
	Eddy Merckx (Bel)	Faema		24
King of the Mountains				
	Eddy Merckx (Bel)	Faema		24
Combined				
	Eddy Merckx (Bel)	Faema		24
Super Combativité				
	Eddy Merckx (Bel)	Faema		24
Team				
		Faema		

1970: Red Harvest

Having been thrown off the 1969 Giro d'Italia while wearing the leader's pink jersey, Merckx returned to the Italian Grand Tour in 1970 and took the win, his second Giro title. Three weeks later he was starting the Tour. His Faemino team once again squeezed the life out of the race, Merckx taking the yellow jersey on the opening stage and then passing the lead to team-mate Italo Zilioli, retaking the *maillot jaune* at the end of Stage Six, in Valenciennes. He then held it all the way to Paris. The Giro/Tour double was done, and Merckx joined Fausto Coppi and Jacques Anquetil in an elite club of people who had pulled off that feat.

This was a Tour without any real drama. Merckx's Faemino squad ended the race with 11 stage wins (out of 29 in 23 days of racing). Merckx won eight of those stages, matching Charles Pélissier's record in the 1930 Tour. A Faemino rider wore the *maillot jaune* on every stage of the race. Merckx took the King of the Mountains, the combination and the Super Combativité titles. It wasn't quite a whitewash for Faemino: Salvarani won the team competition and Walter Godefroot took the points classification for them too. For the fans, though, there was no real reason to buy a newspaper to find out what was going on, everyone knew: Merckx was crushing the life out of the Tour.

In fact, the only bit of real drama in the whole race was somewhat exaggerated, if not manufactured: atop the Ventoux, while talking to the media, the Cannibal collapsed in a faint and had to be given oxygen. He and another rider were ambulanced off the mountain. This had the advantage of getting them to their team hotel ahead of most other riders, who were delayed in their descent of the bald mountain by the hoards of fans also making their way down.

In the offices of Émilien Amaury's *L'Équipe* and *Le Parisien Libéré* newspapers the lack of drama did not go down very well. Goddet, in private, called it a catastrophe. But what could Goddet do to change the situation? It wasn't as if Merckx was without rivals: Lucien Aimar (Sonolor), Roger Pingeon (Peugeot) and Jan Janssen (Bic) were all at the race, as was Raymond Poulidor (Fagor). None of them, though, could challenge the authority of Merckx and his Faemino red guard.

Even the riders' agents were powerless to break Merckx's control: he didn't use the services of either of the two French agents, Daniel Dousset and Roger Piel, and instead let the Belgian Jan Van Buggenhout manage his critérium appearances.

The Tour didn't even have any major drug scandals to get people excited. It wasn't that doping had stopped, far from it, doping was actually entering a new scientific era, with amphetamines being passed over in favour of new drugs like cortisone. But the powerlessness of the Tour's authorities between the two terrible days on the Ventoux – Jean Malléjac's collapse in 1955 and Tom Simpson's death in 1967 – was over, with dopers being caught through the daily controls, and punished.

That punishment had changed following Merckx's positive at Savona. Then, when a rider tested positive, they were immediately suspended from competition. That changed to being a suspended suspension, only having to be served if a rider tested positive a second time within two years. For the first offence, all he got was a time and financial penalty. So while José Samyn and Jean Stablinski had been thrown off the 1968 Tour when they tested positive, when Rudi Altig (Salvarani), Bernard Guyot (Sonolor), Pierre Matignon (Frimatic), Henk Nijdam (Willem II) and Joseph Timmermann (Willem II) were all caught by the doping controls at the 1970 race, they suffered no more than time and financial penalties, their suspensions left hanging over them.

But at least punishment was being handed out, and was seen to be handed out. Justice was being done and being seen to be done; riders were no longer getting away with doping. Except, of course, for the inconvenient fact that there were many, many drugs which the authorities had yet to develop techniques to detect.

Stage-by-Stage Results for the 1970 Tour de France			Stage Winner	Maillot Jaune
Prologue Sat 27 Jun	Limoges (ITT) 150 finishers	7.4 km 9'57" 44.6 kph	Eddy Merckx (Bel) Faemino	Eddy Merckx (Bel) Faemino
Stage 1 Sat 27 Jun	Limoges to La Rochelle 150 finishers	224.5 km 5h50'24" 38.4 kph	Cyrille Guimard (Fra) Fagor	Eddy Merckx (Bel) Faemino
Stage 2 Sun 28 Jun	La Rochelle to Angers 148 finishers	200 km 4h41'19" 42.7 kph	Italo Zilioli (Ita) Faemino	Italo Zilioli (Ita) Faemino
Stage 3a Mon 29 Jun	Angers (TTT) 148 finishers	10.7 km 13'25" 47.9 kph	Faemino	Italo Zilioli (Ita) Faemino
Stage 3b Mon 29 Jun	Angers to Rennes 147 finishers	140 km 3h20'06" 42 kph	Marino Basso (Ita) Molteni	Italo Zilioli (Ita) Faemino
Stage 4 Tue 30 Jun	Rennes to Lisieux 142 finishers	229 km 5h27'07" 42 kph	Walter Godefroot (Bel) Salvarani	Italo Zilioli (Ita) Faemino
Stage 5a Wed 1 Jul	Lisieux to Rouen 141 finishers	94.5 km 2h05'02" 45.3 kph	Walter Godefroot (Bel) Salvarani	Italo Zilioli (Ita) Faemino
Stage 5b Wed 1 Jul	Rouen to Amiens 137 finishers	113 km 2h32'34" 44.4 kph	Jozef Spruyt (Bel) Faemino	Italo Zilioli (Ita) Faemino
Stage 6 Thu 2 Jul	Amiens to Valenciennes 132 finishers	135.5 km 3h05'50" 43.7 kph	Roger de Vlaeminck (Bel) Mars	Eddy Merckx (Bel) Faemino
Stage 7a Fri 3 Jul	Valenciennes to Forest 124 finishers	119 km 2h51'11" 41.7 kph	Eddy Merckx (Bel) Faemino	Eddy Merckx (Bel) Faemino
Stage 7b Fri 3 Jul	Forest (ITT) 122 finishers	7.2 km 10'01" 43.1 kph	José Antonio González (Esp) KAS	Eddy Merckx (Bel) Faemino
Stage 8 Sat 4 Jul	Ciney to Felsberg 117 finishers	232.5 km 6h04'16" 38.3 kph	Alain Vasseur (Fra) Bic	Eddy Merckx (Bel) Faemino
Stage 9 Sun 5 Jul	Saarlouis to Mulhouse 116 finishers	269.5 km 7h44'14" 34.8 kph	Mogens Frey (Sui) Frimatic	Eddy Merckx (Bel) Faemino
Major climbs: Col de la Schlucht (1,139m) Silvano Schiavon (Ita) Salvarani; Col du Grand Ballon (1,343m) Mogens Frey (Den) Frimatic				
Stage 10 Mon 6 Jul	Belfort to Divonne-les-Bains 115 finishers	241 km 5h52'36" 41 kph	Eddy Merckx (Bel) Faemino	Eddy Merckx (Bel) Faemino
Major climbs: Côte des Rousses (1,140m) Guerrino Tosello (Ita) Molteni				
Stage 11a Tue 7 Jul	Divonne-les-Bains (ITT) 115 finishers	8.8 km 10'35" 49.9 kph	Eddy Merckx (Bel) Faemino	Eddy Merckx (Bel) Faemino

Stage-by-Stage Results for the 1970 Tour de France			Stage Winner	Maillot Jaune
Stage 11b Tue 7 Jul	Divonne-les-Bains to Thonon-les-Bains 112 finishers	139.5 km 3h42'43" 37.6 kph	Marino Basso (Ita) Molteni	Eddy Merckx (Bel) Faemino
	Major climbs: Col des Mouilles (1,103m) Cyrille Guimard (Fra) Fagor; Col de Cou (1,916m) Italo Zilioli (Ita) Faemino			
Stage 12 Wed 8 Jul	Thonon-les-Bains to Grenoble 109 finishers	194 km 6h01'49" 32.2 kph	Eddy Merckx (Bel) Faemino	Eddy Merckx (Bel) Faemino
	Major climbs: Col de Leschaux (897m) Cyrille Guimard (Fra) Fagor; Col de Plainpalais (1,173m) Primo Mori (Ita) Salvarani; Col du Granier (1,134m) Andrés Gandarias (Esp) KAS; Col du Cucheron (1,139m) Andrés Gandarias (Esp) KAS; Col de Porte (1,326m) Eddy Merckx (Bel) Faemino			
Stage 13 Thu 9 Jul	Grenoble to Gap 107 finishers	195.5 km 5h52'16" 33.3 kph	Primo Mori (Ita) Salvarani	Eddy Merckx (Bel) Faemino
	Major climbs: Côte de Laffrey (900m) Andrés Gandarias (Esp) KAS; Lholme (1,207m) Andrés Gandarias (Esp) KAS; Col du Noyer (1,664m) Raymond Delisle (Fra) Peugeot; Le Festre (1,441m) Primo Mori (Ita) Salvarani; Col de la Sentinelle (980m) Primo Mori (Ita) Salvarani			
Stage 14 Fri 10 Jul	Gap to Mont Ventoux 105 finishers	170 km 5h47'44" 29.3 kph	Eddy Merckx (Bel) Faemino	Eddy Merckx (Bel) Faemino
	Major climbs: Col de Macuènge (1,068m) Mario Anni (Ita) Molteni; Col Saint-Jean (1,332m) Silvano Schiavon (Ita) Salvarani; Mont Ventoux (1,909m) Eddy Merckx (Bel) Faemino			
Stage 15 Sat 11 Jul	Carpentras to Montpellier 105 finishers	144.5 km 3h53'58" 37.1 kph	Rini Wagtmans (Ned) Willem II	Eddy Merckx (Bel) Faemino
Stage 16 Sun 12 Jul	Montpellier to Toulouse 105 finishers	259.5 km 8h21'12" 31.1 kph	Albert Van Vlierberghe (Bel) Ferretti	Eddy Merckx (Bel) Faemino
Stage 17 Mon 13 Jul	Toulouse to Saint-Gaudens 105 finishers	190 km 5h20'47" 35.5 kph	Luis Ocaña (Esp) Bic	Eddy Merckx (Bel) Faemino
Stage 18 Tue 14 Jul	Saint-Gaudens to La Mongie (Tourmalet) 105 finishers	135.5 km 4h49'36" 28.1 kph	Bernard Thévenet (Fra) Peugeot	Eddy Merckx (Bel) Faemino
	Major climbs: Col de Menté (1,349m) Guerrino Tosello (Ita) Molteni; Col de Peyresourde (1,569m) Raymond Delisle (Fra) Peugeot; Col d'Aspin (1,489m) Primo Mori (Ita) Salvarani; La Mongie (1,715m) Bernard Thévenet (Fra) Peugeot			
Stage 19 Wed 15 Jul	Bagnères-de-Bigorre to Mourenx (Ville Nouvelle) 102 finishers	185.5 km 5h27'25" 34 kph	Christian Raymond (Fra) Peugeot	Eddy Merckx (Bel) Faemino
	Major climbs: Col du Tourmalet (2,115m) Andrés Gandarias (Esp) KAS; Col d'Aubisque (1,709m) Raymond Delisle (Fra) Peugeot			
Stage 20a Thu 16 Jul	Mourenx to Bordeaux 102 finishers	231 km 6h26'49" 35.8 kph	Rolf Wolfshohl (FRG) Fagor	Eddy Merckx (Bel) Faemino
Stage 20b Thu 16 Jul	Bordeaux (ITT) 102 finishers	8.2 km 10'32" 46.7 kph	Eddy Merckx (Bel) Faemino	Eddy Merckx (Bel) Faemino

Stage-by-Stage Results for the 1970 Tour de France			Stage Winner	Maillot Jaune
Stage 21 Fri 17 Jul	Ruffec to Tours 102 finishers	191.5 km 5h24'55" 35.4 kph	Marino Basso (Ita) Molteni	Eddy Merckx (Bel) Faemino
Stage 22 Sat 18 Jul	Tours to Versailles 102 finishers	238.5 km 6h43'13" 35.5 kph	Jean-Pierre Danguillaume (Fra) Peugeot	Eddy Merckx (Bel) Faemino
Stage 23 Sun 19 Jul	Versailles to Paris (La Cipale) (ITT) 100 finishers	54 km 1h09'39" 46.5 kph	Eddy Merckx (Bel) Faemino	Eddy Merckx (Bel) Faemino

Prize fund: 605,535 francs (first prize: 20,000 francs)

Final Classification				
Place	**Rider**	**Team**	**Time**	**Age**
1	Eddy Merckx (Bel)	Faemino	4,254 km 119h31'49" 35.589 kph	25
2	Joop Zoetemelk (Ned)	Mars	+ 12'41"	24
3	Gösta Pettersson (Swe)	Ferretti	+ 15'54"	29
4	Martin Van den Bossche (Bel)	Molteni	+ 18'53"	29
5	Rini Wagtmans (Ned)	Willem II	+ 19'54"	23
6	Lucien Van Impe (Bel)	Sonolor	+ 20'34"	23
7	Raymond Poulidor (Fra)	Fagor	+ 20'35"	34
8	Antoon Houbrechts (Bel)	Salvarani	+ 21'34"	26
9	Francisco Galdós (Esp)	KAS	+ 21'45"	23
10	Georges Pintens (Bel)	Mann	+ 23'23"	23
Lanterne Rouge				
100	Frits Hogerheide (Ned)	Willem II	+ 3h52'12"	26
Points				
	Walter Godefroot (Bel)	Salvarani		27
King of the Mountains				
	Eddy Merckx (Bel)	Faemino		25
Combination				
	Eddy Merckx (Bel)	Faemino		25
Youth				
	Mogens Frey (Den)	Frimatic		29
Team				
		Salvarani		
Super Combativité				
	Roger Pingeon (Fra)	Peugeot		29

1971: A Rival?

Whatever gods Jacques Goddet and Félix Lévitan prayed to for some solution to Eddy Merckx's dominance, they were answered in 1971 when Luis Ocaña stepped up to the plate and gave the Cannibal a run for his money. Across eight days the Tour saw a race that kept everyone on the edge of their seats.

The race had begun in Mulhouse with the now standard prologue and Eddy Merckx in yellow following his new Molteni team's performance in a team time trial. The jersey was briefly passed to team-mate Rini Wagtmans, during a day in which the riders had to squeeze three stages into one day of racing, before passing back to Merckx. So far, so dull. But on the eighth stage, finishing atop the Puy de Dôme, things began to warm up.

Four kilometres from the summit of the Puy, close to where Julio Jiménez and Federico Bahamontes had left Jacques Anquetil and Raymond Poulidor to fight their private duel in 1964, Luis Ocaña (Bic) rode away from Merckx. A kilometre from the summit and Joop Zoetemelk (Mars/Flandria) and Joaquim Agostinho (Hoover) did the same. Merckx only lost 15 seconds to Ocaña on the road, and seven and 13 to Zoetemelk and Agostinho. But the psychological impact was important. Not for the negative effect it had on Merckx – for the positive effect it had on Ocaña.

Two stages later, on the road from Saint-Étienne to Grenoble, Ocaña attacked on the Col de Porte and took Zoetemelk, Bernard Thévenet (Peugeot) and Thomas Petterson (Ferretti) with him and put a minute and a half into Merckx. Thévenet took the stage, Zoetemelk the yellow jersey (the first time since the fifth stage of the 1969 Tour that someone other than Merckx or one of his team-mates was leading the race). Zoetemelk's lead? One second over Ocaña – who took the *maillot jaune* the next day when he put more than eight minutes into Merckx.

The attacking began almost as soon as the stage, a group of riders going clear on the Côte de Laffrey. Present, Ocaña; absent, Merckx. By the time the riders reached the Col du Noyer Ocaña was alone and had five minutes on Merckx. By the time he arrived at the summit finish in Orcières-Merlette Merckx was on the brink of abandoning and Ocaña looked like he might actually win the Tour. And then came the twist. Merckx was down, but he was not out, and after a rest day, he was reinvigorated and ready for war.

Starting stage 12 the Belgian was 9'46" off yellow. Merckx looked human, and his Tour looked to be over. Merckx ended the day still 7'34" down, but the Tour was back on and the Cannibal was looking far from human.

From the start of the stage – 250 kilometres taking the riders from Orcières-Merlette to Marseille – Merckx and his Molteni team-mates attacked. Quite literally from the start, on the descent, from the flag, no time to roll along and warm the legs up. They reached Marseille so far ahead of schedule that the safety barriers were still being put out. The Mayor was so angered by this – Marseille was paying a pretty penny to host the Tour, the least it could do was to arrive on time – that he ruled out further visits from the race as long as he was in charge.

Marseille was followed by a long transfer and a short time trial, 16.3 kilometres around Albi, which Merckx won, with Ocaña putting in a strong performance and ceding just 11 seconds. And then the race was into the Pyrenees. And after already providing two stages that would live long in Tour memory – Orcières-Merlette and Marseille – the riders in the 1971 Tour served up a third. The one in which they crossed the Col de Menté.

It wasn't on the climb that the decisive moment came, but on the descent. José Manuel Fuente (KAS) was off on his own, winning the stage. Behind him Merckx was putting Ocaña under the cosh. On the Col de Portet d'Aspet he'd tried to break the Spaniard, to no effect. The same on the ascent of the Menté, where the weather

Luis Ocaña leads Lucien van Impe and Joop Zoetemelk on the road to Orcières-Merlette in the 1971 Tour.

turned Biblical, a hailstorm lashing the race and roads turning into rivers. Over the summit of the Menté, coming around a rain-soaked bend at speed, Merckx crashed. Ocaña was behind him and also went down. Merckx picked himself up and remounted. Ocaña picked himself up and readied himself to climb back on his bike … when another rider crashed into him. Who is not clear. Zoetemelk thought it was he, others thought it was Agostinho. It matters not. What matters is that Ocaña was down, and this time injured. And Merckx had remounted and was pushing on alone, unaware of what was happening behind him. Which involved Ocaña being taken down off the mountain to a nearby hospital. For the first time since Fiorenzo Magni in 1950, the *maillot jaune* was forced out of the race.

As a mark of respect to his fallen rival Merckx refused to wear the yellow jersey the next day, which he was now the rightful owner of, with a lead of 2'21" over Zoetemelk and 2'51 over Lucien Van Impe (Sonolor).

Merckx added to that lead on a seemingly innocuous stage leading the riders from Mont-de-Marsan to Bordeaux, taking the thick end of three minutes as if from nowhere. Because he could. Because he was the Cannibal.

Stage-by-Stage Results for the 1971 Tour de France			Stage Winner	Maillot Jaune
Prologue Sat 26 Jun	Mulhouse (TTT) 130 finishers	11 km 13'24" 49.3 kph	Molteni	Eddy Merckx (Bel) Molteni
Stage 1a Sun 27 Jun	Mulhouse to Bâle 130 finishers	59.5 km 1h24'36" 42.2 kph	Eric Leman (Bel) Mars	Eddy Merckx (Bel) Molteni
Stage 1b Sun 27 Jun	Bâle to Fribourg 130 finishers	90 km 2h28'26" 36.4 kph	Gerben Karstens (Ned) Goudsmit	Rini Wagtmans (Ned) Molteni
	Major climbs: Happach (1,040m) Joop Zoetemelk (Ned) Mars; Notschrei (1,120m) Joop Zoetemelk (Ned) Mars			
Stage 1c Sun 27 Jun	Fribourg to Mulhouse 130 finishers	74 km 1h43'32" 42.9 kph	Albert Van Vlierberghe (Bel) Ferretti	Eddy Merckx (Bel) Molteni
Stage 2 Mon 28 Jun	Mulhouse to Strasbourg 127 finishers	144 km 3h05'27" 46.6 kph	Eddy Merckx (Bel) Molteni	Eddy Merckx (Bel) Molteni
	Major climbs: Col du Firstplan (722m) Joop Zoetemelk (Ned) Mars			

Stage-by-Stage Results for the 1971 Tour de France			Stage Winner	Maillot Jaune
Stage 3￼Tue 29 Jun	Strasbourg to Nancy￼127 finishers	165.5 km￼4h14'21"￼39 kph	Rini Wagtmans (Ned)￼Molteni	Eddy Merckx (Bel)￼Molteni
	Major climbs: Mont Donon (727m) Joop Zoetemelk (Ned) Mars; Côte de Chapelotte (446m) Joop Zoetemelk (Ned) Mars			
Stage 4￼Wed 30 Jun	Nancy to￼Marche-en-Famenne￼127 finishers	242 km￼6h45'03"￼35.8 kph	Jean-Pierre Genêt (Fra)￼Fagor	Eddy Merckx (Bel)￼Molteni
Stage 5￼Thu 1 Jul	Dinant to Roubaix￼127 finishers	208.5 km￼5h13'56"￼39.8 kph	Pietro Guerra (Ita)￼Salvarani	Eddy Merckx (Bel)￼Molteni
	Major climbs: Mur de Grammont (143m) Joaquim Agostinho (Por) Hoover			
Stage 6a￼Fri 2 Jul	Roubaix to Amiens￼126 finishers	127.5 km￼3h03'19"￼41.7 kph	Eric Leman (Bel)￼Mars	Eddy Merckx (Bel)￼Molteni
Stage 6b￼Fri 2 Jul	Amiens to Le Touquet￼126 finishers	133.5 km￼3h47'56"￼35.1 kph	Mauro Simonetti (Ita)￼Ferretti	Eddy Merckx (Bel)￼Molteni
Sat 3 Jul	Rest Day			
Stage 7￼Sun 4 Jul	Rungis to Nevers￼126 finishers	257.5 km￼6h45'33"￼38.1 kph	Eric Leman (Bel)￼Mars	Eddy Merckx (Bel)￼Molteni
Stage 8￼Mon 5 Jul	Nevers to Puy de Dôme￼126 finishers	221 km￼6h21'10"￼34.8 kph	Luis Ocaña (Esp)￼Bic	Eddy Merckx (Bel)￼Molteni
	Major climbs: La Cratère (780m) Bernard Labourdette (Fra) Bic; Puy de Dôme (1,415m) Luis Ocaña (Esp) Bic			
Stage 9￼Tue 6 Jul	Clermont-Ferrand to￼Saint-Étienne￼121 finishers	153 km￼4h02'18"￼37.9 kph	Walter Godefroot (Bel)￼Peugeot	Eddy Merckx (Bel)￼Molteni
	Major climbs: Col des Fourches (970m) Jean-Pierre Danguillaume (Fra) Peugeot; Col des Pradeaux (1,196m) Jean-Pierre Danguillaume (Fra) Peugeot; Col de la Croix de l'Homme Mort (1,163m) Jean-Pierre Danguillaume (Fra) Peugeot			
Stage 10￼Wed 7 Jul	Saint-Étienne to Grenoble￼114 finishers	188.5 km￼5h24'33"￼34.8 kph	Bernard Thévenet (Fra)￼Peugeot	Joop Zoetemelk (Ned)￼Mars
	Major climbs: Col de la République (1,161m) Cyrille Guimard (Fra) Fagor; Col du Cucheron (1,139m) Désiré Letort (Fra) Bic; Col de Porte (1,326m) Luis Ocaña (Esp) Bic			
Stage 11￼Thu 8 Jul	Grenoble to￼Orcières-Merlette￼106 finishers	134 km￼4h02'49"￼33.1 kph	Luis Ocaña (Esp)￼Bic	Luis Ocaña (Esp)￼Bic
	Major climbs: Côte de Laffrey (900m) Joaquim Agostinho (Por) Hoover; Col du Noyer (1,664m) Luis Ocaña (Esp) Bic; Orcières-Merlette (1,838m) Luis Ocaña (Esp) Bic			

Stage-by-Stage Results for the 1971 Tour de France			Stage Winner	Maillot Jaune
Fri 9 Jul	Rest Day			
Stage 12 Sat 10 Jul	Orcières-Merlette to Marseille 105 finishers	251 km 5h25'28" 46.3 kph	Luciano Armani (Ita) SCIC	Luis Ocaña (Esp) Bic
Stage 13 Sun 11 Jul	Albi (ITT) 105 finishers	16.3 km 22'57" 42.6 kph	Eddy Merckx (Bel) Molteni	Luis Ocaña (Esp) Bic
Stage 14 Mon 12 Jul	Revel to Luchon 99 finishers	214.5 km 6h11'54" 34.6 kph	José Manuel Fuente (Esp) KAS	Eddy Merckx (Bel) Molteni
	Major climbs: Col de Portet d'Aspet (1,069m) José Manuel Fuente (Esp) KAS; Col de Menté (1,349m) José Manuel Fuente (Esp) KAS; Col du Portillon (1,298m) José Manuel Fuente (Esp) KAS			
Stage 15 Tue 13 Jul	Luchon to Superbagnères 99 finishers	19.6 km 47'42" 24.7 kph	José Manuel Fuente (Esp) KAS	Eddy Merckx (Bel) Molteni
	Major climbs: Superbagnères (1,804m) José Manuel Fuente (Esp) KAS			
Stage 16a Wed 14 Jul	Luchon to Gourette (Eaux-Bonnes) 96 finishers	145 km 5h08'36" 28.2 kph	Bernard Labourdette (Fra) Bic	Eddy Merckx (Bel) Molteni
	Major climbs: Col de Peyresourde (1,569m) Lucien Van Impe (Bel) Sonolor; Col d'Aspin (1,489m) Lucien Van Impe (Bel) Sonolor; Col du Tourmalet (2,115m) Lucien Van Impe (Bel) Sonolor; Col d'Aubisque (1,709m) Bernard Labourdette (Fra) Bic			
Stage 16b Wed 14 Jul	Gourette (Eaux-Bonnes) to Pau 96 finishers	57.5 km 1h17'58" 44.2 kph	Herman Van Springel (Bel) Molteni	Eddy Merckx (Bel) Molteni
Stage 17 Thu 15 Jul	Mont-de-Marsan to Bordeaux 95 finishers	188 km 5h32'31" 33.9 kph	Eddy Merckx (Bel) Molteni	Eddy Merckx (Bel) Molteni
Stage 18 Fri 16 Jul	Bordeaux to Poitiers 95 finishers	244 km 6h30'33" 37.5 kph	Jean-Pierre Danguillaume (Fra) Peugeot	Eddy Merckx (Bel) Molteni
Stage 19 Sat 17 Jul	Blois to Versailles 94 finishers	185 km 5h21'06" 34.6 kph	Jan Krekels (Ned) Goudsmit	Eddy Merckx (Bel) Molteni
Stage 20 Sun 18 Jul	Versailles to Paris (La Cipale) (ITT) 94 finishers	53.8 km 1h10'32" 45.8 kph	Eddy Merckx (Bel) Molteni	Eddy Merckx (Bel) Molteni

Prize fund: 470,600 francs (first prize: 20,000 francs)

Final Classification

Place	Rider	Team	Time	Age
1	Eddy Merckx (Bel)	Molteni	3,608 km 96h45'14" 38.084 kph	26
2	Joop Zoetemelk (Ned)	Mars	+ 9'51"	25
3	Lucien Van Impe (Bel)	Sonolor	+ 11'06"	24
4	Bernard Thévenet (Fra)	Peugeot	+ 14'50"	23
5	Joaquim Agostinho (Por)	Hoover	+ 21'00"	28
6	Leif Mortensen (Den)	Bic	+ 21'38"	24
7	Cyrille Guimard (Fra)	Fagor	+ 22'58"	24
8	Bernard Labourdette (Fra)	Bic	+ 30'07"	24
9	Lucien Aimar (Fra)	Sonolor	+ 32'45"	30
10	Vicente López (Esp)	KAS	+ 36'00"	28

Lanterne Rouge

94	Georges Chappe (Fra)	Fagor	+ 3h04'54"	27

Points

	Eddy Merckx (Bel)	Molteni		26

King of the Mountains

	Lucien Van Impe (Bel)	Sonolor		24

Intermediate Sprints

	Pieter Nassen (Bel)	Mars		27

Combination

	Eddy Merckx (Bel)	Molteni		26

Youth

	Joop Zoetemelk (Ned)	Mars		25

Team

		Bic		

Super Combativité

	Luis Ocaña	Bic		26

1972: The Legend of Cyrille Guimard, Part One

When Eddy Merckx attacked Luis Ocaña on the road to Marseille that day in the 1971 Tour, it had been an awful lot of effort for very little time gain. Two-hundred-fifty kilometres of flat-out riding for what, two minutes slashed off a nine-minute deficit? It was one of the most brilliant stages the Tour had seen, and yet Merckx was not happy. And one reason he was not happy was that other teams had helped Ocaña and his Bic team-mates.

One man who came to Ocaña's aid that day was Fagor-Mercier's Cyrille Guimard. He said he did it to protect his own position in the points competition. Merckx wasn't so sure. And so, later in the Tour, he made it a point to take the green jersey from the Frenchman.

The two were separated by two years in age – Merckx the senior – and a vast gulf in their *palmarès*. Guimard had come up through the Tour de l'Avenir, where he won a couple of stages in 1967, and his biggest wins had come at the 1970 Tour, where he took a stage, and the following year's Vuelta, where he took two stages and the points and combined classifications.

At the 1972 Tour, Merckx – gunning for his second Giro/Tour double, having just won the Italian tour – took the yellow jersey in the prologue and was relieved of it the next day by Guimard, who won the stage into Saint-Brieuc. After the Merlin Plage team time trial (in the second part of stage three) Merckx was back in yellow, only for Guimard to win the next day and retake the jersey, which he was then able to hold until the race reached the Pyrenees, even the individual time trial in Bordeaux not ending his time in yellow.

That little tussle between the Belgian and the Frenchman in the opening week of the race hid some of the real damage done by

Merckx to his key rivals. On the stage after the Merlin Plage team time trial, taking the riders to Royan, across the Vendée, all bar Luis Ocaña had been eliminated, Roger Pingeon (Peugeot), Raymond Poulidor (GAN), Lucien Van Impe (Sonolor) and Joop Zoetemelk (Beaulieu – Flandria) all having been forced to concede several minutes.

Going into the Pyrenees, then, Guimard was in yellow with Merckx second at 11 seconds and Ocaña fourth at 1'02". Coming out, the Belgian was in command, with Guimard second at 2'33", Ocaña having failed to mount a serious challenge in the high mountains and slipped to 2'48", though now up to third. A crash on the descent of the Aubisque had helped derail the Spaniard's challenge.

Merckx then man-marked the Spaniard through to the Alps, not giving his opponent any ground and padding his advantage, to 3'02" over Ocaña and 4'05" over Guimard, who had slipped to third. On the road to Briançon, crossing the Izoard, Merckx rode like a champion, crossing the Casse Déserte alone and taking the stage win. Ocaña was by now visibly ailing, with signs of a chest infection. His Tour was as good as over, and he duly climbed off and went home two stages later.

Merckx's double was secured, as was his fourth Tour title. It had taken Philippe Thys five attempts to win his three Tours. Louison Bobet, had taken eight. Jacques Anquetil did it in five, like Thys. Eddy Merckx did it in three – then a year later equalled Anquetil's record of four Tours on the trot.

But, while the race for yellow was over, the race for green was still on-going, and in that Merckx had a challenger, Guimard. The Belgian had doubled yellow and green in two of his three previous victories (Walter Godefroot taking the jersey in 1970) and the Frenchman looked like he was going to deny the Belgian his third green-and-yellow double.

But Guimard was in trouble. He was by now riding with injured knees – tendonitis, some claimed from having pushed too big a gear – and was receiving daily injections of painkillers from his GAN/Mercier medic Bernard Sainz, just to stay in the race. Two days away from Paris the pain was too much and, still second overall and wearing the green jersey, Guimard was forced to climb off in tears and go home.

Knowing the fans were in mixed minds about Merckx – some liked him, many disliked the way he was throttling the life out of the Tour – Jacques Goddet and Félix Lévitan engineered a show of kindness in La Cipale, Merckx presenting Guimard with the green jersey he had denied him in 1971 (because of the help given to Ocaña) and which injury had now just stopped the Frenchman from winning. For the fans, a good loser was better than a brilliant winner.

Stage-by-Stage Results for the 1972 Tour de France			Stage Winner	Maillot Jaune
Prologue Sat 1 Jul	Angers (ITT) 131 finishers	7.2 km 8'51" 48.8 kph	Eddy Merckx (Bel) Molteni	Eddy Merckx (Bel) Molteni
Stage 1 Sun 2 Jul	Angers to Saint-Brieuc 131 finishers	235.5 km 6h00'31" 39.2 kph	Cyrille Guimard (Fra) GAN	Cyrille Guimard (Fra) GAN
Stage 2 Mon 3 Jul	Saint-Brieuc to La Baule 131 finishers	206.5 km 5h09'43" 40 kph	Rik van Linden (Bel) De Gribaldy	Cyrille Guimard (Fra) GAN
Stage 3a Tue 4 Jul	Pornichet to Saint-Jean-de-Monts 130 finishers	161 km 3h56'33" 40.8 kph	Ercole Gualazzini (Ger) Lotto	Cyrille Guimard (Fra) GAN
Stage 3b Tue 4 Jul	Circuit de Merlin-Plage (TTT) 129 finishers	16.2 km 19'20" 50.3 kph	Molteni	Eddy Merckx (Bel) Molteni
Stage 4 Wed 5 Jul	Merlin-Plage to Royan 128 finishers	236 km 5h22'43" 43.9 kph	Cyrille Guimard (Fra) GAN	Cyrille Guimard (Fra) GAN
Stage 5a Thu 6 Jul	Royan to Bordeaux 128 finishers	133.5 km 2h59'33" 44.6 kph	Walter Godefroot (Bel) Peugeot	Cyrille Guimard (Fra) GAN
Stage 5b Thu 6 Jul	Bordeaux (Circuit du Lac) (ITT) 127 finishers	12.7 km 16'05" 47.4 kph	Eddy Merckx (Bel) Molteni	Cyrille Guimard (Fra) GAN
Stage 6 Fri 7 Jul	Bordeaux to Bayonne 127 finishers	205 km 5h44'10" 35.7 kph	Leo Duyndam (Ned) Goudsmit	Cyrille Guimard (Fra) GAN
Sat 8 Jul	Rest Day			

Stage-by-Stage Results for the 1972 Tour de France			Stage Winner	Maillot Jaune
Stage 7 Sun 9 Jul	Bayonne to Pau 118 finishers	220.5 km 6h02'19" 36.5 kph	Yves Hézard (Fra) Sonolor	Cyrille Guimard (Fra) GAN
	Major climbs: Col d'Aubisque (1,709m) Wilfried David (Bel) Peugeot			
Stage 8 Mon 10 Jul	Pau to Luchon 115 finishers	163.5 km 4h54'48" 33.3 kph	Eddy Merckx (Bel) Molteni	Eddy Merckx (Bel) Molteni
	Major climbs: Col du Tourmalet (2,115m) Roger Swerts (Bel) Molteni; Col d'Aspin (1,489m) Roger Swerts (Bel) Molteni; Col de Peyresourde (1,569m) Lucien Van Impe (Bel) Sonolor			
Stage 9 Tue 11 Jul	Luchon to Colomiers 109 finishers	179 km 4h43'01" 37.9 kph	Jozef Huysmans (Bel) Molteni	Eddy Merckx (Bel) Molteni
	Major climbs: Col des Ares (797m) Christian Raymond (Fra) Peugeot; Col de Portet d'Aspet (1,069m) Christian Raymond (Fra) Peugeot			
Stage 10 Wed 12 Jul	Castres to La Grande-Motte 108 finishers	210 km 6h08'19" 34.2 kph	Willy Teirlinck (Bel) Sonolor	Eddy Merckx (Bel) Molteni
	Major climbs: Col de la Fontasse (537m) Mathieu Pustjens (Ned) Sonolor; Col des Treize Vents (600m) Lucien Van Impe (Bel) Sonolor			
Stage 11 Thu 13 Jul	Carnon-Plage to Mont Ventoux 105 finishers	207 km 7h13'45" 28.6 kph	Bernard Thévenet (Fra) Peugeot	Eddy Merckx (Bel) Molteni
	Major climbs: Mont Ventoux (1,909m) Bernard Thévenet (Fra) Peugeot			
Stage 12 Fri 14 Jul	Carpentras to Orcières-Merlette 101 finishers	192 km 5h38'33" 34 kph	Lucien Van Impe (Bel) Sonolor	Eddy Merckx (Bel) Molteni
	Major climbs: Col de Perty (1,303m) Lucien Van Impe (Bel) Sonolor; Col de Manse (1,268m) Joaquim Agostinho (Por) de Gribaldy; Orcières-Merlette (1,838m) Lucien Van Impe (Bel) Sonolor			
Sat 15 Jul	Rest Day			
Stage 13 Sun 16 Jul	Orcières-Merlette to Briançon 96 finishers	201 km 6h26'12" 31.2 kph	Eddy Merckx (Bel) Molteni	Eddy Merckx (Bel) Molteni
	Major climbs: Col de Vars (2,110m) Raymond Delisle (Fra) Peugeot; Col d'Izoard (2,360m) Eddy Merckx (Bel) Molteni			
Stage 14a Mon 17 Jul	Briançon to Valloire (Galibier) 96 finishers	51 km 1h32'02" 33.2 kph	Eddy Merckx (Bel) Molteni	Eddy Merckx (Bel) Molteni
	Major climbs: Col du Lautaret (2,058m) Joaquim Agostinho (Por) de Gribaldy; Col du Galibier (2,556m) Joop Zoetemelk (Ned) Beaulieu			

Stage-by-Stage Results for the 1972 Tour de France			Stage Winner	Maillot Jaune
Stage 14b Mon 17 Jul	Valloire to Aix-les-Bains 94 finishers	151 km 4h48'53" 31.4 kph	Cyrille Guimard (Fra) GAN	Eddy Merckx (Bel) Molteni
	Major climbs: Col du Télégraphe (1,566m) Pietro Campagnari (Ita) Salvarani; Col du Grand Cucheron (1,188m) Eddy Merckx (Bel) Molteni; Col du Granier (1,134m) Lucien Van Impe (Bel) Sonolor			
Stage 15 Tue 18 Jul	Aix-les-Bains to Le Revard 91 finishers	28 km 1h09'49" 24.1 kph	Cyrille Guimard (Fra) GAN	Eddy Merckx (Bel) Molteni
	Major climbs: Mont Revard (1,537m) Cyrille Guimard (Fra) GAN			
Stage 16 Wed 19 Jul	Aix-les-Bains to Pontarlier 89 finishers	198.5 km 6h08'17" 32.3 kph	Willy Teirlinck (Bel) Sonolor	Eddy Merckx (Bel) Molteni
	Major climbs: Col de la Faucille (1,323m) Lucien Van Impe (Bel) Sonolor			
Stage 17 Thu 20 Jul	Pontarlier to Belfort (Ballon d'Alsace) 89 finishers	213 km 5h59'08" 35.6 kph	Bernard Thévenet (Fra) Peugeot	Eddy Merckx (Bel) Molteni
	Major climbs: Col de Schirm (600m) Joaquim Agostinho (Por) de Gribaldy; Col du Hundsruck (752m) Joaquim Agostinho (Por) de Gribaldy; Col d'Oderen (884m) Joaquim Agostinho (Por) de Gribaldy; Ballon d'Alsace (1,178m) Bernard Thévenet (Fra) Peugeot			
Stage 18 Fri 21 Jul	Belfort to Auxerre 88 finishers	257.5 km 7h38'21" 33.7 kph	Rini Wagtmans (Ned) Goudsmit	Eddy Merckx (Bel) Molteni
Stage 19 Sat 22 Jul	Auxerre to Versailles 88 finishers	230 km 6h41'55" 34.3 kph	Joseph Bruyère (Bel) Molteni	Eddy Merckx (Bel) Molteni
Stage 20a Sun 23 Jul	Versailles (ITT) 88 finishers	42 km 55'27" 45.4 kph	Eddy Merckx (Bel) Molteni	Eddy Merckx (Bel) Molteni
Stage 20b Sun 23 Jul	Versailles to Paris (La Cipale) 88 finishers	89 km 2h32'14" 35.1 kph	Willy Teirlinck (Bel) Sonolor	Eddy Merckx (Bel) Molteni

Prize fund: 552,000 francs (first prize: 20,000 francs)

Final Classification

Place	Rider	Team	Time	Age
1	Eddy Merckx (Bel)	Molteni	3,846 km 108h17'18" 35.514 kph	27
2	Felice Gimondi (Ita)	Salvarani	+ 10'41"	29
3	Raymond Poulidor (Fra)	GAN	+ 11'34"	36
4	Lucien Van Impe (Bel)	Sonolor	+ 16'45"	25
5	Joop Zoetemelk (Ned)	Beaulieu	+ 19'09"	26
6	Mariano Martínez (Fra)	De Gribaldy	+ 21'31"	23
7	Yves Hézard (Fra)	Sonolor	+ 21'52"	23
8	Joaquim Agostinho (Por)	De Gribaldy	+ 34'16"	29
9	Bernard Thévenet (Fra)	Peugeot	+ 37'11"	24
10	Edouard Janssens (Bel)	De Gribaldy	+ 42'33"	26

Lanterne Rouge

88	Alain Bellouis (Fra)	Gitane	+ 4h03'33"	24

Points

	Eddy Merckx (Bel)	Molteni		27

King of the Mountains

	Lucien Van Impe (Bel)	Sonolor		25

Intermediate Sprints

	Willy Teirlinck (Bel)	Sonolor		24

Combination

	Eddy Merckx	Molteni		27

Team

		GAN		

Super Combativité

	Cyrille Guimard (Fra)	GAN		25

1973: Ocaña

With four Tour de France wins on his *palmarès*, Eddy Merckx set about adding new achievements to his roll of honour. In the autumn of 1972, following his Tour win, he added the Hour record, joining a list that included Tour champions Lucien Petit-Breton, Fausto Coppi and Jacques Anquetil, as well as the Father of the Tour himself, Henri Desgrange. The following spring Merckx succeeded in equalling Anquetil's feat of doubling the Vuelta a España and the Giro d'Italia (making him the reigning champion in all three Grand Tours (a new first) and only the third to have won all three Grand Tours, Felice Gimondi being the other). The impossible treble – all three Grand Tours in the one season – was a possibility but even the Cannibal resisted the lure of that challenge and opted to sit out the *grande boucle*.

Lucien Aimar (De Kova) was the only previous Tour winner to start the sixtieth Tour. He was joined by the Tour's great nearly-man, Raymond Poulidor (GAN/Mercier), who by now had racked up five visits to the Tour's podium (third once, second four times) without ever wearing the *maillot jaune*. And then there was Joop Zoetemelk (Gitane), second in 1970 and 1971, fifth in 1972. There were also Cyrille Guimard (GAN/Mercier) and Bernard Thévenet (Peugeot), both seen as rising stars. But it was the man who had challenged Merckx hardest in 1972 who was the out-and-out pre-race favourite, the only man who had come close to making Merckx look human at the Tour, Luis Ocaña (Bic).

As early as the third stage, taking the riders over some of the same roads raced in Paris-Roubaix, the wheat was being separated from the chaff, with Ocaña and Guimard getting away in a break that the other contenders missed. Guimard took the stage, and Ocaña's chief rivals lost two and a half minutes. The Frenchman's challenge ended on the sixth stage, with his knees again troubling him, and he lost 20 minutes as the race tackled its first major climb, the Côte des Rousses.

After a rest day, Ocaña stamped his authority on the race as the riders tackled two stages in one day, 80-odd kilometres from Divonne-les-Bains to Gaillard, followed by another 150 kilometres from Gaillard to Méribel-les-Allues. On Mont Salève in the first part Ocaña rode away from the *peloton* and soloed to victory and the race lead. Zoetemelk looked like being the Spaniard's closest challenger, just under three minutes off yellow. But the next day that changed, and a new challenger briefly emerged, another Spaniard, José Manuel Fuente (KAS).

Fuente launched his attack on the Télégraphe, shortly after the race had crossed the Madeleine, and his compatriot Ocaña was the only rider capable of following his wheel. Over the Galibier and the Izoard the two rode together, until 30 kilometres from the finish Fuente punctured and Ocaña rode on alone up the day's final climb, Les Orres, where he took the stage win with just under a minute's lead on Fuente. Zoetemelk had lost more than 20 minutes, and Fuente was now in second place, 9'08" off yellow.

Ocaña added more time in the individual time trial, 28.3 kilometres from Perpignan to Thuir, pushing Fuente back to 10'47". When the race entered the Pyrenees, Fuente attacked on the same Col de Menté where he had crossed while winning a stage in 1971 and where Ocaña crashed out of the Tour, but only put 20 seconds into Ocaña. Zoetemelk went next, but the Spaniard was quickly across to him, and the two began to put some daylight between themselves and the chasers behind. On the Portet d'Aspet the Dutchman was dropped and Ocaña once again soloed to a stage win, his fourth of the race, with a 15-second gap back to Zoetemelk and Fuente losing more than four minutes. Fuente maintained the pressure the next day, but there was just no getting away from Ocaña, who was ruling the race with an iron fist – ruling it the way Merckx had done.

Ocaña put a ribbon round his Tour victory with another two stage wins, bringing his tally to six, and Thévenet usurped Fuente's second place, relegating him to the bottom step of the podium. The fans had got what they wanted, a win for someone other than Merckx, and they cheered Ocaña. Even though his victory was as dominating as any of the Belgian's.

Stage-by-Stage Results for the 1973 Tour de France			Stage Winner	Maillot Jaune
Prologue Sat 30 Jun	Scheveningen (ITT) 132 finishers	7.1 km 9'58" 42.7 kph	Joop Zoetemelk (Ned) Gitane	Joop Zoetemelk (Ned) Gitane
Stage 1a Sun 1 Jul	Scheveningen to Rotterdam 132 finishers	84 km 1h47'44" 46.8 kph	Willy Teirlinck (Bel) Sonolor	Willy Teirlinck (Bel) Sonolor
Stage 1b Sun 1 Jul	Rotterdam to Saint-Niklaas 132 finishers	137.5 km 3h33'41" 38.6 kph	Jose Catieau (Fra) Bic	Herman Van Springel (Bel) Rokado
Stage 2a Mon 2 Jul	Sint-Niklaas (TTT) 132 finishers	12.4 km 14'29" 51.4 kph	Watney	Herman Van Springel (Bel) Rokado
Stage 2b Mon 2 Jul	Sint-Niklaas to Roubaix 130 finishers	138 km 3h34'49" 38.5 kph	Eddy Verstraeten (Bel) Watney	Herman Van Springel (Bel) Rokado
Stage 3 Tue 3 Jul	Roubaix to Reims 127 finishers	226 km 5h41'54" 39.7 kph	Cyrille Guimard (Fra) GAN	José Catieau (Fra) Bic
Stage 4 Wed 4 Jul	Reims to Nancy 126 finishers	214 km 6h09'42" 34.7 kph	Joop Zoetemelk (Ned) Gitane	José Catieau (Fra) Bic
Stage 5 Thu 5 Jul	Nancy to Mulhouse 123 finishers	188 km 5h12'19" 36.1 kph	Walter Godefroot (Bel) Carpenter	José Catieau (Fra) Bic
	Major climbs: Col de la Schlucht (1,139m) Charly Grosskost (Fra) GAN; Col du Grand Ballon (1,343m) Charly Grosskost (Fra) GAN; Siberloch (904m) Charly Grosskost (Fra) GAN			
Stage 6 Fri 6 Jul	Belfort to Divonne-les-Bains 123 finishers	244.5 km 6h53'02" 35.5 kph	Jean-Pierre Danguillaume (Fra) Peugeot	José Catieau (Fra) Bic
	Major climbs: Côte des Rousses (1,140m) Vicente López (Esp) KAS			
Sat 7 Jul	Rest Day			

Stage-by-Stage Results for the 1973 Tour de France			Stage Winner	Maillot Jaune
Stage 7a Sun 8 Jul	Divonne-les-Bains to Gaillard 123 finishers	86.5 km 2h20'39" 36.9 kph	Luis Ocaña (Esp) Bic	Luis Ocaña (Esp) Bic
	Major climbs: Mont Salève (1,283m) Luis Ocaña (Esp) Bic			
Stage 7b Sun 8 Jul	Gaillard to Méribel-les-Allues 123 finishers	150.5 km 4h44'30" 31.7 kph	Bernard Thévenet (Fra) Peugeot	Luis Ocaña (Esp) Bic
	Major climbs: Col de Tamié (907m) Pedro Torres (Esp) La Casera; Méribel-les-Allues (1,750m) Bernard Thévenet (Fra) Peugeot			
Stage 8 Mon 9 Jul	Moutiers to Les Orres 107 finishers	237.5 km 7h55'47" 30 kph	Luis Ocaña (Esp) Bic	Luis Ocaña (Esp) Bic
	Major climbs: Col de la Madeleine (2,000m) Jean-Pierre Danguillaume (Fra) Peugeot; Col du Galibier (2,556m) Luis Ocaña (Esp) Bic; Col d'Izoard (2,360m) José Manuel Fuente (Esp) KAS; Les Orres (1,496m) Luis Ocaña (Esp) Bic			
Stage 9 Tue 10 Jul	Embrun to Nice 99 finishers	234.5 km 8h20'29" 28.1 kph	Vicente López (Esp) KAS	Luis Ocaña (Esp) Bic
	Major climbs: Col de la Cayolle (2,326m) Vicente López (Esp) KAS; Col de Valberg (1,669m) Pedro Torres (Esp) La Casera; Col de Saint-Martin (1,500m) Pedro Torres (Esp) La Casera; Col de Turini (1,607m) Vicente López (Esp) KAS; Côte de Châteauneuf-de-Contes (628m) Vicente López (Esp) KAS			
Stage 10 Wed 11 Jul	Nice to Aubagne 99 finishers	222.5 km 7h18'34" 30.4 kph	Michael Wright (GBr) Gitane	Luis Ocaña (Esp) Bic
	Major climbs: Col de Saint-Arnoux (643m) Pedro Torres (Esp) La Casera; Col de l'Espigoulier (728m) Michael Wright (GBr) Gitane			
Stage 11 Thu 12 Jul	Montpellier to Argelès-sur-Mer 96 finishers	238 km 7h45'21" 30.7 kph	Barry Hoban (GBr) GAN	Luis Ocaña (Esp) Bic
Stage 12a Fri 13 Jul	Perpignan to Thuir (ITT) 96 finishers	28.3 km 37'24" 45.4 kph	Luis Ocaña (Esp) Bic	Luis Ocaña (Esp) Bic
Stage 12b Fri 13 Jul	Thuir to Pyrenees 2000 96 finishers	76 km 2h35'02" 29.4 kph	Lucien Van Impe (Bel) Sonolor	Luis Ocaña (Esp) Bic
	Major climbs: Font-Romeu (1,800m) Lucien Van Impe (Bel) Sonolor			
Sat 14 Jul	Rest Day			

Stage-by-Stage Results for the 1973 Tour de France			Stage Winner	Maillot Jaune
Stage 13 Sun 15 Jul	Bourg-Madame to Luchon 92 finishers	235 km 6h51'50" 34.2 kph	Luis Ocaña (Esp) Bic	Luis Ocaña (Esp) Bic
	Major climbs: Col du Puymorens (1,915m) Pedro Torres (Esp) La Casera; Col de Portet d'Aspet (1,069m) Raymond Martin (Esp) Gitane; Col de Menté (1,349m) José Manuel Fuente (Esp) KAS; Col du Portillon (1,298m) Luis Ocaña (Esp) Bic			
Stage 14 Mon 16 Jul	Luchon to Pau 89 finishers	227.5 km 7h10'41" 31.7 kph	Pedro Torres (Esp) La Casera	Luis Ocaña (Esp) Bic
	Major climbs: Col d'Aspin (1,489m) José Manuel Fuente (Esp) KAS; Col du Tourmalet (2,115m) Bernard Thévenet (Fra) Peugeot; Col du Soulor (1,474m) Pedro Torres (Esp) La Casera			
Stage 15 Tue 17 Jul	Pau to Fleurance 88 finishers	137 km 3h44'34" 36.6 kph	Wilfried David (Bel) Carpenter	Luis Ocaña (Esp) Bic
Stage 16a Wed 18 Jul	Fleurance to Bordeaux 88 finishers	210 km 6h23'50" 32.8 kph	Walter Godefroot (Bel) Carpenter	Luis Ocaña (Esp) Bic
Stage 16b Wed 18 Jul	Bordeaux (Circuit du Lac) (ITT) 88 finishers	12.4 km 16'23" 45.4 kph	Joaquim Agostinho (Por) Bic	Luis Ocaña (Esp) Bic
Stage 17 Thu 19 Jul	Sainte-Foy-la-Grande to Brive-la-Gaillarde 88 finishers	248 km 6h34'45" 37.7 kph	Claude Tollet (Fra) Sonolor	Luis Ocaña (Esp) Bic
Stage 18 Fri 20 Jul	Brive to Puy de Dôme 87 finishers	216.5 km 6h36'21" 32.8 kph	Luis Ocaña (Esp) Bic	Luis Ocaña (Esp) Bic
	Major climbs: Puy de Dôme (1,415m) Luis Ocaña (Esp) Bic			
Stage 19 Sat 21 Jul	Bourges to Versailles 87 finishers	233.5 km 6h59'28" 33.4 kph	Barry Hoban (GBr) GAN	Luis Ocaña (Esp) Bic
Stage 20a Sun 22 Jul	Versailles (ITT) 87 finishers	16 km 20'57" 45.8 kph	Luis Ocaña (Esp) Bic	Luis Ocaña (Esp) Bic
Stage 20b Sun 22 Jul	Versailles to Paris (La Cipale) 87 finishers	89 km 2h21'37" 37.7 kph	Bernard Thévenet (Fra) Peugeot	Luis Ocaña (Esp) Bic

Prize fund: 660,000 francs (first prize: 20,000 francs)

Final Classification

Place	Rider	Team	Time	Age
1	Luis Ocaña (Esp)	Bic	4,090 km 122h25'34" 33.407 kph	28
2	Bernard Thévenet (Fra)	Peugeot	+ 15'51"	25
3	José Manuel Fuente (Esp)	KAS	+ 17'15"	27
4	Joop Zoetemelk (Ned)	Gitane	+ 26'22"	27
5	Lucien Van Impe (Bel)	Sonolor	+ 30'20"	26
6	Herman Van Springel (Bel)	Rokado	+ 32'01"	29
7	Michel Périn (Fra)	GAN	+ 33'02"	26
8	Joaquim Agostinho (Por)	Bic	+ 35'51"	30
9	Vicente López (Esp)	KAS	+ 36'18"	30
10	Régis Ovion (Fra)	Peugeot	+ 36'59"	24
Lanterne Rouge				
87	Jacques Hochart (Fra)	De Kova	+ 4h51'09"	24
Points				
	Herman Van Springel (Bel)	Rokado		29
King of the Mountains				
	Pedro Torres (Esp)	La Casera		24
Intermediate Sprints				
	Marc Demeyer (Bel)	Carpenter		23
Combination				
	Joop Zoetemelk (Ned)	Gitane		27
Team				
		Bic		
Team (Points)				
		GAN		
Super Combativité				
	Luis Ocaña (Esp)	Bic		28

1974: Hands Across the Water

When the Tour de France returned from its wartime hiatus in 1947, its organisation was the responsibility of the La Société du Parc des Princes. With the Parc gone, the Tour was passed into new ownership and in 1973 was put in the charge of La Société d'Exploitation du Tour de France. And exploitation was very much on Félix Lévitan's mind. While some may have felt that Eddy Merckx's dominance was strangling the life out of the Tour, the Tour was actually doing quite well financially, with towns, cities and regions still queuing up to host the event. For beyond the sporting aspect of the race the Tour was also a part of the French social fabric, people watched it on TV or on the roadside not just because they were fans of the sport and cared who won: they did it because it was the Tour de France.

For the 1974 Tour, Lévitan was able to squeeze 1,800,000 francs out of Brittany's market gardeners and vegetable growers in return for granting them the Tour's *grand départ* (this at a time when the Tour's total prize fund was less than half that, 802,650 francs). In return, Brittany was granted the prologue and two stages while a third, up-and-down a dual-carriageway in Plymouth, across the Channel in England, was paid for by the operators of a ferry service between Roscoff and Plymouth. The two transfers required for the British stage didn't please the riders greatly and the first four days of the race were far from a sporting success (the wags at the *Daily Mirror* correctly summed it up with the headline 'Can Forty Million Frenchmen Be Wrong?') but financially, this was just the sort of thing the Tour needed.

On the sporting side of things, defending champion Luis Ocaña was ruled out of participation following a crash earlier in the season at the Tour de l'Aude, as was Joop Zoetemelk, who had suffered a horrific crash during the Midi-Libre stage race. Present, though, was Eddy Merckx who decided to go for this third Giro/Tour double. Less than three weeks after he'd won the *corsa rosa* he was taking the start in the *grande boucle*. And donning the yellow jersey after the prologue.

That lead was then passed to team-mate Jos Bruyère, briefly back to Merckx and then on to Bic's Garben Karstens after the fifth stage. That Karstens was still in contention at that stage owed a little to luck: he had failed to present himself for a doping control after the second stage and so was handed a 10-minute time penalty. But the next day the commissaires decided to give the guy the benefit of the doubt and accept his argument that it was a simple mistake and so overturned his punishment. The policing of doping at the Tour – and at other races – was now so commonplace that such events raised very little interest. The days when doping scandals could bring the race low already seemed to be in the past.

Karstens briefly relinquished the race lead to Brooklyn's Patrick Sercu before taking it back. At this point he was tied on time with Merckx, and so the rule books had to be consulted: was it to be multiple *maillots jaune* as it had in the past or was there a way to separate the two riders? Eventually it was decided that their points tallies should be the decider, and Karstens won out. For one more day. For on the seventh stage Merckx took control of the yellow jersey. In winning the seventh stage – Mons to Chalons-sur-Marne – the Belgian took his tally of stage wins above the 25 recorded by André Leducq over the course of his Tour career in the 1920s and 1930s.

Out of the first phase of mountains, down through the Alps and over the easy side of the Ventoux, Merckx held his lead, exiting with a two-minute advantage over his nearest challenger, Gonzalo Aja (KAS). On the second of four days in the Pyrenees, that nearly-great of the Tour, Raymond Poulidor (GAN) – now 38 years old – took a stage win following an attack that actually dropped the yellow jersey and took the better part of two minutes out of him. But, even with that, the Frenchman was still six minutes behind Merckx, down in fifth place overall.

Raymond Poulidor, Eddy Merckx and Vicente López Carril do a lap of honour in La Cipale at the end of the 1974 Tour.

Many things have disrupted the Tour de France: riders, fans, even journalists. The amount of media coverage the race generated also attracted unions and trade associations, who protested as the Tour passed. Since 1967 the Basque terrorist group ETA had turned their eyes to the Spanish Tour, the Vuelta a España, starting with tack attacks and moving on to high explosives (a bomb went off during the 1968 race). In 1974 the Basque separatists turned their attention to the Tour, threatening disruption. Fortunately for all, that never materialised, but it heightened the tension of the race's passage through the mountains on France's southern border.

With that tension in the background, the race was finally – though only briefly – serving up excitement, with Poulidor again going on the attack and again putting time into Merckx, this time another minute.

But it was all too little and too late and, really, the riders behind Merckx were just scrapping over who would be on the podium alongside the Belgian.

On the twenty-first stage – two races in one day, a road stage followed by an individual time trial – with the yellow jersey sown up Merckx attacked in the first part when wiser heads would have rested and prepared themselves for the time trial. The Belgian took his seventh stage win of the race. For the man who seemed to be able to break records at will, the record of eight stages won by Charles Pélissier at the 1930 Tour (and equalled by Merckx in 1970) was again in his sights. Two stages remained: a time trial around Orléans and then the finale to Paris and the victory laps on La Cipale's track.

In that time trial, though, Merckx was usurped by Michel Pollentier (Carpenter). Breaking Pélissier's record was now impossible. But Merckx could still equal it again, and that he did by taking the sprint in La Cipale. Even so, that took the intervention of the commissaires, for Patrick Sercu (Brooklyn) had actually crossed the line first. He, though, was relegated to third, having moved off his line in the sprint.

Stage-by-Stage Results for the 1974 Tour de France			Stage Winner	Maillot Jaune
Prologue Thu 27 Jun	Brest (ITT) 129 finishers	7.1 km 8'54" 47.9 kph	Eddy Merckx (Bel) Molteni	Eddy Merckx (Bel) Molteni
Stage 1 Fri 28 Jun	Brest to Saint-Pol-de-Léon 129 finishers	144 km 3h25'30" 42 kph	Ercole Gualazzini (Ita) Brooklyn	Joseph Bruyère (Bel) Molteni
Stage 2 Sat 29 Jun	Plymouth to Plymouth 129 finishers	163.7 km 3h53'44" 42 kph	Henk Poppe (Ned) Frisol	Joseph Bruyère (Bel) Molteni
Stage 3 Sun 30 Jun	Morlaix to Saint-Malo 129 finishers	190 km 4h45'57" 39.9 kph	Patrick Sercu (Bel) Brooklyn	Joseph Bruyère (Bel) Molteni
Stage 4 Mon 1 Jul	Saint-Malo to Caen 128 finishers	184.5 km 4h48'54" 38.3 kph	Patrick Sercu (Bel) Brooklyn	Eddy Merckx (Bel) Molteni
Stage 5 Tue 2 Jul	Caen to Dieppe 127 finishers	165 km 4h15'34" 38.7 kph	Ronald de Witte (Bel) Carpenter	Gerben Karstens (Ned) Bic
Stage 6a Wed 3 Jul	Dieppe to Harelbeke 127 finishers	239 km 6h18'56" 37.8 kph	Jean-Luc Molinéris (Fra) Bic	Patrick Sercu (Bel) Brooklyn
Stage 6b Wed 3 Jul	Harelbeke (TTT) 127 finishers	9 km 10'54" 49.5 kph	Molteni	Gerben Karstens (Ned) Bic
Stage 7 Thu 4 Jul	Mons to Chalons-sur-Marne 127 finishers	221.5 km 6h38'37" 33.3 kph	Eddy Merckx (Bel) Molteni	Eddy Merckx (Bel) Molteni
Stage 8a Fri 5 Jul	Chalons-sur-Marne to Chaumont 127 finishers	136 km 3h44'08" 36.4 kph	Cyrille Guimard (Fra) Flandria	Eddy Merckx (Bel) Molteni
Stage 8b Fri 5 Jul	Chaumont to Besançon 127 finishers	152 km 4h25'04" 34.4 kph	Patrick Sercu (Bel) Brooklyn	Eddy Merckx (Bel) Molteni
Stage 9 Sat 6 Jul	Besançon to Gaillard 123 finishers	241 km 7h09'58" 33.6 kph	Eddy Merckx (Bel) Molteni	Eddy Merckx (Bel) Molteni
	Major climbs: Côte des Rousses (1,140m) Andrés Oliva (Esp) La Casera; Mont Salève (1,283m) Gonzalo Aja (Esp) KAS			
Stage 10 Sun 7 Jul	Gaillard to Aix-les-Bains 122 finishers	131.5 km 3h46'44" 34.8 kph	Eddy Merckx (Bel) Molteni	Eddy Merckx (Bel) Molteni
	Major climbs: Mont du Chat (1,504m) Gonzalo Aja (Esp) KAS			
Mon 8 Jul	Rest Day			
Stage 11 Tue 9 Jul	Aix-les-Bains to Serre Chevalier 115 finishers	199 km 6h55'36" 28.7 kph	Vicente López (Esp) KAS	Eddy Merckx (Bel) Molteni
	Major climbs: La Cochette (505m) Domingo Perurena (Esp) KAS; Col du Grand Cucheron (1,188m) Domingo Perurena (Esp) KAS; Col du Télégraphe (1,566m) Herman Van Springel (Bel) Mic; Col du Galibier (2,556m) Vicente López (Esp) KAS			

Stage-by-Stage Results for the 1974 Tour de France			Stage Winner	Maillot Jaune
Stage 12 Wed 10 Jul	Savines-le-Lac to Orange 113 finishers	231 km 7h15'12" 31.8 kph	Jozef Spruyt (Bel) Molteni	Eddy Merckx (Bel) Molteni
	Major climbs: Mont Ventoux (1,909m) Gonzalo Aja (Esp) KAS			
Stage 13 Thu 11 Jul	Avignon to Montpellier 113 finishers	126 km 3h15'42" 38.6 kph	Barry Hoban (GBr) GAN	Eddy Merckx (Bel) Molteni
Stage 14 Fri 12 Jul	Lodève to Colomiers 111 finishers	248.5 km 7h12'50" 34.4 kph	Jean-Pierre Genêt (Fra) GAN	Eddy Merckx (Bel) Molteni
	Major climbs: Col de la Baraque de Bral (610m) Lucien Van Impe (Bel) Sonolor			
Sat 13 Jul	Rest Day			
Stage 15 Sun 14 Jul	Colomiers to Seo de Urgel 110 finishers	225 km 6h42'29" 33.5 kph	Eddy Merckx (Bel) Molteni	Eddy Merckx (Bel) Molteni
	Major climbs: Port d'Envalira (2,407m) Raymond Delisle (Fra) Peugeot			
Stage 16 Mon 15 Jul	Seo de Urgel to Saint-Lary-Soulan 108 finishers	209 km 7h53'29" 26.5 kph	Raymond Poulidor (Fra) GAN	Eddy Merckx (Bel) Molteni
	Major climbs: Puerta del Canto (1,725m) Domingo Perurena (Esp) KAS; Puerto de Bonaiga (2,072m) Domingo Perurena (Esp) KAS; Col du Portillon (1,298m) Domingo Perurena (Esp) KAS; Col de Peyresourde (1,569m) Vicente López (Esp) KAS; Pla d'Adet (2,680m) Raymond Poulidor (Fra) GAN			
Stage 17 Tue 16 Jul	Saint-Lary-Soulan to La Mongie 107 finishers	119 km 3h58'44" 29.9 kph	Jean-Pierre Danguillaume (Fra) Peugeot	Eddy Merckx (Bel) Molteni
	Major climbs: Col d'Aspin (1,489m) Jean-Pierre Danguillaume (Fra) Peugeot; La Mongie (1,715m) Jean-Pierre Danguillaume (Fra) Peugeot			
Stage 18 Wed 17 Jul	Bagnères-de-Bigorre to Pau 107 finishers	141.5 km 4h19'20" 32.7 kph	Jean-Pierre Danguillaume (Fra) Peugeot	Eddy Merckx (Bel) Molteni
	Major climbs: Col du Tourmalet (2,115m) Gonzalo Aja (Esp) KAS; Col du Soulor (1,474m) Andrés Oliva (Esp) La Casera			
Stage 19a Thu 18 Jul	Pau to Bordeaux 107 finishers	195.5 km 4h51'56" 40.2 kph	Francis Campaner (Fra) Lejeune	Eddy Merckx (Bel) Molteni
Stage 19b Thu 18 Jul	Bordeaux (Circuit du Lac) (ITT) 107 finishers	12.4 km 16'15" 45.8 kph	Eddy Merckx (Bel) Molteni	Eddy Merckx (Bel) Molteni
Stage 20 Fri 19 Jul	Saint-Gilles-Croix-de-Vie to Nantes 106 finishers	117 km 2h53'21" 40.5 kph	Gérard Vianen (Ned) GAN	Eddy Merckx (Bel) Molteni
Stage 21a Sat 20 Jul	Vouvray to Orléans 105 finishers	112.5 km 2h19'05" 48.5 kph	Eddy Merckx (Bel) Molteni	Eddy Merckx (Bel) Molteni
Stage 21b Sat 20 Jul	Orléans (ITT) 105 finishers	37.5 km 48'23" 46.5 kph	Michel Pollentier (Bel) Carpenter	Eddy Merckx (Bel) Molteni

Stage-by-Stage Results for the 1974 Tour de France			Stage Winner	Maillot Jaune
Stage 22 Sun 21 Jul	Orléans to Paris (La Cipale) 105 finishers	146 km 3h49'29" 38.2 kph	~~Patrick Sercu (Bel) Brooklyn~~ (1)	Eddy Merckx (Bel) Molteni
			Eddy Merckx (Bel) Molteni	

(1) Patrick Sercu was relegated to third on the stage having come off his line in the sprint

Prize fund: 802,650 francs (first prize: 30,000 francs)

Final Classification				
Place	**Rider**	**Team**	**Time**	**Age**
1	Eddy Merckx (Bel)	Molteni	4,098 km 116h16'58" 35.241 kph	29
2	Raymond Poulidor (Fra)	GAN	+ 8'04"	38
3	Vicente López (Esp)	KAS	+ 8'09"	31
4	Wladimiro Panizza (Ita)	Brooklyn	+ 10'59"	29
5	Gonzalo Aja (Esp)	KAS	+ 11'24"	28
6	Joaquim Agostinho (Por)	Bic	+ 14'24"	31
7	Michel Pollentier (Bel)	Carpenter	+ 16'34"	23
8	Mariano Martínez (Fra)	Sonolor	+ 18'33"	25
9	Alain Santy (Fra)	GAN	+ 19'55"	24
10	Herman Van Springel (Bel)	Mic	+ 24'11"	30
Lanterne Rouge				
105	Lorenzo Alaimo (Ita)	Frisol	+ 3h55'46"	22
Points				
	Patrick Sercu (Bel)	Brooklyn		30
King of the Mountains				
	Domingo Perurena (Esp)	KAS		30
Intermediate Sprints				
	Barry Hoban (GBr)	GAN		34
Combination				
	Eddy Merckx (Bel)	Molteni		29
Team				
		KAS		
Team (Points)				
		GAN		
Super Combativité				
	Eddy Merckx (Bel)	Molteni		29

1975: A God Made Mortal

By the time the 1975 Tour de France came around, Eddy Merckx had started 13 Grand Tours and been undefeated in all bar two: his début Giro d'Italia in 1967, and the 1969 Giro, when events at Savona had seen him thrown off the race with the *maglia rosa* on his back and the win in the bag. There was one victory in the Vuelta a España (1973), five in the Giro (1967, 1970, 1972, 1973 and 1974) and five in the Tour (1969, 1970, 1971, 1972, 1974). And he had four Grand Tour doubles on his role of honour: the Giro/Tour double three times, the Vuelta/Tour double once.

Merckx was the champion of the Hour, he was the reigning World Champion, his *palmarès* was bulging with wins in Classics and stage races. And now, having equalled Jacques Anquetil's record of five wins in the Tour, he set about taking a step above Maître Jacques and went for win number six. He was 30 years old, still young. He was unstoppable.

But, of course, he wasn't. Louis Ocaña had exposed chinks in his armour in 1971. At the 1974 Tour Raymond Poulidor had been able to ride away from him in the Pyrenees. Merckx was human. But his reputation wasn't, and that often protected him: riders defeated themselves before he defeated them. He rode shielded by an aura of invincibility that concealed the man beneath. And on the road from Nice to Pra Loup, Stage 15 of the sixty-second Tour, that shield cracked and the man beneath was fully revealed. And he was just a man, no longer a God.

The race had begun in Charleroi with some new additions to the Tour's wardrobe: the white jersey, which had been used to recognise the leader of the combined category (which competition was now being rested), was now being awarded to the best young rider, while the leader of the King of the Mountains category was granted the privilege of wearing a white jersey with red polka dots. Or, as the French call it, the *maillot à pois rouge*, the jersey with red peas. More sponsors, more cash for the Tour's coffers.

Italy's Francesco Moser (Filotex) took the honours in the prologue and led the race through to the first individual time trial, in Merlin-Plage, where Merckx – still riding for Molteni – won the day and swapped his rainbow jersey for the *maillot jaune*. Moser was 31 seconds back in second, Michel Pollentier (Flandria) just over a minute back, with Bernard Thévenet (Peugeot), Herman Van Springel (Flandria), Raymond Poulidor (GAN), Felice Gimondi (Bianchi) and Lucien Van Impe (Gitane) all within three minutes of the lead.

Three days later came the second race against the clock and again Merckx triumphed. Thévenet moved up to third, with Gimondi, Poulidor, and Van Springel still in the top 10. After two days in the Pyrenees, it was Merckx leading Thévenet, by 1'31", with Joop Zoetemelk (GAN) now the best of the rest, 3'53" behind and in third.

Nothing changed on the transition stages taking the riders up to the Puy de Dôme summit finish, but on the Puy the race got ugly, with a fan stepping out of the crowd just before the summit and landing a punch on Merckx's side. Thévenet was already up the road, with Van Impe, having already exposed Merckx's climbing weakness in the Pyrenees and now fully taking advantage of it on the extinct volcano. Van Impe took the stage win, Thévenet in second. Merckx came in third, ceding 34 seconds to his French rival. Nanard – Thévenet's nickname – was now within a minute of the *maillot jaune*.

Merckx had a rest day in Nice in which to recover from the punches landed on him on the Puy de Dôme, the mental blow landed by Nanard and the physical blow landed by the fan. The latter had landed near the Belgian's liver, and he vomited bile at the stage end and his doctor put him on medication to treat the problem.

When the race resumed the Belgian launched his fight back, jumping clear of Thévenet as they crossed the Col d'Allos and pressing on alone. The gap between the champion and the challenger widened and the Tour seemed to be being decided, in Merckx's favour. Merckx was more than a minute up the road after the descent. With barely six kilometres remaining Nanard seemed not to be challenging as the Belgian – and the Tour title – rode away from him.

And then it happened. Merckx began to weaken. Thévenet, one moment riding to protect his place on the lower steps of the podium, was closing in on the yellow jersey as the gap between champion and challenger narrowed. And then disappeared as Nanard caught up to Merckx. And rode passed him. Merckx was now pedalling squares and bleeding time. At the finish line he was just under two minutes behind the Frenchman, who had taken the stage win. And the *maillot jaune*, which he now held with a lead of 58 seconds over the five-time Tour champion.

Merckx refused to lie down and play dead and tried to fight back the next day, as the race crossed the Vars and the Izoard. This time Nanard was ready for him, and this time he put more than two minutes into Merckx. The race was lost; pretty much all Thévenet had to do now was stay upright and reach Paris. Merckx could have quit the race, citing the after-effects of the punch on the Puy de Dôme as an excuse to go home. But that was not the Belgian's way, so he rode on.

At the start of the next stage Merckx's Tour went from bad to worse when he crashed in the opening kilometres of the stage and broke his cheekbone. But even that wouldn't stop the Belgian; he rode on and reached Paris and, for the first time in his Tour career, stood on one of the lower steps of the podium, second overall.

For the French, Nanard's win was the end of a eight-year drought dating back to Roger Pingeon's win in 1967. And France was really able to celebrate Thévenet's win (the first for a Peugeot rider since Firmin Lambot in 1922), the Tour's finale coming out of the vélodrome and onto the streets of Paris, with the finish line drawn across the Champ-Élysées. Even the French president graced the race with his presence, with Valéry Giscard d'Estaing presenting Thévenet with his trophy. An era had drawn to a close, and a new one began.

Stage-by-Stage Results for the 1975 Tour de France			Stage Winner	Maillot Jaune
Prologue Thu 26 Jun	Charleroi (ITT) 140 finishers	6.25 km 8'49" 42.5 kph	Francesco Moser (Ita) Filotex	Francesco Moser (Ita) Filotex
Stage 1a Fri 27 Jun	Charleroi to Molenbeek 140 finishers	94 km 2h09'27" 43.6 kph	Cees Priem (Ned) Frisol	Francesco Moser (Ita) Filotex
Stage 1b Fri 27 Jun	Molenbeek to Roubaix 138 finishers	108.5 km 2h28'30" 43.8 kph	Rik van Linden (Bel) Bianchi	Francesco Moser (Ita) Filotex
	Major climbs: Mur de Grammont (143m) Lucien Van Impe (Bel) Gitane			
Stage 2 Sat 28 Jun	Roubaix to Amiens 138 finishers	121.5 km 2h37'17" 46.3 kph	Ronald de Witte (Bel) Flandria	Francesco Moser (Ita) Filotex
Stage 3 Sun 29 Jun	Amiens to Versailles 137 finishers	169.5 km 4h04'04" 41.7 kph	Karel Rottiers (Bel) Molteni	Francesco Moser (Ita) Filotex
Stage 4 Mon 30 Jun	Versailles to Le Mans 134 finishers	223 km 5h26'32" 41 kph	Jacques Esclassan (Fra) Peugeot	Francesco Moser (Ita) Filotex
Stage 5 Tue 1 Jul	Sable-sur-Sarthe to Merlin-Plage 134 finishers	222.5 km 5h39'25" 39.3 kph	Theo Smit (Ned) Frisol	Francesco Moser (Ita) Filotex
Stage 6 Wed 2 Jul	Circuit Merlin-Plage (ITT) 134 finishers	16 km 19'33" 49.1 kph	Eddy Merckx (Bel) Molteni	Eddy Merckx (Bel) Molteni
Stage 7 Thu 3 Jul	Saint-Gilles-Croix-de-Vie to Angoulême 131 finishers	235.5 km 6h25'16" 36.7 kph	Francesco Moser (Ita) Filotex	Eddy Merckx (Bel) Molteni
Stage 8 Fri 4 Jul	Angoulême to Bordeaux 130 finishers	134 km 3h25'54" 39 kph	Barry Hoban (GBr) GAN	Eddy Merckx (Bel) Molteni
Stage 9a Sat 5 Jul	Langon to Fleurance 129 finishers	131 km 3h15'32" 40.2 kph	Theo Smit (Ned) Frisol	Eddy Merckx (Bel) Molteni
Stage 9b Sat 5 Jul	Fleurance to Auch (ITT) 129 finishers	37.4 km 49'42" 45.2 kph	Eddy Merckx (Bel) Molteni	Eddy Merckx (Bel) Molteni
Sun 6 Jul	Rest Day			
Stage 10 Mon 7 Jul	Auch to Pau 126 finishers	206 km 5h59'52" 34.3 kph	Felice Gimondi (Ita) Bianchi	Eddy Merckx (Bel) Molteni
	Major climbs: Col du Soulor (1,474m) Lucien Van Impe (Bel) Gitane; Côte de l'Esquillot (325m) Roberto Poggiali (Ita) Filotex			
Stage 11 Tue 8 Jul	Pau to Saint-Lary-Soulan 119 finishers	160 km 5h27'18" 29.3 kph	Joop Zoetemelk (Ned) GAN	Eddy Merckx (Bel) Molteni
	Major climbs: Col du Tourmalet (2,115m) Lucien Van Impe (Bel) Gitane; Col d'Aspin (1,489m) Lucien Van Impe (Bel) Gitane; Pla d'Adet (1,680m) Joop Zoetemelk (Ned) GAN			

Stage-by-Stage Results for the 1975 Tour de France			Stage Winner	Maillot Jaune
Stage 12 Wed 9 Jul	Tarbes to Albi 118 finishers	242 km 7h17'25" 33.2 kph	Gerrie Knetemann (Ned) GAN	Eddy Merckx (Bel) Molteni
Stage 13 Thu 10 Jul	Albi to Super-Lioran 110 finishers	260 km 8h58'44" 29 kph	Michel Pollentier (Bel) Flandria	Eddy Merckx (Bel) Molteni
	Major climbs: Côte de Salgues (950m) Lucien Van Impe (Bel) Gitane; Plomb du Cantal (1,383m) Eddy Merckx (Bel) Molteni; Super-Lioran (1,326m) Michel Pollentier (Bel) Flandria			
Stage 14 Fri 11 Jul	Aurillac to Puy-de-Dôme 107 finishers	173.5 km 5h26'51" 31.8 kph	Lucien Van Impe (Bel) Gitane	Eddy Merckx (Bel) Molteni
	Major climbs: Col du Pas de Péyrol (1,588m) Lucien Van Impe (Bel) Gitane; Puy de Dôme (1,415m) Lucien Van Impe (Bel) Gitane			
Sat 12 Jul	Rest Day			
Stage 15 Sun 13 Jul	Nice to Pra-Loup 99 finishers	217.5 km 7h46'35" 28 kph	Bernard Thévenet (Fra) Peugeot	Bernard Thévenet (Fra) Peugeot
	Major climbs: Saint-Martin (1,500m) Lucien Van Impe (Bel) Gitane; Route de la Couillole (1,678m) Lucien Van Impe (Bel) Gitane; Col des Champs (2,095m) Eddy Merckx (Bel) Molteni; Col d'Allos (2,250m) Eddy Merckx (Bel) Molteni; Pra-Loup (1,630m) Bernard Thévenet (Fra) Peugeot			
Stage 16 Mon 14 Jul	Barcelonnette to Serre Chevalier 97 finishers	107 km 3h16'17" 32.7 kph	Bernard Thévenet (Fra) Peugeot	Bernard Thévenet (Fra) Peugeot
	Major climbs: Col de Vars (2,110m) Joop Zoetemelk (Ned) GAN; Col d'Izoard (2,360m) Bernard Thévenet (Fra) Peugeot			
Stage 17 Tue 15 Jul	Valloire to Morzine-Avoriaz 94 finishers	225 km 7h23'38" 30.4 kph	Vicente López (Esp) KAS	Bernard Thévenet (Fra) Peugeot
	Major climbs: Col de la Madeleine (2,000m) Francisco Galdos (Esp) KAS; Col des Aravis (1,498m) Lucien Van Impe (Bel) Gitane; Col de la Colombière (1,618m) Vicente López (Esp) KAS; Avoriaz (1,800m) Vicente López (Esp) KAS			
Stage 18 Wed 16 Jul	Morzine to Chatel (ITT) 93 finishers	40 km 1h03'15" 37.9 kph	Lucien Van Impe (Bel) Gitane	Bernard Thévenet (Fra) Peugeot
Stage 19 Thu 17 Jul	Thonon-les-Bains to Chalon-sur-Saône 93 finishers	229 km 6h53'59" 33.2 kph	Rik van Linden (Bel) Bianchi	Bernard Thévenet (Fra) Peugeot
	Major climbs: Col de la Faucille (1,323m) Mariano Martínez (Esp) Gitane; Mijoux (1,182m) José Casas (Esp) Super			
Stage 20 Fri 18 Jul	Pouilly-en-Auxois to Melun 90 finishers	256 km 7h39'45" 33.4 kph	Giacinto Santambrogio (Ita) Bianchi	Bernard Thévenet (Fra) Peugeot
Stage 21 Sat 19 Jul	Melun to Senlis 89 finishers	220.5 km 6h36'51" 33.3 kph	Rik van Linden (Bel) Bianchi	Bernard Thévenet (Fra) Peugeot
Stage 22 Sun 20 Jul	Paris (Champs-Élysées) to 86 finishers	163.5 km 3h45'29" 43.5 kph	Walter Godefroot (Bel) Flandria	Bernard Thévenet (Fra) Peugeot

Prize fund: 842,695 francs (first prize: 30,000 francs)

Final Classification

Place	Rider	Team	Time	Age
1	Bernard Thévenet (Fra)	Peugeot	4,000 km 114h35'31" 34.906 kph	27
2	Eddy Merckx (Bel)	Molteni	+ 2'47"	30
3	Lucien Van Impe (Bel)	Gitane	+ 5'01"	28
4	Joop Zoetemelk (Ned)	GAN	+ 6'42"	29
5	Vicente López (Esp)	KAS	+ 19'29"	32
6	Felice Gimondi (Ita)	Bianchi	+ 23'05"	32
7	Francesco Moser (Ita)	Filotex	+ 24'13"	24
8	Josef Fuchs (Sui)	Filotex	+ 25'51"	26
9	Edouard Janssens (Bel)	Molteni	+ 32'01"	29
10	Pedro Torres (Esp)	Super	+ 35'36"	26
Lanterne Rouge				
86	Jacques Boulas (Fra)	Jobo	+ 3h31'21"	26
Points				
	Rik van Linden (Bel)	Bianchi		25
King of the Mountains				
	Lucien Van Impe (Bel)	Gitane		28
Intermediate Sprints				
	Marc Demeyer (Bel)	Flandria		25
Youth				
	Francesco Moser (Ita)	Filotex		24
Team				
		GAN		
Team (Points)				
		GAN		
Super Combativité				
	Eddy Merckx (Bel)	Molteni		30

1976: The Legend of Cyrille Guimard, Part Two

In the first four days of the sixty-third Tour de France, Belgium's Freddy Maertens (Velda/Flandria) won three stages. Over the rest of the Tour Maertens added another five. In his Tour debut, the twenty-four-year-old Belgian had equalled the record held by Charles Pélissier (1930) and Eddy Merckx (1970 and 1974). Belgium had a new hero, just as the old one started to slide off into the wings.

Merckx wasn't retired, he was just sitting the Tour out as he recovered from saddle sores which had afflicted him at the Giro d'Italia (which he lost to Felice Gimondi). The defending champion Bernard Thévenet, again leading the Peugeot lion cubs, came into the race hot off a victory at the Critérium du Dauphiné Libéré, normally a good indicator of pre-Tour form.

The first week of the race was a sprintfest, as Maertens showed, the riders setting off from Saint-Jean-de-Monts in the Vendée and travelling north to Caen and – with the help of transfers between stages – crossing into Belgium before turning south and down to Divonne-les-Baines. From there, the race was handed over to the *grimpeurs*, with the next seven stages all featuring major climbs. And it was in those mountains that the Tour was won and the legend of Cyrille Guimard was born.

Having briefly played the foil to Merckx – and twice seen the Belgian riding away with a green jersey that should have been his – Guimard was transitioning into team management, having finished his road career the year before and raced the pre-season cyclo-cross races in a Gitane jersey, before becoming the team's *directeur sportif*. And he was about to start his managerial career with a bang.

Coming into the mountains Maertens was in yellow, with his Velda team-mate Michel Pollentier in second, just over two minutes back. Behind them was a queue of riders all within three minutes of the yellow jersey, including Raymond Poulidor (GAN) and Lucien Van Impe (Gitane).

The climbing began with the return of the mountain that had hosted the Tour's first summit finish back in 1952, l'Alpe d'Huez. The Alpe had been overlooked by the Tour since its début, even when the race passed by its doorstep in Bourg-d'Oisans. And it was almost overlooked again in 1976, until Félix Lévitan was left with a gap to fill in the race's itinerary (and finances) when a planned visit to Grenoble fell through. The businesses atop the Alpe were offered the race if they could come up with 100,000 francs, which they duly did. And were amply rewarded, the Tour paying dividends in a stage full of excitement.

The *peloton* was 50 strong approaching the base of the Alpe and from the first hairpin the attacks began, with Raymond Delisle (Peugeot) starting the offensive and Van Impe giving chase. He was joined by Joop Zoetemelk (GAN) and the two challenged each other all the way up the mountain, with the Dutchman taking the stage and the Belgian the *maillot jaune*. The first selection had been made and the likely challengers for the Tour victory emerged: Van Impe in yellow, Zoetemelk eight seconds behind him, Poulidor and Thévenet still within two minutes.

Van Impe held on to the *maillot jaune* as the Tour completed the first part of its run of mountains and transferred directly from Manosque to Port-Baracès without any of the traditional transition stages between the Alps and the Pyrenees. And in those latter mountains Thévenet's *directeur sportif* Maurice de Muer played his trump card: as well as having Thévenet within two minutes of Van Impe, the Peugeot boss also had Raymond Delisle, the man who had initiated hostilities on the Alpe and was now just over four minutes off yellow. If he sent Delisle up the road and Van Impe chased, Thévenet would be able to launch a counter-attack once the catch was made. And if Van Impe didn't react, Delisle would be riding himself into an even stronger position and his card could be played again another day.

But Van Impe didn't just fail to react. He let Delisle get away and take just under seven minutes. And the *maillot jaune*. While the next stage didn't disrupt the general classification greatly, de Muer was still a happy man, with another of his lion cubs taking the stage win, Régis Ovion. By the time the results of the anti-doping tests came through five days had passed and the race had reached Bordeaux: Ovion was positive, stripped of his stage win, given a 10-minute time penalty, a one month suspended suspension (only to come into effect if he tested positive again within the next two years) and a fine of 1,000 Swiss francs (anti-doping was the responsibility of the sport's governing body, the Swiss-based UCI). But by the time all that happened the smile was already well and truly wiped off de Muer's face, with his two trump cards – Thévenet and Delisle – having failed him, and Van Impe having won the Tour.

It happened on the stage to the Pla d'Adet, above Saint-Lary-Soulan, the day after Ovion's stage win. Guimard wanted Van Impe to win the stage with a long solo effort and advised his rider to attack on the Col de Peyresourde, about halfway through the stage. When the time came he sent one rider up to Van Impe with the order to attack. No attack came. He sent a second rider up to Van Impe with the order to attack. Again no attack came. So Guimard pressed down on the accelerator of the teamcar and drove up alongside Van Impe to give the order himself: attack now, or I'll drive you off the road. Van Impe attacked and duly won the stage and took back the *maillot jaune*.

But he didn't just take it back: Delisle was relegated to third, more than nine minutes back, Thévenet was twice as far back. And Zoetemelk, who only chased after Van Impe when he realised that the yellow jersey was about to change hands, while he was second overall, it was with a three minute deficit.

And so the fourth man named Lucien won the Tour (after Petit-Breton, Buysse and Aimar) and a three-time King of the Mountains winner became a one-time Tour victor. And Cyrille Guimard sealed his reputation as being both a tactical genius and tough as nails.

* * * * *

While the new regime of doping tests saved the Tour from scandals – even Ovion's positive was not that big an affair, not compared to the reaction to events in the 1950s and 1960s – all was not well elsewhere in the sport. As the journalists at *L'Équipe* revealed when they published a story about a Peugeot rider, Rachel Dard, who had gone to extreme lengths to avoid being declared positive at the Jean Leulliot-organised Étoile des Espoirs.

Dard had tried to avoid testing positive by taking a condom full of someone else's urine into the doping control. Substituting someone else's urine for your own was a standard ruse to beat the testers and the means of doing it varied. Most times the testers failed to notice. But not this time, and the doctor in charge spotted the ruse. Dard and another rider were busted. But, after the two riders poured out a sob story, the doctor decided to forget about what had just happened and not report the riders. And so everyone got on with getting in. Until Dard realised there was a flaw in this cunning plan: while the doctor had agreed to forget about the attempted cheating, he had forgotten to actually collect a sample, and the authorities would realise something was going on once they noticed this.

Dard went in search of the doctor, but he had already left the race and returned to Paris, by train. So Dard hopped in a car and raced the train to Paris, catching the doctor and sorting things out. The doctor, though ... his conscience got the better of him and he took the story to *L'Équipe*. And once they had that, Dard decided to spill all too. The public were given the whole sorry story, about how easy it was to evade the testers.

It was a minor scandal from a minor race concerning a minor rider (albeit one on a major team). But the day was coming when it would be a major rider, at a major race, causing a major scandal. It was just a question of time.

Stage-by-Stage Results for the 1976 Tour de France			Stage Winner	Maillot Jaune
Prologue Thu 24 Jun	Saint-Jean-de-Monts (ITT) 130 finishers	8 km 11'03" 43.4 kph	Freddy Maertens (Bel) Velda	Freddy Maertens (Bel) Velda
Stage 1 Fri 25 Jun	Saint-Jean-de-Monts to Angers 130 finishers	173 km 4h43'37" 36.6 kph	Freddy Maertens (Bel) Velda	Freddy Maertens (Bel) Velda
Stage 2 Sat 26 Jun	Angers to Caen 130 finishers	236.5 km 6h43'49" 35.1 kph	Giovanni Battaglin (Ita) Jolly Ceramica	Freddy Maertens (Bel) Velda
Stage 3 Sun 27 Jun	Le Touquet (ITT) 130 finishers	37 km 47'08" 47.1 kph	Freddy Maertens (Bel) Velda	Freddy Maertens (Bel) Velda
Stage 4 Mon 28 Jun	Le Touquet to Bornem 129 finishers	258 km 7h31'25" 34.3 kph	Hennie Kuiper (Ned) TI-Raleigh	Freddy Maertens (Bel) Velda
Stage 5a Tue 29 Jun	Louvain (TTT) 125 finishers	4.3 km 5'21" 48.2 kph	TI-Raleigh	Freddy Maertens (Bel) Velda
Stage 5b Tue 29 Jun	Louvain to Verviers 125 finishers	144 km 3h51'17" 37.4 kph	Miguel María Lasa (Esp) SCIC	Freddy Maertens (Bel) Velda
Stage 6 Wed 30 Jun	Bastogne to Nancy 123 finishers	209 km 5h22'32" 38.9 kph	Aldo Parecchini (Ita) Brooklyn	Freddy Maertens (Bel) Velda
Stage 7 Thu 1 Jul	Nancy to Mulhouse 121 finishers	205.5 km 5h41'12" 36.1 kph	Freddy Maertens (Bel) Velda	Freddy Maertens (Bel) Velda
	Major climbs: Col du Calvaire (1,144m) Luciano Conati (Ita) SCIC; Col du Grand Ballon (1,343m) Giancarlo Bellini (Ita) Brooklyn			
Stage 8 Fri 2 Jul	Valentigney to Divonne-les-Bains 120 finishers	220.5 km 5h54'11" 37.4 kph	Jacques Esclassan (Fra) Peugeot	Freddy Maertens (Bel) Velda
	Major climbs: Maiche (1,140m) José Martins (Esp) KAS; Côte des Rousses (1,140m) Giancarlo Bellini (Ita) Brooklyn			
Sat 3 Jul	Rest Day			
Stage 9 Sun 4 Jul	Divonne-les-Bains to l'Alpe d'Huez 120 finishers	258 km 8h31'49" 30.2 kph	Joop Zoetemelk (Ned) GAN	Lucien Van Impe (Bel) Gitane
	Major climbs: Col du Luitel (1,262m) Giancarlo Bellini (Ita) Brooklyn; l'Alpe d'Huez (1,860m) Joop Zoetemelk (Ned) GAN			
Stage 10 Mon 5 Jul	Bourg-d'Oisans to Montgenèvre 106 finishers	166 km 5h02'20" 32.9 kph	Joop Zoetemelk (Ned) GAN	Lucien Van Impe (Bel) Gitane
	Major climbs: Col du Lautaret (2,058m) Luciano Conati (Ita) SCIC; Col d'Izoard (2,360m) Lucien Van Impe (Bel) Gitane; Col de Montgenèvre (1,860m) Joop Zoetemelk (Ned) GAN			
Stage 11 Tue 6 Jul	Montgenèvre to Manosque 105 finishers	224 km 5h42'34" 39.2 kph	José Luis Viejo (Esp) Super	Lucien Van Impe (Bel) Gitane
	Major climbs: Col Saint-Jean (1,332m) José-Luis Viejo (Esp) Super; Porteau de Telle (639m) José-Luis Viejo (Esp) Super; Mont d'Or (660m) José-Luis Viejo (Esp) Super			

Stage-by-Stage Results for the 1976 Tour de France			Stage Winner	Maillot Jaune
Wed 7 Jul	Rest Day			
Stage 12 Thu 8 Jul	Port Barcares to Pyrenees 2000 99 finishers	205.5 km 6h47'32" 30.3 kph	Raymond Delisle (Fra) Peugeot	Raymond Delisle (Fra) Peugeot
	Major climbs: Aussières (1,057m) Giancarlo Bellini (Ita) Brooklyn; Col de Jau (1,513m) Raymond Delisle (Fra) Peugeot; Pyrenees 2000 (1,800m) Raymond Delisle (Fra) Peugeot			
Stage 13 Fri 9 Jul	Font-Romeu to Saint-Gaudens 98 finishers	188 km 4h57'23" 37.9 kph	~~Régis Ovion (Fra) Peugeot (1)~~ Willy Teirlinck (Bel) Gitane	Raymond Delisle (Fra) Peugeot
	Major climbs: Col du Puymorens (1,915m) Domingo Perurena (Esp) KAS; Col de Port (1,249m) Roland Smet (Fra) Lejeune			
Stage 14 Sat 10 Jul	Saint-Gaudens to Saint-Lary-Soulan 95 finishers	139 km 4h20'50" 32 kph	Lucien Van Impe (Bel) Gitane	Lucien Van Impe (Bel) Gitane
	Major climbs: Col de Menté (1,349m) Lucien Van Impe (Bel) Gitane; Font-Romeu (1,800m) Raymond Delisle (Fra) Peugeot; Col du Portillon (1,298m) Pedro Torres (Esp) Super; Col de Peyresourde (1,569m) Luis Ocaña (Esp) Super; Saint-Lary-Soulan (1,680m) Lucien Van Impe (Bel) Gitane; Pla d'Adet (1,680m) Lucien Van Impe (Bel) Gitane			
Stage 15 Sun 11 Jul	Saint-Lary-Soulan to Pau 88 finishers	195 km 6h01'37" 32.4 kph	Wladimiro Panizza (Ita) SCIC	Lucien Van Impe (Bel) Gitane
	Major climbs: Col d'Aspin (1,489m) Gerben Karstens (Ned) TI-Raleigh; Col du Tourmalet (2,115m) Francisco Galdos (Esp) KAS; Col d'Aubisque (1,709m) Wladimiro Panizza (Ita) SCIC			
Stage 16 Mon 12 Jul	Pau to Fleurance 88 finishers	152 km 4h38'33" 32.7 kph	Michel Pollentier (Bel) Velda	Lucien Van Impe (Bel) Gitane
Stage 17 Tue 13 Jul	Fleurance to Auch (ITT) 88 finishers	38.75 km 52'41" 44.1 kph	Ferdinand Bracke (Bel) Lejeune	Lucien Van Impe (Bel) Gitane
Stage 18a Wed 14 Jul	Auch to Langon 88 finishers	86 km 2h34'37" 33.4 kph	Freddy Maertens (Bel) Velda	Lucien Van Impe (Bel) Gitane
Stage 18b Wed 14 Jul	Langon to Lacanau-Océan 88 finishers	123 km 3h27'00" 35.7 kph	Freddy Maertens (Bel) Velda	Lucien Van Impe (Bel) Gitane
Stage 18c Wed 14 Jul	Lacanau-Océan to Bordeaux 88 finishers	70.5 km 1h42'13" 41.4 kph	Gerben Karstens (Ned) TI-Raleigh	Lucien Van Impe (Bel) Gitane
Stage 19 Thu 15 Jul	Sainte-Foy-la-Grande to Tulle 87 finishers	219.5 km 6h46'00" 32.4 kph	Hubert Mathis (Fra) Miko	Lucien Van Impe (Bel) Gitane
Stage 20 Fri 16 Jul	Tulle to Puy-de-Dôme 87 finishers	220 km 6h52'52" 32 kph	Joop Zoetemelk (Ned) GAN	Lucien Van Impe (Bel) Gitane
	Major climbs: Puy de Dôme (1,415m) Joop Zoetemelk (Ned) GAN			
Stage 21 Sat 17 Jul	Montargis to Versailles 87 finishers	145.5 km 4h16'07" 34.1 kph	Freddy Maertens (Bel) Velda	Lucien Van Impe (Bel) Gitane

Stage-by-Stage Results for the 1976 Tour de France			Stage Winner	Maillot Jaune
Stage 22a Sun 18 Jul	Paris (Champs-Élysées) (ITT) 87 finishers	6 km 7'46" 46.4 kph	Freddy Maertens (Bel) Velda	Lucien Van Impe (Bel) Gitane
Stage 22b Sun 18 Jul	Paris (Champs-Élysées) 87 finishers	90.7 km 1h58'48" 45.8 kph	Gerben Karstens (Ned) TI-Raleigh	Lucien Van Impe (Bel) Gitane

(1) Régis Ovion was stripped of his stage win he failed a dope test.

Prize fund: 1,004,500 francs (first prize: 100,000 francs)

Final Classification				
Place	**Rider**	**Team**	**Time**	**Age**
1	Lucien Van Impe (Bel)	Gitane	4,017 km 116h22'23" 34.518 kph	29
2	Joop Zoetemelk (Ned)	GAN	+ 4'14"	30
3	Raymond Poulidor (Fra)	GAN	+ 12'08"	40
4	Raymond Delisle (Fra)	Peugeot	+ 12'17"	33
5	Walter Riccomi (Ita)	SCIC	+ 12'39"	26
6	Francisco Galdós (Esp)	KAS	+ 14'50"	29
7	Michel Pollentier (Bel)	Velda	+ 14'59"	25
8	Freddy Maertens (Bel)	Velda	+ 16'09"	24
9	Fausto Bertoglio (Ita)	Jolly Ceramica	+ 16'36"	27
10	Vicente López (Esp)	KAS	+ 19'28"	33
Lanterne Rouge				
87	Aad van den Hoek (Ned)	TI-Raleigh	+ 3h12'54"	24
Points				
	Freddy Maertens (Bel)	Velda		24
King of the Mountains				
	Giancarlo Bellini (Ita)	Brooklyn		30
Intermediate Sprints				
	Robert Mintkiewicz (Fra)	Gitane		28
Youth				
	Enrique Martínez Heredia (Esp)	KAS		23
Team				
		KAS		
Team (Points)				
		GAN		
Super Combativité				
	Raymond Delisle	Peugeot		33

1977: Dark Days

This was the year the Belgian anti-doping authorities pulled a real fast one, not letting the riders know they could test for Stimul – a widely available amphetamine – until after they'd carried out a load of tests. While the rules against doping were the responsibility of the sport's governing body, the UCI (which generally followed the IOC's lead, though usually a year behind), it was down to individual national federations to actually conduct most of the testing. In some countries, those federations warned their riders ahead of new tests being rolled out. But in Belgium, in 1977, there was no warning. A test was developed and it was implemented during the Classics season. The first the riders knew about it was when they got letters telling them they'd tested positive. And the riders caught in 1977 were no small fry, they included some of the sports biggest stars.

Freddy Maertens – the man who had won eight stages in his début Tour – managed to get three strikes that Classics season – Het Volk (5 March), the Ronde van Vlaanderen (3 April) and the Flèche Wallonne (7 April). Others to fall included Willy Teirlinck (Gitane), Willy Planckaert (Maes), Michel Pollentier (a team-mate of Maertens at Flandria) and Joaquim Agostinho (Teka). And then there was Eddy Merckx (FIAT France). Who, like Maertens, popped a positive at the Flèche Wallonne.

For Merckx, the fading champion, this was his third positive in eight years, following Savona in 1969 and the Giro di Lombardia in 1973. The first two the Belgian had been able to brush off, Savona was a conspiracy, a plot to make him lose the Giro d'Italia, while the Lombardia positive was down to a mistake by his team doctor. This third strike, though, that was harder to dismiss. So Merckx blamed the testing, said it was in error and declared that he had no confidence in the system.

Maertens, he came up with a more novel excuse: the authorities had no right to change the list of banned products during the course of a season. But they hadn't. They had simply developed a new test during the course of the season. Maertens's defence, though, revealed the reality of riders' attitudes to doping: it wasn't against the rules if you couldn't test for it. At a time when testing was still in its infancy and products like cortisone and testosterone couldn't be tested for, this allowed riders to use an awful lot of doping products without actually believing they were doping.

Those products also included the sport's first, tentative steps into the era of blood doping. Ahead of the 1977 Tour Joop Zoetemelk revealed that he had made use of blood transfusions at the previous year's Tour, during which he had won three stages, including those to Alpe d'Huez and the Puy de Dôme. Since crashing out of the Midi-Libre in 1974 the Dutchman had been suffering from anaemia, and his doctor had prescribed transfusions as a solution. Jacques Anquetil was said to have used a form of transfusion – taking out a small amount of blood and treating it with ozone before re-injecting it – in the 1967 Giro d'Italia, but Zoetemelk's transfusions were a step above that, using untreated whole blood.

Transfusions were in the news at this time because of the exploits of Finnish athletes, in particular Lasse Virén. The IOC had not banned their use – their logic being that, as they had no test for transfusions, banning them would be pointless – but the public attitude seemed to be against them. You could maybe justify the use of medicines banned by the sporting authorities, but blood? Ethically, that was questionable.

* * * * *

In was in this atmosphere that Bernard Thévenet won his second Tour title. The race had begun with a bang, in Fleurance, with the Pyrenees thrown at the riders as early as the second stage. Once out of those mountains the race then spent two weeks wheeling up through Bordeaux, Angers and Rouen before running up to Roubaix and across to Charleroi before jumping on (via a long transfer) to the Vosges and the Alps. In the Alps, after the time trial in Morzine, Nanard seized the yellow jersey from TI-Raleigh's Dietrich Thurau, who had held it since Fleurance, and set about winning the Tour.

In doing so he saw off challenges from a fading Eddy Merckx (FIAT) and Lucien Van Impe, who had decamped from Gitane to Lejeune, not quite liking Cyrille Guimard's style of man-management. He also had to fend off Hennie Kuiper, whose TI-Raleigh team-mate Thurau had held the yellow jersey for so long, and from Thurau himself, who wasn't going down without making a fight of it.

The challenge from Merckx – riding his last Tour – faded swiftly, on the road to Chamonix, with the Belgian losing minutes and dropping down the general classification. Van Impe faded on the Alpe, as did Thurau, where Kuiper took the stage win and climbed to within eight seconds of Thévenet. The race, though, was now more or less done with the mountains and Kuiper was going to have to make time on the roads to Saint-Étienne and Dijon, and make quite a bit of it, for after Dijon came a time trial, a short stage into Paris, and another time trial before the race's finale on the Champs-Élysées. With Nanard the better performer against the clock the TI-Raleigh man had a lot of work to do,

With a team like TI-Raleigh around him, he should have been able to do it. But they were down three riders after the Alpe, when 33 riders arrived outside the time limit and were sent home. Among those 33 were stars like Patrick Sercu (FIAT) who was wearing the green jersey, and former Hour record-holder Ferdinand Bracke (Lejeune). The previous year TI-Raleigh's *directeur sportif* Peter Post had been successful when he pressured the commissaires to keep his riders in the race when they were eliminated by the time cut in a similarly large group. But this time the judges weren't listening and Post's riders and the rest stayed out. As for the surviving TI-Raleigh riders, they were exhausted from having defended Thurau's jersey for so long and were of little help in trying to relieve Thévenet of the *maillot jaune*. Kuiper did try a solo move on the road to Dijon but Thévenet was awake to the danger and effortlessly closed him down.

And so the race came down to two time trials. In these Thévenet put first 28 seconds into his rival and then another 12 seconds in Paris. It was a tight victory – 48 seconds – but it was enough. Nanard's celebrations, though, took place in the shadow of more doping positives. Through the race six riders had tested positive: Zoetemelk (Miko/Mercier) in Avoriaz on Stage 15; Sebastien Pozo (KAS) in Chamonix on Stage 16; Antonio Menéndez (KAS) at Alpe d'Huez on Stage 17; and Joaquim Agostinho (Teka), Menéndez (again) and Luis Ocaña (Frisol) all in Saint-Étienne on Stage 18 (Agostinho and Menéndez had finished first and second, with Merckx third, though he was not granted the victory, the stage having no winner). All were handed 10-minute time penalties, given the standard suspended suspension and a financial slap on the wrist.

With Thévenet himself having tested positive earlier in the season at Paris-Nice, it was a tainted victory.

Stage-by-Stage Results for the 1977 Tour de France			Stage Winner	Maillot Jaune
Prologue Thu 30 Jun	Fleurance (ITT) 100 finishers	5 km 6'16" 47.9 kph	Dietrich Thurau (FRG) TI-Raleigh	Dietrich Thurau (FRG) TI-Raleigh
Stage 1 Fri 1 Jul	Fleurance to Auch 100 finishers	237 km 7h09'01" 33.1 kph	Pierre-Raymond Villemiane (Fra) Gitane	Dietrich Thurau (FRG) TI-Raleigh
Stage 2 Sat 2 Jul	Auch to Pau 98 finishers	253 km 8h11'08" 30.9 kph	Dietrich Thurau (FRG) TI-Raleigh	Dietrich Thurau (FRG) TI-Raleigh
	Major climbs: Col d'Aspin (1,489m) Luis Balagué (Esp) Teka; Col du Tourmalet (2,115m) Lucien Van Impe (Bel) Lejeune; Col d'Aubisque (1,709m) Hennie Kuiper (Ned) TI-Raleigh			
Stage 3 Sun 3 Jul	Oloron-Sainte-Marie to Vitoria 98 finishers	248.2 km 7h35'30" 32.7 kph	José Nazabal (Esp) KAS	Dietrich Thurau (FRG) TI-Raleigh
	Major climbs: Ispeguy (673m) Lucien Van Impe (Bel) Lejeune; Leiza (605m) José Nazabal (Esp) KAS; Huici (660m) José Nazabal (Esp) KAS			
Stage 4 Mon 4 Jul	Vitoria to Seignosse-le-Penon 98 finishers	256 km 7h35'49" 33.7 kph	Régis Delépine (Fra) Peugeot	Dietrich Thurau (FRG) TI-Raleigh
	Major climbs: Jaizkibel (1,190m) Jean-Pierre Danguillaume (Fra) Peugeot; Alto de Ibardin (315m) Pedro Torres (Esp) Teka			
Stage 5a Tue 5 Jul	Morcenx to Bordeaux 97 finishers	138.5 km 3h38'05" 38.1 kph	Jacques Esclassan (Fra) Peugeot	Dietrich Thurau (FRG) TI-Raleigh

Stage-by-Stage Results for the 1977 Tour de France			Stage Winner	Maillot Jaune
Stage 5b Tue 5 Jul	Bordeaux (Circuit du Lac) (ITT) 97 finishers	30.2 km 39'24" 46 kph	Dietrich Thurau (FRG) TI-Raleigh	Dietrich Thurau (FRG) TI-Raleigh
Wed 6 Jul	Rest Day			
Stage 6 Thu 7 Jul	Bordeaux to Limoges 97 finishers	225.5 km 6h00'40" 37.5 kph	Jan Raas (Ned) Frisol	Dietrich Thurau (FRG) TI-Raleigh
Stage 7a Fri 8 Jul	Jaunay-Clan to Angers 97 finishers	139.5 km 3h45'24" 37.1 kph	Patrick Sercu (Bel) FIAT	Dietrich Thurau (FRG) TI-Raleigh
Stage 7b Fri 8 Jul	Angers (TTT) 97 finishers	4 km 4'49" 49.8 kph	FIAT	Dietrich Thurau (FRG) TI-Raleigh
Stage 8 Sat 9 Jul	Angers to Lorient 97 finishers	246.5 km 6h32'41" 37.7 kph	Giacinto Santambrogio (Ita) Bianchi	Dietrich Thurau (FRG) TI-Raleigh
Stage 9 Sun 10 Jul	Lorient to Rennes 97 finishers	187 km 5h07'36" 36.5 kph	Klaus-Peter Thaler (FRG) Teka	Dietrich Thurau (FRG) TI-Raleigh
	Major climbs: Côte de Mûr-de-Bretagne (295m) Lucien Van Impe (Bel) Lejeune			
Stage 10 Mon 11 Jul	Bagnoles-de-l'Orne to Rouen 95 finishers	174 km 4h49'38" 36 kph	Fedor den Hertog (Ned) Frisol	Dietrich Thurau (FRG) TI-Raleigh
Stage 11 Tue 12 Jul	Rouen to Roubaix 95 finishers	242.5 km 7h07'03" 34.1 kph	Jean-Pierre Danguillaume (Fra) Peugeot	Dietrich Thurau (FRG) TI-Raleigh
Stage 12 Wed 13 Jul	Roubaix to Charleroi 95 finishers	192.5 km 4h32'38" 42.4 kph	Patrick Sercu (Bel) FIAT	Dietrich Thurau (FRG) TI-Raleigh
	Major climbs: Mûr de Grammont (143m) Patrick Sercu (Bel) Fiat			
Stage 13a Thu 14 Jul	Freibourg Im Breisgau (ITT) 94 finishers	46 km 56'42" 48.7 kph	Patrick Sercu (Bel) FIAT	Dietrich Thurau (FRG) TI-Raleigh
Stage 13b Thu 14 Jul	Altkirch to Besançon 94 finishers	159.5 km 4h06'00" 38.9 kph	Jean-Pierre Danguillaume (Fra) Peugeot	Dietrich Thurau (FRG) TI-Raleigh
Fri 15 Jul	Rest Day			
Stage 14 Sat 16 Jul	Besançon to Thonon-les-Bains 91 finishers	230 km 6h15'46" 36.7 kph	Bernard Quilfen (Fra) Gitane	Dietrich Thurau (FRG) TI-Raleigh
	Major climbs: Côte des Rousses (1,140m) Bernard Quilfen (Fra) Gitane; Col de Cou (1,116m) Bernard Quilfen (Fra) Gitane			

Stage-by-Stage Results for the 1977 Tour de France			Stage Winner	Maillot Jaune
Stage 15a Sun 17 Jul	Thonon-les-Bains to Morzine 89 finishers	105 km 2h55'59" 35.8 kph	Paul Wellens (Bel) Frisol	Dietrich Thurau (FRG) TI-Raleigh
	Major climbs: Pas de Morgins (1,369m) Paul Wellens (Bel) Frisol; Col du Corbier (1,325m) Paul Wellens (Bel) Frisol			
Stage 15b Sun 17 Jul	Morzine to Avoriaz (ITT) 89 finishers	14 km 33'49" 24.8 kph	Lucien Van Impe (Bel) Lejeune	Bernard Thévenet (Fra) Peugeot
	Major climbs: Avoriaz (1,800m) Lucien Van Impe (Bel) Lejeune			
Stage 16 Mon 18 Jul	Morzine to Chamonix 87 finishers	121 km 3h29'52" 34.6 kph	Dietrich Thurau (FRG) TI-Raleigh	Bernard Thévenet (Fra) Peugeot
	Major climbs: Col du Corbier (1,325m) Pedro Torres (Esp) Teka; Col de la Forclaz de Montmin (1,150m) Antonio Menendez (Por) KAS; Col des Montets (1,461m) Lucien Van Impe (Bel) Lejeune			
Stage 17 Tue 19 Jul	Chamonix to l'Alpe d'Huez 56 finishers	184.5 km 6h00'20" 30.7 kph	Hennie Kuiper (Ned) TI-Raleigh	Bernard Thévenet (Fra) Peugeot
	Major climbs: Col de la Madeleine (2,000m) André Chalmel (Fra) Gitane; Col du Glandon (1,924m) Lucien Van Impe (Bel) Lejeune; l'Alpe d'Huez (1,860m) Hennie Kuiper (Ned) TI-Raleigh			
Stage 18 Wed 20 Jul	Rossignol Voiron to Saint-Étienne 55 finishers	199.5 km 5h56'05" 33.6 kph	~~Joaquim Agostinho (Por) Teka (1)~~ Vacated	Bernard Thévenet (Fra) Peugeot
	Major climbs: La Louvesc (1,120m) Joaquim Agostinho (Por) Teka; Col de la Croix de Chaubouret (1,230m) Joaquim Agostinho (Por) Teka			
Stage 19 Thu 21 Jul	Saint-Trivier to Dijon 55 finishers	171.5 km 4h29'17" 38.2 kph	Gerrie Knetemann (Ned) TI-Raleigh	Bernard Thévenet (Fra) Peugeot
Stage 20 Fri 22 Jul	Dijon (ITT) 54 finishers	50 km 1h10'45" 42.4 kph	Bernard Thévenet (Fra) Peugeot	Bernard Thévenet (Fra) Peugeot
	Major climbs: Côte de Sombernon (590m) Bernard Thévenet (Fra) Peugeot			
Stage 21 Sat 23 Jul	Montereau to Versailles 54 finishers	141.5 km 3h59'22" 35.5 kph	Gerrie Knetemann (Ned) TI-Raleigh	Bernard Thévenet (Fra) Peugeot
Stage 22a Sun 24 Jul	Paris (Champs-Élysées) (ITT) 54 finishers	6 km 7'52" 45.8 kph	Dietrich Thurau (FRG) TI-Raleigh	Bernard Thévenet (Fra) Peugeot
Stage 22b Sun 24 Jul	Circuit des Champs-Élysées 53 finishers	90.7 km 2h09'04" 42.2 kph	Alain Meslet (Fra) Gitane	Bernard Thévenet (Fra) Peugeot

(1) Joaquim Agostinho was stripped of the stage win after failing an anti-doping test. The stage victory was not awarded to anyone else, as the rider who finished second (Antonio Menéndez, from KAS) also tested positive.

Prize fund: 1,168,490 francs (first prize: 100,000 francs)

Final Classification

Place	Rider	Team	Time	Age
1	Bernard Thévenet (Fra)	Peugeot	4,096 km 115h38'30" 35.419 kph	29
2	Hennie Kuiper (Ned)	TI-Raleigh	+ 0'48"	28
3	Lucien Van Impe (Bel)	Lejeune	+ 3'32"	30
4	Francisco Galdós (Esp)	KAS	+ 7'45"	30
5	Dietrich Thurau (FRG)	TI-Raleigh	+ 12'24"	22
6	Eddy Merckx (Bel)	FIAT	+ 12'38"	32
7	Michel Laurent (Fra)	Peugeot	+ 17'42"	23
8	Joop Zoetemelk (Ned)	Miko	+ 19'22"	31
9	Raymond Delisle (Fra)	Miko	+ 21'32"	34
10	Alain Meslet (Fra)	Gitane	+ 27'31"	27

Lanterne Rouge

53	Roger Loysch (Bel)	Frisol	+ 2h24'08"	29

Points

	Jacques Esclassan (Fra)	Peugeot		28

King of the Mountains

	Lucien Van Impe (Bel)	Lejeune		30

Intermediate Sprints

	Pierre-Raymond Villemiane (Fra)	Gitane		26

Youth

	Dietrich Thurau (FRG)	TI-Raleigh		22

Team

		TI-Raleigh		

Team (Points)

		Peugeot		

Super Combativité

	Gerrie Knetemann (Ned)	TI-Raleigh		26

1978: Yet More Doping

The Amaury Empire, owner of the Tour de France, was thrown into chaos in 1977 when the 67-year-old Émilien Amaury, the man who built it up from nothing after the end of the Second World War, died. His will left the empire to his daughter, Francine, but was being disputed by his son, Philippe, and it was down to the courts to decide who was really in charge. In the interim no one knew who was really in charge.

In addition to losing their patriarch, the Amaury empire was only slowly recovering from having spent much of the past two years in a battle with printers at *Le Parisien Libéré*, who had been striking over redundancies imposed upon them. The dispute had led to protests at the Tour de France but they were minor compared to what else was happening during the strike. An attempt was made on the life of *Le Parisien Libéré*'s editor, Bernard Cabanes, in the form of a bomb outside his home. But the people who planted the explosives picked the wrong Bernard Cabanes and murdered instead the editor-in-chief of Agence France Presse, who happened to have the same name. André Bergeron, the leader of the socialist print union whose workers were helping Amaury break the strike by printing *Le Parisien*, was injured in a second attack that same night. Following the death of Amaury, the strike was brought to a conclusion with the help of Jean-Luc Lagardère, who helped find jobs for the striking workers elsewhere in Paris's newspaper publishing industry.

And it wasn't just the print workers who were feeling truculent, for the Tour's riders were getting fed up with the way things were going on. Since the end of the 1950s Félix Lévitan had been needing more and longer transfers between stages in order to join up the towns and cities willing to pay to host the race. (The Tour had actually had its first transfer as far back as 1906, when the riders had to travel the short distance from Lille to Douai, but they only became a regular feature after 1958.) And Lévitan was also packing in split stages, two and sometimes three stages in one day of racing. The riders were being pushed to the limit, often arriving at team hotels – which sometimes weren't actually hotels and were in fact school dormitories – late in the evening after race traffic had delayed their journey.

On 12 July, on what was the second split stage of the race, the riders struck. A 7.30 start was required in order to pack in all the day's riding, and that meant an even earlier rise for the riders, which itself came after the race had transferred by car the night before from Saint-Lary-Soulan to Tarbes (a distance of about 60 kilometres, give or take). In the morning the *peloton* was meant to race from Tarbes to Valence-d'Agen (158 kilometres) and then, after a brief rest, remount and race on to Toulouse (98 kilometres). And then transfer up to Figeac (about 150 kilometres north) that evening.

The riders travelled the road to Valence-d'Agen at touring pace, with the plan being for the *peloton* to dismount and walk the final kilometre. Jacques Goddet implored the riders to race, if only that final kilometre, so the fans in Valance-d'Agen would still get the spectacle. But the riders were deaf to his entreaties.

All the riders participated in the strike. But, singled out as their spokesman, was France's 23-year-old national champion, Bernard Hinault (Renault). Hinault was a mercurial talent, having won Ghent-Wevelgem, Liège-Bastogne-Liège, the Critérium du Dauphiné Libéré and the GP des Nations in 1977. Coming into the Tour he was the winner of the 1978 edition of the Vuelta a España.

There were shades of Henri Pélissier about Hinault in the way he stood up to race organisers – and the agents, Daniel Dousset and Roger Piel, who still held considerable sway in the sport – but he was more in the model of Jacques Anquetil, a man who felt he was doing a professional's job and deserved to be treated as a professional and not a mere chattel.

Hinault was forceful, direct and uncompromising. Having taken the local mayor to task for criticising the riders' action, he even managed to be apologetic to the people of Valence-d'Agen, who had paid handsomely to host the race but been denied the spectacle of any racing, promising to return to them during the critérium season. He spoke and acted like a leader of men, a true *patron*.

One of the ironies of that riders' strike was that, in the month after the Tour, those same riders travelled vast distances around France and the Low Countries packing in 30 or 40 critériums in as many days, sometimes riding two or even three races in the one day. But on that shadow Tour the riders set their own itinerary, organised their own transport and collected substantial appearance fees. At the Tour, they were simply cogs in a wheel – not in charge – and they were only racing for prize money, which was as little as 10 per cent of the Tour's overall budget, and was generally shared among the team.

The strike was a one-off, Goddet and Lévitan appeasing the *peloton* and promising more consultation and better conditions in the future. And so the race resumed, nothing ever breaking the rhythm of the Tour for long.

By this point in the race the *maillot jaune* had been passing from shoulder to shoulder, TI-Raleigh's Jan Raas taking it in the prologue, passing it to Peugeot's Jacques Bossis, back to Raleigh on the shoulders of Klaus-Peter Thaler and Gerrie Knetemann before Eddy Merckx's old *super domestique* Jos Bruyère took charge of it. That's where it was in Valence d'Agen, and where it still was four days later when the Tour arrived at the foot of Alpe d'Huez and rode into a new scandal. A new doping scandal. Or, rather, an old scandal, repeated on a bigger stage, with a bigger star.

Joop Zoetemelk (Miko/Mercier) started the day in second place overall, 1'03" down on Bruyère, with Hinault in third at 1'40 and Michel Pollentier (Velda/Lano/Flandria) fourth, at 2'38". The rest of the field was six minutes and more back. Pollentier was gunning for the overall win and planning to set that up with a victory on the Alpe. He had prepared himself thoroughly for the Tour, training on the Alpe ahead of the race, familiarising himself with the place he wanted to seal his destiny. And take the stage win and the yellow jersey is just what Pollentier did.

As the stage winner, Pollentier was required to provide a sample for the doping testers. But here he had a problem: he thought he was going to test positive. So he relied on that decade-old old ploy of submitting someone else's urine, using a complicated contraption to hide his deceit. Two years after Rachel Dard's use of such a ruse had been exposed, riders were still getting away with it. And maybe Pollentier would have got away with it that day on the Alpe, had not the rider ahead of him at the doping control also needed to cheat the system – and been quite inept in pulling off his deception. When Pollentier arrived the testers were taking great care, and they spotted his attempt to cheat the control.

For a rider testing positive, the normal punishment was a 10-minute time penalty, a one-month suspended suspension and a small financial fine. The Tour authorities, though, took a very dim view of what Pollentier had attempted to do. Ordinary riders, even stage winners, could be handed the paltry penalties, but Pollentier was now the wearer of the *maillot jaune*, the man on whom all eyes fell. He needed a punishment that fitted his stature, if not his crime. So they threw him off the race.

For some, there was more to Pollentier's disqualification than just his transgression in the doping control. Some felt that Goddet and Lévitan simply didn't like him, didn't think him a fitting champion for their Tour. He had been dubbed by one writer *l'Antipédaleur de Charme*, the opposite of the handsome and elegant Hugo Koblet. Pollentier rode with his knees all over the place and his body flailing all over the bike, and (Pierre Chany said) making the riders behind him seasick. Maybe there is some truth in this, and the Tour's bosses feared that even a 10-minute time penalty wouldn't stop the Belgian from donning the yellow jersey again. Or, perhaps, they were finally showing some backbone in the face of a problem that had now been plaguing the Tour continuously for more than two decades, since that day on the Ventoux in 1955.

Whatever the reasons for Pollentier's exclusion the *maillot jaune* passed to Zoetemelk (himself no stranger to problems with the testers), with Hinault just 14 seconds in arrears and all the rest five minutes and more back. It was now a two-man race. And Hinault won, waiting until the time trial in Nancy to don the jersey, Zoetemelk ceding four minutes in 72 kilometres and falling to 3'56" behind. The champion of France, in his first attempt at both, had just pulled off the Vuelta/Tour double, a feat previously only achieved by Anquetil (1963) and Eddy Merckx (1973).

* * * * *

For Peugeot's Bernard Thévenet, the defending Tour champion, it was a Tour to forget: he exited the race in the Pyrenees. He'd had a season to forget too, riding like a shadow of his former self. Late in the year he was hospitalised and then confessed to the journalist Pierre Chany that he'd ruined his career with cortisone abuse (there was no test for cortisone at the time, and riders had been using it freely since the end of the 1960s).

The doctor at Peugeot, François Bellocq, believed that using cortisone shouldn't count as doping, as it was a natural hormone and all his riders were doing was topping up the tank as the fuel ran out. That the drug was banned was neither here nor there: the rules were for others to worry about and, when you're using a drug that can't be tested for, why worry about them?

Stage-by-Stage Results for the 1978 Tour de France			Stage Winner	Maillot Jaune
Prologue Thu 29 Jun	Leiden (ITT) 109 finishers	5.2 km 6'38" 47 kph	Jan Raas (Ned) TI-Raleigh	Jan Raas (Ned) TI-Raleigh
Stage 1a Fri 30 Jun	Leiden to Saint-Willebrord 108 finishers	135 km 3h24'21" 39.6 kph	Jan Raas (Ned) TI-Raleigh	Jan Raas (Ned) TI-Raleigh
Stage 1b Fri 30 Jun	Saint-Willebrord to Brussels 106 finishers	100 km 2h22'14" 42.2 kph	Walter Planckaert (Bel) C&A	Jan Raas (Ned) TI-Raleigh
Stage 2 Sat 1 Jul	Brussels to Saint-Amand-les-Eaux 106 finishers	199 km 5h21'31" 37.1 kph	Jacques Esclassan (Fra) Peugeot	Jan Raas (Ned) TI-Raleigh
Stage 3 Sun 2 Jul	Saint-Amand-les-Eaux to Saint-Germain-en-Laye 106 finishers	243.5 km 7h25'42" 32.8 kph	Klaus-Peter Thaler (Ned) TI-Raleigh	Jacques Bossis (Fra) Peugeot
Stage 4 Mon 3 Jul	Evreux to Caen (TTT) 106 finishers	153 km 3h39'07" 41.9 kph	TI-Raleigh	Klaus-Peter Thaler (Ned) TI-Raleigh

Stage-by-Stage Results for the 1978 Tour de France			Stage Winner	Maillot Jaune
Stage 5 Tue 4 Jul	Caen to Mazé-Montgeoffroy 106 finishers	244 km 6h00'16" 40.6 kph	Freddy Maertens (Bel) Velda	Klaus-Peter Thaler (Ned) TI-Raleigh
Stage 6 Wed 5 Jul	Mazé-Montgeoffroy to Poitiers 106 finishers	166.2 km 4h02'24" 41.1 kph	Sean Kelly (Irl) Velda	Gerrie Knetemann (Ned) TI-Raleigh
Stage 7 Thu 6 Jul	Poitiers to Bordeaux 106 finishers	242 km 7h01'08" 34.5 kph	Freddy Maertens (Bel) Velda	Gerrie Knetemann (Ned) TI-Raleigh
Stage 8 Fri 7 Jul	Saint-Émilion to Saint-Foye-la-Grande (ITT) 106 finishers	59.3 km 1h22'01" 43.4 kph	Bernard Hinault (Fra) Renault	Joseph Bruyère (Bel) C&A
Stage 9 Sat 8 Jul	Bordeaux to Biarritz 106 finishers	233 km 6h43'10" 34.7 kph	Miguel María Lasa (Esp) Teka	Joseph Bruyère (Bel) C&A
Sun 9 Jul	Rest Day			
Stage 10 Mon 10 Jul	Biarritz to Pau 103 finishers	191.5 km 5h46'54" 33.1 kph	Henk Lubberding (Ned) TI-Raleigh	Joseph Bruyère (Bel) C&A
	Major climbs: Col de Marie-Blanque (1,035m) Michel Pollentier (Bel) Velda			
Stage 11 Tue 11 Jul	Pau to Saint-Lary-Soulan 99 finishers	161 km 5h47'26" 27.8 kph	Mariano Martínez (Fra) Jobo	Joseph Bruyère (Bel) C&A
	Major climbs: Col du Tourmalet (2,115m) Michel Pollentier (Bel) Velda; Col d'Aspin (1,489m) Michel Laurent (Fra) Peugeot; Saint-Lary-Soulan (1,680m) Mariano Martínez (Esp) Jobo			
Stage 12a Wed 12 Jul	Tarbes to Valence-d'Agen 99 finishers	158 km	annulled	Joseph Bruyère (Bel) C&A
Stage 12b Wed 12 Jul	Valence-d'Agen to Toulouse 99 finishers	96 km 2h19'12" 41.4 kph	Jacques Esclassan (Fra) Peugeot	Joseph Bruyère (Bel) C&A
Stage 13 Thu 13 Jul	Figeac to Super Besse 96 finishers	221 km 6h43'49" 32.8 kph	Paul Wellens (Bel) TI-Raleigh	Joseph Bruyère (Bel) C&A
	Major climbs: Sainte-Anastaise (1,161m) Paul Wellens (Bel) TI-Raleigh; Super-Besse (1,275m) Paul Wellens (Bel) TI-Raleigh			
Stage 14 Fri 14 Jul	Besse-en-Chandesse to Puy de Dôme (ITT) 96 finishers	52.5 km 1h25'51" 36.7 kph	Joop Zoetemelk (Ned) Miko	Joseph Bruyère (Bel) C&A
	Major climbs: Puy de Dôme (1,415m) Joop Zoetemelk (Ned) Miko			

Stage-by-Stage Results for the 1978 Tour de France			Stage Winner	Maillot Jaune
Stage 15 Sat 15 Jul	Saint-Dier-d'Auvergne to Saint-Étienne 93 finishers	196 km 5h49'48" 33.6 kph	Bernard Hinault (Fra) Renault	Joseph Bruyère (Bel) C&A
	Major climbs: Col des Fourches (970m) Michel Pollentier (Bel) Velda; Col de la Croix de Chaubouret (1,230m) Michel Pollentier (Bel) Velda			
Stage 16 Sun 16 Jul	Saint-Étienne to l'Alpe d'Huez 90 finishers	240.5 km 7h23'45" 32.5 kph	~~Michel Pollentier (Bel)~~ ~~Velda~~ (1)	~~Michel Pollentier (Bel)~~ ~~Velda~~ (1)
			Hennie Kuiper (Ned) TI-Raleigh	Joop Zoetemelk (Ned) Miko
	Major climbs: Col de la République (1,161m) Jean-Jacques Fussien (Fra) Fiat; Col du Luitel (1,262m) Mariano Martínez (Esp) Jobo; l'Alpe d'Huez (1,860m) Hennie Kuiper (Ned) TI-Raleigh			
Mon 17 Jul	Rest Day			
Stage 17 Tue 18 Jul	Grenoble to Morzine 81 finishers	225 km 7h13'34" 31.1 kph	Christian Seznec (Fra) Miko	Joop Zoetemelk (Ned) Miko
	Major climbs: Col de Porte (1,326m) André Romero (Fra) Jobo; Col du Cucheron (1,139m) Hennie Kuiper (Ned) TI-Raleigh; Col du Granier (1,134m) Hennie Kuiper (Ned) TI-Raleigh; Col de Plainpalais (1,173m) René Bittinger (Fra) Velda; Col de la Colombière (1,618m) René Bittinger (Fra) Velda; Col de Joux-Plane (1,700m) Christian Seznec (Fra) Miko			
Stage 18 Wed 19 Jul	Morzine to Lausanne 78 finishers	137.5 km 3h36'52" 38 kph	Gerrie Knetemann (Ned) TI-Raleigh	Joop Zoetemelk (Ned) Miko
	Major climbs: Col du Corbier (1,325m) Mariano Martínez (Esp) Jobo; Pas de Morgins (1,369m) Mariano Martínez (Esp) Jobo			
Stage 19 Thu 20 Jul	Lausanne to Belfort 78 finishers	181.5 km 5h05'57" 35.6 kph	Marc Demeyer (Bel) Velda	Joop Zoetemelk (Ned) Miko
Stage 20 Fri 21 Jul	Metz to Nancy (ITT) 78 finishers	72 km 1h39'29" 43.4 kph	Bernard Hinault (Fra) Renault	Bernard Hinault (Fra) Renault
Stage 21 Sat 22 Jul	Épernay to Senlis 78 finishers	207.5 km 5h58'49" 34.7 kph	Jan Raas (Ned) TI-Raleigh	Bernard Hinault (Fra) Renault
Stage 22 Sun 23 Jul	Saint-Germain-en-Laye to Paris (Champs-Élysées) 78 finishers	161.5 km 4h22'46" 36.9 kph	Gerrie Knetemann (Ned) TI-Raleigh	Bernard Hinault (Fra) Renault

(1) Michel Pollentier was stripped of his stage win and thrown off the Tour for attempting to cheat at the doping control

Prize fund: 1,227,545 francs (first prize: 100,000 francs)

Final Classification

Place	Rider	Team	Time	Age
1	Bernard Hinault (Fra)	Renault	3,908 km 112h03'02" 36.085 kph	23
2	Joop Zoetemelk (Ned)	Miko	+ 3'56"	32
3	Joaquim Agostinho (Por)	Velda	+ 6'54"	35
4	Joseph Bruyère (Bel)	Domo	+ 9'04"	29
5	Christian Seznec (Fra)	Miko	+ 12'50"	25
6	Paul Wellens (Bel)	TI-Raleigh	+ 14'38"	26
7	Francisco Galdós (Esp)	KAS	+ 17'08"	31
8	Henk Lubberding (Ned)	TI-Raleigh	+ 17'26"	24
9	Lucien Van Impe (Bel)	C&A	+ 21'01"	31
10	Mariano Martínez (Fra)	Jobo	+ 22'58"	29

Lanterne Rouge

78	Philippe Tesnière (Fra)	Boston	+ 3h52'26"	23

Points

	Freddy Maertens (Bel)	Velda		26

King of the Mountains

	Mariano Martínez (Fra)	Jobo		29

Intermediate Sprints

	Jacques Bossis (Fra)	Renault		25

Youth

	Henk Lubberding (Ned)	TI-Raleigh		24

Team

		Miko		

Team (Points)

		TI-Raleigh		

Super Combativité

	Paul Wellens (Bel)	TI-Raleigh		26

1979: A Man Called Hinault

Since Jacques Anquetil in the 1960s, French cycling had lacked a consistent, dominating rider. Bernard Thévenet had blazed a trail across the heavens before burning out. Outside of his two Tour wins, he'd won the Tour de Romandie (1972), the French national championships (1973), the Critérium National (1974), the Critérium du Dauphiné Libéré (1975 and 1976), and that was pretty much it in terms of major victories. None of the Classics, no victories in either of the other two Grand Tours, no rainbow jerseys.

Raymond Poulidor was still the real hero of French cycling, even in retirement, the great nearly-man of the Tour, forged in the mould of Eugène Christophe, a man who could win Milan-Sanremo (1961), the Flèche Wallonne (1963), the GP des Nations (1963), the Critérium National (1964, 1966, 1968, 1971, 1972), the Vuelta a España (1964), the Dauphiné Libéré (1966, 1969) and Paris-Nice (1972, 1973). But it was really his eight visits to the Tour's podium that people seemed to love him for, and the fact that in a Tour career that stretched from 1962 to 1976 – across the eras of Maître Jacques and the Cannibal – he never once wore the *maillot jaune*, though a couple of times coming within a tenth of a tenth of a second of donning it. The French, they love a good loser, especially if he can also win. But really, the French wanted a winner, a real winner. A man for all seasons. Their own Eddy Merckx. They got the next best thing: Bernard Hinault (aka *le Blaireau*, the Badger).

After winning his début Tour in 1978, Hinault went on to bag his second GP des Nations title, and then went into the 1979 race with the Flèche Wallonne and another win in the Dauphiné Libéré on his record of victories. And he went into the Tour declaring he was going to strangle the life out of the race by taking the *maillot jaune* on the first day and sap the morale of his rivals. But despite tackling the prologue on an innovative aerodynamic bike – one of the benefits of riding for a team sponsored by France's national car maker, Renault – the best he could do was finish fourth, four seconds off TI-Raleigh's Gerrie Knetemann and one place behind his key rival for the overall win, Joop Zoetemelk (Miko/Mercier) though tied with him on time.

With the prologue out of the way the *peloton* was immediately launched into the Pyrenees, where the first selection of the real favourites would be made. Knetemann passed the jersey to Hinault's team-mate Jean-René Bernadeau, with *le Blaireau* usurping him the next day in a 23.9-kilometre time trial from Luchon to Superbagnères and – in the process – putting 53 seconds into Zoetemelk. Three days later than he planned, Hinault was in yellow and in control.

The rest of the Pyrenees passed peacefully and the next selection came in Stage Four, 86.6 kilometres of team time trialling from Captieux to Bordeaux. During this Renault's aerodynamic time trial bikes let the riders down, mechanical problems hampering their progress. The result? TI-Raleigh dominated the stage and Zoetemelk claimed back 41 seconds. Far from cowing his opponents, Hinault was looking vulnerable.

Bonus seconds pushed Zoetemelk back to 24 seconds off yellow by the time the riders had to tackle a second team time trial, 90.2 kilometres from Deauville to Le Havre. Peter Post's TI-Raleigh boys again dominated, but this time the Renaults weren't far behind, and Hinault was able to strengthen his lead over Zoetemelk, pushing the Dutchman back to 1'18". And then came a taste of Hell.

Roubaix has been part of the Tour's itinerary since 1907 and many riders have seen their Tour dreams shattered on the rough roads of northern France – roads which the *grande boucle* shared with Paris-Roubaix, a little bit of *l'enfer du nord* being good for the Tour. And in 1979 it was Hinault's turn to feel the pain felt by so many down the years, on a stage that included 32 kilometres of *pavé* incorporating Pévèle and Carrefour de l'Arbre. The *maillot jaune* punctured on the first *pavé* section, and Zoetemelk put the boot in, riding off and away with Hinault's yellow jersey. Three and a half minutes after Zoetemelk rode into the little vélodrome in Roubaix Hinault and his Renault helpmates rolled in, dropping the Badger to second, 2'08" off yellow.

Hinault had a chance to take some time back from Zoetemelk two stages later, a 33.4-kilometre individual time trial around Brussels, and he closed to 1'32". As the race approached the Alps that fell back to 49 seconds. Zoetemelk was making a race of it.

The second phase of mountains opened with yet another race against the clock, a 54.2-kilometre individual time trial from Évian to Morzine-Avoriaz. Hinault stormed it. A race of two halves – opening half flat, closing half climbing – Hinault was already 53 seconds up on Zoetemelk before the climb began, the *maillot jaune virtuel*. At the top of the mountain the gap was 2'37" and Hinault's yellow jersey went from being virtual to very real. With the Dutchman now 1'38" back on GC and all the rest more than 11 minutes off the pace, the fun had begun.

And so too had the doping news. Giovanni Battaglin (Inoxpran) was declared positive, from a sample he'd provided five days earlier. Wearing the polka-dot jersey he got the usual speeding ticket. (The yellow jersey you throw off; the others, they just get slapped wrists.) And a few more wrists would be slapped before the race was over.

In the race itself, the fun saw Hinault taking a few more seconds out of Zoetemelk and then Zoetemelk taking them back a couple of days later when the race tackled Alpe d'Huez for the second time in two days. And then, despite crashing into his *directeur sportive* Cyrille Guimard's car while reconnoitring the Dijon time trial course, Hinault added another minute. Zoetemelk just never got the chance to put up a sustained fight. But the Dutchman was not for giving up, even with Paris practically in sight. And on the final run in to the City of Lights he attacked.

Attacking on the last day of the Tour and spoiling the party was, even by 1979, a real no no. And Zoetemelk was 3'07" off the yellow jersey, the sort of time you take back in the mountains, not on a flat road with a sprint finish. But Zoetemelk went for it anyway. And Hinault pounced after him and caught up. But, instead of the pair sitting up and slipping back into the *peloton*, they pressed on, Hinault himself now attacking. It was Zoetemelk's turn to chase. But again, when the catch was made, the pair didn't just sit up and slip back into the *peloton*. Now they started to work together, arriving into the city a minute clear of the *peloton*.

And then it all came down to the final 150 metres, the two having promenaded up and down, up and down the Champs-Élysées and the bunch behind not closing in on them. The pair had had their fun and given the crowd a spectacle, the champion and his challenger still battling at the last, the yellow jersey leading the Tour de France into Paris. Now it was time for the kill. Zoetemelk dutifully led the sprint out and Hinault duly came flying around him to take the stage, his seventh of the Tour.

In the weeks after the race ended, Hinault's winning margin of three minutes was extended to 13. Zoetemelk had failed another dope test and was again handed a speeding ticket. It mattered little. He and Hinault had been in a class of their own throughout the race and even a 10-minute time penalty couldn't take the Dutchman's second place away from him. In terms of punishing those who broke the rules – in terms of actively discouraging doping – the sport had a long way to go.

Stage-by-Stage Results for the 1979 Tour de France			Stage Winner	Maillot Jaune
Prologue Wed 27 Jun	Fleurance (ITT) 150 finishers	5 km 5'59" 50.1 kph	Gerrie Knetemann (Ned) TI-Raleigh	Gerrie Knetemann (Ned) TI-Raleigh
Stage 1 Thu 28 Jun	Fleurance to Luchon 147 finishers	225 km 6h51'12" 32.8 kph	René Bittinger (Fra) Flandria	Jean-René Bernaudeau (Fra) Renault
	Major climbs: Col de Menté (1,420m) Bernard Hinault (Fra) Renault; Col du Portillon (1,298m) Jean-René Bernaudeau (Fra) Renault			
Stage 2 Fri 29 Jun	Luchon to Superbagnères (ITT) 143 finishers	23.9 km 53'59" 26.6 kph	Bernard Hinault (Fra) Renault	Bernard Hinault (Fra) Renault
	Major climbs: Superbagnères (1,804m) Bernard Hinault (Fra) Renault			

Stage-by-Stage Results for the 1979 Tour de France			Stage Winner	Maillot Jaune
Stage 3 Sat 30 Jun	Luchon to Pau 131 finishers	180.5 km 4h58'29" 36.3 kph	Bernard Hinault (Fra) Renault	Bernard Hinault (Fra) Renault
	Major climbs: Col de Peyresourde (1,569m) Bernard Hinault (Fra) Renault; Col d'Aspin (1,489m) René Bittinger (Fra) Flandria; Col du Soulor (1,474m) Mariano Martínez (Fra) La Redoute			
Stage 4 Sun 1 Jul	Captieux to Bordeaux (TTT) 131 finishers	86.6 km 1h47'15" 48.4 kph	TI-Raleigh	Bernard Hinault (Fra) Renault
Stage 5 Mon 2 Jul	Neuville-de-Poitou to Angers 130 finishers	145.5 km 3h38'00" 40 kph	Jan Raas (Ned) TI-Raleigh	Bernard Hinault (Fra) Renault
Stage 6 Tue 3 Jul	Angers to Saint-Brieuc 129 finishers	238.5 km 6h24'15" 37.2 kph	Joseph Jacobs (Bel) Ijsboerke	Bernard Hinault (Fra) Renault
Stage 7 Wed 4 Jul	Saint-Hilaire-du-Harcouët to Deauville 129 finishers	158.2 km 4h05'51" 38.6 kph	Leo van Vliet (Ned) TI-Raleigh	Bernard Hinault (Fra) Renault
Stage 8 Thu 5 Jul	Deauville to Le Havre (TTT) 129 finishers	90.2 km 1h50'27" 49 kph	TI-Raleigh	Bernard Hinault (Fra) Renault
Stage 9 Fri 6 Jul	Amiens to Roubaix 125 finishers	201.2 km 4h49'03" 41.8 kph	Ludo Delcroix (Bel) Ijsboerke	Joop Zoetemelk (Ned) Miko
Stage 10 Sat 7 Jul	Roubaix to Brussels 120 finishers	124 km 2h44'02" 45.4 kph	Jo Maas (Ned) DAF Trucks	Joop Zoetemelk (Ned) Miko
Stage 11 Sun 8 Jul	Brussels (ITT) 119 finishers	33.4 km 43'01" 46.6 kph	Bernard Hinault (Fra) Renault	Joop Zoetemelk (Ned) Miko
Stage 12 Mon 9 Jul	Rochefort to Metz 113 finishers	193 km 4h42'40" 41 kph	Christian Seznec (Fra) Miko	Joop Zoetemelk (Ned) Miko
Stage 13 Tue 10 Jul	Metz to Ballon d'Alsace 112 finishers	202 km 4h56'23" 40.9 kph	Pierre-Raymond Villemiane (Fra) Renault	Joop Zoetemelk (Ned) Miko
	Major climbs: Ballon d'Alsace (1,178m) Pierre-Raymond Villemiane (Fra) Renault			
Stage 14 Wed 11 Jul	Belfort to Évian 111 finishers	248.2 km 6h45'10" 36.8 kph	Marc Demeyer (Bel) Flandria	Joop Zoetemelk (Ned) Miko
Stage 15 Thu 12 Jul	Evian to Morzine-Avoriaz (ITT) 107 finishers	54.2 km 1h33'35" 34.7 kph	Bernard Hinault (Fra) Renault	Bernard Hinault (Fra) Renault
	Major climbs: Avoriaz (1,800m) Bernard Hinault (Fra) Renault			

Stage-by-Stage Results for the 1979 Tour de France			Stage Winner	Maillot Jaune
Stage 16 Fri 13 Jul	Morzine to Les Menuires 101 finishers	201.3 km 6h05'16" 33.1 kph	Lucien Van Impe (Bel) KAS	Bernard Hinault (Fra) Renault
	Major climbs: Col des Saisies (1,633m) Henk Lubberding (Ned) TI-Raleigh; Cormet de Roselend (1,968m) Henk Lubberding (Ned) TI-Raleigh; Les Ménuires (1,809m) Lucien Van Impe (Bel) KAS			
Sat 14 Jul	Rest Day			
Stage 17 Sun 15 Jul	Les Menuires to l'Alpe d'Huez 97 finishers	166.5 km 6h12'55" 26.8 kph	Joaquim Agostinho (Por) Flandria	Bernard Hinault (Fra) Renault
	Major climbs: Col de la Madeleine (2,000m) Lucien Van Impe (Bel) KAS; Col du Télégraphe (1,566m) Giovanni Battaglin (Ita) Inoxpran; Col du Galibier (2,645m) Lucien Van Impe (Bel) KAS; l'Alpe d'Huez (1,860m) Joaquim Agostinho (Por) Flandria			
Stage 18 Mon 16 Jul	L'Alpe d'Huez to l'Alpe d'Huez 92 finishers	118.5 km 4h23'28" 27 kph	Joop Zoetemelk (Ned) Miko	Bernard Hinault (Fra) Renault
	Major climbs: Colle del Morte (1,360m) Mariano Martínez (Fra) La Redoute; l'Alpe d'Huez (1,860m) Joop Zoetemelk (Ned) Miko			
Stage 19 Tue 17 Jul	L'Alpe d'Huez to Saint-Priest 92 finishers	162 km 4h48'40" 33.7 kph	Dietrich Thurau (FRG) Ijsboerke	Bernard Hinault (Fra) Renault
Stage 20 Wed 18 Jul	Saint-Priest to Dijon 92 finishers	239.6 km 6h52'26" 34.9 kph	~~Gerrie Knetemann (Ned) TI-Raleigh (1)~~ Sergio Parsani (Ita) Bianchi	Bernard Hinault (Fra) Renault
Stage 21 Thu 19 Jul	Dijon (ITT) 91 finishers	48.8 km 1h08'53" 42.5 kph	Bernard Hinault (Fra) Renault	Bernard Hinault (Fra) Renault
Stage 22 Fri 20 Jul	Dijon to Auxerre 91 finishers	189 km 5h32'22" 34.1 kph	Gerrie Knetemann (Ned) TI-Raleigh	Bernard Hinault (Fra) Renault
Stage 23 Sat 21 Jul	Auxerre to Nogent-sur-Marne 91 finishers	205 km 5h52'56" 34.9 kph	Bernard Hinault (Fra) Renault	Bernard Hinault (Fra) Renault
Stage 24 Sun 22 Jul	Le Perreux-sur-Marne to Paris (Champs-Élysées) 90 finishers	180.3 km 4h47'45" 37.6 kph	Bernard Hinault (Fra) Renault	Bernard Hinault (Fra) Renault

(1) Gerrie Knetemann was stripped of his stage win having taken a tow off a team car to get up to the breakaway.

Prize fund: 1,338,120 francs (first prize: 100,000 francs)

Final Classification

Place	Rider	Team	Time		Age
1	Bernard Hinault (Fra)	Renault	3,765 km 103h06'50" 36.513 kph		24
2	Joop Zoetemelk (Ned) (2)	Miko	~~+ 3'07"~~	+ 13'07"	33
3	Joaquim Agostinho (Por)	Flandria	+ 26'53"		36
4	Hennie Kuiper (Ned)	Peugeot	+ 28'02"		30
5	Jean-René Bernaudeau (Fra)	Renault	+ 32'43"		23
6	Giovanni Battaglin (Ita)	Inoxpran	+ 38'12"		28
7	Jo Maas (Ned)	DAF	+ 38'38"		24
8	Paul Wellens (Bel)	TI-Raleigh	+ 39'06"		27
9	Claude Criquiélion (Bel)	KAS	+ 40'38"		22
10	Dietrich Thurau (FRG)	Ijsboerke	+ 44'35"		24

Lanterne Rouge

90	Gerhard Schönbacher (Aut)	Vermeer	+ 4h19'21"	25

Points

	Bernard Hinault (Fra)	Renault		24

King of the Mountains

	Giovanni Battaglin (Ita)	Inoxpran		28

Intermediate Sprints

	Willy Teirlinck (Bel)	KAS		31

Youth

	Jean-René Bernaudeau (Fra)	Renault		23

Team

		Renault		

Team (Points)

		Renault		

Super Combativité

	~~Joop Zoetemelk (Ned) (2)~~	~~Miko~~		33
	Hennie Kuiper (Ned)	Peugeot		30

(2) Joop Zoetemelk was stripped of the Super Combativité title after failing an anti-doping test

1980: Always the Bridesmaid?

It was said by some of Joop Zoetemelk that he came out of the Tour de France every year without a suntan, having spent the three weeks racing around France riding in someone else's shadow. Which is partly true on two levels: Zoetemelk did have a tendency to suck wheels and wait for riders to break; and he was overshadowed by others.

Starting his career in the era of Eddy Merckx and stretching through to what already was clearly the era of Bernard Hinault the Dutchman had five times finished second in the Tour: to Merckx in 1970 and 1971; to Van Impe in 1976; and then to Hinault in 1978 and 1979 (in his other four Tours he was always inside the top 10). Like Raymond Poulidor – who also had five second places at the Tour – Zoetemelk was becoming the eternal second. Always the bridesmaid and never the bride. And then, in 1980, the bride did a moonlight flit, and the 33-year-old Zoetemelk – now riding for Peter Post's all-powerful TI-Raleigh squad – got to step in at the last minute.

The race had opened in Frankfurt with Renault getting their time trial bikes right and Hinault – who had already raced and won the Giro d'Italia and was looking for the second Grand Tour double of his career – duly taking the win in the prologue, only to then lose the *maillot jaune* to TI-Raleigh's Gerrie Knetemann, Peter Post's boys again dominating the team time trials. The jersey briefly passed back to Renault, with Yvon Bertin sporting it, before Rudy Pevenage (DAF Trucks) took control and things settled down until the mountains arrived.

The Pyrenees opened on Stage 13, Pau to Luchon. By the time the *peloton* arrived in Pau Hinault was in yellow, having taken the jersey from Pevenage the day before. Zoetemelk was 21 seconds behind him. The story of most of the previous week had been Hinault's knee. The Badger was suffering from tendonitis – as had his mentor Cyrille Guimard during his career – and there was a big question mark over whether the Badger would make it back to Paris, let alone do so wearing the yellow jersey. A near four-minute lead over Zoetemelk had been chip-chip-chipped away at already, and there was little hope of things improving quickly.

Right up to the end Hinault was talking things up, saying his knee was recovering, promising to attack. But it was all a bluff, and the decision had already been made: Hinault was quitting the Tour. But he wasn't going to quit on the road, climb off with all the press photographers capturing his pain. He did it his way, leaving the team hotel in Pau in the night and hiding out in a team-mate's house in Lourdes. (Two Renault team-mates would later follow Hinault out of the race with tendonitis, Bertin and Jean-René Bernaudeau. Whatever they were doing wrong, it was infectious.)

For Zoetemelk, the yellow jersey was now his – though he followed tradition and declined to start the next stage wearing it – but the race was far from run, he still had Hennie Kuiper (Peugeot) snapping at his heels, 70 seconds behind him. But Kuiper didn't challenge and fell away in the Alps. The bridesmaid became the bride, said 'I do' and lifted the trophy.

* * * * *

Every Tour is made up of a multitude of races: the race to wear yellow, the race to be the last man wearing yellow; the race to win stages; the races for the polka-dot jersey and for the green jersey; the race for the team prize; the races for the other categories. You even have races to be the best rider from your region, the local hero. And you also have the race for last place, the race for the lanterne rouge.

Officially, the Tour doesn't know where it is with the *lanterne rouge*. Technically, it's an honour which doesn't exist. But check out the Tour's *Guide Historique* and, each year, there he is, given his due and singled out among the podium fillers and the jersey winners. The *lanterne rouge*: the last man home. He's not the last man, for many will have fallen along the way by the time the race has reached Paris. He's the last of the men still standing. And that's what makes him so special. He's the last man who didn't fall, the representative of those who couldn't complete the journey.

The *lanterne rouge*'s status within the Société du Tour de France (the Exploitation part of the name having been dropped) reached its nadir in 1980. The previous year Philippe Tesnière (FIAT) and Gerhard Schönbacher (DAF Trucks) had had a ding-dong battle to finish last (the honour of being the *lanterne rouge* generating critérium appearances and the fees that went with them). Tesnière was defending the *lanterne rouge* title he'd won in 1978 but Schönbacher was determined to see he didn't make it back-to-back victories at the bottom of the rankings (you had to go all the way back to 1923 and Daniel Masson to find someone who'd 'won' the *lanterne rouge* more than once).

If either rider stopped for a bladder break, the other stopped with him. If one was halted with a puncture, the other halted too. Where one went, the other followed. They still had to finish within the time limit every day – this wasn't about dawdling along at the back and coming home hours after everyone else. And that race against the cut-off was their real Tour de France, a long, long race against the clock, always avoiding the man with the stopwatch while finishing as far down on the day as they could.

The cut-off was where Tesnière's defence of his *lanterne rouge* title ended. With time trials run off in reverse order, he and Schönbacher had to gamble on what the winning time would be, calculate the cut-off time that would generate and gauge their effort accordingly. Tesnière's calculations failed to consider just how fast Hinault could be on a time trial bike and his red lantern challenge was cut off. The man with the stopwatch sent him home.

Félix Lévitan disliked the publicity accruing to the *lanterne rouge*, especially when it encouraged the sort of shenanigans Schönbacher and Tesnière had engaged in. He felt it demeaned the race. A race he was selling to as many buyers as he could. Which is why, in 1980, Lévitan introduced a new rule. Or, more precisely, he brought back an old rule, the one tried by Jacques Goddet way back in 1939 when

Goddet wanted to eliminate the *lanterne rouge* every day once the race got going.

The rule itself was a borrowing from track cycling's elimination race, the Devil Take the Hindmost, in which the last rider is eliminated on designated laps. It was an apt borrowing for a race which itself borrowed its original format from the track's Six Day races. In Lévitan's hands, from the fifth stage to the pre-penultimate, the axe was to fall on the last man in the general classification. There was to be no race for the *lanterne rouge*.

But what the rule change actually did was to make the race for the *lanterne rouge* all the more exciting, with riders attacking to try and avoid the axe, and Schönbacher treating the Tour as if it was a gigantic Devil Take the Hindmost, gauging his effort so that he was always near the back but never the last man, and then swooping for the win once the axe stopped falling. Lévitan learned a valuable lesson: the same one Goddet had learned in 1939. Don't mess with the last man in the Tour de France. He's got a lot more guts than you can imagine.

Stage-by-Stage Results for the 1980 Tour de France			Stage Winner	Maillot Jaune
Prologue Thu 26 Jun	Frankfurt (ITT) 130 finishers	7.6 km 9'13" 49.5 kph	Bernard Hinault (Fra) Renault	Bernard Hinault (Fra) Renault
Stage 1a Fri 27 Jun	Frankfurt to Wiesbaden 130 finishers	133 km 3h19'39" 40 kph	Jan Raas (Ned) TI-Raleigh	Bernard Hinault (Fra) Renault
Stage 1b Fri 27 Jun	Wiesbaden to Frankfurt (TTT) 126 finishers	45.8 km 53'45" 51.1 kph	TI-Raleigh	Gerrie Knetemann (Ned) TI-Raleigh
Stage 2 Sat 28 Jun	Frankfurt to Metz 125 finishers	276 km 7h36'18" 36.3 kph	Rudy Pevenage (Bel) Ijsboerke	Yvon Bertin (Fra) Renault
Stage 3 Sun 29 Jun	Metz to Liège 122 finishers	282.5 km 7h58'37" 35.4 kph	Henk Lubberding (Ned) TI-Raleigh	Rudy Pevenage (Bel) DAF Trucks
Stage 4 Mon 30 Jun	Circuit de Spa (ITT) 122 finishers	34.6 km 47'28" 43.7 kph	Bernard Hinault (Fra) Renault	Rudy Pevenage (Bel) DAF Trucks
Stage 5 Tue 1 Jul	Liège to Lille 120 finishers	249.6 km 8h03'22" 31 kph	Bernard Hinault (Fra) Renault	Rudy Pevenage (Bel) DAF Trucks

Stage-by-Stage Results for the 1980 Tour de France			Stage Winner	Maillot Jaune
Stage 6 Wed 2 Jul	Lille to Compiègne 119 finishers	215.8 km 5h57'11" 36.3 kph	Jean-Louis Gauthier (Fra) Miko	Rudy Pevenage (Bel) DAF Trucks
Stage 7a Thu 3 Jul	Compiègne to Beauvais (TTT) 118 finishers	65 km 1h24'09" 46.3 kph	TI-Raleigh	Rudy Pevenage (Bel) DAF Trucks
Stage 7b Thu 3 Jul	Beauvais to Rouen 118 finishers	92 km 2h15'33" 40.7 kph	Jan Raas (Ned) TI-Raleigh	Rudy Pevenage (Bel) DAF Trucks
Stage 8 Fri 4 Jul	Flers to Saint-Malo 118 finishers	164.2 km 4h21'04" 37.7 kph	Bert Oosterbosch (Ned) TI-Raleigh	Rudy Pevenage (Bel) DAF Trucks
Sat 5 Jul	Rest Day			
Stage 9 Sun 6 Jul	Saint-Malo to Nantes 118 finishers	205.3 km 5h28'27" 37.5 kph	~~Sean Kelly (Irl)~~ ~~Splendor~~ (1) Jan Raas (Ned) TI-Raleigh	Rudy Pevenage (Bel) DAF Trucks
Stage 10 Mon 7 Jul	Rochefort-sur-Mer to Bordeaux 115 finishers	203 km 4h42'58" 43 kph	Cees Priem (Ned) TI-Raleigh	Rudy Pevenage (Bel) DAF Trucks
Stage 11 Tue 8 Jul	Damazan to Laplume (iTT) 114 finishers	51.8 km 1h10'24" 44.1 kph	Joop Zoetemelk (Ned) TI-Raleigh	Bernard Hinault (Fra) Renault
Stage 12 Wed 9 Jul	Agen to Pau 113 finishers	194.1 km 5h45'24" 33.7 kph	Gerrie Knetemann (Ned) TI-Raleigh	Bernard Hinault (Fra) Renault
Stage 13 Thu 10 Jul	Pau to Bagnères-de-Luchon 101 finishers	200.4 km 6h27'32" 31 kph	Raymond Martin (Fra) Miko	Joop Zoetemelk (Ned) TI-Raleigh
Major climbs: Col d'Aubisque (1,709m) Maurice le Guilloux (Fra) Renault; Col du Tourmalet (2,115m) Raymond Martin (Fra) Miko; Col d'Aspin (1,489m) Raymond Martin (Fra) Miko; Col de Peyresourde (1,569m) Raymond Martin (Fra) Miko				
Stage 14 Fri 11 Jul	Lézignan-Corbières to Montpellier 95 finishers	189.5 km 5h34'49" 34 kph	Ludo Peeters (Bel) Ijsboerke	Joop Zoetemelk (Ned) TI-Raleigh
Stage 15 Sat 12 Jul	Montpellier to Martigues 93 finishers	160 km 3h57'43" 40.4 kph	Bernard Vallet (Fra) La Redoute	Joop Zoetemelk (Ned) TI-Raleigh
Stage 16 Sun 13 Jul	Trets to Pra-Loup 92 finishers	208.6 km 6h25'31" 32.5 kph	Jos Deschoenmaecker (Bel) Marc	Joop Zoetemelk (Ned) TI-Raleigh
Major climbs: Col Saint-Jean (1,332m) Jos de Schoenmacker (Bel) Marc; Pra-Loup (1,630m) Jos de Schoenmacker (Bel) Marc				

Stage-by-Stage Results for the 1980 Tour de France			Stage Winner	Maillot Jaune
Stage 17 Mon 14 Jul	Serre Chevalier to Morzine 90 finishers	242 km 7h09'07" 33.8 kph	Mariano Martínez (Fra) La Redoute	Joop Zoetemelk (Ned) TI-Raleigh
	Major climbs: Col du Galibier (2,645m) Johan de Muynck (Bel) Splendor; Col de la Madeleine (2,000m) Mariano Martínez (Fra) La Redoute; Col de Joux-Plane (1,700m) Mariano Martínez (Fra) La Redoute			
Tue 15 Jul	Rest Day			
Stage 18 Wed 16 Jul	Morzine to Prapoutel-les-Sept-Laux 86 finishers	198.8 km 5h52'46" 33.8 kph	Ludo Loos (Bel) Marc	Joop Zoetemelk (Ned) TI-Raleigh
	Major climbs: Col de la Colombière (1,618m) Ludo Loos (Bel) Marc; Col des Aravis (1,498m) Ludo Loos (Bel) Marc; Champlaurent (1,118m) Ludo Loos (Bel) Marc; Barioz (1,048m) Ludo Loos (Bel) Marc; Prapoutel-les-Sept-Laux (1,358m) Ludo Loos (Bel) Marc			
Stage 19 Thu 17 Jul	Voreppe to Saint-Étienne 85 finishers	139.7 km 4h00'33" 34.8 kph	Sean Kelly (Irl) Splendor	Joop Zoetemelk (Ned) TI-Raleigh
	Major climbs: Le Fayet (611m) Jo Maas (Ned) DAF Trucks; Col de la Croix de Chaubouret (1,230m) Ismaël Lejarreta (Esp) Teka			
Stage 20 Fri 18 Jul	Saint-Étienne (ITT) 85 finishers	34.5 km 45'38" 45.4 kph	Joop Zoetemelk (Ned) TI-Raleigh	Joop Zoetemelk (Ned) TI-Raleigh
Stage 21 Sat 19 Jul	Auxerre to Fontenay-sous-Bois 85 finishers	208 km 5h48'33" 35.8 kph	Sean Kelly (Irl) Splendor	Joop Zoetemelk (Ned) TI-Raleigh
Stage 22 Sun 20 Jul	Fontenay-sous-Bois to Paris (Champs-Élysées) 85 finishers	186.1 km 5h12'27" 35.7 kph	Pol Verschuere (Bel) Ijsboerke	Joop Zoetemelk (Ned) TI-Raleigh

(1) Sean Kelly was relegated for an irregular sprint

Prize fund: 1,487,930 francs (first prize: 100,000 francs)

Final Classification

Place	Rider	Team	Time	Age
1	Joop Zoetemelk (Ned)	TI-Raleigh	3,842 km 109h19'14" 35.144 kph	34
2	Hennie Kuiper (Ned)	Peugeot	+ 6'55"	31
3	Raymond Martin (Fra)	Miko	+ 7'56"	31
4	Johan de Muynck (Bel)	Splendor	+ 12'24"	32
5	Joaquim Agostinho (Por)	Puch	+ 15'37"	37
6	Christian Seznec (Fra)	Miko	+ 16'16"	27
7	Sven Åke Nilsson (Swe)	Miko	+ 16'33"	28
8	Ludo Peeters (Bel)	Ijsboerke	+ 20'45"	26
9	Pierre Bazzo (Fra)	La Redoute	+ 21'03"	26
10	Henk Lubberding (Ned)	TI-Raleigh	+ 21'10"	26
Lanterne Rouge				
85	Gerhard Schönbacher (Aut)	Marc	+ 2h10'52"	26
Points				
	Rudy Pevenage (Bel)	Ijsboerke		26
King of the Mountains				
	Raymond Martin (Fra)	Miko		31
Intermediate Sprints				
	Rudy Pevenage (Bel)	Ijsboerke		26
Combination				
	Ludo Peeters (Bel)	Ijsboerke		26
Youth				
	Johan van der Velde (Ned)	TI-Raleigh		23
Team				
		Miko		
Team (Points)				
		TI-Raleigh		
Super Combativité				
	Christian Levavasseur (Fra)	Miko		24

1981: The Badger Bites Back

After his midnight flit from the 1980 Tour de France Bernard Hinault went home, licked his wounds, and let his knee recover. And at the World Championships he struck back, taking the rainbow jersey. And then, as if he was set on proving points, in the spring of 1981 he went to Paris-Roubaix – a race he'd called a *con* – and won. The rest of the early season he also won the Critérium International and the Amstel Gold Race, and then added the Critérium du Dauphiné Libéré prior to tackling the Tour. And at the *grande boucle* he made clear to everyone that he was back and back to win, by taking the *maillot jaune* in the prologue.

Peter Post's TI-Raleigh boys again bossed the team time trials and again Gerrie Knetemann relieved Hinault of the yellow jersey. When the race reached its sole day in the Pyrenees (Stage 5, Saint-Gaudens to Saint-Lary-Soulan), Hinault took charge and went on the attack. With him went an Australian rider, Phil Anderson (Peugeot). Various riders caught up to the break, including Lucien Van Impe (Boston), now limiting his horizons to another victory in the King of the Mountains competition. Van Impe broke away to take the stage, but Anderson held Hinault's wheel and the two arrived atop the Pla d'Adet together. And it was the Australian who donned the *maillot jaune*, the first for an Antipodean. It had been a long road since Don Kirkham and Iddo Snowy had set out on the 1914 Tour and the rewards along the way had been few and far between (Richard Lamb's *lanterne rouge* in 1931 being a highpoint), but at last the Aussies had a rider capable of challenging the best.

Not that Anderson's tenure in yellow lasted long: the very next day Hinault took over, winning the individual time trial to Pau, scene of his withdrawal the year before. And from there on home it was a one-man race. Anderson was the only rider within four minutes of Hinault, and the Australian could not yet be considered a challenger for the Tour title. The race was as good as in the bag.

Over the rest of the race, Hinault imposed himself upon what passed for opposition and arrived in Paris more than 14 minutes up on Van Impe. His third Tour title won, Hinault looked well capable of matching Anquetil and Merckx in the five-times club.

* * * * *

Anderson's yellow jersey was a sign of the internationalisation of the sport, and he wasn't the only English-speaker shaking the race up. Ireland's Sean Kelly (Wickes/Splendor) took his fourth Tour stage win. The British had Graham Jones riding support for Anderson at Peugeot, and they also had Paul Sherwen at La Redoute. And there had very nearly been a full American team, Félix Lévitan bending heaven and earth to give the growing US TV audience something to root for. Mike Neel (who had raced in Europe in the 1970s) and Mike Fraysse (who was involved with coaching young US riders) were courted to get a group of US amateurs to go professional and come to the Tour, with sponsorship from RTL lined up for them. Those plans, though, got parked, when Cyrille Guimard and Renault delivered their own fully-fledged American pro, Jock Boyer. Lévitan was so happy – and so determined that the Stateside TV audience would be able to pick their man out among the kaleidoscope of colour in the *peloton* – that normal rules were waived and Boyer's Renault jersey was swapped for a stars and stripes affair.

Stage-by-Stage Results for the 1981 Tour de France			Stage Winner	Maillot Jaune
Prologue Thu 25 Jun	Nice (ITT) 150 finishers	5.8 km 6'48" 51.1 kph	Bernard Hinault (Fra) Renault	Bernard Hinault (Fra) Renault
Stage 1a Fri 26 Jun	Nice to Nice 150 finishers	97 km 2h23'19" 40.6 kph	Freddy Maertens (Bel) Sunair	Bernard Hinault (Fra) Renault
	Major climbs: Côte de Roquette (570m) Bernard Hinault (Fra) Renault			
Stage 1b Fri 26 Jun	Nice to Antibes-Nice (TTT) 150 finishers	40 km 46'20" 51.8 kph	TI-Raleigh	Gerrie Knetemann (Ned) TI-Raleigh
Stage 2 Sat 27 Jun	Nice to Martigues 148 finishers	254 km 6h32'27" 38.8 kph	Johan van der Velde (Ned) TI-Raleigh	Gerrie Knetemann (Ned) TI-Raleigh
Stage 3 Sun 28 Jun	Martigues to Narbonne 148 finishers	232 km 6h33'50" 35.3 kph	Freddy Maertens (Bel) Sunair	Gerrie Knetemann (Ned) TI-Raleigh
Stage 4 Mon 29 Jun	Narbonne to Carcassonne (TTT) 148 finishers	77.2 km 1h41'03" 45.8 kph	TI-Raleigh	Gerrie Knetemann (Ned) TI-Raleigh
Stage 5 Tue 30 Jun	Saint-Gaudens to Saint-Lary-Soulan 147 finishers	117.5 km 3h32'32" 33.2 kph	Lucien Van Impe (Bel) Boston	Phil Anderson (Aus) Peugeot
	Major climbs: Col de Peyresourde (1,569m) Bernard Hinault (Fra) Renault; Pla d'Adet (1,680m) Lucien Van Impe (Bel) Boston			
Stage 6 Wed 1 Jul	Nay to Pau (ITT) 146 finishers	26.7 km 35'52" 44.7 kph	Bernard Hinault (Fra) Renault	Bernard Hinault (Fra) Renault
Stage 7 Thu 2 Jul	Pau to Bordeaux 145 finishers	227 km 5h37'24" 40.4 kph	Urs Freuler (Esp) TI-Raleigh	Bernard Hinault (Fra) Renault
Stage 8 Fri 3 Jul	Rochefort-sur-Mer to Nantes 145 finishers	182 km 4h35'37" 39.6 kph	Ad Wijnands (Ned) TI-Raleigh	Bernard Hinault (Fra) Renault
Fri 4 Jul	Rest Day			
Stage 9 Sun 5 Jul	Nantes to Le Mans 145 finishers	196.5 km 4h23'09" 44.8 kph	René Martens (Bel) DAF Trucks	Bernard Hinault (Fra) Renault
Stage 10 Mon 6 Jul	Le Mans to Aulnay-sous-Bois 145 finishers	264 km 6h30'41" 40.5 kph	Ad Wijnands (Ned) TI-Raleigh	Bernard Hinault (Fra) Renault
Stage 11 Tue 7 Jul	Compiègne to Roubaix 144 finishers	246 km 6h18'34" 39 kph	Daniel Willems (Bel) Capri Sonne	Bernard Hinault (Fra) Renault
Stage 12a Wed 8 Jul	Roubaix to Brussels 139 finishers	107.3 km 2h25'48" 44.2 kph	Freddy Maertens (Bel) Sunair	Bernard Hinault (Fra) Renault

Stage-by-Stage Results for the 1981 Tour de France			Stage Winner	Maillot Jaune
Stage 12b Wed 8 Jul	Brussels to Zolder 139 finishers	137.8 km 3h22'31" 40.8 kph	Eddy Planckaert (Bel) Wickes	Bernard Hinault (Fra) Renault
Stage 13 Thu 9 Jul	Beringen to Hasselt 139 finishers	157 km 4h01'20" 39 kph	Freddy Maertens (Bel) Sunair	Bernard Hinault (Fra) Renault
Stage 14 Fri 10 Jul	Mulhouse (ITT) 138 finishers	38.5 km 50'30" 45.7 kph	Bernard Hinault (Fra) Renault	Bernard Hinault (Fra) Renault
Stage 15 Sat 11 Jul	Besançon to Thonon-les-Bains 128 finishers	231 km 5h47'07" 39.9 kph	Sean Kelly (Irl) Wickes	Bernard Hinault (Fra) Renault
Major climbs: Col de Cou (1,116m) Vicente Belda (Esp) Kelme				
Stage 16 Sun 12 Jul	Thonon-les-Bains to Morzine 127 finishers	199.5 km 6h14'29" 32 kph	Robert Alban (Fra) La Redoute	Bernard Hinault (Fra) Renault
Major climbs: Mont Salève (1,283m) Hendrik Devos (Bel) DAF Trucks; Col de la Ramaz (1,616m) Hubert Linard (Fra) Peugeot; Col de Joux-Plane (1,718m) Robert Alban (Fra) La Redoute; Col de Joux-Verte (1,760m) Robert Alban (Fra) La Redoute				
Mon 13 Jul	Rest Day			
Stage 17 Tue 14 Jul	Morzine to l'Alpe d'Huez 125 finishers	230.5 km 7h36'18" 30.3 kph	Peter Winnen (Ned) Capri Sonne	Bernard Hinault (Fra) Renault
Major climbs: Col de la Madeleine (2,000m) Lucien Van Impe (Bel) Boston; Col du Glandon (1,924m) Lucien Van Impe (Bel) Boston; l'Alpe d'Huez (1,860m) Peter Winnen (Ned) Capri Sonne				
Stage 18 Wed 15 Jul	Bourg-d'Oisans to Le Pleynet 124 finishers	131 km 4h16'43" 30.6 kph	Bernard Hinault (Fra) Renault	Bernard Hinault (Fra) Renault
Major climbs: Col du Luitel (1,262m) Roger de Cnijf (Bel) Boston; Saint-Martin d'Uriage (626m) Lucien Van Impe (Bel) Boston; Col des Mouilles (1,016m) Juan Fernández (Esp) Kelme; Barioz (1,041m) Jean-René Bernaudeau (Fra) Peugeot; Le Pleynet (1,445m) Bernard Hinault (Fra) Renault				
Stage 19 Thu 16 Jul	Veurey to Saint-Priest 123 finishers	117.5 km 3h07'02" 37.7 kph	Daniel Willems (Bel) Capri Sonne	Bernard Hinault (Fra) Renault
Major climbs: Veuray-Montaud (689m) Lucien Van Impe (Bel) Boston				
Stage 20 Fri 17 Jul	Saint-Priest (ITT) 123 finishers	46.5 km 1h01'16" 45.5 kph	Bernard Hinault (Fra) Renault	Bernard Hinault (Fra) Renault
Stage 21 Sat 18 Jul	Auxerre to Fontenay-sous-Bois 121 finishers	207 km 5h32'36" 37.3 kph	Johan van der Velde (Ned) TI-Raleigh	Bernard Hinault (Fra) Renault
Stage 22 Sun 19 Jul	Fontenay-sous-Bois to Paris (Champs-Élysées) 121 finishers	186.8 km 4h45'24" 39.3 kph	Freddy Maertens (Bel) Sunair	Bernard Hinault (Fra) Renault

Prize fund: 2,324,000 francs (first prize: 130,000 francs)

Final Classification

Place	Rider	Team	Time	Age
1	Bernard Hinault (Fra)	Renault	3,753 km 96h19'38" 38.960 kph	26
2	Lucien Van Impe (Bel)	Boston	+ 14'34"	34
3	Robert Alban (Fra)	La Redoute	+ 17'04"	29
4	Joop Zoetemelk (Ned)	TI-Raleigh	+ 18'21"	35
5	Peter Winnen (Ned)	Capri Sonne	+ 20'26"	23
6	Jean-René Bernaudeau (Fra)	Peugeot	+ 23'02"	25
7	Johan de Muynck (Bel)	Wickes	+ 24'25"	33
8	Sven Åke Nilsson (Swe)	Miko	+ 24'37"	29
9	Claude Criquiélion (Bel)	Wickes	+ 26'18"	24
10	Phil Anderson (Aus)	Peugeot	+ 27'00"	23

Lanterne Rouge

121	Faustino Cueli (Esp)	Teka	+ 4h29'54"	24

Points

	Freddy Maertens (Bel)	Sunair		29

King of the Mountains

	Lucien Van Impe (Bel)	Boston		34

Intermediate Sprints

	Freddy Maertens (Bel)	Sunair		29

Combination

	Bernard Hinault (Fra)	Renault		26

Youth

	Peter Winnen (Ned)	Capri Sonne		23

Team

		Peugeot		

Team (Points)

		Peugeot		

Super Combativité

	Bernard Hinault (Fra)	Renault		26

1982: The Simple Art of Winning

As he had in 1980, Bernard Hinault again arrived at the Tour de France with a win in the Giro d'Italia in his pocket, still trying for his second Grand Tour double, still trying to join Fausto Coppi, Jacques Anquetil and Eddy Merckx in what was then an elite club of Giro/Tour double winners.

As if working to a set script, Hinault again won the prologue and the Renault man again passed the jersey to TI-Raleigh, this time Ludo Peeters relieving him of the early burden in a road stage. Then it was the turn of Phil Anderson (Peugeot) to again wear yellow, taking Australia's first stage win (in Nancy, on Stage Three) and this time holding the jersey all the way to the individual time trial in Valence-d'Agen on Stage 10.

With Valence-d'Agen again part of the Tour's itinerary it was only fitting that there were more protests disrupting the race, but this time they weren't coming from within the *peloton*, they were coming from without, striking steel workers disrupting the Stage Five team time trial between Orchies and Fontaine-au-Pire, causing the stage to be cancelled after several teams had already taken to the road. That team time trial was hastily rescheduled and packed into a now split Stage Nine, and Peter Post's TI-Raleigh squad again dominated.

It was also only fitting that Hinault, the spokesman for the striking *peloton* in 1978, donned the *maillot jaune* after the individual time trial in Valence-d'Agen, though it was Gerrie Knetemann (TI-Raleigh) who won the stage. Hinault now led Knet by 14 seconds on the general classification, and the rest of the field was already two minutes and more back.

Bernard Hinault takes in his fourth Tour
title in 1982.

Knetemann was no GC contender, and, with two more time trials – and the mountains – still to come, Hinault already looked to have his Giro/Tour double sown up, and his fourth Tour title as good as won. And the rest of the *peloton* seemed to realise this, and the only race that followed was for the right to stand on the podium alongside the unstoppable Hinault.

As if to make up for what was otherwise an unexciting – though nonetheless satisfying – Tour, Hinault took on the sprinters in the finale on the Champs-Élysées and, as when duelling with Joop Zoetemelk in 1979, the *maillot jaune* was first across the line.

* * * * *

With its eightieth birthday – and its seventieth edition – just around the corner, the Tour was on a high. But not all were happy. Some objected to the level of commercialisation at the race – Félix Lévitan had been a very busy man and had more sponsors than he knew what to do with – but the Société du Tour de France wasn't hearing complaints. The Société du Tour was looking to the future, and in that future the Tour wouldn't just be the biggest sporting event in France, wouldn't just be the biggest bike race in the world. The Tour wanted to take on the Olympics and the World Cup.

Taking his lead from Félix Lévitan's long-held dream to internationalise the Tour by opening its doors to amateur teams from the non-traditional cycling nations, Jacques Goddet wrote in *L'Équipe* of the Tour's plans for *mondialisation*. Every four years, he wrote, the Tour would embrace globalisation and revert to national teams, nine from the traditional cycling nations fielding the day's best professional riders, and nine from the emerging nations, fielding amateur riders. The route itself would be international, with nearly half the race taking place outside of France's borders. And it wasn't just the usual suspects that Goddet talked of taking the Tour to, countries that had already hosted stages of the race (Belgium, Germany, Great Britain, Italy, Luxemburg, Monaco, the Netherlands, Spain and Switzerland). No, this would be a truly international Tour, with even a visit to the USA somehow being slotted into the race's schedule.

The promised return to national teams never happened, not with Goddet at the helm at least, and *mondialisation* was already a reality (as well as Anderson again wearing the yellow jersey, Ireland's Sean Kelly came out tops at the end in the race for the *maillot vert*). But the door was now open for Lévitan to bring in the amateurs he had long dreamed of getting into the Tour and for whom he had created the Tour de l'Avenir. Races like the Jean Leulliot-organised Paris-Nice had already got the professionals used to sharing the road with amateurs and now Lévitan had the green light to bring them into the Tour.

Stage-by-Stage Results for the 1982 Tour de France			Stage Winner	Maillot Jaune
Prologue Fri 2 Jul	Bâle (ITT) 169 finishers	7.4 km 9'31" 46.7 kph	Bernard Hinault (Fra) Renault	Bernard Hinault (Fra) Renault
Stage 1 Sat 3 Jul	Circuit de Schupfart-Möhlin 167 finishers	207 km 5h20'23" 38.8 kph	Ludo Peeters (Bel) TI-Raleigh	Ludo Peeters (Bel) TI-Raleigh
Stage 2 Sun 4 Jul	Bâle to Nancy 162 finishers	250 km 6h31'33" 38.3 kph	Phil Anderson (Aus) Peugeot	Phil Anderson (Aus) Peugeot
Major climbs: Ballon d'Alsace (1,178m) Bernard Vallet (Fra) La Redoute				
Stage 3 Mon 5 Jul	Nancy to Longwy 161 finishers	134 km 3h18'07" 40.6 kph	Daniel Willems (Bel) Sunair	Phil Anderson (Aus) Peugeot
Stage 4 Tue 6 Jul	Beauraing to Mouscron 160 finishers	219 km 5h46'16" 37.9 kph	Gerrie Knetemann (Ned) TI-Raleigh	Phil Anderson (Aus) Peugeot
Stage 5 Wed 7 Jul	Orchies to Fontaine-au- Pire (TTT) 160 finishers	73 km	Cancelled	Phil Anderson (Aus) Peugeot
Stage 6 Thu 8 Jul	Lille to Lille 160 finishers	233 km 5h55'42" 39.3 kph	Jan Raas (Ned) TI-Raleigh	Phil Anderson (Aus) Peugeot
Fri 9 Jul	Rest Day			
Stage 7 Sat 10 Jul	Cancale to Concarneau 158 finishers	234.5 km 6h07'12" 38.3 kph	Pol Verschuere (Bel) Vermeer	Phil Anderson (Aus) Peugeot
Stage 8 Sun 11 Jul	Concarneau to Châteaulin 155 finishers	200.8 km 5h03'30" 39.7 kph	Frank Hoste (Bel) TI-Raleigh	Phil Anderson (Aus) Peugeot
Stage 9a Mon 12 Jul	Lorient to Plumelec (TTT) 154 finishers	69 km 1h29'38" 46.2 kph	TI-Raleigh	Phil Anderson (Aus) Peugeot
Stage 9b Mon 12 Jul	Plumelec to Nantes 154 finishers	138.5 km 3h07'32" 44.3 kph	Stefan Mutter (Sui) Puch	Phil Anderson (Aus) Peugeot

Stage-by-Stage Results for the 1982 Tour de France			Stage Winner	Maillot Jaune
Stage 10 Tue 13 Jul	Saintes to Bordeaux 154 finishers	147.2 km 3h16'51" 44.9 kph	Pierre-Raymond Villemiane (Fra) Wolber	Phil Anderson (Aus) Peugeot
Stage 11 Wed 14 Jul	Valence-d'Agen (ITT) 154 finishers	57.3 km 1h17'29" 44.4 kph	Gerrie Knetemann (Ned) TI-Raleigh	Bernard Hinault (Fra) Renault
Stage 12 Thu 15 Jul	Fleurance to Pau 153 finishers	249 km 6h55'47" 35.9 kph	Sean Kelly (Irl) SEM	Bernard Hinault (Fra) Renault
	Major climbs: Col du Soulor (1,474m) André Chalmel (Fra) Peugeot; Col d'Aubisque (1,709m) Beat Breu (Sui) Cilo			
Stage 13 Fri 16 Jul	Pau to Saint-Lary-Soulan 152 finishers	122 km 3h40'27" 33.2 kph	Beat Breu (Sui) Cilo	Bernard Hinault (Fra) Renault
	Major climbs: Saint-Lary-Soulan (1,680m) Beat Breu (Sui) Cilo; Col d'Aspin (1,489m) Michel Laurent (Fra) Peugeot; Pla d'Adet (1,680m) Beat Breu (Sui) Cilo			
Sat 17 Jul	Rest Day			
Stage 14 Sun 18 Jul	Martigues (ITT) 152 finishers	32.5 km 45'12" 43.1 kph	Bernard Hinault (Fra) Renault	Bernard Hinault (Fra) Renault
Stage 15 Mon 19 Jul	Manosque to Orcières-Merlette 150 finishers	208 km 6h34'41" 31.6 kph	Pascal Simon (Fra) Peugeot	Bernard Hinault (Fra) Renault
	Major climbs: Espreaux (1,160m) Pascal Simon (Fra) Peugeot; Le Festre (1,440m) Pascal Simon (Fra) Peugeot; Col du Noyer (1,664m) Pascal Simon (Fra) Peugeot; Chaillolet (1,560m) Pascal Simon (Fra) Peugeot; Serre-Heyraud (1,614m) Pascal Simon (Fra) Peugeot; Orcières-Merlette (1,838m) Pascal Simon (Fra) Peugeot			
Stage 16 Tue 20 Jul	Orcières-Merlette to l'Alpe d'Huez 147 finishers	123 km 3h24'22" 36.1 kph	Beat Breu (Sui) Cilo	Bernard Hinault (Fra) Renault
	Major climbs: Col d'Ornon (1,367m) Bernard Vallet (Fra) La Redoute; l'Alpe d'Huez (1,860m) Beat Breu (Sui) Cilo			
Stage 17 Wed 21 Jul	Bourg-d'Oisans to Morzine 130 finishers	251 km 7h34'20" 33.1 kph	Peter Winnen (Ned) Capri Sonne	Bernard Hinault (Fra) Renault
	Major climbs: Fort de Montperché (1,745m) Bernard Vallet (Fra) La Redoute; Col des Aravis (1,498m) Marino Lejarreta (Esp) Teka; Col de la Colombière (1,618m) Jean-René Bernaudeau (Fra) Peugeot; Col de Joux-Plane (1,700m) Peter Winnen (Ned) Capri Sonne			
Stage 18 Thu 22 Jul	Morzine to Saint-Priest 127 finishers	233 km 6h32'51" 35.6 kph	Adri van Houwelingen (Ned) Kwantum	Bernard Hinault (Fra) Renault
Stage 19 Fri 23 Jul	Saint-Priest (ITT) 126 finishers	48 km 1h04'29" 44.7 kph	Bernard Hinault (Fra) Renault	Bernard Hinault (Fra) Renault
Stage 20 Sat 24 Jul	Sens to Aulnay-sous-Bois 125 finishers	161 km 4h22'21" 36.8 kph	Daniel Willems (Bel) Sunair	Bernard Hinault (Fra) Renault
Stage 21 Sun 25 Jul	Fontenay-sous-Bois to Paris (Champs-Élysées) 125 finishers	186.8 km 5h01'24" 37.2 kph	Bernard Hinault (Fra) Renault	Bernard Hinault (Fra) Renault

Prize fund: 2,207,220 francs (first prize: 150,000 francs)

Final Classification

Place	Rider	Team	Time	Age
1	Bernard Hinault (Fra)	Renault	3,507 km 92h08'46" 38.059 kph	27
2	Joop Zoetemelk (Ned)	Coop	+ 6'21"	36
3	Johan van der Velde (Ned)	TI-Raleigh	+ 8'59"	25
4	Peter Winnen (Ned)	Capri Sonne	+ 9'24"	24
5	Phil Anderson (Aus)	Peugeot	+ 12'16"	24
6	Beat Breu (Sui)	Cilo	+ 13'21"	24
7	Daniel Willems (Bel)	Sunair	+ 15'33"	25
8	Raymond Martin (Fra)	Miko	+ 15'35"	33
9	Hennie Kuiper (Ned)	DAF Trucks	+ 17'01"	33
10	Alberto Fernández (Esp)	Teka	+ 17'19"	27

Lanterne Rouge

125	Werner Devos (Bel)	Sunair	+ 3h04'44"	25

Points

	Sean Kelly (Irl)	SEM		26

King of the Mountains

	Bernard Vallet (Fra)	La Redoute		28

Intermediate Sprints

	Sean Kelly (Irl)	SEM		26

Combination

	Bernard Hinault (Fra)	Renault		27

Youth

	Phil Anderson (Aus)	Peugeot		24

Team

		Coop		

Team (Points)

		TI-Raleigh		

Super Combativité

	Régis Clère (Fra)	Coop		25

1983: The Curse of the Yellow Jersey

July 10th 1983. Pau. The edge of the Pyrenees. A stage win for France, Philippe Chevalier (Renault), with a Dutchman, Gerard Veldscholten (TI-Raleigh), second. Ireland's Sean Kelly (SEM) wins the sprint for third. A year ago he'd won the stage into Pau, the fifth of his Tour career so far, a sprinter winning in a stage that took in the Soulor and the Aubisque. And now here he is again, toward the front of the *peloton* as the mountains rise up on the horizon. Denmark's Kim Andersen (Coop) started the day in yellow, the first Dane ever to lead the Tour, and finishes safely with the bunch. But the bonifications fall in Kelly's favour, and the extra 10 seconds they give him push him ahead of Andersen on GC. The Dane's stint in yellow ends six days after it began.

Kelly's not the first Irishman to wear the Tour's *maillot jaune*. Jacques Anquetil's *domestique* Shay Elliott beat him to that 20 years earlier, when the reigning World Champion Jean Stablinski repaid a debt from the previous year's Worlds. But today Kelly is certainly the most fêted Irishman in the Tour's history. His yellow jersey goes well with his green one. Add the two to the white jersey being sported by Stephen Roche (Peugeot) and you can make as close to the Irish tricolour out of the three jerseys as the Tour allows you.

Kelly's happiness is shared by all on his team, *domestiques* and support staff alike, not least Kelly's *soigneur*, Willy Voet. But happiest of all – perhaps even happier than Kelly himself – is his SEM *directeur sportif* Jean de Gribaldy. This is vindication of De Gri's belief in Kelly. He's proven that the one-time sprint specialist is really a true all-rounder. Two victories in Paris-Nice (1982 and 1983) and now this, leading the Tour de France. And, in a year with no big star dominant in the Tour, Kelly is now among the favourites for overall victory.

No big stars? It's true. The reigning champion, four-time winner Bernard Hinault (Renault) is laid low with a recurrence of his knee problem, in a year that has already seen him win the Vuelta a España. Leaderless, his Renault team has fielded a squad that's gunning for stage wins, and maybe the white jersey for their star of the future, the 22-year-old Tour debutant Laurent Fignon. The bespectacled neophyte had been blooded in Grand Tours, he was at Hinault's side in Spain in the spring and had also helped *le Blaireau* to victory at the Giro d'Italia the year before, but the Tour de France is a step up, bigger and harder, with considerably more media pressure. So this is about Fignon learning lessons for the future, laying the foundations for victories to come.

The next day the heat is up. The *peloton* has four major climbs ahead of it as it enters the Pyrenees. The Aubisque. The Tourmalet. The Aspin. The Peyresourde. Kelly has a *jour sans*. From the start of the stage he's in trouble. At times he seems to need both feet to get one pedal to move. By the top of the Aubisque, the *maillot jaune* is six minutes off the pace. Kelly pulls back time on the descent and in the valley before the Tourmalet. By the summit of the Tourmalet that time regained has been frittered away and, unable to hold a wheel, the *maillot jaune* is 15 minutes down. Kelly again pulls back time lost on the descent. By the summit of the Aspin he is only 13 minutes adrift. By the time the race rolls into Luchon his deficit is down to 10 minutes.

Scotland's Robert Millar has won the stage. Kelly's *maillot jaune* is usurped by his Peugeot team-mate Pascal Simon, who is having a marvellous year, with victory in the Dauphiné Libéré in the run-up to the Tour (soon to be stripped from him for a doping infraction – though at least he doesn't get caught doping at the Tour: five others will return positive samples over the course of the race – including yet again – Coop's Joop Zoetemelk). Fignon lies second, four minutes back, waiting for his time to come, and now wears the white jersey (Roche has had an even bigger mare of a day than Kelly, losing three minutes more than his compatriot and surrendering the best young rider jersey to the rising French star. Another mare in the Pyrenees and a mare in the Alps will help teach Roche how tough the Tour can be).

Simon's own tenure in yellow is not to be blessed by good fortune. He cracks his shoulder blade in a *chute* early in the next day's stage, but he perseveres in yellow. His team-mates Millar, Roche and Phil Anderson – Australia's rising hope – sacrifice their own Tour hopes to nurse Simon through each day until the Alpe d'Huez stage, six days after his crash, when the *maillot jaune* is finally forced to abandon, before getting to the Alpe. Fignon's time has come.

Simon's riding on with his shoulder cracked and the yellow jersey on his back has been a blessing for Fignon, granting him time to rest and recover and prepare for the Alps to come. Others think the race is theirs for the taking: the Spaniards Ángel Arroyo and Pedro Delgado (both Reynolds), 1976-winner Lucien Van Impe (Metauromobili), Peter Winnen (TI-Raleigh). Fignon's a kid, and kids crack easy. But Fignon's a kid growing in self-belief. Hidden in the shadow of Hinault at the Giro and the Vuelta, where his job was to work for *le Blaireau* and not himself, his potential is not yet realised. Even his *directeur sportif* Cyrille Guimard – who knows that Fignon has the potential to win big in the future – is not sure how the kid will do in this final week of the Tour.

At the top of the Alpe Fignon's lead is 1'08" over Delgado, 2'33" over Jean-René Bernaudeau (Wolber) and 3'31" over Winnen. All the rest are four minutes and more back, including team-mate Marc Madiot, at 4'52". The riders have one day of rest before tackling the final mountain stage, with that followed by a transition stage to Dijon and the race's last *rendezvous*, the race against the clock in Dijon on the last-but-one stage, and then the promenade into Paris. Three days in which Fignon can either win or lose the Tour.

The attacks come in the mountains, Winnen and Arroyo (6'26" down at the start of the stage) escaping on the Colombière, with a large group to keep them company and help share the pace. Fignon's grasp on the *maillot jaune* gets weaker and weaker as the gap opens, two minutes, three minutes, four minutes. And still the Joux-Plane to come. But the race is not only Fignon's to lose, the attackers have to stay away too. And Winnen fails, slipping out of the back of the break, as Fignon launches his fight back. The two come together and the Frenchman's grip on the jersey tightens again. At the stage end Arroyo has only taken two minutes out of him: not nearly enough.

Even with a relatively poor time trial – tenth on the stage – Fignon does enough against the clock to tie up the win and ride into Paris, a debutant in yellow. He and all of France are already looking forward to 1984 – Fignon and Hinault, head to head in the Tour.

Stage-by-Stage Results for the 1983 Tour de France			Stage Winner	Maillot Jaune
Prologue Fri 1 Jul	Fontenay-sous-Bois (ITT) 140 finishers	5.5 km 7'01" 47 kph	Eric Vanderaerden (Bel) J Aernoudt	Eric Vanderaerden (Bel) J Aernoudt
Stage 1 Sat 2 Jul	Nogent-sur-Marne to Créteil 140 finishers	163 km 3h49'38" 42.6 kph	Frits Pirard (Ned) Metauromobili	Eric Vanderaerden (Bel) J Aernoudt
Stage 2 Sun 3 Jul	Soissons to Fontaine-au- Pire (TTT) 140 finishers	100 km 2h18'59" 43.2 kph	Coop	Jean-Louis Gauthier (Fra) Coop
Stage 3 Mon 4 Jul	Valenciennes to Roubaix 137 finishers	152 km 3h46'06" 40.3 kph	Rudy Matthijs (Bel) Boule d'Or	Kim Andersen (Den) Coop
Stage 4 Tue 5 Jul	Roubaix to Le Havre 133 finishers	300 km 7h58'11" 37.6 kph	Serge Demierre (Sui) Cilo	Kim Andersen (Den) Coop
Stage 5 Wed 6 Jul	Le Havre to Le Mans 132 finishers	257 km 7h09'53" 35.9 kph	Dominique Gaigne (Fra) Renault	Kim Andersen (Den) Coop
Stage 6 Thu 7 Jul	Chateaubriand to Nantes (ITT) 132 finishers	58.5 km 1h18'34" 44.7 kph	Bert Oosterbosch (Ned) TI-Raleigh	Kim Andersen (Den) Coop
Stage 7 Fri 8 Jul	Nantes to Île d'Oléron 132 finishers	216 km 5h45'37" 37.5 kph	Ricardo Magrini (Ita) Inoxpran	Kim Andersen (Den) Coop
Stage 8 Sat 9 Jul	La Rochelle to Bordeaux 131 finishers	222 km 6h16'00" 35.4 kph	Bert Oosterbosch (Ned) TI-Raleigh	Kim Andersen (Den) Coop
Stage 9 Sun 10 Jul	Bordeaux to Pau 131 finishers	207 km 5h46'42" 35.8 kph	Philippe Chevallier (Fra) Renault	Sean Kelly (Irl) SEM

Stage-by-Stage Results for the 1983 Tour de France			Stage Winner	Maillot Jaune
Stage 10 Mon 11 Jul	Pau to Bagnères de Luchon 115 finishers	201 km 6h23'27" 31.5 kph	Robert Millar (GBr) Peugeot	Pascal Simon (Fra) Peugeot
	Major climbs: Col d'Aubisque (1,709m) Lucien Van Impe (Bel) Metaurmobili; Col du Tourmalet (2,115m) Patrocinio Jiménez (Col) Colombia; Col d'Aspin (1,489m) Patrocinio Jiménez (Col) Colombia; Col de Peyresourde (1,569m) Robert Millar (GBr) Peugeot			
Stage 11 Tue 12 Jul	Bagnères-de-Luchon to Fleurance 113 finishers	177 km 4h27'06" 39.8 kph	Régis Clère (Esp) Saunier Duval	Pascal Simon (Fra) Peugeot
Stage 12 Wed 13 Jul	Fleurance to Roquefort-sur-Soulzon 112 finishers	261 km 7h17'49" 35.8 kph	Kim Andersen (Den) Coop	Pascal Simon (Fra) Peugeot
Stage 13 Thu 14 Jul	Roquefort-sur-Soulzon to Aurillac 108 finishers	210 km 6h00'06" 35 kph	Henk Lubberding (Ned) TI-Raleigh	Pascal Simon (Fra) Peugeot
	Major climbs: Montjaux (1,030m) Robert Millar (GBr) Peugeot; Côte de Montsalvy (780m) Henk Lubberding (Ned) TI-Raleigh			
Stage 14 Fri 15 Jul	Aurillac to Issoire 103 finishers	149 km 3h39'16" 40.8 kph	Pierre le Bigaut (Fra) Coop	Pascal Simon (Fra) Peugeot
	Major climbs: Col du Pas de Péyrol (Le Puy Mary) (1,588m) Lucien Van Impe (Bel) Metaurmobili			
Stage 15 Sat 16 Jul	Clermont-Ferrand to Puy de Dôme (ITT) 103 finishers	15.6 km 40'43" 23 kph	Ángel Arroyo (Esp) Reynolds	Pascal Simon (Fra) Peugeot
	Major climbs: Puy de Dôme (1,415m) Ángel Arroyo (Esp) Reynolds			
Stage 16 Sun 17 Jul	Issoire to Saint-Étienne 101 finishers	144.5 km 3h49'38" 37.8 kph	~~Henk Lubberding (Ned)~~ ~~TI-Raleigh~~ (1) Michel Laurent (Fra) Coop	Pascal Simon (Fra) Peugeot
	Majór climbs: Côte de Lavet (1,030m) Michel Laurent (Fra) Coop			
Stage 17 Mon 18 Jul	La Tour-du-Pin to l'Alpe d'Huez 96 finishers	223 km 7h21'32" 30.3 kph	Peter Winnen (Ned) TI-Raleigh	Laurent Fignon (Fra) Renault
	Major climbs: Col du Cucheron (1,139m) Christian Jourdan (Fra) La Redoute; Col du Granier (1,134m) Christian Jourdan (Fra) La Redoute; Côte de la Table (915m) Christian Jourdan (Fra) La Redoute; Col du Grand Cucheron (1,188m) Serge Demierre (Sui) Cilo; Col du Glandon (1,924m) Lucien Van Impe (Bel) Metaurmobili; l'Alpe d'Huez (1,860m) Peter Winnen (Ned) TI-Raleigh			
Tue 19 Jul	Rest Day			

Stage-by-Stage Results for the 1983 Tour de France			Stage Winner	Maillot Jaune
Stage 18 Wed 20 Jul	Bourg-d'Oisans to Morzine 89 finishers	247 km 7h45′25″ 31.8 kph	Jacques Michaud (Fra) Coop	Laurent Fignon (Fra) Renault
	Major climbs: Col du Glandon (1,924m) Lucien Van Impe (Bel) Metaurmobili; Col de la Madeleine (2,000m) Lucien Van Impe (Bel) Metaurmobili; Col des Aravis (1,498m) Jacques Michaud (Fra) Coop; Col de la Colombière (1,618m) Jacques Michaud (Fra) Coop; Col de Joux-Plane (1,700m) Jacques Michaud (Fra) Coop			
Stage 19 Thu 21 Jul	Morzine to Avoriaz (ITT) 89 finishers	15 km 35′09″ 25.6 kph	Lucien Van Impe (Bel) Metauromobili	Laurent Fignon (Fra) Renault
	Major climbs: Avoriaz (1,800m) Lucien Van Impe (Bel) Metaurmobili			
Stage 20 Fri 22 Jul	Morzine to Dijon 88 finishers	291 km 7h22′56″ 39.4 kph	Philippe Leleu (Fra) Wolber	Laurent Fignon (Fra) Renault
Stage 21 Sat 23 Jul	Dijon (ITT) 88 finishers	50 km 1h11′37″ 41.9 kph	Laurent Fignon (Fra) Renault	Laurent Fignon (Fra) Renault
Stage 22 Sun 24 Jul	Alfortville to Paris (Champs-Élysées) 88 finishers	195 km 5h30′56″ 35.4 kph	Gilbert Glaus (Sui) Cilo	Laurent Fignon (Fra) Renault

(1) Henk Lubberding was stripped of the stage win following an irregular sprint

Prize fund: 2,304,260 francs (first prize: 160,000 francs)

Final Classification

Place	Rider	Team	Time	Age
1	Laurent Fignon (Fra)	Renault	3,809 km 105h07'52" 36.230 kph	22
2	Ángel Arroyo (Esp)	Reynolds	+ 4'04"	26
3	Peter Winnen (Ned)	TI-Raleigh	+ 4'09"	25
4	Lucien Van Impe (Bel)	Metauromobili	+ 4'16"	36
5	Robert Alban (Fra)	La Redoute	+ 7'53"	31
6	Jean-René Bernaudeau (Fra)	Wolber	+ 8'59"	27
7	Sean Kelly (Irl)	SEM	+ 12'09"	27
8	Marc Madiot (Fra)	Renault	+ 14'55"	24
9	Phil Anderson (Aus)	Peugeot	+ 16'56"	25
10	Henk Lubberding (Ned)	TI-Raleigh	+ 18'55"	29
Lanterne Rouge				
88	Marcel Laurens (Bel)	J Aernoudt	+ 4h02'46"	31
Points				
	Sean Kelly (Irl)	SEM		27
King of the Mountains				
	Lucien Van Impe (Bel)	Metauromobili		36
Intermediate Sprints				
	Sean Kelly (Irl)	SEM		27
Youth				
	Laurent Fignon (Fra)	Renault		22
Team				
		TI-Raleigh		
Team (Points)				
		TI-Raleigh		
Super Combativité				
	Serge Demierre (Sui)	Cilo		27

1984: Changes

Orwell's year proved to be an odd one for cycling, with so many things happening and so much changing. At Liège-Bastogne-Liège the podium was Irish, Australian and American. Flèche Wallonne went Danish. It was an Irish one-two at Paris-Nice. The Foreign Legion were strutting their stuff at the Tour too: an American, an Irishman and a Scotsman finished third, fourth and fifth. And in Paris on the day the Tour ended an American was standing on the podium, waving to the crowds while wearing a yellow jersey. The Tour had just got itself a baby sister, the Tour Cycliste Féminin (Félix Lévitan borrowing from history and the Jean Leulliot-organised Tour de France Féminine of the 1950s). Like the Tour de l'Avenir before it, the Tour Cycliste Féminin was raced on some of the same roads as the main race, the women sharing the road ahead of the main *peloton*. And at the end of the inaugural women's Tour America's Marianne Martin had come out tops.

The Tour wasn't the only race moving toward parity for women in 1984: the IOC had finally begun making moves towards an equal number of cycling events for men and women at the Olympics, giving the women a road race at the Los Angeles Games. But the Tour Cycliste Féminin wasn't about parity. It was yet another part of the Tour's grand *mondialisation* project, the women's race reaching parts the men couldn't touch and dragging nations like China into the fold. In the Tour itself, Lévitan's attempts to speed up the internationalisation of the *peloton* had not been the success he had hoped they would be. Despite inviting many, only one team of amateurs turned up for the 1983 Tour, the Colombians. Natural born climbers, they faltered on the flats, and most of them had been burned out even before the race reached the Pyrenees. But they would learn. And they would be back.

While Lévitan's attempts to push *mondialisation* upon the sport were never as successful as he wished them to be, change was happening without his direct influence. The Tour's attempts to bring in an American team had never succeeded but at the 1984 Giro d'Italia, the organisers, *La Gazzetta dello Sport*, were courted by a Robin Morton-bossed and Gianni Motta-sponsored team of American professionals.

On top of all this, the sport was about to receive something that would speed up the rate at which it was changing itself: money. The 1980s saw cycling become sexy and new money pour into the sport. Hollywood thought the sport sexy and had a film crew at the 1984 Tour, capturing footage for *The Yellow Jersey*, a film being directed by Michael Cimino and starring Dustin Hoffman (like many cycling-related films, it would never get made). Sponsors were queuing up to get a slice of cycling's action, with new teams appearing to challenge the old. And there was also new sponsorship interest in the Tour too: the men from Coca-Cola wanted to push Perrier aside and shower their black gold on the Société du Tour de France.

For the Société du Tour, all this change couldn't have been better timed, for at last the Amaury empire had a leader, the six-year-long legal battle over the estate of Émilien Amaury having reached a conclusion the year before. The preferred daughter and the overlooked son – Francine and Philippe – had reached a settlement in which she took the empire's weekly publications and he kept the dailies. And with them went the sporting events they organised, which included the Tour de France. The Tour had a new step-father.

Philippe Amaury's victory over his sister – and his father's wishes – did not come cheap. As well as the legal fees he also had to foot the bill for the inheritance tax due on his share of his father's estate. And to find the money to pay his bills he turned to the man who had helped bail out his father's striking print workers in the 1970s, Jean-Luc Lagardère. And his generosity was rewarded with a 25% stake in the Amaury empire. As Goddet had had to cede a portion of the Tour to secure its ownership in 1947, so too did Philippe Amaury have to cede a share of his newly secured empire.

The Tour was of no immediate interest to Philippe Amaury, it was the newspapers he had fought for, and he immediately set about taking them in hand and left Félix Lévitan and Jacques Goddet to keep doing what they had been doing for so long over on the sporting side of the empire. They may have been his father's men, but they knew what they were doing and could be trusted. One day he would take an interest in what they were up to, but for now it was the newspapers that mattered.

On the back of all this new interest in the sport, the doping arms race stepped up a gear. In January Francesco Moser – the man who had won the first white jersey for the best young rider in the 1975 Tour – broke the record for the Hour, which had stood since 1972, when Eddy Merckx set it. And Moser did it in style, twice setting new records in the space of five days. The appliance of science was part of the key to the Italian's record. And it was not just aerodynamics that the men in the white coats worked on. They also worked on Moser's blood, a fact he admitted to *L'Équipe* in 1999. And when Moser returned to the road for the rest of the 1984 season, he took with him lessons learned in his Hour.

The Italians weren't the only ones playing with blood that year. With the Olympics in Los Angeles, American cyclists wanted to put on a performance. And so they too turned to transfusions to fuel them, a fact that would be revealed by *Rolling Stone* and others just months after the Games ended. It was only following the scandal of the US Olympians, and significant pressure put on the IOC in Italy, that blood doping was actually banned. What Moser and the US Olympians had done, it hadn't been illegal. It wasn't doping. And then suddenly it was. Only there was no test to detect it. Everyone was just supposed to forget they once knew how to do it and promise never to do it again.

* * * * *

All of this is the background against which the 1984 Tour took place. Laurent Fignon, the 23-year-old defending champion, versus

Bernard Hinault, the 29-year-old four-time champion. Both were protégés of the by now legendary Cyrille Guimard who had now bossed three riders to six successes at the Tour, making him the Tour's most successful *directeur sportif* since the days of Alphonse Baugé.

Hinault and Guimard, once a marriage made in heaven, had by now divorced, *le Blaireau* decamping to La Vie Claire, the plaything of the *nouveau riche* businessman Bernard Tapie, where the enigmatic Paul Köchli became his *directeur sportif*. Fignon was still in a Renault jersey.

Fignon had come into the Tour on the back of defeat at the Giro d'Italia, Francesco Moser taking a victory in the *corsa rosa* that even the *tifosi* didn't deny relied on cheating by everyone from the race director down. Hinault too came into the race on the back of defeats, but they seemed to have more to do with the time taken off while his knee healed than anything else.

It was the Badger who drew first blood, winning the prologue and donning the *maillot jaune*. The old script would have required Peter Post's Panasonic/Raleigh squad to take over, but Post had a rival, his rider Jan Raas having just split from him and taken half the team to Kwantum. And it was Kwantum's Ludo Peeters who took the jersey from Hinault, and then passed it to team-mate Jacques Hanegraaf.

Even come the team time trial the old script was out the window, with the best Peter Post's boys could do being second. And ahead of them it wasn't Kwantum. It was Renault. Three stages into the race and Guimard now had Marc Madiot just four seconds off yellow, Greg LeMond at 10 and Fignon at 13. Which of them would get to wear the *maillot jaune*?

Vincent Barteau. It was Vincent Barteau who got to don the *maillot jaune* for Renault. On the fifth stage. He, Maurice le Guilloux (La Vie Claire) and Paulo Ferreira (Sporting Lisboa) were sent on a suicide mission, a break with more than 200 kilometres to ride. With one of their own in the break neither Renault nor La Vie Claire had to chase and could just rest for the day. It was the duty of Kwantum – who held the race lead – to police the break. But they didn't want to, they were more concerned with making sure they got more stage wins than Panasonic. And so the trio of kamikazes were allowed built up a lead. Five minutes. Ten minutes. Fifteen minutes. At the stage end, 17 minutes and change.

Barteau held the jersey for two weeks, through the Pyrenees and into the Alps. He bled time in the time trials but held in own in the mountains. Exiting the Pyrenees Fignon had climbed up to third overall, 10'33" back, with Hinault in fifth, at 12'38". As the race approached the Alps the positions altered subtly following the time trial from Les Echelles to La Ruchère, with Fignon closing to 6'29" and Hinault at 9'15". The phoney war was now over and it was time for the real fighting to begin. It was time to tackle the Alpe.

Alpe d'Huez itself isn't a particularly hard climb. But it typically comes at the end of a stage that has seen the *peloton* cross three, four, even five other major passes, In 1984 it came after passages of the Saint-Pierre de Chevreuse, the Col du Coq and the Côte de Laffrey. Hinault launched his first attack on the Col du Coq and then, when they hit the Laffrey, he fired off attack after attack after attack. And then he attacked again at the foot of the Alpe. Each time, Fignon had brought him back. But Hinault just wouldn't give up, give in. Fignon was going to have to break him, make him realise it was over, for this year at least. This he duly did as the two climbed the Alpe, Fignon ending the day three minutes up on Hinault and, at last, sporting the *maillot jaune*.

The win on the Alpe hadn't gone to France, though. It went international, with Colombia's Lucho Herrera (Café de Colombia) taking the victory salute. It was a moment of celebration not just for the Colombians (even the president called to congratulate Herrera) but also for Félix Lévitan. *Mondialisation* was paying dividends.

From the Alpe back to Paris it was a tough race but there was no one racing against Fignon at this stage. The young pretender had shown his win the year before was no fluke, and he'd done so by defeating *le Blaireau*, something very few others could claim to have ever done. Now France had two super champions and the future was bright. And the Tour was going to grow and grow and grow on the back of their popularity.

Stage-by-Stage Results for the 1984 Tour de France			Stage Winner	Maillot Jaune
Prologue Fri 29 Jun	Montreuil to Noisy-le-Sec (ITT) 170 finishers	5.4 km 6'39" 48.7 kph	Bernard Hinault (Fra) La Vie Claire	Bernard Hinault (Fra) La Vie Claire
Stage 1 Sat 30 Jun	Bondy to Saint-Denis 170 finishers	148.5 km 3h27'18" 43 kph	Frank Hoste (Bel) Europ Décor	Ludo Peeters (Bel) Kwantum
Stage 2 Sun 1 Jul	Bobigny to Louvroil 170 finishers	249.5 km 7h00'31" 35.6 kph	Marc Madiot (Fra) Renault	Jacques Hanegraaf (Ned) Kwantum
Stage 3 Mon 2 Jul	Louvroil to Valenciennes (TTT) 168 finishers	51 km 1h03'54" 47.9 kph	Renault	Jacques Hanegraaf (Ned) Kwantum
Stage 4 Mon 2 Jul	Valenciennes to Béthune 168 finishers	83 km 2h19'03" 35.8 kph	Ferdi van den Haute (Bel) La Redoute	Adrie van der Poel (Ned) Kwantum
Stage 5 Tue 3 Jul	Béthune to Cergy-Pontoise 167 finishers	207 km 4h49'45" 42.9 kph	Paulo Ferreira (Por) Sporting Lisboa	Vincent Barteau (Fra) Renault
Stage 6 Wed 4 Jul	Cergy-Pontoise to Alençon 167 finishers	202 km 5h15'13" 38.4 kph	Frank Hoste (Bel) Europ Décor	Vincent Barteau (Fra) Renault
Stage 7 Thu 5 Jul	Alençon to Le Mans (ITT) 164 finishers	67 km 1h27'33" 45.9 kph	Laurent Fignon (Fra) Renault	Vincent Barteau (Fra) Renault
Stage 8 Fri 6 Jul	Le Mans to Nantes 164 finishers	192 km 4h18'55" 44.5 kph	Pascal Jules (Fra) Renault	Vincent Barteau (Fra) Renault
Stage 9 Sat 7 Jul	Nantes to Bordeaux 163 finishers	338 km 9h40'11" 35 kph	Jan Raas (Ned) Kwantum	Vincent Barteau (Fra) Renault
Stage 10 Sun 8 Jul	Langon to Pau 160 finishers	198 km 4h51'02" 40.8 kph	Eric Vanderaerden (Bel) Panasonic	Vincent Barteau (Fra) Renault
Stage 11 Mon 9 Jul	Pau to Guzet-Neige 150 finishers	226.5 km 7h03'41" 32.1 kph	Robert Millar (GBr) Peugeot	Vincent Barteau (Fra) Renault
	Major climbs: Col de Portet d'Aspet (1,069m) Théo de Rooy (Ned) Panasonic; Col de la Core (1,395m) Jean-René Bernaudeau (Fra) Renault; Col de Latrape (1,100m) Jean-René Bernaudeau (Fra) Renault; Col de Latrape (1,100m) Jean-René Bernaudeau (Fra) Renault; Guzet-Neige (1,480m) Robert Millar (GBr) Peugeot			
Stage 12 Tue 10 Jul	Saint-Girons to Blagnac 147 finishers	111 km 2h39'46" 41.7 kph	Pascal Poisson (Fra) Renault	Vincent Barteau (Fra) Renault
Stage 13 Wed 11 Jul	Blagnac to Rodez 147 finishers	220.5 km 6h03'23" 36.4 kph	Pierre-Henri Menthéour (Fra) Renault	Vincent Barteau (Fra) Renault
Stage 14 Thu 12 Jul	Rodez to Domaine-du-Rouret 142 finishers	227.5 km 6h00'45" 37.8 kph	Fons de Wolf (Bel) Europ Décor	Vincent Barteau (Fra) Renault
	Major climbs: Côte des Vignes (860m) Celestino Prieto (Esp) Reynolds			

Stage-by-Stage Results for the 1984 Tour de France			Stage Winner	Maillot Jaune
Stage 15 Fri 13 Jul	Domaine-du-Rouret to Grenoble 140 finishers	241.5 km 7h05'42" 34 kph	Frédéric Vichot (Fra) Skil	Vincent Barteau (Fra) Renault
	Major climbs: Col du Rousset (1,254m) Jean-René Bernaudeau (Fra) Renault; Côte de Chalimont (1,350m) Pascal Simon (Fra) Peugeot			
Sat 14 Jul	Rest Day			
Stage 16 Sun 15 Jul	Les Echelles to La Ruchère (ITT) 140 finishers	22 km 42'11" 31.3 kph	Laurent Fignon (Fra) Renault	Vincent Barteau (Fra) Renault
	Major climbs: La Ruchère (1,160m) Luis Herrera (Col) Colombia			
Stage 17 Mon 16 Jul	Grenoble to l'Alpe d'Huez 134 finishers	151 km 4h39'24" 32.4 kph	Luis Herrera (Col) Colombia	Laurent Fignon (Fra) Renault
	Major climbs: Saint-Pierre de Chevreuse (880m) Patrocinio Jiménez (Esp) Teka; Col du Coq (1,430m) Ángel Arroyo (Esp) Reynolds; Côte de Laffrey (900m) Luis Herrera (Col) Colombia; l'Alpe d'Huez (1,860m) Luis Herrera (Col) Colombia			
Stage 18 Tue 17 Jul	Bourg-d'Oisans to La Plagne 129 finishers	185 km 6h12'45" 29.8 kph	Laurent Fignon (Fra) Renault	Laurent Fignon (Fra) Renault
	Major climbs: Col du Galibier (2,645m) Jean-François Rodriguez (Fra) Renault; Col de la Madeleine (2,000m) Pedro Delgado (Esp) Reynolds; La Plagne (1,970m) Laurent Fignon (Fra) Renault			
Stage 19 Wed 18 Jul	La Plagne to Morzine 127 finishers	186 km 6h16'25" 29.6 kph	Ángel Arroyo (Esp) Reynolds	Laurent Fignon (Fra) Renault
	Major climbs: Cormet de Roselend (1,968m) Francis Castaing (Fra) Peugeot; Col des Saisies (1,633m) Pedro Delgado (Esp) Reynolds; Col des Aravis (1,498m) Robert Millar (GBr) Peugeot; Col de la Colombière (1,618m) Jérôme Simon (Fra) La Redoute; Col de Joux-Plane (1,700m) Ángel Arroyo (Esp) Reynolds			
Stage 20 Thu 19 Jul	Morzine to Crans-Montana 125 finishers	140.5 km 4h09'16" 33.8 kph	Laurent Fignon (Fra) Renault	Laurent Fignon (Fra) Renault
	Major climbs: Col du Corbier (1,325m) Patrocinio Jiménez (Esp) Teka; Crans-Montana (1,670m) Laurent Fignon (Fra) Renault			
Stage 21 Fri 20 Jul	Crans-Montana to Villefranche-en-Beaujolais 124 finishers	320.5 km 9h28'08" 33.8 kph	Frank Hoste (Bel) Europ Décor	Laurent Fignon (Fra) Renault
Stage 22 Sat 21 Jul	Villié-Morgon to Villefranche-en-Beaujolais (ITT) 124 finishers	51 km 1h07'19" 45.5 kph	Laurent Fignon (Fra) Renault	Laurent Fignon (Fra) Renault
Stage 23 Sun 22 Jul	Pantin to Paris (Champs-Élysées) 124 finishers	196.5 km 5h23'37" 36.4 kph	Eric Vanderaerden (Bel) Panasonic	Laurent Fignon (Fra) Renault

Prize fund: 2,561,450 francs (first prize: 160,000 francs)

Final Classification

Place	Rider	Team	Time	Age
1	Laurent Fignon (Fra)	Renault	4,021 km 112h03'40" 35.882 kph	23
2	Bernard Hinault (Fra)	La Vie Claire	+ 10'32"	29
3	Greg LeMond (USA)	Renault	+ 11'46"	23
4	Robert Millar (GBr)	Peugeot	+ 14'42"	25
5	Sean Kelly (Irl)	Skil	+ 16'35"	28
6	Ángel Arroyo (Esp)	Reynolds	+ 19'22"	27
7	Pascal Simon (Fra)	Peugeot	+ 21'17"	27
8	Pedro Muñoz (Esp)	Teka	+ 26'17"	25
9	Claude Criquiélion (Bel)	Mondial Moquette	+ 29'12"	27
10	Phil Anderson (Aus)	Panasonic	+ 29'16"	26

Lanterne Rouge

124	Gilbert Glaus (Sui)	Cilo	4h01'17"	28

Points

	Frank Hoste (Bel)	Europ Décor		28

King of the Mountains

	Robert Millar (GBr)	Peugeot		25

Intermediate Sprints

	Jacques Hanegraaf (Ned)	Kwantum		23

Youth

	Greg LeMond (USA)	Renault		23

Team

		Renault		

Team (Points)

		Panasonic		

Super Combativité

	Bernard Hinault (Fra)	La Vie Claire		29

1985: The Promise

It was the fourteenth stage of the seventy-second Tour de France. The Alps were behind the *peloton*, the Pyrenees to come. Bernard Hinault (La Vie Claire) was in the *maillot jaune*. His team-mate Greg LeMond was 5'23" back, with Stephen Roche (La Redoute) in third at 6'08" and Sean Kelly (Skil) fourth at 6'35". All the rest were eight minutes and more back. The two Irishmen represented no real threat to Hinault, nor did his American team-mate. The win was in the bag and all he had to do was to stay upright and ride into Paris, his fifth Tour title and his second Giro/Tour double sewn up.

LeMond had joined Hinault at La Vie Claire at the end of previous season. He wanted to win but could see that Laurent Fignon was flavour of the hour at Renault and so followed the money to La Vie Claire, in a highly publicised deal that was supposed to net him a million dollars over three seasons (less publicised, Phil Anderson was reported to have joined Panasonic for a similar amount). With Hinault having just lost the Tour his career seemed to be at an end, and LeMond expected to be La Vie Claire's team-leader at the Tour. Then, as if the fates were mocking the American, Hinault recovered, with the help of La Vie Claire *directeur sportif* Paul Köchli, while over at Renault Fignon fell victim to a knee injury that required surgery.

So there LeMond was in Saint-Étienne that July Saturday afternoon, riding support for Hinault on the day Colombia's Lucho Herrera (Café de Colombia) bagged the third Tour stage win of his career and the second of this race. And it was a win on the flat at that, Herrera having escaped alone over the Crêt de l'Oeillon and

– even after a fall that saw him needing stitches above his left eye after the stage ended – held off his pursuers all the way to the finish line. Eight riders followed Herrera home less than a minute down, with the *peloton* arriving nearly two minutes later and sprinting for tenth place. And it was in that sprint for tenth place that LeMond saw Hinault's hopes of a fifth Tour title seeming to get blown away on the wind.

Three hundred metres from the line, six riders went down, the *maillot jaune* among them. Dazed and confused, Hinault sat on the ground for two minutes as blood from his nose stained his yellow jersey. Finally the badger stood and, gingerly, remounted and crossed the line. The time lost was immaterial, the clock had effectively stopped at the kilometre to go kite, to protect riders against accidents such as this. What mattered was how injured Hinault was and whether he would be able to ride on, with the Pyrenees still to come. Later that night, the extent of the yellow jersey's injuries was revealed: a broken nose. Raymond Poulidor had only lasted a couple of days after sustaining a similar injury in 1968.

The two stages that followed were relatively tame, transition stages taking the race to the edge of the Pyrenees. In those mountains Roche put the boot in and went in search of victory. LeMond, doing his job as Hinault's henchman, dutifully followed the Irishman, marking him: with the American ahead of him by three minutes, Roche was racing for second place. And with Hinault suffering behind, LeMond now saw his chance for the win. But Köchli, his La Vie Claire *directeur sportif* ordered him not to work with Roche, to just mark him. If LeMond wanted to win the Tour, Köchli told him, he could do so, but only by attacking and dropping Roche.

Köchli's thinking was this: La Vie Claire started the day with LeMond 3'38" behind Hinault and Roche at 6'14". The team had a six-minute margin of safety, and either Hinault or LeMond could win. But if LeMond and Roche rode together, that would fall to below three minutes and LeMond would be the team's only ace.

LeMond wanted to win, but he didn't attack Roche and, at the stage end, Hinault had limited his losses and still led LeMond, now 2'25" off yellow, with Roche at five minutes.

The following stage was a split affair, both parts crossing the Aubisque, and Roche took back another 1'30" in the morning by turning the race into a time trial and just riding away from the *peloton*. He was now just 3'33" off yellow – with LeMond still second, at 2'13" – but now the race was out of the Pyrenees. The best chance to beat the battered and bruised Badger had passed.

Hinault rode into Paris and joined Jacques Anquetil and Eddy Merckx in the pantheon of greats, members of the five times club. LeMond took the first Tour stage of his career, winning the final individual time trial on the eve of the promenade into Paris. Acknowledging the work done by the American to help him win the race Hinault promised to return to the Tour the next year and to reverse their roles, he helping the American to victory.

Stage-by-Stage Results for the 1985 Tour de France			Stage Winner	Maillot Jaune
Prologue Fri 28 Jun	Plumelec (ITT) 179 finishers	6.8 km 8'47" 46.4 kph	Bernard Hinault (Fra) La Vie Claire	Bernard Hinault (Fra) La Vie Claire
Stage 1 Sat 29 Jun	Vannes to Lanester 178 finishers	256 km 6h32'52" 39.1 kph	Rudy Matthijs (Bel) Hitachi	Eric Vanderaerden (Bel) Panasonic
Stage 2 Sun 30 Jun	Lorient to Vitré 178 finishers	242 km 6h29'21" 37.3 kph	Rudy Matthijs (Bel) Hitachi	Eric Vanderaerden (Bel) Panasonic
Stage 3 Mon 1 Jul	Vitré to Fougères (TTT) 178 finishers	73 km 1h30'09" 48.6 kph	La Vie Claire	Eric Vanderaerden (Bel) Panasonic
Stage 4 Tue 2 Jul	Fougères to Pont-Audemer 175 finishers	239 km 6h31'46" 36.6 kph	Gerrit Solleveld (Ned) Kwantum	Kim Andersen (Den) La Vie Claire
Stage 5 Wed 3 Jul	Neufchatel-en-Bray to Roubaix 173 finishers	224 km 6h27'25" 34.7 kph	Henri Manders (Ned) Kwantum	Kim Andersen (Den) La Vie Claire
Stage 6 Thu 4 Jul	Roubaix to Reims 169 finishers	221.5 km 6h29'34" 34.1 kph	Francis Castaing (Fra) Peugeot	Kim Andersen (Den) La Vie Claire
Stage 7 Fri 5 Jul	Reims to Nancy 168 finishers	217.5 km 5h55'07" 36.7 kph	Ludwig Wijnants (Bel) Tonissteiner	Kim Andersen (Den) La Vie Claire
Stage 8 Sat 6 Jul	Sarrebourg to Strasbourg (ITT) 166 finishers	75 km 1h34'55" 47.4 kph	Bernard Hinault (Fra) La Vie Claire	Bernard Hinault (Fra) La Vie Claire

Stage-by-Stage Results for the 1985 Tour de France			Stage Winner	Maillot Jaune
Stage 9 Sun 7 Jul	Strasbourg to Épinal 163 finishers	173.5 km 4h13'40" 41 kph	Maarten Ducrot (Ned) Kwantum	Bernard Hinault (Fra) La Vie Claire
	Major climbs: Côte du Champ du Feu (1,100m) Luis Herrera (Col) Café de Colombia; Mont Donon (727m) Niki Ruttimann (Sui) La Vie Claire			
Stage 10 Mon 8 Jul	Épinal to Pontarlier 161 finishers	204.5 km 5h06'27" 40 kph	Jørgen Pedersen (Den) Carrera	Bernard Hinault (Fra) La Vie Claire
	Major climbs: Côte du Désert (810m) Adrie van der Poel (Ned) Kwantum; Côte de Larmont (1,201m) Jørgen Pedersen (Den) Carrera			
Stage 11 Tue 9 Jul	Pontarlier to Morzine-Avoriaz 161 finishers	195 km 5h19'04" 36.7 kph	Luis Herrera (Col) Café de Colombia	Bernard Hinault (Fra) La Vie Claire
	Major climbs: Pas de Morgins (1,369m) Luis Herrera (Col) Café de Colombia; Col du Corbier (1,325m) Luis Herrera (Col) Café de Colombia; Avoriaz (1,800m) Luis Herrera (Col) Café de Colombia			
Stage 12 Wed 10 Jul	Morzine to Lans-en-Vercors 158 finishers	269 km 8h25'31" 31.9 kph	Fabio Parra (Col) Café de Colombia	Bernard Hinault (Fra) La Vie Claire
	Major climbs: Col de la Colombière (1,618m) Luis Herrera (Col) Café de Colombia; Col de Leschaux (898m) Laurent Biondi (Fra) Hitachi; Col de Plainpalais (1,173m) Luis Herrera (Col) Café de Colombia; Col du Granier (1,134m) Reynel Montoya (Col) Café de Colombia; Côte de Montaud (1,687m) Eduardo Chozas (Esp) Reynolds; Côte de Saint-Nizier de Moucherotte (1,180m) Eduardo Chozas (Esp) Reynolds; Lans-en-Vercors (1,410m) Fabio Parra (Col) Café de Colombia			
Stage 13 Thu 11 Jul	Villard-de-Lans (ITT) 158 finishers	38 km 41'04" 55.5 kph	Eric Vanderaerden (Bel) Panasonic	Bernard Hinault (Fra) La Vie Claire
Fri 12 Jul	Rest Day			
Stage 14 Sat 13 Jul	Autrans to Saint-Étienne 157 finishers	179 km 4h56'32" 36.2 kph	Luis Herrera (Col) Café de Colombia	Bernard Hinault (Fra) La Vie Claire
	Major climbs: Crêt de l'Oeillon (1,210m) Luis Herrera (Col) Café de Colombia			
Stage 15 Sun 14 Jul	Saint-Étienne to Aurillac 151 finishers	237.5 km 7h08'42" 33.2 kph	Eduardo Chozas (Esp) Reynolds	Bernard Hinault (Fra) La Vie Claire
	Major climbs: Col du Pas de Péyrol (Le Puy Mary) (1,588m) Eduardo Chozas (Esp) Reynolds			
Stage 16 Mon 15 Jul	Aurillac to Toulouse 146 finishers	247 km 6h31'54" 37.8 kph	Frédéric Vichot (Fra) Skil	Bernard Hinault (Fra) La Vie Claire

Stage-by-Stage Results for the 1985 Tour de France			Stage Winner	Maillot Jaune
Stage 17 Tue 16 Jul	Toulouse to Luz-Ardiden 145 finishers	209.5 km 6h57'21" 30.1 kph	Pedro Delgado (Esp) Seat	Bernard Hinault (Fra) La Vie Claire
	Major climbs: Col d'Aspin (1,489m) José Del Ramo (Esp) Seat; Col du Tourmalet (2,115m) Pello Ruiz (Esp) Seat; Luz-Ardiden (1,715m) Pedro Delgado (Esp) Seat			
Stage 18a Wed 17 Jul	Luz-Saint-Sauveur to Col d'Aubisque 145 finishers	52.5 km 1h39'19" 31.7 kph	Stephen Roche (Irl) La Redoute	Bernard Hinault (Fra) La Vie Claire
	Major climbs: Col du Soulor (1,474m) Stephen Roche (Irl) La Redoute; Col d'Aubisque (1,709m) Stephen Roche (Irl) La Redoute			
Stage 18b Wed 17 Jul	Laruns to Pau 145 finishers	83.5 km 2h22'55" 35.1 kph	Régis Simon (Fra) La Redoute	Bernard Hinault (Fra) La Vie Claire
	Major climbs: Col d'Aubisque (1,709m) Reynel Montoya (Col) Café de Colombia			
Stage 19 Thu 18 Jul	Pau to Bordeaux 145 finishers	203 km 5h42'13" 35.6 kph	Eric Vanderaerden (Bel) Panasonic	Bernard Hinault (Fra) La Vie Claire
Stage 20 Fri 19 Jul	Montpon-Ménestérol to Limoges 144 finishers	225 km 5h53'10" 38.2 kph	Johan Lammerts (Ned) Panasonic	Bernard Hinault (Fra) La Vie Claire
Stage 21 Sat 20 Jul	Circuit du Lac de Vassivière (ITT) 144 finishers	45.7 km 1h02'51" 43.6 kph	Greg LeMond (USA) La Vie Claire	Bernard Hinault (Fra) La Vie Claire
Stage 22 Sun 21 Jul	Orléans to Paris (Champs-Élysées) 144 finishers	196 km 5h13'56" 37.5 kph	Rudy Matthijs (Bel) Hitachi	Bernard Hinault (Fra) La Vie Claire

Prize fund: 3,003,050 francs (first prize: 120,000 francs)

Final Classification

Place	Rider	Team	Time	Age
1	Bernard Hinault (Fra)	La Vie Claire	4,109 km 113h24'23" 36.232 kph	30
2	Greg LeMond (USA)	La Vie Claire	+ 1'42"	24
3	Stephen Roche (Irl)	La Redoute	+ 4'29"	25
4	Sean Kelly (Irl)	Skil	+ 6'26"	29
5	Phil Anderson (Aus)	Panasonic	+ 7'44"	27
6	Pedro Delgado (Esp)	Seat	+ 11'53"	25
7	Luis Herrera (Col)	Café de Colombia	+ 12'53"	24
8	Fabio Parra (Col)	Café de Colombia	+ 13'35"	25
9	Eduardo Chozas (Esp)	Reynolds	+ 13'56"	25
10	Steve Bauer (Can)	La Vie Claire	+ 14'57"	26

Lanterne Rouge

144	Manrico Ronchiato (Ita)	Santini	+ 4h13'48"	24

Points

	Sean Kelly (Irl)	Skil		29

King of the Mountains

	Luis Herrera (Col)	Café de Colombia		24

Intermediate Sprints

	Jozef Lieckens (Bel)	Lotto		26

Combination

	Greg LeMond (USA)	La Vie Claire		24

Youth

	Fabio Parra (Col)	Café de Colombia		25

Team

		La Vie Claire		

Team (Points)

		La Vie Claire		

Super Combativité

	Maarten Ducrot (Ned)	Kwantum		27

1986: The Americans

Friday, 4 July 1986. Boulogne-Billancourt, Paris, France. Canadian 7-Eleven rider Alex Stieda was first to set off on the prologue of the 1986 Tour de France, a 4.6-kilometre *contre-la-montre*. Stieda rode it in 5'33". Until another rider bettered that time, the Canadian was the virtual leader of the Tour de France, wearing an imaginary *maillot jaune*. It took more than a hour for someone to unseat him. That hour, that was just the starters in what was to prove to be a very important Tour for North American cycling.

Following manager Robin Morton's assault on the Giro with a team of American professionals in 1984, she returned the following year to take on the Vuelta a España. And this time she wasn't alone in taking on the European professionals, the 7-Elevens following in her wheel tracks and going to the Giro. Another year on, the 7-Elevens made the list of Tour teams, the last of 21 10-man teams chosen, the most riders the Tour had ever seen.

For most riders in their first Tour, even a virtual yellow jersey would be an accomplishment to cherish. But the next morning, on the first part of a split stage through the suburbs of Paris (Nanterre to Sceaux) Stieda pushed for more. At 85 kilometres, the distance to be raced was comparable to riding critériums back in the States. And, back in the US, the 7-Elevens were the kings of crits. Only 20 riders had bettered Stieda's time the day before, and he was just 12 seconds off the lead. Stieda dared to dream.

Just over 20 kilometres into the ride, the Canuck rode off the front of the race. And kept riding, putting time into the *peloton* – three minutes at one point. Once more the Canadian was resplendent in a virtual *maillot jaune*. With just 17 kilometres to go a group of five riders caught up with him. In the dash for the line Stieda finished fifth of the six. Looking over his shoulder as he crossed the line, the Canuck could see the *peloton* stretched across the road, two seconds back, barrelling for the finish. So close.

Before the chasers had caught him, though, Stieda had picked up 36 seconds in bonifications. When the Tour's bean counters totted everything up the Canadian 7-Eleven rider was found to be leading the Tour de France, eight seconds to the good. Before he could step up to the podium to collect North America's first ever yellow jersey, Stieda had to step up to the podium to collect the white jersey as the best-placed young rider ... then again to collect the red jersey for leader of the intermediate sprints category ... then again to collect the polka-dot jersey of the best climber ... and then again to collect the multi-coloured jersey for the leader of the combination category. By the time he finally stepped up to collect his yellow jersey, the guy was exhausted from all the walking he'd had to do and needed a new suitcase for all his new jerseys.

Then Stieda had to fulfil his media obligations, which were many, an American in yellow being a rarity and more and more English-speaking journalists adding the Tour to their summer schedules. So the Canadian wasn't particularly prepared for the team time trial that followed in the afternoon. Nor, for that matter, were his team-mates. The Americans hadn't even driven the 56 kilometre course, all they'd done was look at it on a map – which proved to be the start of their undoing.

Just 18 kilometres into the ride, Davis Phinney led them round a downhill bend, clocking close to 70 kilometres an hour, only to find a traffic island splitting the road. Phinney made it past the obstacle safely, as did the first few riders behind him. Eric Heiden fluffed it and went down. In attempting to avoid him, several 7-Elevens either went down or scraped their tyres against the kerb and flatted. Chaos followed. The riders ahead didn't know whether to press on or wait and regroup. Eventually, they waited and were all together and back into flying formation.

Then, at the front of the pace line, Alexi Grewal and Doug Shapiro got into a shouting match over who was wrongly positioned

to ride the cross-wind blowing at them. Echelons weren't big in US
critérium racing and Shapiro – who'd ridden the Tour the previous
year as part of the Kwantum squad – thought he knew more about
them than Grewal did. Grewal, who'd ridden the previous season
with Panasonic (Kwantum's great rival), begged to differ. Still
blasting along at nigh on 50 kilometres an hour, Shapiro sought to
settle the argument by pulling his *bidon* from its cage and launching
it at Grewal's head.

Then Stieda got the hunger knock, the dreaded *fringale* and with
still 20 kilometres to go the leader of the Tour de France couldn't
hold the wheel of the team-mate in front of him. The 7-Elevens
slowed for him. Stieda still couldn't hold the wheel in front. A
decision had to be made: jettison the anchor or risk having the
whole team go down with the ship. The big clock was tick-tick-
tocking and the 7-Elevens were in danger of being caught by the cut
off, being sent home in disgrace with not even 150 of the race's
4,000 kilometres run.

The order came to drop the anchor. Three hours after having
donned the yellow jersey, aided by team-mates Chris Carmichael
and Jeff Pierce, Stieda was left to beat the cut-off time while the rest
of the team rode on. Stieda won, but lost four of his five jerseys in
the process, retaining only the polka-dots.

Having done so much to earn the respect of the Continental
professionals, the 7-Elevens had just played true to the stereotype of
a bunch of know-nothing amateurs, a danger to themselves as much
as to the riders around them. Only one team finished slower than
them in the TTT – Félix Lévitan's beloved Colombians. Even three
years on from their first appearance at the Tour, the Colombians
were still the *peloton*'s whipping boys. On the upside, the Colombians
had lost four riders that day to the cut-off, other teams another
eight, but despite their ineptitude, all the 7-Elevens made it across
the finish line in time (30 seconds in time, in Stieda's case).

It was a chastened 7-Eleven team that took to the road the next
day as the Tour headed north toward Belgium, crossing the Somme
in a long, flat 214-kilometre haul up to Liévin, near Lille. With
about a third of the stage still to run, Phinney was dawdling near the

back of the pack when a Swiss rider, Robert Dill-Bundi (Malvor), came riding up the outside of the *peloton* and past Phinney. Phinney decided to latch onto his wheel for a free ride toward the front of the densely packed group of riders.

But when Dill-Bundi got to the front he just kept riding. The road had just narrowed and it was the perfect place to launch an attack. Phinney hardly even thought about it and kept following the wheel in front. Another 10 riders latched onto them. There was some class in the break. Charly Mottet and his Système U team-mate Laurent Biondi, for instance. And there was Dag Otto Lauritzen (Peugeot) and Henk Boeve (PDM). Even the unheralded Dill-Bundi had been an Olympic pursuit champion. There was class enough to build the break and maybe – just maybe – stay away. In 10 kilometres the dozen escapees built up a two-minute lead.

Having been cartoonish the day before, 7-Eleven now had a man up the road animating the race. The day before the world had witnessed two sides of 7-Eleven, the good and the bad. What were they going to deliver next, the ugly? Not with Phinney they weren't. Phinney oozed cool. Phinney oozed charm. Phinney oozed sexiness. Oh yeah, and Phinney had a sprint. Not the best in the *peloton*, but definitely the best in that break. As he proved by taking the stage win.

For the Americans, this Tour was already serving up oodles of entertainment. But the real fun was still to come. And it wouldn't involve the 7-Elevens. The real fun was about to be provided by the man who had finished third on his début two years before and second the year after that. The real fun was about to be provided by the man who Bernard Hinault said he'd help win the 1986 Tour. The 25-year-old Greg LeMond.

The first real GC selection didn't come until Stage 9, a 61.5-kilometre individual time trial around Nantes. Hinault won the stage, with La Vie Claire team-mate LeMond 44 seconds in arrears, moving the Badger up to third overall. Three days later Hinault made that first with an attack that LeMond was unable – by virtue of team orders – to follow, giving him an advantage of more than five minutes over the American team-mate he'd said he was there to help, with the rest of the challengers already falling away.

Bernard Hinault and Greg LeMond in the 1986 Tour.

With a five minute lead and the yellow jersey on his back and the race not even half done, an ordinary rider would have raced conservatively, protected his lead. But Hinault was no ordinary rider. He decided to attack on the road from Pau to Luchon, taking in the Tourmalet, Aspen and Peyresourde before finishing at Superbagnères. Roads made famous by Eddy Merckx in 1969, with a similar exploit while wearing the *maillot jaune*.

Like Merckx before him Hinault opened a gap on the descent of the Tourmalet, this time with still 90 kilometres to go before the sprint through Luchon and the slog up the final climb to the ski-station at Superbagnères. Like Merckx before him Hinault put minutes into the *peloton* as he soloed toward the stage finish. If it had worked out for Hinault like it had for Merckx before the Frenchman would have won not just the stage – and maybe the Tour with it – but new coinage, 'Hinaultissimo,' to go with the 'Merckissimo' Jacques Goddet coined to describe Merckx's solo ride through the Pyrenees 17 years earlier.

Hinault's attack didn't succeed, though, and *le Blaireau* lost all bar 40 seconds of the 5'25" lead over LeMond he had started the day with. Like Merckx before him he ran out of fuel. But unlike Merckx before him he was unable to recover. LeMond took the stage win and Hinault lost a major battle in the psychological war between the two La Vie Claire team-mates.

Whether it really was a war between two team-mates is the great unanswered question from the 1986 Tour de France. Hinault justified his attacking by saying he was riding the other contenders out of the race, helping LeMond to victory by disposing of his challengers. But it seems clear that the lure of a sixth Tour win was too much for Hinault to resist. Riding his last Tour – Hinault lad long promised to retire come his thirty-second birthday – Hinault was riding to win.

With the Pyrenees behind them, things settled down in the *peloton* as the race headed across to the Alps. And on the first day in the Alps Hinault blew a gasket and bled time. LeMond donned the *maillot jaune*, Urs Zimmermann (Carrera) 2'24" behind him on GC, Hinault in third at 2'47" and the rest six minutes and more back. LeMond now had just one man to beat, Zimmermann.

Or was it two? For Hinault was back on the attack the very next day as the *peloton* raced toward Alpe d'Huez. LeMond covered the move, but Zimmermann missed the bus and surrendered what little chance he had of winning that Tour. The two La Vie Claire riders arrived in Bourg d'Oisans with a near five-minute advantage over their Carrera rival. The Badger's attack had burned off the Swiss star, and he and LeMond were able to ride the Alpe looking almost as if they were two friends out for a training ride. And, in a symbolically loaded show of friendship, they crossed the finish line arm in arm, the champion and the champion elect. LeMond's Tour was won, Zimmermann was now nearly eight minutes back.

But Hinault was still just 2'45" off yellow. Too close to give up, too close to deny the dream, to resist the lure of stepping out of the five-times club and being a man alone with six Tour titles. Hinault still challenged LeMond, talked of taking the jersey in the last race against the clock, 58 kilometres around Saint-Étienne. And Hinault did take the stage. But he only took 25 seconds out of his team-mate, and that was after LeMond had crashed and needed to change bikes.

Just five years after Jock Boyer had become the first American to ride the Tour, and two years after Marianne Martin had worn yellow on the Champs-Élysées by winning the Tour Cycliste Féminin, Greg LeMond wore the *maillot jaune* in Paris. The Americans had come and the Americans had conquered. And LeMond had had to do it the hard way, being granted no coronation ride around France, being made work for the win, stage after stage after stage. And for that he – and the Tour itself – had Hinault to thank. Hinault may have broken his word, but in so doing he crafted one of the most exciting Tours ever – if not the most exciting.

For the French, on top of the pain of seeing Hinault defeated they also had to cope with Jeannie Longo again finishing second in the women's Tour, again behind Italy's Maria Canins. The era of French dominance – an era that dated back to Hinault's first Tour win in 1978 – seemed to be over, and the French would have to wait for a new generation to come along and rise to the challenge.

Stage-by-Stage Results for the 1986 Tour de France			Stage Winner	Maillot Jaune
Prologue Fri 4 Jul	Boulogne Billancourt (ITT) 210 finishers	4.6 km 5'21" 51.6 kph	Thierry Marie (Fra) Système U	Thierry Marie (Fra) Système U
Stage 1 Sat 5 Jul	Nanterre to Sceaux 210 finishers	85 km 1h58'33" 43 kph	Pol Verschuere (Bel) Fagor	Alex Stieda (Can) 7-Eleven
Stage 2 Sat 5 Jul	Meudon to Saint-Quentin- en-Yveline (TTT) 198 finishers	56 km 1h10'27" 47.7 kph	Système U	Thierry Marie (Fra) Système U
Stage 3 Sun 6 Jul	Levallois-Perret to Liévin 197 finishers	214 km 5h45'31" 37.2 kph	Davis Phinney (USA) 7-Eleven	Thierry Marie (Fra) Système U
Stage 4 Mon 7 Jul	Liévin to Évreux 195 finishers	243 km 6h57'05" 35 kph	Pello Ruíz (Esp) Seat	Dominique Gaigne (Fra) Système U
Stage 5 Tue 8 Jul	Évreux to Villers-sur-Mer 194 finishers	124.5 km 3h04'05" 40.6 kph	Johan van der Velde (Ned) Panasonic	Johan van der Velde (Ned) Panasonic
Stage 6 Wed 9 Jul	Villers-sur-Mer to Cherbourg 191 finishers	200 km 4h47'01" 41.8 kph	Guido Bontempi (Ita) Carrera	Johan van der Velde (Ned) Panasonic
Stage 7 Thu 10 Jul	Cherbourg to Saint-Hilaire-du-Harcouët 191 finishers	201 km 4h57'00" 40.6 kph	Ludo Peeters (Bel) Kwantum	Jørgen Pedersen (Den) Carrera
Stage 8 Fri 11 Jul	Saint-Hilaire-du-Harcouët to Nantes 191 finishers	204 km 4h39'55" 43.7 kph	Eddy Planckaert (Bel) Panasonic	Jørgen Pedersen (Den) Carrera
Stage 9 Sat 12 Jul	Nantes (ITT) 191 finishers	61.5 km 1h18'46" 46.8 kph	Bernard Hinault (Fra) La Vie Claire	Jørgen Pedersen (Den) Carrera
Stage 10 Sun 13 Jul	Nantes to Futuroscope 191 finishers	183 km 4h27'16" 41.1 kph	Ángel José Sarrapio (Esp) Teka	Jørgen Pedersen (Den) Carrera
Stage 11 Mon 14 Jul	Poitiers to Bordeaux 191 finishers	258.3 km 6h12'40" 41.6 kph	Rudy Dhaenens (Bel) Hitachi	Jørgen Pedersen (Den) Carrera
Stage 12 Tue 15 Jul	Bayonne to Pau 174 finishers	217.5 km 6h03'18" 35.9 kph	Pedro Delgado (Esp) PDM	Bernard Hinault (Fra) La Vie Claire
Major climbs: Col de Burdincurutcheta (1,135m) Ronan Pensec (Fra) Peugeot; Bagargui (1,327m) Ronan Pensec (Fra) Peugeot; Col d'Ichère (680m) Pedro Delgado (Esp) PDM; Col de Marie- Blanque (1,035m) Pedro Delgado (Esp) PDM				
Stage 13 Wed 16 Jul	Pau to Luchon (Superbagnères) 164 finishers	186 km 6h06'37" 30.4 kph	Greg LeMond (USA) La Vie Claire	Bernard Hinault (Fra) La Vie Claire
Major climbs: Col du Tourmalet (2,115m) Dominique Arnaud (Fra) TS Batteries; Col d'Aspin (1,489m) Dominique Arnaud (Fra) TS Batteries; Col de Peyresourde (1,569m) Bernard Hinault (Fra) La Vie Claire; Superbagnères (1,804m) Greg LeMond (USA) La Vie Claire				

Stage-by-Stage Results for the 1986 Tour de France			Stage Winner	Maillot Jaune
Stage 14 Thu 17 Jul	Luchon to Blagnac 162 finishers	154 km 3h47'44" 40.6 kph	Niki Rüttimann (Sui) La Vie Claire	Bernard Hinault (Fra) La Vie Claire
Stage 15 Fri 18 Jul	Carcassonne to Nîmes 157 finishers	225.5 km 5h52'31" 38.4 kph	Frank Hoste (Bel) Fagor	Bernard Hinault (Fra) La Vie Claire
Stage 16 Sat 19 Jul	Nîmes to Gap 152 finishers	246.5 km 7h39'54" 32.2 kph	Jean-François Bernard (Fra) La Vie Claire	Bernard Hinault (Fra) La Vie Claire
Major climbs: Espreaux (1,160m) Julián Gorospe (Esp) TS Batteries				
Stage 17 Sun 20 Jul	Gap to Serre Chevalier 144 finishers	190 km 5h52'52" 32.3 kph	Eduardo Chozas (Esp) Teka	Greg LeMond (USA) La Vie Claire
Major climbs: Col de Vars (2,110m) Eduardo Chozas (Esp) Teka; Col d'Izoard (2,360m) Eduardo Chozas (Esp) Teka; Col du Granon (2,413m) Eduardo Chozas (Esp) Teka				
Stage 18 Mon 21 Jul	Briançon to l'Alpe d'Huez 135 finishers	162.5 km 5h03'03" 32.2 kph	Bernard Hinault (Fra) La Vie Claire	Greg LeMond (USA) La Vie Claire
Major climbs: Col du Galibier (2,645m) Luis Herrera (Col) Café de Colombia; Col de la Croix de Fer (2,067m) Bernard Hinault (Fra) La Vie Claire; l'Alpe d'Huez (1,860m) Bernard Hinault (Fra) La Vie Claire				
Tue 22 Jul	Rest Day			
Stage 19 Wed 23 Jul	Villard-de-Lans to Saint-Étienne 135 finishers	179.5 km 5h06'10" 35.2 kph	Julián Gorospe (Esp) TS Batteries	Greg LeMond (USA) La Vie Claire
Major climbs: Notre Dame (575m) Julián Gorospe (Esp) TS Batteries; Crêt de l'Oeillon (1,210m) Julián Gorospe (Esp) TS Batteries				
Stage 20 Thu 24 Jul	Saint-Étienne (ITT) 134 finishers	58 km 1h15'36" 46 kph	Bernard Hinault (Fra) La Vie Claire	Greg LeMond (USA) La Vie Claire
Stage 21 Fri 25 Jul	Saint-Étienne to Puy-de-Dôme 132 finishers	190 km 5h32'40" 34.3 kph	Erich Mächler (Sui) Carrera	Greg LeMond (USA) La Vie Claire
Major climbs: Col de la Croix de l'Homme Mort (1,163m) Bernard Hinault (Fra) La Vie Claire; Col des Fourches (970m) Bernard Hinault (Fra) La Vie Claire; Toutée (996m) Marino Lejarreta (Esp) Seat; Nadaillat (850m) Ludo Peeters (Bel) Kwantum; Puy de Dôme (1,415m) Erich Mächler (Sui) Carrera				
Stage 22 Sat 26 Jul	Clermont-Ferrand to Nevers 132 finishers	194 km 5h12'55" 37.2 kph	Guido Bontempi (Ita) Carrera	Greg LeMond (USA) La Vie Claire
Stage 23 Sun 27 Jul	Cosne-sur-Loire to Paris (Champs-Élysées) 132 finishers	255 km 6h51'55" 37.1 kph	Guido Bontempi (Ita) Carrera	Greg LeMond (USA) La Vie Claire

Prize fund: 4,500,680 francs (first prize: 300,000 francs)

Final Classification

Place	Rider	Team	Time	Age
1	Greg LeMond (USA)	La Vie Claire	4,094 km 110h35'19" 37.020 kph	25
2	Bernard Hinault (Fra)	La Vie Claire	+ 3'10"	31
3	Urs Zimmermann (Sui)	Carrera	+ 10'54"	26
4	Andy Hampsten (USA)	La Vie Claire	+ 18'44"	24
5	Claude Criquiélion (Bel)	Hitachi	+ 24'36"	29
6	Ronan Pensec (Fra)	Peugeot	+ 25'59"	23
7	Niki Rüttimann (Sui)	La Vie Claire	+ 30'52"	23
8	Álvaro Piño (Esp)	Zor	+ 33'00"	29
9	Steven Rooks (Ned)	PDM	+ 33'22"	26
10	Yvon Madiot (Fra)	Système U	+ 33'27"	24
Lanterne Rouge				
132	Ennio Salvador (Ita)	Gis	+ 2h55'51"	26
Points				
	Eric Vanderaerden (Bel)	Panasonic		24
King of the Mountains				
	Bernard Hinault (Fra)	La Vie Claire		31
Intermediate Sprints				
	Gerrit Solleveld (Ned)	Kwantum		25
Combination				
	Greg LeMond (USA)	La Vie Claire		25
Youth				
	Andy Hampsten (USA)	La Vie Claire		24
Team				
		La Vie Claire		
Team (Points)				
		Panasonic		
Super Combativité				
	Bernard Hinault (Fra)	La Vie Claire		31

1987: The Nouvelle Éire

Sunday, 19 July 1987. The Ventoux. Roland Barthes' God of Evil, Antoine Blondin's witch's cauldron, Jacques Goddet's condemned spot. The third Sunday of the seventy-seventh Tour de France. Eighteen days down, a full week still to go. The Pyrenees were behind the *peloton*, the Alps still to come. Thoughts could soon turn to Paris. But first, *le géant de Provence* had to be overcome.

Absent from the Ventoux were the two men who'd made the 1986 race a classic. Bernard Hinault was refusing to countenance talk of returning from retirement; in that at least he had kept his word. Greg LeMond was recovering from gunshot wounds that had almost killed him. In the early season Tirreno-Adriatico race LeMond had crashed and broken his wrist. Returning to America to recuperate he'd been out hunting with some friends and family when he was accidentally shot, nearly dying as he waited for the emergency services to arrive. Few, if any, expected him to ever return to top flight bicycle racing.

That left his La Vie Claire squad – now renamed Toshiba – without a leader. The 25-year-old Jean-François Bernard was fast-tracked into a team leadership role. And on that third Sunday of the 1987 Tour, on the Ventoux, Bernard gave those who doubted his abilities something to chew over as he blasted up the bald mountain.

In the 1987 Tour Mont Ventoux was used as the location for the race's second of three individual time trial stages. It was a real race of two halves: a flat 18-kilometre section from Carpentras to the base of the Ventoux, and then 18 kilometres up to the weather station at the summit of the climb. For Bernard that's exactly how it would be tackled: in two halves.

Bernard rolled down the starting ramp in Carpentras on a low-profile carbon fibre Look time-trial bike with a rear disc wheel. He reached the weather station on the Ventoux's summit on a light-weight road bike. The change from one to the other cost him maybe a dozen seconds but the loss was more than made up by the aggregation of the marginal gains across the two sections.

The man who had been dubbed the new Bernard Hinault gave the rest of the *peloton* a master class in time trialling, putting 1'39" into Café de Colombia's mountain goat Lucho Herrera, 1'51" into PDM's Pedro Delgado, 2'19" into Carrera's Stephen Roche and 3'58" into the man who had climbed the Ventoux in the *maillot jaune*, Système U's Charly Mottet. At the end of the stage Bernard was the man in yellow, with more than two minutes' advantage on his closest rivals.

In the immediate aftermath of that time trial two things happened which would impact events the following day on the road to Villard-de-Lans. One involved Système U's Laurent Fignon, who had yet to rediscover the form that had won him the Tour in 1983 and 1984. A journalist approached Fignon after the stage had finished, asking if Bernard was his natural successor. Fignon asked if that meant the journalist already had him dead and buried. The journalist said maybe. Fignon told him he was just going to have to demonstrate how wrong that assumption was.

The other involved Roche, who had come into the 1987 Tour as the leading favourite, hot off victory in a contentious Giro d'Italia which had finished just 18 days before the Tour started. That Giro was a race in which Roche's biggest rivals had been his Carrera team-mate and co-leader Roberto Visentini and the Italian fans. The *tifosi* were less than pleased at the thought of a foreigner beating an Italian in their national tour and took a few days to calm down and get used to it, taking their ire out on Roche until they did.

The evening after the Tour's Ventoux time trial the Irishman was in the Carrera team's hotel watching reporting of the day's events on TV. There he saw Bernard doing an interview in which he declared himself the strongest rider in the Tour and claimed that the remaining stages offered no great threat to him. Roche resolved to teach Bernard a lesson in humility.

Earlier in the 1987 season Fignon and Roche were involved in another day's racing in which Bernard had to the taught a lesson, during Paris-Nice. On the stage finishing atop Mont Faron, overlooking the naval dockyards in Toulouse, Bernard had stormed up the final climb looking imperious, taking the race-leader's white jersey off the shoulders of Roche. The day after, on the road to Saint-Tropez, Roche went for a long one in an effort to retake the race lead.

This was one of the features of Roche's riding career, the exploits, those days when he pulled something magic out of the bag, did the unexpected, something daring that made you smile at his audacity. The road to Saint-Tropez wasn't quite magic for Roche, the *peloton* letting him roll away from them and open up a sizable gap before – having given him enough rope to hang himself with, 100 kilometres out on his own – they started to pull him back in. But Roche, when he was caught, was able to sit in, didn't get spat out the back of the speeding *peloton*. Unlike Bernard.

The Toshiba star was hung that day by the speed set by the Système U squad. Cyrille Guimard – the Système U *directeur sportif* – hadn't forgiven Bernard Tapie for luring Hinault and then LeMond away from him to La Vie Claire. That day in the race to the sun, on the road to St-Trop, Fignon and his team-mates made Bernard suffer. He ended the day out of the white jersey, which reverted to Roche's shoulders, he having held his own as Système U drove the pace. Someone should have warned Bernard that days like that could become habit-forming.

Back in the 1987 Tour, as Bernard celebrated taking the yellow jersey, the opening Fignon and Roche were looking for was on the next day's route. Independently of each other they'd both identified the small, bumpy roads through the Vercors as the perfect place to hurt Bernard. The first feed zone, in Léoncel, just after the descent off the Col de Tourniol, was where their ambush would take place. Bernard, and everyone writing Fignon off, would be made eat their words.

On the first of the day's big climbs, the Tourniol, Bernard punctured and fluffed the wheel change before shipping his chain as the *peloton* raced away from him. Down the descent he chased and had just about regained the back of the race when the Système U boys put their plan into action, blasting through the feed zone. What was it Tim Krabbé said in *The Rider*?

"Road racing imitates life, the way it would be without the corruptive influence of civilisation. When you see an enemy lying on the ground, what's your first reaction? To help him to his feet. In road racing, you kick him to death."

Joining the Système U gang in kicking Bernard were Roche, Delgado, Herrera and others. As the break raced away from Bernard, Herrera – who had won the Vuelta a España earlier in the season – attacked out of it, taking with him Delgado, Roche, Mottet and a few others. By the base of the final climb, the Côte de Chalimont, Bernard was three minutes back down the road. Delgado made a move before the summit of the Chalimont and only Roche went with him. The Spaniard and the Irishman raced together toward Villard-de-Lans, Delgado taking the stage and Roche riding into the *maillot jaune*. Bernard was more than four minutes down at the end of the day, out of yellow, and left eating humble pie. (As had Charly Gaul back in 1958, after he had won on the Ventoux only to be ambushed the day after. The Tour, it repeats, but with new twists.)

The day following the *coup d'état* on the road to Villard-de-Lans the Tour tackled the 21 switchbacks of l'Alpe d'Huez. Roche was an unhappy wearer of the *maillot jaune* as the race to the Alpe got underway, figuring a week was too long for his Carrera team to defend yellow. His team-mates had tired themselves out defending Erich Mächler after he took over the jersey on the fourth stage, not losing it until the first individual time trial at Futuroscope on Stage 10, where Mottet had taken over the lead.

Going into the stage to the Alpe Roche had a 1'19" advantage over Delgado, who looked like the rider most likely to deny him victory. Most everyone figured the Irishman was good for a minute over the Spaniard in the penultimate stage's time trial in Dijon. That gave Roche just under two and a half minutes to play with over the Alpe and the next day's summit finish on La Plagne. Lose little more than a minute to Delgado on the Alpe and Roche would still be in with a shout of pulling off the Giro-Tour double and joining Fausto Coppi, Jacques Anquetil, Eddy Merckx and Bernard Hinault in the pantheon of the greats. Lose more and he'd likely lose the race.

On the climb up the Alpe Delgado turned his 1'19" deficit on Roche into a 25 second advantage, finishing the day in yellow. The race was now as finely balanced as it could be: Delgado could secure victory on his own terrain, the summit finish at La Plagne, while Roche could still, conceivably, win the race on his terrain, the final race against the clock in Dijon.

For the three days since the Ventoux time trial the 1987 Tour had thrown up the sort of drama fans want from a Tour, the lead switching from Mottet to Bernard to Roche and then to Delgado. The chief architect of the race, Félix Lévitan, should have been proud of the script he'd outlined and the manner in which the riders had played their parts. Without Hinault and LeMond to steal all the limelight the supporting cast were putting in award-winning performances.

But the man Émilien Amaury had installed to keep an eye on Jacques Goddet as part of the deal to secure the Tour for *L'Équipe* after the war was not on hand to witness how the race was playing out. Four months earlier Lévitan was summarily dismissed from the Amaury empire after a small black hole in the Tour's accounts had been discovered. Lévitan, the man who had been tasked with turning the Tour from a publicity stunt for an ailing newspaper into a profit-making business in its own right, had lost money, $500,000, in a failed attempt to launch a Tour of America in 1983. And he had buried that loss in the Tour's accounts. Four years later, when Philippe Amaury finally found out – when Amaury finally took his eyes off his empire's newspapers and started looking at the Tour – Lévitan was sacked.

It took Amaury until June to get Lévitan's replacement, Jean-François Naquet-Radiguet, in place. Rather than a new boy who had barely got his feet under the desk what the 1987 Tour most needed was a safe pair of hands to manage things day-by-day. So

Jacques Goddet came out of semi-retirement to see that the Tour went off without a hitch.

Goddet had always been more in touch with the sporting side of the race than his ousted co-director and it was through Goddet that an English team of professionals got to ride the 1987 Tour, a polite nod by him to the memory of Tom Simpson who had died on the Tour – on the Ventoux – 20 years earlier. That team was the ANC-Halfords squad owned by Tony Capper.

ANC's Shane Sutton had been the first rider to set off on the prologue of the 1987 Tour de France, a six-kilometre time trial up and down West Berlin's Kurfürstendamm. Until the next rider came home, Sutton was the virtual leader of the Tour de France, wearing an imaginary *maillot jaune*. Three seconds after Sutton crossed the finish line that next rider arrived, Supermacati's Milan Jurčo. Those three seconds were the high point of ANC's Tour de France.

Between Stages Three and 13 three ANC riders had shared ownership of the *lanterne rouge*, Paul Watson falling to the bottom of the general classification first, Guy Gallopin taking it over when Watson retired on the sixth stage along with Graham Jones, and then Shane Sutton carrying it through Stages 11 and 12. At the end of Stage 21 – the team having already seen Sutton and Stephen Swart leave the race – it was the turn of the team owner to leave the race shortly after it arrived at La Plagne. Capper's business was going belly up: riders' salaries hadn't been paid and the bailiffs had been around to the company's office in Stoke. In Capper's absence the remaining riders were reduced to hocking some carbon frames to fund themselves through the last week of the race.

That is just one of the stories of what was happening at the back of the race. At the front the 1987 Tour had just thrown up a day that has gone down in cycling history for a snippet of TV commentary from British broadcaster Channel 4's Phil Liggett, as Delgado approached the finish at La Plagne:

"Again Pedro Delgado has slipped Stephen Roche on the climb. Remember that at one point he had a minute and a half ... and just who is that rider coming up behind? Because that looks like Stephen Roche. That looks like Stephen Roche! It's Stephen Roche who's

Stephen Roche and Jeannie Longo share the podium in Paris at the end of the Tour and the Tour Cycliste Féminin in 1987.

come over the line! He almost caught Pedro Delgado! I don't believe it! What a finish by Stephen Roche! Stephen Roche has risen to the occasion so, so well! He almost caught Pedro Delgado on the line! Surely, now, Stephen Roche is going to win this Tour de France!"

Earlier in the stage Roche had attempted – and failed at – one of those do-or-die exploits he was fond off. Joining a breakaway on the Col de la Madeline the Irishman had escaped Delgado, getting at one point a gap of 1'40" and becoming the *maillot jaune virtuel*, the leader of the race on the road. For 100 kilometres the breakaways hung in there but by the time the race reached the feed zone at Argelès-Gazost, 40 kilometres from the stage end, Roche had been reeled in again. As on that day in Paris-Nice earlier in the season, though, Roche held on as the chasers swept past him and stayed with Delgado until they hit the early ramps of La Plagne.

When the chasers caught Roche Fignon attacked out of the group and began closing down on BH's Anselmo Fuerte, who had won the day before on the Alpe and was up the road on his own. The Spaniard and the Frenchman went up the final climb together. In the sprint for the line the glory went to France, and Fignon crossed the line first, arms punching the air in triumph.

All eyes, though, were on what was happening down the climb. Delgado had jumped clear of Roche early into the climb, figuring the Irishman was running on empty after his fruitless exertions between the Madeleine and Argèles-Gazost. Rather that trying to ride Delgado's pace Roche did as he'd done on the Alpe and let Delgado go as he settled into riding his own race. Then, five kilometres from the summit and with Delgado more than a minute up the road, Roche launched his fight-back, turning those final five kilometres into a handicapped pursuit race. With one TV motorbike having followed Fignon, the next Delgado, and the next one back with the bunch, Roche was in TV no-man's land, lost in the fog of war. He knew how much he had to claw back from Delgado but Delgado didn't know that Roche had launched a counter-attack.

Thirty-nine seconds after Fignon had led Fuerte over the line Café de Colombia's Fabio Parra rolled home. Eighteen seconds after him came Delgado. Cue the commentary from Liggett. Delgado preparing to cross the line. Liggett mentally preparing Roche's obituary. Time skipping a beat. And Roche appearing around the final bend, sprinting for the summit, pouring every ounce of energy he had left into the rush for the line, throwing his Battaglin bike from side to side. Every second counted. One one thousand. Two one thousand. Three one thousand. Four one thousand. Roche crossed the line, Delgado's advantage hacked back to four measly seconds. Twenty-nine seconds now separated the two on GC.

And then the real drama. As Eddy Merckx had on the Ventoux 17 years earlier, Roche's legs went from under him and he collapsed to the ground. The medics arrived with an oxygen mask. The media forgot all about Fignon, all about Delgado, and descended on the fallen Roche. The drama passed but, before it ended, Roche wrapped it up and put a ribbon round it with one of his better *bon mots*. Asked by a TV crew if he could say something to comfort the fans watching, Roche – a man who knew how to play to the media – gave them a priceless line: "Everything's okay, *mais pas de femme ce soir*."

Having limited Delgado's GC lead to just 29 seconds Roche got smacked with a time penalty from the race commissaires. The men in blazers added 10 seconds to his time, pushing Delgado's advantage out to 39 seconds and giving the Spaniard faint hope that victory could still be his. Was Roche really good for a minute over Delgado in Dijon, or could the yellow jersey give the Spaniard wings enough to actually hold onto a slim advantage when the dust had settled?

What had Roche done to merit a 10-second time penalty? Before reaching La Plagne he'd been handed a bottle from his team car. That bottle wasn't one of the official Coca Cola-branded *bidons* which all Tour riders were supposed to feed from. Having ousted Perrier as the Tour's official drink supplier the men from Atlanta were awake to the threats of ambush marketing and made sure that only their red *bidons* were to be used on the race. Albert Londres and Henri Pélissier would have laughed like loons at such a penalty.

Over the two remaining stages taking the race over to Dijon Roche clawed back a few more seconds from Delgado and then sealed the deal on the penultimate day's time trial, beating his rival by just over a minute and taking the *maillot jaune* by 40 seconds, the smallest winning margin since 1968. In Paris the next day even the Irish premier, Charles Haughey, was in attendance to congratulate Roche on his win.

* * * * *

Five weeks later, on a rain-soaked circuit in Villach, Austria, Roche closed out his magical season by adding the World Champion's rainbow jersey to his pink jersey from the Giro d'Italia and the yellow jersey from the Tour. Only one other rider had won all three jerseys in one season: Eddy Merckx. Maybe cycling really had found a new star.

As the year drew to a close the Tour lost another old star when, on November 18, Jacques Anquetil died of stomach cancer. Myth has it that Raymond Poulidor spoke to Maître Jacques on his deathbed and Anquetil laughed that once more the Eternal Second had been beaten. It's not a true story. But it perfectly fits the myth of one of the Tour's greatest rivalries.

Stage-by-Stage Results for the 1987 Tour de France			Stage Winner	Maillot Jaune
Prologue Wed 1 Jul	Berlin (ITT) 207 finishers	6.1 km 7'06" 51.5 kph	Jelle Nijdam (Ned) Superconfex	Jelle Nijdam (Ned) Superconfex
Stage 1 Thu 2 Jul	Berlin to Berlin 206 finishers	105.5 km 2h11'33" 48.1 kph	Nico Verhoeven (Ned) Superconfex	Lech Piasecki (Pol) Del Tongo
Stage 2 Thu 2 Jul	Berlin (TTT) 205 finishers	40.5 km 44'50" 54.2 kph	Carrera	Lech Piasecki (Pol) Del Tongo
Stage 3 Sat 4 Jul	Karlsruhe to Stuttgart 202 finishers	219 km 5h27'35" 40.1 kph	Acácio da Silva (Por) KAS	Erich Mächler (Sui) Carrera
Stage 4 Sun 5 Jul	Stuttgart to Pforzheim 202 finishers	79 km 1h49'23" 43.3 kph	Herman Frison (Bel) Roland	Erich Mächler (Sui) Carrera
Stage 5 Sun 5 Jul	Pforzheim to Strasbourg 202 finishers	112.5 km 2h32'29" 44.3 kph	Marc Sergeant (Bel) Joker	Erich Mächler (Sui) Carrera

Stage-by-Stage Results for the 1987 Tour de France			Stage Winner	Maillot Jaune
Stage 6 Mon 6 Jul	Strasbourg to Épinal 199 finishers	179 km 4h12'57" 42.5 kph	Christophe Lavainne (Fra) Système U	Erich Mächler (Sui) Carrera
	Major climbs: Côte du Champ du Feu (1,100m) Hendrik Devos (Bel) Roland; Mont Donon (727m) Raúl Alcalá (Mex) 7-Eleven			
Stage 7 Tue 7 Jul	Épinal to Troyes 197 finishers	211 km 5h08'17" 41.1 kph	~~Guido Bontempi (Ita)~~ ~~Carrera~~ Manuel Jorge Domínguez (Esp) BH	Erich Mächler (Sui) Carrera
Stage 8 Wed 8 Jul	Troyes to Epinay-sous-Sénart 197 finishers	205.5 km 5h23'53" 38.1 kph	Jean-Paul van Poppel (Ned) Superconfex	Erich Mächler (Sui) Carrera
Stage 9 Thu 9 Jul	Orléans to Rénazé 197 finishers	260 km 7h05'54" 36.6 kph	Adrie van der Poel (Ned) PDM	Erich Mächler (Sui) Carrera
Stage 10 Fri 10 Jul	Saumur to Futuroscope (ITT) 197 finishers	87.5 km 1h58'11" 44.4 kph	Stephen Roche (Irl) Carrera	Charly Mottet (Fra) Système U
Stage 11 Sat 11 Jul	Poitiers to Chaumeil 190 finishers	255 km 7h06'55" 35.8 kph	Martial Gayant (Fra) Système U	Martial Gayant (Fra) Système U
Stage 12 Sun 12 Jul	Brive to Bordeaux 189 finishers	228 km 5h46'21" 39.5 kph	Davis Phinney (USA) 7-Eleven	Martial Gayant (Fra) Système U
Stage 13 Mon 13 Jul	Bayonne to Pau 177 finishers	219 km 6h19'56" 34.6 kph	Erik Breukink (Ned) Panasonic	Charly Mottet (Fra) Système U
	Major climbs: Col de Burdincurutcheta (1,135m) Raúl Alcalá (Mex) 7-Eleven; Bagargui (1,327m) Raúl Alcalá (Mex) 7-Eleven; Col du Soudet (1,540m) Robert Forest (Fra) Fagor; Col de Marie- Blanque (1,035m) Luis Herrera (Col) Café de Colombia			
Stage 14 Tue 14 Jul	Pau to Luz-Ardiden 170 finishers	166 km 5h14'28" 31.7 kph	Dag Otto Lauritzen (Nor) 7-Eleven	Charly Mottet (Fra) Système U
	Major climbs: Col de Marie-Blanque (1,035m) Gilbert Duclos-Lassalle (Fra) Z; Col d'Aubisque (1,709m) Thierry Claveyrolat (Fra) RMO; Les Bordères (1,150m) Teun van Vliet (Ned) Panasonic; Luz-Ardiden (1,715m) Dag-Otto Lauritzen (Nor) 7-Eleven			
Stage 15 Wed 15 Jul	Tarbes to Blagnac 168 finishers	164 km 3h57'59" 41.3 kph	Rolf Gölz (FRG) Superconfex	Charly Mottet (Fra) Système U
Stage 16 Thu 16 Jul	Blagnac to Millau (Le Cade) 166 finishers	216.5 km 5h58'21" 36.2 kph	Régis Clère (Esp) Saunier Duval	Charly Mottet (Fra) Système U
	Major climbs: Millau-Causse Noir/Le Cade (835m) Régis Clère (Fra) Teka			

Stage-by-Stage Results for the 1987 Tour de France			Stage Winner	Maillot Jaune
Stage 17 Fri 17 Jul	Millau to Avignon 164 finishers	239 km 6h17'44" 38 kph	Jean-Paul van Poppel (Ned) Superconfex	Charly Mottet (Fra) Système U
	Major climbs: Col du Perjuret (1,028m) Frédéric Brun (Fra) Z; Mont Aigoual (1,560m) Silvano Contini (Ita) Del Tongo			
Sat 18 Jul	Rest Day			
Stage 18 Sun 19 Jul	Carpentras to Mont Ventoux (ITT) 164 finishers	36.5 km 1h19'44" 27.5 kph	Jean-François Bernard (Fra) Toshiba	Jean-François Bernard (Fra) Toshiba
	Major climbs: Mont Ventoux (1,909m) Jean-François Bernard (Fra) Toshiba			
Stage 19 Mon 20 Jul	Valréas to Villard-de-Lans 152 finishers	185 km 4h53'34" 37.8 kph	Pedro Delgado (Esp) PDM	Stephen Roche (Irl) Carrera
	Major climbs: Col de Tourniol (1,145m) Teun van Vliet (Ned) Panasonic; Col de la Bataille (1,340m) Juan Carlos Castillo (Col) Café de Colombia; Col de la Chau (1,430m) Laurent Fignon (Fra) Système U; Côte de Chalimont (1,300m) Pedro Delgado (Esp) PDM			
Stage 20 Tue 21 Jul	Villard-de-Lans to l'Alpe d'Huez 146 finishers	201 km 5h52'11" 34.2 kph	Federico Echave (Esp) BH	Pedro Delgado (Esp) PDM
	Major climbs: Col du Cucheron (1,139m) Federico Echave (Esp) BH; Col du Coq (1,430m) Denis Roux (Fra) Z; Côte de Laffrey (900m) Federico Echave (Esp) BH; l'Alpe d'Huez (1,860m) Federico Echave (Esp) BH			
Stage 21 Wed 22 Jul	Bourg-d'Oisans to La Plagne 139 finishers	185.5 km 6h07'05" 30.3 kph	Laurent Fignon (Fra) Système U	Pedro Delgado (Esp) PDM
	Major climbs: Col du Galibier (2,645m) Pedro Muñoz (Esp) Fagor; Col de la Madeleine (2,000m) Anselmo Fuerte (Esp) BH; La Plagne (1,970m) Laurent Fignon (Fra) Système U			
Stage 22 Thu 23 Jul	La Plagne to Morzine 137 finishers	186 km 6h13'48" 29.9 kph	Eduardo Chozas (Esp) Teka	Pedro Delgado (Esp) PDM
	Major climbs: Cormet de Roselend (1,968m) Mathieu Hermans (Ned) Caja Rural; Col des Saisies (1,633m) Omar Hernández (Col) Ryalcao; Col des Aravis (1,498m) Eduardo Chozas (Esp) Teka; Col de la Colombière (1,618m) Eduardo Chozas (Esp) Teka; Col de Joux-Plane (1,700m) Eduardo Chozas (Esp) Teka			
Stage 23 Fri 24 Jul	Saint-Julien-en-Genevois to Dijon 137 finishers	224.5 km 6h41'22" 33.6 kph	Régis Clère (Fra) Saunier Duval	Pedro Delgado (Esp) PDM
Stage 24 Sat 25 Jul	Dijon (ITT) 135 finishers	38 km 48'17" 47.2 kph	Jean-François Bernard (Fra) Toshiba	Stephen Roche (Irl) Carrera
Stage 25 Sun 26 Jul	Créteil to Paris (Champs-Élysées) 135 finishers	192 km 4h57'26" 38.7 kph	Jeff Pierce (USA) 7-Eleven	Stephen Roche (Irl) Carrera

Prize fund: 6,284,700 francs (first prize: 300,000 francs)

Final Classification

Place	Rider	Team	Time	Age
1	Stephen Roche (Irl)	Carrera	4,231 km 115h27'42" 36.645 kph	27
2	Pedro Delgado (Esp)	PDM	+ 0'40"	27
3	Jean-François Bernard (Fra)	Toshiba	+ 2'13"	25
4	Charly Mottet (Fra)	Système U	+ 6'40"	24
5	Luis Herrera (Col)	Café de Colombia	+ 9'32"	26
6	Fabio Parra (Col)	Café de Colombia	+ 16'53"	27
7	Laurent Fignon (Fra)	Système U	+ 18'24"	26
8	Anselmo Fuerte (Esp)	BH	+ 18'33"	25
9	Raúl Alcalá (Mex)	7-Eleven	+ 21'49"	23
10	Marino Lejarreta (Esp)	Caja Rural	+ 26'13"	30

Lanterne Rouge

135	Mathieu Hermans (Ned)	Caja Rural	+ 4h23'30"	24

Points

	Jean-Paul van Poppel (Ned)	Superconfex		24

King of the Mountains

	Luis Herrera (Col)	Café de Colombia		26

Intermediate Sprints

	Gilbert Duclos-Lassalle (Fra)	Peugeot		32

Combination

	Jean-François Bernard (Fra)	Toshiba		25

Youth

	Raúl Alcalá (Mex)	7-Eleven		23

Team

		Système U		

Team (Points)

		Système U		

Super Combativité

	Pedro Delgado (Esp)	PDM		27

1988: A Stained Yellow Jersey

The seventy-fifth Tour began with a novelty *préface* in which the competing squads set off for a six-kilometre team time trial, at the end of which a nominated rider would do a flying kilo. None of the time counted toward GC, though the fastest team over the first section trousered a pocketful of cash while the winner of the solo section started the race proper in the *maillot jaune*. Another novelty added for the 1988 Tour was the village *départ*, a gathering area at the start of each stage where riders, journalists and VIPs could mingle and relax.

These novelties came about even as the turmoil at the Société du Tour de France continued. A month before the race Jean-Pierre Courcol took over as race director after Jean-François Naquet-Radiguet went the way of the man he had replaced only a year earlier, Félix Lévitan.

And there was turmoil at the race itself too. For the first time in a decade the racing was overshadowed by a doping scandal. That's not to say that there had been no doping at the Tour over the past few years, just that that doping at the Tour over the past few years had not really been seen to be scandalous. The cycling world had got used to riders being caught and handed speeding tickets. And the riders themselves – generally speaking – had got used to what the authorities could and could not test for, and preferred the latter over the former.

The 1988 Tour de France was into the home straight when the doping scandal erupted. The Alps were a distant memory and the Pyrenees were just fading into the rear-view mirror. The sprinters were back in control as the Tour barrelled into Bordeaux. The race was just five days out from Paris. The Spaniard Pedro Delgado (Reynolds) was wrapped up in the *maillot jaune* and it looked like it would take a major upset for anyone to take it away from him.

On the evening the race arrived in Bordeaux, Jacques Chancel's *après*-Tour TV show hinted at things to come, the host telling his audience he had a hunch something was going to happen and stir up a storm. A few hours later Antenne 2's Patrick Chêne broke the news: 'We've learned that in the hours to come, in the days to come, it will be announced that Pedro Delgado has tested positive for drugs.'

Journalists immediately descended upon Delgado's hotel. The Spaniard, eating his dinner at the time, was asked by reporters for his response and he denied knowledge of any problem with the testers. But was already on the defensive, suggesting he must have drunk from a spiked bottle passed up by a spectator.

The news was made official the following morning, before the start of the stage from Ruelle-sur-Touvre to Limoges: at the end of Stage 13's Grenoble to Villard-de-Lans time trial – where Delgado had won the stage and cemented his claim to the *maillot jaune* – Perico had tested positive for an unnamed drug. If his B-sample confirmed the result of the A test the Spaniard would get a speeding ticket – the standard 10-minute time penalty, suspended suspension and financial fine – that would drop him down the GC from first to seventh.

The closest the Tour had come to such trouble had been 10 years earlier, in 1978, when Michel Pollentier, the newly installed race leader, had been thrown off the race on l'Alpe d'Huez after being caught trying to cheat the dope control. The *maillot jaune*, though, had never failed a dope test.

Delgado himself had seen the damage a positive dope control could do. In 1982 he had been a member of the Reynolds squad when his team-mate Ángel Arroyo was stripped of his Vuelta a España victory shortly after the race ended, after he was found to have used the stimulant methylphenidate. The 10-minute time penalty Arroyo received dropped him from first to thirteenth on GC and handed the race to Marino Lejarreta. (Arroyo was still a

Reynolds rider in 1988, and had started the Tour in support of Delgado, before dropping out on the road to Luz-Ardiden.)

Steven Rooks (PDM), who was wearing the polka-dot jersey, stood to take the race lead if Delgado was penalised. He vowed that if he did take the win he'd go to Delgado's home in Segovia immediately the race ended and present him the *maillot jaune*.

The following day, as the race wended its way from Limoges to the Puy-de-Dôme, Delgado's B-sample was being tested in the Châtenay-Malabry laboratory in Paris. In the Clermont-Ferrand *salle de presse* the assembled journalists were learning more about what was happening. A Spanish colleague told them that the drug Delgado tested positive for was probenecid, which he had definitely used. But, the Spanish journalist assured his colleagues, while the B-sample would confirm that, Delgado would skate because probenecid was not banned by the UCI. It was banned by the IOC, but the UCI were not due to add it to their list until August.

Late into the evening – well after everyone had forgotten Johnny Weltz's victory on the Puy de Dôme for Fagor – the story told by the Spanish journalist was confirmed in full. Delgado was positive for probenecid. But, while it was banned by the IOC, it was not on the UCI's banned list. Delgado was cleared.

Probenecid is an anti-inflammatory, available over the counter, used in the treatment of gout and similar ailments. However, because of its diuretic properties, it has been known to be used by athletes as a masking agent. The IOC had added it to its banned list the previous year, but the IOC's list and the UCI's list were out of synch, and the UCI wouldn't be updating their list until August.

That this lack of synchronisation in the lists might cause a problem should not have come as news. At the Munich Olympics in 1972, a Dutch rider, Aad van den Hoek, and a Spanish rider, Jaime Huélamo, tested positive for Coramine. At the time this was legal in the *peloton* but banned by the IOC. Had the UCI wished to redress the problem they could have done it after that incident, either by accepting the primacy of the IOC list – something that was anathema to the UCI, seen as being tantamount to surrendering sovereignty of their sport – or by updating their own list before the start of the cycling season, instead of towards its end.

* * * * *

Pedro Delgado was not the only one with a doping problem on the 1988 Tour. PDM's Gert-Jan Theunisse had tested positive after the Morzine stage, where he was one of two riders chosen at random to supply a doping sample. The next day, the PDM rider's doping was confirmed: he was positive for testosterone. The 10-minute time penalty dropped him from fourth to eleventh on GC. He got another two minutes during that day's stage when he took a swing at Paul Köchli, the *directeur sportif* at Weinmann/La Suisse and a man known to be against doping. Apparently Theunisse took offence at the less than sympathetic attitude shown by Köchli to his misfortune.

Theunisse disputed the result of the dope test, claimed that the reason he tested positive for testosterone was that he had naturally high levels of the hormone, that a thyroid problem was the cause. But that there might be doping going on in PDM came as no surprise to many involved with the sport. The team had a reputation. The initials – which officially stood for Philips Dupont Magnetics – were variously mistranslated: in Dutch they were said to mean *Prestaties Door Manipulaties* (performances through manipulation); in French it was *Plein de Manipulation* (full of manipulation). In English it was simply Pills, Drugs and Medicine.

* * * * *

Few – apart from the Spaniards – were happy with Delgado being cleared in such a manner. Jean-Marie Courcol, the newly installed head of the Société du Tour de France, wrote in *L'Équipe* that he was ashamed that the letter of the law could replace its spirit and that athletes – who were role models for children – could play with the rules. In the months after the Tour ended Courcol followed Lévitan and Naquet-Radiguet through the Société du Tour's revolving door and handed the reins to Jean-Marie Leblanc, who, like Courcol, had expressed his displeasure with the manner in which Delgado had been cleared, calling it a dismal verdict that rewarded transgression and encouraged fraud.

Delgado didn't care. Nor did his *directeur sportif*, José-Miguel Echávarri. And Perico had the Spanish media behind him. Even the Spanish sports minister had lobbied the UCI on Delgado's behalf. And Delgado had the support of the UCI, led by Spaniard Luis Puig, who criticised the laboratory for not referring to the correct banned list, and questioned the manner in which the story had leaked.

Perico did defend himself though. He told the media he was only looking after himself, following the advice of his doctor, François Bellocq who, he suggested, had prescribed the drug. Oddly, then, Bellocq wrote to *L'Équipe* claiming that he hadn't treated the Spaniard.

Bellocq was a medic with a reputation, earned in the 1970s when he was team doctor for Peugeot. He was named when the Rachel Dard story was reported by *L'Équipe* in 1976, and he was named when Bernard Thévenet confessed his cortisone use. Within the *peloton*, though, he was generally respected, and many riders beat a path to his door, from Tour winners down (Bernard Hinault told the medical magazine *Tonus* in 1988 that Bellocq had been his doctor).

Most famously, Bellocq was an advocate of hormone rebalancing, topping up what exercise depleted. A three-week race like the Tour naturally depletes the body's levels of hormones like testosterone or cortisone. Bellocq believed riders had the right to raise those levels to their normal figure. That the rules said this wasn't right didn't seem to be a problem, and that testosterone and cortisone were banned didn't seem to matter.

That, more or less, was the end of the *affaire*. Delgado rode into Paris in yellow and accepted the applause of the crowd as he was crowned the final victor. The Spanish government and the Spanish royal family congratulated their man. Hinault, even in retirement still the *patron*, gave Delgado his blessing, calling him a classy rider and saying he was pleased by his victory.

Not everyone shared that sentiment. *Figaro* probably summed it up best: "It could be said that the victory is a denial of justice, a shame for cycling, which will probably pay the bill, a bigger one than the world of cycling imagines."

A month later, the UCI's medical commission met at the World Championships in Belgium. As expected, they added probenecid to the banned list.

Stage-by-Stage Results for the 1988 Tour de France			Stage Winner	Maillot Jaune
Préface Part 1 Sun 3 Jul	Pornichet to La Baule (TTT) 198 finishers	6 km 1'14" 48.6 kph	Weinmann	N/A
Préface Part 2 Sun 3 Jul	Pornichet to La Baule (TTT) 198 finishers	1 km 1'14" 48.6 kph	Guido Bontempi (Ita) Carrera	Guido Bontempi (Ita) Carrera
Stage 1 Mon 4 Jul	Pontchateau to Machecoul 198 finishers	91.5 km 2h16'34" 40.2 kph	Steve Bauer (Can) Weinmann	Steve Bauer (Can) Weinmann
Stage 2 Mon 4 Jul	La Haye-Fouassière to Ancenis (TTT) 198 finishers	48 km 55'31" 51.9 kph	Panasonic	Teun van Vliet (Ned) Panasonic
Stage 3 Tue 5 Jul	Nantes to Le Mans 197 finishers	213.5 km 4h52'08" 43.8 kph	Jean-Paul van Poppel (Ned) Superconfex	Teun van Vliet (Ned) Panasonic
Stage 4 Wed 6 Jul	Le Mans to Évreux 196 finishers	158 km 3h25'14" 46.2 kph	Acácio da Silva (Por) KAS	Teun van Vliet (Ned) Panasonic
Stage 5 Thu 7 Jul	Neufchatel-en-Bray to Liévin 185 finishers	147.5 km 3h14'14" 45.6 kph	Jelle Nijdam (Ned) Superconfex	Henk Lubberding (Ned) Panasonic
Stage 6 Fri 8 Jul	Liévin to Wasquehal (ITT) 193 finishers	52 km 1h03'22" 49.2 kph	Sean Yates (GBr) Fagor	Jelle Nijdam (Ned) Superconfex
Stage 7 Sat 9 Jul	Wasquehal to Reims 192 finishers	225.5 km 5h27'10" 41.4 kph	Valerio Tebaldi (Ita) Château d'Ax	Jelle Nijdam (Ned) Superconfex
Stage 8 Sun 10 Jul	Reims to Nancy 192 finishers	219 km 5h24'18" 40.5 kph	Rolf Gölz (FRG) Superconfex	Steve Bauer (Can) Weinmann
Stage 9 Mon 11 Jul	Nancy to Strasbourg 191 finishers	160.5 km 3h47'31" 42.3 kph	Jérôme Simon (Fra) Z	Steve Bauer (Can) Weinmann
Major climbs: Mont Donon (727m) Dominique Garde (Fra) Système U; Le Struthof (1,030m) Frédéric Vichot (Fra) Weinmann				
Stage 10 Tue 12 Jul	Belfort to Besançon 190 finishers	149.5 km 3h28'31" 43 kph	Jean-Paul van Poppel (Ned) Superconfex	Steve Bauer (Can) Weinmann
Major climbs: Ballon de Servance (1,175m) Robert Millar (GBr) Fagor				

Stage-by-Stage Results for the 1988 Tour de France			Stage Winner	Maillot Jaune
Stage 11 Wed 13 Jul	Besançon to Morzine 188 finishers	232 km 6h04'54" 38.1 kph	Fabio Parra (Col) Kelme	Steve Bauer (Can) Weinmann
	Major climbs: Pas de Morgins (1,369m) Ludo Peeters (Bel) Superconfex; Col du Corbier (1,325m) Fabio Parra (Col) Kelme			
Stage 12 Thu 14 Jul	Morzine to l'Alpe d'Huez 179 finishers	227 km 6h55'44" 32.8 kph	Steven Rooks (Ned) PDM	Pedro Delgado (Esp) Reynolds
	Major climbs: Pont d'Arbon (1,110m) Jérôme Simon (Fra) Z; Col de la Madeleine (2,000m) Henri Abadie (Fra) Z; Col du Glandon (1,924m) Steven Rooks (Ned) PDM; l'Alpe d'Huez (1,860m) Steven Rooks (Ned) PDM			
Stage 13 Fri 15 Jul	Grenoble to Villard-de-Lans (ITT) 177 finishers	38 km 1h02'24" 36.5 kph	Pedro Delgado (Esp) Reynolds	Pedro Delgado (Esp) Reynolds
	Major climbs: Côte d'Engins (885m) Pedro Delgado (Esp) Reynolds; Villard-de-Lans (1,150m) Pedro Delgado (Esp) Reynolds			
Sat 16 Jul	Rest Day			
Stage 14 Sun 17 Jul	Blagnac to Guzet-Neige 176 finishers	163 km 4h30'34" 36.1 kph	Massimo Ghirotto (Ita) Carrera	Pedro Delgado (Esp) Reynolds
	Major climbs: Col d'Agnès (1,570m) Robert Millar (GBr) Fagor; Col de Latrape (1,100m) Robert Millar (GBr) Fagor; Guzet-Neige (1,480m) Massimo Ghirotto (Ita) Carrera			
Stage 15 Mon 18 Jul	Saint-Girons to Luz-Ardiden 170 finishers	187.5 km 6h20'44" 29.5 kph	Laudelino Cubino (Esp) BH	Pedro Delgado (Esp) Reynolds
	Major climbs: Col de Portet d'Aspet (1,069m) Steven Rooks (Ned) PDM; Col de Menté (1,349m) Robert Millar (GBr) Fagor; Col de Peyresourde (1,569m) Steven Rooks (Ned) PDM; Col d'Aspin (1,489m) Samuel Cabrera (Col) Café de Colombia; Col du Tourmalet (2,115m) Laudelino Cubino (Esp) BH; Luz-Ardiden (1,715m) Laudelino Cubino (Esp) BH			
Stage 16 Tue 19 Jul	Luz-Ardiden to Pau 165 finishers	38 km 46'36" 48.9 kph	Adri van der Poel (Ned) PDM	Pedro Delgado (Esp) Reynolds
Stage 17 Tue 19 Jul	Pau to Bordeaux 164 finishers	210 km 4h58'03" 42.3 kph	Jean-Paul van Poppel (Ned) Superconfex	Pedro Delgado (Esp) Reynolds
Stage 18 Wed 20 Jul	Ruelle-sur-Touvre to Limoges 159 finishers	93.5 km 2h12'45" 42.3 kph	Gianni Bugno (Ita) Château d'Ax	Pedro Delgado (Esp) Reynolds
Stage 19 Thu 21 Jul	Limoges to Puy-de-Dôme 153 finishers	188 km 5h14'34" 35.9 kph	Johnny Weltz (Den) Fagor	Pedro Delgado (Esp) Reynolds
	Major climbs: Puy de Dôme (1,415m) Johnny Weltz (Den) Fagor			
Stage 20 Fri 22 Jul	Clermont-Ferrand to Chalon-sur-Saône 152 finishers	223.5 km 6h03'45" 36.9 kph	Thierry Marie (Fra) Système U	Pedro Delgado (Esp) Reynolds
Stage 21 Sat 23 Jul	Santenay (ITT) 151 finishers	46 km 1h02'37" 44.1 kph	Juan Martínez Oliver (Esp) Kelme	Pedro Delgado (Esp) Reynolds

Stage-by-Stage Results for the 1988 Tour de France			Stage Winner	Maillot Jaune
Stage 22 Sun 24 Jul	Nemours to Paris (Champs-Élysées) 151 finishers	172.5 km 4h51'29" 35.5 kph	Jean-Paul van Poppel (Ned) Superconfex	Pedro Delgado (Esp) Reynolds

Prize fund: 7,567,250 francs (first prize: 1,300,000 francs)

Final Classification				
Place	**Rider**	**Team**	**Time**	**Age**
1	Pedro Delgado (Esp)	Reynolds	3,286 km 84h27'53" 38.909 kph	28
2	Steven Rooks (Ned)	PDM	+ 7'13"	28
3	Fabio Parra (Col)	Kelme	+ 9'58"	28
4	Steve Bauer (Can)	Weinmann	+ 12'15"	29
5	Éric Boyer (Fra)	Système U	+ 14'04"	24
6	Luis Herrera (Col)	Café de Colombia	+ 14'36"	27
7	Ronan Pensec (Fra)	Z	+ 16'52"	25
8	Álvaro Piño (Esp)	BH	+ 18'36"	31
9	Peter Winnen (Ned)	Panasonic	+ 19'12"	30
10	Denis Roux (Fra)	Z	+ 20'08"	32
Lanterne Rouge				
151	Dirk Wayenberg (Bel)	ADR	+ 3h28'41"	27
Points				
	Eddy Planckaert (Bel)	ADR		29
King of the Mountains				
	Steven Rooks (Ned)	PDM		27
Intermediate Sprints				
	Frans Maassen (Ned)	Superconfex		23
Combination				
	Steven Rooks (Ned)	PDM		27
Youth				
	Erik Breukink (Ned)	Panasonic		24
Team				
		PDM		
Team (Points)				
		PDM		
Super Combativité				
	Jérôme Simon (Fra)	Z		27

1989: A Game of Chess

At both the 1987 and 1988 Tours de France, Laurent Fignon had been the only former winner to take the start, Bernard Hinault having retired and Greg LeMond's recovery from gunshot wounds taking longer than expected. Stephen Roche had been unable to back up his 1987 win following a knee injury. The Fignon who rode those two Tours was a shadow of the man who won in 1983 and 1984. But in 1989 the Professor – now riding in the colours of Super U – seemed to be back to his best and went into the Tour hot off a victory in the Giro d'Italia and having opened the year with a win in Milan-Sanremo.

Also back was LeMond – now riding for ADR – but, unlike his French rival, the American seemed far from his best, having finished the Giro nearly an hour down on Fignon (but – significantly – in a 55-kilometre time trial the American took 1'55" out of Fignon). The man to beat in 1989, though, was surely Pedro Delgado (Reynolds), the defending champion, the man who had to prove that his win in 1988 was no fluke and shouldn't be shrouded in a cloud of suspicion over his use of probenecid.

The Spaniard, though, hamstrung himself from the off, missing his start time in the opening prologue time trial and finishing the day as the *lanterne rouge*, three minutes off the pace. Perico added another four to that when he failed to keep the pace of his team-mates in Stage Two's team time trial. He would spend the rest of the Tour making up that time lost so easily in the opening days of the race but never really challenging for the overall win.

The first real selection among the challengers and would-be challengers came on Stage Five, a 73-kilometre individual time trial from Dinard to Rennes. LeMond aced it, putting 24 seconds into

Delgado and 56 into Fignon. As well as winning the stage the American donned the *maillot jaune*, with Fignon just five seconds back, in second place. Things then settled down until the race reached the Pyrenees on Stage Nine.

The first day in the mountains saw little change, Fignon and LeMond marking one and other and allowing Delgado to slip off up the road and reclaim some of the time he'd surrendered so easily at the start of the race. The stage was won by one of Perico's Reynolds helpmates, Miguel Indurain.

Fignon left it until the closing kilometres of the next stage – the last of the race's mountains until the Alps reared up – before attacking, making a move as they approached Superbagnères and taking 12 seconds out of the American and the yellow jersey off his shoulders. Now it was the Frenchman's turn to lead, and protect a slim margin of just seven seconds back to LeMond. Behind him was Charly Mottet (RMO) at 57 seconds, with Delgado in fourth, already having reduced his deficit to 2'53". After that, the rest of the field was five minutes and more back.

The Alps opened with a time trial to Orcières-Merlette and the positions unchanged since the Pyrenees. The *contre-la-montre* was won by PDM's Steven Rooks, while Fignon ceded 47 seconds to LeMond. The American was back in yellow with a 40-second cushion.

After a rest day the race resumed, with more Alpine climbs thrown at the riders. The Vars and the Izoard on the road to Briançon came next and in the final kilometre – where, in Superbagnères, Fignon took 12 seconds out of LeMond – LeMond took 13 seconds out of Fignon, strengthening his grip on the *maillot jaune*. Three more days in the mountains remained, and then (after a long transfer) the race's finale, a time trial in Paris. The race was far from over yet.

Fignon proved that the next day on the Alpe. PDM's Gert-Jan Theunisse was up the road riding for the stage win when LeMond and Fignon hit the base of the Alpe and their race for the *maillot jaune* really took off. From the first hairpins it was clear that Fignon could take time out of LeMond, the only question was how much. Fignon and his *directeur sportif* Cyrille Guimard had already discussed this – LeMond had been Guimard's discovery and Fignon's former

Greg LeMond time trials to victory in
the 1989 Tour.

team-mate, they both knew his abilities – and it had been agreed that Fignon should attack immediately they hit the Alpe. But Fignon and LeMond had already been attacking one an other incessantly, neither landing a decisive blow.

Six kilometres from the summit of the Alpe Guimard drove up alongside Fignon and told him it was time for the kill, to go and go now. Fignon hesitated. It was only with four kilometres to go that the Frenchman launched his attack, an attack which LeMond could not respond to. In those final four kilometres Fignon put 1'19" into the American and took the *maillot jaune* from his back. Fignon led again, by 26 seconds. Enough with the final time trial to come? Fignon didn't think so. He knew he should have attacked earlier on the Alpe. So, the next day, on the road to Villard-de-Lans, the yellow jersey went for it. And gained 24 seconds.

The two duelled through the final day of climbing, neither gaining the upper hand, and it all came down to the final time trial from Versailles into Paris. Not the traditional promenade into the City of Lights, but a return to the era of Anquetil when a final time trial tied the race up with a neat little ribbon. And this would be a real race of truth, one which would reveal the winner of the 1989 Tour.

Not since Jan Janssen in 1968 had a time trial finale crowned the winner of the Tour. Jean Robic in 1947 was the only other rider to have won the race on its last day. And then it happened again. Riding a Bottecchia bike LeMond turned a 50-second deficit into an eight-second winning margin. Eight seconds. The ghost of Ottavio Bottecchia must have smiled, his name a recognition of his status as his parents' eighth child.

* * * * *

You can go through the whole of the 1989 Tour and find places where Fignon could have picked up another nine seconds and won the Tour. The moments when he hesitated or even failed to press LeMond. For most people, though, those eight seconds can be explained by two things: Fignon rode the final time trial hampered by a boil on his backside; LeMond rode it using revolutionary new handlebar extensions that allowed him to find a more aerodynamic position on his bike.

The irony of LeMond's aerodynamic advantage is that Fignon's *directeur sportif* Cyrille Guimard had been at the forefront of ushering in aerodynamic innovations in time trials at the end of the 1970s. This was not lost on many. Nor was the fact that the handlebar extensions used by LeMond in that final time trial had already been showcased, both earlier in the Tour, and by 7-Eleven at the Tour de Trump in America earlier in the year. Guimard and Fignon knew about them, had even tested them. And then disregarded them.

In the weeks and months that followed Fignon's failure was autopsied. And that's one of the things about the 1989 Tour. It's less about LeMond winning the race by eight seconds and more about Fignon losing it by eight seconds. It's not a story of triumph – though it is that, in part, especially with LeMond returning from gunshot wounds – it's a story of failure. It's a story about lessons that could and should have been learned. And among the people trying to learn a lesson from Fignon's failures in 1989 was one of his *domestiques*, Bjarne Riis.

* * * * *

Outside of the race itself, the turmoil within the Société du Tour de France had subsided. Jean-Marie Leblanc was at the helm and steering a new course. While Henri Desgrange had been a rider with a number of French and world records to his name, and while even Jacques Goddet and Félix Lévitan had briefly dabbled with the sport themselves, Leblanc had the advantage over his predecessors of actually having raced the Tour himself, understood the race the riders rode.

The Tour's dream of *mondialisation* was by now happening even without pressure from the likes of the deposed Félix Lévitan or the retired Jacques Goddet. The Soviets had finally arrived, off their own bat, Ernesto Colnago having helped Sovintersport – the outward-facing arm of the Soviet Ministry of Sports and Physical Culture – bring Soviet cyclists to the Italian Alfa Lum team. While all eyes had been on the Tour's expansion westward, into the English-speaking lands and the Americas, the sport itself was about to expand with a new influx of riders coming in from the east: the Berlin Wall fell in November and the Iron Curtain began to rot away.

Stage-by-Stage Results for the 1989 Tour de France			Stage Winner	Maillot Jaune
Prologue Sat 1 Jul	Luxembourg (ITT) 198 finishers	7.8 km 9'54" 47.3 kph	Erik Breukink (Ned) PDM	Erik Breukink (Ned) PDM
Stage 1 Sun 2 Jul	Luxembourg to Luxembourg 198 finishers	135.5 km 3h21'36" 40.3 kph	Acácio da Silva (Por) Carrera	Acácio da Silva (Por) Carrera
Stage 2 Sun 2 Jul	Luxembourg (TTT) 196 finishers	46 km 53'48" 51.3 kph	Super U	Acácio da Silva (Por) Carrera
Stage 3 Mon 3 Jul	Luxembourg to Spa (Francorchamps) 195 finishers	241 km 6h34'17" 36.7 kph	Raúl Alcalá (Mex) PDM	Acácio da Silva (Por) Carrera
Stage 4 Tue 4 Jul	Liège to Wasquehal 195 finishers	255 km 6h13'58" 40.9 kph	Jelle Nijdam (Ned) Superconfex	Acácio da Silva (Por) Carrera
Wed 5 Jul	Rest Day			
Stage 5 Thu 6 Jul	Dinard to Rennes (ITT) 193 finishers	73 km 1h38'12" 44.6 kph	Greg LeMond (USA) ADR	Greg LeMond (USA) ADR
Stage 6 Fri 7 Jul	Rennes to Futuroscope 191 finishers	259 km 6h57'45" 37.2 kph	Joël Pélier (Ita) SCIC	Greg LeMond (USA) ADR
Stage 7 Sat 8 Jul	Poitiers to Bordeaux 188 finishers	258.5 km 7h21'57" 35.1 kph	Etienne de Wilde (Bel) Histor	Greg LeMond (USA) ADR
Stage 8 Sun 9 Jul	Labastide-d'Armagnac to Pau 188 finishers	157 km 3h51'26" 40.7 kph	Martin Earley (Irl) PDM	Greg LeMond (USA) ADR
Stage 9 Mon 10 Jul	Pau to Cauterets (Cambasque) 185 finishers	147 km 4h32'36" 32.4 kph	Miguel Indurain (Esp) Reynolds	Greg LeMond (USA) ADR
	Major climbs: Cauterets (934m) Miguel Indurain (Esp) Reynolds; Col de Marie-Blanque (1,035m) Robert Forest (Fra) Fagor; Col d'Aubisque (1,709m) Miguel Indurain (Esp) Reynolds; Les Bordères (1,150m) Miguel Indurain (Esp) Reynolds; Le Cambasque (1,320m) Miguel Indurain (Esp) Reynolds			
Stage 10 Tue 11 Jul	Cauterets to Luchon (Superbagnères) 167 finishers	136 km 4h22'19" 31.1 kph	Robert Millar (GBr) Z	Laurent Fignon (Fra) Super U
	Major climbs: Col du Tourmalet (2,115m) Robert Millar (GBr) Z; Col d'Aspin (1,489m) Robert Millar (GBr) Z; Col de Peyresourde (1,569m) Robert Millar (GBr) Z; Superbagnères (1,804m) Robert Millar (GBr) Z			
Stage 11 Wed 12 Jul	Luchon to Blagnac 165 finishers	158.5 km 3h37'47" 43.7 kph	Mathieu Hermans (Ned) Paternina	Laurent Fignon (Fra) Super U

Stage-by-Stage Results for the 1989 Tour de France			Stage Winner	Maillot Jaune
Stage 12 Thu 13 Jul	Toulouse to Montpellier 161 finishers	242 km 5h40'54" 42.6 kph	Valerio Tebaldi (Ita) Château d'Ax	Laurent Fignon (Fra) Super U
Stage 13 Fri 14 Jul	Montpellier to Marseille 155 finishers	179 km 4h17'31" 41.7 kph	Vincent Barteau (Fra) Super U	Laurent Fignon (Fra) Super U
Stage 14 Sat 15 Jul	Marseille to Gap 152 finishers	240 km 6h27'55" 37.1 kph	Jelle Nijdam (Ned) Superconfex	Laurent Fignon (Fra) Super U
	Major climbs: Col du Labouret (1,240m) Jérôme Simon (Fra) Z			
Stage 15 Sun 16 Jul	Gap to Orcières-Merlette (ITT) 150 finishers	39 km 1h10'42" 33.1 kph	Steven Rooks (Ned) PDM	Greg LeMond (USA) ADR
	Major climbs: Col de Manse (1,245m) Steven Rooks (Ned) PDM; Orcières-Merlette (1,838m) Gert-Jan Theunisse (Ned) PDM			
Mon 17 Jul	Rest Day			
Stage 16 Tue 18 Jul	Gap to Briançon 150 finishers	175 km 4h46'45" 36.6 kph	Pascal Richard (Sui) Helvetia	Greg LeMond (USA) ADR
	Major climbs: Col de Vars (2,110m) Bruno Cornillet (Fra) Z; Col d'Izoard (2,360m) Pascal Richard (Sui) Helvetia			
Stage 17 Wed 19 Jul	Briançon to l'Alpe d'Huez 143 finishers	165 km 5h10'39" 31.9 kph	Gert-Jan Theunisse (Ned) PDM	Laurent Fignon (Fra) Super U
	Major climbs: Col du Galibier (2,645m) Gert-Jan Theunisse (Ned) PDM; Col de la Croix de Fer (2,067m) Gert-Jan Theunisse (Ned) PDM; l'Alpe d'Huez (1,860m) Gert-Jan Theunisse (Ned) PDM			
Stage 18 Thu 20 Jul	Bourg-d'Oisans to Villard-de-Lans 139 finishers	91.5 km 2h31'28" 36.2 kph	Laurent Fignon (Fra) Super U	Laurent Fignon (Fra) Super U
	Major climbs: Côte de Laffrey (900m) Laurent Biondi (Fra) Fagor; Côte de Saint-Nizier de Moucherotte (1,180m) Laurent Fignon (Fra) Super U; Villard-de-Lans (150m) Laurent Fignon (Fra) Super U			
Stage 19 Fri 21 Jul	Villard-de-Lans to Aix-les-Bains 138 finishers	125 km 3h17'53" 37.9 kph	Greg LeMond (USA) ADR	Laurent Fignon (Fra) Super U
	Major climbs: Col de Porte (1,326m) Pedro Delgado (Esp) Reynolds; Col du Cucheron (1,139m) Pedro Delgado (Esp) Reynolds; Col du Granier (1,134m) Pedro Delgado (Esp) Reynolds			
Stage 20 Sat 22 Jul	Aix-les-Bains to l'Isle-d'Abeau 138 finishers	130 km 3h26'16" 37.8 kph	Giovanni Fidanza (Ita) Château d'Ax	Laurent Fignon (Fra) Super U
Stage 21 Sun 23 Jul	Versailles to Paris (Champs-Élysées) (ITT) 138 finishers	24.5 km 26'57" 54.5 kph	Greg LeMond (USA) ADR	Greg LeMond (USA) ADR

Prize fund: 8,104,215 francs (first prize: 1,500,000 francs)

Final Classification

Place	Rider	Team	Time	Age
1	Greg LeMond (USA)	ADR	3,285 km 87h38'35" 37.487 kph	28
2	Laurent Fignon (Fra)	Super U	+ 0'08"	28
3	Pedro Delgado (Esp)	Reynolds	+ 3'34"	29
4	Gert-Jan Theunisse (Ned)	PDM	+ 7'30"	26
5	Marino Lejarreta (Esp)	Paternina	+ 9'39"	32
6	Charly Mottet (Fra)	RMO	+ 10'06"	26
7	Steven Rooks (Ned)	PDM	+ 11'10"	28
8	Raúl Alcalá (Mex)	PDM	+ 14'21"	25
9	Sean Kelly (Irl)	PDM	+ 18'25"	33
10	Robert Millar (GBr)	Z	+ 18'46"	30

Lanterne Rouge

138	Mathieu Hermans (Ned)	Paternina	+ 3h04'01"	26

Points

	Sean Kelly (Irl)	PDM		33

King of the Mountains

	Gert-Jan Theunisse (Ned)	PDM		26

Intermediate Sprints

	Sean Kelly (Irl)	PDM		33

Combination

	Steven Rooks (Ned)	PDM		28

Youth

	Fabrice Philipot (Fra)	Toshiba		23

Team

		PDM		

Super Combativité

	Laurent Fignon (Fra)	Super U		28

1990: Breaking Away

The break happened in the sixth kilometre of the second day of the 1990 Tour de France, the first stage proper. The *peloton* was doing a 138.5-kilometre out-and-back loop around the Futuroscope theme park where, the day before, Thierry Marie (Castorama) had won the day and donned the *maillot jaune*. Four riders: Frans Massen (Buckler), Steve Bauer (7-Eleven), Ronan Pensec (Z), Claudio Chiappucci (Carrera). Behind them the pack dawdled as Chiappucci – the instigator of the break – drove the group of four on. Four different teams – including the Z squad of defending champion Greg LeMond – had riders in the break and were happy for one of them to win the stage. The other teams just never got themselves organised. As had happened in 1986 when Bauer donned the yellow jersey on the equivalent day, this was a split stage, the team time trial to come in the afternoon. If the quartet of riders up the road wanted to kill themselves before that, then let them. It was their funeral and they would pay for it.

The question, though, was just how much rope to give the break. None of the four were favourites for the Tour. Six minutes? Seven minutes? Eight minutes? The *peloton* gave them ten. Massen took the stage win. Bauer took the yellow jersey. The race would now take a week to reach the mountains and the script seemed clear: the breakaways would hold on to the jersey and, in the mountains, normal order would be restored.

By the time the Alps arrived on Stage Nine – during which time an individual time trial from Vittel to Épinal had helped put some shape on the general classification behind the escapees – the breakaways were still clear and Raúl Alcalá (PDM) was best placed of the riders behind, 7'19" off Bauer's yellow jersey time. Greg LeMond was in seventh, 10'09" off the pace. In the Alps Bauer slipped back within the breakaways and Ronan Pensec came out on top wearing yellow.

On the road to Alpe d'Huez – the eleventh stage – Massen and Bauer faded, and only Pensec and Chiappucci survived of the original quartet of escapees. LeMond climbed up to third, 9'04" off yellow. After a bumpy time trial to Villard-de-Lans, which Erik Breukink (PDM) won, LeMond slipped to fourth but climbed to within 7'27" of yellow (which had now slipped from Pensec's shoulders and was being sported by Chiappucci). It was still early, the first phase of Alpine climbs now gave way to bumpy roads taking the riders down to the Pyrenees. But people still dared to speak of 1956 and Roger Walkowiak's unexpected win. Could history be about to repeat?

Chiappucci was a real danger. An old school *grimpeur* – prone to launching unexpected attacks, the sort of rider who shook things up by doing the unexpected – Chiappucci had a team around him that knew how to win Grand Tours. And, with the yellow jersey on his back, he dared to believe he could win the Tour.

But on the thirteenth stage – a relatively easy ride to Saint-Étienne, after a rest day – the Italian did the unexpected: he went out the back. LeMond and his Z team-mates took advantage of the Italian's bad day and pressed hard, the American taking back five minutes and clawing his way to within 2'34" of yellow. That fell by another 10 seconds before the Pyrenees reared up.

Over the Aspin and Tourmalet on the road to Luz-Ardiden Chiappucci, in the yellow jersey, gambled all. He attacked out of the *peloton* on the Aspin, setting off after the day's early break and, by the summit of the Tourmalet, opening up a two-minute lead – a lead that was growing with each pedal stroke. But it had all been too much, the attack made too early. On the climb to Luz-Ardiden the Italian cracked. LeMond got back up to him. And rode past him. At the end of the stage the American was six seconds down on that day's victor (Banesto's Miguel Indurain) but 2'15" up on the *maillot jaune*. Chiappucci still held the yellow jersey, but LeMond was now just five seconds behind him. With a time trial to come in Lac de Vassivière on the penultimate day of the Tour the American's third Tour victory was almost certainly assured.

LeMond took more than two minutes out of the yellow jersey in that time trial and joined the three-times club of Tour winners, alongside Philippe Thys and Louison Bobet. At 28 years old he still had time enough to step above them and join Jacques Anquetil, Eddy Merckx and Bernard Hinault in the five-times club.

Stage-by-Stage Results for the 1990 Tour de France			Stage Winner	Maillot Jaune
Prologue Sat 30 Jun	Futuroscope (ITT) 198 finishers	6.3 km 7'49" 48.4 kph	Thierry Marie (Fra) Castorama	Thierry Marie (Fra) Castoroma
Stage 1 Sun 1 Jul	Futuroscope to Futuroscope 198 finishers	138.5 km 3h19'01" 41.8 kph	Frans Maassen (Ned) Buckler	Steve Bauer (Can) 7-Eleven
Stage 2 Sun 1 Jul	Futuroscope (TTT) 198 finishers	44.5 km 53'24" 50 kph	Panasonic	Steve Bauer (Can) 7-Eleven
Stage 3 Mon 2 Jul	Poitiers to Nantes 197 finishers	233 km 5h46'13" 40.4 kph	Moreno Argentin (Ita) Ariostea	Steve Bauer (Can) 7-Eleven
Stage 4 Tue 3 Jul	Nantes to Mont Saint-Michel 197 finishers	203 km 5h23'33" 37.6 kph	Johan Museeuw (Bel) Lotto	Steve Bauer (Can) 7-Eleven
Stage 5 Wed 4 Jul	Avranches to Rouen 194 finishers	301 km 7h43'07" 39 kph	Gerrit Solleveld (Ned) Buckler	Steve Bauer (Can) 7-Eleven
Thu 5 Jul	Rest Day			
Stage 6 Fri 6 Jul	Sarrebourg to Vittel 191 finishers	202.5 km 5h23'56" 37.5 kph	Jelle Nijdam (Ned) Buckler	Steve Bauer (Can) 7-Eleven
Stage 7 Sat 7 Jul	Vittel to Épinal (ITT) 190 finishers	61.5 km 1h17'05" 47.9 kph	Raúl Alcalá (Mex) PDM	Steve Bauer (Can) 7-Eleven
Stage 8 Sun 8 Jul	Épinal to Besançon 186 finishers	181.5 km 4h26'53" 40.8 kph	Olaf Ludwig (FRG) Panasonic	Steve Bauer (Can) 7-Eleven
Stage 9 Mon 9 Jul	Besançon to Geneva 184 finishers	196 km 4h46'07" 41.1 kph	Massimo Ghirotto (Ita) Carrera	Steve Bauer (Can) 7-Eleven
Major climbs: Côte des Rousses (1,140m) Eduardo Chozas (Ita) ONCE				

Stage-by-Stage Results for the 1990 Tour de France			Stage Winner	Maillot Jaune
Stage 10 Tue 10 Jul	Geneva to Saint-Gervais (Mont Blanc) 182 finishers	118.5 km 3h24′31″ 34.8 kph	Thierry Claveyrolat (Fra) RMO	Ronan Pensec (Fra) Z
	Major climbs: Col de la Colombière (1,618m) Thierry Claveyrolat (Fra) RMO; Col des Aravis (1,498m) Thierry Claveyrolat (Fra) RMO; Saint-Gervais Mont-Blanc (1,400m) Thierry Claveyrolat (Fra) RMO; Le Bettex, Saint-Gervais Mont-Blanc (1,400m) Thierry Claveyrolat (Fra) RMO			
Stage 11 Wed 11 Jul	Saint-Gervais to l'Alpe d'Huez 170 finishers	182.5 km 5h37′51″ 32.4 kph	Gianni Bugno (Ita) Château d'Ax	Ronan Pensec (Fra) Z
	Major climbs: Col du Glandon (1,924m) Thierry Claveyrolat (Fra) RMO; l'Alpe d'Huez (1,860m) Gianni Bugno (Ita) Château d'Ax			
Stage 12 Thu 12 Jul	Fontaine to Villard-de-Lans (ITT) 170 finishers	33.5 km 56′52″ 35.3 kph	Erik Breukink (Ned) PDM	Claudio Chiappucci (Ita) Carrera
	Major climbs: Côte d'Engins (860m) Erik Breukink (Ned) PDM			
Fri 13 Jul	Rest Day			
Stage 13 Sat 14 Jul	Villard-de-Lans to Saint-Étienne 168 finishers	149 km 3h20′12″ 44.7 kph	Eduardo Chozas (Esp) ONCE	Claudio Chiappucci (Ita) Carrera
	Major climbs: Col de la Croix de Chaubouret (1,230m) Greg LeMond (USA) Z			
Stage 14 Sun 15 Jul	Le Puy-en-Velay to Millau (Causse Noir) 164 finishers	205 km 5h12′03″ 39.4 kph	Marino Lejarreta (Esp) ONCE	Claudio Chiappucci (Ita) Carrera
	Major climbs: Côte de Choizal (940m) Jean-Claude Bagot (Fra) RMO; Millau-Causse Noir/Le Cade (835m) Marino Lejarreta (Esp) ONCE			
Stage 15 Mon 16 Jul	Millau to Revel 161 finishers	170 km 4h13′56″ 40.2 kph	Charly Mottet (Fra) RMO	Claudio Chiappucci (Ita) Carrera
	Major climbs: Col de Sie (1,020m) Thierry Claveyrolat (Fra) RMO			
Stage 16 Tue 17 Jul	Blagnac to Luz-Ardiden 161 finishers	215 km 7h04′38″ 30.4 kph	Miguel Indurain (Esp) Banesto	Claudio Chiappucci (Ita) Carrera
	Major climbs: Col d'Aspin (1,489m) Claudio Chiappucci (Ita) Carrera; Col du Tourmalet (2,115m) Miguel Ángel Martínez (Esp) ONCE; Luz-Ardiden (1,715m) Miguel Indurain (Esp) Banesto			
Stage 17 Wed 18 Jul	Lourdes to Pau 157 finishers	150 km 4h08′25″ 36.2 kph	Dimitri Konychev (Rus) Alfa-Lum	Claudio Chiappucci (Ita) Carrera
	Major climbs: Col d'Aubisque (1,709m) Óscar Vargas (Esp) Ryalco; Col de Marie-Blanque (1,035m) Dominique Arnaud (Fra) Banesto			
Stage 18 Thu 19 Jul	Pau to Bordeaux 157 finishers	202 km 5h41′33″ 35.5 kph	Gianni Bugno (Ita) Château d'Ax	Claudio Chiappucci (Ita) Carrera
Stage 19 Fri 20 Jul	Castillon-la-Bataille to Limoges 156 finishers	182.5 km 5h16′04″ 34.6 kph	Guido Bontempi (Ita) Carrera	Claudio Chiappucci (Ita) Carrera

Stage-by-Stage Results for the 1990 Tour de France			Stage Winner	Maillot Jaune
Stage 20 Sat 21 Jul	Lac de Vassivière (ITT) 156 finishers	45.5 km 1h02'40" 43.6 kph	Eric Breukink (Ned) ONCE	Greg LeMond (USA) Z
Stage 21 Sun 22 Jul	Brétigny to Paris (Champs-Élysées) 156 finishers	182.5 km 4h53'52" 37.3 kph	Johan Museeuw (Bel) Lotto	Greg LeMond (USA) Z

Prize fund: 10,073,450 francs (first prize: 2,000,000 francs)

Final Classification				
Place	**Rider**	**Team**	**Time**	**Age**
1	Greg LeMond (USA)	Z	3,504 km 90h43'20" 38.621 kph	29
2	Claudio Chiappucci (Ita)	Carrera	+ 2'16"	27
3	Erik Breukink (Ned)	PDM	+ 2'29"	26
4	Pedro Delgado (Esp)	Banesto	+ 5'01"	30
5	Marino Lejarreta (Esp)	ONCE	+ 5'05"	33
6	Eduardo Chozas (Esp)	ONCE	+ 9'14"	30
7	Gianni Bugno (Ita)	Château d'Ax	+ 9'39"	26
8	Raúl Alcalá (Mex)	PDM	+ 11'14"	26
9	Claude Criquiélion (Bel)	Lotto	+ 12'04"	33
10	Miguel Indurain (Esp)	Banesto	+ 12'47"	26
Lanterne Rouge				
156	Rodolfo Massi (Ita)	Ariostea	+ 3h16'26"	24
Points				
	Olaf Ludwig (FRG)	Panasonic		30
King of the Mountains				
	Thierry Claveyrolat (Fra)	RMO		31
Youth				
	Gilles Delion (Fra)	Helvetia		23
Team				
		Z		
Super Combativité				
	Eduardo Chozas (Esp)	ONCE		30

1991: The Rise of EPO

That cycling had a culture of doping – and had always had a culture of doping – was impossible to deny. The speed tickets being handed out throughout the season was proof that. That the authorities were fighting doping seemed impossible to deny too, just look at those speed tickets. But, when their actions are actually looked at, it is harder to say that with certainty. Take the case of Kim Andersen as an example.

In 1987 Andersen – while riding for the Toshiba squad (La Vie Claire as was) – landed his third doping infraction in the space of two years and was handed a lifetime ban (it was actually more than his third infraction in two years, as he had survived multiple other instances where he'd caught the testers' attention). With a rider now on the naughty step for life, the UCI set about changing the rules. At the end of 1988 new ones came into force. You still got a suspended suspension for a first offence, and you still served that suspension if you tested positive a second time, but now within the space of one year, not two. If a third offence was committed – again, now within the space of twelve months – the time on the naughty step would be one year. With the cycling season pretty much running from March to October you would need to be a very dedicated – and very unlucky – rider to cop a twelve-month ban. And even if you were that dedicated – and that unlucky – you would still be welcomed back into the sport after a year out.

An even bigger issue at the time was that many of the doping products being used could not be tested for. Doping can more or less be broken down into two major eras: the era of products which affected the brain's perception of pain (drugs from the strychnine and cocaine of the early years through to the amphetamines of the post-WWII generation); and drugs that affected the body and the rider's abilities (the hormones that came in the 1960s and 1970s, cortisone and testosterone, and the blood transfusions that came in the 1970s and 1980s). For the latter category of drugs, the testers were way behind the curve, it being difficult to tell the difference between, say, testosterone taken to dope and testosterone naturally occurring in the body. A testosterone test didn't arrive until the mid-1980s. In 1991 there was no test for cortisone, and none for blood transfusions.

And there was now a new drug on the market, a synthetic hormone, EPO, that achieved the same effects as blood doping (increasing the number of oxygen-carrying red blood cells in the body) but without the logistical drawbacks of transfusions (no need to extract blood, separate out the red cells, store them and re-transfuse them).

EPO was known about from as early as the late 1980s. In 1988 Les Earnest, a director of the US cycling federation and a critic of the transfusions used in 1984, suggested that a study group be set up to look at the possible benefits of EPO and whether it would be a safer alternative to transfusions. The US federation turned him down. A Danish physician, Søren Kragbak, claimed that in 1989 a Swedish medical company had contacted the Danish cycling federation requesting to be allowed carry out secret EPO tests. That request too was turned down. A drug that was developed for patients with kidney ailments was immediately being seen as having sporting applications, across the globe.

Quite when EPO arrived in the professional *peloton* is not clear. There is much about the sport's doping history that isn't known. We don't know with any degree of certainty when blood transfusions became popular within the professional *peloton*, for instance. Joop Zoetemelk had talked of using them in the 1970s – before they were banned – but it wasn't really until 1984, Moser's Hour and the American Olympians, that cycling really seems to have sat up and paid attention to the possible benefits of blood boosting.

That blood transfusions were being used within the professional *peloton* through the 1980s is pretty clear. While writing his 2012 biography of Eddy Merckx, Daniel Friebe was told by Roger de Vlaeminck that transfusions had been offered to him in 1984, when he was a member of Moser's Gis/Tu Luc squad, where Michele Ferrari was on the medical staff. In 2013 the Dutch daily *De Volksrant* published details of doping within the PDM team at the 1988 Tour de France, with some of the riders reported to have used transfusions. Between those two dates and those two teams, though, little is known as to how widespread the use of transfusions was.

What is known – or at least believed – is that by the early 1990s transfusions had become passé as EPO took over. Who the early adopters were is not known, nor is it known when the majority of the professional *peloton* turned to EPO. But it was out there and being used as early as 1991. And its arrival was linked to a spate of deaths that shook the sport, old professionals dying with heart problems, young amateurs dying in their sleep. How many of those deaths were really the result of EPO is not known, old professionals and young amateurs die all the time, you only really notice the deaths when you get a cluster of them. But at least one of them, the 1990 death of the 27-year-old PDM rider Johannes Draaijer, was blamed on EPO, by his widow.

Rightly or wrongly, that spate of deaths became linked to the use of EPO. And that in itself is the important issue with those deaths, not whether they were really caused by EPO, but that people believed something was changing within the professional *peloton*, that a new drug was being taken up, and seized on a cluster of cycling deaths to press for action. EPO was banned.

But, as with other hormones like cortisone, and as with other practices such as blood transfusions, there was no test for EPO. And cycling's doping culture was such that, even if a product was on the banned list, it wasn't really cheating if it couldn't be tested for.

* * * * *

Symbolically, there was a passing of the crown in 1991, when Greg LeMond's run of Tour titles came to an end and Miguel Indurain's reign began. Indurain was riding for the Banesto squad, the Reynolds team created by José-Miguel Echávarri (a one-time team-mate of Jacques Anquetil) in 1980 but with a different sponsor.

In 1982 Echavárri's team had won the Vuelta a España with Ángel Arroyo, only to have the victory stripped from him when Arroyo failed a dope test. Pedro Delgado gave Echávarri victory in the 1988 Tour de France and then again at the 1989 Vuelta a España. Perico's chances of victory were blown in the 1989 Tour when he missed his start in the prologue and spent the rest of the race making up time but never in contention for the overall win.

Indurain had started out as Delgado's *domestique* but as early as the 1989 Paris-Nice was showing he was a winner of the future, winning *la course au soleil*, ending an eight-year Irish reign at Paris-Nice. He won the race to the sun again in 1990. Indurain had by this stage been checked out by Francesco Conconi and his staff at the University of Ferrara – the men behind Moser's Hour – and his potential was clear. At the 1990 Tour, where Delgado again failed to mount much of a challenge, Echávarri realised that Indurain was ready for greatness and gave him his chance the following year.

It was LeMond, the defending champion, who first took control of the 1991 Tour, winning Stage Eight's individual time trial between Argentin and Alençon and taking the *maillot jaune*. With Erik Breukink (PDM) in second at 1'13" and the sprinter Djamolidine Abdoujaparov (Carrera) in third at 1'21" thoughts were already turning to victory number four for the American. Indurain was best of the rest, in fourth, 2'17" down.

The Pyrenees loomed up on Stage 12 but before the *peloton* got there they had a new doping scandal to deal with, the PDM squad coming down with food poisoning. There were shades of the bad fish episodes in Tours of old, when doping accidents were blamed on food poisoning. But this time it does actually seem to have been food poisoning, the PDM squad using an intravenous food supplement, Intralipid, which had been incorrectly stored and gone off. That the *peloton* was so hooked on needles that they even took their food through them came as a shock to some. For others – such as the Irish journalist David Walsh, Boswell to PDM's Sean Kelly and the ghost in the machine of Stephen Roche's autobiography

– it was just a case of the realities of modern sport and syringes didn't always mean doping. And, since Intralipid wasn't banned, it couldn't be classed as doping, regardless of your view of the ethics of having to inject food every night just to win a bike race. Ethics didn't come into the equation.

When the southern mountains did arrive, they came with a big surprise. A group of riders got away on the opening day of the first phase of mountains. And they stayed away, Luc Leblanc (Castorama) dispossessing LeMond of the *maillot jaune* and taking a lead of 2'35" over the American, with Indurain slipping to fifth, 4'44" off the pace.

Leblanc's possession of the yellow jersey didn't last long though. The next day LeMond lit the blue-touch paper on the Tourmalet and took off, a group of riders latching onto his move, including the yellow jersey of Leblanc, Indurain, and the unpredictable Claudio Chiappucci (Carrera). LeMond, though, faltered before the summit of the climb and Indurain then launched a new attack. He was joined at the foot of the Aspin by Chiappucci. The Italian took the stage, the Spaniard the *maillot jaune*. LeMond dropped like a stone, down to sixth, nearly six minutes off yellow.

With Indurain having a three-minute lead over the erratic Charly Mottet (RMO) the rest of the field was already racing for second place – a race won by Gianni Bugno (Gatorade) who triumphed on Alpe d'Huez and jumped up to second, 3'09" off Indurain's pace.

Indurain sealed the deal with victory in the pre-penultimate day's race against the clock and rode into Paris in yellow, the fourth Spaniard – after Federico Bahamontes, Luis Ocaña and Pedro Delgado – to have won the Tour. And – PDM's Intralipid *faux pas* aside – he did so without any of the scandal associated with Delgado's win three years earlier. Spain had a Tour winner the world could believe in, a Tour winner who didn't trip positives in doping control.

Stage-by-Stage Results for the 1991 Tour de France			Stage Winner	Maillot Jaune
Prologue Sat 6 Jul	Lyon (ITT) 198 finishers	5.4 km 6'11" 52.4 kph	Thierry Marie (Fra) Castorama	Thierry Marie (Fra) Castorama
Stage 1 Sun 7 Jul	Lyon to Lyon 198 finishers	114.5 km 2h28'54" 46.1 kph	Djamolidine Abdoujaparov (Uzb) Carrera	Greg LeMond (USA) Z
Stage 2 Sun 7 Jul	Bron to Chassieu (TTT) 197 finishers	36.5 km 41'23" 52.9 kph	Ariostea	Rolf Sørensen (Den) Ariostea
Stage 3 Mon 8 Jul	Villeurbanne to Dijon 197 finishers	210.5 km 5h15'11" 40.1 kph	Etienne de Wilde (Bel) Histor	Rolf Sørensen (Den) Ariostea
Stage 4 Tue 9 Jul	Dijon to Reims 197 finishers	286 km 7h49'14" 36.6 kph	Djamolidine Abdoujaparov (Uzb) Carrera	Rolf Sørensen (Den) Ariostea
Stage 5 Wed 10 Jul	Reims to Valenciennes 197 finishers	149.5 km 3h17'38" 45.4 kph	Jelle Nijdam (Ned) Buckler	Rolf Sørensen (Den) Ariostea
Stage 6 Thu 11 Jul	Arras to Le Havre 195 finishers	259 km 6h38'27" 39 kph	Thierry Marie (Fra) Castorama	Thierry Marie (Fra) Castorama
Stage 7 Fri 12 Jul	Le Havre to Argentan 194 finishers	167 km 4h02'18" 41.4 kph	Jean-Paul van Poppel (Ned) PDM	Thierry Marie (Fra) Castorama
Stage 8 Sat 13 Jul	Argentan to Alençon (ITT) 194 finishers	73 km 1h35'44" 45.8 kph	Miguel Indurain (Esp) Banesto	Greg LeMond (USA) Z
Stage 9 Sun 14 Jul	Alençon to Rennes 194 finishers	161 km 3h40'51" 43.7 kph	Mauro Ribeiro (Bra) RMO	Greg LeMond (USA) Z
Stage 10 Mon 15 Jul	Rennes to Quimper 189 finishers	207.5 km 5h23'23" 38.5 kph	Phil Anderson (Aus) Motorola	Greg LeMond (USA) Z
Stage 11 Tue 16 Jul	Quimper to Saint-Herblain 185 finishers	246 km 5h12'31" 47.2 kph	Charly Mottet (Fra) RMO	Greg LeMond (USA) Z
Wed 17 Jul	Rest Day			
Stage 12 Thu 18 Jul	Pau to Jaca 181 finishers	192 km 5h15'52" 36.5 kph	Charly Mottet (Fra) RMO	Luc Leblanc (Fra) Castorama
Major climbs: Col du Soudet (1,540m) Pascal Richard (Fra) Helvetia; Col d'Ichère (680m) Pascal Richard (Fra) Helvetia; Col du Somport (1,632m) Luc Leblanc (Fra) Castorama				

Stage-by-Stage Results for the 1991 Tour de France			Stage Winner	Maillot Jaune
Stage 13 Fri 19 Jul	Jaca to Val Louron 173 finishers	232 km 7h11'16" 32.3 kph	Claudio Chiappucci (Ita) Carrera	Miguel Indurain (Esp) Banesto
	Major climbs: Pourtalet (1,794m) Peter Declercq (Bel) Lotto; Col d'Aubisque (1,709m) Guido Winterberg (Sui) Helvetia; Col du Tourmalet (2,115m) Claudio Chiappucci (Ita) Carrera; Col d'Aspin (1,489m) Claudio Chiappucci (Ita) Carrera; Val-Louron (Col d'Azet) (1,579m) Miguel Indurain (Esp) Banesto			
Stage 14 Sat 20 Jul	Saint-Gaudens to Castres 172 finishers	172.5 km 4h15'51" 40.5 kph	Bruno Cenghialta (Ita) Ariostea	Miguel Indurain (Esp) Banesto
Stage 15 Sun 21 Jul	Albi to Alès 171 finishers	235 km 6h21'22" 37 kph	Moreno Argentin (Ita) Ariostea	Miguel Indurain (Esp) Banesto
Stage 16 Mon 22 Jul	Alès to Gap 169 finishers	215 km 6h06'39" 35.2 kph	Marco Lietti (Ita) Ariostea	Miguel Indurain (Esp) Banesto
Stage 17 Tue 23 Jul	Gap to l'Alpe d'Huez 163 finishers	125 km 3h25'48" 36.4 kph	Gianni Bugno (Ita) Gatorade	Miguel Indurain (Esp) Banesto
	Major climbs: Col Bayard (1,246m) Pello Ruiz (Esp) CLAS; Col d'Ornon (1,367m) Pello Ruiz (Esp) CLAS; l'Alpe d'Huez (1,860m) Gianni Bugno (Ita) Gatorade			
Stage 18 Wed 24 Jul	Bourg-d'Oisans to Morzine 159 finishers	255 km 7h26'47" 34.2 kph	Thierry Claveyrolat (Fra) RMO	Miguel Indurain (Esp) Banesto
	Major climbs: Col des Aravis (1,498m) Thierry Claveyrolat (Fra) RMO; Col de la Colombière (1,618m) Thierry Claveyrolat (Fra) RMO; Col de Joux-Plane (1,700m) Thierry Claveyrolat (Fra) RMO			
Stage 19 Thu 25 Jul	Morzine to Aix-les-Bains 158 finishers	177 km 4h18'28" 41.1 kph	Dimitri Konychev (Rus) TVM	Miguel Indurain (Esp) Banesto
	Major climbs: Mont Revard (1,537m) Pascal Richard (Fra) Helvetia			
Stage 20 Fri 26 Jul	Aix-les-Bains to Mâcon 158 finishers	160 km 4h12'52" 38 kph	Viatcheslav Ekimov (Rus) Panasonic	Miguel Indurain (Esp) Banesto
	Major climbs: Col du Berthiand (780m) Claudio Chiappucci (Ita) Carrera			
Stage 21 Sat 27 Jul	Lugny to Mâcon (ITT) 158 finishers	57 km 1h11'45" 47.7 kph	Miguel Indurain (Esp) Banesto	Miguel Indurain (Esp) Banesto
Stage 22 Sun 28 Jul	Melun to Paris (Champs-Élysées) 158 finishers	178 km 4h43'36" 37.7 kph	Dimitri Konychev (Rus) TVM	Miguel Indurain (Esp) Banesto

Prize fund: 9.017,850 francs (first prize: 2,000,000 francs)

Final Classification

Place	Rider	Team	Time	Age
1	Miguel Indurain (Esp)	Banesto	3,914 km 101h01'20" 38.747 kph	27
2	Gianni Bugno (Ita)	Gatorade	+ 3'36"	27
3	Claudio Chiappucci (Ita)	Carrera	+ 5'56"	28
4	Charly Mottet (Fra)	RMO	+ 7'37"	28
5	Luc Leblanc (Fra)	Castorama	+ 10'10"	24
6	Laurent Fignon (Fra)	Castorama	+ 11'27"	30
7	Greg LeMond (USA)	Z	+ 13'13"	30
8	Andy Hampsten (USA)	Motorola	+ 13'40"	29
9	Pedro Delgado (Esp)	Banesto	+ 20'10"	31
10	Gérard Rué (Fra)	Helvetia	+ 20'13"	26
Lanterne Rouge				
158	Rob Harmeling (Ned)	TVM	+ 3h25'51"	26
Points				
	Djamolidine Abdoujaparov (Uzb)	Carrera		27
King of the Mountains				
	Claudio Chiappucci (Ita)	Carrera		28
Youth				
	Álvaro Mejía (Col)	Ryalco		28
Team				
		Banesto		
Super Combativité				
	Claudio Chiappucci (Ita)	Carrera		28

1992: The King in Yellow

It was time for more changes in the way the Tour de France was being run. Jean-Marie Leblanc had rationalised the Tour's wardrobe, realising that less is more and doing away with some of the minor jerseys and other competitions that had appeared during the reign of Félix Lévitan and Jacques Goddet. The *voiture balai* was even stripped of its symbolic broom as the Tour tried to be as modern as it could be, doing away with the toys of its past. Leblanc had even jettisoned the Tour Cycliste Féminin after its 1989 edition, cutting the women free from the Tour – as Lévitan had cut free the Tour de l'Avenir – and leaving the race to sink or swim on its own merits.

Now it was time to change how the Tour itself was organised. And in this latest change it was Leblanc's predecessor Jean-Pierre Courcol who took the lead. A confidant of Philippe Amaury, king of the Amaury empire, Courcol decided to do away with the Société du Tour the France and create a new body to run the *grande boucle* and the rest of the Amaury group's sporting competitions. That new entity was the Amaury Sport Organisation, ASO. To head it Courcol brought in the former skier Jean-Claude Killy – triple Olympic champion in 1968 – who had successfully turned his sporting fame to his financial advantage.

Killy had retired from sport at the age of 25 and become a client of Mark McCormack's global sports marketing agency, International Marketing Group (IMG). With IMG's help Killy became a star of Madison Avenue, 'loaning' his name and image to clients like Canon, Chevrolet, General Motors, Moët et Chandon, Rolex, Schwinn and United Airlines. By the time he joined ASO his personal wealth was estimated at 120 million French francs: four times what the Société du Tour de France had squirrelled away. As co-chair of the Organizing Committee of the Olympic Games in Albertville in 1992 Killy had an address book to die for. And Philippe Amaury was willing to pay generously for it, with ASO's future plans involving closer links with the IOC. With the help of Alain Krzentowski, Killy set about taking the Tour by the scruff of the neck and shaking it.

Within the Tour itself, it was time to celebrate its new Spanish conqueror and San Sebastián hosted the *grand départ*. Fittingly, Miguel Indurain (still flying the colours of Spanish banking giant Banesto) won the day and donned the *maillot jaune*. Fresh off a victory in the Giro d'Italia the Spaniard was gunning for the Giro/ Tour double.

After the prologue, the yellow jersey passed to ONCE's Alex Zülle and on to RMO's Richard Virenque, who then passed it to team-mate Pascal Lino. Indurain waited until the thirteenth stage, to Sestriere, to re-take control.

Coming into the stage from Saint-Gervais to Sestriere Indurain was trailing Lino by 1'27" with three former Tour winners immediately behind him: Stephen Roche (now back in the Carrera fold) a surprising third, 1'58" off the pace; Pedro Delgado (Banesto) fourth at 4'08"; and Greg LeMond (Z) in fifth at 4'27". Behind them, in seventh place and 4'54" off yellow, was Claudio Chiappucci (Carrera), and it was the Italian who kicked life into the race.

This was an old-school stage, 254.5 kilometres of racing which required the riders to hit the road before nine o'clock in the morning – at a time when the typical Tour stage didn't roll off until mid-to-late morning – for a seven or eight hour day at the office. And the finish in Sestriere recalled history, particularly its first appearance, when it was the Tour's second summit finish, the day it overshadowed the first (Alpe d'Huez). The day when Fausto Coppi pulled off a solo exploit. And here we were 40 years on from that. On many of the same roads. And with an Italian rider who could claim a connection (of sorts) to *il Campionissimo*: back in the day, Claudio Chiappucci's father had known Coppi, they served in the Italian army together, and were prisoners of war together in North Africa. The young

Chiappucci had grown up with his father telling him stories about Coppi.

On the road to Sestriere in 1992 Chiappucci went for broke on the Col de Saissies, not even a couple of dozen kilometres into the stage, apparently looking for points to solidify his hold on the polka-dot jersey. He was quickly joined by Virenque and Thierry Claveyrolat (Z). On the descent, the trio of escapees became 11 as others bridged across to them. Over the Cormet de Roselend they rode. As they neared the Iseran – about 120 kilometres into the stage – the break shed members, until at the foot of the Iseran it was just Chiappucci and Virenque, and still 135 kilometres to race.

And that's where the solo ride began, Chiappucci dropping Virenque and crossing the Iseran two minutes up on his chasers, three on the main *peloton*. For more than 100 kilometres Chiappucci held off his pursers, pushing his gap out to five minutes as he approached Mont Cenis. Then Indurain began a chase and Chiappucci's advantage faded. At the base of the final climb it was less than two minutes, and falling with every pedal stroke. But somehow Chiappucci held on, found that fire within that only seemed to burn on certain days, let himself be lifted by the *tifosi* as the Tour crossed into Italy. And he won the stage. Trailing him home, Indurain donned the *maillot jaune* as Lino dropped from first to seventh.

Chiappucci's stage win jumped him up to second as the other challengers for Indurain's crown faded, the Italian just 1'42" off yellow, the rest of the field four minutes and more back. But, now that the Italian posed a real threat to Indurain, the Spaniard marked the life out of him. That was his way: mark the enemy, win in the time trials.

On the Alpe, Chiappucci failed to follow up his Sestriere victory. That was his way: one exploit, rarely ever followed by the killer punch needed to bring total victory.

Through the rest of the mountains Indurain followed where the Italian went, arriving in Tours for the last race of truth with Chiappucci still stuck 1'42" in arrears. On the road from Tours to Blois Indurain blitzed the field, with only Gianni Bugno finishing within a minute of him, all the rest two and more behind.

After having passed through seven countries – the Tour was celebrating the signing of the Maastricht treaty which turned the European Economic Community (EEC) of old into the modern European Union (EU) and put Europe on the road towards a common currency – Indurain arrived in Paris, his second win and his first Giro/Tour double sealed. Coldly, clinically, efficiently. Regally.

Stage-by-Stage Results for the 1992 Tour de France			Stage Winner	Maillot Jaune
Prologue Sat 4 Jul	San Sebastián (ITT) 198 finishers	8 km 9'22" 51.2 kph	Miguel Indurain (Esp) Banesto	Miguel Indurain (Esp) Banesto
	Major climbs: Alto de Jaizkibel (460m) Franco Chioccioli (Ita) GB			
Stage 1 Sun 5 Jul	San Sebastián to San Sebastián 197 finishers	194.5 km 4h37'39" 42 kph	Dominique Arnould (Fra) Castorama	Alex Zülle (Sui) ONCE
	Major climbs: Ispeguy (690m) Richard Virenque (Fra) RMO; Col de Marie-Blanque (1,035m) Richard Virenque (Fra) RMO			
Stage 2 Mon 6 Jul	San Sebastián to Pau 195 finishers	255 km 6h41'56" 38.1 kph	Javier Murguialday (Esp) Amaya Seguros	Richard Virenque (Fra) RMO
Stage 3 Tue 7 Jul	Pau to Bordeaux 195 finishers	210 km 5h45'17" 36.5 kph	Rob Harmeling (Ned) TVM	Pascal Lino (Fra) RMO
Stage 4 Wed 8 Jul	Libourne (TTT) 195 finishers	63.5 km 1h13'15" 52 kph	Panasonic	Pascal Lino (Fra) RMO
Stage 5 Thu 9 Jul	Nogent-sur-Oise to Wasquehal 193 finishers	196 km 4h06'01" 47.8 kph	Guido Bontempi (Ita) Carrera	Pascal Lino (Fra) RMO
Stage 6 Fri 10 Jul	Roubaix to Brussels 192 finishers	167 km 3h37'06" 46.2 kph	Laurent Jalabert (Fra) ONCE	Pascal Lino (Fra) RMO
Stage 7 Sat 11 Jul	Brussels to Valkenburg 184 finishers	196.5 km 4h21'47" 45 kph	Gilles Delion (Fra) Helvetia	Pascal Lino (Fra) RMO
Stage 8 Sun 12 Jul	Valkenburg to Koblenz 179 finishers	206.5 km 4h45'23" 43.4 kph	Jan Nevens (Bel) Lotto	Pascal Lino (Fra) RMO
Stage 9 Mon 13 Jul	Luxembourg to Luxembourg (ITT) 179 finishers	65 km 1h19'31" 49 kph	Miguel Indurain (Esp) Banesto	Pascal Lino (Fra) RMO
Stage 10 Tue 14 Jul	Luxembourg to Strasbourg 177 finishers	217 km 5h02'45" 43 kph	Jean-Paul van Poppel (Ned) PDM	Pascal Lino (Fra) RMO

Stage-by-Stage Results for the 1992 Tour de France			Stage Winner	Maillot Jaune
Stage 11 Wed 15 Jul	Strasbourg to Mulhouse 172 finishers	249.5 km 6h30'49" 38.3 kph	Laurent Fignon (Fra) Gatorade	Pascal Lino (Fra) RMO
	Major climbs: Bagenelles (915m) Rolf Gölz (Ger) Ariostea; Col de la Schlucht (1,139m) Fabio Roscioli (Ita) Carrera; Col du Grand Ballon (1,343m) Laurent Fignon (Fra) Gatorade			
Stage 12 Thu 16 Jul	Dôle to Saint-Gervais 166 finishers	267.5 km 7h10'56" 37.2 kph	Rolf Järmann (Sui) Ariostea	Pascal Lino (Fra) RMO
	Major climbs: Côte d'Echalon (1,010m) Franco Chioccioli (Ita) GB; Mont Salève (1,283m) Fabrice Philippot (Fra) Banesto; Saint-Gervais Mont-Blanc (970m) Pedro Delgado (Esp) Banesto			
Fri 17 Jul	Rest Day			
Stage 13 Sat 18 Jul	Saint-Gervais to Sestriere 147 finishers	254.5 km 7h44'51" 32.8 kph	Claudio Chiappucci (Ita) Carrera	Miguel Indurain (Esp) Banesto
	Major climbs: Col des Saisies (1,633m) Claudio Chiappucci (Ita) Carrera; Cormet de Roselend (1,968m) Claudio Chiappucci (Ita) Carrera; Col de l'Iseran (2,770m) Claudio Chiappucci (Ita) Carrera; Col du Mont Cenis (2,083m) Claudio Chiappucci (Ita) Carrera; Colle del Sestriere (2,035m) Claudio Chiappucci (Ita) Carrera			
Stage 14 Sun 19 Jul	Sestriere to l'Alpe d'Huez 135 finishers	186.5 km 5h41'58" 32.7 kph	Andy Hampsten (USA) Motorola	Miguel Indurain (Esp) Banesto
	Major climbs: Col de Montgenèvre (1,860m) Richard Virenque (Fra) RMO; Col du Galibier (2,645m) Franco Chioccioli (Ita) GB; Col de la Croix de Fer (2,067m) Eric Boyer (Fra) Z; l'Alpe d'Huez (1,860m) Andy Hampsten (USA) Motorola			
Stage 15 Mon 20 Jul	Bourg-d'Oisans to Saint-Étienne 133 finishers	198 km 4h43'59" 41.8 kph	Franco Chioccioli (Ita) GB	Miguel Indurain (Esp) Banesto
	Major climbs: Col de la Croix de Chaubouret (1,230m) Franco Chioccioli (Ita) GB			
Stage 16 Tue 21 Jul	Saint-Étienne to La Bourboule 131 finishers	212 km 5h52'14" 36.1 kph	Stephen Roche (Irl) Carrera	Miguel Indurain (Esp) Banesto
	Major climbs: Col de la Croix-Morand (1,401m) Stephen Roche (Irl) Carrera			
Stage 17 Wed 22 Jul	La Bourboule to Montluçon 130 finishers	189 km 4h34'55" 41.2 kph	Jean-Claude Colotti (Fra) Z	Miguel Indurain (Esp) Banesto
Stage 18 Thu 23 Jul	Montluçon to Tours 130 finishers	212 km 5h07'15" 41.4 kph	Thierry Marie (Fra) Castorama	Miguel Indurain (Esp) Banesto
Stage 19 Fri 24 Jul	Tours to Blois (ITT) 130 finishers	64 km 1h13'21" 52.4 kph	Miguel Indurain (Esp) Banesto	Miguel Indurain (Esp) Banesto
Stage 20 Sat 25 Jul	Blois to Nanterre 130 finishers	222 km 6h03'36" 36.6 kph	Peter de Clercq (Bel) Lotto	Miguel Indurain (Esp) Banesto
Stage 21 Sun 26 Jul	La Défense to Paris (Champs-Élysées) 130 finishers	141 km 3h28'37" 40.6 kph	Olaf Ludwig (Ger) Panasonic	Miguel Indurain (Esp) Banesto

Prize fund: 10,162,950 francs (first prize: 2,000,000 francs)

Final Classification

Place	Rider	Team	Time	Age
1	Miguel Indurain (Esp)	Banesto	3,983 km 100h49'30" 39.504 kph	28
2	Claudio Chiappucci (Ita)	Carrera	+ 4'35"	29
3	Gianni Bugno (Ita)	Gatorade	+ 10'49"	28
4	Andy Hampsten (USA)	Motorola	+ 13'40"	30
5	Pascal Lino (Fra)	RMO	+ 14'37"	25
6	Pedro Delgado (Esp)	Banesto	+ 15'16"	32
7	Erik Breukink (Ned)	PDM	+ 18'51"	28
8	Giancarlo Perini (Ita)	Carrera	+ 19'16"	32
9	Stephen Roche (Irl)	Carrera	+ 20'23"	32
10	Jens Heppner (Ger)	Telekom	+ 25'30"	27
Lanterne Rouge				
130	Fernando Quevedo (Esp)	Amaya Seguros	+ 4h12'11"	27
Points				
	Laurent Jalabert (Fra)	ONCE		23
King of the Mountains				
	Claudio Chiappucci (Ita)	Carrera		29
Youth				
	Eddy Bouwmans (Ned)	Panasonic		24
Team				
		Carrera		
Super Combativité				
	Claudio Chiappucci (Ita)	Carrera		29
Europe Sans Frontières				
	Viatcheslav Ekimov (Rus)	Panasonic		26

1993: A Back-to-Back Double

Miguel Indurain went into the eightieth Tour de France yet again fresh off another win in the Giro d'Italia, gunning for his third Tour crown and his second Giro/Tour double. And he pulled it off with indecent ease, only one rider seeming to challenge him: Tony Rominger (CLAS), who had won the third Grand Tour, the Vuelta a España, in the spring.

Indurain (still with Banesto's backing) took the opening prologue, surrendered the *maillot jaune* on Stage Two, fluffed the team time trial on Stage Four (his Banesto squad finished seventh, 1'22" down on the day) and then took control after the individual time trial at Lac de Madine on Stage Nine, putting two minutes and more into his rivals. It was that easy for him.

Rominger tried making a fight of it on the road to Serre Chevalier on Stage 10, following Indurain when he upped the pace on the Galibier, with the Colombian Álvaro Mejía and the American Andy Hampsten (both Motorola) following his lead, along with the Pole Zenon Jaskula (GB/MG Maglificio) also joining in. Hampsten and Jaskula were quickly burned off. Indurain ceded a couple of seconds in the sprint for the finish and Rominger took the stage. Indurain's attack had burnt off key rivals and he now held the *maillot jaune* with a comfortable margin of 3'08" over Mejía, with Rominger down in fifth, 5'44" off the pace.

The next day it was Rominger attacking, in the closing kilometre of the climb to Isola 2000. But Indurain was all over him like a rash, giving no quarter. The Vuelta winner made it back-to-back stage wins but didn't even dent Indurain's lead.

On the second day in the Pyrenees Rominger lit another match, again saving his attack until the closing kilometres of the final climb, but this time was beaten to the stage win by Jaskula, taking the first Polish stage win in the Tour, while Indurain ceded just three seconds. Crumbs from his bountiful feast.

Claudio Chiappucci (Carvera) again took a shot at glory, launching a challenge on the road to Pau and taking the stage win. But behind Indurain only had eyes for one man, Rominger, who didn't even try for crumbs this time.

As the race exited the Pyrenees and sprinted toward Bordeaux, members of the Tour's press caravan sped ahead, to witness the resurrection of the Hour record. In the decade since Moser's Hour in 1984 the one-time blue riband event had been allowed to just sit there and gather dust, as it had in the 12 years after Merckx's Hour in 1972. But now it was back, with two stars of the British time trial scene each wanting to add it to their otherwise Spartan *palmarès*: Scotland's Graeme Obree and England's Chris Boardman. Obree struck first, setting a new record on 17 July, as the Tour raced from Marseille to Montpellier. But he did that in Norway, with few there to witness the feat. Boardman, on the other hand, had scheduled his Hour for the race's arrival in Bordeaux, riding in the Vélodrome du Lac. And so twice in the space of six days the Hour fell, both times by little heralded riders. The professionals were made to sit up and pay attention: the Hour was back.

After Bordeaux came the penultimate day's time trial, 48 kilometres from Bretigny-sur-Orge to Monthléry. This time there were no gifts for Rominger and he won the race of truth clearly, 42 seconds up on Indurain. If nothing else it offered hope that Indurain's challenge for a fourth Tour title in 1993 would actually be a real race and not just another coronation.

Miguel Indurain arrives in Paris at the end of win number three in 1993.

Stage-by-Stage Results for the 1993 Tour de France			Stage Winner	Maillot Jaune
Prologue Sat 3 Jul	Puy du Fou (ITT) 180 finishers	6.8 km 8'12" 49.8 kph	Miguel Indurain (Esp) Banesto	Miguel Indurain (Esp) Banesto
Stage 1 Sun 4 Jul	Luçon to Les Sables-d'Olonne 180 finishers	215 km 4h52'29" 44.1 kph	Mario Cipollini (Ita) GB	Miguel Indurain (Esp) Banesto
Stage 2 Mon 5 Jul	Les Sables-d'Olonne to Vannes 177 finishers	227.5 km 5h41'09" 40 kph	Wilfried Nelissen (Bel) Novemail	Wilfried Nelissen (Bel) Novemail
Stage 3 Tue 6 Jul	Vannes to Dinard 176 finishers	189.5 km 4h41'53" 40.3 kph	Djamolidine Abdoujaparov (Uzb) Lampre	Wilfried Nelissen (Bel) Novemail
Stage 4 Wed 7 Jul	Dinard to Avranches (TTT) 175 finishers	81 km 1h34'10" 51.6 kph	GB	Mario Cipollini (Ita) GB
Stage 5 Thu 8 Jul	Avranches to Évreux 175 finishers	225.5 km 5h11'57" 43.4 kph	Jesper Skibby (Den) TVM	Wilfried Nelissen (Bel) Novemail
Stage 6 Fri 9 Jul	Evreux to Amiens 174 finishers	158 km 3h11'50" 49.4 kph	Johan Bruyneel (Bel) ONCE	Mario Cipollini (Ita) GB
Stage 7 Sat 10 Jul	Péronne to Chalons-sur-Marne 172 finishers	199 km 4h28'11" 44.5 kph	Bjarne Riis (Den) Ariostea	Johan Museeuw (Bel) GB
Stage 8 Sun 11 Jul	Chalons-sur-Marne to Verdun 171 finishers	184.5 km 4h22'23" 42.2 kph	Lance Armstrong (USA) Motorola	Johan Museeuw (Bel) GB
Stage 9 Mon 12 Jul	Lac de Madine (ITT) 171 finishers	59 km 1h12'50" 48.6 kph	Miguel Indurain (Esp) Banesto	Miguel Indurain (Esp) Banesto
Tue 13 Jul	Rest Day			
Stage 10 Wed 14 Jul	Villard-de-Lans to Serre Chevalier 166 finishers	203 km 5h28'52" 37 kph	Tony Rominger (Sui) CLAS	Miguel Indurain (Esp) Banesto
	Major climbs: Col du Glandon (1,924m) Stefano Colagè (Ita) ZG; Col du Télégraphe (1,566m) Thierry Claveyrolat (Fra) GAN; Col du Galibier (2,645m) Tony Rominger (Sui) CLAS			
Stage 11 Thu 15 Jul	Serre Chevalier to Isola 2000 151 finishers	179 km 5h41'03" 31.5 kph	Tony Rominger (Sui) CLAS	Miguel Indurain (Esp) Banesto
	Major climbs: Col d'Izoard (2,360m) Claudio Chiappucci (Ita) Carrera; Col de Vars (2,110m) Davide Cassani (Ita) Ariostea; La Bonette-Restefond (2,802m) Robert Millar (GBr) TVM; Isola 2000 (1,900m) Tony Rominger (Sui) CLAS			

Stage-by-Stage Results for the 1993 Tour de France			Stage Winner	Maillot Jaune
Stage 12 Fri 16 Jul	Isola to Marseille 149 finishers	286.5 km 7h29'44" 38.2 kph	Fabio Roscioli (Ita) Carrera	Miguel Indurain (Esp) Banesto
Stage 13 Sat 17 Jul	Marseille to Montpellier 145 finishers	181.5 km 4h13'10" 43 kph	Olaf Ludwig (Ger) Telekom	Miguel Indurain (Esp) Banesto
Stage 14 Sun 18 Jul	Montpellier to Perpignan 143 finishers	223 km 5h28'51" 40.7 kph	Pascal Lino (Fra) Festina	Miguel Indurain (Esp) Banesto
Stage 15 Mon 19 Jul	Perpignan to Andorra 139 finishers	231.5 km 7h20'19" 31.5 kph	Oliverio Rincón (Col) Amaya Seguros	Miguel Indurain (Esp) Banesto
	Major climbs: Col de Jau (1,513m) Richard Virenque (Fra) Festina; Garabel (1,256m) Leonardo Sierra (Ita) ZG; Côte de Puyvalador (1,370m) Olivero Rincon (Col) Amaya; Col du Puymorens (1,915m) Olivero Rincon (Col) Amaya; Port d'Envalira (2,407m) Leonardo Sierra (Ita) ZG; Coll d'Ordino (1,910m) Olivero Rincon (Col) Amaya; Montée de Pal (1,870m) Olivero Rincon (Col) Amaya			
Tue 20 Jul	Rest Day			
Stage 16 Wed 21 Jul	Andorra to Saint-Lary-du-Soulan 138 finishers	230 km 7h21'01" 31.3 kph	Zenon Jaskula (Pol) GB	Miguel Indurain (Esp) Banesto
	Major climbs: Collado del Canto (1,725m) Tony Rominger (Sui) CLAS; Puerto de Bonaiga (2,072m) Tony Rominger (Sui) CLAS; Col du Portillon (1,298m) Tony Rominger (Sui) CLAS; Col de Peyresourde (1,569m) Claudio Chiappucci (Ita) Carrera; Pla d'Adet (1,670m) Zenon Jaskula (Pol) GB; Saint-Lary-Soulan (1,680m) Zenon Jaskula (Pol) GB			
Stage 17 Thu 22 Jul	Tarbes to Pau 136 finishers	190 km 5h05'33" 37.3 kph	Claudio Chiappucci (Ita) Carrera	Miguel Indurain (Esp) Banesto
	Major climbs: Col du Tourmalet (2,115m) Tony Rominger (Sui) CLAS; Col d'Aubisque (1,709m) Claudio Chiappucci (Ita) Carrera			
Stage 18 Fri 23 Jul	Orthez to Bordeaux 136 finishers	199.5 km 5h09'04" 38.7 kph	Djamolidine Abdoujaparov (Uzb) Lampre	Miguel Indurain (Esp) Banesto
Stage 19 Sat 24 Jul	Bretigny-sur-Orge to Monthléry (ITT) 136 finishers	48 km 57'02" 50.5 kph	Tony Rominger (Sui) CLAS	Miguel Indurain (Esp) Banesto
Stage 20 Sun 25 Jul	Viry-Chatillon to Paris (Champs-Élysées) 136 finishers	196.5 km 5h27'20" 36 kph	Djamolidine Abdoujaparov (Uzb) Lampre	Miguel Indurain (Esp) Banesto

Prize fund: 11,000,000 francs (first prize: 2,000,000 francs)

Final Classification

Place	Rider	Team	Time	Age
1	Miguel Indurain (Esp)	Banesto	3,714 km 95h57'09" 38.709 kph	29
2	Tony Rominger (Sui)	CLAS	+ 4'59"	32
3	Zenon Jaskula (Pol)	GB	+ 5'48"	31
4	Álvaro Mejía (Col)	Motorola	+ 7'29"	26
5	Bjarne Riis (Den)	Ariostea	+ 16'26"	29
6	Claudio Chiappucci (Ita)	Carrera	+ 17'18"	30
7	Johan Bruyneel (Bel)	ONCE	+ 18'04"	28
8	Andy Hampsten (USA)	Motorola	+ 20'14"	31
9	Pedro Delgado (Esp)	Banesto	+ 23'57"	33
10	Vladimir Poulnikov (Ukr)	Carrera	+ 25'29"	28

Lanterne Rouge

136	Edwig van Hooydonck (Bel)	Wordperfect	+ 3h30'15"	26

Points

	Djamolidine Abdoujaparov (Uzb)	Lampre		29

King of the Mountains

	Tony Rominger (Sui)	CLAS		32

Youth

	Antonio Martín (Esp)	Amaya Seguros		23

Team

		Carrera		

Super Combativité

	Massimo Ghirotto (Ita)	ZG Mobili		32

1994: Orange Juice

Cementing the return of the Hour record to cycling's schedule, Graeme Obree took back the record from Chris Boardman, riding on the Vélodrome du Lac in Bordeaux in April. By the end of the year three new marks would be set for the Hour, first by Miguel Indurain in September, and then twice by Tony Rominger in October and November. The record made famous by Henri Desgrange – and set by Tour winners from Lucien Petit-Breton through Fausto Coppi and Jacques Anquetil and on to Eddy Merckx – was back as the sport's true test of a rider.

But it was a cruel spring for the sport, especially for those who believed that doping was under control, that the lack of major riders falling foul of the testers meant there was a lack of doping – conveniently ignoring the fact that there were no tests for some of the most serious products and procedures believed to be in use. In April the Gewiss squad of Moreno Argentin, Giorgio Furlan and Evgeni Berzin landed a podium lockout at the Flèche Wallonne and, following it, the team's doctor, Michelle Ferrari, compared the dangers of EPO to those of orange juice.

That podium lockout alone merited raised eyebrows but it had come on the back of a season which had already seen Furlan win Tirreno-Adriatico, with Berzin just behind him in second. Furlan then added Milan-Sanremo and the Critérium International to his tally. Three days before their podium lock-out at the Flèche he was on the bottom step at Liège-Bastogne-Liège, with Berzin taking the victory. And now the media had the team's doctor going on the record and dismissing the dangers of EPO. A drug that had been banned since 1991. But for which there was still no test.

Francesco Conconi – the chief of Moser's medical crew back in 1984 – was by now charged with developing an EPO test and the IOC even supplied him with EPO to experiment with on amateurs in order to develop that test. Until it arrived, nothing – the authorities said – could be done, except implore the riders to obey the rules and not dope. Which they had been doing since before drug testing was forced upon the sport in the 1960s.

As for Ferrari's orange juice comment, the UCI responded with alarm and alacrity. And they leapt to the good doctor's defence – he was a respected physician, part of the team that had helped Francesco Moser set his Hour record in 1984 and had since then been working with various cycling teams – and claimed that the media had misquoted him. But they hadn't. Ferrari had said what he was reported to have said. And in so doing let the cat out of the bag as to what was really going on in the sport.

Ferrari was fired by Gewiss but continued working with some of the team's riders. And he also signed new clients, including Tony Rominger. And it was with Ferrari's help that Rominger set his Hour records – and broke Indurain's – after the Tour had ended.

Beyond that cloud, there was much sunshine. For the British, it was a time to celebrate, two Hour men and now one of them was riding with the professionals, Boardman having secured a slot at the GAN squad, alongside Greg LeMond. And, as if to celebrate with the British, Jean-Marie Leblanc took the Tour across the Channel for the first time in 20 years, with the race getting two stages in Great Britain, from Dover to Brighton and an out and back loop around Portsmouth. The newly opened Channel Tunnel ferried the riders across to Britain, while ferries took them back to France, where the Tour could resume its loop of the country in Cherbourg.

For the British, the Tour had brought much success since their first foray in 1937. British riders had won stages, one had won the King of the Mountains competition (Robert Millar, in 1984), two had even won the *lanterne rouge* (Tony Hoar in 1955 and John Clarey in 1968). But only one had ever worn the *maillot jaune*, Tom Simpson, in 1962. Then, like British buses, two more came along together, Boardman and Sean Yates (Motorola).

Boardman was the first to don the jersey, taking the race's opening prologue and losing it only on the eve of the race's transfer under the Channel, at the end of stage three. Then when the race returned to France – after Johan Museeuw and Flavio Vanzella (both GB/MG Technogym) had sported it – Yates picked the *maillot jaune* up in Rennes. Then Museeuw took it back and warmed it up for Miguel Indurain, who took control in Stage Nine's Périgueux to Bergerac individual time trial.

Indurain held the jersey with a 2'28 lead over Tony Rominger, whose CLAS squad of the year before had been beefed up with fresh sponsorship from Giorgio Squinzi and was now known as Mapei/CLAS. Some had blamed Rominger's failure the year before on his having a weak team behind him. Now, with money no object, it was time for the Swiss star to step up to the plate and prove he had the beating of Indurain in him. Instead, Rominger abandoned once the race exited the Pyrenees, Indurain had already put more than two minutes into him on the road to the Hautacam, and then Rominger lost another three minutes the next day.

Indurain's fourth victory was then, like his third, a coronation parade.

Stage-by-Stage Results for the 1994 Tour de France			Stage Winner	Maillot Jaune
Prologue Sat 2 Jul	Lille (ITT) 189 finishers	7.2 km 7'49" 55.3 kph	Chris Boardman (GBr) GAN	Chris Boardman (GBr) GAN
Stage 1 Sun 3 Jul	Lille to Armentières 189 finishers	234 km 5h46'16" 40.5 kph	Djamolidine Abdoujaparov (Uzb) Polti	Chris Boardman (GBr) GAN
Stage 2 Mon 4 Jul	Roubaix to Boulogne-sur-Mer 186 finishers	203.5 km 5h05'40" 39.9 kph	Jean-Paul van Poppel (Ned) Festina	Chris Boardman (GBr) GAN
Stage 3 Tue 5 Jul	Calais to Eurotunnel (TTT) 185 finishers	66.5 km 1h20'31" 49.6 kph	GB	Johan Museeuw (Bel) GB
Stage 4 Wed 6 Jul	Dover to Brighton 185 finishers	204.5 km 5h12'53" 39.2 kph	Francisco Cabello (Esp) Kelme	Flavio Vanzella (Ita) GB
Stage 5 Thu 7 Jul	Portsmouth to Portsmouth 182 finishers	187 km 4h10'49" 44.7 kph	Nicola Minali (Ita) Gewiss	Flavio Vanzella (Ita) GB
Stage 6 Fri 8 Jul	Cherbourg to Rennes 181 finishers	270.5 km 6h58'47" 38.8 kph	Gianluca Bortolami (Ita) Mapei	Sean Yates (GBr) Motorola

Stage-by-Stage Results for the 1994 Tour de France			Stage Winner	Maillot Jaune
Stage 7 Sat 9 Jul	Rennes to Futuroscope 177 finishers	259.5 km 5h56'50" 43.6 kph	Ján Svorada (SVK) Lampre	Johan Museeuw (Bel) GB
Stage 8 Sun 10 Jul	Poitiers to Trélissac 176 finishers	218.5 km 5h09'27" 42.4 kph	Bo Hamburger (Den) TVM	Johan Museeuw (Bel) GB
Stage 9 Mon 11 Jul	Périgueux to Bergerac (ITT) 175 finishers	64 km 1h15'58" 50.5 kph	Miguel Indurain (Esp) Banesto	Miguel Indurain (Esp) Banesto
Stage 10 Tue 12 Jul	Bergerac to Cahors 175 finishers	160.5 km 3h38'11" 44.1 kph	Jacky Durand (Fra) Castorama	Miguel Indurain (Esp) Banesto
Stage 11 Wed 13 Jul	Cahors to Lourdes (Hautacam) 173 finishers	263.5 km 6h58'04" 37.8 kph	Luc Leblanc (Fra) Festina	Miguel Indurain (Esp) Banesto
	Major climbs: Hautacam (1,560m) Luc Leblanc (Fra) Festina			
Thu 14 Jul	Rest Day			
Stage 12 Fri 15 Jul	Lourdes to Luz-Ardiden 161 finishers	204.5 km 6h08'32" 33.3 kph	Richard Virenque (Fra) Festina	Miguel Indurain (Esp) Banesto
	Major climbs: Col de Peyresourde (1,569m) Roberto Torres (Esp) Festina; Col d'Aspin (1,489m) Richard Virenque (Fra) Festina; Col du Tourmalet (2,115m) Richard Virenque (Fra) Festina; Luz-Ardiden (1,715m) Richard Virenque (Fra) Festina			
Stage 13 Sat 16 Jul	Bagnères-de-Bigorre to Albi 159 finishers	223 km 5h14'48" 42.5 kph	Bjarne Riis (Den) Gewiss	Miguel Indurain (Esp) Banesto
Stage 14 Sun 17 Jul	Castres to Montpellier 140 finishers	202 km 5h11'04" 39 kph	Rolf Sørensen (Den) GB	Miguel Indurain (Esp) Banesto
	Major climbs: Col de la Fontasse (537m) Peter Declercq (Bel) Lotto			
Stage 15 Mon 18 Jul	Montpellier to Carpentras 135 finishers	231 km 6h31'59" 35.4 kph	Eros Poli (Ita) Mercatone Uno	Miguel Indurain (Esp) Banesto
	Major climbs: Mont Ventoux (1,909m) Eros Poli (Ita) Mercatone Uno			
Stage 16 Tue 19 Jul	Valréas to l'Alpe d'Huez 128 finishers	224.5 km 6h06'45" 36.7 kph	Roberto Conti (Ita) Lampre	Miguel Indurain (Esp) Banesto
	Major climbs: Menée (1,402m) Ronan Pensec (Fra) Novemail; Col d'Ornon (1,367m) Ángel Camargo (Col) Kelme; l'Alpe d'Huez (1,860m) Roberto Conti (Ita) Lampre			
Stage 17 Wed 20 Jul	Bourg-d'Oisans to Val Thorens 126 finishers	149 km 5h13'52" 28.5 kph	Nelson Rodríguez (Col) ZG Mobili	Miguel Indurain (Esp) Banesto
	Major climbs: Col du Glandon (1,924m) Richard Virenque (Fra) Festina; Col de la Madeleine (2,000m) Piotr Ugrumov (Lat) Gewiss; Val Thorens (2,275m) Nelson Rodriguez (Col) ZG			
Stage 18 Thu 21 Jul	Moutiers to Cluses 119 finishers	174.5 km 4h52'19" 35.8 kph	Piotr Ugrumov (Lat) Gewiss	Miguel Indurain (Esp) Banesto
	Major climbs: Col des Saisies (1,633m) Peter Declercq (Bel) Lotto; Col de la Croix-Fry (1,467m) Piotr Ugrumov (Lat) Gewiss; Col de la Colombière (1,618m) Piotr Ugrumov (Lat) Gewiss			

Stage-by-Stage Results for the 1994 Tour de France			Stage Winner	Maillot Jaune
Stage 19 Fri 22 Jul	Cluses to Avoriaz (ITT) 119 finishers	47.5 km 1h22'59" 34.3 kph	Piotr Ugrumov (Lat) Gewiss	Miguel Indurain (Esp) Banesto
	Major climbs: Côte de les Gets (1,155m) Piotr Ugrumov (Lat) Gewiss; Avoriaz (1,800m) Piotr Ugrumov (Lat) Gewiss			
Stage 20 Sat 23 Jul	Morzine to Lac Saint-Point 117 finishers	208.5 km 5h50'37" 35.7 kph	Djamolidine Abdoujaparov (Uzb) Polti	Miguel Indurain (Esp) Banesto
	Major climbs: Col de la Faucille (1,323m) Peter Declercq (Bel) Lotto			
Stage 21 Sun 24 Jul	Disneyland Paris to Paris (Champs-Élysées) 117 finishers	175 km 4h43'34" 37 kph	Eddy Seigneur (Fra) GAN	Miguel Indurain (Esp) Banesto

Prize fund: 11,597,450 francs (first prize: 2,200,000 francs)

Final Classification				
Place	Rider	Team	Time	Age
1	Miguel Indurain (Esp)	Banesto	3,978 km 103h38'38" 38.282 kph	30
2	Piotr Ugrumov (Lit)	Gewiss	+ 5'39"	33
3	Marco Pantani (Ita)	Carrera	+ 7'19"	23
4	Luc Leblanc (Fra)	Festina	+ 10'03"	27
5	Richard Virenque (Fra)	Festina	+ 10'10"	24
6	Roberto Conti (Ita)	Lampre	+ 12'29"	29
7	Alberto Elli (Ita)	GB	+ 20'17"	30
8	Alex Zülle (Sui)	ONCE	+ 20'35"	26
9	Udo Bölts (Ger)	Telekom	+ 25'19"	27
10	Vladimir Poulnikov (Ukr)	Carrera	+ 25'28"	29
Lanterne Rouge				
117	John Talen (Ned)	Mercatone Uno	+ 3h39'03"	29
Points				
	Djamolidine Abdoujaparov (Uzb)	Polti		30
King of the Mountains				
	Richard Virenque (Fra)	Festina		24
Youth				
	Marco Pantani (Ita)	Carrera		23
Team				
		Festina		
Super Combativité				
	Eros Poli (Ita)	Mercatone Uno		30

1995: A Death in the Family

No rider had yet got to four Tour titles and stopped, and, with Miguel Indurain appearing to have no challengers, no one was betting against him becoming the first rider to win five in a row.

For the first week of the eighty-second Tour the yellow jersey was swapped around from one rider to another as the race approached its first full-length individual time trial, on Stage Eight, from Huy to Seraing. Indurain appeared to be on the way to an unchallenged victory. Any excitement would have to come from exploits. And then Indurain pulled a surprise. He gave the Tour an exploit, going on the attack, on the flat, on the day before the time trial.

It was the stage from Charleroi to Liège, on roads similar to those raced in Liège-Bastogne-Liège. Bjarne Riis (Gewiss) was wearing the yellow jersey when it started. On the Côte de Mont Theux, 25 kilometres out from the stage end, Indurain launched an attack that only Eric Boyer (Polti) and Johan Bruyneel (ONCE) were able to respond to. Doing all the pace-making Indurain soon burned Boyer off. But Bruyneel clung on tenaciously. Five kilometres out from the finish they had – Indurain had – built up a lead of 49 seconds. Sportingly, Indurain didn't contest the sprint, allowing Bruyneel to take the stage. And, with it, the yellow jersey from Riis.

His point made on the road to Liège, Indurain assumed full control in the time trial the next day, with Riis conceding only 12 seconds and Rominger 58. Riis was Indurain's nearest challenger, 23 seconds off yellow, with everyone else two minutes and more back.

The rest of those rivals may have been down, but not all were out, and Alex Zülle (ONCE) attacked on the road to La Plagne on the next stage (after a rest day). After attacking on the Saisies, with still

100 kilometres to go to the summit of the Roselend, Zülle was five minutes up on the yellow jersey and in danger of dethroning the king and taking yellow. Indurain, calm as he always was, bided his time, only launching a fight-back just over 10 kilometres out from home. In those 10 kilometres the Spaniard slashed Zülle's lead to just two minutes. For Zülle it was nonetheless a profitable day, he took the stage win and climbed to second overall, 2'27" back.

Then it was the turn of Marco Pantani (Carrera) to go for one on the Alpe, Stage 10, storming up the hill at an unbelievable pace. Indurain didn't need to chase, Pantani was no threat. Firstly, he was just returning from a major injury and nearly 15 minutes in arrears. Secondly, he was just another crazy Italian *grimpeur* who tried to shake things up once or twice with some crazy moves and fan-pleasing exploits. Unchased, but riding up the Alpe like he had the hounds of hell snapping at his heels, Pantani took the stage win.

And this was the way the rest of the Tour unfolded, Indurain safely in yellow, with Zülle seeming content to ride for second, while the rest of the *peloton's* stars and would-be stars mopped up the stage wins. Laurent Jalabert (ONCE) took a victory salute in Mende after a 200-kilometre breakaway. He took five minutes out of Indurain and was, for a time, even leading the Tour on the road. But then Indurain found friends in the *peloton* – favours given were returned, all those crumbs passed down from his table remembered and repaid – and they helped him close Jalabert down. Still, the Frenchman climbed up to third and 3'35" down, with his team-mate Zülle still second, at 2'44".

For ONCE the Tour should have been just beginning. They now had two riders capable of playing tag with Indurain, attacking and counter-attacking him until he broke. But then the racing was brought to a halt.

On the fifteenth stage, on the road from Saint-Girons to Cauterets, as the *peloton* swooped down the Col de Portet d'Aspet early in the stage, riders went down like skittles. One of them didn't get up: Motorola's Fabio Casartelli, gold medallist in the 1992 Olympic road race. Twenty-eight years after Tom Simpson's death on the

Ventoux, 60 years after Francisco Cepeda died on the Galibier, the Tour had just suffered the third racing fatality in its 82 editions.

At a time when the sport's doping problem seemed to be out of control and it was easy to lose faith in the professional *peloton*, the Tour responded by showing its heart. The day after Casartelli's death the *peloton* rode at funereal pace along the scheduled route from Tarbes to Pau. As they approached the finish line they ushered Casartelli's Motorola team-mates to the front and let them cross the line alone. Two days later Casartelli's team-mate Lance Armstrong took the second Tour stage win of his career, winning into Limoges and saluting the sky as he coasted to the finish. For all that was wrong with the sport, for all that the sport was out of control, it still had a soul. And in that soul there was still some goodness.

For ONCE, the tag tactics never came, Jalabert cracked on the Tourmalet and fell back, leaving Zülle defending his podium place. After that no one challenged Indurain. He added more time in the *contre-la-montre* and sailed into Paris a fully paid up member of the five-times club.

Stage-by-Stage Results for the 1995 Tour de France			Stage Winner	Maillot Jaune
Prologue Sat 1 Jul	Saint-Brieuc (ITT) 188 finishers	7.3 km 9'00" 48.7 kph	Jacky Durand (Fra) Castorama	Jacky Durand (Fra) Castorama
Stage 1 Sun 2 Jul	Dinan to Lannion 188 finishers	233.5 km 5h49'18" 40.1 kph	Fabio Baldato (Ita) MG	Jacky Durand (Fra) Castorama
Stage 2 Mon 3 Jul	Perros-Guirrec to Vitré 186 finishers	235.5 km 5h26'35" 43.3 kph	Mario Cipollini (Ita) Mercatone Uno	Laurent Jalabert (Fra) ONCE
Stage 3 Tue 4 Jul	Mayenne to Alençon (TTT) 181 finishers	67 km 1h13'10" 54.9 kph	Gewiss	Laurent Jalabert (Fra) ONCE
Stage 4 Wed 5 Jul	Alençon to Le Havre 177 finishers	162 km 3h40'23" 44.1 kph	Mario Cipollini (Ita) Mercatone Uno	Ivan Gotti (Ita) Gewiss
Stage 5 Thu 6 Jul	Fécamp to Dunkerque 175 finishers	261 km 5h51'46" 44.5 kph	Jeroen Blijlevens (Ned) TVM	Ivan Gotti (Ita) Gewiss
Stage 6 Fri 7 Jul	Dunkerque to Charleroi 174 finishers	202 km 4h30'57" 44.7 kph	Erik Zabel (Ger) Telekom	Bjarne Riis (Den) Gewiss
Stage 7 Sat 8 Jul	Charleroi to Liège 170 finishers	203 km 4h48'14" 42.3 kph	Johan Bruyneel (Bel) ONCE	Johan Bruyneel (Bel) ONCE

Stage-by-Stage Results for the 1995 Tour de France			Stage Winner	Maillot Jaune
Stage 8 Sun 9 Jul	Huy to Seraing (ITT) 169 finishers	54 km 1h04'16" 50.4 kph	Miguel Indurain (Esp) Banesto	Miguel Indurain (Esp) Banesto
Mon 10 Jul	Rest Day			
Stage 9 Tue 11 Jul	Le Grand-Bornand to La Plagne 154 finishers	160 km 4h41'18" 34.1 kph	Alex Zülle (Sui) ONCE	Miguel Indurain (Esp) Banesto
	Major climbs: Côte de Hery (1,030m) Laurent Brochard (Fra) Festina; Col des Saisies (1,633m) Federico Muñoz (Col) Kelme; Cormet de Roselend (1,968m) Alex Zülle (Sui) ONCE; La Plagne (1,970m) Alex Zülle (Sui) ONCE			
Stage 10 Wed 12 Jul	Aime-La Plagne to l'Alpe d'Huez 143 finishers	162.5 km 5h13'14" 31.1 kph	Marco Pantani (Ita) Carrera	Miguel Indurain (Esp) Banesto
	Major climbs: Col de la Madeleine (2,000m) Richard Virenque (Fra) Festina; Col de la Croix de Fer (2,067m) Richard Virenque (Fra) Festina; l'Alpe d'Huez (1,860m) Marco Pantani (Ita) Carrera			
Stage 11 Thu 13 Jul	Bourg-d'Oisans to Saint-Étienne 141 finishers	199 km 4h43'15" 42.2 kph	Maximilian Sciandri (GBr) MG	Miguel Indurain (Esp) Banesto
	Major climbs: La Forteresse (660m) Hernán Buenahora (Col) Kelme; Crêt de l'Oeillon (1,210m) Hernán Buenahora (Col) Kelme			
Stage 12 Fri 14 Jul	Saint-Étienne to Mende 134 finishers	222.5 km 5h19'05" 41.8 kph	Laurent Jalabert (Fra) ONCE	Miguel Indurain (Esp) Banesto
	Major climbs: Côte de la Croix Neuve (1,045m) Laurent Jalabert (Fra) ONCE			
Stage 13 Sat 15 Jul	Mende to Revel 129 finishers	245 km 5h50'45" 41.9 kph	Serguei Outschakov (Ukr) Polti	Miguel Indurain (Esp) Banesto
	Major climbs: Col de Sie (1,020m) Bruni Cenghialta (Ita) Gewiss			
Stage 14 Sun 16 Jul	Saint-Orens-de-Gameville to Guzet-Neige 129 finishers	164 km 4h29'08" 36.6 kph	Marco Pantani (Ita) Carrera	Miguel Indurain (Esp) Banesto
	Major climbs: Port de Lers (1,516m) Marco Pantani (Ita) Carrera; Guzet-Neige (1,480m) Marco Pantani (Ita) Carrera			
Mon 17 Jul	Rest Day			
Stage 15 Tue 18 Jul	Saint-Girons to Cauterets (Crêtes-du-Lys) 119 finishers	206 km 6h20'48" 32.5 kph	Richard Virenque (Fra) Festina	Miguel Indurain (Esp) Banesto
	Major climbs: Col de Portet d'Aspet (1,069m) Richard Virenque (Fra) Festina; Col de Menté (1,349m) Richard Virenque (Fra) Festina; Col de Peyresourde (1,569m) Richard Virenque (Fra) Festina; Col d'Aspin (1,489m) Richard Virenque (Fra) Festina; Col du Tourmalet (2,115m) Richard Virenque (Fra) Festina; Cauterets (Crêtes du Lys) (1,301m) Richard Virenque (Fra) Festina			
Stage 16 Wed 19 Jul	Tarbes to Pau 117 finishers	237 km	neutralised	Miguel Indurain (Esp) Banesto
Stage 17 Thu 20 Jul	Pau to Bordeaux 117 finishers	246 km 6h29'49" 37.9 kph	Erik Zabel (Ger) Telekom	Miguel Indurain (Esp) Banesto
Stage 18 Fri 21 Jul	Montpon-Ménestérol to Limoges 115 finishers	166.5 km 3h47'53" 43.8 kph	Lance Armstrong (USA) Motorola	Miguel Indurain (Esp) Banesto

Stage-by-Stage Results for the 1995 Tour de France			Stage Winner	Maillot Jaune
Stage 19 Sat 22 Jul	Lac de Vassivière (ITT) 115 finishers	46.5 km 57'34" 48.5 kph	Miguel Indurain (Esp) Banesto	Miguel Indurain (Esp) Banesto
Stage 20 Sun 23 Jul	Sainte-Geneviève-des-Bois to Paris (Champs-Élysées) 115 finishers	155 km 3h39'46" 42.3 kph	Djamolidine Abdoujaparov (Uzb) Novell	Miguel Indurain (Esp) Banesto

Prize fund: 12,091,250 francs (first prize: 2,200,000 francs)

Final Classification				
Place	**Rider**	**Team**	**Time**	**Age**
1	Miguel Indurain (Esp)	Banesto	3,635 km 92h44'59" 39.193 kph	31
2	Alex Zülle (Sui)	ONCE	+ 4'35"	27
3	Bjarne Riis (Den)	Gewiss	+ 6'47"	31
4	Laurent Jalabert (Fra)	ONCE	+ 8'24"	26
5	Ivan Gotti (Ita)	Gewiss	+ 11'33"	26
6	Melcior Mauri (Esp)	ONCE	+ 15'20"	29
7	Fernando Escartin (Esp)	Mapei	+ 15'49"	27
8	Tony Rominger (Sui)	Mapei	+ 16'46"	34
9	Richard Virenque (Fra)	Festina	+ 17'31"	25
10	Hernán Buenahora (Col)	Kelme	+ 18'50"	28
Lanterne Rouge				
115	Bruno Cornillet (Fra)	Chazal	+ 3h36'26"	32
Points				
	Laurent Jalabert (Fra)	ONCE		26
King of the Mountains				
	Richard Virenque (Fra)	Festina		25
Youth				
	Marco Pantani (Ita)	Carrera		26
Team				
		ONCE		
Super Combativité				
	Hernán Buenahora (Col)	Kelme		28

1996: The Dane Curse

When the end came, it came with a whimper, not a bang. The *peloton* just rode away from Miguel Indurain on the first day in the Alps, a week into the Tour on the road to Les Arcs, the phoney war done and the real fighting just begun. The five-time Tour champion lost four minutes on the stage and gave his chief rivals an unexpected advantage.

A day later, on the first full time trial, Stage Eight, 30.5 kilometres from Bourg-Saint-Maurice to Val d'Isère, on what was traditionally the day Indurain took control of the Tour, the Spaniard lost more time. And then, on a snow-shortened stage to Sestriere (Stage Nine), it became clear who was about to inherit the Banesto star's crown: Deutsche Telekom's Bjarne Riis.

With the Dane in yellow and Indurain slipping further and further out of contention, the Telekoms took control of the race and began to eliminate Riis's challengers. Coming into the Pyrenees on stage 16, Abraham Olano (Mapei) was second at 56 seconds, Evgeni Berzin (Gewiss) at 1'08" and Tony Rominger (Mapei) fourth at 1'21", the rest two minutes and more back.

On the Hautacam, at the end of Stage 16's first day in the Pyrenees, Riis just rode away from the *peloton* and sealed the deal. Or, more precisely, he didn't just ride away from the *peloton* and seal the deal. He taunted them before tying up the win.

It was 16 July, Indurain's thirty-second birthday. Riis was one of a group of a dozen riders that hit the base of the Hautacam together, TVM's Laurent Roux up the road hoping to win the stage. Alex Zülle (ONCE) jumped away and went in pursuit of Roux with about 12 kilometres to go. The Festina riders Richard Virenque and

Laurent Brochard pulled the bunch back up to Zülle, who had already caught Roux. In so doing, they shed some members out the back of the bunch.

Riis's team-mate Jan Ullrich took over the pace-making, the front group now in Indian file, eight or nine riders wheel on wheel. Behind them the rest were bunched and spread across the road. Riis was second wheel when he suddenly swung out and eased off the power. He was still flying up the hill but relativity made it look like he was standing still, cat and mousing as if in a track sprint. As the others passed, the Dane turned his head to the left and eyed them up. Indurain, Olano, Virenque, and Dufaux all passed him. Then the yellow jersey slotted back into the file of riders, seventh wheel, behind Luc Leblanc (Polti) and ahead of the bunching group of riders behind.

The metres were counting down and the riders were belting up the climb. Ullrich was pulling them along at a vicious pace, the seven percent gradient no impediment. Then, as the climb ramped up toward eight, nine and 10 percent, Riis again swung wide and was again on the outside of the line of riders. Then he stood on his pedals and blasted past his rivals. Now it was they who looked like they were standing still.

Then, as sudden as Riis's burst of speed came, it went and the yellow jersey eased back. Indurain, Dufaux, Virenque and Leonardo Piepoli (Reffin) were onto his wheel. Behind, the injection of speed was having an impact, more riders were going out the back.

A group of riders, pulled along by Ullrich, bridged up to the front group and Riis went again. Virenque matched him as Indurain struggled to cope with the changes in pace. Then it was just Riis, Virenque and Dufaux alone at the front. Soon Riis was alone, going for the stage win and sealing his Tour victory. At the end of the stage, no rider was within two minutes of him on general classification, and the Tour had a new champion.

Riis rode on into Paris without much of a challenge. The Dane, a *domestique* for Laurent Fignon back in the 1980s and a witness to Fignon's defeat in 1989, had finally completed the transformation from helpmate to Tour challenger and then from Tour challenger into Tour winner.

Arrival of the 1996 Tour on the Champs-Élysées.

That was the story then, Riis won by powerful riding in the mountains as Indurain suffered a *Tour sans*. In 2007, spurred by a tell-all autobiography published by their former *soigneur* Jeff d'Hont, various Telekom riders confessed to doping. Riis eventually joined them and admitted what most people already knew: he'd doped. His 2010 autobiography added detail to that confession. A decade after the high-water mark of Gen-EPO, the reality of those years began to become clearer.

Stage-by-Stage Results for the 1996 Tour de France			Stage Winner	Maillot Jaune
Prologue Sat 29 Jun	'S-Hertogenbosch (ITT) 197 finishers	9.4 km 10'53" 51.8 kph	Alex Zülle (Sui) ONCE	Alex Zülle (Sui) ONCE
Stage 1 Sun 30 Jun	'S-Hertogenbosch to 'S-Hertogenbosch 195 finishers	209 km 5h00'01" 41.8 kph	Frédéric Moncassin (Fra) GAN	Alex Zülle (Sui) ONCE
Stage 2 Mon 1 Jul	'S-Hertogenbosch to Wasquehal 192 finishers	247.5 km 6h29'22" 38.1 kph	Mario Cipollini (Ita) Saeco	Alex Zülle (Sui) ONCE
Stage 3 Tue 2 Jul	Wasquehal to Nogent-sur-Oise 191 finishers	195 km 5h29'21" 35.5 kph	Erik Zabel (Ger) Deutsche Telekom	Frédéric Moncassin (Fra) GAN
Stage 4 Wed 3 Jul	Soissons to Lac de Madine 188 finishers	232 km 5h43'50" 40.5 kph	Cyril Saugrain (Fra) Aubervilliers 93	Stéphane Heulot (Fra) GAN
Stage 5 Thu 4 Jul	Lac de Madine to Besançon 183 finishers	242 km 6h55'53" 34.9 kph	Jeroen Blijlevens (Ned) TVM	Stéphane Heulot (Fra) GAN
Stage 6 Fri 5 Jul	Arc-et-Senans to Aix-les-Bains 166 finishers	207 km 5h05'38" 40.6 kph	Michael Boogerd (Ned) Rabobank	Stéphane Heulot (Fra) GAN
Major climbs: Col de la Croix de la Serre (1,049m) Leon van Bon (Ned) Rabobank				
Stage 7 Sat 6 Jul	Chambéry to Les Arcs 159 finishers	200 km 5h47'22" 34.5 kph	Luc Leblanc (Fra) Polti	Evgeni Berzin (Rus) Gewiss
Major climbs: Col de la Madeleine (2,000m) Richard Virenque (Fra) Festina; Cormet de Roselend (1,968m) Udo Bölts (Ger) Deutsche Telekom; Les Arcs (1,700m) Luc Leblanc (Fra) Polti				
Stage 8 Sun 7 Jul	Bourg-Saint-Maurice to Val d'Isère (ITT) 157 finishers	30.5 km 51'53" 35.3 kph	Evgeni Berzin (Rus) Gewiss	Evgeni Berzin (Rus) Gewiss
Major climbs: Val d'Isère (1,810m) Bjarne Riis (Den) Deutsche Telekom				
Stage 9 Mon 8 Jul	Le Monêtier-les-Bains to Sestriere 157 finishers	46 km 1h10'44" 39 kph	Bjarne Riis (Den) Deutsche Telekom	Bjarne Riis (Den) Deutsche Telekom
Major climbs: Col de l'Iseran (2,770m) n/a; Col du Galibier (2,645m) n/a; Col de Montgenèvre (1,860m) Bjarne Riis (Den) Deutsche Telekom; Colle del Sestriere (2,035m) Bjarne Riis (Den) Deutsche Telekom				

Stage-by-Stage Results for the 1996 Tour de France			Stage Winner	Maillot Jaune
Stage 10 Tue 9 Jul	Turin to Gap 151 finishers	208.5 km 5h08'10" 40.6 kph	Erik Zabel (Ger) Deutsche Telekom	Bjarne Riis (Den) Deutsche Telekom
	Major climbs: Col de Montgenèvre (1,860m) Richard Virenque (Fra) Festina; Col de la Sentinelle (980m) Rolf Sørensen (Swe) Rabobank			
Wed 10 Jul	Rest Day			
Stage 11 Thu 11 Jul	Gap to Valence 146 finishers	202 km 5h09'12" 39.2 kph	José Jaime González (Col) Kelme	Bjarne Riis (Den) Deutsche Telekom
	Major climbs: Col de Cabre (1,180m) Richard Virenque (Fra) Festina; Faucile (Col du Rousset) (1,254m) Laurent Brochard (Fra) Festina; Le Chaux (1,350m) Laurent Brochard (Fra) Festina			
Stage 12 Fri 12 Jul	Valence to Le Puy-en-Velay 145 finishers	143.5 km 3h29'19" 41.1 kph	Pascal Richard (Sui) MG	Bjarne Riis (Den) Deutsche Telekom
	Major climbs: Col de Lachamp (1,320m) Mirko Gualdi (Ita) Polti			
Stage 13 Sat 13 Jul	Le Puy-en-Velay to Super Besse 143 finishers	177 km 4h03'56" 43.5 kph	Rolf Sørensen (Den) Rabobank	Bjarne Riis (Den) Deutsche Telekom
	Major climbs: Saint-Anastaise (1,160m) Paolo Savoldelli (Ita) Roslotto; Super-Besse (1,275m) Orlando Sergio Rodrigues (Por) Banesto			
Stage 14 Sun 14 Jul	Besse to Tulle 137 finishers	186.5 km 4h06'29" 45.4 kph	Djamolidine Abdoujaparov (Uzb) Refin	Bjarne Riis (Den) Deutsche Telekom
	Major climbs: Col de la Croix-Morand (1,401m) Richard Virenque (Fra) Festina			
Stage 15 Mon 15 Jul	Brive-la-Gaillarde to Villeneuve-sur-Lot 135 finishers	176 km 3h54'52" 45 kph	Massimo Podenzana (Ita) Carrera	Bjarne Riis (Den) Deutsche Telekom
Stage 16 Tue 16 Jul	Agen to Lourdes (Hautacam) 134 finishers	199 km 4h56'16" 40.3 kph	Bjarne Riis (Den) Deutsche Telekom	Bjarne Riis (Den) Deutsche Telekom
	Major climbs: Hautacam (1,560m) Bjarne Riis (Den) Deutsche Telekom			
Stage 17 Wed 17 Jul	Argelès-Gazost to Pamplona 129 finishers	262 km 7h07'08" 36.8 kph	Laurent Dufaux (Sui) Festina	Bjarne Riis (Den) Deutsche Telekom
	Major climbs: Col du Soulor (1,474m) Pascal Hervé (Fra) Festina; Col d'Aubisque (1,709m) Neil Stephens (Aus) ONCE; Col de Marie-Blanque (1,100m) Neil Stephens (Aus) ONCE; Col du Soudet (1,540m) Neil Stephens (Aus) ONCE; Port de Larrau (1,573m) Richard Virenque (Fra) Festina			
Stage 18 Thu 18 Jul	Pamplona to Hendaye 129 finishers	154.5 km 4h11'02" 36.9 kph	Bart Voskamp (Ned) TVM	Bjarne Riis (Den) Deutsche Telekom
	Major climbs: Ispéguy (672m) Pascal Hervé (Fra) Festina; Puerto-Otxondo (602m) Cristian Salvato (Ita) Refin			
Stage 19 Fri 19 Jul	Hendaye to Bordeaux 129 finishers	226.5 km 5h25'11" 41.8 kph	Frédéric Moncassin (Fra) GAN	Bjarne Riis (Den) Deutsche Telekom
Stage 20 Sat 20 Jul	Bordeaux to Saint-Émilion (ITT) 129 finishers	63.5 km 1h15'31" 50.5 kph	Jan Ullrich (Ger) Deutsche Telekom	Bjarne Riis (Den) Deutsche Telekom

Stage-by-Stage Results for the 1996 Tour de France			Stage Winner	Maillot Jaune
Stage 21 Sun 21 Jul	Palaiseau to Paris (Champs-Élysées) 129 finishers	147.5 km 3h30'44" 42 kph	Fabio Baldato (Ita) MG	Bjarne Riis (Den) Deutsche Telekom

Prize fund: 12,002,250 francs (first prize: 2,200,000 francs)

Final Classification				
Place	**Rider**	**Team**	**Time**	**Age**
1	Bjarne Riis (Den)	Deutsche Telekom	3,765 km 95h57'16" 39.227 kph	32
2	Jan Ullrich (Ger)	Deutsche Telekom	+ 1'41"	22
3	Richard Virenque (Fra)	Festina	+ 4'37"	26
4	Laurent Dufaux (Sui)	Festina	+ 5'53"	27
5	Peter Luttenberger (Aut)	Carrera	+ 7'07"	23
6	Luc Leblanc (Fra)	Polti	+ 10'03"	29
7	Piotr Ugrumov (Lat)	Roslotto	+ 10'04"	35
8	Fernando Escartin (Esp)	Kelme	+ 10'26"	28
9	Abraham Olano (Esp)	Mapei	+ 11'00"	26
10	Tony Rominger (Sui)	Mapei	+ 11'53"	35
Lanterne Rouge				
129	Jean-Luc Masdupuy (Fra)	Agrigel	+ 3h49'52"	27
Points				
	Erik Zabel (Ger)	Deutsche Telekom		26
King of the Mountains				
	Richard Virenque (Fra)	Festina		26
Youth				
	Jan Ullrich (Ger)	Deutsche Telekom		22
Team				
		Festina		
Super Combativité				
	Richard Virenque (Fra)	Festina		26

1997: The Gathering Storm

The reality of the Gen-EPO years was already becoming clear in the 1990s. In 1996, NAS – Italy's *Nucleo antisofisticazione*, the branch of the Carabinieri dealing with health and hygiene matters – became aware of unusually high sales of EPO in Tuscany in the weeks leading up to the Giro d'Italia. Somehow they linked this to the race itself. They decided to investigate.

The 1996 *corsa rosa* started in Greece, with a prologue in Athens followed by two stages before the race returned to Italy. The plan was for everyone on the Giro to return to Italy by ferry, across the Aegean, landing at the port of Brindisi. NAS decided that that was where they would hit the race and search everyone. When checking the exact details, NAS enquired of CONI – the Italian Olympic committee – when the ferries were due to arrive in Brindisi.

Somehow NAS's plans leaked and everyone was aware of the welcoming committee waiting for them in Brindisi, especially when *La Gazzetta dello Sport* (organisers of the Giro) published details of the proposed raid. For some reason, 12 unmarked team vehicles decided to return to Italy overland, via Montenegro, Albania and Croatia. They could have saved the petrol money: because of the leak, the Brindisi raid was cancelled.

EPO could still be used freely by the *peloton*, despite being banned. The EPO test Francesco Conconi was searching for was still no closer to reality. In 1996 a Canadian professor, Guy Brisson, Director of the Montréal anti-doping laboratory, floated a new idea for an EPO test to the UCI, proposing that he carry out blood tests at the Tour de Romandie as part of his research. The UCI gave Brisson the go ahead but the riders objected and refused to co-operate.

Eventually, assured that the testing would be anonymous and for research purposes only, the riders relented and Brisson carried out his tests at the Tour de Suisse.

As far as the UCI were concerned, Brisson's EPO research came to nothing. The UCI, in principle, opposed blood tests, on ethical grounds. The Tour de Suisse testing did reveal an unusually high haematocrit level – the volume of oxygen-carrying red blood cells – within the *peloton*, 46% when other research suggested a level closer to 42% should have been expected.

In October of 1996, after the Tour and the Vuelta a España (which had now switched to being the last of the three Grand Tours), a trio of French cycling officials called upon the UCI to bring in blood testing as a means of combating the EPO epidemic. Riders joined in the chorus. As did Conconi, who was supposed to be developing that EPO test, he now suggesting that the UCI could 'rest' riders who had abnormally high – and therefore unhealthy – haematocrit levels.

But the real revelations came in the pages of La Gazzetta dello Sport and L'Équipe, both papers running major doping exposés. Late in 1996 La Gazzetta revealed the existence of an Italian doping report that had been suppressed by the authorities and which suggested that the Italian *peloton* was "pumped to the gills with shit like EPO, hGH and testosterone." L'Équipe ran with stories from riders who said they were quitting the sport as they didn't want to have to dope to keep up with the others. The UCI's inaction on the matter was heavily criticised. The UCI – led by Hein Verbruggen – struck back and criticised the retiring riders, saying that they were simply at the end of their careers and could no longer hold on.

A week after L'Équipe's articles ran in early 1997, the UCI formally voted to introduce blood tests and set an haematocrit level of 50% (47% for women), above which riders would be rested, for the benefit of their health. Even Jean-Marie Leblanc, boss of the Tour de France, later admitted that the haematocrit test was a compromise, there to protect riders from their own excesses. It was something that levelled the playing field somewhat, putting an upper limit on how much EPO a rider could use. But it didn't just level the playing field downwards. It also set a target to aspire to.

And then, having been stymied in their attempts to raid the 1996 Giro, NAS had the element of surprise in 1997 and hit the *corsa rosa*, searching the team hotel of MG Technogym and finding doping products. If the cycling authorities were going to drag their heels on solving the sport's doping problems, the judicial authorities would just have to do their job for them.

* * * * *

Against this toxic background the 1997 Tour took place. Bjarne Riis returned to defend his crown but was usurped by his young Deutsche Telekom team-mate Jan Ullrich, who took control of the race in the Pyrenees as Riis faded. The young German already had a GC lead of 2'58" over Festina's Richard Virenque, with everyone else more than four minutes back. If the Tour was to be contested and Ullrich denied a coronation ride back to Paris, the Festina riders were going to have to take the fight to Telekom.

They passed on the opportunity on the last day in the Pyrenees and the following day – Stage 12's individual time trial in Saint-Étienne – the German crushed the opposition, pushing his general classification lead out to 5'42" over Virenque, with the rest of the field eight minutes and more back.

As he had in 1995 and 1997, Marco Pantani bossed the Alpe d'Huez stage the next day, scorching up the switch-backed mountain. Behind him, Ullrich showed his power, finishing 47 seconds behind the Italian and nearly a minute and a half up on Virenque. The Festina riders were being shamed. So they mounted a fight back, attacking the next day over the Glandon. But Ullrich held their pace, matched them pedal stroke for pedal stroke. The stage end was an uncontested sprint, Virenque getting the glory, Ullrich safe and sure of his first Tour win.

The 23-year-old German looked set to lead the sport into the twenty-first century in a new era of dominance.

Stage-by-Stage Results for the 1997 Tour de France			Stage Winner	Maillot Jaune
Prologue Sat 5 Jul	Rouen (ITT) 198 finishers	7.3 km 8'20" 52.6 kph	Chris Boardman (GBr) GAN	Chris Boardman (GBr) GAN
Stage 1 Sun 6 Jul	Rouen to Forges-les-Eaux 197 finishers	192 km 4h39'59" 41.1 kph	Mario Cipollini (Ita) Saeco	Mario Cipollini (Ita) Saeco
Stage 2 Mon 7 Jul	Saint-Valéry-en-Caux to Vire 196 finishers	262 km 6h27'47" 40.5 kph	Mario Cipollini (Ita) Saeco	Mario Cipollini (Ita) Saeco
Stage 3 Tue 8 Jul	Vire to Plumelec 195 finishers	224 km 4h54'33" 45.6 kph	Erik Zabel (Ger) Deutsche Telekom	Mario Cipollini (Ita) Saeco
Stage 4 Wed 9 Jul	Plumelec to Puy du Fou 193 finishers	223 km 5h46'42" 38.6 kph	Nicola Minali (Ita) Batik	Mario Cipollini (Ita) Saeco
Stage 5 Thu 10 Jul	Chantonnay to La Châtre 192 finishers	261.5 km 6h16'14" 41.7 kph	Cédric Vasseur (Fra) GAN	Cédric Vasseur (Fra) GAN
Stage 6 Fri 11 Jul	Le Blanc to Marennes 190 finishers	215.5 km 5h58'09" 36.1 kph	Jeroen Blijlevens (Ned) TVM	Cédric Vasseur (Fra) GAN
Stage 7 Sat 12 Jul	Marennes to Bordeaux 186 finishers	194 km 4h11'15" 46.3 kph	Erik Zabel (Ger) Deutsche Telekom	Cédric Vasseur (Fra) GAN
Stage 8 Sun 13 Jul	Sauternes to Pau 186 finishers	161.5 km 3h22'42" 47.8 kph	Erik Zabel (Ger) Deutsche Telekom	Cédric Vasseur (Fra) GAN
Stage 9 Mon 14 Jul	Pau to Loudenvielle 179 finishers	182 km 5h24'57" 33.6 kph	Laurent Brochard (Fra) Festina	Cédric Vasseur (Fra) GAN
	Major climbs: Col du Soulor (1,474m) Laurent Brochard (Fra) Festina; Col du Tourmalet (2,115m) Javier Pascual Rodríguez (Esp) Kelme; Col d'Aspin (1,489m) Pascal Hervé (Fra) Festina; Col de Val-Louron (Col d'Azet) (1,580m) Marco Pantani (Ita) Mercatone Uno			
Stage 10 Tue 15 Jul	Luchon to Arcalis 178 finishers	252.5 km 7h46'06" 32.5 kph	Jan Ullrich (Ger) Deutsche Telekom	Jan Ullrich (Ger) Deutsche Telekom
	Major climbs: Col de Portet d'Aspet (1,069m) Laurent Brochard (Fra) Festina; Col de Port (1,249m) Laurent Brochard (Fra) Festina; Port d'Envalira (2,407m) Richard Virenque (Fra) Festina; Coll d'Ordino (1,910m) Jean-Philippe Dojwa (Fra) La Mutuelle de Seine et Marne; Arcalis (Andorra) (2,240m) Jan Ullrich (Ger) Deutsche Telekom			
Stage 11 Wed 16 Jul	Andorra to Perpignan 175 finishers	192 km 5h05'05" 37.8 kph	Laurent Desbiens (Fra) Cofidis	Jan Ullrich (Ger) Deutsche Telekom
	Major climbs: Port d'Envalira (2,407m) Richard Virenque (Fra) Festina; Col du Chioula (1,450m) Richard Virenque (Fra) Festina			

Stage-by-Stage Results for the 1997 Tour de France			Stage Winner	Maillot Jaune
Thu 17 Jul	Rest Day			
Stage 12 Fri 18 Jul	Saint-Étienne (ITT) 172 finishers	55.5 km 1h16′24″ 43.6 kph	Jan Ullrich (Ger) Deutsche Telekom	Jan Ullrich (Ger) Deutsche Telekom
	Major climbs: Col de la Croix de Chaubouret (1,230m) Jan Ullrich (Ger) Deutsche Telekom			
Stage 13 Sat 19 Jul	Saint-Étienne to l'Alpe d'Huez 171 finishers	203.5 km 5h02′42″ 40.3 kph	Marco Pantani (Ita) Mercatone Uno	Jan Ullrich (Ger) Deutsche Telekom
	Major climbs: Col du Grand Bois (1,161m) Richard Virenque (Fra) Festina; l'Alpe d'Huez (1,860m) Marco Pantani (Ita) Mercatone Uno			
Stage 14 Sun 20 Jul	Bourg-d'Oisans to Courchevel 155 finishers	148 km 4h34′16″ 32.4 kph	Richard Virenque (Fra) Festina	Jan Ullrich (Ger) Deutsche Telekom
	Major climbs: Col du Glandon (1,924m) Richard Virenque (Fra) Festina; Col de la Madeleine (2,000m) Richard Virenque (Fra) Festina; Courchevel (2,004m) Richard Virenque (Fra) Festina			
Stage 15 Mon 21 Jul	Courchevel to Morzine 148 finishers	208.5 km 5h57′16″ 35 kph	Marco Pantani (Ita) Mercatone Uno	Jan Ullrich (Ger) Deutsche Telekom
	Major climbs: Col de la Forclaz de Montmin (1,150m) Laurent Jalabert (Fra) ONCE; Col de la Croix-Fry (1,477m) Laurent Jalabert (Fra) ONCE; Col de la Colombière (1,618m) Richard Virenque (Fra) Festina; Col de Joux-Plane (1,700m) Marco Pantani (Ita) Mercatone Uno			
Stage 16 Tue 22 Jul	Morzine to Freiburg in Breisgau 143 finishers	181 km 4h30′11″ 40.2 kph	Christophe Mengin (Fra) La Francaise des Jeux	Jan Ullrich (Ger) Deutsche Telekom
	Major climbs: Col de la Croix (1,778m) José Jaime González (Col) Kelme			
Stage 17 Wed 23 Jul	Freiburg in Breisgau to Colmar 143 finishers	218.5 km 4h54′38″ 44.5 kph	Neil Stephens (Aus) Festina	Jan Ullrich (Ger) Deutsche Telekom
Stage 18 Thu 24 Jul	Colmar to Montbéliard 139 finishers	175.5 km 4h24′48″ 39.8 kph	Didier Rous (Fra) Festina	Jan Ullrich (Ger) Deutsche Telekom
	Major climbs: Côte de Gueberschwihr (560m) Laurent Jalabert (Fra) ONCE; Col du Grand Ballon (1,343m) Francesco Casagrande (Ita) Saeco; Col du Hundsruck (748m) Richard Virenque (Fra) Festina; Ballon d'Alsace (1,060m) Didier Rous (Fra) Festina			
Stage 19 Fri 25 Jul	Montbéliard to Dijon 139 finishers	172 km 4h03′17″ 42.4 kph	Mario Traversoni (Ita) Carrera	Jan Ullrich (Ger) Deutsche Telekom
Stage 20 Sat 26 Jul	Disneyland (ITT) 139 finishers	63 km 1h15′57″ 49.8 kph	Abraham Olano (Esp) Banesto	Jan Ullrich (Ger) Deutsche Telekom
Stage 21 Sun 27 Jul	Dysneyland to Paris (Champs-Élysées) 139 finishers	149.5 km 3h54′36″ 38.2 kph	Nicola Minali (Ita) Batik	Jan Ullrich (Ger) Deutsche Telekom

Prize fund: 11,972,150 francs (first prize: 2,200,000 francs)

Final Classification

Place	Rider	Team	Time	Age
1	Jan Ullrich (Ger)	Deutsche Telekom	3,950 km 100h30'35" 39.237 kph	23
2	Richard Virenque (Fra)	Festina	+ 9'09"	27
3	Marco Pantani (Ita)	Mercatone Uno	+ 14'03"	26
4	Abraham Olano (Esp)	Banesto	+ 15'55"	27
5	Fernando Escartin (Esp)	Kelme	+ 20'32"	29
6	Francesco Casagrande (Ita)	Saeco	+ 22'47"	26
7	Bjarne Riis (Den)	Deutsche Telekom	+ 26'34"	33
8	José María Jiménez (Esp)	Banesto	+ 31'17"	26
9	Laurent Dufaux (Sui)	Festina	+ 31'55"	28
10	Roberto Conti (Ita)	Mercatone Uno	+ 32'26"	32

Lanterne Rouge

139	Philippe Gaumont (Fra)	Cofidis	+ 4h26'09"	24

Points

	Erik Zabel (Ger)	Deutsche Telekom		27

King of the Mountains

	Richard Virenque (Fra)	Festina		27

Youth

	Jan Ullrich (Ger)	Deutsche Telekom		23

Team

		Deutsche Telekom		

Super Combativité

	Richard Virenque (Fra)	Festina		27

1998: The Tour de France is Decadent and Depraved

It all began like something out of Hunter S Thompson's *Fear & Loathing In Las Vegas*. Willy Voet was somewhere around Neuville-en-Ferrain when the customs officers pulled him over. His car looked like a mobile police narcotics lab. It was almost a quarter to seven in the morning, and Voet still had a hundred kilometres to drive before reaching Calais, where he was to board a ferry to the UK. Then would follow the long drive up to Holyhead and another ferry ride, this one taking him to Dublin, where the 1998 Tour de France was due to start in a little over three and a half days time.

What Voet hadn't known when he decided on his route from Brussels to Calais was that the quiet little back-road he'd chosen to use to cross the Franco-Belgian border was also a route used by small-time drug dealers. Maybe that's why French customs officers were waiting on this quiet little back-road. Not that Voet looked like a drug dealer, not in his official Tour-issued FIAT. Voet was the *soigneur* for the Festina squad, the leading team in the French *peloton*. Festina was home to Richard Virenque, the favourite cyclist of French housewives, four-time winner of the climbers' polka-dot jersey in the Tour, the man who had finished second to Telekom's Jan Ullrich in the previous year's race and one of the favourites for this year's Tour.

Realistically, this customs stop was nothing to be afraid of. Realistically, given the car, given the team, given the race, this would be little more than a formality, a quick stop and a wave-through. Realistically though, Voet had plenty of reasons to fear these customs officers. For one, he shouldn't have been at the wheel of a car, his licence having been revoked for six months following a fourth speeding offence. Then there were the phials of *pot Belge* – a mix of amphetamines, caffeine, cocaine, heroin, painkillers and corticosteroids – in his rucksack on the passenger seat, from which Voet had charged up that morning as preparation for the long journey to Dublin ahead of him. And then there was the fact that the car was a pharmacy on wheels.

Voet's own inventory of the contents of the two refrigerated bags behind the driver's seat was: "234 doses of EPO, 80 flasks of human growth hormone, 160 capsules of male hormone, testosterone and 60 pills called Asaflow, a product based on aspirin, which makes the blood more fluid."

Realistically, Voet was screwed. Once the customs officials looked inside those two refrigerated bags behind the driver's seat there was no way he was going to make it to the Tour's start in Dublin. And his Festina squad wasn't going to make it to the Tour's finish in Paris.

* * * * *

The World Cup was on, being hosted by France, and France were looking good for a win. So Jean-Marie Leblanc and his team at ASO decided to get the Tour out of France. The Irish taxpayers having generously offered to pay the fee, the honour of hosting the *grand départ* fell to Dublin. The Tour could claim to be honouring the Irish who'd raced in the Tour: Stephen Roche, who won it in 1987; Sean Kelly who briefly wore the yellow jersey and won four green jerseys; Martin Earley who won a stage; Paul Kimmage and Laurence Roche who were *géants de la route*; Ian Moore who started the 1961 Tour; and Shay Elliott, who set the ball rolling for the Irish, winning a stage and wearing the yellow jersey in the 1950s and 1960s. But really it was all about getting out of France and giving the media a story that could compete with the World Cup.

The folk at ASO needn't have bothered putting themselves to all the trouble of taking the Tour to Dublin. Willy Voet's arrest gave the media a story that more than held its own against the World Cup. The reality of doping at the Tour was about to be revealed in a way that no one could ignore. The *peloton* was about to be shown to be a pharmacy on wheels. The riders were about to be reduced to common criminals and rounded up by the *gendarmerie*.

Through the first week of the race the authorities dithered. At first, Voet was said to have acted alone, then it became clear that he was in charge of a team-run doping programme. It was only at the start of the individual time trial to Corrèze – Stage Seven – that the Festina riders were expelled from the Tour, despite their continued protestations of innocence.

The Corrèze time trial should have been a high point for the Tour. The day the race's phoney war ended and the real contenders for the final *maillot jaune* revealed themselves. Politically, it was also an important stage, Corrèze being the heartland of support for French president Jacques Chirac.

Breaking with the traditions of Henri Desgrange and Jacques Goddet – who were avowedly apolitical as far as the race and its sponsoring newspapers (*L'Auto* before the war, *L'Équipe* after) were concerned – Philippe Amaury, head of the Amaury empire that controlled the Tour, had come out in favour of Chirac in the 1995 presidential elections. Chirac himself was willing to show his support for the media baron and the Tour by attending the jersey presentations at the end of the Corrèze time trial.

Chirac, in fact, was playing the Corrèze time trial for every vote it was worth and had been putting in the groundwork for this day. When the Festina squad visited the area in June, to preview the course of the time trial, Chirac's wife Bernadette insisted on being allowed join them. She also insisted on a camera crew from state-owned France 2 being on hand to film the occasion. Some in Festina were happy with the request. Like Philippe Amaury, Richard Virenque was another high-profile supporter of Chirac. Festina team-boss Bruno Roussel, though, claimed it took the intervention of Jean-Marie Leblanc himself before he acceded to the request from the President's wife. France 2 was scheduled to broadcast the footage from the training session on the evening of the Corrèze time trial. In light of Festina's expulsion from the race, it never made it to air.

Chirac though did attend the post-stage jersey presentation, where he spoke to the press, telling them it was a pity that the Festina riders had to be sent home, but that they had to go, that doping was cheating and must be condemned and punished.

It was only with the expulsion of the Festina riders that the reality of their situation finally began to sink in with all the riders: they had thought themselves untouchable, thought themselves too big to be taken down. Now they saw they were not. No one was too big to be taken down. Not even the Tour de France.

Some defended the Festina riders, saying they shouldn't have been sent home, that they hadn't failed any drugs tests (conveniently ignoring the fact that there was still no test for EPO and some of the other drugs found in Voet's car). The *peloton* began to unite. They knew that they could be next to face the chop. And another team had by now become a part of the Festina *affaire*. In March, a TVM vehicle had been stopped and searched. A large quantity of EPO had been found. In Reims, the local magistrate had decided to re-open the case against the team.

As the race rolled on and as Jan Ullrich began to take control and set about winning his second Tour title, more and more riders began to leave the Tour. Some called for the Tour to be stopped, *L'Équipe* and *Le Parisien*'s press rivals making hay while the sun shone. On the rest day between Stages 11 and 12 the TVM team hotel was raided, and team-boss Cees Priem was taken into custody along with a few other members of the support staff. When the race resumed the riders brought the Tour to a halt, climbing off their bikes. For an hour race director Leblanc pleaded with them to go on – nothing breaks the rhythm of the Tour – and, after an hour, the race resumed. But only at touring pace, until some teams had had enough and tried to make a race of it.

As the race reached the Alps the noise of the Festina *affaire* diminished to a background hum and the real racing began, Marco Pantani (Mercatone Uno) launching an attack on the road to Les Deux Alps (Stage 15) that won him the stage and dethroned Ullrich, giving the Italian the *maillot jaune*.

It was one of those days when you look out the window and just want to go back to bed. It was certainly not the sort of day when you'd want to be crossing the roof of the Tour de France. But that was what was in front of the riders on the road to Les Deux Alps, 189 kilometres that more or less climbed from the off to the 2,067-metre summit of the Col de la Croix de Fer and then threw the double climb of the Cols du Télégraphe and Galibier at the riders. After the descent off the Galibier – at 2,645 metres, the high point of the Tour – all that lay ahead for the survivors was the nine-kilometre climb to the ski-station at Les Deux Alpes.

Pantani – who came into the Tour on the back of victory in the Giro d'Italia – had publicly targeted this day for a stage win following his victory in the Pyrenees at Plateau de Beille. Four kilometres before the summit of the Galibier, Pantani backed up his words with action. Ullrich had dropped the last of his Telekom team-mates and was without support and surrounded by his key rivals in the race. Pantani watched and waited as the German wore himself out trying to control the race alone. And then the Italian simply rode off the front of the group and disappeared into the fog and the drizzle and the crowds lining the climb. In those four kilometres Pantani put almost three minutes into Ullrich.

On the roof of the Tour Pantani paused to don a rain cape before facing into the 15 kilometre descent to the foot of Les Deux Alpes, surrendering a good 30 seconds of the lead he'd just carved out for himself. Having started the day with a three-minute deficit on Ullrich, Pantani may well have been riding himself into the *maillot jaune* but, with the penultimate day's 52-kilometre time trial to come, even if he did take the jersey he would only be keeping it warm. On a good day Ullrich could comfortably put four minutes into Pantani in that final race of truth. At best then, Pantani was riding for yet another stage win and the glory of a few days in yellow. He certainly wasn't going to put another four minutes plus into the German on the descent off the Galibier and the relatively short climb up to Les Deux Alpes.

When Pantani rode into the ski-station at Les Deux Alpes – arms spread, head raised, eyes closed, a picture of Christ on the cross

– Ullrich was still four kilometres down the climb. By the time he crossed the line the German had ceded almost nine minutes to the Italian. Pantani was leading the Tour by four seconds short of six minutes.

The next night more team hotels were raided and more riders taken into custody. The morning after, the *peloton* was in the mood for more protests. Thirty-two kilometres into the stage the riders once again dismounted and protested. When the race resumed it was without the ONCE squad, who'd had enough and decided to go home. And again it was only at touring pace. ONCE were followed home to Spain by Banesto. Other teams decamped the Tour as the day progressed. It was 7.30 in the evening before the riders arrived in Aix-les-Bains. No results were issued for the stage. That night, more hotels were raided and more riders withdrew from the race.

Eventually, limping ever onwards, the Tour arrived at its last major showdown, the individual time trial from Montceau-les-Mines to Le Creusot, 52 kilometres in which Pantani would either win or lose the Tour. Ullrich needed to make up 5'56". He got 2'35". Pantani did the Giro/Tour double, winning a Tour described by race director Leblanc as being "at the same time a magnificent race and one poisoned by scandal."

Cycling had been given a wake-up call, as it had on the Ventoux in 1955 and 1967. Many believed that this time it would be different, that this time the change would come and the doping would stop.

* * * * *

Among the many revelations during the Festina Tour was one that, at the time, was barely noticed: the Canadian Guy Brisson, who in 1996 had attempted to develop a test for EPO which the UCI said was unsuccessful, claimed that he had in fact developed a test, one that relied on indirect evidence of doping rather than direct evidence of specific doping products. And Brisson revealed that the sport's authorities had rejected this. They felt it left them vulnerable to legal challenges. At a time when some riders had deeper pockets than the UCI that was a situation which could bring down the sport of cycling.

Stage-by-Stage Results for the 1998 Tour de France			Stage Winner	Maillot Jaune
Prologue Sat 11 Jul	Dublin (ITT) 189 finishers	5.6 km 6'12" 54.2 kph	Chris Boardman (GBr) GAN	Chris Boardman (GBr) GAN
Stage 1 Sun 12 Jul	Dublin to Dublin 189 finishers	180.5 km 4h29'58" 40.1 kph	Tom Steels (Bel) Mapei	Chris Boardman (GBr) GAN
Stage 2 Mon 13 Jul	Enniscorthy to Cork 186 finishers	205.5 km 5h45'10" 35.7 kph	Ján Svorada (Cze) Mapei	Erik Zabel (Ger) Telekom
Stage 3 Tue 14 Jul	Roscoff to Lorient 186 finishers	169 km 3h33'36" 47.5 kph	Jens Heppner (Ger) Telekom	Bo Hamburger (Den) Casino
Stage 4 Wed 15 Jul	Plouay to Cholet 184 finishers	252 km 5h48'32" 43.4 kph	Jeroen Blijlevens (Ned) TVM	Stuart O'Grady (Aus) GAN
Stage 5 Thu 16 Jul	Cholet to Châteauroux 183 finishers	228.5 km 5h18'49" 43 kph	Mario Cipollini (Ita) Saeco	Stuart O'Grady (Aus) GAN
Stage 6 Fri 17 Jul	La Châtre to Brive-la-Gaillarde 181 finishers	204.5 km 5h05'32" 40.2 kph	Mario Cipollini (Ita) Saeco	Stuart O'Grady (Aus) GAN
Stage 7 Sat 18 Jul	Meyrignac to Corrèze (ITT) 172 finishers	58 km 1h15'25" 46.1 kph	Jan Ullrich (Ger) Telekom	Jan Ullrich (Ger) Telekom
Stage 8 Sun 19 Jul	Brive-la-Gaillarde to Montauban 170 finishers	190.5 km 4h40'55" 40.7 kph	Jacky Durand (Fra) Casino	Laurent Desbiens (Fra) Cofidis
Stage 9 Mon 20 Jul	Montauban to Pau 168 finishers	210 km 5h21'10" 39.2 kph	Leon van Bon (Ned) Rabobank	Laurent Desbiens (Fra) Cofidis
Stage 10 Tue 21 Jul	Pau to Luchon 151 finishers	196.5 km 5h49'40" 33.7 kph	Rodolfo Massi (Ita) Casino	Jan Ullrich (Ger) Telekom
	Major climbs: Col d'Aubisque (1,709m) Cédric Vasseur (Fra) GAN; Col du Tourmalet (2,115m) Alberto Elli (Ita) Casino; Col d'Aspin (1,489m) Rodolfo Massi (Ita) Casino; Col de Peyresourde (1,569m) Rodolfo Massi (Ita) Casino			
Stage 11 Wed 22 Jul	Luchon to Plateau de Beille 148 finishers	170 km 5h15'27" 32.3 kph	Marco Pantani (Ita) Mercatone Uno	Jan Ullrich (Ger) Telekom
	Major climbs: Col de Menté (1,349m) Alberto Elli (Ita) Casino; Col de Portet d'Aspet (1,069m) Alberto Elli (Ita) Casino; Col de la Core (1,395m) Roland Meier (Sui) Cofidis; Col de Port (1,249m) Roland Meier (Sui) Cofidis; Plateau de Beille (1,780m) Marco Pantani (Ita) Mercatone Uno			

Stage-by-Stage Results for the 1998 Tour de France			Stage Winner	Maillot Jaune
Stage 12 Thu 23 Jul	Tarascon-sur-Ariège to Cap d'Agde 148 finishers	206 km 4h12'51" 48.9 kph	Tom Steels (Bel) Mapei	Jan Ullrich (Ger) Telekom
Fri 24 Jul	Rest Day			
Stage 13 Sat 25 Jul	Frontignan-La Peyrade to Carpentras 147 finishers	196 km 4h32'46" 43.1 kph	Daniele Nardello (Ita) Mapei	Jan Ullrich (Ger) Telekom
	Major climbs: Col de Murs (627m) José Vicente García (Esp) Banesto			
Stage 14 Sun 26 Jul	Valréas to Grenoble 147 finishers	186.5 km 4h30'53" 41.3 kph	Stuart O'Grady (Aus) GAN	Jan Ullrich (Ger) Telekom
	Major climbs: Col du Rousset (1,254m) Stuart O'Grady (Aus) GAN			
Stage 15 Mon 27 Jul	Grenoble to Les Deux Alpes 140 finishers	189 km 5h43'45" 33 kph	Marco Pantani (Ita) Mercatone Uno	Marco Pantani (Ita) Mercatone Uno
	Major climbs: Col de la Croix de Fer (2,067m) Rodolfo Massi (Ita) Casino; Col du Télégraphe (1,566m) Rodolfo Massi (Ita) Casino; Col du Galibier (2,645m) Marco Pantani (Ita) Mercatone Uno; Les Deux-Alpes (1,644m) Marco Pantani (Ita) Mercatone Uno			
Stage 16 Tue 28 Jul	Vizille to Albertville 134 finishers	204 km 5h39'47" 36 kph	Jan Ullrich (Ger) Telekom	Marco Pantani (Ita) Mercatone Uno
	Major climbs: Col de Porte (1,326m) Stéphane Heulot (Fra) La Francaise des Jeux; Col du Grand Cucheron (1,188m) Stéphane Heulot (Fra) La Francaise des Jeux; Col du Granier (1,134m) Stéphane Heulot (Fra) La Francaise des Jeux; Col du Cucheron (1,139m) Stéphane Heulot (Fra) La Francaise des Jeux; Col de la Madeleine (2,000m) Jan Ullrich (Ger) Telekom			
Stage 17 Wed 29 Jul	Albertville to Aix-les-Bains 117 finishers	149 km	Neutralised	Marco Pantani (Ita) Mercatone Uno
Stage 18 Thu 30 Jul	Aix-les-Bains to Neufchatel 101 finishers	218.5 km 4h53'27" 44.7 kph	Tom Steels (Bel) Mapei	Marco Pantani (Ita) Mercatone Uno
	Major climbs: Col de la Faucille (1,323m) Cédric Vasseur (Fra) GAN			
Stage 19 Fri 31 Jul	La Chaux-de-Fonds to Autun 96 finishers	242 km 5h10'14" 46.8 kph	Magnus Bäckstedt (Swe) GAN	Marco Pantani (Ita) Mercatone Uno
Stage 20 Sat 1 Aug	Montceau-les-Mines to Le Creusot (ITT) 96 finishers	52 km 1h03'52" 48.9 kph	Jan Ullrich (Ger) Telekom	Marco Pantani (Ita) Mercatone Uno
Stage 21 Sun 2 Aug	Melun to Paris (Champs-Élysées) 96 finishers	147.5 km 3h44'36" 39.4 kph	Tom Steels (Bel) Mapei	Marco Pantani (Ita) Mercatone Uno

Prize fund: 12,019,650 francs (first prize: 2,200,000 francs)

Final Classification

Place	Rider	Team	Time	Age
1	Marco Pantani (Ita)	Mercatone Uno	3,875 km 92h49'46" 39.983 kph	27
2	Jan Ullrich (Ger)	Telekom	+ 3'21"	24
3	Bobby Julich (USA)	Cofidis	+ 4'08"	26
4	Christophe Rinero (Fra)	Cofidis	+ 9'16"	24
5	Michael Boogerd (Ned)	Rabobank	+ 11'26"	26
6	Jean-Cyril Robin (Fra)	US Postal	+ 14'57"	28
7	Roland Meier (Sui)	Cofidis	+ 15'13"	30
8	Daniele Nardello (Ita)	Mapei	+ 16'07"	25
9	Giuseppe di Grande (Ita)	Mapei	+ 17'35"	24
10	Axel Merckx (Bel)	Polti	+ 17'39"	25

Lanterne Rouge

96	Damien Nazon (Fra)	La Française des Jeux	+ 3h12'15"	24

Points

	Erik Zabel (Ger)	Telekom		28

King of the Mountains

	Christophe Rinero (Fra)	Cofidis		24

Youth

	Jan Ullrich (Ger)	Telekom		24

Team

		Cofidis		

Super Combativité

	Jacky Durand (Fra)	Casino		31

1999: The Modern Prometheus

In 1999 cycling was still reeling from the previous year's Festina *affaire*, which had somehow taken so many by surprise and left them expressing their shock that there was a serious doping problem in cycling, despite all that was known about the sport and all that had happened in the years leading up to 1998. Part of the fallout from Festina was that the media really began shaking the skeletons in cycling's cupboard. They had seen in 1998 that doping sold, that fans were actually interested in it. And so the public learned more and more about what had really been going on in cycling over the previous few years.

Rattling bones is bad enough, but some former riders just didn't seem to be singing from the UCI's approved hymn sheet of a new, clean cycling, a sport responding to events of the year before and walking away from a century and more of doping. Take, for instance, Francesco Moser, who finally admitted that his 1984 Hour record had been built on blood doping and told *L'Équipe* that the sport had to learn to live with doping, that pure cycling was just an illusion. As far as Moser was concerned, riders should simply be told the effects of a medicine and then, if they wanted to, the choice to use it or not should be theirs. It was the same line that riders like Jacques Anquetil had rolled out in the 1960s when anti-doping tests first arrived: it was the riders who should decide what was and was not doping.

In the autumn of 1998, after the Tour had ended, Italian police raided the offices of Francesco Conconi at the University of Ferrara and uncovered records – which they released in 1999 – that suggested Conconi and his staff (which in the early 1990s included

Michele Ferrari) had been treating a large number of athletes with EPO dating back to 1992. Among the cyclists named were members of the Carrera team, including Claudio Chiappucci and Stephen Roche.

In March, shortly after Paris-Nice, Jean-Cyril Robin – now with La Française des Jeux but previously a member of the Festina and US Postal teams – told a French newspaper that there was now a *peloton à deux vitesses*, a two-speed *peloton*. Robin's comments received the support of Daniel Baal, president of the French cycling federation. As the year progressed, others echoed them. Rather than the whole *peloton* having cleaned up in the wake of the 1998 Tour, it was now split into two, part riding doped, part trying to ride clean.

Things got more serious in April, when various different riders and team personnel got caught up in new judicial investigations, one of which centred around the famed veterinarian and doping doctor, Bernard Sainz, aka Dr Mabuse, whose time in the sport dated all the way back to being Cyrille Guimard's medical advisor in the early 1970s.

May brought more bad news when Willy Voet, the *soigneur* at the heart of the Festina *affaire*, published a book that laid bare his 30-year career in the sport and the cheating he had witnessed and been party to. And then came the Giro d'Italia and the downfall of Marco Pantani, champion the year before of the Italian and French Grand Tours

Pantani was taken down by the haematocrit test introduced in 1997. In its first year, nearly 500 blood tests were carried out. Ten riders were told to stop racing for two weeks and rest until their haematocrit levels dropped below 50%. It hadn't taken long for people to work out how to beat the test. All you needed was about 20 minutes notice that you were about to be tested. If you knew your haematocrit count was over the limit, all you had to do was dilute your blood. You could do this by drinking a couple of litres of water. Or you could try something more direct, like an IV drip.

But just because you knew your haematocrit level didn't mean you'd always beat the test. Accidents happened. As Pantani found during the Giro, two days out from the finish and just before the race was due to climb the Gavia, the high-point of that year's race. Before the stage got underway, Pantani fell foul of the UCI's vampires, failed the haematocrit test and got thrown off the race.

* * * * *

There were some serious attempts to clean up the sport following the Festina *affaire*. The French introduced mandatory health checks for their riders. Each rider was required to submit himself to four tests a year. Once a base level was established, a rider would have to explain variances in their biological profile. In other words, longitudinal testing, or a rudimentary biological passport. When the French introduced their health checks a number of high-profile riders removed themselves from France, Laurent Jalabert (then riding for Manolo Sáiz's ONCE squad) decamped to Switzerland, and Richard Virenque (then still proclaiming his innocence in the Festina *affaire*) moved to Italy.

In Italy one branch of the Italian Olympic committee (CONI), began looking at procedures that would reveal attempts to cheat the haematocrit test. They got permission to test Italian riders at the Giro – for research purposes – but this met with considerable resistance from within the *peloton*, similar to the way the riders had attempted to stop Guy Brisson's testing in 1996, with Pantani to the fore in attempting to stymie the testers.

This led to an argument with Mapei's Andrea Tafi, live on Italian TV. The day after that incident, during the race, Tafi was reduced to tears at the back of the *peloton* as he was subjected to a stream of abuse from other riders, led by Pantani. The *peloton* did not take too kindly to riders who failed to toe the line, who failed to adhere to the sport's code of *omertà*

So, by the time the Tour rolled around in July, cycling needed an uplifting story and a hero they could believe in. Lance Armstrong came along and gave it both. Having already won two Tour stages and come back from life-threatening cancer Armstrong was a hero for a new age.

One way or another, the 1999 Tour was going to give the sport a new winner: Bjarne Riis, Jan Ullrich and Marco Pantani were all *in absentia*. And, from the off, Armstrong looked to be the man, winning the prologue and donning the *maillot jaune* before handing it over to Casino's Ján Kirsipuu to keep warm until the first major time trial, Stage Eight in Metz. There Armstrong re-took the lead, two minutes clear of any of his rivals on general classification. And then, after a day of rest, the American secured his Tour victory, in the mountains.

It was the road to Sestriere and Armstrong's US Postal riders bossed the race as they crossed the day's early climbs. Six kilometres from the summit Armstrong, twiddling a low gear, rode away from the *peloton*, taking the stage and pushing his general classification lead out to more than six minutes.

If Armstrong's Tour victory was unchallenged on the road, it was not unchallenged by the media. Word leaked that the American had tested positive for cortisone early in the race and questions were asked (three decades after professional cyclists had begun using the drug, the anti-doping authorities had finally developed a test to detect its use, and the riders had been warned of this fact ahead of the race). A back-dated therapeutic use exemption was produced (contrary to the rules, which required TUEs to be disclosed before the test) and Armstrong's cortisone use was officially excused.

Among the claims made by Willy Voet was one that a Festina rider, Laurent Brochard, had won the World Championships in 1997 and then fallen foul of the testers only for the matter to be swept under the carpet by the production of a back-dated TUE. Voet claimed that Hein Verbruggen himself was the man who provided the solution, telling the French team manager to use a back-dated TUE (Verbruggen chose to sue Voet over this claim, and, the former *soigneur* being unable to provide proof to support his claim, Verbruggen won the case). Back-dated TUEs, people knew, were a great get out of gaol free card.

And while other riders couldn't challenge Armstrong on the road, some chose to speak out against the doping that was still clearly going on within the *peloton*. Chief among these was Christophe Bassons (La Française des Jeux). He was writing a daily diary for *Le Parisien* and in one instalment he noted that the *peloton* was shocked by the performance of Armstrong.

By the time the Tour set off for Alpe d'Huez Bassons was the black sheep of the race, shunned by his fellow professionals, who wanted him to stick to the party line, the one that said the sport was cleaning itself up. Even Basson's own team-mates turned against him, La Française des Jeux's riders not being allowed get into breaks because of him. And, since La Française des Jeux had no overall contender for the *maillot jaune*, the success or failure of their Tour rested on getting into breaks and trying to take a stage win.

On the road to Alpe d'Huez Armstrong, in his yellow jersey, rode up to Bassons and told him it was time to either shut up or go home. His claims, Bassons was told, were not good for cycling. And, after the stage, Armstrong repeated those words to the massed media. And Armstrong wasn't alone. No one in the *peloton* stood up and supported Bassons. And even outside the *peloton* the *patron* himself, Bernard Hinault – now working for ASO – criticised Bassons and claimed it was he, Bassons, who was damaging the sport. Two days later Bassons took Armstrong's advice and went home.

Even *L'Équipe* was asking questions, in a coded way, about what was going on, deploying euphemisms to put a question mark over Armstrong. Pierre Ballester interviewed Armstrong for the paper and asked all the right questions, are you or have you ever been a user of EPO and/or corticosteroids, that sort of thing. When the interview appeared, complete with all of Armstrong's denials and protestations of innocence, Tour director Jean-Marie Leblanc was less than pleased.

Leblanc knew first hand what allegations of doping could do, he had come to power within the Tour on the back of the Delgado *affaire* in 1988. And he was marketing the 1999 Tour as being the Tour of Renewal – in the same way Jacques Goddet and Félix Lévitan had marketed the 1968 race as the Tour of Good Health. Discussing doping was spoiling the image he was trying to create, the image of a sport that had taken control of its doping problem. After first turning on Ballester, Leblanc then turned to *L'Équipe*'s cycling editor Jean-Michel Rouet. He explained to Rouet what the party line was and told him it was time to toe it. And so *L'Équipe*'s tone changed, softened. *L'Équipe* praised Armstrong, and stopped (for a while, at least) trying to bury him.

But the fact was that so many really wanted to believe that the sport had cleaned up, so many really wanted to believe in a hero returned from cancer who could still compete at the highest level in the toughest race. So many really wanted to believe so hard that they were willing to dismiss claims of doping, dismiss those making them as cynics and sceptics. Belief is blind.

* * * * *

1999 was the Tour's eighty-sixth edition. In those 86 races history has been rewritten dozens of times. All the results of the 1904 edition were revised months after the race ended. In the years since, riders had won stages only to immediately have their victory stripped from them for infractions of the sprinting rules. In the years after the 1960s and the advent of doping rules riders had won stages only to have their victory stripped from them days later when it was found they had failed the doping controls. The Tour's history, it is forever being re-written, constantly being revised.

In 2012, more than a decade after Armstrong's win, years after the Armstrong era – which stretched through to 2005 – drew to a close, the United States Anti-Doping Agency (USADA) completed an investigation into doping at Armstrong's teams and declared the American guilty of having doped to win. And they rewrote the history of the Armstrong era, stripping the American of every single result he had achieved in the sport since 1 August, 1998.

Given the state of the *peloton* during the Gen-EPO years, those victories were not reallocated to other riders. As with that stage in the 1977 Tour when the first and second riders across the line in Saint-Étienne had tested positive, all of Armstrong's results through to 2005 were simply left as having been vacated.

Stage-by-Stage Results for the 1999 Tour de France			Stage Winner	Maillot Jaune
Prologue Sat 3 Jul	Puy du Fou (ITT) 180 finishers	6.8 km 8'02" 50.8 kph	~~Lance Armstrong (USA)~~ ~~US Postal~~	~~Lance Armstrong (USA)~~ ~~US Postal~~
				Vacated
Rated climbs: Côte du Fossé (245m) Mariano Piccoli (Ita) Lampre				
Stage 1 Sun 4 Jul	Montaigu to Challans 180 finishers	208 km 4h56'18" 42.1 kph	Ján Kirsipuu (Est) Casino	~~Lance Armstrong (USA)~~ ~~US Postal~~
				Vacated
Rated climbs: Côte de Saint-Michel (Mont Mercure) (264m) Laurent Brochard (Fra) Festina				
Stage 2 Mon 5 Jul	Challans to Saint-Nazaire 178 finishers	176 km 3h45'32" 46.8 kph	Tom Steels (Bel) Mapei	Ján Kirsipuu (Est) Casino
Rated climbs: Côte du Pont de Saint-Nazaire (72m) Francisco Cerezo (Esp) Vitalicio Seguros				
Stage 3 Tue 6 Jul	Nantes to Laval 177 finishers	194.5 km 4h29'27" 43.3 kph	Tom Steels (Bel) Mapei	Ján Kirsipuu (Est) Casino
Rated climbs: Côte de Bel-Air (425m) Massimo Giunti (Ita) Cantina Tollo				
Stage 4 Wed 7 Jul	Laval to Blois 177 finishers	191 km 3h51'45" 49.4 kph	Mario Cipollini (Ita) Saeco	Ján Kirsipuu (Est) Casino
Rated climbs: Côte de Beaumont-la-Ronce (151m) Anthony Morin (Fra) La Française des Jeux				
Stage 5 Thu 8 Jul	Bonneval to Amiens 176 finishers	233.5 km 5h36'28" 41.6 kph	Mario Cipollini (Ita) Saeco	Ján Kirsipuu (Est) Casino
Rated climbs: Côte de Coulombs (130m) Mariano Piccoli (Ita) Lampre; Côte de Limay (126m) Mariano Piccoli (Ita) Lampre				
Stage 6 Fri 9 Jul	Amiens to Maubeuge 176 finishers	171.5 km 4h11'09" 41 kph	Mario Cipollini (Ita) Saeco	Ján Kirsipuu (Est) Casino
Rated climbs: Côte de Cappy (80m) Mariano Piccoli (Ita) Lampre				
Stage 7 Sat 10 Jul	Avesnes to Thionville 176 finishers	227 km 5h26'59" 41.7 kph	Mario Cipollini (Ita) Saeco	Ján Kirsipuu (Est) Casino
Rated climbs: Côte de Thonnelle (254m) Lylian Lebreton (Fra) Big Mat; Côte de Longuyon (273m) Lylian Lebreton (Fra) Big Mat; Côte de Boismont (300m) Jacky Durand (Fra) Lotto				
Stage 8 Sun 11 Jul	Metz (ITT) 175 finishers	56.5 km 1h08'36" 49.4 kph	~~Lance Armstrong (USA)~~ ~~US Postal~~	~~Lance Armstrong (USA)~~ ~~US Postal~~
			Vacated	Vacated
Rated climbs: Côte de Lorry-lès-Metz (256m) Mariano Piccoli (Ita) Lampre; Côte de Gravelotte (323m) Lance Armstrong (USA) US Postal				

Stage-by-Stage Results for the 1999 Tour de France			Stage Winner	Maillot Jaune
Mon 12 Jul	Rest Day			
Stage 9 Tue 13 Jul	Le Grand-Bornand to Sestriere 167 finishers	213.5 km 5h57'11" 35.9 kph	~~Lance Armstrong (USA) US Postal~~	~~Lance Armstrong (USA) US Postal~~
			Vacated	Vacated
	Rated climbs: Col du Marais (843m) Dimitri Konychev (Rus) Mercatone Uno; Col de Tamié (907m) Mariano Piccoli (Ita) Lampre; Col du Télégraphe (1,566m) José Luis Arrieta (Esp) Banesto; Col du Galibier (2,645m) José Luis Arrieta (Esp) Banesto; Col de Montgenèvre (1,860m) Richard Virenque (Fra) Polti; Colle del Sestriere (2,035m) Lance Armstrong (USA) US Postal			
Stage 10 Wed 14 Jul	Sestriere to l'Alpe d'Huez 160 finishers	220.5 km 6h42'31" 32.9 kph	Giuseppe Guerini (Ita) Telekom	~~Lance Armstrong (USA) US Postal~~
				Vacated
	Rated climbs: Col du Mont Cenis (2,083m) Dimitri Konychev (Rus) Mercatone Uno; Col de la Croix de Fer (2,067m) Stéphane Heulot (Fra) La Francaise des Jeux; l'Alpe d'Huez (1,860m) Giuseppe Guerini (Ita) Telekom			
Stage 11 Thu 15 Jul	Bourg-d'Oisans to Saint-Étienne 159 finishers	198.5 km 4h34'03" 43.5 kph	Ludo Dierckxsens (Bel) Lampre	~~Lance Armstrong (USA) US Postal~~
				Vacated
	Rated climbs: Col de Parménie (571m) Rik Verbrugghe (Bel) Lotto; Côte des Barges (372m) Dimitri Konychev (Rus) Mercatone Uno; Col de la Croix de Chaubouret (1,230m) Ludo Dierckxsens (Bel) Lampre			
Stage 12 Fri 16 Jul	Saint-Galmier to Saint-Flour 155 finishers	201.5 km 4h53'50" 41.1 kph	David Etxebarria (Esp) ONCE	~~Lance Armstrong (USA) US Postal~~
				Vacated
	Rated climbs: Col de la Croix de l'Homme Mort (1,163m) Massimiliano Lelli (Ita) Cofidis; Col des Pradeaux (1,196m) Massimiliano Lelli (Ita) Cofidis; Côte du Procureur (1,013m) Massimiliano Lelli (Ita) Cofidis; Col de Fix-Saint-Geneys (1,133m) Gianpaolo Mondeni (Ita) Cantina Tollo; Côte de Lestival (963m) Steve de Wolf (Bel) Cofidis; Côte de Védrines-Saint-Loup (1,117m) David Etxebarria Alkorta (Esp) ONCE			
Stage 13 Sat 17 Jul	Saint-Flour to Albi 154 finishers	236.5 km 5h52'45" 40.2 kph	Salvatore Commesso (Ita) Saeco	~~Lance Armstrong (USA) US Postal~~
				Vacated
	Rated climbs: Côte de Chaudes-Aigues (990m) Roland Meier (Sui) Cofidis; Côte de la Moissetie (598m) Mariano Piccoli (Ita) Lampre; Côte de la Croix du Broual (315m) Paolo Lanfranchi (Ita) Mapei; Côte de Cambargue (340m) Paolo Lanfranchi (Ita) Mapei; Côte de Duron (450m) Paolo Lanfranchi (Ita) Mapei; Côte de Compolibat (692m) Mariano Piccoli (Ita) Lampre; Côte du Port de la Besse (425m) José Vicente García (Esp) Banesto			
Stage 14 Sun 18 Jul	Castres to Saint-Gaudens 152 finishers	199 km 4h37'59" 43 kph	Dimitri Konychev (Rus) Mercatone Uno	~~Lance Armstrong (USA) US Postal~~
				Vacated
	Rated climbs: Côte de Fendeille (351m) Dimitri Konychev (Rus) Mercatone Uno; Côte du Vicaria (449m) Gianni Faresin (Ita) Mapei			

Stage-by-Stage Results for the 1999 Tour de France			Stage Winner	Maillot Jaune
Mon 19 Jul	Rest Day			
Stage 15 Tue 20 Jul	Saint-Gaudens to Piau-Engaly 143 finishers	173 km 5h19'49" 32.5 kph	Fernando Escartin (Esp) Kelme	~~Lance Armstrong (USA)~~ ~~US Postal~~
				Vacated
	Rated climbs: Col des Ares (797m) Mariano Piccoli (Ita) Lampre; Col de Menté (1,349m) Alberto Elli (Ita) Telekom; Col du Portillon (1,298m) Kurt van de Wouwer (Bel) Lotto; Col de Peyresourde (1,569m) Alberto Elli (Ita) Telekom; Col de Val-Louron (Col d'Azet) (1,580m) Fernando Escartin (Esp) Kelme; Piau-Engaly (1,800m) Fernando Escartin (Esp) Kelme			
Stage 16 Wed 21 Jul	Lannemezan to Pau 142 finishers	192 km 5h17'07" 36.3 kph	David Etxebarria (Esp) ONCE	~~Lance Armstrong (USA)~~ ~~US Postal~~
				Vacated
	Rated climbs: Col d'Aspin (1,489m) Mariano Piccoli (Ita) Lampre; Col du Tourmalet (2,115m) Alberto Elli (Ita) Telekom; Col du Soulor (1,474m) Pavel Tonkov (Rus) Mapei; Col d'Aubisque (1,709m) Alberto Elli (Ita) Telekom			
Stage 17 Thu 22 Jul	Mourenx to Bordeaux 141 finishers	200 km 4h22'29" 45.7 kph	Tom Steels (Bel) Mapei	~~Lance Armstrong (USA)~~ ~~US Postal~~
				Vacated
	Rated climbs: Côte d'Arthez-de-Béarn (188m) Elio Aggiano (Ita) Vitalicio Seguros			
Stage 18 Fri 23 Jul	Jonzac to Futuroscope 141 finishers	187 km 4h17'43" 43.5 kph	Gianpaolo Mondini (Ita) Cantina Tollo	~~Lance Armstrong (USA)~~
				Vacated
	Rated climbs: Côte de Pamproux (160m) Frédéric Bessy (Fra) Casino			
Stage 19 Sat 24 Jul	Futuroscope (ITT) 141 finishers	57 km 1h08'17" 50.1 kph	~~Lance Armstrong (USA)~~ ~~US Postal~~	~~Lance Armstrong (USA)~~ ~~US Postal~~
			Vacated	Vacated
Stage 20 Sun 25 Jul	Arpajon to Paris (Champs-Élysées) 141 finishers	143.5 km 3h37'39" 39.6 kph	Robbie McEwen (Aus) Rabobank	~~Lance Armstrong (USA)~~ ~~US Postal~~
				Vacated
	Rated climbs: Côte de Saint-Rémy-lès-Chevreuse (153m) Kurt van de Wouwer (Bel) Lotto; Côte de Châteaufort (190m) Richard Virenque (Fra) Polti			

Prize fund: 14,964,950 francs (first prize: 2,200,000 francs)

Final Classification

Place	Rider	Team	Time	Age
~~1~~	~~Lance Armstrong (USA)~~	~~US Postal~~	~~3,870 km~~ ~~91h32'16"~~ ~~40.276 kph~~	~~27~~
1	Vacated			
2	Alex Zülle (Sui)	ONCE	+ 7'37"	31
3	Fernando Escartin (Esp)	Kelme	+ 10'26"	31
4	Laurent Dufaux (Sui)	Saeco	+ 14'43"	30
5	Ángel Casero (Esp)	Festina	+ 15'11"	26
6	Abraham Olano (Esp)	ONCE	+ 16'47"	29
7	Daniele Nardello (Ita)	Mapei	+ 17'02"	26
8	Richard Virenque (Fra)	Polti	+ 17'28"	29
9	Wladimir Belli (Ita)	Festina	+ 17'37"	28
10	Andrea Peron (Ita)	ONCE	+ 23'10"	27

Lanterne Rouge

141	Jacky Durand (Fra)	Lotto	+ 3h19'09"	32

Points

	Erik Zabel (Ger)	Telekom		29

King of the Mountains

	Richard Virenque (Fra)	Polti		29

Youth

	Benoît Salmon (Fra)	Casino		25

Team

		Banesto		

Super Combativité

	Jacky Durand (Fra)	Lotto		32

Note: In 2012 Lance Armstrong was stripped of all his results dating back to 1 August, 1998, following an investigation by the United States Anti-Doping Agency into doping at his teams. None of his results in the 1999 Tour de France were re-awarded.

2000: Prometheus Unbound

The first Tour of the new millennium opened with a time trial too long to be called a prologue but too short to inflict serious damage on the main contenders, being just 16.5 kilometres around the Futuroscope theme park, situated near Poitiers, which had hosted the Tour on a number of occasions since its opening in 1987 and had now become part of the Amaury empire, at a cost of €42 million. David Millar (Cofidis) trumped the defending champion Lance Armstrong and took the stage, two seconds up on the American.

The next individual time trial not coming until the pre-penultimate day of the race, if Armstrong wanted to take control of the Tour before the mountains reared up, he would have to do so in the team time trial on Stage Four. He didn't, ONCE besting the US Postal squad by 26 seconds leaving Armstrong stuck in third on general classification, 24 seconds behind ONCE's Laurent Jalabert.

The American had to wait until Stage 10, the Tour's sole day in the Pyrenees, before he could assert himself. Appropriately for a man selling the story of a cancer victim restored to full health, that stage ended on the Hautacam, above the Roman Catholic shrine at Lourdes. In a day of Biblical weather, when thoughts turned to building an ark and sailing away, Armstrong rode away from the group of pre-race favourites, twiddling his low gear and pursuing the remnants of the day's early break. Only one of them could hold Armstrong off, Javier Otxoa (Kelme), who hit the base of the Hautacam 10 minutes up on the American and crossed the finish line 16 kilometres later 42 seconds ahead of him.

Armstrong may have been denied a stage win, but he wasn't denied the *maillot jaune*, taking a lead of 4'14" over Jan Ullrich (Deutsche Telekom), the rest five minutes and more back.

After a transition stage taking the riders to Revel, the Tour then transferred to Carpentras for an assault on Mont Ventoux. About four kilometres from the summit Marco Pantani (Mercatone Uno) escaped from the yellow jersey group, gunning for the stage win, any dreams he might have had of winning his second Tour title having already evaporated and he back to the man he used to be, a stage-bagger. Armstrong gave chase, bridging across to the Italian with indecent ease. The American then denied himself the stage win, not contesting the sprint for the summit.

This was the way of champions, to grant others the crumbs from the table. It was the way Indurain had won, the final *maillot jaune* being more important than the number of stages won along the way and the favours given eventually returning, when most needed. But Pantani was no minnow, he was a (former) champion himself. And when Armstrong impolitely told the media he had gifted the stage to the Italian, the American made an enemy in the *peloton*, when the gesture itself should have won him a friend.

And so Pantani set about upsetting Armstrong's victory parade around France (Ullrich had now slipped back to 4'55" and didn't look like he had much of a challenge in him). Three days later, on Stage 15's journey from Briançon to Courchevel, Pantani launched an attack 13 kilometres out from the summit finish. Armstrong went with him, as did Roberto Heras (Kelme). Three kilometres from the summit Pantani left his companions behind and soloed to victory, 50 seconds up on Armstrong and Heras. But once again it was Armstrong who was smiling: Ullrich had now slipped to 7'26" behind.

If no one else was going to defeat Armstrong it fell to the American to defeat himself, and he duly tried to do just that when the race resumed after a rest day, bonking in the closing kilometres of the Col de Joux-Plane. How had the American – famed for being meticulous in his preparation – allowed himself to run out of food? Blame Pantani. During the rest day the war of words between the

Lance Armstrong celebrates win number two. As with the other six, this would be stripped from him in 2012.

Italian and the American had escalated. So when Pantani attacked early into the stage – with 130 kilometres to go – the US Postals were ordered to pursue. Pantani may have been more than nine minutes down at the start of the stage, but this was no longer about the *maillot jaune*, this was personal. And the Postals did chase. For three hours. And when they hit the feed zone they were so intent on their pursuit that Armstrong didn't take on any food.

The pursuit wasn't without result: Pantani was eventually brought to heel, and then shelled out the back of the *peloton*. But the cost was high, for as soon as Armstrong cracked Ullrich started to put time into him, clawing his way back to 5'37" off yellow. After the individual time trial to Morzine, Armstrong pushed that back to 6'02" and sailed on into Paris for his second Tour victory.

* * * * *

As well as adding the Futuroscope theme park to the Amaury empire, 2000 saw Jean-Claude Killy exiting ASO, having helped double the value of its sporting properties since he was installed as head of the newly-formed ASO in 1992. Philippe Amaury now felt that Killy had grown too powerful, and so he paid him off, granting him a very generous golden parachute. Alain Krzentowski, who Killy had brought in with him to help grow ASO, was also shown the door, with an equally generous pay-off. Patrice Clerc was installed to lead the company that owned the Tour into the new millennium.

Stage-by-Stage Results for the 2000 Tour de France			Stage Winner	Maillot Jaune
Stage 1 Sat 1 Jul	Futuroscope (ITT) 177 finishers	16.5 km 19'03" 52 kph	David Millar (GBr) Cofidis	David Millar (GBr) Cofidis
	Rated climbs: Côte de Jaunay-Clan (125m) Marcel Wüst (Ger) Festina			
Stage 2 Sun 2 Jul	Futuroscope to Loudun 177 finishers	194 km 4h46'08" 40.7 kph	Tom Steels (Bel) Mapei	David Millar (GBr) Cofidis
Stage 3 Mon 3 Jul	Loudun to Nantes 177 finishers	161.5 km 3h37'51" 44.5 kph	Tom Steels (Bel) Mapei	David Millar (GBr) Cofidis
Stage 4 Tue 4 Jul	Nantes to Saint-Nazaire (TTT) 177 finishers	70 km 1h25'55" 48.9 kph	ONCE	Laurent Jalabert (Fra) ONCE

Stage-by-Stage Results for the 2000 Tour de France			Stage Winner	Maillot Jaune
Stage 5 Wed 5 Jul	Vannes to Vitré 177 finishers	202 km 4h19'05" 46.8 kph	Marcel Wüst (Ger) Festina	Laurent Jalabert (Fra) ONCE
	Rated climbs: Côte de Cadoudal (170m) Paolo Bettini (Ita) Mapei; Côte de Coët-Bugat Jacky Durand (Fra) Lotto; Côte de Calorguen Sébastien Demarbaix (Bel) Lotto; Mont du Chat (1,504m) Sébastien Demarbaix (Bel) Lotto			
Stage 6 Thu 6 Jul	Vitré to Tours 176 finishers	198.5 km 4h28'06" 44.4 kph	Leon van Bon (Ned) Rabobank	Alberto Elli (Ita) Deutsche Telekom
Stage 7 Fri 7 Jul	Tours to Limoges 174 finishers	205.5 km 5h11'41" 39.6 kph	Christophe Agnolutto (Fra) AG2R	Alberto Elli (Ita) Deutsche Telekom
	Rated climbs: Côte de Maison-Neuve Christophe Agnolutto (Fra) AG2R			
Stage 8 Sat 8 Jul	Limoges to Villeneuve-sur-Lot 171 finishers	203.5 km 4h22'14" 46.6 kph	Erik Dekker (Ned) Rabobank	Alberto Elli (Ita) Deutsche Telekom
	Rated climbs: Côte de Petit Puy-Mathieu Erik Dekker (Ned) Rabobank; Côte de Hautefort Erik Dekker (Ned) Rabobank; Côte de la Bachellerie Erik Dekker (Ned) Rabobank; Côte de Monflanquin Erik Dekker (Ned) Rabobank			
Stage 9 Sun 9 Jul	Agen to Dax 171 finishers	181 km 4h29'06" 40.4 kph	Paolo Bettini (Ita) Mapei	Alberto Elli (Ita) Deutsche Telekom
	Rated climbs: Côte de Montaud (1,687m) Paolo Bettini (Ita) Mapei			
Stage 10 Mon 10 Jul	Dax to Lourdes (Hautacam) 162 finishers	205 km 6h09'32" 33.3 kph	Javier Otxoa (Esp) Kelme	~~Lance Armstrong (USA) US Postal Service~~
				Vacated
	Rated climbs: Côte de Barcus (385m) Javier Otxoa (Esp) Kelme; Col de Marie-Blanque (1,035m) Javier Otxoa (Esp) Kelme; Col d'Aubisque (1,709m) Javier Otxoa (Esp) Kelme; Col du Soulor (1,474m) Javier Otxoa (Esp) Kelme; Hautacam (1,560m) Javier Otxoa (Esp) Kelme			
Stage 11 Tue 11 Jul	Bagnères-de-Bigorre to Revel 160 finishers	218.5 km 5h05'47" 42.9 kph	Erik Dekker (Ned) Rabobank	~~Lance Armstrong (USA) US Postal Service~~
				Vacated
	Rated climbs: Côte de Mauvezin (507m) Erik Dekker (Ned) Rabobank; Côte de Capvern Santiago Botero (Col) Kelme; Côte de Saint-Christaud Santiago Botero (Col) Kelme; Côte de Cabagnous Santiago Botero (Col) Kelme; Côte de Montesquieu Santiago Botero (Col) Kelme; Côte de Saint-Ferréol (363m) Santiago Botero (Col) Kelme			
Wed 12 Jul	Rest Day			
Stage 12 Thu 13 Jul	Carpentras to Mont Ventoux 151 finishers	149 km 4h15'11" 35 kph	Marco Pantani (Ita) Mercatone Uno	~~Lance Armstrong (USA) US Postal Service~~
				Vacated
	Rated climbs: Col de Murs (627m) Christophe Agnolutto (Fra) AG2R; Col de Javon Nico Mattan (Bel) Cofidis; Col de Notre Dame des Abeilles (996m) Nico Mattan (Bel) Cofidis; Côte de Mormoiron Nico Mattan (Bel) Cofidis; Mont Ventoux (1,909m) Marco Pantani (Ita) Mercatone Uno			
Stage 13 Fri 14 Jul	Avignon to Draguignan 145 finishers	185.5 km 4h03'02" 45.8 kph	José Vicente García (Esp) Banesto	~~Lance Armstrong (USA) US Postal Service~~
				Vacated
	Rated climbs: Côte de Saint-Hilaire Jean-Cyril Robin (Fra) Bonjour; Côte de Cadarache Didier Rous (Fra) Bonjour; Côte de l'Esparrus José Vicente García (Esp) Banesto			

Stage-by-Stage Results for the 2000 Tour de France			Stage Winner	Maillot Jaune
Stage 14 Sat 15 Jul	Draguignan to Briançon 141 finishers	249 km 7h56'13" 31.4 kph	Santiago Botero (Col) Kelme	~~Lance Armstrong (USA)~~ ~~US Postal Service~~
				Vacated
	Rated climbs: Côte de Canjuers (840m) Nico Mattan (Bel) Cofidis; Col d'Allos (2,250m) Pascal Hervé (Fra) Polti; Col de Vars (2,110m) Jens Heppner (Ger) Deutsche Telekom; Col d'Izoard (2,360m) Santiago Botero (Col) Kelme			
Stage 15 Sun 16 Jul	Briançon to Courchevel 137 finishers	173.5 km 5h34'46" 31.1 kph	Marco Pantani (Ita) Mercatone Uno	~~Lance Armstrong (USA)~~ ~~US Postal Service~~
				Vacated
	Rated climbs: Col du Galibier (2,645m) Pascal Hervé (Fra) Polti; Col de la Madeleine (2,000m) Massimiliano Lelli (Ita) Cofidis; Courchevel (2,004m) Marco Pantani (Ita) Mercatone Uno			
Mon 17 Jul	Rest Day			
Stage 16 Tue 18 Jul	Courchevel to Morzine 134 finishers	196 km 5h32'20" 35.4 kph	Richard Virenque (Fra) Polti	~~Lance Armstrong (USA)~~ ~~US Postal Service~~
				Vacated
	Rated climbs: Col des Saisies (1,650m) Marco Pantani (Ita) Mercatone Uno; Col des Aravis (1,498m) Marco Pantani (Ita) Mercatone Uno; Col de la Colombière (1,618m) Marco Pantani (Ita) Mercatone Uno; Côte de Châtillon-sur-Cluses (730m) Didier Rous (Fra) Bonjour; Col de Joux-Plane (1,700m) Richard Virenque (Fra) Polti			
Stage 17 Wed 19 Jul	Evian-les-Bains to Lausanne 130 finishers	155 km 3h24'53" 45.4 kph	Erik Dekker (Ned) Rabobank	~~Lance Armstrong (USA)~~ ~~US Postal Service~~
				Vacated
	Rated climbs: Col des Mosses (1,448m) Massimiliano Lelli (Ita) Cofidis; Côte de Lausanne Enrico Zaina (Ita) Mercatone Uno			
Stage 18 Thu 20 Jul	Lausanne to Freiburg im Breisgau 129 finishers	252 km 6h08'15" 41.1 kph	Salvatore Commesso (Ita) Saeco	~~Lance Armstrong (USA)~~ ~~US Postal Service~~
				Vacated
	Rated climbs: Côte de Oberer-Hauenstein Jean-Cyril Robin (Fra) Bonjour; Côte de Fullinsdorf Jens Voigt (Ger) Crédit Agricole; Côte de Waidhof (286m) Salvatore Commesso (Ita) Saeco Côte de Lörrach Salvatore Commesso (Ita) Saeco			
Stage 19 Fri 21 Jul	Freibourg Im Breisgau to Mulhouse (ITT) 129 finishers	59 km 1h05'01" 54.4 kph	~~Lance Armstrong (USA)~~ ~~US Postal Service~~	~~Lance Armstrong (USA)~~ ~~US Postal Service~~
			Vacated	Vacated
Stage 20 Sat 22 Jul	Belfort to Troyes 128 finishers	254.5 km 6h14'13" 40.8 kph	Erik Zabel (Ger) Deutsche Telekom	~~Lance Armstrong (USA)~~ ~~US Postal Service~~
				Vacated
	Rated climbs: Côte de Chagnon Richard Virenque (Fra) Polti; Côte de Chaumont François Simoni (Fra) Bonjour; Côte d'Alun Sébastien Hinault (Fra) Crédit Agricole			
Stage 21 Sun 23 Jul	Paris to Paris (Champs-Élysées) 127 finishers	138 km 3h12'36" 43 kph	Stefano Zanini (Ita) Mapei	~~Lance Armstrong (USA)~~ ~~US Postal Service~~
				Vacated

Prize fund: 15,500,500 francs (first prize: 2,200,000 francs)

Final Classification

Place	Rider	Team	Time	Age
1	~~Lance Armstrong (USA)~~	~~US Postal Service~~	~~3,662 km~~ ~~92h33'08"~~ ~~39.569 kph~~	~~28~~
1	Vacated			
2	Jan Ullrich (Ger)	Deutsche Telekom	+ 6'02"	26
3	Joseba Beloki (Esp)	Festina	+ 10'04"	26
4	Christophe Moreau (Fra)	Festina	+ 10'34"	29
5	Roberto Heras (Esp)	Kelme	+ 11'50"	26
6	Richard Virenque (Fra)	Polti	+ 13'26"	30
7	Santiago Botero (Col)	Kelme	+ 14'18"	27
8	Fernando Escartin (Esp)	Kelme	+ 17'21"	32
9	Francisco Mancebo (Esp)	Banesto	+ 18'09"	24
10	Daniele Nardello (Ita)	Mapei	+ 18'25"	27
Lanterne Rouge				
127	Olivier Perraudeau (Fra)	Bonjour	+ 3h46'37"	27
Points				
	Erik Zabel (Ger)	Deutsche Telekom		30
King of the Mountains				
	Santiago Botero (Col)	Kelme		27
Youth				
	Francisco Mancebo (Esp)	Banesto		24
Team				
		Kelme		
Super Combativité				
	Erik Dekker (Ned)	Rabobank		29

Note: In 2012 Lance Armstrong was stripped of all his results dating back to 1 August, 1998 following an investigation by the United States Anti-Doping Agency into doping at his teams. None of his results in the 2000 Tour de France were re-awarded.

2001: Victor

2000 had been a relatively quiet year for the sport as far as doping was concerned. The skeletons in the cupboard were still rattling as the fallout from the Festina *affaire* continued to rain, but generally things seemed to calm down. There were a few relatively minor scandals, but nothing that rocked the Tour. After the Tour, things began to get rough again. The Festina trial opened in the autumn. And Lance Armstrong and his US Postal team found themselves at the centre of an inquiry into their use of a product called Actovegin, a calf blood extract that some believed had properties similar to EPO.

The team denied using the product, that the only reason they had it was to treat a staff member's diabetes. Whether Actovegin counts as doping is confusing. It's a product that has had an on-and-off relationship with the banned list: at first it wasn't illegal, then it was, then it wasn't again. A French inquiry into the allegations never went anywhere, but it was another cloud over the American's claims to be winning clean. And even if Actovegin wasn't banned, surely the injection of calf blood extract was pushing the boundaries of acceptable behaviour in the pursuit of sporting excellence?

The bigger cloud, though, came when the journalist David Walsh tried to reveal that Armstrong had a working relationship with Michele Ferrari, the Italian doctor who had been part of Francesco Moser's medical team when he broke the Hour record in 1984 and who, since then, had been involved with various teams and riders in the professional *peloton*. Ferrari was the man who, in 1994, compared the dangers of EPO with orange juice. He was the doctor behind Tony Rominger breaking the Hour record in 1994. Ferrari was a doctor with a reputation.

Knowing that Walsh was onto the story, Armstrong outed himself, tried to take control of the narrative by revealing that he had first met the Italian doctor in 1995 and that the two were collaborating for a tilt at the Hour record. Conducting his own Q&A on his relationship with the Italian doctor Armstrong asked and answered the key questions: "Is it questionable? Perhaps. Has Lance Armstrong ever tested positive? No. Has Lance Armstrong been tested? A lot." And in an interview ahead of the Tour Armstrong continued with his much-tested-never-positive line; he revealed that he'd been subjected to anti-doping tests as recently at the recent Tour de Suisse and been found clean.

And Armstrong was now being cleared of EPO use, the authorities finally introducing a test for the drug that had come to the sport's notice more than a dozen years before and had been banned since 1991. The new EPO test was implemented during the spring Classics. And immediately it started getting results. Roland Meier (Team Coast) was positive at the Flèche Wallonne. Bo Hamburger (CSC/Tiscali) was positive from an out-of-competition test the next day, Sergio Barbero (Lampre) and Laurent Chotard (Mercury/ Viatel) at the pre-Giro leg-loosener, the Tour de Romandie. Pascal Hervé (Alexia), Riccardo Forconi (Mercatone Uno) and Dario Frigo (Fassa Bortolo) tested positive during the Giro d'Italia, and Txema del Olmo (Euskaltel/Euskadi), tripped positives at the Tour de France. (Not all of the riders who tripped positives ended up receiving bans, the EPO test having been implemented quickly and the Court of Arbitration for Sport (CAS) dismissing some of the cases.)

Out of 170 tests conducted during the Tour – an average of seven a day – Del Olmo's was the only positive. The UCI concluded that "the problem of EPO no longer influences cycling at the highest level." All that really happened, of course, was that riders modified their use of EPO and backed it up with blood transfusions, which some riders – including Armstrong and his US Postal team-mates – had already turned to the year before.

Armstrong's attempts to put a positive spin on his relationship with Ferrari didn't help much, many expressing their belief that such a relationship raised many questions. Greg LeMond, whose record as the most successful American cyclist at the Tour Armstrong was now challenging, said that he was devastated when he heard the news and disappointed in Armstrong. Jean-Marie Leblanc, still the man in charge of the Tour, was equally unhappy, but said that both Armstrong and Ferrari deserved the benefit of the doubt, until evidence to the contrary could be produced.

As well as questions being asked about Armstrong's relationship with Ferrari the sport had to deal with more judicial investigations and police raids, this time at the Giro d'Italia, with NAS officers hitting the race in Sanremo and the Giro serving up a repeat of the 1998 Tour.

* * * * *

In the shadow of all this, the 2001 Tour went ahead.

Having had just one Pyrenean stage in 2000, for 2001 the Tour served up just one Alpine stage – Alpe d'Huez – which didn't come until the tenth stage of the race. And – once again denied victory on the opening day of the race – Armstrong had to wait until the mountains arrived before he won a stage. But that would be done without donning the *maillot jaune*. For on the eighth stage of the race, Colmar to Pontarlier, a large group of riders got away and put 35 minutes into the *peloton*.

Most were no challengers for the general classification and had already ceded significant time before the race arrived in Colmar. But two riders profited and profited big. Stuart O'Grady (Crédit Agricole) donned the *maillot jaune* and was trailed in the general classification by François Simon (Bonjour), 4'32" back. The next best rider was more than 20 minutes off the pace, with Armstrong 35'19" in arrears.

So come the Alpe Armstrong had a mountain to climb. And set about climbing it by letting his rivals think he was having a repeat of the Col de Joux-Plane the year before and was running on empty. With the American gurning his way up the Glandon, his rivals fell for his deceit, and wore themselves out before the race reached the foot of the Alpe – where Armstrong attacked. Scorching the climb he took the stage, putting just shy of two minutes into Jan Ullrich (Deutsche Telekom). In the race for the yellow jersey Armstrong was still 20 minutes off the pace. That yellow jersey had now passed from O'Grady to Simon. Fittingly, Simon was the younger brother of Pascal Simon, the man who donned the *maillot jaune* in the 1983 Tour only to break his shoulder blade and, after riding on for several days, have to abandon on the road to Alpe d'Huez, still in yellow.

The Alpe was followed by the first major time trial, 32 kilometres between Grenoble and Chamrousse. This Armstrong bossed, putting a minute into Ullrich, his nearest rival, and climbing up to 13'07" off the yellow jersey, still being worn by Simon. Now the race was heading back into the Pyrenees, scene of Pascal Simon's crash all those years ago.

In the Pyrenees, Armstrong finally donned the *maillot jaune* as Simon finally weakened and fell down the general classification. The American took another minute out of Ullrich on the stage to Saint-Lary-Soulan and was 3'54" clear of his nearest GC rival, Andrei Kivilev (Cofidis), with Ullrich back in fourth, 5'13" down.

Armstrong added his fourth stage win, triumphing in the final time trial, during which Ullrich conceded more than a minute but climbed up to second. Armstrong's Tour win was sealed and, for the third year in a row it was an American in Paris taking the applause of the crowds.

Stage-by-Stage Results for the 2001 Tour de France			Stage Winner	Maillot Jaune
Prologue Sat 7 Jul	Dunkerque (ITT) 189 finishers	8.2 km 9'20" 52.7 kph	Christophe Moreau (Fra) Festina	Christophe Moreau (Fra) Festina
Stage 1 Sun 8 Jul	Saint-Omer to Boulogne-sur-Mer 188 finishers	194.5 km 4h55'15" 39.5 kph	Erik Zabel (Ger) Deutsche Telekom	Erik Zabel (Ger) Deutsche Telekom
	Rated climbs: Côte de Desvres (90m) Jacky Durand (Fra) Française Des Jeux; Côte du Cap Gris-Nez (116m) Jacky Durand (Fra) Française Des Jeux			
Stage 2 Mon 9 Jul	Calais to Anvers 187 finishers	218.5 km 4h35'47" 47.5 kph	Marc Wauters (Bel) Rabobank	Marc Wauters (Bel) Rabobank
Stage 3 Tue 10 Jul	Anvers to Seraing 186 finishers	198.5 km 4h34'32" 43.4 kph	Erik Zabel (Ger) Deutsche Telekom	Stuart O'Grady (Aus) Crédit Agricole
	Rated climbs: Côte de Mont-Theux (330m) Nicolas Jalabert (Fra) CSC; Côte des Forges Benoît Salmon (Fra) AG2R; Côte de Sart-Tilman-Tilff Benoît Salmon (Fra) AG2R			

Stage-by-Stage Results for the 2001 Tour de France			Stage Winner	Maillot Jaune
Stage 4 Wed 11 Jul	Huy to Verdun 185 finishers	215 km 5h17'49" 40.6 kph	Laurent Jalabert (Fra) CSC	Stuart O'Grady (Aus) Crédit Agricole
	Rated climbs: Côte de Celles Patrice Halgand (Fra) Jean Delatour; Côte de la Marquisette Patrice Halgand (Fra) Jean Delatour; Ave-et-Auffe Patrice Halgand (Fra) Jean Delatour; Côte de Redu (420m) Patrice Halgand (Fra) Jean Delatour			
Stage 5 Thu 12 Jul	Verdun to Bar-le-Duc (TTT) 185 finishers	67 km 1h21'32" 49.3 kph	Crédit Agricole	Stuart O'Grady (Aus) Crédit Agricole
Stage 6 Fri 13 Jul	Commercy to Strasbourg 183 finishers	211.5 km 4h50'39" 43.7 kph	Ján Kirsipuu (Est) AG2R	Stuart O'Grady (Aus) Crédit Agricole
	Rated climbs: Côte de Void-Vacon (350m) Patrice Halgand (Fra) Jean Delatour; Côte de Chapelotte (446m) Laurent Brochard (Fra) Jean Delatour; Mont Donon (727m) Laurent Brochard (Fra) Jean Delatour			
Stage 7 Sat 14 Jul	Strasbourg to Colmar 177 finishers	162.5 km 4h06'04" 39.6 kph	Laurent Jalabert (Fra) CSC	Jens Voigt (Ger) Crédit Agricole
	Rated climbs: Col du Kreuzweg (768m) Alberto López (Esp) Euskaltel; Col de Fouchy (603m) Alberto López (Esp) Euskaltel; Col d'Adelspach (850m) Laurent Jalabert (Fra) CSC; Col du Calvaire (1,144m) Laurent Jalabert (Fra) CSC; Collet du Linge (983m) Laurent Jalabert (Fra) CSC			
Stage 8 Sun 15 Jul	Colmar to Pontarlier 175 finishers	222.5 km 4h59'18" 44.6 kph	Erik Dekker (Ned) Rabobank	Stuart O'Grady (Aus) Crédit Agricole
	Rated climbs: Côte de Beaucourt (440m) Ludo Dierckxens (Bel) Lampre; Côte de Saint-Hippolyte (786m) Ludovic Turpin (Fra) AG2R			
Stage 9 Mon 16 Jul	Pontarlier to Aix-les-Bains 173 finishers	185 km 3h57'48" 46.7 kph	Sergei Ivanov (Rus) Fassa Bortolo	Stuart O'Grady (Aus) Crédit Agricole
	Rated climbs: Côte de Rousses (1,060m) David Etxebarria (Esp) Euskaltel; Côte de Pralon (469m) Bradley McGee (Aus) Française Des Jeux; Côte de Bossy (520m) David Etxebarria (Esp) Euskaltel			
Stage 10 Tue 17 Jul	Aix-les-Bains to l'Alpe d'Huez 166 finishers	209 km 6h23'47" 32.7 kph	~~Lance Armstrong (USA)~~ ~~US Postal~~ Vacated	François Simon (Fra) Bonjour
	Rated climbs: Col du Frêne (950m) Eladio Jiménez (Esp) Banesto; Col de la Madeleine (2,000m) Laurent Roux (Fra) Jean Delatour; Col du Glandon (1,924m) Laurent Roux (Fra) Jean Delatour; l'Alpe d'Huez (1,860m) Lance Armstrong (USA) US Postal			
Stage 11 Wed 18 Jul	Grenoble to Chamrousse (ITT) 166 finishers	32 km 1h07'27" 28.5 kph	~~Lance Armstrong (USA)~~ ~~US Postal~~ Vacated	François Simon (Fra) Bonjour
	Rated climbs: Chamrousse (1,730m) Lance Armstrong (USA) US Postal			
Thu 19 Jul	Rest Day			

Stage-by-Stage Results for the 2001 Tour de France			Stage Winner	Maillot Jaune
Stage 12 Fri 20 Jul	Perpignan to Ax-les-Thermes 160 finishers	166.5 km 5h03'34" 32.9 kph	Félix Cárdenas (Col) Kelme	François Simon (Fra) Bonjour
	Rated climbs: Col de Coudons (883m) Paolo Bettini (Ita) Mapei; Col des Sept Frères (1,253m) Paolo Bettini (Ita) Mapei; Col du Chioula (1,431m) Paolo Bettini (Ita) Mapei; Ax-Les-Thermes (Plateau de Bonascre) (1,375m) Félix Cárdenas (Col) Kelme			
Stage 13 Sat 21 Jul	Foix to Saint-Lary-Soulan 153 finishers	194 km 5h44'22" 33.8 kph	~~Lance Armstrong (USA)~~ ~~US Postal~~	~~Lance Armstrong (USA)~~ ~~US Postal~~
			Vacated	Vacated
	Rated climbs: Col de Portet d'Aspet (1,069m) Laurent Roux (Fra) Jean Delatour; Col de Menté (1,349m) Laurent Jalabert (Fra) CSC; Col du Portillon (1,298m) Laurent Jalabert (Fra) CSC; Col de Peyresourde (1,569m) Laurent Jalabert (Fra) CSC; Col de Val-Louron (Col d'Azet) (1,580m) Laurent Jalabert (Fra) CSC; Saint-Lary-Soulan (Pla d'Adet) (1,680m) Lance Armstrong (USA) US Postal			
Stage 14 Sun 22 Jul	Tarbes to Luz-Ardiden 152 finishers	144.5 km 4h24'30" 32.8 kph	Roberto Laiseka (Esp) Euskaltel	~~Lance Armstrong (USA)~~ ~~US Postal~~
				Vacated
	Rated climbs: Haut-de-La-Côte (799m) Jens Voigt (Ger) Crédit Agricole; Côte de Mauvezin (507m) Patrice Halgand (Fra) Jean Delatour; Côte de Capvern-les-Bains Jean-Cyril Robin (Fra) Bonjour; Col d'Aspin (1,489m) Bobby Julich (USA) Crédit Agricole; Col du Tourmalet (2,115m) Sven Montgomery (Sui) La Francaise des Jeux; Luz-Ardiden (1,715m) Roberto Laiseka (Esp) Euskaltel			
Mon 23 Jul	Rest Day			
Stage 15 Tue 24 Jul	Pau to Lavaur 151 finishers	232.5 km 5h16'21" 44.1 kph	Rik Verbrugghe (Bel) Lotto	~~Lance Armstrong (USA)~~ ~~US Postal~~
				Vacated
	Rated climbs: Côte de la Tricherie (351m) Alexander Vinokourov (Kaz) Deutsche Telekom; Côte de Lamayou (340m) Piotr Wadecki (Pol) Domo; Côte de Puntous de Laguian (260m) Laurent Brochard (Fra) Jean Delatour; Côte de Bidalon (270m) Michael Boogerd (Ned) Rabobank			
Stage 16 Wed 25 Jul	Castelsarrasin to Sarran 146 finishers	227.5 km 5h27'11" 41.7 kph	Jens Voigt (Ger) Crédit Agricole	~~Lance Armstrong (USA)~~ ~~US Postal~~
				Vacated
	Rated climbs: Côte de Lostanges (500m) Luis Pérez (Esp) Festina; Côte de Saint-Adrian (345m) Luis Pérez (Esp) Festina			
Stage 17 Thu 26 Jul	Brive to Montluçon 145 finishers	194 km 4h13'36" 45.9 kph	Serge Baguet (Bel) Lotto	~~Lance Armstrong (USA)~~ ~~US Postal~~
				Vacated
	Rated climbs: Côte de la Forêt de la Feuillade (670m) Benoît Salmon (Fra) AG2R; Côte de Rozeille (534m) Benoît Salmon (Fra) AG2R			
Stage 18 Fri 27 Jul	Montluçon to Saint-Amand-Montrond (ITT) 145 finishers	61 km 1h14'16" 49.3 kph	~~Lance Armstrong (USA)~~ ~~US Postal~~	~~Lance Armstrong (USA)~~ ~~US Postal~~
			Vacated	Vacated
Stage 19 Sat 28 Jul	Orléans to Évry 144 finishers	149.5 km 3h12'27" 46.6 kph	Erik Zabel (Ger) Deutsche Telekom	~~Lance Armstrong (USA)~~ ~~US Postal~~
				Vacated
	Rated climbs: Côte de Gironville (113m) Laurent Roux (Fra) Jean Delatour			

Stage-by-Stage Results for the 2001 Tour de France			Stage Winner	Maillot Jaune
Stage 20 Sun 29 Jul	Corbeil-Essonnes to Paris (Champs-Élysées) 144 finishers	160.5 km 3h57'28" 40.6 kph	Ján Svorada (Cze) Lampre	~~Lance Armstrong (USA)~~ ~~US Postal~~
				Vacated
	Rated climbs: Côte de Gif-sur-Yvette (153m) Rubens Bertogliati (Sui) Lampre			

Prize fund: 16,470,750 francs (first prize: 2,200,000 francs)

Final Classification				
Place	**Rider**	**Team**	**Time**	**Age**
~~1~~	~~Lance Armstrong (USA)~~	~~US Postal~~	~~3,458 km~~ ~~86h17'28"~~ ~~40.070 kph~~	29
1	Vacated			
2	Jan Ullrich (Ger)	Deutsche Telekom	+ 6'44"	27
3	Joseba Beloki (Esp)	ONCE	+ 9'05"	27
4	Andrei Kivilev (Kaz)	Cofidis	+ 9'53"	27
5	Igor González de Galdeano (Esp)	ONCE	+ 13'28"	27
6	François Simon (Fra)	Bonjour	+ 17'22"	32
7	Óscar Sevilla (Esp)	Kelme	+ 18'30"	24
8	Santiago Botero (Col)	Kelme	+ 20'55"	28
9	Marcos Serrano (Esp)	ONCE	+ 21'45"	28
10	Michael Boogerd (Ned)	Rabobank	+ 22'38"	29
Lanterne Rouge				
144	Jimmy Casper (Fra)	La Francaise des Jeux	+ 3h52'17"	23
Points				
	Erik Zabel (Ger)	Deutsche Telekom		31
King of the Mountains				
	Laurent Jalabert (Fra)	CSC		32
Youth				
	Óscar Sevilla (Esp)	Kelme		24
Team				
		Kelme		
Super Combativité				
	Laurent Jalabert (Fra)	CSC		32

Note: In 2012 Lance Armstrong was stripped of all his results dating back to 1 August, 1998 following an investigation by the United States Anti-Doping Agency into doping at his teams. None of his results in the 2001 Tour de France were re-awarded.

2002: Monstering The Tour

Having had to wait so long to wear the yellow jersey in 2001, Lance Armstrong (US Postal Service) donned the *maillot jaune* on the opening day of the 2002 Tour de France. And then gave it away, not reclaiming it until the race reached the mountains on Stage 11.

Following the now familiar script, the American crushed his opponents on the first day in the mountains, Pau to La Mongie. Armstrong was in yellow, Joseba Beloki (ONCE) was in second place, 1'21" back, Igor González de Galdeano – Beloki's team-mate and the man who warmed up the *maillot jaune* for Armstrong – in third at 1'48".

The next day Armstrong added the second Pyrenean stage, Lannemezan to Plateau de Beille and another minute on his rivals.

Stage 14 saw the *peloton* summit the Ventoux, where Richard Virenque (Domo/Farm Frites) – still the favourite of French housewives, the 1998 Tour notwithstanding – took the win, Armstrong not even bothering to be close enough to him to get into an argument with another rider over gifts. Armstrong now led Beloki by 4'21" and it was Raimondas Rumšas (Lampre) who was in third, at 6'39". The American was being allowed coast to his fourth Tour title.

And coast he continued to do. Win number four was the easiest of the lot so far. This, though, was a win in which Armstrong didn't have to beat Jan Ullrich, the Telekom rider sidelined with a knee injury and, in June, having tripped a positive for amphetamines – Ecstasy – following an out-of-competition test.

Almost as soon as the Tour ended the wife of the man on the bottom step of the podium, Raimondas Rumšas, was arrested on the Franco-Italian border with a car full of performance-enhancing drugs. She claimed they were for personal use. Her husband was safe, for out of the 141 anti-doping tests conducted during the Tour not a single one tripped a positive

Stage-by-Stage Results for the 2002 Tour de France			Stage Winner	Maillot Jaune
Prologue Sat 6 Jul	Luxembourg (ITT) 189 finishers	7 km 9'08" 45.9 kph	~~Lance Armstrong (USA)~~ ~~US Postal Service~~	~~Lance Armstrong (USA)~~ ~~US Postal Service~~
			Vacated	Vacated
Stage 1 Sun 7 Jul	Luxembourg to Luxembourg 189 finishers	192.5 km 4h49'16" 39.9 kph	Rubens Bertogliati (Sui) Lampre	Rubens Bertogliati (Sui) Lampre
	Rated climbs: Côte de Hoscheid Stéphane Bergès (Fra) AG2R; Côte de Vianden (360m) Christophe Mengin (Fra) FDJeux.com; Côte de Wormeldange (200m) Christophe Mengin (Fra) FDJeux.com; Côte de Hostert Laurent Lefèvre (Fra) Jean Delatour			
Stage 2 Mon 8 Jul	Luxembourg to Sarrebrück 189 finishers	181 km 4h19'51" 41.8 kph	Óscar Freire (Esp) Mapei	Rubens Bertogliati (Sui) Lampre
	Rated climbs: Côte de Perl Stéphane Bergès (Fra) AG2R; Côte d'Alsweiler-Heid Stéphane Bergès (Fra) AG2R			
Stage 3 Tue 9 Jul	Metz to Reims 189 finishers	174.5 km 4h13'37" 41.3 kph	Robbie McEwen (Aus) Lotto	Erik Zabel (Ger) Deutsche Telekom
	Rated climbs: Côte de Gravelotte Christophe Mengin (Fra) FDJeux.com; Côte de la Biesme (250m) Franck Rénier (Fra) Bonjour			
Stage 4 Wed 10 Jul	Épernay to Château-Thierry (TTT) 189 finishers	67.5 km 1h19'49" 50.7 kph	ONCE	Igor González de Galdeano (Esp) ONCE
Stage 5 Thu 11 Jul	Soissons to Rouen 187 finishers	195 km 4h13'33" 46.1 kph	Ján Kirsipuu (Est) AG2R	Igor González de Galdeano (Esp) ONCE
Stage 6 Fri 12 Jul	Forges-les-Eaux to Alençon 185 finishers	199.5 km 4h23'07" 45.5 kph	Erik Zabel (Ger) Deutsche Telekom	Igor González de Galdeano (Esp) ONCE
	Rated climbs: Côte du Val d'Any (125m) Christophe Mengin (Fra) FDJeux.com; Côte de Saint-Vigor (136m) Christophe Mengin (Fra) FDJeux.com			
Stage 7 Sat 13 Jul	Bagnoles-de-l'Orne to Avranches 184 finishers	176 km 4h10'56" 42.1 kph	Bradley McGee (Aus) FDJeux.com	Igor González de Galdeano (Esp) ONCE
	Rated climbs: Côte du Mont-Pinçon (366m) Anthony Morin (Fra) Crédit Agricole; Col de l'Embranchement (La Chapelle-Uree) (210m) Leon van Bon (Ned) Domo			

Stage-by-Stage Results for the 2002 Tour de France			Stage Winner	Maillot Jaune
Stage 8 Sun 14 Jul	Saint-Martin-de-Landelles to Plouay 182 finishers	217.5 km 4h36'52" 47.1 kph	Karsten Kroon (Ned) Rabobank	Igor González de Galdeano (Esp) ONCE
	Rated climbs: Côte de Becherel (142m) Ruslan Ivanov (Mol) Alessio; Côte de Kervalan (140m) Raivis Belohvošciks (Lat) Lampre; Côte de Ty-Marrec (129m) Raivis Belohvošciks (Lat) Lampre			
Stage 9 Mon 15 Jul	Lanester to Lorient (ITT) 182 finishers	52 km 1h02'18" 50.1 kph	Santiago Botero (Col) Kelme	Igor González de Galdeano (Esp) ONCE
Tue 16 Jul	Rest Day			
Stage 10 Wed 17 Jul	Bazas to Pau 181 finishers	147 km 3h00'15" 48.9 kph	Patrice Halgand (Fra) Jean Delatour	Igor González de Galdeano (Esp) ONCE
	Rated climbs: Côte d'Eugénie-les-Bains (140m) Patrice Hagland (Fra) Jean Delatour; Côte de Boucoue (163m) Patrice Hagland (Fra) Jean Delatour; Côte d'Auga (238m) Patrice Hagland (Fra) Jean Delatour			
Stage 11 Thu 18 Jul	Pau to La Mongie 177 finishers	158 km 4h21'57" 36.2 kph	~~Lance Armstrong (USA)~~ ~~US Postal Service~~ Vacated	~~Lance Armstrong (USA)~~ ~~US Postal Service~~ Vacated
	Rated climbs: Côte de Louvié-Juzon (501m) Emmanuel Magnien (Fra) Bonjour; Col d'Aubisque (1,709m) Laurent Jalabert (Fra) CSC; La Mongie (1,715m) Lance Armstrong (USA) US Postal Service			
Stage 12 Fri 19 Jul	Lannemezan to Plateau de Beille 166 finishers	199.5 km 6h00'29" 33.2 kph	~~Lance Armstrong (USA)~~ ~~US Postal Service~~ Vacated	~~Lance Armstrong (USA)~~ ~~US Postal Service~~ Vacated
	Rated climbs: Col de Menté (1,349m) Christophe Oriol (Fra) AG2R; Col de Portet d'Aspet (1,069m) Laurent Jalabert (Fra) CSC; Col de la Core (1,395m) Laurent Jalabert (Fra) CSC; Col de Port (1,249m) Laurent Jalabert (Fra) CSC; Plateau de Beille (1,780m) Lance Armstrong (USA) US Postal Service			
Stage 13 Sat 20 Jul	Lavelanet to Béziers 164 finishers	171 km 4h08'18" 41.3 kph	David Millar (GBr) Cofidis	~~Lance Armstrong (USA)~~ ~~US Postal Service~~ Vacated
	Rated climbs: Col de Montségur (1,059m) Laurent Jalabert (Fra) CSC; Col de la Badourade (655m) Laurent Jalabert (Fra) CSC; Col de Saint-Benoît (615m) Laurent Jalabert (Fra) CSC			
Stage 14 Sun 21 Jul	Lodève to Mont Ventoux 163 finishers	221 km 5h43'26" 38.6 kph	Richard Virenque (Fra) Domo	~~Lance Armstrong (USA)~~ ~~US Postal Service~~ Vacated
	Rated climbs: Mont Ventoux (1,909m) Richard Virenque (Fra) Domo			
Mon 22 Jul	Rest Day			

Stage-by-Stage Results for the 2002 Tour de France			Stage Winner	Maillot Jaune
Stage 15 Tue 23 Jul	Vaison-la-Romaine to Les Deux Alpes 162 finishers	226.5 km 5h55'16" 38.3 kph	Santiago Botero (Col) Kelme	~~Lance Armstrong (USA)~~ ~~US Postal Service~~
				Vacated
	Rated climbs: Col de Prémol (963m) Stantiago Botero (Col) Kelme; Col de Grimone (1,318m) Axel Merckx (Bel) Domo; Col de la Croix Haute (1,179m) Axel Merckx (Bel) Domo; Col du Banchet (900m) Axel Merckx (Bel) Domo; Côte de Ponsonas (750m) Axel Merckx (Bel) Domo; Col d'Ornon (1,367m) Axel Merckx (Bel) Domo; Les Deux-Alpes (1,644m) Stantiago Botero (Col) Kelme			
Stage 16 Wed 24 Jul	Les Deux Alpes to La Plagne 156 finishers	179.5 km 5h48'29" 30.9 kph	Michael Boogerd (Ned) Rabobank	~~Lance Armstrong (USA)~~ ~~US Postal Service~~
				Vacated
	Rated climbs: Col du Galibier (2,645m) Stantiago Botero (Col) Kelme; Col de la Madeleine (2,000m) Michael Boogerd (Ned) Rabobank; La Plagne (1,970m) Michael Boogerd (Ned) Rabobank			
Stage 17 Thu 25 Jul	Aime to Cluses 153 finishers	142 km 4h02'27" 35.1 kph	Dario Frigo (Ita) Tacconi Sport	~~Lance Armstrong (USA)~~ ~~US Postal Service~~
				Vacated
	Rated climbs: Cormet de Roselend (1,968m) Mario Aerts (Bel) Lotto; Col des Saisies (1,650m) Mario Aerts (Bel) Lotto; Col des Aravis (1,498m) Mario Aerts (Bel) Lotto; Col de Colombière (1,618m) Mario Aerts (Bel) Lotto			
Stage 18 Fri 26 Jul	Cluses to Bourg-en-Bresse 153 finishers	176.5 km 4h28'28" 39.4 kph	Thor Hushovd (Nor) Crédit Agricole	~~Lance Armstrong (USA)~~ US Postal Service
				Vacated
	Rated climbs: Côte des Bois de Serves (830m) Leon van Bon (Ned) Domo; Côte de Marlioz (580m) Erik Dekker (Ned) Rabobank; Côte de la Sémine (548m) Jakob Piil (Den) CSC; Col de Richemont (1,060m) Nicki Sørensen (Den) CSC; Col de la Cheminée (925m) Jakob Piil (Den) CSC; Côte de Giriat (685m) Jakob Piil (Den) CSC; Col du Berthiand (780m) Jörg Jaksche (Ger) ONCE			
Stage 19 Sat 27 Jul	Régnié Durette to Mâcon (ITT) 153 finishers	50 km 1h03'50" 47 kph	~~Lance Armstrong (USA)~~ ~~US Postal Service~~	~~Lance Armstrong (USA)~~ ~~US Postal Service~~
			Vacated	Vacated
	Rated climbs: Côte du Fût d'Avenas (635m) Raimondas Rumšas (Lit) Lampre			
Stage 20 Sun 28 Jul	Melun to Paris (Champs-Élysées) 153 finishers	144 km 3h30'47" 41 kph	Robbie McEwen (Aus) Lotto	~~Lance Armstrong (USA)~~ ~~US Postal Service~~
				Vacated

Prize fund: 2,664,035 euro (first prize: 335,390 euro)

Final Classification

Place	Rider	Team	Time	Age
~~1~~	~~Lance Armstrong (USA)~~	~~US Postal Service~~	~~3,278 km~~ ~~82h05'12"~~ ~~39.920 kph~~	~~30~~
1	Vacated			
2	Joseba Beloki (Esp)	ONCE	+ 7'17"	28
3	Raimondas Rumšas (Lit)	Lampre	+ 8'17"	30
4	Santiago Botero (Col)	Kelme	+ 13'10"	29
5	Igor González de Galdeano (Esp)	ONCE	+ 13'54"	28
6	José Azevedo (Por)	ONCE	+ 15'44"	28
7	Francisco Mancebo (Esp)	iBanesto.com	+ 16'05"	26
8	~~Levi Leipheimer (USA)~~ (1)	Rabobank	+ 17'11"	~~28~~
8	Vacated			
9	Roberto Heras (Esp)	US Postal Service	+ 17'12"	28
10	Carlos Sastre (Esp)	CSC	+ 19'05"	27
Lanterne Rouge				
153	Igor Flores (Esp)	Euskaltel	+ 3h35'52"	28
Points				
	Robbie McEwen (Aus)	Lotto		30
King of the Mountains				
	Laurent Jalabert (Fra)	CSC		33
Youth				
	Ivan Basso (Ita)	Fassa Bortolo		24
Team				
		ONCE		
Super Combativité				
	Laurent Jalabert (Fra)	CSC		33

Note: In 2012 Lance Armstrong was stripped of all his results dating back to 1 August, 1998 following an investigation by the United States Anti-Doping Agency into doping at his teams. None of his results in the 2002 Tour de France were re-awarded.
(1) During the USADA investigation Levi Leipheimer admitted his doping and was stripped of his results.

2003: Centennial Celebrations

One hundred summers had passed since the Tour de France was born, and the Tour celebrated. Nantes, Bordeaux, Toulouse, Marseille, Lyon, and Paris – the original host towns, in 1903 – were all put on the itinerary for a race that stayed within France's borders.

In the 50 years since the Tour celebrated its half-century – by which time 28 men had won the race – another 25 had added their names to the Tour's roll of honour. At the time that half-century was celebrated, nine Tour champions were in the grave. By 2003 they were joined by another 22: Maurice Garin (winner 1903) died in 1957; Fausto Coppi (1949 and 1952) in 1960; Gustave Garrigou (1911) in 1963; Firmin Lambot (1919 and 1922) and Hugo Koblet (1951) in 1964; Odile Defraye (1912) in 1965; Sylvère Maes (1936 and 1939) in 1966; Léon Scieur (1921) in 1969; Philippe Thys (1913) in 1971; Georges Speicher (1933) in 1978; Lucien Buysse (1926), Gastone Nencini (1960), André Leducq (1930 and 1932), and Jean Robic (1947) in 1980; Romain Maes (1935), Louison Bobet (1953, 1954, 1955) and Antonin Magne (1931 and 1934) in 1983; Nicolas Frantz (1927 and 1928) in 1985; Jacques Anquetil (1957, 1961, 1962, 1963, 1964) in 1987; Luis Ocaña (1973) in 1994; Roger Lapébie (1937) in 1996; and Gino Bartali (1938, 1948) in 2000. Dead also was Jacques Goddet, who passed in 2000. Throughout the course of the race the Tour paid homage to as many of its fallen champions as it could.

As well as celebrating its past, the Tour also had the future to look forward to, with Lance Armstrong looking set to join the five-times club, alongside Jacques Anquetil, Eddy Merckx, Bernard Hinault and Miguel Indurain. That he would join them seemed like an odds-on bet; he had had no challengers the year before. But, returned from his time on the naughty step and with his knee fully recovered was Jan Ullrich. Despite problems with his team – he had left Telekom and joined Team Coast, only for Coast to collapse, and Team Bianchi had to step in and rescue him – the German was flying. In the prologue he drew first blood by putting five seconds into Armstrong (US Postal).

Denied the *maillot jaune* in the prologue – it was taken by FDJeux. com's Bradley McGee – Armstrong didn't even land in yellow on the first day in the mountains: Stage Seven, Lyon to Morzine. Richard Virenque (Quick Step/Davitamon) surprised by taking both the stage and the yellow jersey, 2'37" clear of Armstrong, who was now up to second with Ullrich having slipped back to 3'15" in arrears.

Armstrong did assert himself the next day, on Alpe d'Huez, relieving Virenque of the *maillot jaune*, with a 40-second lead over Joseba Beloki (ONCE), 1'10 over Iban Mayo (Euskaltel/Euskadi) and 1'17" on Alexander Vinokourov (Telekom). The former Telekom star Ullrich was down in eighth, now 2'10" off the pace.

Beloki took himself out of the race the following stage, crashing on the descent of the Côte de la Rochette, tar melted by the heat of the day causing him to go down and sustain serious injuries. Armstrong, marking him as close as he could, had to take evasive action to stay upright, cyclo-crossing across an adjacent field before rejoining the road. Vinokourov took the stage, and 36 seconds out of Armstrong, putting him just 21 seconds off yellow.

Stage 12 saw the first full-length individual time trial, 47 kilometres from Gaillac to Cap Découverte. As he had in the prologue, Ullrich bested Armstrong, cutting 1'36" off his deficit, while Vinokourov showed he had a lot to learn yet, ceding 2'06" to Ullrich and 30 seconds to Armstrong. Now it was the German 1997 Tour winner in second, 34 seconds down with Vino at 51 seconds.

Armstrong followed up his loss in the time trial by ceding yet more time to Ullrich on the road to Plateau de Bonascre, with the German closing to within 15 seconds of yellow. A day after that Armstrong let Vinokourov recoup time lost in the race against the clock and close to 18 seconds. The rest of the field, though, was now four minutes and more back.

Having more or less won four Tours by bossing the life out of the *peloton* on the first day in the mountains, Armstrong was actually looking human in this ninetieth edition of the Tour. And then he finally seemed to wake up and bossed the life out of the race on the last day in the mountains.

It was on the road to Luz-Ardiden, 159.5 kilometres of Pyrenean climbing that took in the Aspin and the Tourmalet before its summit finish. Nine kilometres from the finish line Armstrong made his move, with only Ullrich and Mayo able to follow his change of pace. Then the unthinkable happened: Armstrong went down, having caught his handlebars on a *musette* being carried by a spectator. Mayo went down behind him. Ullrich, rather than putting his head down and going for broke, respected etiquette and paused, waiting for the American to remount. Two years before Armstrong had paused when Ullrich crashed descending the Peyresourde and the German knew that what goes around comes around.

At first Armstrong struggled to clip his shoe back into the pedal after remounting. Then he set off after the riders who'd passed him. And almost fell again when his chain slipped while he was standing on the pedals. But, showing the same bike-handling skills that had taken him through that field when Beloki crashed, the American stayed upright. By now his blood was up. No sooner was he back at the front of the race than he was attacking again. And this time no one was following his wheel. Armstrong flew up the final kilometres like a bat out of hell, mopping up the last of the day's breakaways and taking the stage win, With that sudden burst of speed he pushed Ullrich back to 1'07" on GC, while Vino slipped back to 2'45".

The centenary Tour then came down to the penultimate day's individual time trial, 49 kilometres from Pornic to Nantes. Ullrich had taken five seconds out of Armstrong in the prologue's 6.5-kilometre race against the clock, and then 1'36" in the 47 kilometres to Cap Découverte on Stage 12. And from the opening kilometres of the final race of truth the German seemed to have the advantage, being six seconds up after just four kilometres. The unthinkable seemed possible, the German looked set to deny the American his fifth Tour title. But then Ullrich fluffed it, decking it on a roundabout with 10 kilometres to go. The German remounted but the race was over. Armstrong had equalled Indurain's record of five Tours back-to-back.

* * * * *

Bareley noticed at the time, the seventh stage saw Jesús Manzano (Kelme) exit the Tour after collapsing on the Col de Portes. Dehydration was blamed at the time. Manzano later (in 2004) revealed it had been because of an injection of Oxyglobin that went wrong. While the cycling authorities did their best to dismiss Manzano's claims, the Spanish judicial authorities took an interest and began their own investigation.

Stage-by-Stage Results for the 2003 Tour de France			Stage Winner	Maillot Jaune
Prologue Sat 5 Jul	Paris (Eiffel Tower to Maison de la Radio) (ITT) 198 finishers	6.5 km 7'26" 52.4 kph	Bradley McGee (Aus) FDJeux.com	Bradley McGee (Aus) FDJeux.com
Stage 1 Sun 6 Jul	Saint-Denis to Meaux 198 finishers	168 km 3h44'33" 44.9 kph	Alessandro Petacchi (Ita) Fassa Bortolo	Bradley McGee (Aus) FDJeux.com
	Rated climbs: Côte de Champcueil Christophe Mengin (Fra) FDJeux.com			
Stage 2 Mon 7 Jul	La Ferté-sous-Jouarre to Sedan 196 finishers	204.5 km 5h06'33" 40 kph	Baden Cooke (Aus) FDJeux.com	Bradley McGee (Aus) FDJeux.com
	Rated climbs: Côte de le Charmel Lilian Jégou (Fra) Crédit Agricole; Côte de Longwé Frédéric Finot (Fra) Jean Delatour			
Stage 3 Tue 8 Jul	Charleville-Mézières to Saint-Dizier 196 finishers	167.5 km 3h27'39" 48.4 kph	Alessandro Petacchi (Ita) Fassa Bortolo	Jean-Patrick Nazon (Fra) Jean Delatour
	Rated climbs: Côte de Boutancourt Paolo Bettini (Ita) Quick Step			
Stage 4 Wed 9 Jul	Joinville to Saint-Dizier (TTT) 196 finishers	69 km 1h18'27" 52.8 kph	US Postal	Víctor Hugo Peña (Col) US Postal
Stage 5 Thu 10 Jul	Troyes to Nevers 196 finishers	196.5 km 4h09'47" 47.2 kph	Alessandro Petacchi (Ita) Fassa Bortolo	Víctor Hugo Peña (Col) US Postal
	Rated climbs: Côte de Tonnerre (255m) Frédéric Finot (Fra) Jean Delatour; Côte de Rennebourg (255m) Frédéric Finot (Fra) Jean Delatour			

Stage-by-Stage Results for the 2003 Tour de France			Stage Winner	Maillot Jaune
Stage 6 Fri 11 Jul	Nevers to Lyon 194 finishers	230 km 5h08'35" 44.7 kph	Alessandro Petacchi (Ita) Fassa Bortolo	Víctor Hugo Peña (Col) US Postal
	Rated climbs: Côte des Echarmeaux (712m) Anthony Geslin (Fra) Brioches La Boulangère; Côte de Lozanne (322m) Anthony Geslin (Fra) Brioches La Boulangère			
Stage 7 Sat 12 Jul	Lyon to Morzine 187 finishers	230.5 km 6h06'03" 37.8 kph	Richard Virenque (Fra) Quick Step	Richard Virenque (Fra) Quick Step
	Rated climbs: Col de Portes (1,020m) Paolo Bettini (Ita) Quick Step; Côte du Mont des Princes (690m) Richard Virenque (Fra) Quick Step; Côte de Cruseilles (770m) Richard Virenque (Fra) Quick Step; Col de la Ramaz (1,616m) Richard Virenque (Fra) Quick Step; Côte de les Gets (1,160m) Richard Virenque (Fra) Quick Step			
Stage 8 Sun 13 Jul	Sallanches to l'Alpe d'Huez 179 finishers	219 km 5h57'30" 36.8 kph	Iban Mayo (Esp) Euskaltel	~~Lance Armstrong (USA)~~ ~~US Postal~~
				Vacated
	Rated climbs: Côte de Megève (1,050m) Richard Virenque (Fra) Quick Step; Côte des Rafforts (1,023m) Richard Virenque (Fra) Quick Step; Col du Télégraphe (1,566m) Pierrick Féderigo (Fra) Crédit Agricole; Col du Galibier (2,645m) Stefano Garzelli (Ita) Vini Caldirola; l'Alpe d'Huez (1,860m) Iban Mayo (Esp) Euskaltel			
Stage 9 Mon 14 Jul	Bourg-d'Oisans to Gap 172 finishers	184.5 km 5h02'00" 36.7 kph	Alexander Vinokourov (Kaz) Telekom	~~Lance Armstrong (USA)~~ ~~US Postal~~
				Vacated
	Rated climbs: Col du Lautaret (2,058m) Danilo Di Luca (Ita) Saeco; Col d'Izoard (2,360m) Aitor Garmendia (Esp) Bianchi; Côte de Saint-Apollinaire (1,272m) Jörg Jaksche (Ger) ONCE; Côte de la Rochette (1,120m) Alexander Vinokourov (Kaz) Telekom			
Stage 10 Tue 15 Jul	Gap to Marseille 171 finishers	219.5 km 5h09'33" 42.5 kph	Jakob Piil (Den) CSC	~~Lance Armstrong (USA)~~ ~~US Postal~~
				Vacated
	Rated climbs: Côte de Villedieu (384m) Philippe Gaumont (Fra) Cofidis; Côte du Jaillet Serge Baguet (Bel) Lotto			
Wed 16 Jul	Rest Day			
Stage 11 Thu 17 Jul	Narbonne to Toulouse 167 finishers	153.5 km 3h29'33" 44 kph	Juan Antonio Flecha (Esp) iBanesto.com	~~Lance Armstrong (USA)~~ ~~US Postal~~
				Vacated
	Rated climbs: Côte de Saissac (514m) Iñigo Cuesta (Esp) Cofidis			
Stage 12 Fri 18 Jul	Gaillac to Cap Découverte (ITT) 165 finishers	47 km 58'32" 48.2 kph	Jan Ullrich (Ger) Bianchi	~~Lance Armstrong (USA)~~ ~~US Postal~~
				Vacated

Stage-by-Stage Results for the 2003 Tour de France			Stage Winner	Maillot Jaune
Stage 13 Sat 19 Jul	Toulouse to Plateau de Bonascre 162 finishers	197.5 km 5h16'08" 37.5 kph	Carlos Sastre (Esp) CSC	~~Lance Armstrong (USA)~~ ~~US Postal~~
				Vacated
	Rated climbs: Port de Pailhères (2,001m) Juan Miguel Mercado (Esp) iBanesto.com; Ax 3 Domaines (Plateau de Bonsacre) (1,372m) Carlos Sastre (Esp) CSC			
Stage 14 Sun 20 Jul	Saint-Girons to Loudenvielle 155 finishers	191.5 km 5h31'52" 34.6 kph	Gilberto Simoni (Ita) Saeco	~~Lance Armstrong (USA)~~ ~~US Postal~~
				Vacated
	Rated climbs: Col de Latrape (1,100m) Christophe Mengin (Fra) FDJeux.com; Col de la Core (1,395m) Richard Virenque (Fra) Quick Step; Col de Portet d'Aspet (1,069m) Richard Virenque (Fra) Quick Step; Col de Menté (1,349m) Richard Virenque (Fra) Quick Step; Col du Portillon (1,298m) Richard Virenque (Fra) Quick Step; Col de Peyresourde (1,569m) Gilberto Simoni (Ita) Saeco			
Stage 15 Mon 21 Jul	Bagnères-de-Bigorre to Luz-Ardiden 151 finishers	159.5 km 4h29'26" 35.5 kph	~~Lance Armstrong (USA)~~ ~~US Postal~~	~~Lance Armstrong (USA)~~ ~~US Postal~~
			Vacated	Vacated
	Rated climbs: Côte de Meilhas Sylvain Chavanel (Fra) Brioches La Boulangère; Côte de Bugard Sylvain Chavanel (Fra) Brioches La Boulangère; Côte de Castelbajac Sylvain Chavanel (Fra) Brioches La Boulangère; Col d'Aspin (1,489m) Sylvain Chavanel (Fra) Brioches La Boulangère; Col du Tourmalet (2,115m) Sylvain Chavanel (Fra) Brioches La Boulangère; Luz-Ardiden (1,715m) Lance Armstrong (USA) US Postal			
Tue 22 Jul	Rest Day			
Stage 16 Wed 23 Jul	Pau to Bayonne 149 finishers	197.5 km 4h59'41" 39.5 kph	Tyler Hamilton (USA) CSC	~~Lance Armstrong (USA)~~ ~~US Postal~~
				Vacated
	Rated climbs: Côte des Crêts Salvatore Commesso (Ita) Saeco; Col du Soudet (1,540m) Kurt Van de Wouwer (Bel) Quick Step; Port de Larrau (1,573m) Kurt Van de Wouwer (Bel) Quick Step; Col Bagarguy (1,327m) Tyler Hamilton (USA) CSC; Col de Burdincurutcheta (1,135m) Tyler Hamilton (USA) CSC			
Stage 17 Thu 24 Jul	Dax to Bordeaux 149 finishers	181 km 3h54'23" 46.3 kph	Servais Knaven (Ned) Quick Step	~~Lance Armstrong (USA)~~ ~~US Postal~~
				Vacated
Stage 18 Fri 25 Jul	Bordeaux to Saint-Maixent-l'École 148 finishers	202.5 km 4h03'18" 49.9 kph	Pablo Lastras (Esp) iBanesto.com	~~Lance Armstrong (USA)~~ ~~US Postal~~
				Vacated
Stage 19 Sat 26 Jul	Pornic to Nantes (ITT) 148 finishers	49 km 54'05" 54.4 kph	David Millar (GBr) Cofidis	~~Lance Armstrong (USA)~~ ~~US Postal~~
				Vacated
Stage 20 Sun 27 Jul	Ville-d'Avray to Paris (Champs-Élysées) 147 finishers	152 km 3h38'49" 41.7 kph	Jean-Patrick Nazon (Fra) Jean Delatour	~~Lance Armstrong (USA)~~ ~~US Postal~~
				Vacated

Prize fund: 2,877,705 euro (first prize: 400,000 euro)

Final Classification

Place	Rider	Team	Time	Age
~~1~~	~~Lance Armstrong (USA)~~	~~US Postal~~	~~3,427 km~~ ~~83h41'12"~~ ~~40.940 kph~~	~~31~~
1	Vacated			
2	Jan Ullrich (Ger)	Bianchi	+ 1'01"	29
3	Alexander Vinokourov (Kaz)	Telekom	+ 4'14"	32
4	Tyler Hamilton (USA)	CSC	+ 6'17"	29
5	Haimar Zubeldia (Esp)	Euskaltel	+ 6'51"	26
6	Iban Mayo (Esp)	Euskaltel	+ 7'06"	25
7	Ivan Basso (Ita)	Fassa Bortolo	+ 10'12"	25
8	Christophe Moreau (Fra)	Crédit Agricole	+ 12'28"	32
9	Carlos Sastre (Esp)	CSC	+ 18'49"	28
10	Francisco Mancebo (Esp)	iBanesto.com	+ 19'15"	27
Lanterne Rouge				
147	Hans de Clercq (Bel)	Lotto	+ 4h48'35"	34
Points				
	Baden Cooke (Aus)	FDJeux.com		24
King of the Mountains				
	Richard Virenque (Fra)	Quick Step		33
Youth				
	Denis Menchov (Rus)	iBanesto.com		25
Team				
		CSC		
Super Combativité				
	Alexander Vinokourov (Kaz)	Telekom		29
Le Centenaire				
	Stuart O'Grady (Aus)	Crédit Agricole		29
Prix de l'Europe Enlargie				
	René Andrle (Cze)	ONCE		29

Note: In 2012 Lance Armstrong was stripped of all his results dating back to 1 August, 1998 following an investigation by the United States Anti-Doping Agency into doping at his teams. None of his results in the 2003 Tour de France were re-awarded.

2004: Prometheus in Chains

Count the ways in which 2004 was a rotten year.

Marco Pantani was found dead in a hotel room in Rimini. The former Tour de France and Giro d'Italia champion was 34 and just the latest in a new cluster of cycling deaths that raised fresh questions about the cost of cycling's doping culture, what damage doping had done to the riders who went through Gen-EPO.

The Cofidis *affaire* erupted, an investigation into doping at the French team that, over the course of the six months between January and June, saw a drip-feed of allegations and accusations appear in the media, culminating with the arrest of David Millar shortly before the Tour commenced.

Jesús Manzano made his revelations about doping at Kelme and explained just why it was he was ambulanced out of the 2003 Tour de France. The UCI's president, Hein Verbruggen, dismissed Manzano's revelations.

The Italian 'Oil for Drugs' investigation kicked into gear with police raids and a number of top riders – including Danilo di Luca – being linked to the doping doctor Carlo Santuccione. At the Giro d'Italia, there were more police raids as the judicial authorities continued to be a more effective force in the fight against doping than the sporting authorities who had the most to gain from a clean sport.

And then there was Lance Armstrong, who was now the subject of new book, *LA Confidentiel: Les Secrets de Lance Armstrong*, by the French and Irish journalists Pierre Ballester and David Walsh. In it the two journalists detailed the links between Armstrong and doping. A former Motorola rider, Stephen Swart, said that

Armstrong and other members of the team joined Gen-EPO in 1995. A former USPS *soigneur* Emma O'Reilly offered testimony about the 1999 back-dated TUE at the Tour and other direct knowledge she had of doping at the team. The authors even produced evidence that, while being treated for his cancer, Armstrong had confessed to using performance-enhancing drugs during his cycling career.

Armstrong was put on the back foot, but came out fighting. Extraordinary allegations, he said, needed extraordinary evidence. He sued the French publishers of *LA Confidentiel*. He sued a French newspaper, *L'Express* and the British *Sunday Times* after they repeated allegations made in the book. (The French cases Armstrong eventually dropped, in the British one the *Sunday Times* settled, but then got their money back after the USADA report was published in 2012.)

It was a year in which it was hard to avoid the negative publicity of doping. Perversely, then, it was a year in which everyone should have been able to celebrate a major success in the fight against doping, the World Anti-Doping Agency taking charge of the harmonisation of doping's rules and regulations, WADA taking responsibility for detailing what was banned and what was the correct punishment for committing a doping offence. Created in 1999 by the IOC as a response to the Festina *affaire*, WADA finally took charge ahead of the Athens Olympics. But in the run-up to those Games a number of sports bodies were still in dispute with WADA and had yet to sign their names on the dotted line, including both FIFA and the UCI. They only signed at the eleventh hour, when it was a choice between getting with the programme or leaving the Olympic movement.

Within the ninety-first Tour itself, Armstrong rolled through the opening stages as his key rivals eliminated themselves. Iban Mayo (Euskaltel) blew it on the third stage as the Tour took in some of Paris-Roubaix's pavé sectors, squandering the thick end of four minutes. Tyler Hamilton (Phonak) decked it on stage six and retired from the race a week later as the injuries sustained took their toll.

When the Tour hit the mountains on Stage 12, Castelsarrasin to La Mongie, Thomas Voeckler (Brioches la Boulangère) was in yellow and Armstrong seemed to be in no rush to relieve him of the jersey. The race passed through the Pyrenees with Armstrong only bothering to climb up to second overall and, when the race reached the Alps, it was with Voeckler still in yellow.

Finally, in Villard-de-Lans, on Stage 15, Armstrong shucked off his lethargy and took control, with Ivan Basso (CSC) his closest rival, at 1'25". For the CSCs that seemed to be enough, and they never took the challenge to Armstrong. The American pushed his lead out to 3'48" after a time trial up Alpe d'Huez. The Tour was over and Armstrong had gone where no Tour winner had gone before: six wins.

And then, on what should have been a dull transition day taking the race up to its final time trial, Armstrong finally gave the race a story. On the road to Lons-le-Saunier, the race's eighteenth stage, with just 32 kilometres of racing done, Filippo Simeoni (Domina Vacanze) tried to break out of the *peloton* and bridge across to the break that was a minute up the road. The Italian was 2h42'55" off yellow and looking for a shot at a stage win. Instead of getting that chance he found the *maillot jaune* chasing him down.

This sort of action was almost unheard of. Back in the day a *patron* like Bernard Hinault might close a rider down early in a stage if he was upsetting plans for a quiet day in the saddle, but this? This was personal. Simeoni was testifying in the trial of Michele Ferrari, speaking of his own experience of working with the Italian doctor and his own doping. Armstrong didn't like this. Ferrari was a key part of Armstrong's support staff.

So Armstrong rode up to the break with Simeoni and laid down the law: as long as Simeoni was there, he wasn't leaving and the break would be closed down. Simeoni was forced to drop back to the *peloton*. Where the rest of the riders turned on him, echoing the manner in which they had turned on Andrea Taffi during the 1999 Giro d'Italia, when he went up against Marco Pantani.

Armstrong said he was proud of what he'd done, telling the media that Simeoni was just a guy out to damage the sport and that a lot of riders had patted him on the back for what he had done to bring the Italian to heel. Despite all that was going on in the sport, the deaths and the doping *affaires*, the message just didn't seem to be getting through to the riders. They thought themselves invincible, again.

The scandals continued after the Tour. A new test for blood transfusions was introduced, and among those caught was Tyler Hamilton, first at the Olympics (which offence he got off due to an error in the storage of his B sample) and then at the Vuelta a España. A new weapon had been added to the anti-doping armoury.

Stage-by-Stage Results for the 2004 Tour de France			Stage Winner	Maillot Jaune
Prologue Sat 3 Jul	Liège (ITT) 188 finishers	6.1 km 6'50" 53.6 kph	Fabian Cancellara (Sui) Fassa Bortolo	Fabian Cancellara (Sui) Fassa Bortolo
Stage 1 Sun 4 Jul	Liège to Charleroi 187 finishers	202.5 km 4h40'29" 43.3 kph	Ján Kirsipuu (Est) AG2R	Fabian Cancellara (Sui) Fassa Bortolo
	Rated climbs: Côte de Florzé (295m) Jens Voigt (Ger) CSC; Côte de Awan (227m) Paolo Bettini (Ita) Quick Step; Côte de Werbomont (459m) Janek Tombak (Est) Cofidis; Côte de Borlon (349m) Paolo Bettini (Ita) Quick Step; Côte de Ocquier (321m) Jens Voigt (Ger) CSC			
Stage 2 Mon 5 Jul	Charleroi to Namur 186 finishers	197 km 4h18'39" 45.7 kph	Robbie McEwen (Aus) Lotto	Thor Hushovd (Nor) Crédit Agricole
	Rated climbs: Côte de Bomerée (207m) Paolo Bettini (Ita) Quick Step; Côte de Silenrieux (257m) Jérôme Pineau (Fra) Brioches La Boulangère			
Stage 3 Tue 6 Jul	Waterloo to Wasquehal 184 finishers	210 km 4h36'46" 45.5 kph	Jean-Patrick Nazon (Fra) AG2R	Robbie McEwen (Aus) Lotto
	Rated climbs: Bruineput (118m) Bram de Groot (Ned) Rabobank; Mur Geraardbergen (97m) Bram de Groot (Ned) Rabobank			
Stage 4 Wed 7 Jul	Cambrai to Arras (TTT) 183 finishers	64.5 km 1h12'03" 53.7 kph	US Postal	~~Lance Armstrong (USA)~~ ~~US Postal~~
				Vacated
Stage 5 Thu 8 Jul	Amiens to Chartres 181 finishers	200.5 km 5h05'58" 39.3 kph	Stuart O'Grady (Aus) Cofidis	Thomas Voeckler (Fra) Brioches la Boulangère
	Rated climbs: Mont des Fourches (234m) Sandy Casar (Fra) FDJeux.com			
Stage 6 Fri 9 Jul	Bonneval to Angers 179 finishers	196 km 4h33'41" 43 kph	Tom Boonen (Bel) Quick Step	Thomas Voeckler (Fra) Brioches la Boulangère
Stage 7 Sat 10 Jul	Châteaubriant to Saint-Brieuc 176 finishers	204.5 km 4h31'34" 45.2 kph	Filippo Pozzato (Ita) Fassa Bortolo	Thomas Voeckler (Fra) Brioches la Boulangère
	Rated climbs: Côte de Dinan (74m) Erik Dekker (Ned) Rabobank; Côte de Saint-Aide (62m) Erik Dekker (Ned) Rabobank			

Stage-by-Stage Results for the 2004 Tour de France			Stage Winner	Maillot Jaune
Stage 8￼Sun 11 Jul	Lamballe to Quimper￼176 finishers	168 km￼3h54'22"￼43 kph	Thor Hushovd (Nor)￼Crédit Agricole	Thomas Voeckler (Fra)￼Brioches la Boulangère
	Rated climbs: Côte de Mûr-de-Bretagne (295m) Ronny Scholz (Ger) Gerolsteiner; Côte de Saint-Mayeux (287m) Ronny Scholz (Ger) Gerolsteiner; Côte de Ménez-Kuz (136m) Ronny Scholz (Ger) Gerolsteiner; Côte de l'Enseigne Verte (247m) Jakob Piil (Den) CSC			
Mon 12 Jul	Rest Day			
Stage 9￼Tue 13 Jul	Saint-Léonard-de-Noblat to Guéret￼172 finishers	160.5 km￼3h32'55"￼45.2 kph	Robbie McEwen (Aus)￼Lotto	Thomas Voeckler (Fra)￼Brioches la Boulangère
	Rated climbs: Côte de la Croix de Mapertuis (615m) Richard Virenque (Fra) Quick Step; Côte d'Aubusson (592m) Iñigo Landaluze (Esp) Euskaltel			
Stage 10￼Wed 14 Jul	Limoges to Saint-Flour￼169 finishers	237 km￼6h00'24"￼39.5 kph	Richard Virenque (Fra)￼Quick Step	Thomas Voeckler (Fra)￼Brioches la Boulangère
	Rated climbs: Le Mont Gargan (573m) Richard Virenque (Fra) Quick Step; Côte de Lestards (856m) Richard Virenque (Fra) Quick Step; Côte de Saint-Yrieix le Déjalat (750m) Richard Virenque (Fra) Quick Step; Côte de Soursac (532m) Richard Virenque (Fra) Quick Step; Côte de Chalvignac (568m) Richard Virenque (Fra) Quick Step; Col de Néronne (1,242m) Richard Virenque (Fra) Quick Step; Col du Pas de Péyrol (Le Puy Mary) (1,588m) Richard Virenque (Fra) Quick Step; Col d'Entremont (1,210m) Richard Virenque (Fra) Quick Step; Col de Prat de Bouc (Plomb du Cantal) (1,383m) Richard Virenque (Fra) Quick Step			
Stage 11￼Thu 15 Jul	Saint-Flour to Figeac￼167 finishers	164 km￼3h54'58"￼41.9 kph	David Moncoutié (Fra)￼Cofidis	Thomas Voeckler (Fra)￼Brioches la Boulangère
	Rated climbs: Côte des Ternes (970m) Fabian Wegmann (Ger) Gerolsteiner; Côte de Thérondels (950m) Richard Virenque (Fra) Quick Step; Côte de Mur-de-Barrez (783m) David Moncoutié (Fra) Cofidis; Côte de Montsalvy (780m) David Moncoutié (Fra) Cofidis			
Stage 12￼Fri 16 Jul	Castelsarrasin to La Mongie￼166 finishers	197.5 km￼5h03'58"￼39 kph	Ivan Basso (Ita)￼CSC	Thomas Voeckler (Fra)￼Brioches la Boulangère
	Rated climbs: Col d'Aspin (1,489m) Michael Rasmussen (Den) Rabobank; La Mongie (1,715m) Ivan Basso (Ita) CSC			
Stage 13￼Sat 17 Jul	Lannemezan to Plateau de Beille￼160 finishers	205.5 km￼6h04'38"￼33.8 kph	~~Lance Armstrong (USA)~~￼~~US Postal~~￼Vacated	Thomas Voeckler (Fra)￼Brioches la Boulangère
	Rated climbs: Col des Ares (797m) Sylvain Chavanel (Fra) Brioches La Boulangère; Col de Portet d'Aspet (1,069m) Sylvain Chavanel (Fra) Brioches La Boulangère; Col de la Core (1,395m) Sylvain Chavanel (Fra) Brioches La Boulangère; Col de Latrape (1,100m) Sylvain Chavanel (Fra) Brioches La Boulangère; Col d'Agnès (1,570m) Michael Rasmussen (Den) Rabobank; Port de Lers (1,517m) Michael Rasmussen (Den) Rabobank; Plateau de Beille (1,780m) Lance Armstrong (USA) US Postal			
Stage 14￼Sun 18 Jul	Carcassonne to Nîmes￼160 finishers	192.5 km￼4h18'32"￼44.7 kph	Aitor González (Esp)￼Fassa Bortolo	Thomas Voeckler (Fra)￼Brioches la Boulangère
Mon 19 Jul	Rest Day			

Stage-by-Stage Results for the 2004 Tour de France			Stage Winner	Maillot Jaune
Stage 15 Tue 20 Jul	Valréas to Villard-de-Lans 157 finishers	180.5 km 4h40'30" 38.6 kph	~~Lance Armstrong (USA)~~ ~~US Postal~~	~~Lance Armstrong (USA)~~ ~~US Postal~~
			Vacated	Vacated
Rated climbs: Côte d'Aleyrac (490m) Axel Merckx (Bel) Lotto; Côte de Puy Saint-Martin (326m) Axel Merckx (Bel) Lotto; Col des Limouches (1,075m) Axel Merckx (Bel) Lotto; Col de l'Echarasson (1,146m) Richard Virenque (Fra) Quick Step; Col de Carri (1,215m) Richard Virenque (Fra) Quick Step; Côte de Chalimont (1,374m) Richard Virenque (Fra) Quick Step; Villard-de-Lans (1,150m) Lance Armstrong (USA) US Postal				
Stage 16 Wed 21 Jul	Bourg-d'Oisans to l'Alpe d'Huez (ITT) 155 finishers	15.5 km 39'41" 23.4 kph	~~Lance Armstrong (USA)~~ ~~US Postal~~	~~Lance Armstrong (USA)~~ ~~US Postal~~
			Vacated	Vacated
Rated climbs: l'Alpe d'Huez (1,860m) Lance Armstrong (USA) US Postal				
Stage 17 Thu 22 Jul	Bourg-d'Oisans to Le Grand-Bornand 147 finishers	204.5 km 6h11'52" 33 kph	~~Lance Armstrong (USA)~~ ~~US Postal~~	~~Lance Armstrong (USA)~~ ~~US Postal~~
			Vacated	Vacated
Rated climbs: Col du Glandon (1,924m) Gilberto Simoni (Ita) Saeco; Col de la Madeleine (2,000m) Gilberto Simoni (Ita) Saeco; Col de Tamié (907m) Richard Virenque (Fra) Quick Step; Col de la Forclaz de Montmin (1,150m) Richard Virenque (Fra) Quick Step; Col de la Croix-Fry (1,477m) Floyd Landis (USA) US Postal				
Stage 18 Fri 23 Jul	Annemasse to Lons-le-Saunier 147 finishers	166.5 km 4h04'03" 40.9 kph	Juan Miguel Mercado (Esp) Quick Step	~~Lance Armstrong (USA)~~ ~~US Postal~~
				Vacated
Rated climbs: Côte de Collonges (512m) Dmitri Fofonov (Kaz) Cofidis; Col de la Faucille (1,323m) Juan Miguel Mercado (Esp) Quick Step; Col de Lajoux (1,198m) Juan Miguel Mercado (Esp) Quick Step; Côte des Crozets (998m) Juan Miguel Mercado (Esp) Quick Step; Côte de Nogna (587m) Juan Miguel Mercado (Esp) Quick Step				
Stage 19 Sat 24 Jul	Besançon (ITT) 147 finishers	55 km 1h06'49" 49.4 kph	~~Lance Armstrong (USA)~~ ~~US Postal~~	~~Lance Armstrong (USA)~~ ~~US Postal~~
			Vacated	Vacated
Stage 20 Sun 25 Jul	Montereau to Paris (Champs-Élysées) 147 finishers	163 km 4h08'26" 39.4 kph	Tom Boonen (Bel) Quick Step	~~Lance Armstrong (USA)~~ ~~US Postal~~
				Vacated
Rated climbs: Côte de Montfermeil (103m) Christophe Moreau (Fra) Crédit Agricole				

Prize fund: 3,000,000 euro (first prize: 400,000 euro)

Final Classification

Place	Rider	Team	Time	Age
~~1~~	~~Lance Armstrong (USA)~~	~~US Postal~~	~~3,391 km~~ ~~83h36'02"~~ ~~40.553 kph~~	~~32~~
1	Vacated			
2	Andreas Klöden (Ger)	T-Mobile	+ 6'19"	29
3	Ivan Basso (Ita)	CSC	+ 6'40"	26
4	Jan Ullrich (Ger)	T-Mobile	+ 8'50"	30
5	José Azevedo (Por)	US Postal	+ 14'30"	30
6	Francisco Mancebo (Esp)	Illes Balears	+ 18'01"	28
7	Georg Totschnig (Aut)	Gerolsteiner	+ 18'27"	33
8	Carlos Sastre (Esp)	CSC	+ 19'51"	29
9	~~Levi Leipheimer (USA) (1)~~	~~Rabobank~~	~~+ 20'12"~~	~~30~~
9	Vacated			
10	Óscar Pereiro (Esp)	Phonak	+ 22'54"	26
Lanterne Rouge				
147	Jimmy Casper (Fra)	Cofidis	+ 3h55'49"	26
Points				
	Robbie McEwen (Aus)	Lotto		32
King of the Mountains				
	Richard Virenque (Fra)	Quick Step		34
Youth				
	Vladimir Karpets (Rus)	Illes Balears		23
Team				
		T-Mobile		
Super Combativité				
	Richard Virenque (Fra)	Quick Step		34

Note: In 2012 Lance Armstrong was stripped of all his results dating back to 1 August, 1998 following an investigation by the United States Anti-Doping Agency into doping at his teams. None of his results in the 2004 Tour de France were re-awarded.

(1) During the USADA investigation Levi Leipheimer admitted his doping and was stripped of his results.

2005: The Big Con

When it was all over, when the seventh Tour was won and as he drew the curtain on his cycling career, Lance Armstrong stood on the top step of the podium on the Champs-Élysées for one last time and gave a speech in which he said he was sorry. Sorry for all the cynics and the sceptics: "I'm sorry for you. I'm sorry that you can't dream big. I'm sorry you don't believe in miracles."

A month later, their hero no longer needed, *L'Équipe* bit the hand that had fed it so well for the past seven years. With a front page headline that read '*Le Mensonge Armstrong*' (the Armstrong Lie) they tore down whatever was left of the façade of a clean Tour champion and showed that the foundations of Armstrong's seven Tour titles were built on EPO. For evidence, *L'Équipe* relied on tests that had been carried out for research purposes, using samples stored from the 1999 Tour de France. These showed that samples given by Armstrong contained evidence of EPO use.

These were not official anti-doping tests, and their findings could not lead to sanctions being handed out. Armstrong's doping was not being prosecuted in a court of law. This was all about the court of public opinion. If the authorities weren't going to tackle the American, it was the only way to challenge his cheating. The authorities did respond to *L'Équipe*'s exposé. Not by questioning Armstrong about his use of EPO in 1999 but by questioning how *L'Équipe* got their story.

Some hoped that, with Armstrong retired, this would be the end of it. People had grown weary, they hoped his treachery would be forgotten, as the treachery of others before him had been forgotten. But in the years ahead they were denied relief, as was Armstrong.

His treachery would eventually be revealed. Very slowly. Very painfully. Piece by piece.

* * * * *

Armstrong's seventh Tour title was a relatively easy win. He donned the *maillot jaune* after Stage Four's team time trial to Blois, with his chief rival already down and out, Jan Ullrich – back in the Deutsche Telekom fold, with T-Mobile – having crashed into a car on the eve of the race's opening stage and bleeding time from the off.

Armstrong briefly passed the yellow jersey to CSC's Jens Voigt before fully taking control of the race in the high Alps. At the end of the first day of big mountains – Stage 10, Grenoble to Courchevel – Armstrong led Michael Rasmussen (Rabobank) by 38 seconds, Ivan Basso (CSC) by 2'40", Christophe Moreau (Crédit Agricole) by 2'42" and Alejandro Valverde (Illes Balears – the Banesto team of old with a new sponsor) by 3'16".

By the time the Pyrenees arrived Rasmussen had been pushed back to 1'41" and Basso to 2'46", with all the rest four minutes and more back. Rasmussen fell away as they scaled the Pyrenean peaks, and then fell even further away when they took on the final race against the clock on Stage 20, the Dane twice crashing and three times having to change his bike in a *contre-la-montre* that looked like something out of Wacky Races. It didn't spoil Armstrong's party, and he rode into Paris as the Tour's seven time champion.

Stage-by-Stage Results for the 2005 Tour de France			Stage Winner	Maillot Jaune
Stage 1 Sat 2 Jul	Fromentine to Noirmoutier-en-l'Île (ITT) 189 finishers	19 km 20'51" 54.7 kph	~~David Zabriskie (USA)~~ ~~CSC~~ (1)	~~David Zabriskie (USA)~~ ~~CSC~~ (1)
			Vacated	Vacated
Stage 2 Sun 3 Jul	Challans to Les Essarts 189 finishers	181.5 km 3h51'31" 47 kph	Tom Boonen (Bel) Quick Step	~~David Zabriskie (USA)~~ ~~CSC~~ (1)
				Vacated
Rated climbs: Côte du lac de la Vouraie Thomas Voeckler (Fra) Bouygues Telecom				

Stage-by-Stage Results for the 2005 Tour de France			Stage Winner	Maillot Jaune
Stage 3 Mon 4 Jul	La Châtaigneraie to Tours 189 finishers	212.5 km 4h36'09" 46.2 kph	Tom Boonen (Bel) Quick Step	~~David Zabriskie (USA)~~ ~~CSC~~ (1)
				Vacated
	Rated climbs: Côte de Pouzauges (208m) Fabian Wegmann (Ger) Gerolsteiner; Côte de Chinon (123m) Erik Dekker (Ned) Rabobank; Côte de la Taconnière (102m) Erik Dekker (Ned) Rabobank			
Stage 4 Tue 5 Jul	Tours to Blois (TTT) 189 finishers	67.5 km 1h10'39" 57.3 kph	Discovery Channel	~~Lance Armstrong (USA)~~ ~~Discovery Channel~~
				Vacated
	Rated climbs: Côte de Bellevue (1,056m) Laszlo Bodrogi (Hun) Crédit Agricole			
Stage 5 Wed 6 Jul	Chambord to Montargis 188 finishers	183 km 3h46'00" 48.6 kph	Robbie McEwen (Aus) Davitamon	~~Lance Armstrong (USA)~~ ~~Discovery Channel~~
				Vacated
Stage 6 Thu 7 Jul	Troyes to Nancy 187 finishers	199 km 4h12'52" 47.2 kph	Lorenzo Bernucci (Ita) Fassa Bortolo	~~Lance Armstrong (USA)~~ ~~Discovery Channel~~
				Vacated
	Rated climbs: Côte de Joinville (338 m) Stéphane Augé (Fra) Cofidis; Côte de Brouthières (387m) Karsten Kroon (Ned) Rabobank; Côte de Montigny (364m) Karsten Kroon (Ned) Rabobank; Côte de Maron (398m) Christophe Mengin (Fra) Française Des Jeux			
Stage 7 Fri 8 Jul	Lunéville to Karlsruhe 185 finishers	228.5 km 5h03'45" 45.1 kph	Robbie McEwen (Aus) Davitamon	~~Lance Armstrong (USA)~~ ~~Discovery Channel~~
				Vacated
	Rated climbs: Col de la Chipotte (458m) Fabian Wegmann (Ger) Gerolsteiner; Col du Hantz (637m) Fabian Wegmann (Ger) Gerolsteiner			
Stage 8 Sat 9 Jul	Pforzheim to Gérardmer 180 finishers	231.5 km 5h03'54" 45.7 kph	Pieter Weening (Ned) Rabobank	~~Lance Armstrong (USA)~~ ~~Discovery Channel~~
				Vacated
	Rated climbs: Côte de Dobel (702m) Michael Rasmussen (Den) Rabobank; Côte de Bad-Herrenalb (537m) Michael Rasmussen (Den) Rabobank; Côte de Nachtigal (382m) Michael Rasmussen (Den) Rabobank; Côte de Zimmerplatz (363m) Michael Rasmussen (Den) Rabobank; Col de la Schlucht (1,139m) Andreas Klöden (Ger) T-Mobile			
Stage 9 Sun 10 Jul	Gérardmer to Mulhouse 175 finishers	171 km 4h08'20" 41.3 kph	Michael Rasmussen (Den) Rabobank	Jens Voigt (Ger) CSC
	Rated climbs: Col de la Grosse Pierre (955m) Michael Rasmussen (Den) Rabobank; Col des Feignes (922m) Michael Rasmussen (Den) Rabobank; Col de Bramont (956m) Michael Rasmussen (Den) Rabobank; Col du Grand Ballon (1,338m) Michael Rasmussen (Den) Rabobank; Col de Bussang (731m) Michael Rasmussen (Den) Rabobank; Ballon d'Alsace (1,171m) Michael Rasmussen (Den) Rabobank			
Mon 11 Jul	Rest Day			

Stage-by-Stage Results for the 2005 Tour de France			Stage Winner	Maillot Jaune
Stage 10 Tue 12 Jul	Grenoble to Courchevel 173 finishers	192.5 km 4h50'35" 39.7 kph	Alejandro Valverde (Esp) Illes Balears	~~Lance Armstrong (USA)~~ ~~Discovery Channel~~
				Vacated
	Rated climbs: Cormet de Roselend (1,968m) Laurent Brochard (Fra) Bouygues Telecom; Courchevel (2,004m) Alejandro Valverde (Esp) Illes Balears			
Stage 11 Wed 13 Jul	Courchevel to Briançon 167 finishers	173 km 4h47'38" 36.1 kph	Alexander Vinokourov (Kaz) T-Mobile	~~Lance Armstrong (USA)~~ ~~Discovery Channel~~
				Vacated
	Rated climbs: Col de la Madeleine (2,000m) Stantiago Botero (Col) Phonak; Col du Télégraphe (1,566m) Stantiago Botero (Col) Phonak; Col du Galibier (2,645m) Alexander Vinokourov (Kaz) T-Mobile			
Stage 12 Thu 14 Jul	Briançon to Digne-les-Bains 162 finishers	187 km 4h20'06" 43.1 kph	David Moncoutié (Fra) Cofidis	~~Lance Armstrong (USA)~~ ~~Discovery Channel~~
				Vacated
	Rated climbs: Côte des Demoiselles Coiffées (1,067m) Michael Boogerd (Ned) Rabobank; Col Saint-Jean (1,332m) Juan Manuel Garate (Esp) Saunier Duval; Col du Labouret (1,240m) Juan Manuel Garate (Esp) Saunier Duval; Col du Corobin (1,230m) David Moncoutié (Fra) Cofidis; Col de l'Orme (734m) David Moncoutié (Fra) Cofidis			
Stage 13 Fri 15 Jul	Miramas to Montpellier 161 finishers	173.5 km 3h43'14" 46.6 kph	Robbie McEwen (Aus) Davitamon	~~Lance Armstrong (USA)~~ ~~Discovery Channel~~
				Vacated
	Rated climbs:			
Stage 14 Sat 16 Jul	Agde to Ax 3 Domaines 160 finishers	220.5 km 5h43'43" 38.5 kph	~~Georg Totschnig (Aut)~~ ~~Gerolsteiner~~	~~Lance Armstrong (USA)~~ ~~Discovery Channel~~
				Vacated
	Rated climbs: Col de Villerouge (404m) Yuri Krivtsov (Ukr) AG2R; Col de Bedos (485m) Juan Manuel Garate (Esp) Saunier Duval; Col des Fourches (970m) Juan Manuel Garate (Esp) Saunier Duval; Col du Paradis (622m) Juan Manuel Garate (Esp) Saunier Duval; Port de Pailhères (2,001m) Georg Totschnig (Aut) Gerolsteiner; Ax 3 Domaines (1,372m) Georg Totschnig (Aut) Gerolsteiner			
Stage 15 Sun 17 Jul	Lézat-sur-Lèze to Saint-Lary-Soulan (Pla d'Adet) 158 finishers	205.5 km 6h06'38" 33.6 kph	~~George Hincapie (USA)~~ ~~Discovery Channel~~ Vacated	~~Lance Armstrong (USA)~~ ~~Discovery Channel~~ Vacated
	Rated climbs: Col de Portet d'Aspet (1,069m) Erik Dekker (Ned) Rabobank; Col de Menté (1,349m) Erik Dekker (Ned) Rabobank; Col du Portillon (1,298m) Karsten Kroon (Ned) Rabobank; Col de Peyresourde (1,569m) Laurent Brochard (Fra) Bouygues Telecom; Val-Louron (Col d'Azet) (1,579m) Laurent Brochard (Fra) Bouygues Telecom; Saint-Lary-Soulan (Pla d'Adet) (1,680m) Gilberto Hincapie (USA) Discovery Channel			
Mon 18 Jul	Rest Day			

Stage-by-Stage Results for the 2005 Tour de France			Stage Winner	Maillot Jaune
Stage 16 Tue 19 Jul	Mourenx to Pau 156 finishers	180.5 km 4h38'40" 38.9 kph	Óscar Pereiro (Esp) Phonak	~~Lance Armstrong (USA)~~ ~~Discovery Channel~~
				Vacated
Rated climbs: Col d'Ichère (674m) Jérôme Pineau (Fra) Bouygues Telecom; Col de Marie-Blanque (1,035m) Jörg Ludewig (Ger) Domina Vacanze; Col d'Aubisque (1,709m) Cadel Evans (Aus) Davitamon; Côte de Pardiès (Côte de Notre-Dame-de-Piétat) (380m) Óscar Pereiro (Esp) Phonak				
Stage 17 Wed 20 Jul	Pau to Revel 155 finishers	239.5 km 5h41'19" 42.1 kph	Paolo Savoldelli (Ita) Discovery Channel	~~Lance Armstrong (USA)~~ ~~Discovery Channel~~
				Vacated
Rated climbs: Côte de Baleix (348m) Bobby Julich (USA) CSC; Côte de Betbèze (407m) Andrei Grivko (Ukr) Domina Vacanze; Côte de Capens (285m) Andrei Grivko (Ukr) Domina Vacanze; Côte de Saint-Ferréol (363m) Paolo Savoldelli (Ita) Discovery Channel				
Stage 18 Thu 21 Jul	Albi to Mende 155 finishers	189 km 4h37'36" 40.9 kph	Marcos Serrano (Esp) ONCE	~~Lance Armstrong (USA)~~ ~~Discovery Channel~~
				Vacated
Rated climbs: Côte de la Béssède (610m) Xabier Zandio (Esp) Illes Balears; Côte de Raujolles (517m) Carlos da Cruz (Fra) Française des Jeux; Côte de Boyne (903m) Carlos da Cruz (Fra) Française des Jeux; Côte de Chabrits (924m) Axel Merckx (Bel) Davitamon; Côte de la Croix Neuve (montée Laurent Jalabert) (1,045m) Marcos Serrano (Esp) Liberty Seguros				
Stage 19 Fri 22 Jul	Issoire to Le Puy-en-Velay 155 finishers	153.5 km 3h33'04" 43.2 kph	Giuseppe Guerini (Ita) T-Mobile	~~Lance Armstrong (USA)~~ ~~Discovery Channel~~
				Vacated
Rated climbs: Côte des Gerbaudias (681m) Christophe Moreau (Fra) Crédit Agricole; Côte de Saint-Eloy-la-Glacière (1,046m) Óscar Pereiro (Esp) Phonak; Col des Pradeaux (1,196m) Óscar Pereiro (Esp) Phonak; Côte des Terrasses (925m) Óscar Pereiro (Esp) Phonak; Côte de Malaveille (918m) Óscar Pereiro (Esp) Phonak				
Stage 20 Sat 23 Jul	Saint-Étienne (ITT) 155 finishers	55.5 km 1h11'46" 46.4 kph	~~Lance Armstrong (USA)~~ ~~Discovery Channel~~	~~Lance Armstrong (USA)~~ ~~Discovery Channel~~
			Vacated	Vacated
Rated climbs: Col de la Gachet (731m) Lance Armstrong (USA) Discovery Channel				
Stage 21 Sun 24 Jul	Corbeil-Essonnes to Paris (Champs-Élysées) 155 finishers	144.5 km 3h40'57" 39.2 kph	Alexander Vinokourov (Kaz) T-Mobile	~~Lance Armstrong (USA)~~ ~~Discovery Channel~~
				Vacated
Rated climbs: Côte de Gif-sur-Yvette (153m) Lance Armstrong (USA) Discovery Channel				

Prize fund: 3,000,000 euro (first prize: 400,000 euro)

Final Classification

Place	Rider	Team	Time	Age
~~1~~	~~Lance Armstrong (USA)~~	~~Discovery Channel~~	~~3,593 km~~ ~~86h15'02"~~ ~~41.654 kph~~	~~33~~
1	Vacated			
2	Ivan Basso (Ita)	CSC	+ 4'40"	27
3	~~Jan Ullrich (Ger)~~ (2)	~~T-Mobile~~	~~+ 6'21"~~	~~29~~
3	Vacated			
4	Francisco Mancebo (Esp)	Illes Balears	+ 9'59"	31
5	Alexander Vinokourov (Kaz)	T-Mobile	+ 11'01"	31
6	~~Levi Leipheimer (USA)~~ (1)	~~Gerolsteiner~~	~~+ 11'21"~~	~~31~~
6	Vacated			
7	Michael Rasmussen (Den)	Rabobank	+ 11'33"	31
8	Cadel Evans (Aus)	Davitamon	+ 11'55"	28
9	Floyd Landis (USA)	Phonak	+ 12'44"	29
10	Óscar Pereiro (Esp)	Phonak	+ 16'04"	27
Lanterne Rouge				
155	Iker Flores (Esp)	Euskaltel	+ 4h20'24"	28
Points				
	Thor Hushovd (Nor)	Crédit Agricole		27
King of the Mountains				
	Michael Rasmussen (Den)	Rabobank		31
Youth				
	Yaroslav Popovych (Ukr)	Discovery Channel		25
Team				
		T-Mobile		
Super Combativité				
	Óscar Pereiro (Esp)	Phonak		27

Note: In 2012 Lance Armstrong was stripped of all his results dating back to 1 August, 1998 following an investigation by the United States Anti-Doping Agency into doping at his teams. None of his results in the 2005 Tour de France were re-awarded.
(1) During the USADA investigation in 2012 David Zabriskie and Levi Leipheimer admitted their doping and were stripped of their results.
(2) Jan Ullrich was found guilty in 2012 of having worked with Eufemiano Fuentes and stripped of results dating back to May 2005.

2006: For the Loser Now Will Be Later to Win

In 2006, for cycling at least, the times really were a changing. Lance Armstrong was gone, and a new generation of riders was about to step up to the plate. Some dared to hope that they would clean up their act, but that was too much to ask for. It would take something serious, something very serious, to make them realise that the public was getting tired of their doping. In 2006 two very serious somethings were delivered. The first was a major Spanish doping case, Operación Puerto, in which the doping practices of Eufemiano Fuentes were laid bare. The second was the new champion of the Tour, Floyd Landis, being busted for doping while en route to his Tour victory.

Puerto arose on the back of Jesús Manzano's 2004 claims about drug use in the Kelme squad during his time as a member of the team, claims which – at the time – the UCI dismissed out of hand. In May 2006 Spanish police raided the offices of Fuentes and took custody of more than 100 bags of stored blood, each labelled with a codename. Various teams and riders found themselves excluded from the 2006 Tour on the back of the Puerto investigation, among them likely favourites Jan Ullrich (T-Mobile) and Ivan Basso (CSC). One sponsor – Liberty Seguros, funding the team than once was ONCE – pulled the plug immediately. Finally, the *peloton* was shown that there were real consequences, real financial consequences, arising from their doping – not just time off on the naughty step but the possibility of other teams walking away from the sport and crashing cycling's already precarious economy.

The Puerto investigation would rumble on and on for several years, with Fuentes – who had facilitated blood transfusions for dozens of riders, as well as many unnamed athletes from other sports – being handed a one-year suspended sentence after being found guilty of public health offences. But, while the case itself would never produce a satisfactory outcome, the fallout from it, coupled with events at the Tour, had a major impact on the sport, and for once there was real evidence of real change as cycling finally understood that its culture of chemical dependence was no longer sustainable and the sport would have to change with the times.

* * * * *

The Tour itself, stripped of some major pre-race favourites, became a two-way battle, between former Armstrong lieutenant Floyd Landis (Phonak) and Óscar Pereiro (Caisse d'Épargne – the latest iteration of the old Reynolds and Banesto squads).

Landis took control when the race reached the Pyrenees, donning the *maillot jaune* at the end of the second day in the high hills, Tarbes to Pla de Beret, with a slim eight-second lead over Cyril Dessel (AG2R) and the next three riders all within two minutes: Denis Menchov (Rabobank) at 1'01", Cadel Evans (Davitamon/Lotto) at 1'17" and Carlos Sastre (CSC) at 1'52".

The three transition stages taking the race over to the Alps should have changed nothing, should have been more chances for the sprinters, but on the second of the three a break got away that was allowed build up a lead of nearly 30 minutes with just 40 kilometres to go. The sprinters' teams surrendered, and Landis's Phonak squad seemed happy to see the break go. At the end of the stage, in Montélimar, the breakaways had an advantage of 29'57" over the *peloton* and the Tour had a new leader, Pereiro, who had started the day 28'50" down and now led Landis by 1'29". With the Alps still to come the Phonaks seemed to have acted wisely by treating the stage as a rest day and letting the breakaways have their moment in the sun, and Pereiro a couple of days in yellow.

That belief was strengthened on the first day in the Alps, when Landis took the jersey back at the top of Alpe d'Huez, with Pereiro pushed back to 10 seconds off yellow and the rest of the *peloton* two minutes and more back. All Landis had to do now was dispatch

Pereiro back to the depths of the general classification and the Tour win was in the bag.

And then the American blew it, and blew it big time. Cracking in the closing kilometres of the road to La Toussuire Landis lost 10 minutes and had to be dragged to the line by team-mate Axel Merckx (son of the Cannibal). Pereiro was back in yellow, with Sastre at 1'50". But Landis – now 8'08" off yellow – refused to bow down. There was still one more day in the mountains in which to mount a fight back. One more spin of the wheel. One last chance.

One last chance, that's all it was. There was still a time trial to come, and Landis was good for time in that, but not eight minutes. So Landis took his chance. Attacking on the Col de Saisses, just over 80 kilometres into the 200-kilometre stage Landis took off and went in pursuit of the day's early breakaways. Recalling Charly Gaul's exploits in 1958 – a shot at victory blown away by one bad day, only for Gaul to charge back into contention and steal the win – Landis charged on to Morzine, mopping up the escapees, while the *peloton* behind dawdled, giving him rope and hoping he would hang himself. At the finish, though, Landis was five minutes clear of Sastre, with Pereiro another two minutes back. The Spanish pretender maintained his hold on the yellow jersey, but now Landis was up to third, 30 seconds behind, with Sastre sandwiched between the two at 12 seconds off yellow.

As it had for Gaul in 1958, it would all come down to the final time trial. The race's earlier race against the clock – covering 52 kilometres – had seen Sastre losing 2'10" and Pereiro 2'40" to stage winner Serhiy Honchar (T-Mobile) while Landis was within 1'01" of the Ukrainian. This final time trial covered 57 kilometres to Montceau-les-Mines. Honchar again took the win, with Landis within 1'11" of his time while Pereiro was 1'29" behind that. Landis was back in yellow. For the eighth year in a row it was an American standing on the top step of the podium in Paris.

* * * * *

Four days after the Tour ended, as the shadow Tour kicked on and riders set out on the critérium circuit, the news broke: Landis was positive. The sample given after his stage win in Morzine showed evidence of testosterone use. Landis, naturally, challenged the test result and took his case all the way, leaving it unclear who had won the 2006 Tour until shortly before the 2008 race commenced. Landis was officially stripped of the win. After Maurice Garin in 1904 he was only the second Tour winner to be stripped of his victory (the Armstrong Tours were not vacated until 2012). Almost forgotten in it all was Óscar Pereiro, who won the Tour two years after he lost it.

Stage-by-Stage Results for the 2006 Tour de France			Stage Winner	Maillot Jaune
Prologue Sat 1 Jul	Strasbourg (ITT) 176 finishers	7.1 km 8'17" 51.4 kph	Thor Hushovd (Nor) Crédit Agricole	Thor Hushovd (Nor) Crédit Agricole
Stage 1 Sun 2 Jul	Strasbourg to Strasbourg 176 finishers	184.5 km 4h10'00" 44.3 kph	Jimmy Casper (Fra) Cofidis	~~George Hincapie (USA) Discovery Channel (2)~~
				Vacated
Rated climbs: Côte de Heiligenstein (290m) Fabian Wegmann (Ger) Gerolsteiner				
Stage 2 Mon 3 Jul	Obernai to Esch-sur-Alzette 175 finishers	228.5 km 5h36'14" 40.8 kph	Robbie McEwen (Aus) Davitamon	Thor Hushovd (Nor) Crédit Agricole
Rated climbs: Col des Pandours (662m) Aitor Hernández (Esp) Euskaltel; Col de Valsberg (652m) Aitor Hernández (Esp) Euskaltel; Côte de Kédange-sur-Canner (253m) David de la Fuente (Esp) Saunier Duval; Côte de Kanfen (325m) David de la Fuente (Esp) Saunier Duval; Côte de Volmerange-les-Mines (410m) Fabian Wegmann (Ger) Gerolsteiner				
Stage 3 Tue 4 Jul	Esch-sur-Alzette to Valkenburg 172 finishers	216.5 km 4h57'54" 43.6 kph	Matthias Kessler (Ger) T-Mobile	Tom Boonen (Bel) Quick Step
Rated climbs: Côte de la Haute-Levée (502m) Jérôme Pineau (Fra) Bouygues Telecom Côte de Oneux (327m) Jérôme Pineau (Fra) Bouygues Telecom Côte de Petit-Rechain (270m) Jérôme Pineau (Fra) Bouygues Telecom Côte de Loorberg (216m) Jérôme Pineau (Fra) Bouygues Telecom Côte de Trintelen (195m) José Luis Arrieta (Esp) AG2R Le Cauberg (135m) Matthias Kessler (Ger) T-Mobile				
Stage 4 Wed 5 Jul	Huy to Saint-Quentin 172 finishers	207 km 4h59'50" 41.4 kph	Robbie McEwen (Aus) Davitamon	Tom Boonen (Bel) Quick Step
Rated climbs: Côte de Peu d'Eau (215m) Jérôme Pineau (Fra) Bouygues Telecom; Côte de Falaën (217m) Laurent Lefèvre (Fra) Bouygues Telecom				
Stage 5 Thu 6 Jul	Beauvais to Caen 172 finishers	225 km 5h18'50" 42.3 kph	Óscar Freire (Esp) Rabobank	Tom Boonen (Bel) Quick Step
Rated climbs: Mont des Fourches (234m) Jérôme Pineau (Fra) Bouygues Telecom Côte du Buquet (116m) Björn Schröder (Ger) Milram Côte de Saint-Grégoire-du-Vièvre (153m) Björn Schröder (Ger) Milram Côte du Boulay (145m) Björn Schröder (Ger) Milram				

Stage-by-Stage Results for the 2006 Tour de France			Stage Winner	Maillot Jaune
Stage 6 Fri 7 Jul	Lisieux to Vitré 171 finishers	189 km 4h10'17" 45.3 kph	Robbie McEwen (Aus) Davitamon	Tom Boonen (Bel) Quick Step
	Rated climbs: Côte de la Hunière (231m) Giuseppe Guerini (Ita) T-Mobile			
Stage 7 Sat 8 Jul	Saint-Grégoire to Rennes (ITT) 170 finishers	52 km 1h01'43" 50.6 kph	Serhiy Honchar (Ukr) T-Mobile	Serhiy Honchar (Ukr) T-Mobile
Stage 8 Sun 9 Jul	Saint-Méen Le Grand to Lorient 170 finishers	181 km 4h13'18" 42.9 kph	Sylvain Calzati (Fra) AG2R	Serhiy Honchar (Ukr) T-Mobile
	Rated climbs: Côte de Mûr-de-Bretagne (295m) Sylvain Calzati (Fra) AG2R Côte de Saint-Mayeux (287m) Sylvain Calzati (Fra) AG2R Côte de Gouarec (234m) Sylvain Calzati (Fra) AG2R			
Mon 10 Jul	Rest Day			
Stage 9 Tue 11 Jul	Bordeaux to Dax 170 finishers	169.5 km 3h35'24" 47.2 kph	Óscar Freire (Esp) Rabobank	Serhiy Honchar (Ukr) T-Mobile
Stage 10 Wed 12 Jul	Cambo-les-Bains to Pau 168 finishers	190.5 km 4h49'10" 39.5 kph	Juan Miguel Mercado (Esp) Agritubel	Cyril Dessel (Fra) AG2R
	Rated climbs: Col d'Osquich (500m) Cyril Dessel (Fra) AG2R Col du Soudet (1,540m) Cyril Dessel (Fra) AG2R Col de Marie-Blanque (1,035m) Cyril Dessel (Fra) AG2R			
Stage 11 Thu 13 Jul	Tarbes Val d'Aran to Pla de Beret 165 finishers	206.5 km 6h06'25" 33.8 kph	Denis Menchov (Rus) Rabobank	Floyd Landis (USA) Phonak
	Rated climbs: Col du Tourmalet (2,115m) David de la Fuente (Esp) Saunier Duval Col d'Aspin (1,489m) Fabian Wegmann (Ger) Gerolsteiner Col de Peyresourde (1,569m) David de la Fuente (Esp) Saunier Duval Col du Portillon (1,298m) David de la Fuente (Esp) Saunier Duval Puerto de Beret (1,860m) Denis Menchov (Rus) Rabobank			
Stage 12 Fri 14 Jul	Luchon to Carcassonne 160 finishers	211.5 km 4h34'58" 46.2 kph	Yaroslav Popovych (Ukr) Discovery Channel	Floyd Landis (USA) Phonak
	Rated climbs: Col des Ares (796m) Michael Rasmussen (Den) Rabobank; Côte de Pujos (520m) David Millar (GBr) Garmin; Côte du Pâl de Pailhes (445m) Christophe le Mével (Fra) Crédit Agricole; Côte de Pamiers (407m) Yaroslav Popovych (Ukr) Discovery Channel			
Stage 13 Sat 15 Jul	Béziers to Montélimar 160 finishers	230 km 5h24'36" 42.5 kph	Jens Voigt (Ger) CSC	Óscar Pereiro (Esp) Caisse d'Épargne
	Rated climbs: Côte de Puéchabon (290m) Sylvain Chavanel (Fra) Cofidis Col de la Cardonille (330m) Andriy Grivko (Ukr) Milram Côte de l'Arbousset (230m) Sylvain Chavanel (Fra) Cofidis Côte de Saint-Maurice d'Ibie (306m) Andriy Grivko (Ukr) Milram Côte de Villeneuve de Berg (398m) Jens Voigt (Ger) CSC			

Stage-by-Stage Results for the 2006 Tour de France			Stage Winner	Maillot Jaune
Stage 14 Sun 16 Jul	Montélimar to Gap 156 finishers	180.5 km 4h14'23" 42.6 kph	Pierrick Fédrigo (Fra) Bouygues Telecom	Óscar Pereiro (Esp) Caisse d'Épargne
Rated climbs: Côte du Bois de Salles (443m) Michael Boogerd Col de Peyruergue (820m) Salvatore Commesso (Ita) Lampre Col de Perty (1,303m) David Cañada (Esp) Saunier Duval Col de la Sentinelle (980m) Salvatore Commesso (Ita) Lampre				
Mon 17 Jul	Rest Day			
Stage 15 Tue 18 Jul	Gap to l'Alpe d'Huez 152 finishers	187 km 4h52'22" 38.4 kph	Fränk Schleck (Lux) CSC	Floyd Landis (USA) Phonak
Rated climbs: Col d'Izoard (2,360m) Stefano Garzelli (Ita) Liquigas Col du Lautaret (2,058m) David de la Fuente (Esp) Saunier Duval l'Alpe d'Huez (1,860m) Fränk Schleck (Lux) CSC				
Stage 16 Wed 19 Jul	Bourg-d'Oisans to La Toussuire 147 finishers	182 km 5h36'04" 32.5 kph	Michael Rasmussen (Den) Rabobank	Óscar Pereiro (Esp) Caisse d'Épargne
Rated climbs: Col du Galibier (2,645m) Michael Rasmussen (Den) Rabobank Col de la Croix de Fer (2,067m) Michael Rasmussen (Den) Rabobank Col du Mollard (1,638m) Michael Rasmussen (Den) Rabobank La Toussuire (1,690m) Michael Rasmussen (Den) Rabobank				
Stage 17 Thu 20 Jul	Saint-Jean-de-Maurienne to Morzine 143 finishers	200.5 km 5h23'36" 37.2 kph	~~Floyd Landis (USA)~~ ~~Phonak~~ (1)	Óscar Pereiro (Esp) Caisse d'Épargne
			Carlos Sastre (Esp) CSC	
Rated climbs: Col des Saisies (1,633m) Patrice Halgand (Fra) Crédit Agricole Col des Aravis (1,498m) Patrice Halgand (Fra) Crédit Agricole Col de la Colombière (1,618m) Floyd Landis (USA) Phonak Côte de Châtillon-sur-Cluses (730m) Floyd Landis (USA) Phonak Col de Joux-Plane (1,700m) Floyd Landis (USA) Phonak				
Stage 18 Fri 21 Jul	Morzine to Mâcon 141 finishers	197 km 4h16'15" 46.1 kph	Matteo Tosatto (Ita) Quick Step	Óscar Pereiro (Esp) Caisse d'Épargne
Rated climbs: Côte de Châtillon-en-Michaille (535m) Mario Aerts (Bel) Davitamon; Col du Berthiand (780m) Sylvain Calzati (Fra) AG2R; Côte de Chambod (437m) Levi Leipheimer (USA) Gerolsteiner				
Stage 19 Sat 22 Jul	Le Creusot to Montceau-les-Mines (ITT) 140 finishers	57 km 1h07'45" 50.5 kph	Serhiy Honchar (Ukr) T-Mobile	~~Floyd Landis (USA)~~ ~~Phonak~~ (1)
				Óscar Pereiro (Esp) Caisse d'Épargne
Stage 20 Sun 23 Jul	Sceaux (Antony) to Paris (Champs-Élysées) 139 finishers	154.5 km 3h56'52" 39.1 kph	Thor Hushovd (Nor) Crédit Agricole	~~Floyd Landis (USA)~~ ~~Phonak~~ (1)
				Óscar Pereiro (Esp) Caisse d'Épargne
Rated climbs: Côte de Gif-sur-Yvette (153m) Michael Rasmussen (Den) Rabobank; Mont Valérien (129m) Victor Hugo Peña (Col) Phonak				

Prize fund: 3,200,000 euro (first prize: 450,000 euro)

Final Classification

Place		Rider	Team	Time	Age
1		~~Floyd Landis (USA)~~ (1)	Phonak	~~3,657 km~~ ~~89h39'30"~~ ~~40.784 kph~~	~~30~~
2	1	Óscar Pereiro (Esp)	Caisse d'Épargne	+ 0'57"	28
3	2	Andreas Klöden (Ger)	T-Mobile	+ 1'29"	31
4	3	Carlos Sastre (Esp)	CSC	+ 3'13"	31
5	4	Cadel Evans (Aus)	Davitamon	+ 5'08"	29
6	5	Denis Menchov (Rus)	Rabobank	+ 7'06"	28
7	6	Cyril Dessel (Fra)	AG2R	+ 8'41"	31
8	7	Christophe Moreau (Fra)	AG2R	+ 9'37"	35
9	8	Haimar Zubeldia (Esp)	Euskaltel	+ 12'05"	29
~~10~~	9	Michael Rogers (Aus)	T-Mobile	+ 15'07"	26
~~11~~	10	Fränk Schleck (Lux)	CSC	+ 17'46"	26

Lanterne Rouge

~~139~~	139	Wim Vansevenant (Bel)	Davitamon	+ 4h02'01"	34

Points

		Robbie McEwen (Aus)	Davitamon		34

King of the Mountains

		Michael Rasmussen (Den)	Rabobank		32

Youth

		Damiano Cunego (Ita)	Lampre		24

Team

			T-Mobile		

Super Combativité

		Aitor Hernández (Esp)	Euskaltel		24

(1) Floyd Landis was stripped of his Morzine stage win and overall Tour title after failing an anti-doping control.
(2) During the USADA investigation George Hincapie admitted his doping and was stripped of his result.

2007: The Year of Living Dangerously

Between Operación Puerto and Floyd Landis, cycling got yet another wake up call in 2006. And as early as 2007 there was some evidence that some teams were actually heeding it this time. Jonathan Vaughters at Slipstream and Bjarne Riis at CSC implemented independent anti-doping programmes at their teams, programmes that would go further than the basic UCI testing and look at longitudinal details. They were joined by Bob Stapleton at T-Mobile (the latest iteration of Deutsche Telekom), following confessions from various former riders that they had doped during their time with the German team. Suddenly the sport went from having one or two riders you could dare to believe raced clean to having one or two teams you could dare to believe the same of. On the back of those independent anti-doping programmes, the UCI introduced its own longitudinal testing, the Biological Passport, which – though imperfect, being limited in its scope to looking just for evidence of blood doping – was a major step forward in the battle to beat doping, relying as it does on indirect evidence of drug use. The sort of indirect evidence Guy Brisson wanted the UCI to look at back in 1996.

Among those former Telekom riders realising that confession was good for the soul was Riis, who finally admitted that EPO had played a role in his 1996 Tour win. The authorities at ASO were shocked. Immediately they decided to strip the Dane of his Tour victory, neglecting the legal niceties such as the statute of limitations (eight years) and the fact that ASO didn't have the authority to strip victories from past winners. Also conveniently forgotten was the fact that, when Bernard Thévenet confessed that his 1975 and 1977 Tour victories owed more than a little to his use of cortisone, the

Tour bosses were deaf to his words and simply pretended they weren't spoken. They remain deaf to them to this day and warmly welcome the French champion to the Tour.

Helping drive home the message that doping was damaging the sport was the news that Addidas – one of T-Mobile's co-sponsors – was withdrawing its €500,000 funding. They joined other sponsors such as Liberty Seguros, Würth, and Communidad Valenciana, who had pulled out from other teams on the back of Operación Puerto. Doping was clearly impacting the sport's economy.

But, while some clearly did get the message, many didn't, and things were going to have get worse before they got better. And at the 2007 Tour they got a lot worse.

* * * * *

A few weeks before the Tour started the UCI's Anne Gripper – the woman in charge of the UCI's handling of anti-doping – informed the media that she had a special watch-list of six or seven riders, dubbed the Men in Black, who were messing around with the recently introduced whereabouts system and evading out-of-competition tests, an offence that could trigger the equivalent of a test failure.

The UCI were so concerned by what was going on in the sport that all top-tier riders were asked to voluntarily sign a Rider's Commitment to a New Cycling, in which they pledged to pay a year's salary should they test positive. The voluntary nature of this Commitment was somewhat undermined by the diktat that only riders who'd put their name to it could ride the Tour.

The Tour itself actually started in good spirits, in London, England, with the British pushing out the boat to celebrate the race's third visit to Great Britain and its first start there. After the usual opening week of sprinters having fun, things warmed up when the race hit the mountains and Rabobank's Michael Rasmussen – known to fans as the Chicken – took control on the road from Le Grand-Bornand to Tignes, Stage Eight. The Dane led T-Mobile's Linus Gerdemann by 43 seconds (having taken the yellow jersey from him), with the rest of the field two minutes and more back.

A few days later, as the race transitioned across to the Pyrenees, news broke that Rasmussen had missed a number of out-of-competition tests over the previous two years. The basic case against Rasmussen is quite simple, though somewhat complicated by cycling's alphabet soup of differing agencies with responsibility for carrying out doping controls. The key agencies involved here are the UCI and the ADD (Anti Doping Denmark, the Danish arm of WADA).

The timeline of events runs as follows: on 24 March 2006 the UCI issued Rasmussen a recorded warning for having failed to provide whereabouts information for the second quarter of 2006 (April to June), which information should have been submitted by 17 March; ADD attempted to test Rasmussen on 6 April 2007, failed, and issued a recorded warning (8 May 2007); on 29 June 2007 the UCI issued a further recorded warning, this time concerning Rasmussen's late filing of changes to his whereabouts during the periods 4-12 and 12-28 June 2007; ADD again attempted to test Rasmussen on 21 June 2007 and again failed and again issued a recorded warning (10 July 2007).

Under the relevant rules, a rider needed three recorded warnings from the same agency within a rolling 18-month period in order to trigger a doping violation. On 10 July then – four days into the Tour – Rasmussen was in receipt of four separate recorded warnings, two from the UCI for late filing of whereabouts information and two from ADD for missed tests. Under the relevant rules the Dane was sailing close to the wind but had not yet triggered an anti-doping violation. How many other riders in the *peloton* were in similarly choppy waters is not known; generally it's not something riders talk about and, while someone felt it necessary to leak Rasmussen's whereabouts problems, no one was talking about other riders.

While out-of-competition testing had been available to the UCI for some time (Bo Hamburger had been caught by the newly introduced EPO test in 2001 following an out-of-competition test after the Flèche Wallonne, and you can find riders failing out-of-competition tests in the 1990s) it did not really become a proper tool in the anti-doping arsenal until after the whereabouts system was implemented. That only came into being following the UCI's acceptance the World

Anti-Doping Code prior to the 2004 Athens Olympics (the previous out-of-competition system was used at World Championships and on rest days in stage races, along with those occasions when the UCI actually knew – or could guess – a rider's whereabouts).

The Chicken's whereabouts weren't the only doping problem rocking the Tour. Two days after the Dane donned the *maillot* jaune T-Mobile's Patrik Sinkewitz was pulled from the race having been informed he'd failed an out-of-competition test before the Tour commenced. Following the Telekom confessions earlier in the year this prompted German TV channels ZDF and ARD to pull the plug on their broadcasts.

In the atmosphere of the time there was little sympathy for anyone suspected of doping. And little regard for the letter of the law either: no one questioned how or why Rasmussen's whereabouts problems had been leaked, what real purpose was being served by embarrassing him. If the dopers were going to pay scant regard to the rules, well the anti-doping side could do the same too. All that mattered was cleaning the sport up.

Things were bad enough for Rasmussen as they were, with questions being asked about his whereabouts violations. Then they got worse. For several years a story had been floating around in cycling circles concerning a shoe box that contained a blood substitute. Shortly before the Tour commenced the story had appeared in David Walsh's *From Lance to Landis*. No one had been able to stand the story up before; it was the word of one man, Whitney Richards, against another, and heretofore Richards had insisted on keeping his name out of the story. But then Richards decided to go public with it, naming Rasmussen. *VeloNews*'s Neal Rogers confronted Rasmussen with the question in a post-stage press conference: were you the rider Richards was talking about? Rasmussen claimed to be unable to confirm the story.

That press conference came at the end of Stage 12 and the following day delivered the individual time trial, where Rasmussen's 2'35" lead over Caisse d'Épargne's Alejandro Valverde in the general classification was expected to evaporate. Instead, the Dane raised eyebrows with a ride that saw him holding onto the yellow

Tom Boonen with Alberto Contador, winner of the 2007 Tour de France.

jersey on the day most everyone expected him to lose it, ending the day with a 1'00" GC lead over Cadel Evans (Predictor/Lotto). The Chicken was a mountain goat better known for falling off his bike a lot in time trials. While he clearly had room for improvement the level by which he'd stepped up surprised many. Still, they do say that the yellow jersey gives you wings and Rasmussen attributed much of his performance on the day to weather conditions that had improved by the time he shot down the start ramp.

Nothing much changed over the next few days, save for a comment from UCI president Pat McQuaid that he would feel uncomfortable were Rasmussen to win the Tour (McQuaid had already said he'd be uncomfortable with an Alexander Vinokourov (Astana) victory after he'd revealed he was working with Michele Ferrari). On the 24 July rest day – separating Stages 15 and 16 – Vinokourov was bounced out of the race when he tested positive for a heterologous blood transfusion, and the whole of his Astana team withdrew from the race.

On that rest day Rasmussen had given the usual press conference for the wearer of the yellow jersey. A lot of the questions he faced concerned the doping cloud hanging over him. Rasmussen's answers managed to make a bad situation worse. Given that cycling is, in reality, as much about marketing as it is about sport, and athletes act as brand ambassadors for their sponsors, it is remarkable how little media training they receive. As fans, we quite like this, it makes them, if not more honest and open, then at least more human in their answers. Sometimes, though, they are all too human.

Rasmussen's first mistake was to try and explain away the recorded warnings he had received. The first recorded warning, he claimed, had been issued without the normal step of a written warning having been issued (a rider is supposed to receive a written warning, to which he can provide an explanation and it is only if that explanation is not accepted that a recorded warning gets issued). The Dane tried to explain that he had phoned the UCI at the time about this. Asked by the media who had taken his call Rasmussen said it was Anne Gripper. The problem here was that, when Rasmussen had claimed to have called the UCI in spring 2006, Gripper was not yet in situ, not having taken up her position with the UCI until later in the year.

That proved to be the least of the problems Rasmussen caused for himself that day. In explaining the missed test from ADD and his second late-filing error with the UCI, Rasmussen made reference to the fact that he had been training in Mexico. Rasmussen was a man of the world: a Dane married to a Mexican who lived in Italy and rode under a racing licence issued in Monaco. That he was known to train in Mexico had led some to speculate that he was one of Gripper's half-dozen Men in Black.

The problem with the Mexico story, though, was that earlier in the race, during a TV transmission, Italian commentator and former professional Davide Cassani had made a reference to having seen Rasmussen training in Italy, Cassani making the point that Rasmussen was taking his preparation for the Tour seriously. Rasmussen was now saying that, at the time Cassani said he saw him in Italy, he was actually in Mexico. When a Danish journalist, DR's Niels Christian, got Cassani to go on the record with his sighting of the Dane in the Dolomites the Chicken's goose was well and truly cooked.

When the Tour resumed on Stage 16 some riders decided to stage a sit-down protest at the start, against the dopers in their midst. The day ended with Cofidis joining Astana in withdrawing from the race when Cristian Moreni was revealed to have failed a doping control. It also ended with Rasmussen having taken the stage and all but assured his overall victory, now having a lead of 3'10" over Alberto Contador (Discovery Channel). A few hours later Rabobank withdrew Rasmussen from the race, claiming the Dane had lied to them about his whereabouts.

After that, Contador inherited the Dane's lead and went on to win a Tour that had been shrouded in a cloud of suspicion and fear.

* * * * *

Four months later the UCI issued Rasmussen with a written warning concerning incorrect whereabouts information for the period 21-29 June. Early in January 2008 that became a recorded warning. The Chicken now had three strikes against him from the UCI and consequently won a two-year suspension as the booby prize.

Stage-by-Stage Results for the 2007 Tour de France			Stage Winner	Maillot Jaune
Prologue Sat 7 Jul	London (ITT) 189 finishers	7.9 km 8'50" 53.7 kph	Fabian Cancellara (Sui) CSC	Fabian Cancellara (Sui) CSC
Stage 1 Sun 8 Jul	London to Canterbury 188 finishers	203 km 4h39'01" 43.7 kph	Robbie McEwen (Aus) Predictor	Fabian Cancellara (Sui) CSC
Stage 2 Mon 9 Jul	Dunkerque to Ghent 188 finishers	168.5 km 3h48'22" 44.3 kph	Gert Steegmans (Bel) Quick Step	Fabian Cancellara (Sui) CSC
Stage 3 Tue 10 Jul	Waregem to Compiègne 187 finishers	236.5 km 6h36'15" 35.8 kph	Fabian Cancellara (Sui) CSC	Fabian Cancellara (Sui) CSC
	Rated climbs: Côte de Blérancourt (142m) Stéphane Augé (Fra) Cofidis			
Stage 4 Wed 11 Jul	Villers-Cotterêts to Joigny 186 finishers	193 km 4h37'47" 41.7 kph	Thor Hushovd (Nor) Crédit Agricole	Fabian Cancellara (Sui) CSC
	Rated climbs: Côte de Veuilly la Poterie (125m) Aleksandr Kuchynski (Blr) Liquigas; Côte de Doucy (170m) Sylvain Chavanel (Fra) Cofidis; Côte de Galbaux (173m) Sylvain Chavanel (Fra) Cofidis; Côte de Bel-Air (170m) Christian Knees (Ger) Milram			
Stage 5 Thu 12 Jul	Chablis to Autun 184 finishers	182.5 km 4h39'01" 39.2 kph	Filippo Pozzato (Ita) Liquigas	Fabian Cancellara (Sui) CSC
	Rated climbs: Côte des Grandes-Châtelaines (284m) Sylvain Chavanel (Fra) Cofidis; Côte de Domecy-sur-Cure (238m) Sylvain Chavanel (Fra) Cofidis; Côte de Champignolles-le-Bas (338m) Sylvain Chavanel (Fra) Cofidis; Côte de Coulon (275m) Sylvain Chavanel (Fra) Cofidis; Côte de Saint-Maurice (389m) Sylvain Chavanel (Fra) Cofidis; Côte de Château-Chinon (519m) Sylvain Chavanel (Fra) Cofidis; Haut-Folin (867m) Sylvain Chavanel (Fra) Cofidis; Côte de la Croix de la Libération (586m) Laurent Lefèvre (Fra) Bouygues Telecom			
Stage 6 Fri 13 Jul	Semur-en-Auxois to Bourg-en-Bresse 183 finishers	199.5 km 5h20'59" 37.3 kph	Tom Boonen (Bel) Quick Step	Fabian Cancellara (Sui) CSC
	Rated climbs: Côte de Grandmont (479m) Bradley Wiggins (GBr) Cofidis; Col de Brancion (354m) Bradley Wiggins (GBr) Cofidis			
Stage 7 Sat 14 Jul	Bourg-en-Bresse to Le Grand-Bornand 180 finishers	197.5 km 4h53'13" 40.4 kph	Linus Gerdemann (Ger) T-Mobile	Linus Gerdemann (Ger) T-Mobile
	Rated climbs: Côte de Corlier (753m) Michael Rasmussen (Den) Rabobank; Côte de Cruseilles (770m) David de la Fuente (Esp) Saunier Duval; Côte Peguin (874m) David de la Fuente (Esp) Saunier Duval; Col de la Colombière (1,618m) Linus Gerdemann (Ger) T-Mobile			

Stage-by-Stage Results for the 2007 Tour de France			Stage Winner	Maillot Jaune
Stage 8 Sun 15 Jul	Le Grand-Bornand to Tignes 172 finishers	165 km 4h49'40" 34.2 kph	Michael Rasmussen (Den) Rabobank	Michael Rasmussen (Den) Rabobank
	Rated climbs: Col du Marais (843m) Stefan Schumacher (Ger) Gerolsteiner; Côte du Bouchet-Mont-Charvin (931m) Stefan Schumacher (Ger) Gerolsteiner; Col de Tamié (907m) Thomas Voeckler (Fra) Bouygues; Cormet de Roselend (1,968m) Michael Rasmussen (Den) Rabobank; Montée d'Hauteville (1,639m) Michael Rasmussen (Den) Rabobank; Tignes (2,068m) Michael Rasmussen (Den) Rabobank			
Mon 16 Jul	Rest Day			
Stage 9 Tue 17 Jul	Val d'Isère to Briançon 171 finishers	159.5 km 4h14'24" 37.6 kph	Mauricio Soler (Col) Barloworld	Michael Rasmussen (Den) Rabobank
	Rated climbs: Col de l'Iseran (2,770m) Yaroslav Popovych (Ukr) Discovery Channel; Col du Télégraphe (1,566m) Mikel Astarloza (Esp) Euskaltel; Col du Galibier (2,645m) Mauricio Soler (Col) Barloworld			
Stage 10 Wed 18 Jul	Tallard to Marseille 171 finishers	229.5 km 5h20'24" 43 kph	Cédric Vasseur (Fra) Quick Step	Michael Rasmussen (Den) Rabobank
	Rated climbs: Côte de Châteauneuf-Val-Saint Donat (666m) Marcus Burghardt (Ger) T-Mobile; Côte de Villedieu (384m) Patrice Halgand (Fra) Crédit Agricole; Côte des Bastides (354m) Patrice Halgand (Fra) Crédit Agricole; Col de la Gineste (324m) Patrice Halgand (Fra) Crédit Agricole			
Stage 11 Thu 19 Jul	Marseille to Montpellier 168 finishers	182.5 km 3h47'50" 48.1 kph	Robbie Hunter (RSA) Barloworld	Michael Rasmussen (Den) Rabobank
	Rated climbs: Côte de Calissanne (136m) Kanstantsin Sivtsov (Blr) Barloworld			
Stage 12 Fri 20 Jul	Montpellier to Castres 166 finishers	178.5 km 4h25'32" 40.3 kph	Tom Boonen (Bel) Quick Step	Michael Rasmussen (Den) Rabobank
	Rated climbs: Côte de Cantagal (171m) Philippe Gilbert (Bel) Française des Jeux; Côte du Mas-Rouet (380m) Amets Txurruka (Esp) Euskaltel; Col du Buis (340m) Amets Txurruka (Esp) Euskaltel; Montée de la Jeante (958m) Amets Txurruka (Esp) Euskaltel			
Stage 13 Sat 21 Jul	Albi (ITT) 166 finishers	54 km 1h06'34" 48.7 kph	~~Alexander Vinokourov~~ ~~(Kaz)~~ ~~Astana~~ (1) Cadel Evans (Aus) Predictor	Michael Rasmussen (Den) Rabobank
Stage 14 Sun 22 Jul	Mazamet to Plateau de Beille 165 finishers	197 km 5h25'48" 36.3 kph	Alberto Contador (Esp) Discovery Channel	Michael Rasmussen (Den) Rabobank
	Rated climbs: Côte de Saint-Sarraille (810m) David de la Fuente (Esp) Saunier Duval; Port de Pailhères (2,001m) Rubén Pérez (Esp) Euskaltel; Plateau de Beille (1,780m) Alberto Contador Velasco (Esp) Discovery Channel			

Stage-by-Stage Results for the 2007 Tour de France				Stage Winner	Maillot Jaune
Stage 15 Mon 23 Jul	Foix to Loudenvielle (Le Louron) 160 finishers	196 km 5h34'28" 35.2 kph		~~Alexander Vinokourov~~ ~~(Kaz)~~ ~~Astana~~ (1)	Michael Rasmussen (Den) Rabobank
				Kim Kirchen (Lux) T-Mobile	
	Rated climbs: Col de Port (1,249m) Juan Manuel Garate (Esp) Quick Step; Col de Portet d'Aspet (1,069m) Laurent Lefèvre (Fra) Bouygues Telecom; Col de Menté (1,349m) Juan Manuel Garate (Esp) Quickstep; Port de Balès (1,755m) Kim Kirchen (Lux) T-Mobile; Col de Peyresourde (1,569m) Alexander Vinokourov (Kaz) Astana				
Tue 24 Jul	Rest Day				
Stage 16 Wed 25 Jul	Orthez to Gourette (Col d'Aubisque) 150 finishers	218.5 km 6h23'21" 34.2 kph		Michael Rasmussen (Den) Rabobank	Michael Rasmussen (Den) Rabobank
	Rated climbs: Port de Larrau (1,573m) José Vicente García (Esp) Caisse d'Épargne; Alto Laza (1,129m) José Vicente García (Esp) Caisse d'Épargne; Col de la Pierre-Saint-Martin (1,760m) Mauricio Soler (Col) Barloworld; Col de Marie-Blanque (1,035m) Mauricio Soler (Col) Barloworld; Col d'Aubisque (1,709m) Michael Rasmussen (Den) Rabobank				
Stage 17 Thu 26 Jul	Pau to Castelsarrasin 141 finishers	188.5 km 4h14'04" 44.5 kph		Daniele Bennati (Ita) Lampre	Alberto Contador (Esp) Discovery Channel
	Rated climbs: Côte de Baleix (348m) Matteo Tosatto (Ita) Quickstep; Côte de Villecomtal (335m) Markus Fothen (Ger) Gerolsteiner; Côte de Miélan (283m) Markus Fothen (Ger) Gerolsteiner; Côte de Sainte-Dode aux Croix (328m) David Millar (GBr) Saunier Duval; Côte de Mont-Theux (330m) David Millar (GBr) Saunier Duval; Côte de la Montagnère (177m) Jens Voigt (Ger) CSC				
Stage 18 Fri 27 Jul	Cahors to Angoulême 141 finishers	211 km 5h13'31" 40.4 kph		Sandy Casar (Fra) Française des Jeux	Alberto Contador (Esp) Discovery Channel
	Rated climbs: Côte de Salvezou (246m) Frederik Willems (Bel) Liquigas; Côte de Lavercantière (288m) Laurent Lefèvre (Fra) Bouygues Telecom; Côte de Saint-Martial-de-Nabirat (235m) Laurent Lefèvre (Fra) Bouygues Telecom; Côte de Saint-Cyprien (277m) Michael Boogerd (Ned) Rabobank				
Stage 19 Sat 28 Jul	Cognac to Angoulême (ITT) 141 finishers	55.5 km 1h02'44" 53.1 kph		~~Levi Leipheimer (USA)~~ ~~Discovery Channel~~ (2)	Alberto Contador (Esp) Discovery Channel
				Vacated	
Stage 20 Sun 29 Jul	Marcoussis to Paris (Champs-Élysées) 141 finishers	146 km 3h51'03" 37.9 kph		Daniele Bennati (Ita) Lampre	Alberto Contador (Esp) Discovery Channel
	Rated climbs: Côte de Saint-Rémy-les-Chevreuse (153m) Gert Steegmans (Bel) Quickstep; Côte de Châteaufort (190m) Gert Steegmans (Bel) Quickstep				

(1) Alexander Vinokourov was stripped of his stage wins after testing positive for a blood transfusion.
(2) During the USADA investigation Levi Leipheimer admitted his doping and was stripped of his results.

Prize fund: 3,200,000 euro (first prize: 450,000 euro)

Final Classification

Place	Rider	Team	Time	Age
1	Alberto Contador (Esp)	Discovery Channel	3,570 km 91h00'26" 39.228 kph	24
2	Cadel Evans (Aus)	Predictor	+ 0'23"	30
3	~~Levi Leipheimer (USA)~~ (2)	Discovery Channel	+ 0'31"	33
3	Vacated			
4	Carlos Sastre (Esp)	CSC	+ 7'08"	32
5	Haimar Zubeldia (Esp)	Euskaltel	+ 8'17"	30
6	Alejandro Valverde (Esp)	Caisse d'Épargne	+ 11'37"	27
7	Kim Kirchen (Lux)	T-Mobile	+ 12'18"	29
8	Yaroslav Popovych (Ukr)	Discovery Channel	+ 12'25"	27
9	Mikel Astarloza (Esp)	Euskaltel	+ 14'14"	27
10	Óscar Pereiro (Esp)	Caisse d'Épargne	+ 14'25"	29

Lanterne Rouge

141	Wim Vansevenant (Bel)	Predictor	+ 3h52'54"	35

Points

	Tom Boonen (Bel)	Quick Step		26

King of the Mountains

	Mauricio Soler (Col)	Barloworld		24

Youth

	Alberto Contador (Esp)	Discovery Channel		24

Team

		Discovery Channel		

Super Combativité

	Amets Txurruka (Esp)	Euskaltel		24

2008: The ProTour Wars

Doping was not the only thing causing headaches within the cycling community in 2007. There was also a bit of a brouhaha between the sport's governing body, the UCI, and the major race organiser, ASO, over the shape and nature of the cycling calendar.

Problems with the cycling calendar date back to the earliest days of the sport. It wasn't until the 1940s that anyone really bothered trying to put some shape on the calendar, with the creation in 1948 of the Challenge Desgrange-Colombo. That lasted through to 1958, when the organising newspapers – principally *L'Équipe* in France and *La Gazzetta dello Sport* in Italy – had a falling out. Into the void created by the disappearance of the Challenge Desgrange-Colombo stepped the French drinks company Pernod, with the Super Prestige Pernod trophy, which awarded points to riders based on their performance in key one-day and stage races throughout the season. That lasted through to 1987 but disappeared following a change in French legislation which effectively stopped drinks companies sponsoring sport.

A few years before the demise of the Super Prestige Pernod trophy the UCI introduced a ranking system for riders. At this time the sport was split between amateurs and professionals. The professional side of the sport was governed by the FICP (Fédération Internationale de Cyclisme Professionnel) while the Fédération Internationale Amateur de Cyclisme (FIAC) looked after the amateurs. These two arms of the UCI had been created in the 1960s to oversee the two sides of the sport. When Hein Verbruggen took charge of the FICP in the early 1980s he set about making the professional side of the sport more professional, and the FICP points system was brought in.

In 1989 Verbruggen decided to fill the gap created by the demise of the Super Prestige Pernod trophy by creating the World Cup, which was made up of only the key one-day races (and a few that were not very key but helped the sport's internationalisation agenda). Entry to the World Cup races was governed by the points accumulated by teams in the FICP rankings. From the outset, the Tour de France's organisers – who also organised a number of key one-day races – objected to the World Cup, seeing it as an attempt by the UCI to muscle in on the revenues their races generated, particularly TV rights. The World Cup, though, was not very successful. Perrier sponsored it in its initial years but it then ran without a major sponsor and little interest in who won it.

In 2005 the UCI – by now fully united, the amateur and professional division having ended with the Cold War and the IOC's admittance to the Olympics of professionals – decided to remake the World Cup and create the ProTour. Verbruggen, who took over the UCI presidency in 1991, wanted to create a clear league system within the sport, with the top teams riding all the top races and not having to rely on invitations from race organisers. Unlike the World Cup it replaced, the ProTour incorporated multi-day races, particularly the Grand Tours. Licences were to be given to a fixed number of teams, and those licences guaranteed participation in all the ProTour's races. This was a problem for the Grand Tour organisers – ASO in France, RCS Sport in Italy and Unipublic in Spain – who wanted the final say on who rode, or did not ride, their races.

In 2007, under the leadership of Patrice Clerc (the man who replaced Jean-Claude Killy at the head of ASO) and Christian Prudhomme (also replaced Jean-Marie Leblanc as Tour Director in 2007) ASO banned one of the new ProTour teams from their races. The team was Unibet.com, and ASO claimed that French gambling legislation blocked their participation in French races. This created a showdown with the UCI, which had happily taken Unibet.com's ProTour registration fee. The first battlefield was the early season Paris-Nice, which by now was part of the Amaury empire. A peace deal was eventually cobbled together, but by the time 2008's

Paris-Nice came around the UCI and the race organisers were again arguing. This time ASO and the other Grand Tour organisers withdrew all their races from the ProTour, taking 11 of the 27 races on the calendar with them.

The main upshot of this was that the 2008 Tour was organised under the aegis of the French cycling federation, not the UCI itself, and that dope testing at the race was conducted by the AFLD (Agence Française de Lutte Contre le Dopage), the French arm of WADA. Stung by events in 2006 (Floyd Landis's positive and the events surrounding riders and teams linked to Operación Puerto) and 2007 (the various positives announced during the race and the problems with Michael Rasmussen's whereabouts failures), Clerc and ASO were determined to take control of the Tour's doping problem. And they did so by confronting it head on.

In this they were blessed by the advent of a new test for an EPO-like drug, CERA. Without forewarning the teams the test was rolled out at the Tour. Riders, caught unawares, fell foul of the testers, with Manuel Beltrán (Liquigas), Moisés Dueñas (Barloworld) and Riccardo Riccò (Saunier Duval) all getting caught for blood boosting during the race. But the AFLD didn't stop there. After the race ended they retested samples, and Bernhard Kohl (Gerolsteiner), Leonardo Piepoli (Saunier Duval) and Stefan Schumacher (Gerolsteiner) joined the list of riders caught blood boosting at the Tour. Schumacher, Riccò and Piepoli had all won stages in the race, and Kohl had finished on the bottom step of the podium.

Such high-profile positives would normally be a major scandal, and questions would be asked about the Tour's future. But, because of the manner in which the tests were done – a new test introduced without warning, riders being targeted for testing, samples re-tested after the race ended – this was all actually good news, clear evidence that someone was trying to tackle the sport's doping problem head on. The Tour could actually claim to be on the road to recovery and to have really done something to help break the sport's dependence on chemical assistance.

In among all of this, there was a race going on, and it was race that came down to a battle on Alpe d'Huez just a few days before the race reached Paris.

Defending champion Alberto Contador was absent, his Discovery Channel team having more or less merged with Astana, and Astana being told by ASO to spend some time on the naughty step because of Alexander Vinokourov's problems at the 2007 Tour. That left a somewhat open race and, coming into Stage 17's assault on the Alpe, it was CSC's Fränk Schleck who was wearing yellow with Bernhard Kohl (Gerolsteiner) in second, at seven seconds, Cadel Evans (Silence/Lotto) third at eight seconds, Carlos Sastre (CSC/ Saxo Bank) fourth at 49 seconds and Denis Menchov (Rabobank) fifth at 1'13", all the rest two minutes and more in arrears.

Evans and Menchov were the better time trial riders, and a final race against the clock was looming on Stage 20. For one of the others – Schleck, Kohl or Sastre – to win the Tour they were going to have to do it on the Alpe.

Hitting the base of the Alpe the five challengers were all together. CSC held the whip hand, two riders who could tag team the others, Schleck and Sastre attacking and counter-attacking until one of them got away. In the end, all it took was one attack, Sastre going early in the Alpe and only Menchov able to respond to his sudden burst of speed. Behind, Schleck marked Evans, ready to go with him if he tried to bridge across. Sastre quickly rode Menchov off his wheel and sailed to a stage victory that netted him the *maillot jaune*, with team-mate Schleck in second at 1'24", Kohl at 1'33", Evans at 1'34" and Menchov at 2'39". Now all Sastre had to do was defend the jersey in the final time trial and he would be able to ride into Paris as the winner of the Tour.

Evans and Menchov performed as expected in the race against the clock, but not well enough to unseat Sastre, who ended the day with a 1'05" advantage over Evans on GC. The race was run and Sastre had won.

* * * * *

The Tour was followed by the Beijing Olympics and, during those Games, ASO and the UCI kissed and made up. Heading up the Amaury empire was Marie-Odile Amaury, widow of Émilien Amaury's son Philippe (who had died in 2006) and the new matriarch of the Amaury empire. In 2007 she had brought Alain Krzentowski back into the ASO fold, seven years after he and Jean-Claude Killy had been paid off by Philippe Amaury and replaced by Patrice Clerc. ASO was being buffeted by a perfect storm: an advertising market that was in decline, a succession of Tours that had been blighted by doping scandals, and its on-going war with the UCI over the ProTour. Old hands, Marie-Odile Amaury decided, were needed at the wheel.

ASO's fight with the UCI was turning into a tussle with the IOC, with threats of secession being bandied about. For the Olympic movement the idea of a major event organiser stepping away from the UCI was not pleasant, it challenged the IOC's supremacy at the top of the sporting pyramid. If cycling suffered a schism, would other sports follow? Whither the IOC then? But ASO couldn't really split with the UCI and abandon the Olympic movement; other parts of the Amaury empire made a profit re-selling TV rights to the Olympics and other Olympic sports. It was clear that a solution to the struggle with the UCI was needed.

And that's where Krzentowski was a major asset. He was able to call on Killy, now working for the IOC, to facilitate negotiations with the UCI, who at the time were reluctant to actually sit down and work out a mutually agreeable solution. Killy called on his IOC boss, Jacques Rogge, to put some stick about and force UCI president Pat McQuaid to sit down and talk (the UCI holding a somewhat weakened hand within the IOC following all the drugs scandals cycling was going through).

Amaury and McQuaid talked and thrashed out a deal that would see ASO and the UCI working closely together to reshape the sport. Patrice Clerc – the man most closely associated with ASO's fight with the UCI – was shown the door within ASO and things settled down. The ProTour wars were over. There finally seemed to be an efficient and effective attempt to tackle doping. The Tour de France would sail into the future free from the problems of the past.

Stage-by-Stage Results for the 2008 Tour de France			Stage Winner	Maillot Jaune
Stage 1 Sat 5 Jul	Brest to Plumelec 179 finishers	197.5 km 4h36'07" 42.9 kph	Alejandro Valverde (Esp) Caisse d'Épargne	Alejandro Valverde (Esp) Caisse d'Épargne
	Rated climbs: Côte de Ty-Jopic (Pont-de-Buis-les-Quimerch) (160m) Björn Schröder (Ger) Milram; Côte de Kerivarc'h (144m) Thomas Voeckler (Fra) Bouygues Telecom; Col de Toullaëron (266m) Lilian Jégou (Fra) Française des Jeux; Côte de Guenervé (116m) David de la Fuente (Esp) Saunier Duval			
Stage 2 Sun 6 Jul	Auray to Saint-Brieuc 179 finishers	164.5 km 3h45'13" 43.8 kph	Thor Hushovd (Nor) Crédit Agricole	Alejandro Valverde (Esp) Caisse d'Épargne
	Rated climbs: Côte de Bieuzy-Lanvaux (143m) Sylvain Chavanel (Fra) Cofidis; Côte de Kergroix (159m) Thomas Voeckler (Fra) Bouygues Telecom; Côte de Mûr-de-Bretagne (295m) Sylvain Chavanel (Fra) Cofidis; Côte de Saint-Mayeux (287m) Thomas Voeckler (Fra) Bouygues Telecom			
Stage 3 Mon 7 Jul	Saint-Malo to Nantes 178 finishers	208 km 5h05'27" 40.9 kph	Samuel Dumoulin (Fra) Cofidis	Romain Feillu (Fra) Agritubel
Stage 4 Tue 8 Jul	Cholet (ITT) 178 finishers	29.5 km 35'44" 49.5 kph	~~Stefan Schumacher (Ger) Gerolsteiner (1)~~	~~Stefan Schumacher (Ger) Gerolsteiner (1)~~
			Kim Kirchen (Lux) Columbia	Kim Kirchen (Lux) Columbia
Stage 5 Wed 9 Jul	Cholet to Châteauroux 177 finishers	232 km 5h27'52" 42.5 kph	Mark Cavendish (GBr) Columbia	~~Stefan Schumacher (Ger) Gerolsteiner (1)~~
				Kim Kirchen (Lux) Columbia
Stage 6 Thu 10 Jul	Aigurande to Super Besse 176 finishers	195.5 km 4h57'52" 39.4 kph	~~Riccardo Riccò (Ita) Saunier Duval (1)~~	Kim Kirchen (Lux) Columbia
			Alejandro Valverde (Esp) Caisse d'Épargne	
	Rated climbs: Côte de l'Armelle (602m) Sylvain Chavanel (Fra) Cofidis; Côte de Crocq (740m) Sylvain Chavanel (Fra) Cofidis; Col de la Croix-Morand (1,401m) Sylvain Chavanel (Fra) Cofidis; Super-Besse (1,275m) Riccardo Riccò (Ita) Saunier Duval			
Stage 7 Fri 11 Jul	Brioude to Aurillac 171 finishers	159 km 3h52'53" 41 kph	Luis León Sánchez (Esp) Caisse d'Épargne	Kim Kirchen (Lux) Columbia
	Rated climbs: Côte de Fraisse (912m) David Millar (GBr) Garmin; Côte de Villedieu (384m) Jens Voigt (Ger) CSC; Col d'Entremont (1,210m) David de la Fuente (Esp) Saunier Duval; Col du Pas de Péyrol (Le Puy Mary) (1,588m) David de la Fuente (Esp) Saunier Duval; Côte de Saint-Jean-de-Donne (822m) David de la Fuente (Esp) Saunier Duval			

Stage-by-Stage Results for the 2008 Tour de France			Stage Winner	Maillot Jaune
Stage 8 Sat 12 Jul	Figeac to Toulouse 170 finishers	172.5 km 4h02'54" 42.6 kph	Mark Cavendish (GBr) Columbia	Kim Kirchen (Lux) Columbia
	Rated climbs: Côte de Loupiac (333m) David de la Fuente (Esp) Saunier Duval; Côte de Macarou (512m) Laurent Lefèvre (Fra) Bouygues Telecom; Côte de la Guionie (583m) Laurent Lefèvre (Fra) Bouygues Telecom; Côte du Port de la Besse (425m) Laurent Lefèvre (Fra) Bouygues Telecom			
Stage 9 Sun 13 Jul	Toulouse to Bagnères-de-Bigorre 170 finishers	224 km 5h39'28" 39.6 kph	~~Riccardo Riccò (Ita)~~ ~~Saunier Duval~~ (1) Vladimir Efimkin (Rus) AG2R	Kim Kirchen (Lux) Columbia
	Rated climbs: Côte de Saint-Pey (324m) Sebastian Lang (Ger) Gerolsteiner; Côte de Sainte-Quitterie (325m) Sebastian Lang (Ger) Gerolsteiner; Côte de Mane (418m) Sebastian Lang (Ger) Gerolsteiner; Col de Buret (599m) Sebastian Lang (Ger) Gerolsteiner; Col des Ares (797m) Sebastian Lang (Ger) Gerolsteiner; Col de Peyresourde (1,569m) Sebastian Lang (Ger) Gerolsteiner; Col d'Aspin (1,489m) Riccardo Riccò (Ita) Saunier Duval			
Stage 10 Mon 14 Jul	Pau to Lourdes (Hautacam) 169 finishers	156 km 4h19'27" 36.1 kph	~~Leonardo Piepoli (Ita)~~ ~~Saunier Duval~~ (1) Juan José Cobo (Esp) Saunier Duval	Cadel Evans (Aus) Silence
	Rated climbs: Côte de Benejacq (469m) David de la Fuente (Esp) Saunier Duval; Côte de Loucrup (540m) Leonardo Duque (Col) Cofidis; Col du Tourmalet (2,115m) Rémy di Grégorio (Fra) Française des Jeux; Hautacam (1,520m) Leonardo Piepoli (Ita) Saunier Duval			
Tue 15 Jul	Rest Day			
Stage 11 Wed 16 Jul	Lannemezan to Foix 166 finishers	167.5 km 3h58'13" 42.2 kph	Kurt-Asle Arvesen (Nor) CSC	Cadel Evans (Aus) Silence
	Rated climbs: Col de Larrieu (662m) Alexander Botcharov (Rus) Cofidis; Col du Portel (1,432m) Amaël Moinard (Fra) Cofidis; Col del Bouich (597m) Amaël Moinard (Fra) Cofidis			
Stage 12 Thu 17 Jul	Lavelanet to Narbonne 158 finishers	168.5 km 3h40'52" 45.8 kph	Mark Cavendish (GBr) Columbia	Cadel Evans (Aus) Silence
	Rated climbs: Col du Camperié (534m) Samuel Dumoulin (Fra) Cofidis			
Stage 13 Fri 18 Jul	Narbonne to Nîmes 158 finishers	182 km 4h25'42" 41.1 kph	Mark Cavendish (GBr) Columbia	Cadel Evans (Aus) Silence
	Rated climbs: Côte de la Resclauze (236m) Florent Brard (Fra) Cofidis; Côte de Puéchabon (290m) Florent Brard (Fra) Cofidis; Pic Saint-Loup (240m) Florent Brard (Fra) Cofidis			
Stage 14 Sat 19 Jul	Nîmes to Digne-les-Bains 157 finishers	194.5 km 4h13'08" 46.1 kph	Óscar Freire (Esp) Rabobank	Cadel Evans (Aus) Silence
	Rated climbs: Côte de Mane (490m) José Iván Gutiérrez (Esp) Caisse d'Épargne; Col de l'Orme (734m) Roman Kreuziger (Cze) Liquigas			

Stage-by-Stage Results for the 2008 Tour de France			Stage Winner	Maillot Jaune
Stage 15 Sun 20 Jul	Embrun to Prato Nevoso 153 finishers	183 km 4h50'44" 37.8 kph	Simon Gerrans (Aus) Crédit Agricole	Fränk Schleck (Lux) CSC
	Rated climbs: Col d'Agnel (2,744m) Egoi Martínez (Esp) Euskaltel; Colle del Morte (1,360m) José Luis Arrieta (Esp) AG2R; Prato Nevoso (1,440m) Simon Gerrans (Aus) Crédit Agricole			
Mon 21 Jul	Rest Day			
Stage 16 Tue 22 Jul	Cuneo to Jauziers 151 finishers	157 km 4h31'27" 34.7 kph	Cyril Dessel (Fra) AG2R	Fränk Schleck (Lux) CSC
	Rated climbs: Col de la Lombarde (2,351m) Stefan Schumacher (Ger) Gerolsteiner; Cime de la Bonette-Restefond (2,802m) John-Lee Augustyn (RSA) Barloworld			
Stage 17 Wed 23 Jul	Embrun to l'Alpe d'Huez 150 finishers	210 km 6h07'58" 34.2 kph	Carlos Sastre (Esp) CSC	Carlos Sastre (Esp) CSC
	Rated climbs: Côte de Sainte-Marguerite (1,185m) Stefan Schumacher (Ger) Gerolsteiner; Col du Galibier (2,645m) Stefan Schumacher (Ger) Gerolsteiner; Col de la Croix de Fer (2,067m) Peter Velits (Slo) Milram; l'Alpe d'Huez (1,860m) Carlos Sastre (Esp) CSC			
Stage 18 Thu 24 Jul	Bourg-d'Oisans to Saint-Étienne 150 finishers	196.5 km 4h30'21" 43.6 kph	Marcus Burghardt (Ger) Columbia	Carlos Sastre (Esp) CSC
	Rated climbs: Col de Parmenie (571m) Carlos Barredo (Esp) Quick Step; Col de la Croix de Montvieux (811m) Carlos Barredo (Esp) Quick Step; Côte de Sorbiers (503m) Carlos Barredo (Esp) Quick Step			
Stage 19 Fri 25 Jul	Roanne to Montluçon 145 finishers	163 km 3h37'09" 45 kph	Sylvain Chavanel (Fra) Cofidis	Carlos Sastre (Esp) CSC
	Rated climbs: La Croix-du-Sud (760m) Stefan Schumacher (Ger) Gerolsteiner; Côte de la Croix-Rouge (532m) Stefan Schumacher (Ger) Gerolsteiner			
Stage 20 Sat 26 Jul	Cérilly to Saint-Amand-Montrond (ITT) 145 finishers	53 km 1h03'50" 49.8 kph	~~Stefan Schumacher (Ger) Gerolsteiner (1)~~	Carlos Sastre (Esp) CSC
			Fabian Cancellara (Sui) CSC	
Stage 21 Sun 27 Jul	Etampes to Paris (Champs-Élysées) 145 finishers	143 km 3h51'38" 37 kph	Gert Steegmans (Bel) Quick Step	Carlos Sastre (Esp) CSC
	Rated climbs: Côte de Saint-Rémy-lès-Chevreuse (153m) Bernard Kohl (Aus) Gerolsteiner; Côte de Châteaufort (190m) Freddy Bichot (Fra) Agributel			

Prize fund: 3,200,000 euro (first prize: 450,000 euro)

Final Classification

Place		Rider	Team	Time	Age
~~1~~	1	Carlos Sastre (Esp)	CSC	3,559 km 87h52'52" 40.492 kph	33
~~2~~	2	Cadel Evans (Aus)	Silence	+ 0'58"	31
3		~~Bernhard Kohl (Aut)~~ (1)	~~Gerolsteiner~~	~~+ 1'13"~~	~~25~~
4	3	Denis Menchov (Rus)	Rabobank	+ 2'10"	30
5	4	Christian Vandevelde (USA)	Garmin	+ 3'05"	32
6	5	Fränk Schleck (Lux)	CSC	+ 4'28"	28
~~7~~	6	Samuel Sánchez (Esp)	Euskaltel	+ 6'25"	30
8	7	Kim Kirchen (Lux)	Columbia	+ 6'55"	30
9	8	Alejandro Valverde (Esp)	Caisse d'Épargne	+ 7'12"	28
~~10~~	9	Tadej Valjavec (Slo)	AG2R	+ 9'05"	31
~~11~~	10	Vladimir Efimkin (Rus)	AG2R	+ 9'55"	26

Lanterne Rouge

| ~~145~~ | 145 | Wim Vansevenant (Bel) | Silence | + 3h55'45" | 36 |

Points

| | | Óscar Freire (Esp) | Rabobank | | 32 |

King of the Mountains

| | | Vacated | | | |
| | | ~~Bernhard Kohl (Aut)~~ (1) | ~~Gerolsteiner~~ | | ~~25~~ |

Youth

| | | Andy Schleck (Lux) | CSC | | 23 |

Team

| | | | CSC | | |

Super Combativité

| | | Sylvain Chavanel (Fra) | Française Des Jeux | | 29 |

(1) Results re-allocated (or vacated) because of anti-doping violations revealed during and after the Tour.

2009: Life's a Riot with Team-Mate versus Team-Mate

Following the ending of the UCI and ASO's battles over the shape and nature of the professional cycling colander – and the Tour de France's status within that calander – everything looked good for the sport, and the years ahead held out the promise of Tours free from scandals over doping or who really ran the sport. And then Lance Armstrong decided to come out of retirement and try for win number eight.

That, financially, the sport had grown during the Armstrong era is not disputed. It was growing before the Armstrong era but really took off during his reign, his successes catching the eyes of new sponsors in the US who were only too happy to link themselves with the sport, catch a piece of the limelight of Armstrong's fairytale story. And it's equally true that the sport suffered after Armstrong retired, buffeted as it was by a string a doping stories and the downturn in the global economy. So, when Armstrong came back he was welcomed with open arms by many, who hoped that with him he would bring more money. Instead, they got more scandal. And, by coming out of retirement, Armstrong set in motion the events that would finally lead to his downfall in 2012.

Before that downfall happened though, there was the 2009 Tour de France to be dealt with. Armstrong decided to return to the sport with his former *directeur sportif* Johan Bruyneel – now bossing the Astana squad, where 2007 Tour champion Alberto Contador was the team leader. Excluded from the 2008 Tour, Contador had added the Giro d'Italia and the Vuelta a España to his *palmarès* and was an odds-on favourite for the win in the 2009 Tour until. Until Armstrong joined him as a team-mate.

Two top dogs on the same team, both gunning for Tour victory. It was 1986 all over again, Bernard Hinault versus Greg LeMond, Armstrong as Hinault, the boss of the *peloton*, Contador as the more fragile LeMond, the man who felt he deserved the win. A race full of *polemica*, real and manufactured animosity. And the organisers tried to deliver a Tour route that would keep the tension alive right until the end, with the Ventoux served up on the penultimate stage.

In the battle between Armstrong and Contador, the Spaniard drew first blood, finishing the opening stage – a 15-kilometre race against the clock – just 18 seconds behind Fabian Cancellara (Saxo Bank) and 22 seconds ahead of Armstrong.

Before arriving at Stage Four's team time trial in Montpellier, the race crossed the Camargue, and Armstrong got the drop on Contador when cross-winds broke the *peloton* into echelons as the HTC – Colombia squad (the old Telekom/T-Mobile team minus its German telecoms sponsor) ripped the race apart in their quest for a stage win for their sprint specialist Mark Cavendish. The American was toward the pointy end of the bunch at the decisive moment, while his Spanish rival was dawdling further back. Contador lost 41 seconds. Not major, but a blow in the psychological war waging between the two Tour champions.

That move put Armstrong in with a shout of donning the *maillot jaune* after Stage Four's team time trial in Montpellier. But, while the Astana riders bossed the race against the clock, the American missed out on the jersey by two tenths of a second, with Cancellara doing enough to hold onto the race lead. He was still holding it a few days later when the race arrived on the edge of the Pyrenees.

There – on Stage Seven, finishing in Andorra – AG2R's Rinaldo Nocentini seized his moment and the yellow jersey, while Contador took 21 seconds out of Armstrong by fleeing his company on the final climb. Behind Nocentini in the general classification it was now Contador second at six seconds and Armstrong third at eight.

Things then settled down until the thirteenth stage, two days out from the Alps, when Armstrong's former US Postal lieutenant George Hincapie (HTC) took a shot at Nocentini's yellow jersey but fell short by five seconds. That, though, moved him up to second overall, with Contador and Armstrong as they were at six and eight seconds.

The first day in the Alps, Stage 15's journey from Pontarlier to Verbier, Contador showed his climbing legs again, jumping clear of Armstrong six kilometres from the summit finish and taking the stage win, a minute and a half out of Armstrong and the *maillot jaune*. Armstrong seemed to concede defeat, acknowledging that the Spaniard had bested him. But the team was by now split between riders siding with Armstrong and riders siding with Contador, with Armstrong having the weight of numbers on his side. Contador may have been in yellow and with a 1'37" advantage over Armstrong but the American could still attempt to unseat him, at which point the Spaniard would be relying on friends on other teams to help him protect himself.

So Contador continued to fight, not yet believing the win was in the bag, and on Stage 17, Bourg-Saint-Maurice to Le Grand-Bornant, he put Armstrong to the sword. The American was in trouble on the penultimate climb of the day, the Col de Romme, and on the final climb, the Col de la Colombière, Contador put the boot in and rode away, taking with him the two Schleck brothers, Fränk and Andy (both Saxo Bank), dropping his Astana team-mate Andreas Klöden in the process. The elder Schleck brother, Fränk, took the stage win and Contador was able to celebrate a little, his attack having demoted Armstrong to fourth, at 3'25", with the two Schlecks filling out the podium places, Fränk in third at 3'26" and Andy second at 2'26".

The Annecy time trial on Stage 18 saw Contador taking another stage win and Armstrong climbing back up to third, as Fränk Schleck slipped down the general classification.

All of which made the final visit to the Ventoux a bid of a damp squib, with its real significance being not who stood on the top step of the podium but who stood on the bottom: Andy Schleck was in second at 4'11" with Armstrong in third at 5'21". Snapping at the American's heels were Garmin's Bradley Wiggins in fourth at 5'36", Contador and Armstrong's Astana team-mate Klöden in fifth at 5'38" and Fränk Schleck in sixth at 5'59". High winds made the fight for third pretty tedious, and the only change the day produced was Fränk Schleck displacing Klöden and taking fifth.

* * * * *

Three years later, the USADA investigation caused a minor re-write of the results: Wiggins and everyone behind him were elevated one place as Armstrong was stripped of his eighth and final visit to the Tour's podium.

Stage-by-Stage Results for the 2009 Tour de France			Stage Winner	Maillot Jaune
Stage 1￼Sat 4 Jul	Monaco (ITT)￼180 finishers	15.5 km￼19'32"￼47.6 kph	Fabian Cancellara (Sui)￼Saxo Bank	Fabian Cancellara (Sui)￼Saxo Bank
	Rated climbs: Cote de Beausoleil (205m) Alberto Contador (Esp) Astana			
Stage 2￼Sun 5 Jul	Monaco to Brignoles￼180 finishers	187 km￼4h30'02"￼41.6 kph	Mark Cavendish (GBr)￼Columbia	Fabian Cancellara (Sui)￼Saxo Bank
	Rated climbs: La Turbie (555m) Tony Martin (Ger) Columbia; Côte de Roquefort-les-Pins (218m) Jussi Veikkanen (Fin) Française des Jeux; Côte de Tournon (270m) Jussi Veikkanen (Fin) Française des Jeux; Col de l'Ange (241m) Jussi Veikkanen (Fin) Française des Jeux			
Stage 3￼Mon 6 Jul	Marseille to La￼Grande-Motte￼179 finishers	196.5 km￼5h01'24"￼39.1 kph	Mark Cavendish (GBr)￼Columbia	Fabian Cancellara (Sui)￼Saxo Bank
	Rated climbs: Côte de Calissanne (136m) Koen de Kort (Ned) Skil; Col de la Vayède (179m) Koen de Kort (Ned) Skil			
Stage 4￼Tue 7 Jul	Montpellier (TTT)￼178 finishers	39 km￼46'29"￼50.3 kph	Astana	Fabian Cancellara (Sui)￼Saxo Bank
Stage 5￼Wed 8 Jul	Cap d'Agde to Perpignan￼178 finishers	196.5 km￼4h29'35"￼43.7 kph	Thomas Voeckler (Fra)￼Bbox Bouygues￼Telecom	Fabian Cancellara (Sui)￼Saxo Bank
	Rated climbs: Col de Feuilla (250m) Anthony Geslin (Fra) Française des Jeux; Côte de Treilles (219m) Anthony Geslin (Fra) Française des Jeux			
Stage 6￼Thu 9 Jul	Gerone to Barcelona￼177 finishers	181.5 km￼4h21'33"￼41.6 kph	Thor Hushovd (Nor)￼Cervélo	Fabian Cancellara (Sui)￼Saxo Bank
	Rated climbs: Côte de Sant-Feliu de Guixols (120m) Alexandre Botcharov (Rus) Katusha; Côte de Tossa de Mar (176m) Stéphane Augé (Fra) Cofidis; Côte de Sant-Vicenc de Montalt (202m) Stéphane Augé (Fra) Cofidis; Collsacreu (345m) Stéphane Augé (Fra) Cofidis; Côte de la Conreria (330m) David Millar (GBr) Garmin			

Stage-by-Stage Results for the 2009 Tour de France			Stage Winner	Maillot Jaune
Stage 7 Fri 10 Jul	Barcelona to Andorra-Arcalis 176 finishers	224 km 6h11'31" 36.2 kph	Brice Feillu (Fra) Agritubel	Rinaldo Nocentini (Ita) AG2R
	Rated climbs: Côte de Montserrat (435m) Christophe Riblon (Fra) AG2R; Port de Solsona (708m) Christophe Riblon (Fra) AG2R; Col du Serra-Seca (1,160m) Christophe Riblon (Fra) AG2R; Port del Comte (1,249m) Christophe Riblon (Fra) AG2R; Arcalis (Andorra) (2,240m) Brice Feillu (Fra) Agributel			
Stage 8 Sat 11 Jul	Andorra la Vella to Saint-Girons 172 finishers	176.5 km 4h31'50" 39 kph	Luis León Sánchez (Esp) Caisse d'Épargne	Rinaldo Nocentini (Ita) AG2R
	Rated climbs: Port d'Envalira (2,407m) Sandy Casar (Fra) Française des Jeux; Col de Port (1,249m) Sandy Casar (Fra) Française des Jeux; Col d'Agnès (1,570m) Samuel Sánchez			
Stage 9 Sun 12 Jul	Saint-Gaudens to Tarbes 171 finishers	160.5 km 4h05'31" 39.2 kph	Pierrick Fédrigo (Fra) Bbox Bouygues Telecom	Rinaldo Nocentini (Ita) AG2R
	Rated climbs: Col d'Aspin (1,489m) Franco Pellizotti (Ita) Liquigas; Col du Tourmalet (2,115m) Franco Pellizotti (Ita) Liquigas			
Mon 13 Jul	Rest Day			
Stage 10 Tue 14 Jul	Limoges to Issoudun 171 finishers	194.5 km 4h46'43" 40.7 kph	Mark Cavendish (GBr) Columbia	Rinaldo Nocentini (Ita) AG2R
	Rated climbs: Côte de Salvanet (340m) Mikhail Ignatiev (Rus) Katusha; Côte de Saint-Laurent-les-Eglises (396m) Mikhail Ignatiev (Rus) Katusha; Côte de Bénévent-l'Abbaye (465m) Thierry Huppond (Fra) Skil			
Stage 11 Wed 15 Jul	Vatan to Saint-Fargeau 170 finishers	192 km 4h17'55" 44.7 kph	Mark Cavendish (GBr) Columbia	Rinaldo Nocentini (Ita) AG2R
	Rated climbs: Côte d'Allogny (267m) Johan van Summeren (Bel) Silence; Côte de Perreuse (342m) Marcin Sapa (Pol) Lampre			
Stage 12 Thu 16 Jul	Tonnerre to Vittel 166 finishers	211.5 km 4h52'24" 43.4 kph	Nicki Sørensen (Den) Saxo Bank	Rinaldo Nocentini (Ita) AG2R
	Rated climbs: Côte de Baon (257m) David Millar (GBr) Garmin; Côte de Gye-sur-Seine (281m) Franco Pellizotti (Ita) Liquigas; Côte d'Essoyes (298m) Laurent Lefèvre (Fra) Bbox Bouygues Telecom; Côte des Grands-Bois (413m) Franco Pellizotti (Ita) Liquigas; Côte de Morlaix (432m) Franco Pellizotti (Ita) Liquigas; Côte de Bourmont (500m) Franco Pellizotti (Ita) Liquigas			
Stage 13 Fri 17 Jul	Vittel to Colmar 164 finishers	200 km 4h56'26" 40.5 kph	Heinrich Haussler (Ger) Cervélo	Rinaldo Nocentini (Ita) AG2R
	Rated climbs: Côte de Xertigny (588m) Juan Manuel Garate (Esp) Rabobank; Col de la Schlucht (1,139m) Rubén Pérez (Esp) Euskaltel; Col de Platzerwasel (1,155m) Sylvain Chavanel (Fra) Quick Step; Col du Bannstein (483m) Heinrich Haussler (Ger) Cervélo; Col du Firstplan (722m) Heinrich Haussler (Ger) Cervélo			

Stage-by-Stage Results for the 2009 Tour de France			Stage Winner	Maillot Jaune
Stage 14 Sat 18 Jul	Colmar to Besançon 164 finishers	199 km 4h37'46" 43 kph	Sergei Ivanov (Rus) Katusha	Rinaldo Nocentini (Ita) AG2R
Rated climbs: Côte de Lebetain (490m) Frederik Willems (Bel) Liquigas; Côte de Blamont (558m) Sébastien Minard (Fra) Cofidis				
Stage 15 Sun 19 Jul	Pontarlier to Verbier 162 finishers	207.5 km 5h03'58" 41 kph	Alberto Contador (Esp) Astana	Alberto Contador (Esp) Astana
Rated climbs: Côte du Rafour (1,084m) Franco Pellizotti (Ita) Liquigas; Col des Etroits (1, 153m) Franco Pellizotti (Ita) Liquigas; Côte de la Carrière (791m) Christophe Kern (Fra) Cofidis; Côte de Prévonloup (760m) Ryder Hesjedal (Can) Garmin; Col des Mosses (1,448m) Pierrick Féderigo (Fra) Bbox Bouygues Telecom; Monteé de Verbier (1,468m) Alberto Contador (Esp) Astana				
Mon 20 Jul	Rest Day			
Stage 16 Tue 21 Jul	Martigny to Bourg-Saint-Maurice 161 finishers	159 km 4h14'20" 37.5 kph	~~Mikel Astarloza (Esp) Euskaltel (1)~~ Sandy Casar (Fra) Française Des Jeux	Alberto Contador (Esp) Astana
Rated climbs: Col du Grand Saint-Bernard (2,470m) Franco Pellizotti (Ita) Liquigas; Col du Petit Saint-Bernard (2,188m) Franco Pellizotti (Ita) Liquigas				
Stage 17 Wed 22 Jul	Bourg-Saint-Maurice to Le Grand-Bornant 158 finishers	169.5 km 4h53'54" 34.6 kph	Fränk Schleck (Lux) Saxo Bank	Alberto Contador (Esp) Astana
Rated climbs: Cormet de Roselend (1,968m) Franco Pellizotti (Ita) Liquigas; Col des Saisies (1,633m) Thor Hushovd (Nor) Cervélo; Côte d'Araches (964m) Thor Hushovd (Nor) Cervélo; Col de Romme (1,297m) Fränk Schleck (Lux) Saxo Bank; Col de la Colombière (1,618m) Fränk Schleck (Lux) Saxo Bank				
Stage 18 Thu 23 Jul	Annecy (ITT) 158 finishers	40.5 km 48'30" 50.1 kph	Alberto Contador (Esp) Astana	Alberto Contador (Esp) Astana
Stage 19 Fri 24 Jul	Bourgoin-Jallieu to Aubenas 156 finishers	178 km 3h50'35" 46.3 kph	Mark Cavendish (GBr) Columbia	Alberto Contador (Esp) Astana
Rated climbs: Côte de Culin (512m) Thierry Huppond (Fra) Skil; Côte de la Forêt de Chambaran (650m) Geoffroy Lequatre (Fra) Agributel; Col de l'Escrinet (787m) Alessandro Ballan (Ita) Lampre				
Stage 20 Sat 25 Jul	Montélimar to Mont Ventoux 156 finishers	167 km 4h39'21" 35.9 kph	Juan Manuel Gárate (Esp) Rabobank	Alberto Contador (Esp) Astana
Rated climbs: Côte de Citelle (428m) Alberto Timmer (Ned) Skil; Col d'Ey (718m) Aleksander Kuschynski (Blr) Liquigas; Col de Fontaube (648m) Daniele Righi (Ita) Lampre; Col des Abeilles (998m) Juan Manuel Gárate (Esp) Rabobank; Mont Ventoux (1,912m) Juan Manuel Gárate (Esp) Rabobank				
Stage 21 Sun 26 Jul	Montereau-Fault-Yonne to Paris (Champs-Élysées) 156 finishers	164 km 4h02'18" 40.6 kph	Mark Cavendish (GBr) Columbia	Alberto Contador (Esp) Astana

Prize fund: 3,200,000 euro (first prize:450,000 euro)

The Tour was followed by the Beijing Olympics and, during those Games, ASO and the UCI kissed and made up. Heading up the Amaury empire was Marie-Odile Amaury, widow of Émilien Amaury's son Philippe (who had died in 2006) and the new matriarch of the Amaury empire. In 2007 she had brought Alain Krzentowski back into the ASO fold, seven years after he and Jean-Claude Killy had been paid off by Philippe Amaury and replaced by Patrice Clerc. ASO was being buffeted by a perfect storm: an advertising market that was in decline, a succession of Tours that had been blighted by doping scandals, and its on-going war with the UCI over the ProTour. Old hands, Marie-Odile Amaury decided, were needed at the wheel.

ASO's fight with the UCI was turning into a tussle with the IOC, with threats of secession being bandied about. For the Olympic movement the idea of a major event organiser stepping away from the UCI was not pleasant, it challenged the IOC's supremacy at the top of the sporting pyramid. If cycling suffered a schism, would other sports follow? Whither the IOC then? But ASO couldn't really split with the UCI and abandon the Olympic movement; other parts of the Amaury empire made a profit re-selling TV rights to the Olympics and other Olympic sports. It was clear that a solution to the struggle with the UCI was needed.

And that's where Krzentowski was a major asset. He was able to call on Killy, now working for the IOC, to facilitate negotiations with the UCI, who at the time were reluctant to actually sit down and work out a mutually agreeable solution. Killy called on his IOC boss, Jacques Rogge, to put some stick about and force UCI president Pat McQuaid to sit down and talk (the UCI holding a somewhat weakened hand within the IOC following all the drugs scandals cycling was going through).

Amaury and McQuaid talked and thrashed out a deal that would see ASO and the UCI working closely together to reshape the sport. Patrice Clerc – the man most closely associated with ASO's fight with the UCI – was shown the door within ASO and things settled down. The ProTour wars were over. There finally seemed to be an efficient and effective attempt to tackle doping. The Tour de France would sail into the future free from the problems of the past.

In among all of this, there was a race going on, and it was race that came down to a battle on Alpe d'Huez just a few days before the race reached Paris.

Defending champion Alberto Contador was absent, his Discovery Channel team having more or less merged with Astana, and Astana being told by ASO to spend some time on the naughty step because of Alexander Vinokourov's problems at the 2007 Tour. That left a somewhat open race and, coming into Stage 17's assault on the Alpe, it was CSC's Fränk Schleck who was wearing yellow with Bernhard Kohl (Gerolsteiner) in second, at seven seconds, Cadel Evans (Silence/Lotto) third at eight seconds, Carlos Sastre (CSC/Saxo Bank) fourth at 49 seconds and Denis Menchov (Rabobank) fifth at 1'13", all the rest two minutes and more in arrears.

Evans and Menchov were the better time trial riders, and a final race against the clock was looming on Stage 20. For one of the others – Schleck, Kohl or Sastre – to win the Tour they were going to have to do it on the Alpe.

Hitting the base of the Alpe the five challengers were all together. CSC held the whip hand, two riders who could tag team the others, Schleck and Sastre attacking and counter-attacking until one of them got away. In the end, all it took was one attack, Sastre going early in the Alpe and only Menchov able to respond to his sudden burst of speed. Behind, Schleck marked Evans, ready to go with him if he tried to bridge across. Sastre quickly rode Menchov off his wheel and sailed to a stage victory that netted him the *maillot jaune*, with team-mate Schleck in second at 1'24", Kohl at 1'33", Evans at 1'34" and Menchov at 2'39". Now all Sastre had to do was defend the jersey in the final time trial and he would be able to ride into Paris as the winner of the Tour.

Evans and Menchov performed as expected in the race against the clock, but not well enough to unseat Sastre, who ended the day with a 1'05" advantage over Evans on GC. The race was run and Sastre had won.

* * * * *

Paris-Nice came around the UCI and the race organisers were again arguing. This time ASO and the other Grand Tour organisers withdrew all their races from the ProTour, taking 11 of the 27 races on the calendar with them.

The main upshot of this was that the 2008 Tour was organised under the aegis of the French cycling federation, not the UCI itself, and that dope testing at the race was conducted by the AFLD (Agence Française de Lutte Contre le Dopage), the French arm of WADA. Stung by events in 2006 (Floyd Landis's positive and the events surrounding riders and teams linked to Operación Puerto) and 2007 (the various positives announced during the race and the problems with Michael Rasmussen's whereabouts failures), Clerc and ASO were determined to take control of the Tour's doping problem. And they did so by confronting it head on.

In this they were blessed by the advent of a new test for an EPO-like drug, CERA. Without forewarning the teams the test was rolled out at the Tour. Riders, caught unawares, fell foul of the testers, with Manuel Beltrán (Liquigas), Moisés Dueñas (Barloworld) and Riccardo Riccò (Saunier Duval) all getting caught for blood boosting during the race. But the AFLD didn't stop there. After the race ended they retested samples, and Bernhard Kohl (Gerolsteiner), Leonardo Piepoli (Saunier Duval) and Stefan Schumacher (Gerolsteiner) joined the list of riders caught blood boosting at the Tour. Schumacher, Riccò and Piepoli had all won stages in the race, and Kohl had finished on the bottom step of the podium.

Such high-profile positives would normally be a major scandal, and questions would be asked about the Tour's future. But, because of the manner in which the tests were done – a new test introduced without warning, riders being targeted for testing, samples re-tested after the race ended – this was all actually good news, clear evidence that someone was trying to tackle the sport's doping problem head on. The Tour could actually claim to be on the road to recovery and to have really done something to help break the sport's dependence on chemical assistance.

In 1989 Verbruggen decided to fill the gap created by the demise of the Super Prestige Pernod trophy by creating the World Cup, which was made up of only the key one-day races (and a few that were not very key but helped the sport's internationalisation agenda). Entry to the World Cup races was governed by the points accumulated by teams in the FICP rankings. From the outset, the Tour de France's organisers – who also organised a number of key one-day races – objected to the World Cup, seeing it as an attempt by the UCI to muscle in on the revenues their races generated, particularly TV rights. The World Cup, though, was not very successful. Perrier sponsored it in its initial years but it then ran without a major sponsor and little interest in who won it.

In 2005 the UCI – by now fully united, the amateur and professional division having ended with the Cold War and the IOC's admittance to the Olympics of professionals – decided to remake the World Cup and create the ProTour. Verbruggen, who took over the UCI presidency in 1991, wanted to create a clear league system within the sport, with the top teams riding all the top races and not having to rely on invitations from race organisers. Unlike the World Cup it replaced, the ProTour incorporated multi-day races, particularly the Grand Tours. Licences were to be given to a fixed number of teams, and those licences guaranteed participation in all the ProTour's races. This was a problem for the Grand Tour organisers – ASO in France, RCS Sport in Italy and Unipublic in Spain – who wanted the final say on who rode, or did not ride, their races.

In 2007, under the leadership of Patrice Clerc (the man who replaced Jean-Claude Killy at the head of ASO) and Christian Prudhomme (also replaced Jean-Marie Leblanc as Tour Director in 2007) ASO banned one of the new ProTour teams from their races. The team was Unibet.com, and ASO claimed that French gambling legislation blocked their participation in French races. This created a showdown with the UCI, which had happily taken Unibet.com's ProTour registration fee. The first battlefield was the early season Paris-Nice, which by now was part of the Amaury empire. A peace deal was eventually cobbled together, but by the time 2008's

Final Classification

Place		Rider	Team	Time	Age
~~1~~	1	Alberto Contador (Esp)	Astana	3,459.5 km 85h48'35" 40.315 kph	26
~~2~~	2	Andy Schleck (Lux)	Saxo Bank	+ 4'11"	24
3		~~Lance Armstrong (USA)~~ (2)	~~Astana~~	~~+ 5'24"~~	~~37~~
4	3	Bradley Wiggins (GBr)	Garmin	+ 6'01"	29
5	4	Fränk Schleck (Lux)	Saxo Bank	+ 6'04"	29
6	5	Andreas Klöden (Ger)	Astana	+ 6'42"	34
~~7~~	6	Vincenzo Nibali (Ita)	Liquigas	+ 7'35"	24
8	7	Christian Vandevelde (USA)	Garmin	+ 12'04"	33
9	8	Roman Kreuziger (Cze)	Liquigas	+ 14'16"	23
~~10~~	9	Christophe le Mével (Fra)	Française des Jeux	+ 14'25"	28
~~11~~	10	Mikel Astarloza (Esp)	Euskaltel	+ 14'44"	29

Lanterne Rouge

~~156~~	155	Yauheni Hutarovich (Blr)	Française des Jeux	+ 4h16'27"	25

Points

		Thor Hushovd (Nor)	Cervélo		31

King of the Mountains

		Vacated			
		~~Franco Pellizotti (Ita)~~ (3)	~~Liquigas~~		31

Youth

		Andy Schleck (Lux)	Saxo Bank		24

Team

			Astana		

Super Combativité

		Vacated			
		~~Franco Pellizotti (Ita)~~ (3)	~~Liquigas~~		31

(1) Mikel Astarloza was stripped of his stage win having failed an anti-doping test ahead of the Tour.
(2) In 2012 Lance Armstrong was stripped of his podium placing following the USADA report, with the position being re-awarded to Bradley Wiggins.
(3) In 2011 Franco Pellizotti was stripped of all results dating back to 2009 after he was caught by the UCI's biological passport.

2010: A Steak Through the Heart of the Tour

Just when it was all going so well, just when the Tour de France had got through a whole edition without any major doping scandals, and with the minor ones barely raising an eyebrow, it all went wrong again. On 25 July Alberto Contador, still riding in Astana's colours, stood on the top step of the Tour's podium on the Champs-Élysées and celebrated his third Tour title. Two months after the race ended German media broke the news that the Spaniard was being investigated by the UCI, having tested positive for clenbuterol. Contador claimed the drug must have come from a tainted steak eaten during the race and was initially cleared by the Spanish federation. The UCI then appealed the case to CAS and in 2011 they delivered a guilty verdict. The men with the Tipp-Ex were called out to rewrite the Tour's results one more time and Andy Schleck (Saxo Bank) joined Henri Cornet (1904) and Óscar Pereiro (2006) in the list of riders who won Tours they lost.

The race itself, well that was another centennial celebration for the Tour, this time the century since the Pyrenees were added to the race's itinerary. Four days in the mountains on France's southern border were scheduled, a veritable feast of Pyrenean climbs, with just two days in the Alps having preceded them as appetizers.

Fabian Cancellara (Saxo Bank) again donned the first *maillot jaune* of the race, with a win in the opening prologue time trial in Rotterdam. Two days later, on rain- and oil-slicked roads, riders fell like skittles with 30 kilometres to go, and the bosses in the *peloton* decided to neutralise the finale of the stage, which allowed early breakaway Sylvain Chavanel (Quick Step) to take the stage win and the jersey from Cancellara.

Chavanel's time in yellow, though, was brief, with Cancellara taking the jersey back the following day and looking set to lead the race in the Alps. Chavanel had other ideas, and just ahead of the race's entry into the high mountains he took his second win, on Stage Seven, and once again relieved Cancellara of the weight of the *maillot jaune*. Then the real racing began.

That was on Stage Eight, Station des Rousses to Morzine-Avoriaz. There the younger Schleck brother showed he wasn't as timorous as he looked and attacked the defending champion, Contador ceding 10 seconds after Schleck launched an attack in the closing kilometre of the stage. The big winner on the day was Cadel Evans (BMC), who donned the yellow jersey, with Schleck at 20 seconds, and Contador third at 1'01". For Evans, though, his time in yellow would be brief and painful. He rode on with a cracked elbow and lost the *maillot jaune* to Schleck, who now had Contador 41 seconds behind him and everyone else two minutes and more back.

The two days in the Alps done, the race transitioned across to the Pyrenees by way of four relatively easy days, at the end of which Contador had pulled back 10 seconds. Stage 14 – Revel to Ax 3 Domaines – served as an entrée to the high mountains in which little changed. Stage 15, though, was different.

The riders were travelling from Pamiers to Bagnères-de-Luchon, with the Port de Balès coming as the final climb, its summit arriving just 20 kilometres out from the stage end. Up the road, the day's break was off the leash and having fun but, as the summit of the Port de Balès loomed up, Contador's Astana troops began massing at the front of the chase group and poured on the power. Almost as soon as all of Contador's booster rockets burned out on the climb, Schleck took the initiative and launched an attack that took him, Contador and Denis Menchov (Rabobank), Samuel Sánchez (Euskaltel/Euskadi) and Jürgen van den Broeck (Omega Pharma/Lotto) clear, with Alexander Vinokourov (Astana) later rejoining his team leader.

Contador seemed happy to sit in and let Schleck do all the work. Two kilometres from the summit Schleck tried to attack and was brought to standstill: he'd slipped his chain. Contador, Menchov,

Sánchez and Vinokourov powered past him. Meanwhile Schleck fumbled with his chain, trying to remount it. Thirty-nine seconds after Contador, Menchov and Sánchez crossed the finish line – 2'50" down on stage winner Thomas Voeckler (Bbox Bouygues Telecom) – Schleck crossed the line. And Contador donned the *maillot jaune*, with an eight-second lead.

Questions were asked about race etiquette – should or shouldn't the yellow jersey's rivals wait when he's in trouble – but the answers were hard to find. There are times when it is clearly fair to respect the misfortune of a fallen rival, but there are other times when the misfortune is self inflicted, and the yellow jersey should be made to suffer. You don't wait if the *maillot jaune* bonks, you do wait if he gets taken out by a spectator. Where a slipped chain fitted few could agree.

The race then came down to Stage 17, what was scheduled to be the key day in the mountains, the riders finishing atop the Col du Tourmalet. Fittingly, the finale of the stage came down to Contador and Schleck, who attacked 10 kilometres from the summit of the Tourmalet. But, despite attempt after attempt by Schleck to open a gap between himself and the *maillot jaune* Contador was not for dropping and matched his rival pedal stroke for pedal stroke.

Generously, Contador didn't contest the sprint for the line and Schleck had to settle for seconds: the stage win, and second place on the podium come Paris. Ironically, Contador added another 31 seconds to his winning margin in the final race against the clock, meaning Schleck missed out on the yellow jersey by 39 seconds. The same amount of time he lost on the Port de Balès.

Then came the clenbuterol positive, which Contador tried to explain as having been caused by eating a tainted steak (clenbuterol being known to be illegally used by some cattle farmers to beef up their stock). WADA's strict liability rules, though, tend to be unsympathetic when it comes to questions of contamination, and the Spaniard was, eventually, after a long-drawn-out affair, stripped of the win.

Stage-by-Stage Results for the 2010 Tour de France			Stage Winner	Maillot Jaune
Prologue Sat 3 Jul	Rotterdam (ITT) 197 finishers	8.9 km 10'00" 53.4 kph	Fabian Cancellara (Sui) Saxo Bank	Fabian Cancellara (Sui) Saxo Bank
Stage 1 Sun 4 Jul	Rotterdam to Brussels 195 finishers	223.5 km 5h09'38" 43.3 kph	Alessandro Petacchi (Ita) Lampre	Fabian Cancellara (Sui) Saxo Bank
Stage 2 Mon 5 Jul	Brussels to Spa 193 finishers	201 km 4h40'48" 42.9 kph	Sylvain Chavanel (Fra) Quick Step	Sylvain Chavanel (Fra) Quick Step
	Rated climbs: Côte de France (244m) Jérôme Pineau (Fra) Quick Step; Côte de Filot (297m) Jérôme Pineau (Fra) Quick Step; Côte de Werbomont (459m) Jérôme Pineau (Fra) Quick Step; Côte d'Aisomont (488m) Jérôme Pineau (Fra) Quick Step; Col de Stockeu (506m) Sylvain Chavanel (Fra) Quick Step; Col du Rosier (564m) Sylvain Chavanel (Fra) Quick Step			
Stage 3 Tue 6 Jul	Wanze to Arenberg (Porte-du-Hainaut) 189 finishers	213 km 4h49'38" 44.1 kph	Thor Hushovd (Nor) Cervélo	Fabian Cancellara (Sui) Saxo Bank
	Rated climbs: Côte de Bothey (148m) Ryder Hesjedal (Can) Garmin			
Stage 4 Wed 7 Jul	Cambrai to Reims 189 finishers	153.5 km 3h34'55" 42.9 kph	Alessandro Petacchi (Ita) Lampre	Fabian Cancellara (Sui) Saxo Bank
	Rated climbs: Côte de Vadencourt (158m) Iban Mayo (Esp) Footon			
Stage 5 Thu 8 Jul	Épernay to Montargis 188 finishers	187.5 km 4h30'50" 41.5 kph	Mark Cavendish (GBr) HTC	Fabian Cancellara (Sui) Saxo Bank
	Rated climbs: Côte d'Orbais-l'Abbaye (205m) Jurgen van de Waele (Bel) Quick Step; Côte de Mécringes (184m) Jurgen van de Waele (Bel) Quick Step			
Stage 6 Fri 9 Jul	Montargis to Gueugnon 188 finishers	227.5 km 5h37'42" 40.4 kph	Mark Cavendish (GBr) HTC	Fabian Cancellara (Sui) Saxo Bank
	Rated climbs: Côte de Bouhy (349m) Mathieu Perget (Fra) Caisse d'Épargne; Côte de la Chapelle-Saint-André (305m) Mathieu Perget (Fra) Caisse d'Épargne; Côte des Montarons (400m) Mathieu Perget (Fra) Caisse d'Épargne; Côte de la Croix de l'Arbre (418m) Mathieu Perget (Fra) Caisse d'Épargne			
Stage 7 Sat 10 Jul	Tournus to Station des Rousses 186 finishers	165.5 km 4h22'52" 37.8 kph	Sylvain Chavanel (Fra) Quick Step	Sylvain Chavanel (Fra) Quick Step
	Rated climbs: Côte de l'Aubépin (541m) Jérôme Pineau (Fra) Quick Step; Côte des Granges (581m) Jérôme Pineau (Fra) Quick Step; Côte d'Arinthod (730m) Jérôme Pineau (Fra) Quick Step; Côte du Barrage de Vouglans (710m) Jérôme Pineau (Fra) Quick Step; Col de la Croix de la Serre (1,049m) Jérôme Pineau (Fra) Quick Step; Côte de Lamoura (1,145m) Sylvain Chavanel (Fra) Quick Step			

Stage-by-Stage Results for the 2010 Tour de France			Stage Winner	Maillot Jaune
Stage 8 Sun 11 Jul	Station des Rousses to Morzine-Avoriaz 186 finishers	189 km 4h54'11" 38.5 kph	Andy Schleck (Lux) Saxo Bank	Cadel Evans (Aus) BMC
	Rated climbs: Côte de la Petite Joux (1,174m) Rein Taaramae (Est) Cofidis; Côte de Grésin (523m) Christophe Riblon (Fra) AG2R; Col de la Ramaz (1,616m) Mario Aerts (Bel) Omega Pharma; Côte de les Gets (1,619m) Mario Aerts (Bel) Omega Pharma; Morzine-Avoriaz (1,800m) Andy Schleck (Lux) Saxo Bank			
Mon 12 Jul	Rest Day			
Stage 9 Tue 13 Jul	Morzine-Avoriaz to Saint-Jean-de-Maurienne 181 finishers	204.5 km 5h38'10" 36.3 kph	Sandy Casar (Fra) FDJ	Andy Schleck (Lux) Saxo Bank
	Rated climbs: Côte de Châtillon-sur-Cluses (741m) Jérôme Pineau (Fra) Quick Step; Col de la Colombière (1,618m) Christophe Moreau (Fra) Caisse d'Épargne; Col des Aravis (1,498m) Jérôme Pineau (Fra) Quick Step; Col de la Madeleine (2,000m) Anthony Charteau (Fra) Bbox Bouygues Telecom; Col des Saisies (1,633m) Jérôme Pineau (Fra) Quick Step			
Stage 10 Wed 14 Jul	Chambéry to Gap 181 finishers	179 km 5h10'56" 34.5 kph	Sergio Miguel Paulinho (Por) RadioShack	Andy Schleck (Lux) Saxo Bank
	Rated climbs: Côte de Laffrey (900m) Mario Aerts (Bel) Omega Pharma; Col du Noyer (1,664m) Mario Aerts (Bel) Omega Pharma			
Stage 11 Thu 15 Jul	Sisteron to Bourg-lès-Valence 178 finishers	184.5 km 4h42'29" 39.2 kph	Mark Cavendish (GBr) HTC	Andy Schleck (Lux) Saxo Bank
	Rated climbs: Col de Cabre (1,177m) Jose Alberto Benitez (Esp) Footon			
Stage 12 Fri 16 Jul	Bourg-de-Péage to Mende 176 finishers	210.5 km 4h58'26" 42.3 kph	Joaquim Rodríguez (Esp) Katusha	Andy Schleck (Lux) Saxo Bank
	Rated climbs: Côte de Saint-Barthélémy-le-Plain (489m) Pierrick Féderigo (Fra) Bbox Bouygues Telecom; Col des Nonières (670m) Anthony Charteau (Fra) Bbox Bouygues Telecom; Le Suc de Montivernoux (1,315m) Sandy Casar (Fra) FDJ; Côte de la Mouline (1,085m) Anthony Charteau (Fra) Bbox Bouygues Telecom; Côte de la Croix Neuve (Montée Laurent Jalabert) (1,045m) Alberto Contador (Esp) Astana			
Stage 13 Sat 17 Jul	Rodez to Revel 175 finishers	196 km 4h26'26" 44.1 kph	Alexander Vinokourov (Kaz) Astana	Andy Schleck (Lux) Saxo Bank
	Rated climbs: Côte de Mergals (637m) Sylvain Chavanel (Fra) Quick Step; Côte de Bégon (698m) Pierrick Féderigo (Fra) Bbox Bouygues Telecom; Côte d'Ambialet (474m) Pierrick Féderigo (Fra) Bbox Bouygues Telecom; Côte de Puylaurens (368m) Sylvain Chavanel (Fra) Quick Step; Côte de Saint-Ferréol (363m) Alessandro Ballan (Ita) BMC			
Stage 14 Sun 18 Jul	Revel to Ax 3 Domaines 175 finishers	184.5 km 4h52'42" 37.8 kph	Christophe Riblon (Fra) AG2R	Andy Schleck (Lux) Saxo Bank
	Rated climbs: Port de Pailhères (2,001m) Christophe Riblon (Fra) AG2R; Ax 3 Domaines (1,372m) Christophe Riblon (Fra) AG2R			

Stage-by-Stage Results for the 2010 Tour de France			Stage Winner	Maillot Jaune
Stage 15 Mon 19 Jul	Pamiers to Bagnères-de-Luchon 174 finishers	187 km 4h44'51" 39.4 kph	Thomas Voeckler (Fra) Bbox Bouygues Telecom	Alberto Contador (Esp) Astana
	Rated climbs: Côte de Carla-Bayle (375m) Pierrick Féderigo (Fra) Bbox Bouygues Telecom; Col de Portet d'Aspet (1,069m) Thomas Voeckler (Fra) Bbox Bouygues Telecom; Col des Ares (797m) Thomas Voeckler (Fra) Bbox Bouygues Telecom; Port de Balès (1,755m) Thomas Voeckler (Fra) Bbox Bouygues Telecom			
Stage 16 Tue 20 Jul	Bagnères-de-Luchon to Pau 172 finishers	199.5 km 5h31'43" 36.1 kph	Pierrick Fédrigo (Fra) Bbox Bouygues Telecom	Alberto Contador (Esp) Astana
	Rated climbs: Col de Peyresourde (1,569m) Sylvester Szmyd (Pol) Liquigas; Col d'Aspin (1,489m) Anthony Charteau (Fra) Bbox Bouygues Telecom; Col du Tourmalet (2,115m) Christophe Moreau (Fra) Caisse d'Épargne; Col d'Aubisque (1,709m) Christophe Moreau (Fra) Caisse d'Épargne			
Wed 21 Jul	Rest Day			
Stage 17 Thu 22 Jul	Pau to Col du Tourmalet 171 finishers	174 km 5h03'29" 34.4 kph	Andy Schleck (Lux) Saxo Bank	~~Alberto Contador (Esp)~~ ~~Astana~~ (1)
				Andy Schleck (Lux) Saxo Bank
	Rated climbs: Côte de Renoir (340m) Alexander Kolobnev (Rus) Katusha; Col de Marie-Blanque (1,035m) Juan Antonio Flecha (Esp) Sky; Col du Soulor (1,474m) Marcus Burghardt (Ger) BMC; Col du Tourmalet (2,115m) Andy Schleck (Lux) Saxo Bank			
Stage 18 Fri 23 Jul	Salies-de-Béarn to Bordeaux 170 finishers	190 km 4h37'09" 41.1 kph	Mark Cavendish (GBr) HTC	~~Alberto Contador (Esp)~~ ~~Astana~~ (1)
				Andy Schleck (Lux) Saxo Bank
Stage 19 Sat 24 Jul	Bordeaux to Pauillac (ITT) 170 finishers	51 km 1h00'56" 50.2 kph	Fabian Cancellara (Sui) Saxo Bank	~~Alberto Contador (Esp)~~ ~~Astana~~ (1)
				Andy Schleck (Lux) Saxo Bank
Stage 20 Sun 25 Jul	Longjumeau to Paris (Champs-Élysées) 170 finishers	105 km 2h42'21" 38.8 kph	Mark Cavendish (GBr) HTC	~~Alberto Contador (Esp)~~ ~~Astana~~ (1)
				Andy Schleck (Lux) Saxo Bank

Prize fund: 3,200,000 euro (first prize: 450,000 euro)

Final Classification

Place		Rider	Team	Time	Age
~~1~~		~~Alberto Contador (Esp) (1)~~	~~Astana~~	~~3,642 km~~ ~~91h58'48"~~ ~~39.594 kph~~	~~27~~
~~2~~	1	Andy Schleck (Lux)	Saxo Bank	+ 0'39"	25
3	2	Denis Menchov (Rus)	Rabobank	+ 2'01"	32
4	3	Samuel Sánchez (Esp)	Euskaltel	+ 3'40"	32
5	4	Jürgen Van Den Broeck (Bel)	Omega Pharma	+ 6'54"	27
6	5	Robert Gesink (Ned)	Rabobank	+ 9'31"	24
~~7~~	6	Ryder Hesjedal (Can)	Garmin	+ 10'15"	29
8	7	Joaquim Rodríguez (Esp)	Katusha	+ 11'37"	31
9	8	Roman Kreuziger (Cze)	Liquigas	+ 11'54"	24
~~10~~	9	Chris Horner (USA)	RadioShack	+ 12'02"	38
~~11~~	10	Luis León Sánchez (Esp)	Caisse d'Épargne	+ 14'21"	26

Lanterne Rouge

~~170~~	170	Adriano Malori (Ita)	Lampre	+ 4h27'03"	22

Points

		Alessandro Petacchi (Ita)	Lampre		36

King of the Mountains

		Anthony Charteau (Fra)	Bbox Bouygues Telecom		31

Youth

		Andy Schleck (Lux)	Saxo Bank		25

Team

			RadioShack		

Super Combativité

		Sylvain Chavanel (Fra)	Quick Step		31

(1) Alberto Contador was stripped of all results after 21 July, when he tested positive for clenbuterol

2011: Cuddles, At Last

When the opening stage of the 2011 Tour rolled off across the Passage du Gois Alberto Contador (Saxo Bank) was still the defending champion, the Court of Arbitration for Sport had not yet stripped him of the title after his positive for clenbuterol. But it wasn't to be Contador's Tour; he went down hard on the opening stage, surrendering 1'14", and never really was able to mount much of a challenge after that.

With Contador out, it was time for Andy Schleck (Leopard) to make up for his defeat the year before. But Schleck wasn't the only one with his eyes on the prize. Cadel Evans (BMC) also had a score to settle: two podium finishes and losing the yellow jersey the previous year after crocking his elbow. And from the off Evans showed he was flying, taking second place on the opening stage's uphill finish and picking up a few seconds on key rivals. And he added more seconds on Stage Four's finish on the Mûr de Bretagne.

By the time the race reached the Pyrenees on Stage 12 the yellow jersey had passed from Philippe Gilbert (Omega Pharma) to Thor Hushovd (Garmin) and on to Thomas Voeckler (Europcar). There, in the closing kilometres of the climb to Luz-Ardiden, it was the turn of Fränk Schleck (Leopard) to be stealing seconds, launching at attack that distanced Evans. Exiting the Pyrenees two days later, little had changed: Voeckler was still in yellow. Fränk Schleck was in second at 1'49", Evans third at 2'06" and Andy Schleck fourth at 2'15".

One transition stage and two transfers took the race across to the Alps, where Andy Schleck showed signs of weakness on Stage 16's haul from Saint-Paul-Trois-Châteaux to Gap, getting a touch of the yips on a tricky, wet descent. Evans profited, taking more time from both of the Schleck brothers, while Voeckler's lead fell. It was now Evans in second at 1'45", Fränk Schleck at 1'49" and Andy Schleck at 3'03".

So far it had all been about seconds here and seconds there, attacks in the closing kilometres or some really iffy descending. Entertaining, but not exactly exciting. And then, on Stage 18, the Tour snapped wide awake. And, fittingly, it was on the road to the scene of this year's centennial celebration, the Galibier.

On what looked like another day of seeing Evans and the Schlecks watching each other until the final kilometres of the Galibier, Andy Schleck launched an attack on the Izoard – with 60 kilometres still to be raced – and bridged across to team-mates Joost Posthuma and Maxime Montfort who were up the road and ready to help their team leader.

Behind, there was squabbling over who should lead the chase, with Voeckler not showing much willingness to defend his jersey. Words were exchanged and Cuddles – the affectionate name for Evans, who can be a bit of a prickly customer – tried to boss his companions into doing some work. But his entreaties were falling on deaf ears. So it fell to the Australian to make the pace alone.

Meanwhile Schleck was up the road with the early breakaways targets for him to aim for and, a couple of times, able to put in some effort for him. To add insult to injury, having sat in and let Evans do all the chase work Fränk Schleck got the drop on the Australian and took back some seconds at the finish line, arriving 2'07" down on his brother, with Evans rolling home eight seconds later. Voeckler did enough (just) to hold his yellow jersey for one more day, with Andy Schleck at 15 seconds, Fränk Schleck at 1'08" and Evans at 1'12". Would one minute be enough of a cushion for Andy Schleck come the Grenoble time trial in two days time?

It would have to be, because the Schlecks failed to crack Evans on the last day in the mountains, to Alpe d'Huez. And it wasn't, Evans putting 2'31" into Andy Schleck and 2'41" into his brother. Cuddles had finally won the Tour.

Stage-by-Stage Results for the 2011 Tour de France			Stage Winner	Maillot Jaune
Stage 1 Sat 2 Jul	Passage du Gois to Mont-des-Alouettes 198 finishers	191.5 km 4h41'31" 40.8 kph	Philippe Gilbert (Bel) Omega Pharma	Philippe Gilbert (Bel) Omega Pharma
	Rated climbs: Mont des Alouettes (Les Herbiers) (215m) Philippe Gilbert (Bel) Omega Pharma-Lotto			
Stage 2 Sun 3 Jul	Les Essarts (TTT) 198 finishers	23 km 24'48" 55.6 kph	Garmin	Thor Hushovd (Nor) Garmin
Stage 3 Mon 4 Jul	Olonne-sur-Mer to Redon 198 finishers	198 km 4h40'21" 42.4 kph	Tyler Farrar (USA) Garmin	Thor Hushovd (Nor) Garmin
	Rated climbs: Côte du Pont de Saint-Nazaire (72m) Mickaël Delage (Fra) FDJ			
Stage 4 Tue 5 Jul	Lorient to Mûr-de-Bretagne 197 finishers	172.5 km 4h11'39" 41.1 kph	Cadel Evans (Aus) BMC	Thor Hushovd (Nor) Garmin
	Rated climbs: Côte de Laz (237m) Johnny Hoogerland (Ned) Vacansoleil; Côte de Mûr-de-Bretagne (295m) Cadel Evans (Aus) BMC			
Stage 5 Wed 6 Jul	Carhaix to Cap Fréhel 195 finishers	164.5 km 3h38'32" 45.2 kph	Mark Cavendish (GBr) HTC	Thor Hushovd (Nor) Garmin
	Rated climbs: Côte de Gurunhuel (281m) Anthony Delaplace (Fra) Saur			
Stage 6 Thu 7 Jul	Dinan to Lisieux 193 finishers	226.5 km 5h13'37" 43.3 kph	Edvald Boasson Hagen (Nor) Sky	Thor Hushovd (Nor) Garmin
	Rated climbs: Côte de Saint-Michel de Montjoie (335m) Johnny Hoogerland (Ned) Vacansoleil; Côte du Bourg d'Ouilly (203m) Anthony Roux (Fra) FDJ			
Stage 7 Fri 8 Jul	Le Mans to Châteauroux 190 finishers	218 km 5h38'53" 38.6 kph	Mark Cavendish (GBr) HTC	Thor Hushovd (Nor) Garmin
Stage 8 Sat 9 Jul	Aigurande to Super Besse (Sancy) 188 finishers	189 km 4h36'46" 41 kph	Rui Costa (Por) Caisse d'Épargne	Thor Hushovd (Nor) Garmin
	Rated climbs: Côte d'Évaux-les-Bains (450m) Julien el Farès (Fra) Cofidis; Côte du Rocher des Trois Tourtes (766m) Alexander Kolobnev (Rus) Katusha; Col de la Croix Saint-Robert (1,451m) Tejay van Garderen (USA) HTC; Super-Besse Sancy (1,275m) Rui Costa (Por) Movistar			

Stage-by-Stage Results for the 2011 Tour de France			Stage Winner	Maillot Jaune
Stage 9 Sun 10 Jul	Issoire to Saint-Flour 180 finishers	208 km 5h27'09" 38.1 kph	Luis León Sánchez (Esp) Rabobank	Thomas Voeckler (Fra) Europcar
	Rated climbs: Côte de Massiac (753m) Thomas Voeckler (Fra) Europcar; Col du Pas de Péyrol (Le Puy Mary) (1,588m) Thomas Voeckler (Fra) Europcar; Col du Perthus (1,309m) Johnny Hoogerland (Ned) Vacansoleil; Col de Cère (1,300m) Johnny Hoogerland (Ned) Vacansoleil; Côte de la Chevade (1,162m) Johnny Hoogerland (Ned) Vacansoleil; Col de Prat de Bouc (Plomb du Cantal) (1,392m) Johnny Hoogerland (Ned) Vacansoleil; Côte du Château d'Alleuze (872m) Thomas Voeckler (Fra) Europcar; Saint-Flour (Montée des Orgues) (882m) Luis Leon Sanchez (Esp) Rabobank			
Mon 11 Jul	Rest Day			
Stage 10 Tue 12 Jul	Aurillac to Carmaux 178 finishers	158 km 3h31'21" 44.9 kph	André Greipel (Ger) Omega Pharma	Thomas Voeckler (Fra) Europcar
	Rated climbs: Côte de Figeac (350m) Marco Marcato (Ita) Vacansoleil; Côte de Loupiac (333m) Marco Marcato (Ita) Vacansoleil; Côte de Villefranche de Rouergue (511m) Marco Marcato (Ita) Vacansoleil; Côte de Mirandol-Bourgnounac (415m) Thomas Voeckler (Fra) Europcar			
Stage 11 Wed 13 Jul	Blaye-les-Mines to Lavaur 177 finishers	167.5 km 3h46'07" 44.4 kph	Mark Cavendish (GBr) HTC	Thomas Voeckler (Fra) Europcar
	Rated climbs: Côte de Tonnac (346m) Lars Boom (Ned) Rabobank; Côte de Puylaurens (368m) Mickaël Delage (Fra) FDJ			
Stage 12 Thu 14 Jul	Cugnaux to Luz-Ardiden 175 finishers	211 km 6h01'15" 35 kph	Samuel Sánchez (Esp) Euskaltel	Thomas Voeckler (Fra) Europcar
	Rated climbs: La Hourquette d'Ancizan (1,538m) Laurent Mangel (Fra) Saur; Col du Tourmalet (2,115m) Jérémy Roy (Fra) FDJ; Luz-Ardiden (1,715m) Samuel Sanchez (Esp) Euskaltel			
Stage 13 Fri 15 Jul	Pau to Lourdes 171 finishers	152.5 km 3h47'36" 40.2 kph	Thor Hushovd (Nor) Garmin	Thomas Voeckler (Fra) Europcar
	Rated climbs: Côte de Cuqueron (265m) Jelle Vanendert (Bel) Omega Pharma; Côte de Bel-Air (425m) Jérémy Roy (Fra) FDJ; Col d'Aubisque (1,709m) Jérémy Roy (Fra) FDJ			
Stage 14 Sat 16 Jul	Saint-Gaudens to Plateau de Beille 170 finishers	168.5 km 5h13'25" 32.3 kph	Jelle Vanendert (Bel) Omega Pharma	Thomas Voeckler (Fra) Europcar
	Rated climbs: Col de Portet d'Aspet (1,069m) Mickaël Delage (Fra) FDJ; Col de la Core (1,395m) Mickaël Delage (Fra) FDJ; Col de Latrape (1,100m) Sandy Casar (Fra) FDJ; Col d'Agnès (1,570m) Sylvain Chavanel (Fra) Quick Step; Port de Lers (1,517m) Gorka Izagirre (Esp) Euskaltel; Plateau de Beille (1,780m) Jelle Vanendert (Bel) Omega Pharma			
Stage 15 Sun 17 Jul	Limoux to Montpellier 170 finishers	192.5 km 4h20'24" 44.4 kph	Mark Cavendish (GBr) HTC	Thomas Voeckler (Fra) Europcar
	Rated climbs: Côte de Villespassans (288m) Mikhail Ignatyev (Rus) Katusha			

Stage-by-Stage Results for the 2011 Tour de France			Stage Winner	Maillot Jaune
Mon 18 Jul	Rest Day			
Stage 16 Tue 19 Jul	Saint-Paul-Trois-Châteaux to Gap 170 finishers	162.5 km 3h31'38" 46.1 kph	Thor Hushovd (Nor) Garmin	Thomas Voeckler (Fra) Europcar
	Rated climbs: Col de Manse (1,272m) Ryder Hesjedal (Can) Garmin			
Stage 17 Wed 20 Jul	Gap to Pinerolo 169 finishers	179 km 4h18'00" 41.6 kph	Edvald Boasson Hagen (Nor) Sky	Thomas Voeckler (Fra) Europcar
	Rated climbs: Côte de Sainte-Marguerite (1,185m) Sylvain Chavanel (Fra) Quick Step; Côte de la Chaussée (1,365m) Sylvain Chavanel (Fra) Quick Step; Col de Montgenèvre (1,860m) Sylvain Chavanel (Fra) Quick Step; Sestriere (2,035m) Rubén Pérez (Esp) Euskaltel ; Colle Pra Martino (916m) Edvald Boasson Hagen (Nor) Sky			
Stage 18 Thu 21 Jul	Pinerolo to Galibier (Serre-Chevalier) 168 finishers	200.5 km 6h07'56" 32.7 kph	Andy Schleck (Lux) Leopard	Thomas Voeckler (Fra) Europcar
	Rated climbs: Col d'Agnel (2,744m) Maxim Iglinskiy (Kaz) Astana; Col d'Izoard (2,360m) Maxim Iglinskiy (Kaz) Astana; Col du Galibier (2,645m) Andy Schleck (Lux) Leopard			
Stage 19 Fri 22 Jul	Modane/Valfréjus to l'Alpe d'Huez 167 finishers	109.5 km 3h13'25" 34 kph	Pierre Rolland (Fra) Europcar	Andy Schleck (Lux) Leopard
	Rated climbs: Col du Télégraphe (1,566m) Gorka Izagirre (Esp) Euskaltel; Col du Galibier (2,645m) Andy Schleck (Lux) Leopard; l'Alpe d'Huez (1,860m) Pierre Rolland (Fra) Europcar			
Stage 20 Sat 23 Jul	Grenoble (ITT) 167 finishers	42.5 km 55'33" 45.9 kph	Tony Martin (Ger) HTC	Cadel Evans (Aus) BMC
Stage 21 Sun 24 Jul	Créteil to Paris (Champs-Élysées) 167 finishers	95 km 2h27'02" 38.8 kph	Mark Cavendish (GBr) HTC	Cadel Evans (Aus) BMC

Prize fund: 3,200,000 euro (first prize: 450,000 euro)

Final Classification

Place		Rider	Team	Time	Age
1	1	Cadel Evans (Aus)	BMC	3,630 km 86h12'22" 39.788 kph	34
2	2	Andy Schleck (Lux)	Leopard	+ 1'34"	26
3	3	Fränk Schleck (Lux)	Leopard	+ 2'30"	31
4	4	Thomas Voeckler (Fra)	Europcar	+ 3'20"	32
5		~~Alberto Contador (Esp)~~ (1)	~~Saxo Bank~~	~~+ 3'57"~~	~~28~~
6	5	Samuel Sánchez (Esp)	Euskaltel	+ 4'55"	33
~~7~~	6	Damiano Cunego (Ita)	Lampre	+ 6'05"	29
~~8~~	7	Ivan Basso (Ita)	Liquigas	+ 7'23"	33
~~9~~	8	Tom Danielson (USA)	Garmin	+ 8'15"	33
~~10~~	9	Jean-Christophe Péraud (Fra)	AG2R	+ 10'11"	34
~~11~~	10	Pierre Rolland (Fra)	Europcar	+ 10'43"	24

Lanterne Rouge

~~167~~	167	Fabio Sabatini (Ita)	Liquigas	+ 3h57'43"	26

Points

		Mark Cavendish (GBr)	HTC		26

King of the Mountains

		Samuel Sánchez (Esp)	Euskaltel		33

Youth

		Pierre Rolland (Fra)	Europcar		24

Team

			Garmin		

Super Combativité

		Jérémy Roy (Fra)	FDJ		28

(1) Alberto Contador was stripped of his fifth place finish when CAS finally reached a decision on his 2010 positive for clenbuterol

2012: A Return to National Teams?

Back at the end of the 1920s when Henri Desgrange finally got fed up with the way trade teams were making a mockery of his desire to see the best rider win the best race, he replaced trade teams with national and regional squads. And immediately they delivered successes to France. But by the early 1960s it was ever harder to keep the trade teams out, not without sacrificing some of the Tour's importance, possibly even ceding its top race status to the Giro d'Italia. So Jacques Goddet and Félix Lévitan re-admitted the trade teams. National teams were, briefly, brought back in 1967 and 1968 but, since then the trade teams have had full access to the Tour's stage.

Every few years someone, especially in France, suggests bringing back national teams. It would be a cure, they say, for the overt commercialism of the race. Which it wouldn't, national teams having carried sponsors' names on their jerseys, shorts and caps, and most of the Tour's commercialism being driven by the race organisers, who want to make a profit.

And, as the years mount up since Bernard Hinault last won the Tour for France in 1985, every few years someone, especially in France, suggests bringing back trade teams as a way of getting a Frenchman standing on the top step of the Tour's podium. That might actually work. But it's worth pointing out here that flying the flag hasn't exactly helped the French bring home many World Championships since the days of Hinault (only Luc Leblanc in 1994 and Laurent Brochard in 1997 have won the road championships while wearing French jerseys).

While the idea of the Tour ever reverting again to national teams seems hard to imagine, the reality is it is already happening. Astana are the national team of Kazakhstan, backed by the country's cycling federation. Katusha are the national team of Russia and are similarly backed by their national federation. Orica/GreenEdge is the de facto Australian national team. Euskaltel/Euskadi flies the flag for the Basques in their quest for an identity separate from Spain. And the British, well the British have Team Sky.

Born on the back of Lottery-funded track success that has seen the British rule the boards, Sky was born in 2010, with the stated objective of landing a Briton on the top step of the podium in Paris within five years. Their timing was perfect, for only the year before Bradley Wiggins had surprised many in the manner in which he transformed himself from an Olympic pursuit champion into a Tour contender, finishing fourth in the 2009 Tour. Sky were able to entice Wiggins away from Garmin but in the two Tours that followed – 2010 and 2011 – he was first a shadow of the man who finished fourth and then a non-finisher, crashing out of the 2011 race with a broken collarbone. 2012, though, right from the moment the race route was announced, that looked like being Wiggins's year.

And it would prove to be his year without two major challengers: Alberto Contador (Saxo Bank), who was spending time on the naughty step, his 2010 clenbuterol case having finally been decided, and Andy Schleck (RadioShack), ruled out through injury. That still left defending champion Cadel Evans (BMC), along with Vincenzo Nibali (Liquigas) as strong rivals.

Coming into the Tour, Sky had shown form by dominating key preparatory races: Paris-Nice, the Tour de Romandie and the Critérium du Dauphiné (Nibali landed Tirreno-Adriatico, Evans the Critérium International). And each time Sky won, they won the same way: wiping the floor with opponents in the time trials and bossing the life out of the *peloton* on the road stages. So, coming into the Tour, it was not as if others weren't aware of Sky's tactics. Forewarned doesn't mean forearmed, for they were in no position to counter Sky's tactics, Wiggins wiping the floor with his opponents in the time trials while his team bossed the life out of the *peloton* on the other stages.

Chris Froome and Bradley Wiggins
during the 2012 Tour.

Wiggins donned the *maillot jaune* old school style, taking control of the race on the first day in the high mountains – Stage Seven to Planche des Belles Filles – and never letting go thereafter. After the finish on Planche des Belle Filles Wiggins led Evans by 10 seconds on general classification and Nibali by 16, with the rest of the top 10 all within two minutes of yellow.

Two days later it was time for Wiggins to crush the opposition in the 41.5 kilometre time trial from Arc-et-Senans to Besançon, and at the end of it Evans was 1'53" off yellow, with Nibali in fourth at 2'23" (Wiggins's team-mate Chris Froome moved up to third, at 2'07").

The next major change came on Stage 11, Albertville to La Toussuire, where Evans fell back after having launched an attack on the Glandon, losing 1'26" at the end of the stage. Now it was a straight fight between Wiggins and Nibali. The Italian went on the attack on Stage 17, on the climb to Peyragudes, but Wiggins and the Sky-train quickly brought him to heel, as they had brought him to heel every other time he'd opened up a gap on earlier stages. This time the attack cost the Italian 18 seconds as Wiggins strengthened his grip on the yellow jersey.

In the final time trial Wiggins pushed Nibali back to 6'19" on general classification, with team-mate Froome in second at 3'21". It was a cold and efficient victory. But a victory nonetheless. And one delivered two years ahead of Sky's 2014 target. The British had done it. They had successfully landed a man on the top step of the Tour's podium. The only question now was: could they bring him back again?

* * * * *

A month after the Tour ended, USADA announced it had imposed a life-time ban on Lance Armstrong and stripped him of all results dating back to 1998. Seven Tour wins were wiped from the record. Add in 1904, 2006 and 2010, that's ten Tours in which the man who won the Tour in Paris later lost that victory. Ten Tours out of 99.

USADA's pursuit of Armstrong was necessary. For too long it had been too clear that something was going on, with evidence unearthed by journalists making it nearly impossible to believe that the American was riding clean, and too much going on in the sport to believe that anyone winning as effortlessly as he did – and beating riders who were later revealed to have doped – could be riding clean.

But USADA's pursuit was also necessary because they had been given evidence of Armstrong's doping and couldn't just dismiss it in the same way, say, the UCI dismissed claims by people like Jesús Manzano. And that evidence came from a former team-mate of Armstrong's, Floyd Landis.

Landis had challenged his own doping case all the way to CAS, never publicly admitting that he had doped. When he returned from his time on the naughty step he found doors closed to him. When Armstrong returned to the professional *peloton* in 2009 Landis thought that his former team-mate might help open some of those doors for him. Landis had, after all, respected the sport's code of silence. But help came there none. And Landis finally realised that it was all pointless and blew the gaff on Armstrong and the whole US Postal doping scheme.

But there is a problem arising from the USADA decision: in singling out Armstrong and blaming all the ills of a whole generation – of the whole sport – on him, there is a danger of our becoming blinkered to the past and too hopeful about the future. The past was rotten, as rotten as the Armstrong era was, and too many riders from the past are today still silent about what really went on during their time in the professional *peloton*. Armstrong's doping – the whole of cycling's doping – can be forgiven, if not forgotten. As fans, we have long since forgiven heroes of the past like Fausto Coppi and Jacques Anquetil who were at least open about their use of doping products.

While doping should be deplored, it is not the doping that is the real crime. It's the code of silence associated with it, the lies and the denials of the many who refuse to acknowledge the role they played in the sport's culture of chemical assistance. And, as long as those lies continue go on, it makes it hard to simply accept someone's word today that they are riding clean, even as it is clear that the *peloton* is cleaning itself up and that the sport is cleaner than it has been at any time since doping was banned in the 1960s, maybe even cleaner than at any time it has been in its history.

And that is the real crime of Lance Armstrong and of all the others who have doped and lied to protect their image: their lies are still damaging the sport today, denying today's riders the right to be believed. Armstrong is the one who has been punished, while others continue to profit from reputations built on lies and doping.

Stage-by-Stage Results for the 2012 Tour de France			Stage Winner	Maillot Jaune
Prologue Sat 30 Jun	Liège (ITT) 198 finishers	6.4 km 7'13" 53.2 kph	Fabian Cancellara (Sui) RadioShack	Fabian Cancellara (Sui) RadioShack
Stage 1 Sun 1 Jul	Liège to Seraing 198 finishers	198 km 4h58'19" 39.8 kph	Peter Sagan (Svk) Liquigas	Fabian Cancellara (Sui) RadioShack
	Rated climbs: Côte de Cokaifagne (543m) Michael Mørkøv (Den) Saxo Bank; Côte de Francorchamps (486m) Pablo Urtasun (Esp) Euskaltel; Côte de Lierneux (527m) Michael Mørkøv (Den) Saxo Bank; Côte de Barvaux (220m) Michael Mørkøv (Den) Saxo Bank; Côte de Seraing (259m) Peter Sagan (Svk) Liquiga			
Stage 2 Mon 2 Jul	Visé to Tournai 198 finishers	207.5 km 4h56'59" 41.9 kph	Mark Cavendish (GBr) Sky	Fabian Cancellara (Sui) RadioShack
	Rated climbs: Côte de la Citadelle de Namur (188m) Michael Mørkøv (Den) Saxo Bank			
Stage 3 Tue 3 Jul	Orchies to Boulogne-sur-Mer 196 finishers	197 km 4h42'58" 41.8 kph	Peter Sagan (Svk) Liquigas	Fabian Cancellara (Sui) RadioShack
	Rated climbs: Côte de l'Éperche (195m) Michael Mørkøv (Den) Saxo Bank; Côte de Mont Violette (173m) Michael Mørkøv (Den) Saxo Bank			
Stage 4 Wed 4 Jul	Abbeville to Rouen 195 finishers	214.5 km 5h18'32" 40.4 kph	André Greipel (Ger) Lotto	Fabian Cancellara (Sui) RadioShack
	Rated climbs: Côte du Mont Huon (99m) David Moncoutié (Fra) Cofidis; Côte de Dieppe (86m) Anthony Delaplace (Fra) Saur; Côte de Pourville-sur-Mer (104m) David Moncoutié (Fra) Cofidis			
Stage 5 Thu 5 Jul	Rouen to Saint-Quentin 194 finishers	196.5 km 4h41'30" 41.9 kph	André Greipel (Ger) Lotto	Fabian Cancellara (Sui) RadioShack
Stage 6 Fri 6 Jul	Épernay to Metz 190 finishers	207.5 km 4h37'00" 44.9 kph	Peter Sagan (Svk) Liquigas	Fabian Cancellara (Sui) RadioShack
	Rated climbs: Côte de Toussaint (118m) Anthony Delaplace (Fra) Saur; Côte de Buxières (398m) David Zabriskie (USA) Garmin			

Stage-by-Stage Results for the 2012 Tour de France			Stage Winner	Maillot Jaune
Stage 7 Sat 7 Jul	Tomblaine to Planche des Belles Filles 181 finishers	199 km 4h58'35" 40 kph	Chris Froome (GBr) Sky	Bradley Wiggins (GBr) Sky
	Rated climbs: Col de la Grosse Pierre (956m) Chris Anker Sörensen (Den) Saxo Bank; Col du Mont de Fourche (633m) Chris Anker Sörensen (Den) Saxo Bank; La Planche des Belles Filles (1,035m) Chris Froome (GBr) Sky			
Stage 8 Sun 8 Jul	Belfort to Porrentruy 178 finishers	157.5 km 3h56'10" 40 kph	Thibaut Pinot (Fra) FDJ	Bradley Wiggins (GBr) Sky
	Rated climbs: Côte de Bondeval (499m) Jens Voigt (Ger) RadioShack; Côte du Passage de la Douleur (806m) Jens Voigt (Ger) RadioShack; Côte de Maison-Rouge (784m) Blel Kadri (Fra) AG2R; Côte de Saignelégier (979m) Jérémy Roy (Fra) FDJ; Côte de Saulcy (928m) Fredrik Kessiakoff (Swe) Astana; Côte de la Caquerelle (834m) Fredrik Kessiakoff (Swe) Astana; Col de la Croix (798m) Thibaut Pinot (Fra) FDJ			
Stage 9 Mon 9 Jul	Arc-et-Senans to Besançon (ITT) 178 finishers	41.5 km 51'24" 48.4 kph	Bradley Wiggins (GBr) Sky	Bradley Wiggins (GBr) Sky
Tue 10 Jul	Rest Day			
Stage 10 Wed 11 Jul	Mâcon to Bellegarde-sur-Valserine 175 finishers	194.5 km 4h46'26" 40.7 kph	Thomas Voeckler (Fra) Europcar	Bradley Wiggins (GBr) Sky
	Rated climbs: Côte de Corlier (762m) Michael Mørkøv (Den) Saxo Bank; Col du Grand Colombière (1,505m) Thomas Voeckler (Fra) Europcar; Col de Richemond (1,061m) Thomas Voeckler (Fra) Europcar			
Stage 11 Thu 12 Jul	Albertville to La Toussuire (Les Sybelles) 167 finishers	148 km 4h43'54" 31.3 kph	Pierre Rolland (Fra) Europcar	Bradley Wiggins (GBr) Sky
	Rated climbs: Col de la Madeleine (2,000m) Peter Velits (Svk) Omega Pharma; Col de la Croix de Fer (2,067m) Fredrik Kessiakoff (Swe) Astana; Col du Mollard (1,638m) Pierre Rolland (Fra) Europcar; La Toussuire (1,703m) Pierre Rolland (Fra) Europcar			
Stage 12 Fri 13 Jul	Saint-Jean-de-Maurienne to Annonay (Davézieux) 164 finishers	226 km 5h42'46" 39.6 kph	David Millar (GBr) Garmin	Bradley Wiggins (GBr) Sky
	Rated climbs: Col du Grand Cucheron (1,188m) Robert Kišerlovski (Cro) Astana; Col du Granier (1,134m) Robert Kišerlovski (Cro) Astana; Côte d'Ardoix (366m) Robert Kišerlovski (Cro) Astana			
Stage 13 Sat 14 Jul	Saint-Paul-Trois-Châteaux to Cap d'Agde 163 finishers	217 km 4h57'59" 43.7 kph	André Greipel (Ger) Lotto	Bradley Wiggins (GBr) Sky
	Rated climbs: Mont Saint-Clair (159m) Jurgen Van Den Broeck (Bel) Lotto			

Stage-by-Stage Results for the 2012 Tour de France			Stage Winner	Maillot Jaune
Stage 14 Sun 15 Jul	Limoux to Foix 162 finishers	191 km 4h50'29" 39.5 kph	Luis León Sánchez (Esp) Rabobank	Bradley Wiggins (GBr) Sky
	Rated climbs: Col du Portel (601m) Thomas Voeckler (Fra) Europcar; Port de Lers (1,517m) Sergio Miguel Paulinho (Por) Saxo Bank; Mûr de Péguère (1,375m) Sandy Casar (Fra) FDJ			
Stage 15 Mon 16 Jul	Samatan to Pau 156 finishers	158.5 km 3h40'15" 43.2 kph	Pierrick Fédrigo (Fra) FDJ	Bradley Wiggins (GBr) Sky
	Rated climbs: Côte de Lahitte-Toupière (298m) Thomas Voeckler (Fra) Europcar; Côte de Simacourbe (312m) Thomas Voeckler (Fra) Europcar; Côte de Monassut-Audiracq (318m) Thomas Voeckler (Fra) Europcar			
Tue 17 Jul	Rest Day			
Stage 16 Wed 18 Jul	Pau to Bagnères-de-Luchon 153 finishers	197 km 5h35'02" 35.3 kph	Thomas Voeckler (Fra) Europcar	Bradley Wiggins (GBr) Sky
	Rated climbs: Col d'Aubisque (1,709m) Thomas Voeckler (Fra) Europcar; Col du Tourmalet (2,115m) Thomas Voeckler (Fra) Europcar; Col d'Aspin (1,489m) Thomas Voeckler (Fra) Europcar; Col de Peyresourde (1,559m) Thomas Voeckler (Fra) Europcar			
Stage 17 Thu 19 Jul	Bagnères-de-Luchon to Peyragudes 153 finishers	143.5 km 4h12'11" 34.1 kph	Alejandro Valverde (Esp) Movistar	Bradley Wiggins (GBr) Sky
	Rated climbs: Col de Menté (1,349m) Thomas Voeckler (Fra) Europcar; Col des Ares (797m) Thomas Voeckler (Fra) Europcar; Côte de Burs (592m) Thomas Voeckler (Fra) Europcar; Port de Balès (1,755m) Alejandro Valverde (Esp) Movistar; Peyragudes (1,603m) Alejandro Valverde (Esp) Movistar			
Stage 18 Fri 20 Jul	Blagnac to Brive-la-Gaillarde 153 finishers	222.5 km 4h54'12" 45.4 kph	Mark Cavendish (GBr) Sky	Bradley Wiggins (GBr) Sky
	Rated climbs: Côte de Saint-Georges (186m) Nick Nuyens (Bel) Saxo Bank; Côte de Cahors (206m) Michael Albasini (Sui) Orica; Côte de Souillac (206m) Yukiya Arashiro (Jpn) Europcar; Côte de Lissac-sur-Couze (290m) Alexander Vinokourov (Kaz) Astana			
Stage 19 Sat 21 Jul	Bonneval to Chartres (ITT) 153 finishers	53.5 km 1h04'13" 50 kph	Bradley Wiggins (GBr) Sky	Bradley Wiggins (GBr) Sky
Stage 20 Sun 22 Jul	Rambouillet to Paris (Champs-Élysées) 153 finishers	120 km 3h08'07" 38.3 kph	Mark Cavendish (GBr) Sky	Bradley Wiggins (GBr) Sky
	Rated climbs: Côte de Saint-Rémy-lès-Chevreuse (153m) Thomas Voeckler (Fra) Europcar; Côte de Châteaufort (190m) Ruben Plaza (Esp) Movistar			

Prize fund: 3,200,000 euro (first prize:450,000 euro)

Final Classification

Place	Rider	Team	Time	Age
1	Bradley Wiggins (GBr)	Sky	3,497 km 87h34'47" 39.883 kph	32
2	Chris Froome (GBr)	Sky	+ 3'21"	27
3	Vincenzo Nibali (Ita)	Liquigas	+ 6'19"	27
4	Jurgen Van Den Broeck (Bel)	Lotto	+ 10'15"	29
5	Tejay van Garderen (USA)	BMC	+ 11'04"	23
6	Haimar Zubeldia (Esp)	RadioShack	+ 15'41"	35
7	Cadel Evans (Aus)	BMC	+ 15'49"	25
8	Pierre Rolland (Fra)	Europcar	+ 16'26"	25
9	Janez Brajkovic (Slo)	Astana	+ 16'23"	28
10	Thibaut Pinot (Fra)	FDJ	+ 17'17"	22

Lanterne Rouge

153	Jimmy Engoulvent (Fra)	Saur	+ 3h57'36"	32

Points

	Peter Sagan (Svk)	Liquigas		22

King of the Mountains

	Thomas Voeckler (Fra)	Europcar		33

Youth

	Tejay van Garderen (USA)	BMC		23

Team

		RadioShack		

Super Combativité

	Chris Anker Sørensen (Den)	Saxo Bank		27

2013: The One Hundredth Tour

Bradley Wiggins almost lost the 2012 Tour de France, and the man who almost beat him was himself. On the stage to La Toussuire, team-mate Chris Froome momentarily dropped Wiggins and had to be called to heel by *directeur sportif* Sean Yates. A few months after the Tour ended, Wiggins wrote in the third volume of his autobiographies that, thereafter, he didn't quite know what to expect from his team-mate. But it was worse than just that, for that night on La Toussuire Wiggins actually wanted to quit the Tour, while wearing the yellow jersey. As Antonin Magne found out in the 1930s, the mental pressure of the Tour can often be harder than the physical.

Relations between the two team-mates soured. And they stayed sour into the new season. Froome had by then been elevated to Sky's leader for the Tour, with Wiggins going to Italy in a quest to add the Giro d'Italia to his *palmarès*. The defending champion would ride the Tour, but only to support Froome, to do as Hinault had done in 1986 and repay a team-mate for help given. And then, ahead of the Giro, the plotline changed: Wiggins talked up going for the Giro/Tour double. Opening – for the second time in five years – the prospect of the Tour serving up a repeat of its epic 1986 edition. In the end, though, it all came to naught. Wiggins didn't survive the Giro and a knee injury sustained there ruled him out of the Tour.

Which then left the way clear for Froome to win. But he would face opposition. Of the 22 teams entered in the race, most were at the Tour for reasons other than the final *maillot jaune*. Omega Pharma/Quick Step were racing for stage wins and the points competition, with Mark Cavendish. Ditto Cannondale (Liquigas with a new name) with Peter Sagan, Lotto with André Greipel and Argos/Shimano with Marcel Kittel. Europcar were looking for stage wins and the King of the Mountains title, with Thomas Voeckler and Pierre Rolland. On and on you could go, eliminating teams from the general classification race until you were left with just six. Sky with Froome; BMC, who had the old warhorse Cadel Evans and the Young Turk Tejay van Garderen; Saxo/Tinkoff with Alberto Contador; Katusha with Joaquim Rodríguez; Movistar with Alejandro Valverde and Nairo Quintana; and Garmin with Ryder Hesjedal. Six teams out of 22 with clear favourites for the final victory.

As early as Stage Eight of the race there was just one favourite for victory: Froome. On the first mountain stage of the race, Castres to Ax 3 Domaines, Sky seemed to have strangled the life out of the Tour, Froome taking the stage win and the *maillot jaune*, all his key rivals already more than a minute back on GC and only team-mate Richie Porte within a minute of his time. A repeat of 2012 seemed to be on the cards, Froome playing Wiggins, Porte as Froome.

But the very next day that script was thrown out the window. Barely 30 kilometres into the stage Froome's Sky workhorses were scattered across the road as Garmin unleashed anarchy, sending riders off the front and taking the fight to Sky. Only Porte was left to protect his team-leader. Valverde launched an attack on the descent of the Col de Menté that dropped him, leaving Froome alone and exposed. Quintana followed that with a succession of attacks but, each time, the Colombian climbing sensation was brought to heel by Froome. At the stage end Froome's rivals seemed content to settle for the damage done to Sky's morale – and Porte's GC standing – while Garmin's Dan Martin got the stage win.

Three days later, on Stage 11, Froome put his foot down in the first individual time trial, pushing his rivals back to three minutes and more on GC. Again the Tour seemed to be over. And again the tables were turned, this time on Stage 13, Tours to Saint-Amand-Montrond, where Froome was again left without team-mates as side-winds split the *peloton* into echelons and Cavendish and Contador's Omega

Pharma and Saxo team-mates caused havoc. Froome was gapped and lost 1'09" to Contador. There are days when you win the Tour and there are days when you don't lose it, and this was the day that Froome didn't lose the Tour, keeping his head and accepting his fate, working carefully to limit his losses. He still finished the day with no rival within two minutes of him on GC.

Stage 15 saw the Tour tackle the Ventoux, by which time the Sky train was firing on all cylinders, setting a fearsome pace to the bottom of the bald mountain and launching Froome to a stage win that recalled the battle between Lance Armstrong and Marco Pantani in the 2000 Tour. Quintana had escaped the lead group with about 12 kilometres of the climb to go, but four kilometres later Froome effortlessly bridged across to him, dropping everyone else as he did so. The Colombian and the Briton briefly rode together before, a kilometre or so from the summit, Froome simply accelerated away from Quintana and took the stage victory. Froome now led by four minutes and more and again the Tour seemed over.

Contador was by now down to 4'25" off yellow and looking beaten, but the Spaniard was not admitting defeat. If he couldn't beat Froome on the bike, he'd just have to do it off and, after a rest day, he took the battle to the Briton on the descents on the road to Gap. Froome, like many climbers of old, could go uphill with indecent haste but coming down them, that was a different matter. Risking everything, Contador did manage to make Froome come to a standstill on a descent. But only to avoid running into the Spaniard, who himself momentarily ran off the road on the same descent that had put an end to Joseba Beloki's Tour dreams ten years earlier and saw Lance Armstrong cyclo-crossing through a field in his efforts to stay upright. Froome may have been riding to what, just looking at the time gaps, was an effortless victory, but he was being put under constant pressure by his rivals who kept hitting him when he least expected it.

That was followed by Stage 17's second race of truth, 32 kilometres from Embrum to Chorges, which Froome again bossed. Then came two ascents of Alpe d'Huez on one stage and this time the problems coming at Froome came from his own squad, a team car breaking down and not being able to pass food to him before the second ascent of the Alpe. Five kilometres from the summit Froome began to bonk and Porte had to drop back to the team car – which had by now caught up with the back of the race – and collect some energy gels for the *maillot jaune*. Quintana and Rodríguez gained a minute on the road, and another 20 seconds when the race commissaires wagged their fingers at the Sky riders over their illegal feed. Even still, Froome was now leading by more than five minutes over all his rivals. Barring an upset, the win was in the bag. But in a race that had already produced more tension than most recent Tours, no one was ruling out an upset.

The upset never came, and, as dusk fell on Paris on the second last Sunday in July, the Tour raced into the City of Lights for an evening finish and the Kenyan-born Briton was crowned the victor of the one hundredth Tour, joining the 58 other men whose names appear on the Tour's role of honour

* * * * *

Celebrating the Tour's second one hundredth birthday – the 11 Tours lost to the two World Wars being the difference between years and races run – ASO pushed the boat out, inviting many of the surviving *géants de la route* to the party in Paris. Absent from the feast was the Tour's own Banquo, Lance Armstrong, but his ghost was present throughout the race, the Tour champion-in-waiting daily having to answer questions about doping. In the light of all that has gone on in cycling across the full span of its history, and until the UCI show the sort of leadership that can leave people confident that doping is really being tackled, such questions are inevitable, and those at the top of the sport have to be willing to answer them.

After the Tour, the UCI took a step that may yet lead to that confidence being generated. Two-term president Pat McQuaid was voted out of office and replaced by Brian Cookson. During McQuaid's time in office, much was done to tackle the sport's doping problem. The Biological Passport was introduced and a no-needles policy was brought in, banning the use of all injections unless medically justified. Tour winners Floyd Landis and Alberto Contador were banned on the back of doping offences. But behind those steps forward McQuaid often pushed the sport backwards through his confrontational management style, getting into needless disputes with teams, with race organisers, with the UCI's own member federations. There was only limited transparency on what was happening within the UCI and how the sport was really being governed. These and many more issues Cookson has promised to address.

Cookson has also agreed to follow up on McQuaid's failed attempt to investigate cycling's past and get some understanding of how the doping problem came about and how it was allowed to get out of control in the manner it did. Maybe if we finally understand the problem we can begin to move forward. We may never be able to believe in the old myth of Angels with winged angles sailing up the Tour's mountains. And maybe we should never believe in fairy stories like that anyway. But perhaps with understanding will come a time when not every stunning performance is immediately met with questions about doping.

Stage-by-Stage Results for the 2013 Tour de France			Stage Winner	Maillot Jaune
Stage 1 Sat 29 Jun	Porto-Vecchio to Bastia 198 finishers	213 km 4h56'52" 43 kph	Marcel Kittel (Ger) Argos	Marcel Kittel (Ger) Argos
	Rated climbs: Côte de Sotta (147m) Juan José Lobato (Esp) Euskaltel			
Stage 2 Sun 30 Jun	Bastia to Ajaccio 198 finishers	156 km 3h43'11" 41.9 kph	Jan Bakelants (Bel) RadioShack	Jan Bakelants (Bel) RadioShack
	Rated climbs: Col de Bellagranajo (723m) Lars Boom (Ned) Belkin; Col de la Serra (807m) Blel Kadri (Fra) AG2R; Col de Vizzavona (1,163m) Pierre Rolland (Fra) Europcar; Côte du Salario (98m) Cyril Gautier (Fra) Europcar			
Stage 3 Mon 1 Jul	Ajaccio to Calvi 196 finishers	145.5 km 3h41'24" 39.4 kph	Simon Gerrans (Aus) Orica	Jan Bakelants (Bel) RadioShack
	Rated climbs: Col de San Bastiano (415m) Simon Clarke (Aus) Orica; Col de San Martino (429m) Simon Clarke (Aus) Orica; Côte de Porto (161m) Simon Clarke (Aus) Orica; Col de Marsolino (443m) Pierre Rolland (Fra) Europcar			
Stage 4 Tue 2 Jul	Nice (TTT) 195 finishers	25 km 25'56" 57.8 kph	Orica	Simon Gerrans (Aus) Orica
Stage 5 Wed 3 Jul	Cagnes-sur-Mer to Marseille 195 finishers	228.5 km 5h31'51" 41.3 kph	Mark Cavendish (GBr) Omega Pharma	Simon Gerrans (Aus) Orica
	Rated climbs: Côte de Châteauneuf-Grasse (388m) Thomas de Gendt (Bel) Vacansoleil; Col de l'Ange (241m) Thomas de Gendt (Bel) Vacansoleil; Côte de la Roquebrussanne (418m) Yukiya Arashiro (Jpn) Europcar; Côte des Bastides (354m) Thomas de Gendt (Bel) Vacansoleil			

Stage-by-Stage Results for the 2013 Tour de France			Stage Winner	Maillot Jaune
Stage 6 Thu 4 Jul	Aix-en-Provence to Montpellier 191 finishers	176.5 km 3h59'02" 44.3 kph	André Greipel (Ger) Lotto	Daryl Impey (RSA) Orica
	Rated climbs: Col de la Vayède (179m) Kanstantsin Sivtsov (Blr) Sky			
Stage 7 Fri 5 Jul	Montpellier to Albi 188 finishers	205.5 km 4h54'12" 41.9 kph	Peter Sagan (Svk) Cannondale	Daryl Impey (RSA) Orica
	Rated climbs: Col des 13 Vents (600m) Blel Kadri (Fra) AG2R; Col de la Croix-de-Mounis (809m) Blel Kadri (Fra) AG2R; Côte de la Quintaine (739m) Jan Bakelants (Bel) RadioShack; Côte de Teillet (491m) Jan Bakelants (Bel) RadioShack			
Stage 8 Sat 6 Jul	Castres to Ax 3 Domaines 186 finishers	195 km 5h03'08" 38.6 kph	Chris Froome (GBr) Sky	Chris Froome (GBr) Sky
	Rated climbs: Côte de Saint-Ferréol (363m) Rudy Molard (Fra) Cofidis; Port de Pailhères (2,001m) Nairo Quintana (Col) Movistar; Ax 3 Domaines (1,350m) Chris Froome (GBr) Sky			
Stage 9 Sun 7 Jul	Saint-Girons to Bagnères-de-Bigorre 182 finishers	168.5 km 4h43'03" 35.7 kph	Daniel Martin (Irl) Garmin	Chris Froome (GBr) Sky
	Rated climbs: Col de Portet d'Aspet (1,069m) Arnold Jeannesson (Fra) FDJ; Col de Menté (1,349m) Thomas Danielson (USA) Garmin; Col de Peyresourde (1,569m) Thomas de Gendt (Bel) Vacansoleil; Col de Val-Louron (Col d'Azet) (1,580m) Simon Clarke (Aus) Orica; La Hourquette d'Ancizan (1,564m) Daniel Martin (Irl) Garmin			
Mon 8 Jul	Rest Day			
Stage 10 Tue 9 Jul	Saint-Gildas-des-Bois to Saint-Malo 182 finishers	197 km 4h53'25" 40.3 kph	Marcel Kittel (Ger) Argos	Chris Froome (GBr) Sky
	Rated climbs: Côte de Dinan (74m) Lieuwe Westra (Ned) Vacansoleil			
Stage 11 Wed 10 Jul	Avranches to Mont Saint-Michel (ITT) 182 finishers	33 km 36'29" 54.3 kph	Tony Martin (Ger) Omega Pharma	Chris Froome (GBr) Sky
Stage 12 Thu 11 Jul	Fougères to Tours 182 finishers	218 km 4h49'49" 45.1 kph	Marcel Kittel (Ger) Argos	Chris Froome (GBr) Sky
Stage 13 Fri 12 Jul	Tours to Saint-Amand-Montrond 181 finishers	173 km 3h40'08" 47.2 kph	Mark Cavendish (GBr) Omega Pharma	Chris Froome (GBr) Sky
	Rated climbs: Côte de Crotz (165m) Pierre Rolland (Fra) Europcar			
Stage 14 Sat 13 Jul	Saint-Pourçain-sur-Sioule to Lyon 181 finishers	191 km 4h15'11" 44.9 kph	Matteo Trentin (Ita) Omega Pharma	Chris Froome (GBr) Sky
	Rated climbs: Côte de Marcigny (371m) Simon Geschke (Ger) Argos; Côte de la Couverte (614m) Blel Kadri (Fra) AG2R; Côte de Thizy-les-Bourgs (536m) Blel Kadri (Fra) AG2R; Col du Pilon (727m) Blel Kadri (Fra) AG2R; Côte de Lozanne (322m) Jens Voigt (Ger) RadioShack; Côte de la Duchère (263m) Michael Albasini (Sui) Orica; Côte de la Croix-Rousse (254m) Julien Simon (Fra) Sojasun			

Stage-by-Stage Results for the 2013 Tour de France			Stage Winner	Maillot Jaune
Stage 15 Sun 14 Jul	Givors to Mont Ventoux 181 finishers	242.5 km 5h48'45" 41.7 kph	Chris Froome (GBr) Sky	Chris Froome (GBr) Sky
	Rated climbs: Côte d'Eyzin-Pinet (436m) Thomas de Gendt (Bel) Vacansoleil; Côte de Primarette (459m) Pierre Rolland (Fra) Europcar; Côte de Lens-Lestang (424m) Julien el Farès (Fra) Sojasun; Côte de Bordeaux (651m) Jérémy Roy (Fra) FDJ.fr; Mont Ventoux (1,912m) Chris Froome (GBr) Sky			
Mon 15 Jul	Rest Day			
Stage 16 Tue 16 Jul	Vaison-la-Romaine to Gap 179 finishers	168 km 3h52'45" 43.3 kph	Rui Costa (Por) Movistar	Chris Froome (GBr) Sky
	Rated climbs: Côte de la Montagne de Bluye (590m) Ryder Hesjedal (Can) Garmin; Col de Macuègne (1,068m) Johnny Hoogerland (Ned) Vacansoleil; Col de Manse (1,268m) Rui Costa (Por) Movistar			
Stage 17 Wed 17 Jul	Embrun to Chorges (ITT) 177 finishers	32 km 51'33" 37.2 kph	Chris Froome (GBr) Sky	Chris Froome (GBr) Sky
	Rated climbs: Côte de Puy-Sanières (1,173m) Alberto Contador (Esp) Saxo; Côte de Réallon (1,227m) Joaquim Rodriguez (Esp) Katusha			
Stage 18 Thu 18 Jul	Gap to l'Alpe d'Huez 175 finishers	172.5 km 4h51'32" 35.5 kph	Christophe Riblon (Fra) AG2R	Chris Froome (GBr) Sky
	Rated climbs: Col de Manse (1,268m) Ryder Hesjedal (Can) Garmin; Rampe du Motty (982m) Thomas Danielson (USA) Garmin; Col d'Ornon (1,371m) Arnold Jeannesson (Fra) FDJ.fr; l'Alpe d'Huez (1,765m) Moreno Moser (Ita) Cannondale; Col de Sarenne (1,999m) Tejay van Garderen (USA) BMC; l'Alpe d'Huez (1,850m) Christophe Riblon (Fra) AG2R			
Stage 19 Fri 19 Jul	Bourg-d'Oisans to Le Grand-Bornand 170 finishers	204.5 km 5h59'01" 34.2 kph	Rui Costa (Por) Movistar	Chris Froome (GBr) Sky
	Rated climbs: Col du Glandon (1,924m) Ryder Hesjedal (Can) Garmin; Col de la Madeleine (2,000m) Ryder Hesjedal (Can) Garmin; Col de Tamié (907m) Pierre Rolland (Fra) Europcar; Col de l'Épine (947m) Pierre Rolland (Fra) Europcar; Col de la Croix-Fry (1,477m) Rui Costa (Por) Movistar			
Stage 20 Sat 20 Jul	Annecy to Mont Semnoz 170 finishers	125 km 3h39'04" 34.2 kph	Nairo Quintana (Col) Movistar	Chris Froome (GBr) Sky
	Rated climbs: Côte de Puget (796m) Pierre Rolland (Fra) Europcar; Col de Leschaux (944m) Igor Antón (Esp) Euskaltel; Côte d'Aillon-le-Vieux (929m) Pierre Rolland (Fra) Europcar; Col des Prés (1,142m) Pierre Rolland (Fra) Europcar; Mont Revard (1,463m) Jens Voigt (Ger) RadioShack; Mont Semnoz (1,655m) Nairo Quintana (Col) Movistar			
Stage 21 Sun 21 Jul	Versailles to Paris (Champs-Élysées) 169 finishers	133.5 km 3h06'14" 43 kph	Marcel Kittel (Ger) Argos	Chris Froome (GBr) Sky
	Rated climbs: Côte de Saint-Rémy-lès-Chevreuse (154m) Gert Steegmans (Bel) Omega Pharma; Côte de Chârueafort (155m) José Rojas (Esp) Movistar			

Prize fund: 3,400,000 Euro (first prize: 450,000 Euro)

Final Classification

Place	Rider	Team	Time	Age
1	Chris Froome (GBr)	Sky	83h56'40"	28
2	Nairo Quintana (Col)	Movistar	+ 4'20"	23
3	Joaquim Rodríguez (Esp)	Katusha	+ 5'04"	34
4	Alberto Contador (Esp)	Saxo	+ 6'27"	30
5	Roman Kreuziger (Cze)	Saxo	+ 7'27"	27
6	Bauke Mollema (Ned)	Belkin	+ 11'42"	26
7	Jakob Fuglsang (Den)	Astana	+ 12'17"	28
8	Alejandro Valverde (Esp)	Movistar	+ 15'26"	33
9	Daniel Navarro (Esp)	Cofidis	+ 15'52"	30
10	Andrew Talansky (USA)	Garmin	+ 17'39"	24
Lanterne Rouge				
169	Svein Tuft (Can)	Orica		36
Points				
	Peter Sagan (Svk)	Cannondale		23
King of the Mountains				
	Nairo Quintana (Col)	Movistar		23
Youth				
	Nairo Quintana (Col)	Movistar		23
Team				
		Saxo		
Super Combativité				
	Christophe Riblon (Fra)	AG2R		32

Statistics

Multiple Overall Victories

~~7: Lance Armstrong 1999, 2000, 2001, 2002, 2003, 2004, 2005~~

5: Jacques Anquetil 1957, 1961, 1962, 1963, 1964; Eddy Merckx 1969, 1970, 1971, 1972, 1974; Bernard Hinault 1978, 1979, 1981, 1982, 1985; Miguel Indurain 1991, 1992, 1993, 1994, 1995

3: Philippe Thys 1913, 1914, 1920; Louison Bobet 1953, 1954, 1955; Greg LeMond 1986, 1989, 1990

2: Lucien Petit-Breton 1907, 1908; Firmin Lambot 1919, 1922; Ottavio Bottecchia 1924, 1925; Nicolas Frantz 1927, 1928; André Leducq 1930, 1932; Antonin Magne 1931, 1934; Sylvère Maes 1936, 1939; Gino Bartali 1938, 1948; Fausto Coppi 1949, 1952; Bernard Thévenet 1975, 1977; Laurent Fignon 1983, 1984; Alberto Contador 2007, 2009

Overall Victories by Nation

36 (from 21 men): France (Maurice Garin 1903; Henri Cornet 1904; Louis Trousselier 1905; René Pottier 1906; Lucien Petit-Breton 1907, 1908; Octave Lapize 1910; Gustave Garrigou 1911; Henri Pélissier 1923; André Leducq 1930, 1932; Antonin Magne 1931, 1934; Georges Speicher 1933; Roger Lapébie 1937; Jean Robic 1947; Louison Bobet 1953, 1954, 1955; Roger Walkowiak 1956; Jacques Anquetil 1957, 1961, 1962, 1963, 1964; Lucien Aimar 1966; Roger Pingeon 1967; Bernard Thévenet 1975, 1977; Bernard Hinault 1978, 1979, 1981, 1982, 1985; Laurent Fignon 1983, 1984)

18 (from 10 men): Belgium (Odile Defraye 1912; Philippe Thys 1913, 1914, 1920; Firmin Lambot 1919, 1922; Léon Scieur 1921; Lucien

Buysse 1926; Maurice Dewaele 1929; Romain Maes 1935; Sylvère
Maes 1936, 1939; Eddy Merckx 1969, 1970, 1971, 1972, 1974;
Lucien Van Impe 1976)

12 (from 7 men): Spain (Federico Bahamontes 1959; Luis Ocaña 1973;
Pedro Delgado 1988; Miguel Indurain 1991, 1992, 1993, 1994, 1995;
Oscar Pereiro 2006; Alberto Contador 2007, 2009; Carlos Sastre
2008)

9 (from 6 men): Italy (Ottavio Bottecchia 1924, 1925; Gino Bartali
1938, 1948; Fausto Coppi 1949, 1952; Gastone Nencini 1960; Felice
Gimondi 1965; Marco Pantani 1998)

5 (from 4 men): Luxembourg (François Faber 1909; Nicolas Frantz 1927,
1928; Charly Gaul 1958; Andy Schleck 2010)

3 (from 1 man): USA (Greg LeMond 1986, 1989, 1990)

2 (from 2 men): Switzerland (Ferdi Kübler 1950; Hugo Koblet 1951)
Netherlands (Jan Janssen 1968; Joop Zoetemelk 1980) Great Britain
(Bradley Wiggins 2012; Chris Froome 2013)

1: Ireland (Stephen Roche 1987); Denmark (Bjarne Riis 1996);
Germany (Jan Ullrich 1997); Australia (Cadel Evans 2011)

Most Podium Finishes

8: Raymond Poulidor (1962 3rd, 1964 2nd, 1965 2nd, 1966 3rd, 1969 3rd,
1972 3rd, 1974 2nd, 1976 3rd); ~~Lance Armstrong (1999 1st, 2000 1st,
2001 1st, 2002 1st, 2003 1st, 2004 1st, 2005 1st, 2009 3rd)~~

7: Joop Zoetemelk (1970 2nd, 1971 2nd, 1976 2nd, 1978 2nd, 1979 2nd, 1980
1st, 1982 2nd); Bernard Hinault (1978 1st, 1979 1st, 1981 1st, 1982 1st,
1984 2nd, 1985 1st, 1986 2nd); Jan Ullrich (1996 2nd, 1997 1st, 1998 2nd,
2000 2nd, 2001 2nd, 2003 2nd, 2005 3rd)

6: Gustave Garrigou (1907 2nd, 1909 2nd, 1910 3rd, 1911 1st, 1912 3rd,
1913 2nd); Jacques Anquetil (1957 1st, 1959 3rd, 1961 1st, 1962 1st,
1963 1st, 1964 1st); Eddy Merckx (1969 1st, 1970 1st, 1971 1st, 1972 1st,
1974 1st, 1975 2nd)

5: Lucien Van Impe (1971 3rd, 1975 3rd, 1976 1st, 1977 3rd, 1981 2nd);
Greg LeMond (1984 3rd, 1985 2nd, 1986 1st, 1989 1st, 1990 1st); Miguel
Indurain (1991 1st, 1992 1st, 1993 1st, 1994 1st, 1995 1st)

Smallest Winning Margins

1989: Greg LeMond beat Laurent Fignon by eight seconds

2007: Alberto Contador beat Cadel Evans by 23 seconds

2006: Óscar Pereiro beat Andreas Klöden by 32 seconds

1968: Jan Janssen beat Herman Van Springel by 38 seconds

1987: Stephen Roche beat Pedro Delgado by 40 seconds

1977: Bernard Thévenet beat Hennie Kuiper by 48 seconds

1964: Jacques Anquetil beat Raymond Poulidor by 55 seconds

2008: Carlos Sastre beat Cadel Evans by 58 seconds

Biggest Winning Margin

Maurice Garin beat Lucien Pothier by two hours, 59 minutes and 31 seconds in 1903.

Victories in the Tour de France and one of the other Grand Tours in the same season

Fausto Coppi: Giro d'Italia + Tour de France 1949, 1952

Jacques Anquetil: Vuelta a España + Tour de France 1963

Jacques Anquetil: Giro d'Italia + Tour de France 1964

Eddy Merckx: Giro d'Italia + Tour de France 1970, 1972, 1974

Bernard Hinault: Vuelta a España + Tour de France 1978

Bernard Hinault: Giro d'Italia + Tour de France 1982, 1985

Stephen Roche: Giro d'Italia + Tour de France 1987

Miguel Indurain: Giro d'Italia + Tour de France 1992, 1993

Marco Pantani: Giro d'Italia + Tour de France 1998

Note: Before 1995 the Vuelta was run in the spring, before the Giro. Three men have doubled the Giro and the Vuelta: Eddy Merckx in 1973, Giovanni Battaglin in 1981, and Alberto Contador in 2008. No one has won all three Grand Tours in a single season. Eddy Merckx and Bernard Hinault have won all three within twelve months, Merckx following his Giro/Tour double of 1972 with victory in the 1973 Vuelta and Bernard Hinault following his 1982 Giro/Tour double with a win in the 1983 Vuelta.

Multiple Maillot Vert Victories (Points)

6: Erik Zabel (1996, 1997, 1998, 1999, 2000, 2001)

4: Sean Kelly (1982, 1983, 1985, 1989)

3: Jan Janssen (1964, 1965, 1967); Eddy Merckx (1969, 1971, 1972); Freddy Maertens (1976, 1978, 1981); Djamolidine Abdoujaparov (1991, 1993, 1994); Robbie McEwen (2002, 2004, 2006)

2: Stan Ockers (1955, 1956); Jean Graczyk (1958, 1960); André Darrigade (1959, 1961); Laurent Jalabert (1992, 1995); Thor Hushovd (2005, 2009); Peter Sagan (2012, 2013)

Maillot Vert Victories by Nation

19 (from 14 men): Belgium (Stan Ockers 1955, 1956; Rik Van Looy 1963; Willy Planckaert 1966; Eddy Merckx 1969, 1971, 1972; Walter Godefroot 1970; Herman Van Springel 1973; Patrick Sercu 1974; Rik Van Linden 1975; Freddy Maertens 1976, 1978, 1981; Rudy Pevenage 1980; Frank Hoste 1984; Eric Vanderaerden 1986; Eddy Planckaert 1988; Tom Boonen 2007)

9 (from 6 men): France (Jean Forestier 1957; Jean Graczyk 1958, 1960; André Darrigade 1959, 1961; Jacques Esclassan 1977; Bernard Hinault 1979; Laurent Jalabert 1992, 1995)

8 (from 3 men): Germany (Rudy Altig 1962; Olaf Ludwig 1990; Erik Zabel 1996, 1997, 1998, 1999, 2000, 2001)

4 (from 2 men): Netherlands (Jan Janssen 1964, 1965, 1967; Jean-Paul van Poppel 1987); Australia (Robbie McEwen 2002, 2004, 2006; Baden Cooke 2003)

4 (from 1 man): Ireland (Sean Kelly 1982, 1983, 1985, 1989)

3 (from 1 man): Uzbekistan (Djamolidine Abdoujaparov 1991, 1993, 1994)

2 (from 2 men): Switzerland (Fritz Schär 1953; Ferdi Kübler 1954); Italy (Franco Bitossi 1968; Alessandro Petacchi 2010)

2 (from 1 man): Norway (Thor Hushovd 2005, 2009); Slovakia (Peter Sagan 2012, 2013)

1: Spain (Óscar Freire 2008); Great Britain (Mark Cavendish 2011)

Multiple Maillot à Pois Victories (King of the Mountains)

7: Richard Virenque 1994, 1995, 1996, 1997, 1999, 2003, 2004

6: Federico Bahamontes 1954, 1958, 1959, 1962, 1962, 1964; Lucien Van Impe 1971, 1972, 1975, 1977, 1981, 1983

3: Julio Jiménez 1965, 1966, 1967

2: Félicien Vervaecke 1935, 1937; Gino Bartali 1938, 1948; Fausto Coppi 1949, 1952; Charly Gaul 1955, 1956; Imerio Massignan 1960, 1961; Eddy Merckx 1969, 1970; Luis Herrera 1985, 1987; Claudio Chiappucci 1991, 1992; Laurent Jalabert 2001, 2002; Michael Rasmussen 2005, 2006

Maillot à Pois Rouge Victories by Nation

20 (from 13 men): France (René Vietto 1934; Louison Bobet 1950; Raphaël Géminiani 1951; Mariano Martínez 1978; Raymond Martin 1980; Bernard Vallet 1982; Bernard Hinault 1986; Thierry Claveyrolat 1990; Richard Virenque 1994, 1995, 1996, 1997, 1999, 2003, 2004; Christophe Rinero 1998; Laurent Jalabert 2001, 2002; Anthony Charteau 2010; Tommy Voeckler 2012)

16 (from 9 men): Spain (Vicente Trueba 1933; Julián Berrendero 1936; Jesús Loroño 1953; Federico Bahamontes 1954, 1958, 1959, 1962, 1963, 1964; Julio Jiménez 1965, 1966, 1967; Aurelio González 1968; Pedro Torres 1973; Domingo Perurena 1974; Samuel Sánchez 2011)

12 (from 8 men): Italy (Gino Bartali 1938, 1948; Pierre Brambilla 1947; Fausto Coppi 1949, 1952; Gastone Nencini 1957; Imerio Massignan 1960, 1961; Giancarlo Bellini 1976; Giovanni Battaglin 1979; Claudio Chiappucci 1991, 1992)

11 (from 4 men): Belgium (Félicien Vervaecke 1935, 1937; Sylvère Maes 1939; Eddy Merckx 1969, 1970; Lucien Van Impe 1971, 1972, 1975, 1977, 1981, 1983)

5 (from 4 men): Colombia (Luis Herrera 1985, 1987; Sergio Botero 2000; Mauricio Soler 2007; Nairo Quintana 2013)

2 (from 1 man): Luxembourg (Charly Gaul 1955, 1956) Denmark (Michael Rasmussen 2005, 2006)

2 (from 2 men): Netherlands (Steven Rooks 1988, Gert-Jan Theunisse 1989)

1: Great Britain (Robert Millar 1984); Switzerland (Tony Rominger 1993)

Multiple Maillot Blanc Victories (Youth)

3: Jan Ullrich 1996, 1997, 1998; Andy Schleck 2008, 2009, 2010

2: Marco Pantani 1994, 1995

Maillot Blanc Victories By Nation

6 (from 6 men) France (Jean-René Bernaudeau 1979; Laurent Fignon 1983; Fabrice Philippot 1989; Gilles Delion 1990; Benoît Salmon 1999; Pierre Rolland 2011)

5 (from 4 men) Italy (Francesco Moser 1975; Marco Pantani 1994, 1995; Ivan Basso 2002; Damiano Cunego 2006)

5 (from 5 men) Spain (Enrique Martínez 1976; Antonio Martín 1993; Francisco Mancebo 2000; Óscar Sevilla 2001; Alberto Contador 2007) Netherlands (Henk Lubberding 1978; Johan van der Velde 1980; Peter Winnen 1981; Erik Breukink 1988; Eddy Bouwmans 1992)

4 (from 2 men) Germany (Dietrich Thurau 1977; Jan Ullrich 1996, 1997, 1998)

3 (from 3 men) United States of America (Greg LeMond 1984; Andy Hampsten 1986; Tejay van Garderen 2012) Colombia (Fabio Parra 1985; Álvaro Mejía 1991; Nairo Quintana 2013)

3 (from 1 man) Luxembourg (Andy Schleck 2008, 2009, 2010)

2 (from 2 men) Russia (Denis Menchov 2003; Vladimir Karpets 2004)

1 Australia (Phil Anderson 1982); Mexico (Raúl Alcalá 1987); Ukraine (Yaroslav Popovych 2005)

Multiple Lanterne Rouge Winners

3: Wim Vansevenant (2006, 2007, 2008)

2: Daniel Masson (1922, 1923); Gerhard Schönbacher (1979, 1980); Mathieu Hermans (1987, 1989); Jimmy Casper (2001, 2004)

Lanterne Rouge Victories by Nation

51 (from 49 men): France (Arsène Millocheau 1903; Antoine Deflotière 1904; Clovis Lacroix 1905; Georges Bronchard 1906; Albert Chartier 1907; Henri Anthoine 1908; Georges Devilly 1909; Constant Collet 1910; Lucien Roquebert 1911; Maurice Dartigue 1912; Henri Alavoine 1913; Henri Leclerc 1914; Jules Nempon 1919; Charles Raboisson 1920; Henri Catelan 1921; Daniel Masson 1922, 1923; Victor Lafosse 1924; Fernand Besnier 1925; André Drobecq 1926; Jacques Pfister 1927; Edouard Persin 1928; André Léger 1929; Marcel Ilpide 1930; Ernest Neuhard 1933; Aldo Bertocco 1936; Armand le Moal 1939; Henri Paret 1952; Claude Rouer 1953; Roger Chaussabel 1956; Guy Million 1957; Louis Bisilliat 1959; André Geneste 1961; Anatole Novak 1964; Joseph Groussard 1965; Jean-Pierre Genet 1967; André Wilhem 1969; Georges Chappe 1971; Alain Bellouis 1972; Jacques Hochart 1973; Jacques Boulas 1975; Philippe Tesnière 1978; Jean-Luc Masdupuy 1996; Bruno Cornillet 1995; Philippe Gaumont 1997; Damien Nazon 1998; Jacky Durand 1999; Olivier Perraudeau 2000; Jimmy Casper 2001, 2004; Jimmy Engoulvent 2012)

11 (from 11 men): Italy (Antonio Folco 1934; Vittorio Seghezzi 1948; Guido de Santi 1949; Augusto Marcaletti 1962; Paolo Manucci 1966; Lorenzo Alaimo 1974; Manrico Ronchiato 1985; Ennio Salvador 1986; Rodolfo Massi 1990; Adriano Malori 2010; Fabio Sabatini 2011)

10 (from 8 men): Belgium (Willy Derboven 1963; Roger Loysch 1977; Werner Devos 1982; Marcel Laurens 1983; Dirk Wayenberg 1988; Edwig Van Hooydonck 1993; Hans de Clerq 2003; Wim Vansevenant 2006, 2007, 2008)

7 (from 6 men): Netherlands (Janus Hellemons 1938; Frits Hogerheide 1970; Aad van der Hoek 1976; Mathieu Hermans 1987, 1989; Rob Harmeling 1991; John Talen 1994)

5 (from 5 men): Spain (José Berrendero 1960; Faustino Cuelli 1981; Fernando Quevedo 1992; Igor Flores 2002; Iker Flores 2005)

4 (from 4 men): Switzerland (Pietro Tarchini 1947; Fritz Zbinden 1950; Walter Favre 1958; Gilbert Glaus 1984)

2 (from 2 men): Germany (Rudolf Risch 1932; Willi Kutschbach 1935); Luxembourg (Aloïs Klensch 1937; Marcel Dierkens 1954); Great Britain (Tony Hoar 1955; John Clarey 1968)

2 (from 1 man): Austria (Gerhard Schönbacher 1979, 1980)

1: Australia (Richard Lamb 1931); Algeria (Abd El Kader Zaaf 1951); Belarus (Yauheni Hutarovich 2009) Canada (Svein Tuft 2013)

Multiple Classification Victories in a Single Tour

1938: Gino Bartali: Overall + King of the Mountains

1939: Sylvère Maes: Overall + King of the Mountains

1948: Gino Bartali: Overall + King of the Mountains

1949: Fausto Coppi: Overall + King of the Mountains

1952: Fausto Coppi: Overall + King of the Mountains

1955: Charly Gaul: King of the Mountains + Super Combativité

1958: Federico Bahamontes: King of the Mountains + Super Combativité

1959: Federico Bahamontes: Overall + King of the Mountains

1960: Jean Graczyk: Points + Super Combativité

1968: Franco Bitossi: Points + Combination

1969: Eddy Merckx: Overall + Points + King of the Mountains + Combination + Super Combativité

1970: Eddy Merckx: Overall + King of the Mountains + Combination + Super Combativité

1971: Eddy Merckx: Overall + Points + Combination + Super Combativité

1972: Eddy Merckx: Overall + Points + Combination

1973: Luis Ocaña: Overall + Super Combativité

1974: Eddy Merckx: Overall + Combination + Super Combativité

1979: Bernard Hinault: Overall + Points

1980: Rudy Pevenage: Points + Intermediate Sprints

1981: Bernard Hinault: Overall + Combination + Super Combativité

1981: Freddy Maertens: Points + Intermediate Sprints

1982: Bernard Hinault: Overall + Combination

1982: Sean Kelly: Points + Intermediate Sprints

1983: Laurent Fignon: Overall + Youth

1983: Sean Kelly: Points + Intermediate Sprints

1986: Greg LeMond: Overall + Combination

1986: Bernard Hinault: King of the Mountains + Super Combativité

1988: Steven Rooks: King of the Mountains + Combination

1989: Sean Kelly: Points + Intermediate Sprints

1991: Claudio Chiappucci: King of the Mountains + Super Combativité

1992: Claudio Chiappucci: King of the Mountains + Super Combativité

1996: Richard Virenque: King of the Mountains + Super Combativité

1997: Jan Ullrich: Overall + Youth

1997: Richard Virenque: King of the Mountains + Super Combativité

2001: Laurent Jalabert: King of the Mountains + Super Combativité

2002: Laurent Jalabert: King of the Mountains + Super Combativité

2004: Richard Virenque: King of the Mountains + Super Combativité

2007: Alberto Contador: Overall + Youth

2010: Andy Schleck: Overall + Youth

2013: Nairo Quintana: King of the Mountains + Youth

Most Stage Wins (including time trials and prologues)

34: Eddy Merckx (1969 6, 1970 8, 1971 4, 1972 6, 1974 8, 1975 2)

28: Bernard Hinault (1978 3, 1979 7, 1980 3, 1981 5, 1982 4, 1984 1, 1985 2, 1986 3)

25: Mark Cavendish (2008 4, 2009 6, 2010 5, 2011 5, 2012 3, 2013 2)

25: André Leducq (1927 3, 1928 4, 1929 5, 1930 2, 1931 1, 1932 6, 1933 2, 1935 1, 1938 1)

22: André Darrigade (1953 1, 1955 1, 1956 1, 1957 3, 1958 5, 1959 2, 1960 1, 1961 4, 1962 1, 1963 1, 1964 2)

22: ~~Lance Armstrong~~ (1993 1, 1995 1, ~~1999 4, 2000 1, 2001 4, 2002 4, 2003 1, 2004 5, 2005 1~~)

20: Nicolas Frantz (1924 2, 1925 4, 1926 4, 1927 3, 1928 5, 1929 2)

Most Stage Wins in a Single Tour

8: Charles Pélissier 1930; Eddy Merckx 1970, 1974; Freddy Maertens 1976

Most Participations in a Career

17 starts, 15 finishes: Stuart O'Grady (Aus) 1997-2013 (DNF 2000, 2007)

17 starts, 13 finishes: George Hincapie (USA) 1996-2012 (DNF 1997, DQ 2004-2006)

16 starts, 16 finishes: Joop Zoetemelk (Ned) 1970-1973, 1975-1986

16 starts, 13 finishes: Jens Voigt (Ger) 1998-2013 (DNF 2003, 2005, 2009)

15 starts, 15 finishes: Lucien Van Impe (Bel) 1969-1981, 1983, 1985; Viatcheslav Ekimov (Rus) 1990-1998, 2000-2004, 2006

15 starts, 13 finishes: Guy Nulens (Bel) 1980-1994 (DNF 1980, 1983)

15 starts, 11 finishes: Christophe Moreau (Fra) 1996-2010 (DQ 1998, DNF 2001-2002, 2008)

International Grands Départs

5: Netherlands (Amsterdam 1954; Scheveningen 1973; Leiden 1978; 's-Hertogenbosch 1996; Rotterdam 2010)

4: Belgium (Brussels 1958; Charleroi 1975; Liège 2004, 2012)

3: Germany (Köln 1965; Frankfurt 1980; Berlin 1987)

2: Luxembourg (Luxembourg 1989, 2002)

1: Switzerland (Basel 1982); Spain (San Sebastián 1992); Ireland (Dublin 1998); Great Britain (London 2007); Monaco (Monaco 2009)

French Grands Départs (by region and départment)

Île-de-France (41):

Paris 1903-1914, 1919-25, 1927-1939, 1947-1950, 2003;

Val-de-Marne – Nogent-sur-Marne 1963; Fontenoy-sur-Bois 1983;

Seine-Saint-Denis – Montreuil 1984; *Hauts-de-Seine* – Boulogne-Billancourt 1986

Pays de la Loire (9):

Loire-Atlantique – Nantes 1957; Pornichet 1988;

Maine-et-Loire – Angers 1967, 1972;

Vendée – St-Jean-de-Monts 1976; Le Puy du Fou 1993, 1999; Fromentine 2005; Passage-du-Gois 2011

Brittany (6):

Finistère – Brest 1952, 1974, 2008;

Ille-et-Vilaine – Rennes 1964;

Côtes-d'Armor – St-Brieuc 1995;

Morbihan – Plumelec 1985

Alsace (4):

Bas-Rhin – Strasbourg 1953, 2006;

Haut-Rhin – Mulhouse 1959, 1971

Nord-Pas-de-Calais (4):

Nord – Lille 1960, 1994; Roubaix 1969; Dunkerque 2001

Lorraine (4):

Moselle – Metz 1951;

Meurthe-et-Moselle – Nancy 1962, 1966;

Vosges – Vittel 1968

Haute Normandy (3):

Seine-Maritime – Le Havre 1955; Rouen 1961, 1997

Poitou-Charentes (2):

Vienne – Futuroscope 1990, 2000

Rhône-Alpes (2):

Haute-Savoie – Évian 1926; Rhône Lyon 1991

Midi-Pyrénées (2):

Gers – Fleurance 1977, 1979

Champagne-Ardenne (1):

Marne – Reims 1956

Limousin (1):

Haute-Vienne – Limoges 1970

Provence-Alpes-Côte d'Azur (1):

Alpes-Maritimes – Nice 1981

Corsica (1):

Corse-du-Sud – Porto-Vecchio (2013)

(8 regions have yet to host the Tour's *grand départ*: Auvergne, Centre, Aquitaine, Languedoc-Roussillon, Picardie, Bourgogne, Franche-Comté and Basse-Normandie.)

Terms and Abbreviations

Countries

Alg – Algeria

Aus – Australia

Aut – Austria

Bel – Belgium

Blr – Belarus

Bra – Brazil

Can – Canada

Col – Colombia

Cro – Croatia

Cze – Czechoslovakia

Den – Denmark

Esp – Spain

Est – Estonia

Fin – Finland

Fra – France

FRG – West Germany (Federal Republic of Germany – 1952-1988)

GBr – Great Britain

Ger – Germany

Hun – Hungary

Irl – Ireland

Ita – Italy

Jpn – Japan

Kaz – Kazakhstan

Lat – Latvia

Lit – Lithuania

Lux – Luxembourg

Mex – Mexico

Mol – Moldavia

Mor – Morocco

Ned – Netherlands

Nor – Norway

Pol – Poland

Por – Portugal

RSA – South Africa

Rus – Russia

Slo – Slovenia

Slq – Slovakia

Sui – Switzerland

Swe – Sweden

Ukr – Ukraine

USA – United States of America

Uzb – Uzbekistan

Lexicon

Bidon – water bottle

Bonifications – time bonuses, deducted form overall elapsed time

Campionissimo – champion of champions (Italian)

Caravanne publicitaire – the publicity caravan that precedes the passage of the riders on the road

Chute – a crash or a fall

Col – a mountain or mountain pass

Côte – a small *Col*

Commissaires – race referees

Contra-la-montre – against the clock, a time trial

Corsa rosa – nickname for the Giro d'Italia

Critérium – a race on a short, closed circuit

Défaillance – a complete physical collapse

Derailleur – mechanism for changing gear

Directeur sportif – team manager

DNF – did not finish

Domestique – team helper

DQ – disqualified

Echelon – the line of riders that forms across the width of the road when the wind is coming from the side

Extra-sportif – a sponsor from outside the traditional cycling industry

Festina *affaire* – the 1998 Tour

Flamme rouge – the flag which indicates the riders have one kilometre to go before the finish

Fringale – the bonk, a lack of blood sugar caused by forgetting to take on food

Géant de la route – giant of the road, originally stars from the road side of the sport, later someone who had finished the Tour

General Classification – table indicating who is leading the race, and how far behind him his rivals are

Grande boucle – the big loop, nickname for the Tour

Gregari – Italian form of *domestiques*

Grimpeur – climber

Jour de répos – a rest day

Jour sans – a day without, a day in which the rider simply can't perform

Lanterne Rouge – the red lantern, nickname for the last rider in the Tour's general classification

Maglia rosa – the pink jersey worn by the leader of the Giro d'Italia

Maillot à pois rouge – the polka-dot jersey worn by the leader of the King of the Mountains competition

Maillot blanc – the white jersey worn by the best-placed young rider

Maillot jaune – the yellow jersey worn by the leader of the Tour

Maillot vert – the green jersey worn by the leader of the points competition

Meilleur grimpeur – the best climber prize, an unofficial King of the Mountains award that ran in early Tours

Mondialisation – globalisation, internationalisation

Palmarès – a rider's list of victories, his roll of honour

Parcours – the race route

Pavé – typically, the cobbled roads of northern France

Peloton – the pack, the bunch of riders that forms on the road

Pistard – track rider

Rouleur – a rider who rides fast on the flat

Salle de presse – press room

Soigneur – carer, masseur

Super Combativité – an award for the most attacking rider

Tifosi – Italian cycling fans

UCI – Union Cycliste Internationale, cycling's governing body

Voiture ballai – The broom wagon which brings up the tail end of the race, following the last rider on the road

WADA – World Anti-Doping Authority

Bibliography

Books

Abt, Samuel – *LeMond: The Incredible Comeback*, 1991; *In High Gear: The World of Professional Bicycle Racing*, 1989; *Champion: Bicycle Racing in the Age of Miguel Indurain*, 1993

Abt, Samuel with James Startt – *In Pursuit of the Yellow Jersey: Bicycle Racing in the Year of the Tortured Tour*, 1999

Albergotti, Reed & Vanessa O'Connell – *Wheelmen: Lance Armstrong, the Tour de France, and the Greatest Sports Conspiracy Ever*, 2013

Allchin, Richard & Adrian Bell – *Golden Stages of the Tour de France*, 2003

Bacon, Ellis – *Mapping Le Tour: The Unofficial History of All 100 Tour de France Races*, 2013

Balf., Todd – *Major: A Black Athlete, A White Era, and the Fight To Be the World's Fastest Human Being*, 2008

Barthes, Roland – *The Eiffel Tower and Other Mythologies* (translation by Richard Howard), 1997

Baugé, Alphonse – *Lettres à Mon Directeur: Le Tour de France 1907*, 1908

Belbin, Giles – *Mountain Kings: Agony and Euphoria on the Peaks of the Tour de France*, 2013

Benson, Daniel & Richard Moore –*Bike!: A Tribute to the World's Greatest Cycling Designers*, 2012

Bobet, Jean – *Tomorrow We Ride* (translation by Adam Berry), 2004

Bruyneel, Johan – *We Might As Well Win* (with Bill Strickland), 2008

Cavendish, Mark – *Boy Racer* (with Daniel Friebe), 2009; *At Speed: My Life in the Fast Lane* (with Daniel Friebe), 2013

Clemitson, Suze – *100 Tours, 100 Tales*, 2013

Connor, Jeff – *Wide Eyed and Legless: Inside the Tour de France,1988; Field of Fire: The Tour de France of '87 and the Rise and Fall of ANC Halfords*, 2012

Cossins, Peter with Isabel Best, Chris Sidwells & Clare Griffith – *Le Tour 100: The Definitive History of the World's Greatest Race*, 2013

Coyle, Daniel – *Lance Armstrong's War: One Man's Battle Against Fate, Fame, Love, Death, Scandal, and a Few Other Rivals on the Road to the Tour de France*, 2005

Dauncey, Hugh & Geoff Hare – *The Tour de France 1903-2003: A Century of Sporting Structures, Meanings and Values*, 2003

Deering, John – *Team on the Run*, 2002

Denson, Vin – *The Full Cycle*, 2008

Dineen, Robert – *Reg Harris: The Rise and Fall of Britain's Greatest Cyclist*, 2012

Drake, Geoff – *Team 7-Eleven*, 2011

Ejnès, Gérard with Philippe Bouvet, Philippe Brunel, Raoul Dufourcq, Serge Laget & Gérard Schaller – *The Official Tour de France Centennial 1903-2003*, 2003

Elliott, Malcolm – *Sprinter: The Life and Times of a Professional Road Racer* (with Jeff Connor), 1989

Evans, Cadel – *Close to Flying*, 2009

Fife Graeme – *Tour de France: The History, the Legend, the Riders*, 1999; *Inside the Peloton: Riding, Winning and Losing the Tour de France*, 2001

Fignon, Laurent – *We Were Young and Carefree* (translation by William Fotheringham), 2009

Foot, John – *Pedalare! Pedalare!: A History of Italian Cycling*, 2011

Fotheringham, Alasdair – *The Eagle of Toledo: The Life and Times of Federico Bahamontes*, 2012

Fotheringham, William – *A Century of Cycling*, 2002; *Put Me Back On My Bike: In Search of Tom Simpson*, 2002; *Roule Britannia: Great Britain and the Tour de France*, 2004; *Fallen Angel: The Passion of Fausto Coppi*, 2009; *Cyclopedia*, 2010; *Merckx: Half Man, Half Bike*, 2012; *Racing Hard: 20 Tumultuous Years in Cycling*, 2013

Fournel, Paul – *Need for the Bike* (translation by Allan Stoekl), 2003

Friebe, Daniel – *Mountain High: Europe's Greatest Cycle Climbs*, 2011; *Eddy Merckx: The Cannibal*, 2012; *Mountain Higher: Europe's Extreme Undiscovered and Unforgettable Cycle Climbs*, 2013

Gilbert, Philippe – *My Year in Top Gear* (translation by Martin Lambert), 2011

Green, Johnny – *Push Yourself Just a Little Bit More*, 2005

Guinness, Rupert – *The Foreign Legion*, 1993; *The Tour: Behind the Scenes of Cadel Evans' Tour de France*, 2012

Hamilton, Tyler – *The Secret Race* (with Daniel Coyle), 2012

Hardie, Martin with David Shilbury, Ianto Ware & Claudio Bozzi – *I Wish I Was Twenty-One: Beyond Doping in the Australian Peloton*, 2010

Healy, Graham with Richard Allchin – *Shay Elliott: The Life and Death of Ireland's First Yellow Jersey*, 2011

Hilton, Tim – *One More Kilometre and We're In the Showers: Memoirs of a Cyclist*, 2005

Homan, Andrew – *Life in the Slipstream: The Legend of Bobby Walthour Sr*, 2011

Houlihan, Barry – *Dying to Win*, 1999

Howard, Paul – *Sex, Lies and Handlebar Tape: The Remarkable Life of Jacques Anquetil, the First Five-Times Winner of the Tour de France*, 2008

Humphreys, Bill & Jerry Dunn – *The Jersey Project*, 2012

Hutchinson Michael – *The Hour*, 2006

Johnson, Mark – *Argyle Armada: Behind the Scenes of the Pro Cycling Life*, 2012

Kelly, Sean – *Hunger: The Autobiography* (with Lionel Birnie), 2013

Kimmage, Paul – *A Rough Ride*, 1990

Krabbé, Tim – *The Rider*, 1978

Laget, Serge with Françoise Laget, Philippe Cazabam, Gilles Montgermont & Peter Cossins – *Tour de France: Official 100th Anniversary Edition* (translation by Peter Cossins) 2013

Laget, Serge with Luke Edwardes-Evans & Andy McGrath – *Le Tour de France 100: The Official Treasures*, 2013

Lazell, Marguerite – *Tour de France: The Complete Illustrated History*, 2003

Lee, Daniel – *The Belgian Hammer: Forging Young Americans Into Professional Cyclists*, 2011

Maertens, Freddy – *Fall From Grace* (with Manu Adrieens, translation by Steve Hawkins), 1993

Maso, Benjo – *Sweat of the Gods: Myths and Legends of Bicycle Racing* (translation by Michiel Horn), 2004

McConnon, Aili & Andres McConnon – *The Lion of Tuscany: Gino Bartali, Tour de France Legend and Italy's Secret World War II Hero*, 2012

McEwen, Robbie – *One Way Road: The Autobiography of Robbie McEwen, Three Time Tour de France Green Jersey Winner* (with Edward Pickering), 2011

McGann, Bill & Carol – *The Story of the Tour de France, Vol 1*, 2006; *The Story of the Tour de France, Vol 2*, 2008

Millar, David – *Racing Through the Dark: The Fall and Rise of David Millar* (with Jeremy Whittle), 2011

Møller, Verner – *The Doping Devil* (translation by John Hoberman), 2008; *The Scapegoat: About the Expulsion of Michael Rasmussen from the Tour de France 2007 and Beyond*, 2011

Moore, Gerry – *The Little Black Bottle: Choppy Warburton, the Question of Doping, and the Deaths of His Bicycle Riders*, 2011

Moore, Richard – *In Search of Robert Millar*, 2007; *Sky's the Limit: British Cycling's Quest to Conquer the Tour de France*, 2011; *Slaying the Badger: LeMond, Hinault and the Greatest Ever Tour de France*, 2011; *Tour de France 100: A Photographic History of Cycling's Most Iconic Race*, 2013; *Mastermind: How Dave Brailsford Reinvented the Wheel*, 2013

Moore, Tim – *French Revolutions: Cycling the Tour de France*, 2001

Nelsson, Richard – *The Tour de France … to the Bitter End*, 2012

Nicholson, Geoffrey – *The Great Bike Race*, 1977; *Le Tour*, 1990

Nye, Peter – *Hearts of Lions: The History of American Bicycle Racing*, 1989; *The Six-Day Bicycle Races: America's Jazz-Age Sport*, 2006

Obree, Graeme – *The Flying Scotsman*, 2003

Parkin, Joe – *A Dog in a Hat*, 2008

Peiper, Allan – *A Peiper's Tale* (with Chris Sidwells), 2005

Penn, Robert – *It's All About the Bike: The Pursuit of Happiness On Two Wheels*, 2010

Phinney, Davis – *The Happiness of Pursuit* (with Austin Murphy), 2011

Pickering, Edward – *The Race Against Time*, 2013

Pinotti, Marco – *The Cycling Professor* (translation by Fabrizio Viani), 2012

Redeker, Robert – *Le Sport Contre les Peuples*, 2002

Rendell, Matt – *Kings of the Mountains*, 2002; *A Significant Other: Riding the Centenary Tour de France with Lance Armstrong*, 2005; *The Death of Marco Pantani*, 2007; *Blazing Saddles: The Cruel and Unusual History of the Tour de France*, 2008; *Olympic Gangster: The Legend of José Beyaert, Cycling Champion, Fortune Hunter and Outlaw*, 2009

Reuman, Ron, Stephan Vanfleteren, Jan Maes, Frederik Backelandt – *Merckx 525* (translation by Ted Costantino), 2012

Ritchie, Andrew – *Major Taylor: The Fastest Bicycle Rider In the World*, 1988

Roche, Nicolas – *Inside the Peloton: My Life as a Professional Cyclist*, 2011

Roche, Stephen – *My Road To Victory (with David Walsh)*, 1987; *The Agony and the Ecstasy: Stephen Roche's World of Cycling* (with David Walsh), 1988; *Born to Ride* (with Peter Cossins), 2012

Rubino, Guido – *Italian Racing Bicycles: The People, the Products, the Passion* (translation by Jay Hyams), 2011

Sergant, Pascal – *Masters of the Pavé: A History of Strongmen*, 2002

Sharp, David – *Va Va Froome: The Remarkable Rise of Chris Froome*, 2013

Simpson, Tommy – *Cycling Is My Life* (with David Saunders), 1966

Smith, Martin – *The Daily Telegraph Book of the Tour de France*, 2009

Strickland, Bill – *Tour de Lance: The Extraordinary Story of Lance Armstrong's Fight to Reclaim the Tour de France*, 2010

Sykes, Herbie – *The Eagle of the Canavese: Franco Balmamion and the Giro d'Italia*, 2008; *Maglia Rosa: Triumph and Tragedy at the Giro d'Italia*, 2011; *Coppi: Inside the Legend of the Campionissimo*, 2012

Thompson, Christopher S – *The Tour de France: A Cultural History*, 2006

Vespini, Jean-Paul – *The Tour is Won on the Alpe: Classic Battles of the Tour de France*, 2008

Voet, Willy – *Breaking the Chain: Drugs and Cycling, the True Story* (with Pierre Ballester, translation by William Fotheringham) 2001

Walsh, David – *Kelly: A Biography of Sean Kelly*, 1986; *Sean Kelly: A Man For All Seasons*, 1991; *Inside the Tour de France*, 1993; *From Lance to Landis*, 2007; *Seven Deadly Sins: My Pursuit of Lance Armstrong*, 2012; *Inside Team Sky: The Inside Story of Team Sky and Their Challenge for the 2013 Tour de France*, 2012

Walsh, David & Pierre Ballester – *LA Confidentiel: Les Secrets de Lance Armstrong*, 2004

Wegelius, Charly – *Domestique: The True Life Ups and Downs of a Tour Pro* (with Tom Southam), 2013

Wheatcroft, Geoffrey – *Le Tour: A History of the Tour de France*, 2004

Whittle, Jeremy – *Yellow Fever*, 1998; *Bad Blood: The Secret Life of the Tour de France*, 2008

Wiggins, Bradley – *In Pursuit of Glory* (with Brendan Gallagher), 2008; *On Tour* (with Scott Mitchell), 2010; *My Time* (with William Fotheringham), 2012

Witherell, James L – *When Heroes Were Giants: 100 Tours de France*, 2013;

Woodland, Les – *Cycling Heroes: The Golden Years*, 1994; *The Unknown Tour de France: The Many Faces of the World's Greatest Bike Race*, 2002; *The Crooked Path to Victory: Drugs and Cheating in Professional Bicycle Racing*, 2003; Yates, Sean – *It's All About the Bike: My Autobiography (with John Deering)*, 2013

Websites

Bicycling.com
BikeRaceInfo.com
CyclingArchives.com
CyclingNews.com
Gallica.bnf.fr
LaGrandeBoucle.com
LeTour.fr
Memoire-Du-Cyclisme.eu
TourFacts.dk
VeloNews.com